W9-BXW-447

THE NEW YORK PUBLIC LIBRARY

AMERICAN HISTORY DESK REFERENCE

THE NEW YORK PUBLIC LIBRARY

AMERICAN HISTORY DESK REFERENCE

A Stonesong Press Book

New York

HYPERION
77 West 66th Street
New York, NY 10023-6298

Copyright © 1997, 2003 by Stonesong Press, LLC and The New York Public Library,
Astor, Lenox and Tilden foundations

All rights reserved. No part of this book may be used or reproduced in any manner whatsoever
without the written permission of the Publisher. Printed in the United States of America.
For information, address: Hyperion, 77 West 66th Street, New York, NY 10023-6298.

 The name "*The New York Public Library*" and the representation of the lion appearing
in this work are trademarks and the property of The New York Public Library, Astor,
Lenox, and Tilden foundations.

Hyperion books are available for special promotions and premiums. For details, contact
Michael Rentas, Manager, Inventory and Premium Sales, Hyperion, 77 West 66th Street,
11th Floor, New York, New York, 10023 or call 212-456-0133.

A Stonesong Press Book

Designed by Laura Smyth
Production by smythtype
Maps created by Netmaps, S. A.
Photo research by Jennifer Woolf and Sarah Parvis

Second Edition

10 9 8 7 6 5 4 3 2 1

Library of Congress Cataloging-in-Publication Data

The New York Public Library American history desk reference / The New York Public
    Library.—2nd edition
        p. cm.
"A Stonesong Press book."
Includes bibliographical references and index.
ISBN 0-7868-6847-3
    1. United States—History—Chronology. 2. United States—History—Dictionaries.
I. Title: American history desk reference. II. The New York Public Library.

E174.5'.N47 2003
973'.02'02—dc22   2003056655

THE NEW YORK PUBLIC LIBRARY PROJECT SPONSOR

Paul LeClerc, *President*

Mary K. Conwell, *Senior Vice President and Director of The Branch Libraries*

William D. Walker, *Senior Vice President and the Andrew W. Mellon Director of The Research Libraries*

Michael J. Zavelle, *Senior Vice President and Chief Administrative Officer*

Karen Van Westering, *Director of Publications*

THE STONESONG PRESS

Series Developer
Paul Fargis

Editor, Second Edition
Sarah Parvis

Managing Editor, Second Edition
Judy Pray

Revising Editor
Jeff Hacker

Contributors
Michele Camardella
Marian Faux
Marilyn Miller
Akim Reinhardt
Alexa Torgerson

Editorial Consultants
Ann Hofstra Grogg, *Chief Editorial Consultant*
Andrew Attaway
Duncan B. Gardiner, Ph.D.

A NOTE FROM THE EDITORS

Every attempt has been made to ensure that this publication is as accurate as possible and as comprehensive as space would allow. We are grateful to the many researchers, librarians, teachers, reference editors, and friends who contributed facts, figures, time, energy, ideas, and opinions. Our choice of what to include was aided by their advice and their voices of experience. The contents, however, remain subjective to some extent, because we could not possibly cover everything that one might look for in one volume. If errors or omissions are discovered, we would appreciate hearing from you as we prepare future editions. Please address suggestions and comments to The Stonesong Press, 11 East 47th Street, New York, NY 10017.

We hope you find this work useful.

How to Use this Book

Sidebars, which appear in boxes throughout the book, highlight people and events featured in the master timelines.

EACH CHAPTER IN THIS BOOK covers a particular topic, such as territorial expansion, military history, or education in America. To investigate a specific area of American history, follow the timelines that make up each chapter. Because the book is arranged by theme, many people, laws, events, and issues will appear in more than one chapter. For example, Dr. Martin Luther King Jr. figures prominently in Chapter Four: Immigration and Minority Life in discussions about civil rights, in Chapter Five: Military History in entries on antiwar protests; and in Chapter Thirteen, which covers religion. For this reason, we encourage the reader to use the extensive **Index** at the back of the book to locate information about people and events whose impact can be felt in more than one area of American History. For further information, consult **Additional Sources,** which is located at the back of the book. Organized by chapter, it includes books, periodicals, and descriptions of useful websites and search engines.

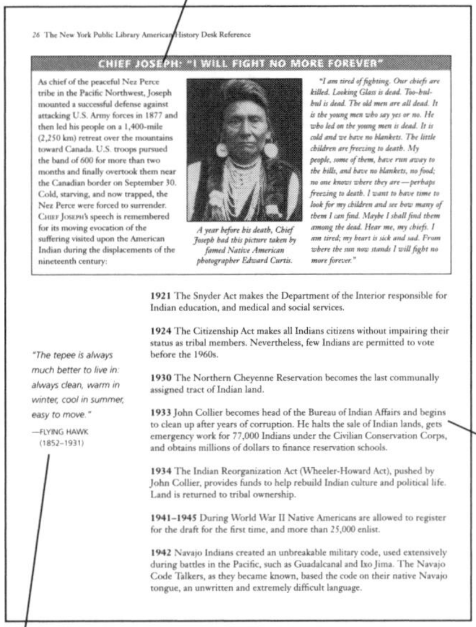
26 The New York Public Library American History Desk Reference

CHIEF JOSEPH: "I WILL FIGHT NO MORE FOREVER"

As chief of the peaceful Nez Perce tribe in the Pacific Northwest, Joseph mounted a successful defense against attacking U.S. Army forces in 1877 and then led his people on a 1,400-mile (2,250 km) retreat over the mountains toward Canada. U.S. troops pursued the band of 600 for more than two months and finally overtook them near the Canadian border on September 30. Cold, starving, and now trapped, the Nez Perce were forced to surrender. CHIEF JOSEPH's speech is remembered for its moving evocation of the suffering visited upon the American Indian during the displacements of the nineteenth century:

A year before his death, Chief Joseph had this picture taken by famed Native American photographer Edward Curtis.

"I am tired of fighting. Our chiefs are killed. Looking Glass is dead. Too-hul-hul is dead. The old men are all dead. It is the young men who say yes or no. He who led on the young men is dead. It is cold and we have no blankets. The little children are freezing to death. My people, some of them, have run away to the hills, and have no blankets, no food; no one knows where they are—perhaps freezing to death. I want to have time to look for my children and see how many of them I can find. Maybe I shall find them among the dead. Hear me, my chiefs. I am tired; my heart is sick and sad. From where the sun now stands I will fight no more forever."

1921 The Snyder Act makes the Department of the Interior responsible for Indian education, and medical and social services.

1924 The Citizenship Act makes all Indians citizens without impairing their status as tribal members. Nevertheless, few Indians are permitted to vote before the 1960s.

"The tepee is always much better to live in: always clean, warm in winter, cool in summer, easy to move."

—FLYING HAWK (1852–1931)

1930 The Northern Cheyenne Reservation becomes the last communally assigned tract of Indian land.

1933 John Collier becomes head of the Bureau of Indian Affairs and begins to clean up after years of corruption. He halts the sale of Indian lands, gets emergency work for 77,000 Indians under the Civilian Conservation Corps, and obtains millions of dollars to finance reservation schools.

1934 The Indian Reorganization Act (Wheeler-Howard Act), pushed by John Collier, provides funds to help rebuild Indian culture and political life. Land is returned to tribal ownership.

1941–1945 During World War II Native Americans are allowed to register for the draft for the first time, and more than 25,000 enlist.

1942 Navajo Indians created an unbreakable military code, used extensively during battles in the Pacific, such as Guadalcanal and Ixo Jima. The Navajo Code Talkers, as they became known, based the code on their native Navajo tongue, an unwritten and extremely difficult language.

Master Timelines are the backbone of the book, featuring the prominent trends and events of the topic covered in each chapter.

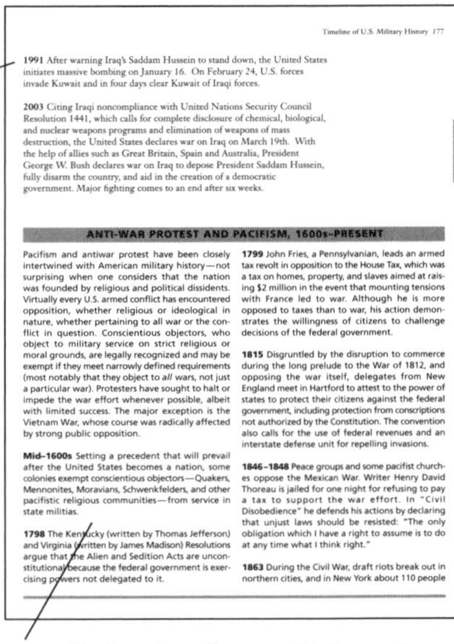
Timeline of U.S. Military History 177

1991 After warning Iraq's Saddam Hussein to stand down, the United States initiates massive bombing on January 16. On February 24, U.S. forces invade Kuwait and in four days clear Kuwait of Iraqi forces.

2003 Citing Iraqi noncompliance with United Nations Security Council Resolution 1441, which calls for complete disclosure of chemical, biological, and nuclear weapons programs and elimination of weapons of mass destruction, the United States declares war on Iraq on March 19th. With the help of allies such as Great Britain, Spain and Australia, President George W. Bush declares war on Iraq to depose President Saddam Hussein, fully disarm the country, and aid in the creation of a democratic government. Major fighting comes to an end after six weeks.

ANTI-WAR PROTEST AND PACIFISM, 1600s–PRESENT

Pacifism and antiwar protest have been closely intertwined with American military history—not surprising when one considers that the nation was founded by religious and political dissidents. Virtually every U.S. armed conflict has encountered opposition, whether religious or ideological in nature, whether pertaining to all war or the conflict in question. Conscientious objectors, who object to military service on strict religious or moral grounds, are legally recognized and may be exempt if they meet narrowly defined requirements (most notably that they object to *all* wars, not just a particular war). Protesters have sought to halt or impede the war effort whenever possible, albeit with limited success. The major exception is the Vietnam War, whose course was radically affected by strong public opposition.

Mid–1600s Setting a precedent that will prevail after the United States becomes a nation, some colonies exempt conscientious objectors—Quakers, Mennonites, Moravians, Schwenkfelders, and other pacifistic religious communities—from service in state militias.

1798 The Kentucky (written by Thomas Jefferson) and Virginia (written by James Madison) Resolutions argue that the Alien and Sedition Acts are unconstitutional because the federal government is exercising powers not delegated to it.

1799 John Fries, a Pennsylvanian, leads an armed tax revolt in opposition to the House Tax, which was a tax on homes, property, and slaves aimed at raising $2 million in the event that mounting tensions with France led to war. Although he is more opposed to taxes than to war, his action demonstrates the willingness of citizens to challenge decisions of the federal government.

1815 Disgruntled by the disruption to commerce during the long prelude to the War of 1812, and opposing the war itself, delegates from New England meet in Hartford to attest to the power of states to protect their citizens against the federal government, including protection from conscriptions not authorized by the Constitution. The convention also calls for the use of federal revenues and an interstate defense unit for repelling invasions.

1846–1848 Peace groups and some pacifist churches oppose the Mexican War. Writer Henry David Thoreau is jailed for one night for refusing to pay a tax to support the war effort. In "Civil Disobedience" he defends his actions by declaring that unjust laws should be resisted: "The only obligation which I have a right to assume is to do at any time what I think right."

1863 During the Civil War, draft riots break out in northern cities, and in New York about 110 people

Quotations and **Factoids** appear in the margins.

Spotlight Timelines, which run in two columns, highlight the evolution of an important trend or event within the chapter topic. **Legislation** and **Supreme Court decisions** appear in Spotlight Timelines as well.

Notable Figures appear at the end of each chapter and includes short biographies of men and women significant to the chapter topic.

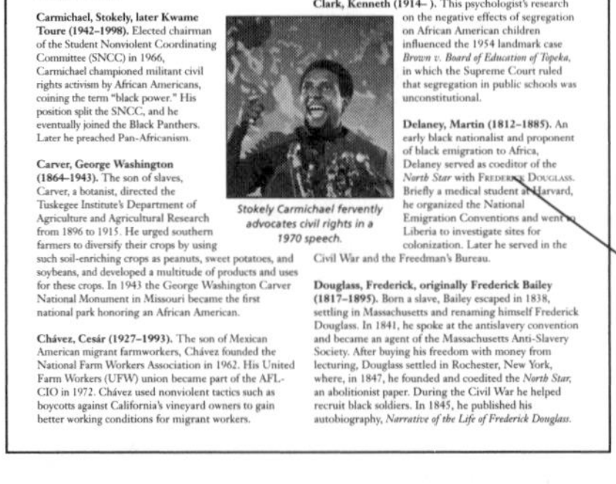
140 The New York Public Library American History Desk Reference

NOTABLE FIGURES, *cont.*

Brown, John (1800–1859). A militant abolitionist, Brown and his five sons moved in 1855 to Kansas, where he and a small group of supporters murdered five supposed proslavery settlers along Pottawatomie Creek. In 1859, he led an attack on the federal arsenal at Harpers Ferry, Virginia. In the ensuing battle with the militia, Brown was wounded and captured; later he was hanged. The raid was widely popular in the North, where some considered Brown a martyr, but enraged and terrified the South.

Bunche, Ralph (1904–1971). The grandson of a slave, Bunche drafted the sections of the U.N. charter on trusteeship territories. In 1948, as chief U.N. mediator in Palestine he arranged for a cease-fire between the Arabs and the Jews, for which he was awarded the 1950 Nobel Peace Prize. From 1967 to 1971 he was undersecretary-general of the United Nations, the highest rank held so far by an American.

Carmichael, Stokely, later Kwame Toure (1942–1998). Elected chairman of the Student Nonviolent Coordinating Committee (SNCC) in 1966, Carmichael championed militant civil rights activism by African Americans, coining the term "black power." His position split the SNCC, and he eventually joined the Black Panthers. Later he preached Pan-Africanism.

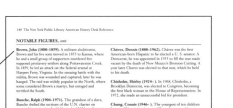

Stokely Carmichael fervently advocates civil rights in a 1970 speech.

Carver, George Washington (1864–1943). The son of slaves, Carver, a botanist, directed the Tuskegee Institute's Department of Agriculture and Agricultural Research from 1896 to 1915. He urged southern farmers to diversify their crops by using such soil-enriching crops as peanuts, sweet potatoes, and soybeans, and developed a multitude of products and uses for these crops. In 1943 the George Washington Carver National Monument in Missouri became the first national park honoring an African American.

Chávez, Cesár (1927–1993). The son of Mexican American migrant farmworkers, Chávez founded the National Farm Workers Association in 1962. His United Farm Workers (UFW) union became part of the AFL-CIO in 1972. Chávez used nonviolent tactics such as boycotts against California's vineyard owners to gain better working conditions for migrant workers.

Chávez, Dennis (1888–1962). Chávez was the first American-born Hispanic to be elected a U. S. senator. A Democrat, he was appointed in 1935 to fill the seat made vacant by the death of New Mexico's Bronson Cutting. A year later Chavez was elected to that seat, which he held to his death.

Chisholm, Shirley (1924–). In 1968, Chisholm, a Brooklyn Democrat, was elected to Congress, becoming the first black woman in the House of Representatives. In 1972, she made an unsuccessful bid for president.

Chung, Connie (1946–). The youngest of ten children born to Chinese immigrants, Chung began working at CBS in 1971 and in 1993 became the first Asian American woman to coanchor a national news program. She remains one of the few Chinese Americans seen regularly on national television.

Clark, Kenneth (1914–). This psychologist's research on the negative effects of segregation on African American children influenced the 1954 landmark case *Brown v. Board of Education of Topeka,* in which the Supreme Court ruled that segregation in public schools was unconstitutional.

Delaney, Martin (1812–1885). An early black nationalist and proponent of black emigration to Africa, Delaney served as coeditor of the *North Star* with FREDERICK DOUGLASS. Briefly a medical student at Harvard, he organized the National Emigration Conventions and went to Liberia to investigate sites for colonization. Later he served in the Civil War and the Freedman's Bureau.

Douglass, Frederick, originally Frederick Bailey (1817–1895). Born a slave, Bailey escaped in 1838, settling in Massachusetts and renaming himself Frederick Douglass. In 1841, he spoke at the antislavery convention and became an agent of the Massachusetts Anti-Slavery Society. After buying his freedom with money from lecturing, Douglass settled in Rochester, New York, where, in 1847, he founded and coedited the *North Star,* an abolitionist paper. During the Civil War he helped recruit black soldiers. In 1845, he published his autobiography, *Narrative of the Life of Frederick Douglass.*

Small Capital Letters indicate the names of the people who appear in the Notable Figures section at the end of the chapter in which they appear.

Contents

Introduction

I was at a luncheon with a group of friends at Casamento's, a traditional New Orleans café on Magazine Street with the best fried oysters in the city. Talk turned to World War I, and on demand I was asked how many American soldiers were killed during the war. By training, I am a Cold War historian, and I had no ready answer. This caused a round of good-natured jokes at my expense; everybody took a shot at me with tweaks like, "So, Mr. Historian doesn't know about World War I?" and "You've got to be kidding, I thought you knew everything about America!" I felt like a physician being accused of malpractice. Slightly embarrassed, I managed to cough up a defense: "What's important is not that I have an immediate answer but when I research it tomorrow morning my verdict will be correct."

The greatest hazard of being a professional historian is that people expect you to be a walking encyclopedia, to have snap answers to obscure questions about the past. They want to imagine you as their "lifeline" on the TV show *Who Wants to Be a Millionaire*, the rough-and-ready scholar they can count on in a pinch. This insistence on immediacy is foolish, another manifestation of the American obsession with quickness over quality. For the truly wise historian is a devotee of the double check. The mind, after all, is a fallible thing, and since our hard currency is cold fact, it's best to be 100 percent positive before spouting out a date or statistic or body count just to satisfy the unrealistic hopes of our various inquirers. Our professional talent lies in knowing where to look for factoids: in the realm of U.S. history, *The New York Public Library American History Desk Reference* shines forth as one of our most trustworthy tools.

Today, history has been largely co-opted by our popular culture. We learn about President John F. Kennedy's assassination from Oliver Stone's movie *JFK*, and D-Day from Steven Spielberg's *Saving Private Ryan*. Students often glean their historical wisdom from fast-paced overviews in documentaries on the History Channel and poorly conceived websites.

This blur between history, myth, and mistake is as old as time. For as Washington Irving noted in his irrepressible *The Sketch Book* (1820): "History fades into fable; fact becomes clouded with doubt and controversy; the imagination molders from the tablet; the statue falls from the pedestal. Columns, arches, pyramids, what are they but heaps of sand; and their epitaphs, but characters written in the dust?"

Our founding fathers fully realized that history making was hard to reclaim in history books. As so-called historians began writing accounts of the Declaration of Independence and Valley Forge, an incredulous John Adams cut to the chase. "I consider the true history of the American Revolution, and the establishment of our present Constitution, as lost forever," he sniffed. "And nothing but misrepresentations, or partial accounts of it, will ever be received." Thomas Jefferson, writing John Adams in early September 1817, similarly concluded that "a morsel of genuine history is a thing so rare as to be always valuable."

The skeptical Adams and Jefferson, however, would have celebrated *The New York Public Library American History Desk Reference* because it offers only the facts surrounding 1776. Revisionist theories, narrative conceits, and clever analyses are left to the working historians to conjure up for themselves. What this volume does offer is an essential timeline of American history—from the Paleo-Indian Era to the war in Afghanistan, where precise dates and important statistics are offered in well-organized abundance. There is an old adage that working historians often use when preparing to write a full-length biography or a battlefield history: "Abandon chronology at your own peril." This sentiment understands we live our lives day by day and hour by hour. Historical events occur—as life itself does—in chronological fashion. Realizing this essential truth, The New York Public Library, one of the world's most noble houses of learning, wisely lent its resources to this reference work, which can assist both professional historians and novices alike. And they made sure it was user-friendly.

Appropriately this book begins with a chapter on "Native American History." Besides the first-rate timeline that opens with the possible migration of people from Siberia during the last Ice Age and ends with the recent return of 84,000 acres of tribal land to the Utes, there are thumbnail "spotlights" on such controversial issues as "Who Is an Indian?" "Slaughter of the Buffalo," and "Reservations: What Are They and How Do They Work?" The chapter also highlights aspects of Native American culture, such as the ghost dance of the Great Plains and the languages and modes of living of the many culture areas across the nation. Another particularly useful essay in this chapter reminds us that Native Americans have contributed such words to the English language as "tepee," "tobacco," "toboggan," and "succotash." And we learn that an astounding twenty-seven states trace their names to Indian origins: Alabama, Alaska, Arizona, Arkansas, Connecticut, Idaho, Illinois, Indiana, Iowa, Kansas, Kentucky, Massachusetts, Michigan, Minnesota, Mississippi, Missouri, Nebraska, North Dakota, Ohio, Oklahoma, Oregon, South Dakota, Tennessee, Texas, Utah, Wisconsin, and Wyoming.

While not a heavily illustrated book, each chapter includes a smattering of well-placed maps, sketches, and photographs. For example, the illustration of the layout of a slave ship makes the horror of the Middle Passage clear, just as the photo of the building of the Panama Canal brings home the enormity of that engineering feat. The maps of major battles during our conflicts around the world illuminate the text and fill in the blanks for the average person whose geography may be lacking. And to anyone who gets confused about where various Indians lived at the time of European migration to the New World, the map demarcating tribes in geographical regions is a godsend.

Few people will read this book from cover to cover. Most will dip into it to look up a specific fact or event. This is a pity. For I can think of few better books to have on a deserted island. This is because, in part, the editors wisely divided the book into broad-based chapters such as "Government, Politics, and Law," "Military History," and "Transportation and Communication." This makes for easy topical reading. In each chapter, the reader can look at related events in the order in which they occurred to see, for example, the dates and facts that contributed to tensions of the Cold War—that the Soviet Union shot down an American spy plane a year before building the Berlin Wall and two years before the Kennedy-Khrushchev

standoff in the Cuban missile crisis. The timelines in this tome show us that the Harley-Davidson motorcycle was devised by William Harley the very same year that Henry Ford founded the Ford Motor Company and that Orville and Wilbur Wright flew their Kitty Hawk for the first time in 1903—a mere twenty-four years before Charles Lindbergh completed his nonstop flight from New York to Paris. Reading history this way allows for remarkable perspective.

By the same token, it is fascinating to flip through the fourteen chapters and read the diverse events taking place in American life in any given year. In 1921, Nicola Sacco and Bartolomeo Vanzetti were sentenced to death for murder in a highly charged case rife with anti-immigrant sentiment. In the very same year, Taft becomes the only former president to hold the position of chief justice of the Supreme Court, Congress creates the Bureau of Public Roads to connect major cities across the country, Eugene O'Neill writes his famous play *Anna Christie*, and the first transcontinental airmail flight from New York to San Francisco takes twenty-seven hours. However the reader chooses to use the book, it places occurrences in their context and also presents a broad view of the accomplishments of Americans and the events that shape our history.

I can testify to the convenience of having this book structured in such a fashion for I used Chapter 9 "Economy, Business, and Labor" as a bible when writing *Wheels for the World: Henry Ford, His Company, and A Century of Progress.* Seeking to place Henry Ford into the proper context of U.S. business history, I used the facts offered on the history of minimum wage, British mercantilism, the gold standard, the national debt, and child labor to provide needed context to my primary research material on the automobile industry. And again, the short biographies offered on such tycoons as Jay Gould, J. P Morgan, and George Westinghouse proved helpful as I wrote my text.

But the real value of *The New York Public Library American History Desk Reference* came to me after I gave a lecture on Dwight D. Eisenhower at the New School for Social Research in front of about 300 people. It was the fiftieth anniversary of President Eisenhower's farewell address in which he warned about the so-called "industrial-military complex" that had developed due to our expensive Cold War showdown with the Soviet Union. A debate ensued as to whether Eisenhower was essentially a hawk or a dove in foreign affairs. I began discussing how in 1953—the first year of Eisenhower's presidency—he created the position of special assistant for National Security Affairs, or National Security Adviser to the president. A woman in the audience quite logically asked me who Eisenhower appointed as his NSC adviser. I offered that there were actually four who served during his eight-year White House tenure. The first was Robert Cutler, the second Dillon Anderson, the third was Robert Cutler—then I drew a blank. For about one minute, I hemmed and hawed at the microphone, racking my brain to conjure up the proper name: it was to no avail. But during a coffee break I cell-phoned my office at the Eisenhower Center for American Studies in New Orleans and told them to quickly look up the history of the NSC in the galley of *The New York Public Library American History Desk Reference* book, which was lying on my messy desk. Within minutes they called back: Gordon Gray took over the post in 1958. Upon returning to the stage, I was able to show off both my memory and diligence by announcing the obscure foreign policy adviser's name.

That being said, *The New York Public Library American History Desk Reference* is a handy and indispensable reference useful for more than just looking up the odd fact. It offers a complete look at the varied aspects of American history. With chapters ranging from "Exploration and Colonization" to "A Rural to an Urban Nation" to "Military History," this book is the book for any reader with an interest in the past or the desire to know how we got to the point where we are today. Each chapter includes a spotlight on major acts of legislation and Supreme Court rulings—a clever arrangement that shows us all the progression of our rights as Americans. At the same time, the text of the chronologies illustrates the events that spurred the changes in our laws. Whether it is America's relation to the Middle East peace process or the background on why taxes are so complex, the chronologies, spotlights on legislation, informative sidebars, notable biographies, and fun factoids in this book can help us all understand the past, and, by extension, the events in the news today.

And as for how many American lives were lost in World War I? I found the answer in the "Military History" chapter: 116,708.

Douglas Brinkley
Director
The Eisenhower Center for American Studies
The University of New Orleans

CHAPTER 1

NATIVE AMERICAN HISTORY

■

HIGHLIGHTS

Timeline of Native American History

NATIVE AMERICANS—the indigenous peoples of the Americas—have a history and culture that stretch from the Paleolithic era to the present, encompassing literally thousands of tribes, or cultural groups, and more than 300 languages in North America alone. Although the dominant image of Indian life has been a composite picture, Native American peoples—even among the so-called Plains Indians—were and remain remarkably diverse.

THE PALEO-INDIAN ERA

c. 50,000–15,000 B.C. During the last great Ice Age, migration is possible from Siberia over the Bering Strait land bridge into North America.

c. 35,000–25,000 B.C. This period yields the earliest archaeological evidence of life in North America in sites as diverse as Meadowcroft Rockshelter (Pennsylvania), Wilson Butte Cave (Idaho), and Folsom and Clovis (New Mexico).

c. 12,000 B.C. Archaeological evidence indicates humans are living throughout North and South America.

c. 11,000–9000 B.C. Ice recedes and land immigration from Asia is no longer possible.
   Clovis technology in New Mexico offers the first indication of an advanced tool, the six-pointed spearhead.
   Old Cordilleran Culture exists in the Pacific Northwest.
   Desert Culture is established in the Great Basin.

c. 7000 B.C. Cochise Culture descends from Desert Culture and is active in the Southwest.

THE PRE-COLUMBIAN ERA

c. 4000 B.C. The first settled communities spring up along the Pacific coast.
   Old Copper Culture forms around the Great Lakes.

c. 3000–1000 B.C. Aleuts and Inuits migrate by boat across the Bering Strait to settle in Alaska.

c. 3000–500 B.C. The Red Paint Culture is active in the Northeast.

1500 B.C. Mexican crops are introduced into the Southwest.

c. 1000 B.C. The first pottery appears along the East Coast.

c. 500 B.C.–A.D. 400 Adena Culture flourishes in Ohio.

300 B.C.–A.D. 500 Hopewell is predominant in the eastern United States, with its center in southern Ohio.

c. 300 B.C.–A.D. 1300 Mogollon Culture is active in the Southwest; by the end of the period it is absorbed into the Anasazi world.

c. 100 B.C.–A.D. 1500 Hohokam Culture is active in the Southwest.

c. 100 B.C. Anasazi Culture takes shape and grows on the Colorado River, where present-day Arizona, New Mexico, Utah, and Colorado meet.

c. A.D. 500–650 The bow and arrow, developed in the Plains, gains widespread use east of the Mississippi River.

c. 700–900 The Mississippi Culture forms in the Mississippi River valley.

ANCIENT INDIAN CULTURES

Because so much of what is known about them remains speculative, ancient Indian cultures are difficult to describe. Generally, these cultures are divided into three broad classifications: Paleo-Indian, Archaic, and Classic (alternately known as Formative).

Beyond this, there is little agreement regarding the specific time periods, or even the terms used to describe them. For example, Paleo-Indians are typically divided into three categories: Preprojectile, Paleo, and Protoarchaic. But sometimes Protoarchaic groups are classified with Archaic ones. The Classic Culture is often divided into two periods, the Formative and the Classic, the latter referring to a golden age that existed in several cultures toward the end of the period.

Finally, the cultures themselves refuse to fit neatly into niches. The Old Cordilleran Culture of the Pacific Northwest is an example of a culture that existed during the Paleo era that was nevertheless advanced enough to be classified as Archaic, while the Desert Culture of the Great Basin was still a foraging society

well into the agriculturally oriented Archaic era.

Since no prehuman remains have been found thus far in the Americas, humans must have migrated there. Most archaeologists agree that the first humans came to North America from Asia by traveling across the Bering Strait land bridge that united Siberia and Alaska during the late Pleistocene era. The most recent evidence indicates that they could have come as early as 50,000 B.C., but more probably arrived somewhere between 35,000 or 25,000 B.C., or even as late as 15,000 B.C.

PALEO-INDIAN CULTURE

Dates: 50,000–30,000 B.C.
Mode of living: Nomadic forager–hunters hunt Pleistocene mammals, such as wooly mammoths, mastodons, lions, tigers, bighorn bison, and tapirs.
Technology: Bone and stone tools; ideas flow through the continent from north to south.
Social organization: Small bands of thirty to forty, probably organized around families with elders making

ANCIENT INDIAN CULTURES, cont.

decisions. Little or no trade. Fairly peaceable with loosely defined territories.
Housing: Lean-tos, cliff overhangs, caves.
Clothes: Animal furs and hides.

DIVISIONS

Preprojectile: Tools and spears have no points. *Sites:* Old Crow Flats, Yukon Territory; Lewisville, Texas.
Projectile: Tools and spears have stone points, with shape determining names of dominant cultures. *Sites:* Clovis (or Llano) and Folsom, New Mexico, and spread to the Great Plains; Plano, throughout North America.

ARCHAIC CULTURE

Dates: 8000 or 6000–1000 B.C.
Mode of living: Nomadic forager–hunters hunt bison, beaver, antelope, elk, and deer.
Technology: Projectile points used to make more specialized tools such as knives, drills, scrapers, and milling stones. Basket weaving and cloth weaving. First to build boats; also to domesticate dogs.
Social organization: Trade widespread, with evidence of gourds from Mesoamerica and copper from the West found in the East. Seminomadic when necessary, but communities becoming localized with a few permanent sites. Burial and occasionally cremation are now ceremonial. Corpses are buried in flexed position.
Housing: Earliest remains of constructed houses date to this period.
Clothes: Animal skins and vegetable materials. Ornaments beginning to appear.

DIVISIONS

Eastern: Denser populations. *Site:* Old Copper in Great Lakes region, unique for using copper.
Western: Also called Cochise Culture, less dense. *Sites:* New Mexico and Arizona.
Arctic and subarctic: Late Archaic (3000–1000 B.C.) Eskimos and Aleuts arrive in small boats, crossing the now-flooded Bering Strait.

CLASSIC CULTURE

Dates: Generally 1000 B.C. to contact with whites at the end of the fifteenth century.
Mode of living: Sedentary farmers and hunters.

Technology: Agriculture develops. Techniques fairly primitive: slash-and-burn, no irrigation, digging stick and hoe are the only implements. Pottery begins and develops. Ideas now typically flow from south to north.
Social organization: Small villages, even city-states by end of period. Groups larger, up to 1,000. Greater differentiation among cultures.
Housing: Varied. *See* Divisions.
Clothes: Varied. *See* Divisions.

DIVISIONS

Early Archaic: Adena (c. 500 B.C.–A.D. 400), located in the Ohio Valley and spreading into Kentucky, West Virginia, Indiana, Pennsylvania, and New York; Hopewell (c. 300 B.C.–A.D. 500), located in the Ohio Valley, spreading as far south as Alabama.

Adena Culture has some agriculture and grows tobacco for ceremonial use. Class divisions are more pronounced than in previous period. Circular wood-and-bark houses. Clothing consists of furs, hides, and woven garments; crafted goods becoming more sophisticated. Introduction of burial mounds in geometric shapes, the largest of which is the Great Serpent Mound in southern Ohio; grave objects rare. *Site:* Great Serpent Mound, Adams County, Ohio.

Hopewell is a larger, more advanced version of Adena. Crafts very refined; clothes ornamental and sophisticated. Mounds are larger; elaborate grave objects now common. Housing consists of nearly rectangular-shaped buildings. Class divisions are still more pronounced, with priests at top, followed by merchants and warriors. *Site:* Enclosure, Newark, Ohio.
Late Archaic: Mississippi, Mogollon, Hohokam, Anasazi.

Mississippi Culture, prevalent A.D.700–900, in the Mississippi River valley. Villages, the dominant form of community, now sometimes surrounded by stockades. Major sites often surrounded by smaller villages. Master mound builders; death-obsessed culture. Cemeteries now used for burial; large platform-shaped mud mounds used ceremonially. Rigid caste system. Crafts, especially pottery, very refined. Elaborate trade network. Influenced by Adena, Hopewell, and Mesoamerica. Modern-day descendants include (Mississippi) Creek, Natchez, Chickasaw, and (Plains)

Hidatsa, Omaha, Mandan, Pawnee, Wichita. *Site:* Cahokia, Illinois, near St. Louis.

Mogollon culture (c. 300 B.C.–A.D. 1300) occupies mountains of southern Arizona and New Mexico. First in Southwest to adopt agriculture, make pottery, and build houses. Housing consists of subterranean pit houses, an excellent adaptation to the hot climate. Excellent weavers. Descended from Cochise Culture; absorbed into Anasazi. *Sites:* Chaco Canyon, New Mexico; Flagstaff, Arizona; Mesa Verde, Colorado.

Hohokam (c. 100 B.C.–A.D. 1500) active in the desert in the Gila and Salt River valleys. Greatest achievement is complex system of irrigation, and possible invention of etching (on shells). Descended from Cochise Culture, perhaps southern tradition; modern-day descendants include Hopi, Zuni, and Pueblo.

Sites: Snaketown, Arizona; Point of Pines, Arizona.

Anasazi (c. 100 B.C.–A.D. 1300) occupy the Four Corners country where Utah, Colorado, Arizona, and New Mexico now converge. The apex of southwestern cultures, it combines characteristics of Mogollon and Hohokam Cultures but is more extensive and more influential. Known to Navajos as the "ancient ones." Produce excellent refined crafts, both pottery and woven; colorful and often ceremonial clothes; many ceremonial objects. Anasazi originally live in pit houses but invent pueblos—mud-constructed, aboveground buildings that eventually evolve into interconnected, terraced villages. First in North America to do terraced farming and to cultivate maize. They abandon their sites, possibly due to drought or invasions from warlike Plains Indians.

In an attempt to document all aspects of Native American life, photographer Edward Curtis captured the traditional Hopi way of preparing cornmeal in this photograph (c. 1920).

Timeline, *cont.*

c. 1000 Tobacco is grown for ceremonial use.

1000–1300 This is the classic period of Mississippi and Anasazi Cultures.

1276–1299 Severe drought in the Southwest changes living patterns for many Indian peoples. Anasazis abandon villages and vanish as a culture.

1300s Early northern migrants, the Athapaskans, arrive in the Southwest; Mandans migrate from the east-central region to the Missouri River, reaching what is now North Dakota by the eighteenth century.

c. 1450 The Iroquois League or Iroquois Confederacy is founded in the Northeast (see below).

Hiawatha, the Iroquois folk hero and subject of Henry Wadsworth Longfellow's poem "Song of Hiawatha," was an actual historical figure credited with founding the Iroquois League in about 1450.

THE POST-COLUMBIAN ERA

1492 Christopher Columbus arrives in the Caribbean.

1516 The first major epidemic (smallpox) occurs in the New World. Most likely brought to the Caribbean and Mexico by Spanish travelers, smallpox spread along trade routes and proved devastating to many Indian tribes.

TRIBAL UNIONS AND CONFEDERATIONS

For purposes of mutual defense, social and cultural communion, and the advancement of common interests, Native Americans have for centuries joined together in loose confederations and formal alliances. Peoples of similar custom and language were part of large regional "nations"—such as the Cherokee, Great Sioux, Mohawk, and Navajo—many of which still survive today. On several notable occasions, tribes banded together to form powerful political, military, and economic unions with common leadership and democratic representation. Notable among these were:

Iroquois League: Built on the principle of representation and majority rule, it was formed in the fifteenth century by five Iroquian-speaking tribes in present-day New York State—Seneca, Cayuga, Oneida, Onondaga, and Mohawk—most likely as a defense against neighboring Huron. The Tuscarora became the league's sixth member in the early eighteenth century. The union remained powerful until its collapse during the American Revolution.

Powhatan Confederacy: Under the leadership of Chief POWHATAN, the father of POCAHONTAS and known for his relationship with Capt. John Smith, the confederacy included more than thirty tribes near the Pamunkey River, in what is now Virginia, during the early seventeenth century.

Five Civilized Tribes: Formed in 1859 in the Indian Territory of Oklahoma, it comprised the Iroquian-speaking Cherokee and the Muskogean-speaking Chickasaw, Choctaw, Creek, and Seminole. Removed from their homelands east of the Mississippi in 1830, they organized autonomous states modeled after the U.S. government and followed many of the customs and practices of neighboring whites.

Indian Peoples at the Time of Early European Settlement

1539 Spanish explorer Hernando de Soto lands in Florida and travels upward through the South, conquering many Indian communities along the way. In Alabama, ancestors of the modern Chickasaws hold him off but are weakened by the epidemic diseases his army introduces.

THE SEVENTEENTH AND EIGHTEENTH CENTURIES: COLONIZATION

Claims and colonization by Europeans initiated three centuries of warfare. For a list of major Indian–white wars, see p. 152.

1607 Jamestown is founded in Virginia by the British. Its leader, John Smith, is captured by the Powhatan Confederacy and, according to legend, saved by POCAHONTAS.

MAJOR INDIAN EPIDEMICS, 1516–1902

Inhabitants of the Western Hemisphere had no exposure to, and therefore no natural immunity to, the diseases Europeans brought with them. Measles and smallpox became plagues that wiped out entire peoples.

1516 The first major smallpox epidemic is introduced when a shipload of colonists carry it to Hispaniola with devastating results. From there it spreads throughout the Caribbean and travels up and down North and South America along trade routes. Pizarro writes that it kills half the Indians it touches.

1531 Measles sweeps through the Southwest.

1545 Bubonic plague surfaces in the Southwest.

1592 Smallpox is found throughout North America east of the Mississippi and in the Southwest.

1602 Smallpox strikes the Southwest.

1615–1660 Several outbreaks of smallpox devastate East Coast and Great Lakes tribes.

1637 Scarlet fever sweeps through Indian communities.

c. 1738 White slave traders spread smallpox to Cherokees in Georgia.

1782–1783 Smallpox introduced into the Northwest.

1837 Smallpox among the Mandans reduces a people who had numbered about 9,000 in 1750 to fewer than 200.

1837–1870 Four major smallpox epidemics devastate western Indian nations.

1847 An outbreak of measles, along with other factors, develops into the Cayuse War of 1847–1850 in the Williamette Valley in Oregon Territory.

1902 The Eskimo population of Southhampton Island in the Hudson Bay is wiped out by typhus.

1620 Pilgrims landing at Plymouth, Massachusetts, are helped by Wampanoag leader Massasoit and Squanto, a Patuxet.

1622 An uprising by the Powhatan Confederacy nearly wipes out the Jamestown settlement, killing some 350 settlers, and initiating a decade of hostilities. By 1645, Indian resistance ends.

1626 Peter Minuit buys Manhattan Island from the Canarsie Indians for 60 guilders (the fabled $24); although that amount was then equal to several thousand dollars, the island was still dramatically underpriced.

1636–1637 The Pequots are wiped out in the Pequot War. This campaign, deliberately waged by the Puritans, occurred along the Thames River in southeastern Connecticut.

1642–1653 The Hurons and Iroquois clash over the fur trade in a war instigated—and supplied—by the Dutch and the French. The defeated Huron withdraw west, to Michigan, Wisconsin, and western Ontario while the victorious Iroquois sign a peace treaty with the French.

1675–1676 King Philip's War pits the New England colonists against the Wampanoags, Narragansetts, and Nipmucks; it is the last major Indian–white war in New England and drives the Indians out of the region, with the exception of Maine.

1676 In Bacon's Rebellion near Jamestown, Virginia, Nathaniel Bacon and a band of vigilante followers eradicate the Pamunkey Indians.

Mid to late 1600s Intermittent warfare on the frontier continues between the Dutch and the Indians and the British and the Indians.

1680 New Mexican Pueblos rebel against the Spanish in the Southwest and drive them out for twelve years. In 1692, the Spanish reconquest of New Mexico ends with the reoccupation of Santa Fe.

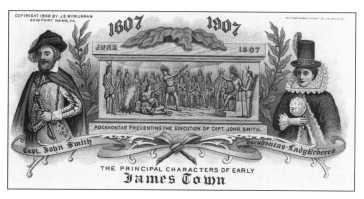

1689–1748 Native Americans play a key role in three wars involving France, Spain, and Britain: King William's War (1689–1697), Queen Anne's War (1702–1713), and King George's War (1744–1748). Various Indian nations ally with either the French or the English. For example, the Iroquois firmly ally themselves with the British against the French, and the Abnaki fight alongside the French in Maine in 1692.

This 1906 postcard illustrates the legendary story of Pocahontas saving Capt. John Smith, while also depicting them both in Elizabethan dress.

c. 1700 The Mississippi Culture fades.

1700s During the golden age of Mandan Culture, the Mandan bands occupy nine villages and maintain a population of approximately 3,500 along the Missouri River in North Dakota.

1711–1713 Following a massacre by Tuscaroras in Carolina, white settlers ally with other tribes. After a defeat in which more than 300 Tuscarora warriors are killed, the tribe's survivors flee north, where they join the Iroquois Confederation.

1712–1737 The French and the Fox tribe in Wisconsin and Illinois fight repeatedly, and the Foxes are almost annihilated. The remnant joins the Sacs, their traditional enemy.

1715–1716 Enraged by the destruction of the Tuscaroras, Yamasee kill more than 200 settlers in South Carolina before the colonists, aided by the Cherokees, defeat them. The Yamasees retreat into Georgia and Florida, where they ally with the Spanish against the English.

Northwest Indians called eulachon fish "candlefish" because the fish's oil could be used as a torch. Because of their high fat content, the dried fish could burn for hours.

1720–1763 The French wage unrelenting war on the Chickasaws using French troops and the Choctaws; lack of coordination between the French and their Indian allies and vagaries of weather are exploited by the Chickasaws so that when the French leave the Mississippi valley at the end of the French and Indian War the Chickasaws remain unconquered.

1723 The first permanent school for Indians is built by colonists in Williamsburg, Virginia.

1729 The Natchez rebel against the French in the Southeast. At first the Natchez enjoy success, but by 1731 they are almost decimated.

1754–1763 During the French and Indian War, several Indian Nations ally with the French, who lose and then cede Canada and Indian lands around the Great Lakes to the British.

INDIAN RELIGION

While there are a number of stereotypes concerning Native American spirituality, the reality is that the diversity and plurality of Indian religions makes it difficult to generalize. Furthermore, as with any other culture, Native religions have continued to evolve and change over time. Just as American Christianity has changed significantly over the last 500 years, so, too, have numerous Native religions.

Before the arrival of Europeans, there were many different religions and belief systems. Some, like the people of the lower Mississippi River valley, developed highly organized religious systems, not unlike the Vatican in terms of hierarchy. Highly stratified societies featured a priestly class at the top, headed by a king or queen who was considered to be a divine entity. Others, like many people in the central and northern plains, were very decentralized and personal in their spirituality. Medicine men offered spiritual counseling and guidance, as well as medical services, but their influence did not have the arbitrary power that accompanies offices in most Western-style institutions. Rather, practices such as prayers and vision quests were personal endeavors. Other ceremonies that featured numerous participants (such as the sweat lodge), or even the entire nation (the annual Sun Dance) conformed to a proscribed set of rituals and customs in terms of organization and other logistical elements. But even within these ceremonies, a premium was placed on the individual religious experiences of given participants. The Pueblos of the Southwest featured strong theocracies in which religious institutions were intimately tied to the national government. Living in the close quarters of their villages, codes of conduct and political procedure were strictly enforced by holders of religious offices.

Almost immediately, Spanish (and to a lesser extent French and English) colonizers began to aggressively proselytize to Native peoples, often resorting to coercive and even violent methods to convert them. During the nineteenth century and early twentieth centuries, the United States was eager but often unfocused in its attempts to convert Indians. Consequently, in addition to the many adherents of various indigenous religions, there are also a number of Native people today who belong to one of many Christian denominations.

There have also been several important pan-Indian religious movements. Incorporating various Native religions, and occasionally even elements of Christianity, these international Native religious movements began gaining momentum as early as the eighteenth century. A number of pan-Indian religions are still thriving today, including the Longhouse Religion (founded by Handsome Lake of the Senecas at the beginning of the nineteenth century), the Ghost Dance Religion (founded by Wovoka of the Paiutes in the late nineteenth century, see p. 29), and the Native American Church, which combines aspects of Christianity with the traditional southwestern use of peyote as a sacrament.

1759–1761 Cherokee War in the southern Appalachian highlands results in Cherokee surrender of land in the Carolinas and Virginia.

1763 Under PONTIAC, the Potawatomis and Ottawas organize a revolt over the seizure of Indian lands by the British in the aftermath of the French and Indian War. In response, the British issue the Proclamation of 1763, which forbids white settlement west of the Appalachians to reserve the area for Indian nations.

1768 The Iroquois relinquish their lands under the Treaty of Fort Stanwix, and under the Treaty of Hard Labor, the war-weary Cherokees do the same.

1774 Dunmore's War, led by Virginia governor John Murray, earl of Dunmore, forces the Shawnees to cede more of their land in the Ohio valley.

1776–1783 During the American Revolution, many Indians fight on the side of the British. When the war ends, the British abandon their Indian allies, allowing the colonists to claim victory over the Native American population as well as the British.

1777–1779 In the Midwest, Gen. George Rogers Clark mounts a series of important campaigns in which he captures Vincennes, a strategic British fort in southern Indiana, then marches northwest to destroy the Shawnees and Delawares.

1790 Little Turtle's War, led by Miami chief LITTLE TURTLE, scuttles the forces of Gen. Josiah Harmar along the Maumee River in Indiana.

1791 LITTLE TURTLE defeats Arthur St. Clair's forces along the Wabash River in Indiana.

1794 Anthony Wayne gets revenge for St. Clair's defeat at the Battle of Fallen Timber, near the western shore of Lake Erie.

1795 In the Treaty of Greenville, Miamis cede most of Ohio (Old Northwest Territory).

THE NINETEENTH CENTURY: RESISTANCE AND DISPLACEMENT

1808 Shawnee chief TECUMSEH forms a confederacy to defend Indian lands in the Old Northwest.

1809 In the Treaty of Fort Wayne, the Delawares and Potawatomis cede lands in Indiana.

Inuits often put small boots made of sealskin on their huskies to protect the dogs' paws from being cut by the sharp arctic ice.

HORSES

Horses were native to North America but had disappeared by about 800 B.C. and were unknown to the Indians when the Spanish arrived. The Indians of Mexico found them terrifying, and they no doubt contributed to the general impression that the Spanish were invincible. By 1700, horses were roaming wild in the Southwest, and they thrived on the grasslands of the plains. Indians quickly adopted the horse, which enabled them to hunt buffalo more efficiently. As Indian peoples were pushed onto the plains by white settlements in the East, they developed a distinctive nomadic culture. Meanwhile, Spanish explorers and missionaries had introduced horses into Florida as well, and horseback riding spread among tribes north into California.

1811 The Battle of Tippecanoe in northwestern Indiana dashes TECUMSEH's hopes for a confederacy.

1812–1815 During the War of 1812, between the British and the Americans, Indians side mostly with the British. TECUMSEH dies at the Battle of the Thames (River), east of Detroit in Ontario, while providing cover for retreating British forces.

1814 Creek resistance in the South is crushed by Andrew Jackson at the Battle of Horseshoe Bend in Alabama.

1815 Indian Country is reestablished west of Missouri and Arkansas, on land regarded as nonarable by whites. President James Madison proposes to relocate all the eastern tribes to the West.

1817–1818 In the first Seminole War, Andrew Jackson captures Pensacola but fails to subdue the Seminoles in Spanish Florida. The United States will install military bases in Pensacola in 1821 that are used during later conflicts with the Seminoles.

1820s The government begins to move tribes into Indian Country, defined as the lands west of the Mississippi River.

1824 The Bureau of Indian Affairs is established in the War Department.

1830 The Indian Removal Act provides for moving all Indians to lands west of the Mississippi River.

1831 The Supreme Court rules that the Cherokee Nation is subject to federal but not state law. Andrew Jackson ignores the ruling and orders the army to remove the Cherokees, Chickasaws, Choctaws, Creeks, and Seminoles. The Choctaws are the first to be moved west of the Mississippi River.

1832 In Black Hawk's War, Sacs and Foxes are decimated defending the Mississippi River Valley in present-day Illinois and Wisconsin.

1834 The federal government formally sets aside land, in present-day Oklahoma, Kansas, and Nebraska, as Indian Territory.

1835–1842 In the second Seminole War, the United States begins moving Seminoles out of Florida to the West.

1836 Creeks are forcibly removed from their southeastern homeland to lands west of the Mississippi River; about 3,500 of the 15,000 tribal members perish.

1838 The Trail of Tears: 16,000 Cherokees are forcibly removed from

---

Captured during King Philip's War, Mary Rowlandson spent three months with the Wampanoag. Released for a ransom of £20, she wrote an account of her captivity that became an instant best-seller in England and the colonies.

Scalping was not a custom native to the Indians. It was an Anglo-Saxon practice brought to America by the Dutch and English in the seventeenth century.

their Georgia land of several centuries and escorted by 7,000 U.S. Army soldiers to a reservation in Oklahoma. En route, about one-quarter of the Cherokees die.

1847 At Taos, Pueblo people resist the American occupation of New Mexico during the Mexican War.

1851 The Sioux hand over large tracts of land on the Great Plains for resettlement by whites.

1854 The U.S. government abolishes about half of Indian Territory to make room for the transcontinental railroad and to accommodate the influx of white settlers to lands west of the Mississippi River.

1855–1858 The Third Seminole War virtually destroys what remains of the tribe.

1855–1858 In the Pacific coast wars (Rogue River War, 1855–1856; Yakima War, 1855–1856; and Spokane War, 1858), the U.S. Army devastates the Indian population in this region and forces the survivors onto reservations.

1861–1865 During the Civil War, the few Indians who do fight side with the Confederacy while taking advantage of the diminished regular forces to continue ongoing skirmishes with southern and northern whites.

1862 The Homestead Act, giving 160 acres of public domain land free to any settler who resides on it for five years, further decimates Indian Territory. The act accelerates white settlement of the West.

1864 The Long Walk, which is actually several walks, takes place after Christopher "Kit" Carson employs a scorched-earth offensive against the Navajos to force them to move 300 miles (480 km) across New Mexico. In all, between 5,000 and 8,000 Navajos are relocated.

In the Sand Creek Massacre of BLACK KETTLE's Cheyennes, volunteer forces kill 28 men and 102 women and children who have gathered near a white fort to sue for peace. Fewer men than women and children are killed because they are hunting at the time of attack.

1865–1868 Red Cloud's War (also called the Sioux War) forces the U.S. Army to abandon the Bozeman Trail in Montana, the Sioux's buffalo-hunting ground.

1867 The Treaty of Medicine Lodge compels more than 100,000 Apaches, Arapahos, Bannocks, Cheyennes, Kiowas, Navajos, Shoshones, and Sioux to accept reservation status in Indian Territory and to agree to relinquish the territory outside of the reservations.

The Choctaw Indian Nation held slaves and signed a treaty of alliance with the Confederacy in 1861.

"Everything the Indian does is in a circle, and that is because the power of the world always works in circles, and everything tries to be round."

—*BLACK ELK SPEAKS,* 1932

The World Eskimo-Indian Olympics is held every year, featuring contests such as the Ear Pull, where two contestants loop twine around each other's ears and compete in a tug-of-war; and the Knuckle Hop, where participants jump forward in the push-up position with their weight landing on their knuckles and the tips of their toes.

1868 The Fourteenth Amendment defines citizenship, stating that "Indians not taxed" are not to be included in population counts for purposes of representation.

1871 The Indian Appropriation Act decrees that Indian tribes no longer enjoy the status of separate nations. The federal government will no longer negotiate treaties with individual tribes.

1872 Apache chief COCHISE, after eleven years' resistance, agrees to live on a reservation in Arizona that includes part of his tribe's ancestral land. After his death in 1874, his tribe is removed.

1872–1873 The Modocs, a northern California tribe, are forced onto land that is not part of their ancestral heritage.

1874 The Battle at Palo Duro Canyon is a U.S. Army victory over the Indians that includes the slaughter of 1,000 Indian ponies.

1874–1875 The Red River War is fought. Following a decade in which Arapahos, Cheyennes, Comanches, and Kiowas successfully wage guerrilla warfare against the U.S. Army, the tribes are conquered during a year of all-out warfare, and forced onto reservations.

1876–1881 In the Sioux War, a coalition of Plains Indians led by CRAZY HORSE and SITTING BULL fights the U.S. Army. An important early Indian victory is the defeat of General George Armstrong Custer's forces at Little Bighorn, known as Custer's Last Stand. By 1877 the Plains Indians are driven into the Dakota Territory, and in 1881 the surrender of Sitting Bull ends the conflict.

1877 In the flight of the Nez Perce, CHIEF JOSEPH leads the U.S. Army on a 1,400-mile (2,250-km) chase under war conditions through Idaho, Wyoming, and Montana to avoid being settled on a reservation. They are finally herded onto a desert reservation in Indian Territory.

1878–1879 In the Bannock-Paiute Uprising in Idaho, Bannocks, Paiutes, Sheepeaters, and Utes resist—in vain—resettlement onto reservations.

1881–1886 Fought in New Mexico and Arizona, Geronimo's Resistance ends with the surrender of Apache leader GERONIMO and effectively terminating Indian–white strife in the Southwest.

1887 The Dawes Severalty Act (General Allotment Act) imposes a system of individual—as opposed to tribal—land ownership on Indians, a serious blow to tribal sovereignty.

THE GREAT BUFFALO SLAUGHTER

With the introduction of the horse, some woodlands tribes moved to the Great Plains, where the buffalo became the mainstay of their new culture as well as their primary means of survival. Buffalo hides were used to make clothing, tepees, furniture, moccasins, religious regalia, and drums. Hoofs were used ceremonially and to make implements, utensils, and glue. The bladder served as a storage pouch. Meat was used for food and in ceremonies. Fat and marrow produced food, paint, and cosmetics. Fur was used ceremonially and to make rope. Buffalo dung provided fuel.

White settlers and adventurers were far less discriminate in their slaughter of the buffalo. While some was for profit (hides and tongue), often it was for sheer fun. Where an estimated 70 million buffalo once roamed, by 1840, only 40 million remained. Between 1872 and 1874, 3.7 million buffalo were destroyed. By 1875, 1 million survived, and a mere decade later that population was reduced to 20,000. By 1895, there were fewer than 1,000 buffalo in North America.

In the late 1880s, a few states passed laws to protect the buffalo, but a more typical attitude was that of Gen. Philip Sheridan, who wrote: "Let them kill, skin, and sell until the buffalo is destroyed…it is the only way to bring lasting peace and allow civilization to advance." Not until the 1970s did pressure from environmentalists lead to serious protection of the animal, whose numbers today hover around 50,000.

1890 In what is now South Dakota, the Battle of Wounded Knee, the last great Indian defeat, marks the end of centuries of Indian–white warfare over lands (see p. 29).

1891 By treaty, effective 1893, the rights of Indians in the Cherokee Outlet are terminated and this area is added to Oklahoma territory.

1898 The Curtis Act overrides treaties promising southeastern tribes that their western lands will never be included in any state or territory without their approval.

THE TWENTIETH CENTURY: THE CONTEMPORARY ERA

1906 The federal government takes the Blue Lake region of New Mexico, an area sacred to Pueblos, to create a national park.

1907 Indian Territory is eliminated when Oklahoma achieves statehood.

1909 The Enlarged Homestead Act increases to 320 acres, the size of a homestead in certain states, encouraging white landholding in areas that have been home to two-thirds of all Indians since 1865.

1913 The Indian head nickel is produced in tribute to the "vanishing red man."

1917–1918 During World War I, although not subject to the draft, many Indians volunteer.

George Armstrong Custer carried out his fatal march on Little Bighorn in June 1876 against the orders of his superior officer. Custer had graduated last in his class at West Point in 1861 and had been court-martialed in 1867 for disobeying orders.

CHIEF JOSEPH: "I WILL FIGHT NO MORE FOREVER"

As leader of the peaceful Nez Perce tribe in the Pacific Northwest, CHIEF JOSEPH mounted a successful defense against attacking U.S. Army forces in 1877 and then led his people on a 1,400-mile (2,250-km) retreat over the mountains toward Canada. U.S. troops pursued the band of 600 for more than two months and finally overtook them near the Canadian border on September 30. Cold, starving, and now trapped, the Nez Perce were forced to surrender. Chief Joseph's speech is remembered for its moving evocation of the suffering visited upon the American Indian during the displacements of the nineteenth century:

A year before his death, Chief Joseph had this picture taken by famed Native American photographer Edward Curtis.

I am tired of fighting. Our chiefs are killed. Looking Glass is dead. Too-hul-hul is dead. The old men are all dead. It is the young men who say yes or no. He who led on the young men is dead. It is cold and we have no blankets. The little children are freezing to death. My people, some of them, have run away to the hills, and have no blankets, no food; no one knows where they are— perhaps freezing to death. I want to have time to look for my children and see how many of them I can find. Maybe I shall find them among the dead. Hear me, my chiefs. I am tired; my heart is sick and sad. From where the sun now stands I will fight no more forever.

"The tepee is always much better to live in: always clean, warm in winter, cool in summer, easy to move."

—FLYING HAWK
(1852–1931)

1921 The Snyder Act makes the Department of the Interior responsible for Indian education, and medical and social services.

1924 The Citizenship Act makes all Indians citizens without impairing their status as tribal members. Nevertheless, few Indians are permitted to vote before the 1960s.

1930 The Northern Cheyenne Reservation becomes the last communally assigned tract of Indian land.

1933 John Collier becomes head of the Bureau of Indian Affairs and begins to clean up after years of corruption. He halts the sale of Indian lands, gets emergency work for 77,000 Indians under the Civilian Conservation Corps, and obtains millions of dollars to finance reservation schools.

1934 The Indian Reorganization Act (Wheeler-Howard Act), pushed by John Collier, provides funds to help rebuild Indian culture and political life. Land is returned to tribal ownership.

1941–1945 During World War II Native Americans are allowed to register for the draft for the first time, and more than 25,000 enlist.

1942 Navajo Indians created an unbreakable military code, used extensively during battles in the Pacific, such as Guadalcanal and Iwo Jima. The Navajo Code Talkers, as they became known, based the code on their native Navajo tongue, an unwritten and extremely difficult language.

1946 The Indian Claims Commission is established to settle land disputes between the U.S. government and Indian nations.

1950 The Utes are compensated $31 million for tribal lands taken from them in Colorado and Utah between 1891 and 1938.

1953 House Concurrent Resolution No. 108 allows Congress to terminate by legislative fiat any tribe as a political unit.

1954–1962 Congress passes twelve termination bills, eliminating more than sixty tribes, all in the West.

1955 The Public Health Service takes over the administration of Indian health programs and subsequently establishes the Indian Health Service. Despite great improvements, Indians today have the highest mortality rates of any ethnic group.

1961 The republication of the 1932 book *Black Elk Speaks* sparks intense interest in Indian literature.

1964 The Civil Rights Act restores tribal law to reservations, and President Lyndon B. Johnson pledges to end paternalism.
    The first conference on Indian poverty is held in Washington, D.C.
    An "Indian desk" is established at the Office of Economic Opportunity.

1968 American Indian Movement (AIM), an organization dedicated to protecting treaty rights, encouraging self-determination, and preserving traditional Native American languages, culture, and spirituality, is founded in Minneapolis.

1969 Militants occupy the federal penitentiary on Alcatraz Island in San Francisco, demanding government funds for a cultural center and a university.
    VINE DELORIA's book *Custer Died for Your Sins* rekindles interest in Indian history, told from the Indians' point of view.

1970 The federal government restores 48,000 acres of New Mexico's Blue Lake region to the Taos Pueblos.
    Dee Brown writes *Bury My Heart at Wounded Knee*, revealing that the historic battle was in fact an Indian massacre.
    The Native American Rights Fund (NARF) is established, eventually winning the return of lands for the Passamaquoddies and Penobscots of Maine, attempting to strengthen the regulations regarding remains and ceremonial objects, and offering assistance to unrecognized tribal entities.

1972 AIM and other Indian activists stage a sit-in at the Bureau of Indian Affairs in Washington, D.C., following a cross-country caravan called the Trail of Broken Treaties.

The Navajo Code Talkers created a word for America which sounds like "Ne-He-Mah" and literally means "Our Mother." It was among the 200 words in the Navajo code used during World War II. Others included *submarine* which sounds like "Besh-Lo" and translates to "iron fish," and *sniper* which sounds like "Oh-Behi" and literally translates to "pick 'em off."

INDIAN MUSIC

The music of Native America is as old and diverse as the many peoples, tribes, and nations that occupied the vast spaces of North America. Common to most native cultures was a belief that musical instruments were living beings, to be used for mediating the human and spiritual realms. Most Native American instruments fell into the percussion family—especially drums and rattles—and were used to create a beat for ritual dancing and conjure spirits. Small percussion instruments were often part of the dance costume worn around the wrists, arms, calves, and ankles. Other common instruments included various kinds of whistles and flutes, made from carved wood, animal shells, reeds, gourds, and rawhide.

Traditional native music was predominantly vocal with percussion accompaniment. Songs were rarely composed or written down, but sprung spontaneously from spiritual inspiration. Those with words were often historical or mythological narratives, drawn from oral tradition. There were also work songs, lullabies, animal tributes, dance songs, and ceremonial songs for war, marriage, and other tribal events. Individual nations and tribes had distinctive musical and dance repertoires which evolved, in part, through contact with neighboring peoples. Music remains an integral part of spiritual and communal life among modern Native Americans.

1973 AIM activists occupy Wounded Knee, South Dakota, demanding that the federal government honor treaties. The FBI, under the direction of J. Edgar Hoover, attacks, and two Indians and one federal marshal are killed.

1978 Passamaquoddy and Penobscot Indians become the first tribes to make a major land claim against the United States when they demand the return of two-thirds of the state of Maine. A tentative settlement is worked out in which they abandon their land claims in return for $27 million in a federal trust and $54.4 million in land acquisitions funds.

Members of a Sioux tribe, some wearing traditional Native American dress, protest on Alcatraz Island in San Francisco.

1979 Seminoles start bingo games, beginning the modern era of gambling on the reservations.

1982 President Ronald Reagan vetoes Congress's water-rights settlement of $112 million to the Papagos. The federal government eventually pays them $40 million.

1988 Congress passes the Indian Gaming Regulatory Act, ending the debate on the legality of gambling on the reservations. The law establishes the National Indian Gaming Commission with oversight responsibilities.

1992 *Time* magazine reveals that 140 tribes operate more than 150 casinos. Revenues in 1993 are in excess of $3.2 billion.

THE WOUNDED KNEE MASSACRE: SITTING BULL AND THE GHOST DANCE

A pan-Indian religious movement that swept the Great Plains in the 1880s and involved a ritual called the Ghost Dance may have started several decades earlier among the Nevada Paiutes. A shaman named Tavibo predicted the coming of a messianic prophet who would help the Indians regain their lost world and cause white people to vanish. Another version of the legend, related by the Pacific Northwest Indians, foretold a return to righteous ways—that is, a return to life as it was before the arrival of the whites. In 1899, the prophecies were tied to the dance when the Paiute prophet Wovoka, ill with scarlet fever, supposedly died and returned to life. He said the Creator had given him a ritual—the Ghost Dance— to perform with his people. Wovoka's prophecies and the Ghost Dance spread rapidly among the Arapahos, northern Cheyennes, and Sioux, indeed through most of the western tribes.

Sitting Bull, a Lakota Sioux holy man and leader, organized resistance movements and fought against the U.S. military at such battles as Little Bighorn.

happen should Sitting Bull openly endorse the Ghost Dance, went to his home at Standing Rock, North Dakota. They tried to arrest him, and in the argument that followed, two Indian policemen shot and killed Sitting Bull.

In a last sad chapter to the life of this great Indian leader, the Miniconjou people, fearing more armed conflict, fled. The army gave chase, and on December 28, 1890, the starving, horseless, and weaponless Indians were surrounded and taken to Wounded Knee, now in South Dakota. The next morning the troops began disarming the Indians. In the confusion a gun fired, and jittery troops fired on the Indian men, women, and children. Many were wearing white shirts that bore the symbols of their movement— an eagle, a buffalo, and the morning star—which they believed would protect them from the soldiers' bullets. More than 200 Indians died; perhaps as many as 300. Many wounded crawled away, hid in the snow, and died of their wounds in the bitter cold. Four men and forty-seven women and children were found alive or wounded after the shooting stopped and were taken to Pine Ridge.

The white settlers on the Great Plains, who were themselves familiar with messianic visions after several decades of fierce Indian–white warfare, feared any teaching that forecast their demise. Their fears flourished in proportion to the Ghost Dance's growing popularity among the Indians. Armed conflicts often broke out between whites and Native Americans wherever the dance was to be performed, and these tensions culminated in the events at Wounded Knee in 1890.

The Miniconjous of the Lakota Sioux at Pine Ridge, South Dakota, led by SITTING BULL, were planning to perform the Ghost Dance. Federal agents, fearful of the Ghost Dance and of Sitting Bull and of what might

Sitting Bull's death and the massacre at Wounded Knee marked the end of the Sioux–white wars and the culture of the Plains Indians that Sitting Bull had hoped to preserve. The Ghost Dance was rarely performed after Wounded Knee, although some Plains Indians, notably the Pawnees, have incorporated parts of the dance, such as the hand game, into other dances that survive today.

Native Americans today suffer the highest rates of poverty, unemployment, disease, and suicide of any ethnic group in America. They are more than twice as likely than any other people to be the victims of violent crime.

Timeline, *cont.*

1994 President Bill Clinton, in recognition of Indians' newfound economic and political power, meets with representatives from 500 Indian tribes to pledge the federal government's support of their culture.

The first National Summit on Indian Health Care takes place.

The Smithsonian National Museum of the American Indian opens in New York City; a permanent site is expected to open in Washington, D.C., in 2003.

1995 Attorney General Janet Reno establishes the Office of Tribal Justice to improve the responsiveness of the Department of Justice to federally recognized Indian tribes.

1996 Federal funding for Indian programs is cut by nearly 10 percent, as the budget of the Bureau of Indian Affairs is slashed by $160 million.

2000 The federal government returns 84,000 acres in northern Utah that it took from the Utes in 1916. It is the largest turnover of public land to American Indians in the continental United States in more than a century.

RESERVATIONS: WHAT THEY ARE AND HOW THEY WORK

Reservation lands set aside for the use of Native Americans at present occupy approximately 50 million acres and take several forms. The quality of the land dedicated to Indian use varies widely, but much of it is fairly remote and otherwise undesirable. Much of the reservation land in the West is nonarable, for example, a factor that has obviously contributed to the persistent poverty that has plagued reservation Indians for two centuries. Indians in the Southwest have been the most successful at continuing to live on land that they consider theirs. The Shinnecocks of Long Island, New York, who inhabit some of the country's richest real estate, are a notable exception.

Reservations, which were first established in the mid-seventeenth century as whites began to take away Indian lands to use for their own purposes, have been created in three different categories: those established by an act of Congress, purchase, or treaty before 1871, those created after 1871, and those created by Executive Order. In the latter instance, for example, the Reno tribe of Nevada bought land for its own colony.

The date establishing a reservation usually refers to when the U.S. government recognized the land as dedicated to Indian use rather than when the Indians began to live on it. Although the U.S. government officially recognized the Pueblo reservation in New Mexico in 1864, for example, Pueblos have lived on this land for hundreds of years.

Initially, reservations were established to "missionize" Indians, that is, to convert them to Christianity and to get them to conform to European ideas of civilization. This was the purpose of the very first reservation, established by the Puritans in 1638 for the Quinnipiacs in New Haven, Connecticut. Since then, they have variously been used to segregate Indians, assimilate them, destroy their culture, preserve their culture, and since the 1970s, to accord tribal Indians a special status. In the 1980s, a series of Supreme Court decisions greatly expanded the rights of reservation tribes by establishing their right to control gaming on Indian lands, an activity that is reducing poverty among many tribes and bringing them wealth. Today Indian tribes have jurisdiction on reservation lands and are not usually subject to state laws or taxes (although individual Indians may be).

As of 2000, there were 556 federally "identified areas," including reservations under Indian jurisdiction and trust lands. Their total area exceeded 56 million acres, home to about one-third of the nation's total Indian population.

INDIAN CULTURE AREAS

Indian cultures have been divided into geographic regions, each exhibiting several common characteristics. Apart from geography, a culture often (but not always) shared tribes, languages, modes of living, and political organization.

THE NORTHEAST CULTURE AREA

Area: Atlantic Ocean to the Mississippi River, uppermost region of the northeast Unites States south to the Tidewater region of Virginia and North Carolina.
Tribes: Descendants of mound builders. Iroquois-speaking: Cayuga, Huron, Mohawk, Oneida, Onondaga, Seneca, Tuscarora, Tobacco. Algonquian-speaking: Delaware, Fox, Illinois, Kickapoo, Mahican, Massachuset, Menominee, Miami, Mohegan, Ottowa, Pequot, Potawatomi, Sauk, Shawnee, Shinnecock, Wampanoag.
Languages: Iroquoian and Algonquian dialects.
Mode of living: Foraging and some horticulture. Small, semisedentary villages. Communal longhouses, gabled or vaulted log-frame structures are unique to the Iroquois. Algonquins live in wigwams; are among the first Indians to be destroyed after contact with the whites.
Political organization: Strong familial and tribal ties; chiefs are leaders. In the mid-fifteenth century the Iroquois organize into a political, intertribal league, whose political symbol is the communal longhouse. Algonquins were less politically organized.
Unusual feature: The Iroquois League is believed by some historians to have been at least a partial model for the federalist form of government of the United States.

THE SOUTHEAST CULTURE AREA

Area: Tidewater region to the Gulf of Mexico; Atlantic Ocean to the Trinity River in Texas, extending into parts of Oklahoma, Arkansas, Missouri, Kentucky, Virginia, and North Carolina.
Tribes: Alabama, Atakapa, Biloxi, Caddo, Cherokee, Chickasaw, Chitimacha, Choctaw, Creek, Natchez, Quapaw, Seminole, Timucua, and Tunica.
Languages: Predominantly Muskogean, Sioux, Iroquoian, Algonquian, and Caddoan; also isolated languages such as Timucuan, Atakapan, Natchez, Chitimacha.
Mode of living: Farming, supplemented with hunting, gathering, and fishing. Wattle-and-daub housing; also

chickees—raised, thatched-roof platform structures unique to the Seminoles.
Political organization: Chiefs and priests rule large groups and villages.
Unusual feature: Considered among the most advanced culturally of any Amerindian group outside Mesoamerica. Cherokees, Choctaws, Chickasaws, Creeks, and Seminoles were referred to as the Five Civilized Tribes because they readily adopted white culture, including farming of large plantations and slaveholding, and frequently intermarried with whites.

This 1873 Timothy O'Sullivan photograph shows a Navajo camp in New Mexico.

THE GREAT PLAINS CULTURE AREA

Area: Mississippi River valley to the Rocky Mountains; south from the northern U.S. border to southern Texas.
Tribes: Arapaho, Arikara, Blackfeet, Cheyenne, Crow, Hidatsa, Iowa, Kiowa–Apache, Mandan, Osage, Pawnee, Plains Cree, Sarci, Sioux, and Wichita.
Languages: Sioux and Caddoan.
Mode of living: Initially nomadic foraging; then forming seminomadic villages; some farming; mainly bison hunting. Tepee is the primary form of housing.
Political organization: Loosely organized initially; then formed hunter–warrior societies.
Unusual feature: Plains Indians, a familiar image often depicted in Western literature, art, and movies,

INDIAN CULTURE AREAS, cont.

are in large part the result of the European presence in North America. In the 1600s the introduction of horses entirely changed their way of life, converting them from seminomadic gatherers to hunting societies. The need to defend their diminishing lands from whites leads a once-peaceable people to form warrior societies. Another important factor that shapes their cultural landscape is the migration, often forced, of many tribes to the Great Plains, which intermingles their cultures with those already living there. Not surprisingly, the Plains Culture Area is the seedbed for the revivalist movements, such as the Ghost Dance religion, that spring up in the mid-nineteenth century.

THE SOUTHWEST CULTURE AREA

Area: Present-day Arizona, New Mexico, and parts of adjoining states.
Tribes: Apache, Havasupai, Seri, Walapai, Yavapai, all of whom are foragers. Cocopa, Hopi, Laguna, Mojave, Navajo, Opata, Papago, Pima, Zuni, all of whom are horticultural.
Languages: Athapaskan family.
Mode of living: Foraging, horticulture. Semisedentary village dwellers. Primary forms of housing are hogans, conical log-and-stick-framed, mud-covered structures, tepees, and pueblos, unique forms of architecture composed of multistoried, flat-roofed, terraced adobe or stone dwellings.
Political organization: Religious organizations dominate social life, which is organized around an active annual ceremonial cycle. Pueblos contain subterranean holy rooms or passageways called kivas, which may be routes to the spirit world. Later some warrior societies, largely defensive, formed.

THE GREAT BASIN CULTURE AREA

Area: Most of Utah and Nevada, parts of Oregon, Colorado, Wyoming, Idaho, and the eastern border of California.
Tribes: Comanche, Klamath, Paiute, Panamint, Shoshone, Ute, and Washo.
Languages: Uto-Aztecan family except for the Washo, who spoke a Hokan dialect.
Mode of living: A harsh environment condemns these Native Americans to a life of gathering and foraging; they are sometimes called "diggers." Some hunting of

small game. Wickiups, domed huts covered with reeds, grasses, or brush, are their homes.
Political organization: Typically one-family units. Leadership is minimal and informal, usually falling to the male elder. Territories are large—50 square miles (130 sq km) to the individual—so there is little warfare. Occasional cooperation for a group hunt.

THE CALIFORNIA CULTURE AREA

Area: Present-day California, including Baja but exclusive of the state's eastern border region.
Tribes: Chumash, Costano, Maidu, Miwok, Modoc, Patwin, Pomo, Salinan, Wintun, Yana, Yokuts, and Yuki.
Languages: More than 200 independent dialects. Hokan dominates in the northern region, Penutium in the middle, and Shoshonean in the south.
Mode of living: Semisedentary, foraging and fishing. Housing is plankhouses, made of hand-split planks over a log frame, and wickiups, domed huts covered with reeds, grass, or brush.
Political organization: Single villages as large as 100 members or more, often composed of related families. Inherited chiefdoms are largely ceremonial.
Unusual feature: Some groups, such as one that becomes known as the Mission Indians, are forced to lead a serflike existence under the hierarchical rule of the Spanish missions between 1769 and the 1860s. Their culture was destroyed in the process.

THE INTERIOR PLATEAU CULTURE AREA

Area: Rocky Mountains to the Cascade Mountains on the west.
Tribes: Cayuse, Chinook, Coeur d'Alene, Flathead, Kootenay, Kutenai, Lillooet, Medoc, Nez Perce, Okanogan, Shuswap, Spokan, Thompson, Umatilla, and Yakima.
Languages: Mosan or Penutian dialects; also the isolated language Kitenai, spoken by the Kutenai; some Algonquian and Athapascan.
Mode of living: Foraging and fishing in riverbank villages. Many of these groups move to the Great Plains after horses are reintroduced. Housing varies from wigwams in Baja to domed, thatched-roof houses in midregion, to plankhouses along the northern coast.
Political organization: Headsmen run the villages.

THE NORTHWEST COAST CULTURE AREA

Area: Pacific Coast in the Northwest; bordered by Columbia and Fraser Rivers on the west.

Tribes: Haida, Hupa, Karok, Kwakiutl, Nootka, Salish, Tlingit, Tsimshian, and Yurok.

Languages: Athapascan, Penutian, Mosan dialects.

Mode of living: Semisedentary; fishing and hunting of small game; live in plankhouses.

Political organization: Independent villages of 100 or more are headed by chiefs. Societies are highly hierarchical with persons ranked by kinship to chiefs. Well-organized, ancestral-based religion involving huge public dramas, spirit quests, and visionary encounters with ancestors.

Unusual features: Noted for totem poles, symbolic representations of ancestors. Wealth is both individual and group and often exhibited at ritualized gift-giving ceremonies called potlatches.

THE SUBARCTIC CULTURE AREA

Area: From interior Alaska across and including most of Canada south of the Arctic coastal plain to Newfoundland.

Tribes: Chilcotin, Chipewyan, Eastern Algonquians, Kaska, Koyukon, Kutchin, Nabesna, Naskapi, Northern Ojibway, Swampy Cree, Tagish, Wood Cree, and Yellowknife.

Languages: Athapaskan, Algonquian, and Beothukan on Newfoundland.

Mode of living: Nomadic, following the seasonal migrations of caribou; lived primarily in log houses, wigwams, and tepees.

Political organizations: Live in small bands bonded by blood and language.

Unusual feature: Very low population in a region marked by long, harsh winters and short, miserable summers with clouds of mosquitoes and black flies.

THE ARCTIC CULTURAL AREA

Area: From coasts of Greenland along Arctic coasts of Canada and Alaska to extreme eastern Siberia.

Tribes: Inuit (Eskimo) and Aleut, who inhabit Aleutian Islands.

Languages: Eskimo-Aleut.

Mode of living: Fishing, hunting of sea mammals and large game such as moose, caribou, and bear. Eskimos live in igloos, conical ice-block dwellings, and Aleuts live in pithouses, subterranean log-frame and mud structures, both unique to the region.

Political organizations: Little political affiliation; a few families or sometimes even one live as a unit, with male elder head of family.

Unusual feature: Remarkably uniform culture.

INDIAN WORDS INTO AMERICAN ENGLISH

Some Indian words that have entered the English language include *tepee, tobacco, toboggan, moccasin, papoose, hominy, wigwam,* and *succotash,* the latter being a vegetarian staple of frontier life.

The biggest single contribution of the Indian languages, though, is the names given to the thousands of lakes, river, towns, counties, and other geographic places in the United States. As early as 1916, one linguistics expert had located 196 Indian place names in California alone, and today there are more than 5,000 just in New England. More than half the states trace their names to Indian origins: Alabama, Alaska, Arizona, Arkansas, Connecticut, Idaho, Illinois, Indiana, Iowa, Kansas, Kentucky, Massachusetts, Michigan, Minnesota, Mississippi, Missouri, Nebraska, North Dakota, Ohio, Oklahoma, Oregon, South Dakota, Tennessee, Texas, Utah, Wisconsin, and Wyoming.

LEGISLATION AFFECTING NATIVE AMERICANS, 1786–PRESENT

1786 An ordinance aims to define the economic relationship between Indians and settlers so that interaction will be as harmonious as possible. Successive acts in 1790, 1793, 1796, 1799, and 1802 continue the authority of the federal government. Shifts in public opinion by 1834 result in a new law, replacing the 1802 act, that provides more protection for persons doing business with Indians than for the Indians or the tribes.

1787 Northwest Ordinance. This states, "the utmost good faith shall always be observed towards the Indians; their lands and property shall never be taken from them without their consent."

1790 Intercourse Act. This multipronged legislation regulates Indian–white trade via licensing arrangements, makes purchases of Indian lands invalid unless approved by the federal government, and punishes whites for crimes in Indian Country.

1802 Intercourse Act. As well as extending the first act, this also establishes Indian Territory and forms the basis for the federal government's "wardship" over Indians until 1834.

1824 The Bureau of Indian Affairs is established by an act of Congress.

1830 Indian Removal Act. This provides for the removal of Indians west of the Mississippi.

1834 Intercourse Act. An expansion of the 1802 act, this redefines the boundaries of Indian Territory and calls for the removal of still more southeastern tribes from their lands to Indian Territory. It also empowers the federal government to intervene in Indian wars.

1868 Fourteenth Amendment. This defines citizenship, stating that "Indians not taxed" are not to be included in population counts for purposes of representation.

1871 Indian Appropriations Act. This terminates the treaty process by forbidding recognition of tribes as nations or independent powers. The federal government will no longer negotiate with Indian tribes before taking over their lands.

1885 Major Crimes Act. Passed in reaction to the *Crow Dog* case, in which the Supreme Court ruled that federal law does not apply to Indian lands unless so specified by Congress, this act affirms that federal law supersedes tribal sovereignty in cases involving specific serious crimes.

1887 General Allotment Act (Dawes Severalty Act). This provides for the dissolution of tribes, changing the status of many Indians from tribal members to individuals by allotting them 160 acres, to be held in trust by the federal government for twenty-five years to prevent exploitation. Although land has been granted to individuals before the act and tribal lands will be allotted after its passage, the act symbolically undermines tribal rights.

1898 Curtis Act. This overrides treaties promising certain tribes that their land will never be included in any state or territory without their approval.

1924 Indian Citizenship Act. All Native Americans born in the United States are defined as U.S. citizens. Few Indians are allowed to vote, but this act is generally accepted as the source of Indian enfranchisement.

1934 Indian Reorganization Act, also known as the Wheeler-Howard Act. This reverses the assimilationist policy that prevailed from the 1800s onward, returns tribal lands, permits the establishment of tribal constitutions, and funds social and welfare programs for Indians.

1946 Indian Claims Commission Act. This authorizes Indians to press claims relating to laws, treaties, Executive Orders, and even "dealings that are not recognized by any existing rule of law or equity" that have harmed them.

1953 Public Law 280. This gives some states jurisdiction over offenses by or against Native Americans.

1954 Termination Resolution. This permits the ending of the tribal status of Indian tribes believed competent to survive without federal assistance. Between 1954 and 1962 Congress passes twelve termination bills affecting more than sixty tribes. Many tribes are left impoverished and have since sued the federal government on grounds that they did not understand what termination involved.

1968 Indian Civil Rights Act. This extends the protections of the Constitution and the Bill of Rights to all Native Americans, including those with tribal status.

1978 American Indian Religious Freedom Act. Establishes measures to protect and preserve traditional religions of Native Americans.

Indian Child Welfare Act. Affirms tribal authority over the adoption of Native American children and regulates placement proceedings. Amended in 1996.

1988 Indian Gaming Regulatory Act. With the idea of promoting economic self-sufficiency, gambling is allowed on Indian land, if not prohibited by federal law. The National Indian Gaming Commission is given the task of overseeing all such activities.

1990 Native American Graves Protection and Repatriation Act. Protects Indian burial sites and human remains, and requires the return of Indian artifacts.

1991 Native American Languages Act. Federal law designed to "preserve, protect, and promote the rights and freedom of Native Americans to use, practice, and develop Native American languages."

1996 Native American Housing Assistance and Self-Determination Act. Creates special public housing programs and federal assistance grants for Indian tribes.

NATIVE AMERICAN RIGHTS TODAY: WHO IS AN INDIAN?

Indian rights today consist of the civil rights Indians assert as individuals as well as the rights they are accorded by virtue of their status as members of a tribe.

• Individual Native Americans have the same rights and obligations as any U.S. citizen. Those who live on reservations are subject to tribal law, which the courts have recognized as being similar to states' powers; that is, reservations are for the most part self-governing, but Congress has the power to regulate them.

• As tribal members, Indians enjoy a special status and are subject to special regulations. Individuals can't, for example, sell tribal lands. They enjoy certain tax exemptions. Tribes have the authority to operate federally funded programs similar to the block grant system, but individual Indians do not automatically qualify for government subsidies.

• Tribal recognition is necessary to claim any subsidy but not to be counted as Indian in the census. Generally, an Indian is a person who is of some degree Indian blood and is recognized as an Indian by a tribe and/or the United States.

INDIAN CONTRIBUTIONS TO AMERICAN CULTURE

Native Americans have rarely been given enough credit for their enormous contribution to American culture. Their inventions and products have influenced what we eat, how we dress, the shapes of our buildings, and even, some historians believe, the federal form of the U.S. government. Among the Indians' most notable contributions are the following (some are from Central and South America):

• **Foods.** Native American staples now eaten around the world include the potato, sweet potato, corn (maize), manioc, tomatoes, beans, artichokes, squash, turkey, maple sugar, vanilla, and cacao (used to make chocolate). Tobacco, not a food, is a New World crop; cotton, so strongly associated with the American South, was also known in Africa and Asia.

• **Medicine.** Indian remedies served as the model for many drugs that are now laboratory made. Since its first publication in 1820, the official United States Pharmacopeia has listed more than 200 drugs used originally by Indians. Coca, for example, was used to make novocaine for pain relief during dental procedures, and quinine was, until the 1940s, the only treatment for malaria. For many years curare was used in surgery to stop breathing long enough to insert rubber tubing into the windpipe to prevent choking, and ipecac is still used as an emetic.

• **Housing and architecture.** Sibley tents, variations on Plains Indians' tepees, have been used by armies around the world. Arctic and Antarctic explorers relied on a unique form of Indian housing known as the igloo. The Pueblo influence on architecture also is seen in many domestic and public buildings in the Southwest. The University of New Mexico, for example, was patterned after Pueblo housing (known as pueblos), and I. M. Pei, the renowned Chinese American architect, acknowledges using the thirteenth-century pueblos at Mesa Verde National Park as inspiration for the laboratories he designed at the National Center for Atmospheric Research in Boulder, Colorado.

• **Lifestyle and recreation.** The hammock, common in many Indian cultures, found its way onto navy and merchant marine ships as a space-saving bed—and into our backyards for relaxation. Toboggans and the sport of lacrosse, both Indian inventions, have been a source of enjoyment for millions.

• **Textiles and clothing.** Parkas, a perennial clothing staple, were first worn by Indians and originally taken up by whites as military garb. Ponchos saw new life during World War I as soldiers' rain gear and have enjoyed spurts of popularity ever since. Indian moccasins have been adapted as house slippers, and people living in snowy climes rely on Indian-originated snowshoes.

• **Federalism.** Some historians believe the United States' unique form of government, in which federal and state governments exist in a delicate balance of power, was inspired by the Iroquois League, an organization of five northeastern tribes.

THE BUREAU OF INDIAN AFFAIRS

The federal government's policies toward Native Americans are one and the same with the policies of the Bureau of Indian Affairs (BIA), the agency that oversees relations between the government and Indians. However misguided they may be judged by today's standards, early administrators believed that their task was to teach Indians English and agriculture and hoped they would become Christians. The reservation system would thus speed them on the way to becoming good citizens. The creation of reservations was largely achieved via a system of treaties negotiated by the BIA, in which Indians often believed they were leasing their land or land rights rather than selling the land outright.

Initially the Bureau of Indian Affairs was located within the Department of War, but in 1849 it was transferred to the newly created Department of the Interior. The BIA was also charged with administering Indian lands, which it did for the most part erratically, restrictively, and in a manner most Indians found denigrating.

During the late nineteenth century a new policy of acculturation was instituted. Its underlying purpose was to reduce the federal government's responsibility for a people it had spent decades making dependent. Reservations were broken up and land allotments turned over to individuals in the belief that land ownership was the basis for the democracy the United States strived to create. Many of the people active in the program were former abolitionists who had used much the same philosophy in that struggle.

With the passage of time, the BIA became one of the more corrupt and graft-ridden agencies of the federal government. Indian agents, on-site representatives of the BIA who were stationed on or near reservations, cheated Indians in countless ways, large and small, including private sales of Indian lands designed primarily for personal gain.

The corruption was not checked until 1933, when John Collier became head of the BIA. For the first time in its history, the bureau was run by someone interested in helping Native Americans. By that time, however, Indians had lost two-thirds of their lands, but Collier set up reform commissions and undertook studies to find ways to improve Indians' lives. He sued to protect Indian lands and establish their rights. A Division of Indian Health was established at the BIA, and other social, educational, and medical services became available. The 1930s and 1940s were an era of tribal restoration. Reservation lands were returned, and tribal law was recognized for the first time. Most important, under Collier, Indians were hired for the first time at the BIA.

The 1950s saw some backsliding as the BIA resumed the tribal-termination policy and began encouraging Indians to relocate to cities. Urbanization was an attempt to end reservation poverty, which for obvious reasons had been growing since the reservation system was initiated. While the policy left Indians free to rebuild their own nations and tribes, it did little to eradicate poverty. Instead, the BIA simply moved poverty off the reservation while eradicating the safety net it had provided.

By the late 1960s, the country was in the midst of a civil rights revolution whose impact was felt on reservations across the country. Indians were at last emboldened to demand control of the BIA, which they were granted after they staged a sit-in at the agency in November 1972.

Indians suffered, as did many other groups, from a reduction in government services under President Ronald Reagan in the 1980s, but this was balanced with a great advance in the early 1990s, when Indians won the right to control gaming on their own lands and were further found to be exempt from paying federal taxes on the profits. With gambling booming around the country, many Indian nations suddenly found themselves rich. Indian nations became self-sufficient in a way they had not been in many decades. The full results of turning to gambling are not yet in. At best gambling may be a mixed blessing, for on some reservations the advent of crime connected to gambling is a potent factor that is not fully understood.

SUPREME COURT DECISIONS AFFECTING NATIVE AMERICANS, 1823–PRESENT

1823 *Johnson v. McIntosh.* The Court rejects the validity of land titles granted to individuals by Indians.

1831 *Cherokee Nation v. Georgia.* This decision establishes the Cherokee Nation as a "domestic dependent nation," not a foreign state.

1870 *Boudinot v. United States* (Cherokee Tobacco case). The Court begins to establish the principle that acts of Congress supersede prior treaties by ruling that Cherokees can be taxed on tobacco profits even though a treaty had specifically exempted this product.

1832 *Worcester v. Georgia.* The Court declares that within the Cherokee Nation "the laws of Georgia can have no force." But Georgia defies the Court, and President Andrew Jackson reportedly quips, "John Marshall has made this decision. Now let him enforce it." With no means to prevent the encroachment of white settlers and state law, the Cherokees, by 1835, are forced to surrender their lands east of the Mississippi and prepare for removal.

1883 *Ex parte Crow Dog.* The Court overturns a death sentence handed down by a federal court, stating that tribal law prevails except when the United States has specifically claimed jurisdiction in a treaty. The case arose when a Sioux chief named Crow Dog murdered a fellow tribe member who had seduced his wife. Despite having been punished by his tribe, the chief was retried in federal court and sentenced to death. See also *United States v. Kagama.*

1884 *Elk v. Wilkins.* In this post–Fourteenth Amendment decision, the Court finds Native American John Elk ineligible to vote.

1886 *United States v. Kagama.* In a case related to *Crow Dog,* the Court finds that federal courts have jurisdiction over certain crimes committed by Indians on reservations. It was able to reverse itself because, in outrage over the 1883 *Crow Dog* decision, Congress passed the Major Crimes Act, extending its legal authority over reservation Indians.

1895 *Talton v. Mayes.* The Court upholds a punishment meted out by the Cherokee Nation court and denies a convicted killer, who claims his due-process rights were violated, the right to appeal the decision in a U.S. court.

1903 *Lone Wolf v. Hitchcock.* The Court rejects a plea that tribal lands were taken without due process and also forecloses any avenue of appeal on grounds that Indians are wards of the federal government and thus cannot sue their own guardian.

1908 *Winters v. United States.* The Court declares that Indian control of water rights is implied in the treaties and agreements that established reservations.

1955 *Tee-Hit-Ton Indians v. United States.* The Court caps interest payments to tribes for the loss of their lands, thus rendering moot several cases that are pending.

1955 *Squire v. Capoeman.* The Court rules that Indians are not subject to capital gains tax accruing from the sale of resources on lands they have been granted by treaty. An apparent victory for Indians, the decision was based on the underlying principle that a ward could not be taxed to benefit the guardian, a view widely held to be denigrating to Indians.

1960 *Federal Power Commission v. Tuscarora Indian Nation.* The Court rules that the federal government can take reservation land—or any land—under the right of eminent domain, which states that the government may acquire private property for public use so long as the owner receives just compensation.

1962 *Organized Village of Kake v. Egan.* The Court upholds Alaska's right to regulate fishing on non-reservation lands on grounds that tribal law does not apply.

1968 *Menominee Tribe v. United States.* The Court says that Wisconsin cannot make Native Americans subject to its conservation laws.

1973 *McClanahan v. Arizona State Tax Commission.* The Court finds that Arizona cannot tax the income of reservation Indians whose entire earnings were derived from reservation resources.

1974 *Morton v. Mancari.* The court rules that provisions of the Indian Reorganization Act of 1934 giving preference to Indians in employment in the Bureau of Indian Affairs are not repealed by the Equal Employment Opportunities Act of 1972 and do not constitute racial discrimination in violation of the due process clause of the Fifth Amendment.

1978 *Oliphant v. Suquamish Indian Tribe.* The Court denies reservation tribes the right to arrest and punish trespassers who violate their laws.

1978 *United States v. Wheeler.* The Court reiterates the supremacy of tribal law except where specifically limited by treaty or act of Congress. (While the decision appeared to be favorable to Native Americans, some experts interpreted it to mean that tribal sovereignty existed, as one legal expert wrote, "only at the sufferance of Congress.")

1978 *United States v. John.* The Court rules that tribes can be dissolved only by their own members, thus negating the policy of termination.

1978 *Santa Clara Pueblo v. Martinez.* The Court rules that an individual tribe may be governed by its traditional laws, even if they conflict with the civil rights of individuals. The writ of habeas corpus is the sole instrument that an individual may use against a tribe.

1980 *Washington v. Confederated Tribes of the Colville Indian Reservation.* The Court rules that reservation Indians are subject to state jurisdiction and state sales tax.

1983 *New Mexico v. Mescalero Apache Tribe.* The Court decides that tribes have regulatory jurisdiction over hunting and fishing rights on their lands.

1985 *County of Oneida, New York v. Oneida Indian Nation of New York State.* The Court says tribes have a right to sue to enforce aboriginal land rights.

1986 *United States v. Dion.* The Court abrogates treaty rights entitling Indians to hunt American eagles at a time when eagles are threatened with extinction.

1987 *California v. Cabazon Band of Mission Indians.* The Court rules that states cannot regulate gaming on Indian lands.

1989 *Mississippi Band of Choctaw Indians v. Holyfield.* The Court confirms tribes' right to regulate adoptions of Native American children.

1996 *Seminole Tribe v. Florida.* The Court rules that the 1988 Indian Gaming Regulatory Act violates state sovereignty under the Eleventh Amendment by permitting tribes to sue states that have failed to negotiate "in good faith" on casino development.

1998 *Kiowa Tribe of Oklahoma v. Manufacturing Technologies, Inc.* The Court upholds tribal sovereign immunity.

1999 *Minnesota v. Mille Lacs Band of Chippewa Indians.* The Court upholds the right of Chippewa Indians to hunt and fish on 13 million acres of Minnesota public land free of state regulation.

NOTABLE FIGURES IN NATIVE AMERICAN HISTORY

Black Elk (1863–1950). This Oglala Lakota author worked to preserve the culture of his people, especially the games, many of which had started as amusement and then taken on a sacred nature. He was the subject of Joseph Epes Brown's classic study, *The Sacred Pipe: Black Elk's Account of the Seven Sacred Rites of the Oglala Sioux* (1953). Black Elk wrote *Black Elk Speaks* in 1932.

Black Hawk (1767–1838). From 1831 to 1832 this Sac chief led the Sacs and Foxes in a resistance movement and outright fighting, known as Black Hawk's War, in Illinois and Wisconsin when the U.S. government sought their land under the terms of an illegal 1804 treaty. Eventually the tribes were forced to cede 6 million acres, and Black Hawk was captured in 1833 by the army. Black Hawk expounded the Indian belief that land could not be sold in his 1833 dictated autobiography, *Life of Ma-ka-tai-me-she-kia-kiak*, or *Black Hawk*.

Black Kettle (?–1868). Known as a peaceful leader, this Cheyenne chief led his people to Sand Creek to sue for peace in 1864. While he and his warriors were out hunting, those who remained in the camp—mostly women and children—were the victims of a vicious massacre by white volunteers. In November 1868, Black Kettle and hundreds of other Cheyennes were killed in their village by Lt. Col. George Custer.

Brant, Joseph (1742–1807). A Mohawk chief whose tribal name was Thayendanegea, he fought on the British side in the French and Indian War and in PONTIAC's Rebellion. During the American Revolution, Brant helped to draw most Iroquois to the British side and led raids in New York State and Pennsylvania. After the Revolution, Brant obtained lands and subsidies in Canada.

Campbell, Ben Nighthorse (1933–). Campbell, whose father was a Cheyenne, was elected to the U.S. House of Representatives from Colorado in 1986 and to the Senate in 1992 and 1998. He became the first Native American chairman of the Senate Indian Affairs Committee.

Chief Joseph (c. 1840–1904). In 1877, this Nez Perce chief led his people on a 1,400-mile (2,250-km) escape under war conditions through Idaho, Wyoming, and Montana to avoid settlement on a reservation. They were finally herded onto a reservation in Indian Territory. Joseph died on the Colville Reservation in eastern Washington.

Cochise (c. 1815–1874). Chiricahua Apache chief Cochise was falsely accused of kidnapping a child in 1861. In response, an army officer Lieutenant George Bascom hanged six Apaches. Cochise escaped, but after the "Bascom Affair" waged a ten-year campaign of guerrilla warfare on the U.S. Army in the Southwest.

Crazy Horse (c. 1842–1877). Along with SITTING BULL and RED CLOUD, he was a forceful Sioux leader in the post–Civil War era and was considered by the U.S. Army to be one of the most effective guerrilla fighters for over a decade as he resisted settlement on a reservation. Crazy Horse was victorious in three actions against U.S. troops in 1876: Powder River (March), Rosebud (June), and Little Bighorn (June). In an altercation at the Red Cloud Agency in Nebraska, he was stabbed.

Curtis, Charles (1860–1936). Curtis was the first senator partly of Indian background and an early activist on behalf of Indian rights. Elected to the House of Representatives from Kansas, he served there from 1892 to 1906, then served as senator from 1907 to 1913 and from 1915 to 1929. From 1929 to 1933 he was vice president under Herbert Hoover. He sponsored the Curtis Act, 1898.

Deganawida (fl. 1560–1570). This legendary Mohawk mystic and leader, along with Hiawatha (another mystic, not to be confused with Henry Wadsworth Longfellow's literary character of the same name), is credited with founding the Iroquois League (c. 1450), a confederacy of five (later six) northeastern tribes that historians believe was one of the models for the federal government.

Deloria, Vine (1933–). This Dakota author wrote *Custer Died for Your Sins* (1969), *God Is Red* (1973), and *Metaphysics for Modern Existence* (1979), books that helped to reawaken interest in Indian culture and history.

Erdrich, Louise (1954–). Born to a French Ojibwa mother and a German American father, Ehrdrich has written several novels chronicling the lives of Native Americans and reservation life, including *Love Medicine* (1984), *The Beet Queen* (1986), *Tracks* (1988), and *The Antelope's Wife* (1998).

Geronimo (1829–1909). Along with Vittorio and COCHISE, this Chiricahua Apache leader was among the last of the great warriors who fought off Mexican and white domination in the American Southwest. Geronimo repeatedly eluded the army's attempts to capture him, and when captured, he often escaped. In 1886 he was forced to surrender at Skelton Canyon, about 25 miles (40 km) from

Apache Pass, where the Apache wars had begun three and a half decades earlier. By then an American folk hero, Geronimo spent the last fourteen years of his life at Fort Sill, Oklahoma. He marched in Theodore Roosevelt's inaugural parade in 1905 and became a member of the Dutch Reformed Church.

Little Turtle (c. 1752–1812). A Miami chief, he organized forces of Miami, Shawnee, and other tribes to resist white settlement.

Mankiller, Wilma (1945–). In 1987, this Cherokee became the first woman ever elected to head a major Indian tribe. Her book, *Mankiller: A Chief and Her People*, was published in 1993.

Martinez, Maria (c. 1881–1980). A San Ildefonso (New Mexico) potter, Martinez, a Pueblo, rediscovered the lost method of making black-on-black pottery. By sharing the formula, she helped to start an economic and artistic renaissance among her people.

Metacom (1639?–1676). Known to the British as King Philip, this Wampanoag chief was the son of Massasoit, who had helped the Pilgrims survive their first winter in America. Metacom organized the last great resistance (also called King Philip's War) against New England colonists, which resulted in the Indians' being driven from the region. The war ended with Metacom's capture and beheading.

Momaday, N. Scott (1934–). A Kiowa Indian, Momaday won the Pulitzer Prize in 1969 for *House Made of Dawn*, sparking a new interest in Native American life and writing. Momaday also founded the Buffalo Trust, dedicated to preserving Native American cultural heritage.

Montezuma, Carlos (c. 1865–1923). A Yavapai physician/activist, he was kidnapped as a child and sold to photographer Carlos Gentile, whose name he assumed. Montezuma reestablished ties with his people as an adult and practiced medicine among them. Convinced that reservations were little more than prisons, he became a national spokesperson on behalf of Indian rights.

Osceola (c. 1800–1838). A Seminole leader, he led a resistance movement, raiding farms, towns, and militia

This 1905 photo of the aging warrior Geronimo was taken the day before he participated in Theodore Roosevelt's inauguration.

posts and often destroying the army's transportation lines, in the early 1880s when the southeastern Indians were resisting removal and resettlement onto reservations. Seized under a flag of truce, he was imprisoned at Fort Moultrie, South Carolina, where he soon died.

Parker, Quanah (c. 1845–1911). This Comanche chief was one of the great post–Civil War warriors who resisted resettlement. On the advice of a mystic, he organized a Sun Dance and used it to recruit a war party of 700. He suffered a serious setback at Palo Duro Canyon when the army killed more than 1,000 of his men's ponies. Parker never signed a treaty until his ultimate surrender in 1875, but then he settled into reservation life at Fort Sill, Oklahoma. Parker also organized a pan-Indian religious movement that became the Native American Church.

Pocahontas (c. 1595–1617). Daughter of the powerful Algonquin leader POWHATAN, Pocahontas is primarily remembered for having saved John Smith, the Jamestown colony's founder, from execution by her father, a story that may be apocryphal. The twelve-year-old girl befriended the English at Jamestown, and when her father, dissatisfied with the settlers' intentions, made plans to starve them out, Pocahontas became an informer. Open warfare soon broke out. In 1613, in hopes of forcing a truce, the British lured Pocahontas to a ship and took her captive. During her captivity she wed colonist John Rolfe, an event that may have contributed to the ensuing truce, which lasted until 1622. In 1616, the Rolfes sailed to England, where Pocahontas was presented at court. In 1617, while en route home, she took ill and died suddenly.

Pontiac (c. 1720–c. 1769). When the French ceded Indian lands around the Great Lakes to the British in the aftermath of the French and Indian War, this Ottawa chief organized a confederacy to reclaim the lands. In response, the British issued the Proclamation of 1763, which decreed that land west of the Appalachians was Indian Country and would not be settled by whites.

Powhatan (c. 1547–1618?). Known as Wahunsonacoch by his people, Powhatan strengthened the confederacy of Tidewater tribes established by his father. He was

NOTABLE FIGURES, *cont.*

instrumental in maintaining peaceful relations with the Jamestown colonists in the early days of the settlement. His daughter POCAHONTAS married the Englishman John Rolfe.

The Prophet (also known as the Shawnee Prophet) (1775?–1837?). Tenskwatawa, the brother of TECUMSEH, claimed to have had a divine revelation from the Native American master of life that urged him to denounce white culture and encourage a return to Native American ways. In 1808 he founded Tippecanoe on the Wabash River in what is now Indiana (later called Prophetstown) where Indians of different tribes could live separate from white society. His influence is said to have helped precipitate the Creek resistance that ended at Horseshoe Bend in 1814.

Red Cloud (1822–1909). A Lakota Sioux chief, Red Cloud, along with SITTING BULL, was a leader in the Sioux War, also called Red Cloud's War, from 1865 to 1867, which reclaimed the Bozeman Trail, the primary hunting ground of the Plains Indians.

Sacajawea (c. 1786–1812?). Also known as Bird Woman, this Shoshone was the guide and only woman on the Lewis and Clark Expedition (1804–1806). Later, she served as an interpreter–liaison with several other tribes. Captured as a child by Mandans, she lived most of her life with them.

Sequoyah (1766–1843). Sequoyah, a Cherokee also known as George Guess, developed a syllabary language for the Cherokee and taught thousands of Native Americans to read and write.

Silko, Leslie Marmon (1948–). Born in Albuquerque, New Mexico, Silko is a writer of Pueblo, Laguna, Mexican, and white ancestry. Her major works, such as *Ceremony* (1977), *Storyteller* (1981), and *Almanac of the Dead* (1991), often focus on preserving Native American oral traditions.

Sitting Bull (1834–1890). A holy man rather than a chief, this Lakota Sioux leader organized the Plains tribes to fight the Great Sioux War (also known as RED CLOUD'S War). The Indians routed the U.S. Army and successfully reclaimed their hunting ground, but in 1868, when the Lakota agreed to move to a reservation, Sitting Bull refused to go and organized a new resistance movement. Sitting Bull and his 2,000 resisters, defeated and killed all the troops under Custer's immediate command (more than 260 men) on June 25–26, 1876. Fearing retribution, Sitting Bull and his warriors fled into Canada, but dwindling food supplies forced them to return to the United States, where Sitting Bull was immediately taken prisoner. On his release two years later, he moved to the Standing Rock reservation in North Dakota, where he hoped to influence his people not to sign away any more of their land. Sitting Bull's last political act was to become involved in the Ghost Dance movement. During a scuffle, when Indian police officers attempted to arrest Sitting Bull, he was shot and killed.

Tallchief, Maria (1925–). An Osage, Tallchief became a classical ballerina who danced with George Balanchine's company (and who was also for a time his wife) and with the Paris Opera Ballet. Her most famous role was the title role in *The Firebird*, which Balanchine created for her.

Tecumseh (1768–1813). The dream of this great Shawnee leader was to forge an Indian state out of the Old Northwest Territory around the Great Lakes. With his brother who was known as THE PROPHET, he organized a confederacy of tribes in the region. At the Battle of Tippecanoe in 1811, his forces (in his absence) were lured into battle by William Henry Harrison and the power of the Confederacy was broken.

Tekakwitha, Kateri (1656–1680). Tekakwitha, a Mohawk, was the first American Indian ever proposed for Roman Catholic sainthood. Converted by Jesuits, she was known for her piousness and bravery in the face of suffering. Pope John Paul II beatified her in 1980.

Thorpe, Jim (1888–1953). Sac athlete Jim Thorpe won the pentathlon and the decathlon at the 1912 Olympic Games. He was later stripped of his medals for playing one season of semipro baseball, but his medals were restored in 1983.

Ward, Nancy (c. 1738–1824). This Cherokee leader was the daughter of a Delaware man and a Cherokee woman. Ward lived with her mother's people and married a fellow Cherokee, a warrior who later died in a skirmish between the Cherokees and the Creeks. Although it was virtually unheard of for a woman to be included in a war party, Ward donned men's clothing and took over her husband's role in battle. Her reward for helping to rout the enemy was a position on the Council of Chiefs, making her possibly the first Cherokee woman ever to wield such power. She was also awarded the title Beloved Woman, with the responsibility of deciding the fates of prisoners.

CHAPTER 2

EXPLORATION AND COLONIZATION

HIGHLIGHTS

Timeline of Exploration and Colonization

ALTHOUGH THE VIKINGS WERE the first Europeans to colonize the New World, more than 500 years elapsed between their journeys and the first voyage of CHRISTOPHER COLUMBUS in 1492. Among the developments that provided the impetus for the European rediscovery of America were the Protestant Reformation, the Catholic Counter-Reformation, and the Renaissance, each of which encouraged the individualism necessary for exploration. In addition, by 1492 Portugal, France, Spain, and England had grown from small territories of warring noble families into nation-states. Their rulers eagerly sought to expand trade, especially with Asia and Africa, by financing overseas exploration and to claim new territories in the rapidly escalating drive for power and domination. Improved maps and new methods for determining latitude and longitude at sea gave sailors the confidence they needed to press forward into uncharted waters. These were people driven by ideas of adventure, by dreams of wealth, and by a deep-seated belief that it was their duty to spread the Christian faith. The same motivations, combined with the desire to start new lives and practice their chosen religions, guided the interior exploration and settlement of the New World.

LANDFALL

c. 982 Norseman ERIC THE RED discovers Greenland.

c. 986 ERIC THE RED leads an expedition to colonize Greenland and, with 500 settlers, establishes the first Viking settlement there.

1000 LEIF ERIKSSON, son of ERIC THE RED, lands on the coast of what is now either Newfoundland or Nova Scotia, Canada, probably becoming the first European to discover America. Finding grapes (probably berries) there, the Vikings call the region Vinland (Wineland).

1492 Sponsored by Isabella of Castile and Ferdinand of Aragon, Italian navigator CHRISTOPHER COLUMBUS lands on the Bahaman island of Guanahani, which he names San Salvador. Columbus also sights Cuba and lands on Haiti.

1493 On his second voyage, CHRISTOPHER COLUMBUS comes upon Puerto Rico, Jamaica, and Dominica.

1497 JOHN CABOT lands on the east coast of North America either at Newfoundland or Canada's Cape Breton Island and claims the region for England's King Henry VII.

1498 On his second voyage, JOHN CABOT's fate is unknown, although some believe he may have reached North America.

On his third voyage, COLUMBUS sails to Trinidad and the Orinoco River in South America.

1499 Italian explorer AMERIGO VESPUCCI sails to the northern and eastern coasts of South America and arrives at the mouth of the Amazon River.

1502–1503 On his fourth and last voyage, COLUMBUS comes upon Saint Lucia, Honduras, Costa Rica, and Panama.

1507 Mapmaker Martin Waldseemüller shows the name "America" on the first map indicating the New World distinct from Asia.

"Then, at two hours after midnight, the Pinta fired a cannon, my prearranged signal for the sighting of land."
—COLUMBUS'S LOG, OCTOBER 12, 1492

SPANISH CONQUEST AND ROUTES WITHIN

1508? Searching for a northwest passage (a short sea route around or through North America to east Asia), British explorer SEBASTIAN CABOT may have reached Hudson Bay. His exploits are debated.

1513 Spaniard JUAN PONCE DE LEÓN, according to legend, searching for the Fountain of Youth, reaches Florida.

VASCO NÚÑEZ DE BALBOA leads an expedition across the Isthmus of Panama and becomes the first European to sight the Pacific Ocean from the New World.

1519–1521 Spanish explorer HERNANDO CORTÉS conquers Mexico, capturing the Aztec capital Tenochtitlán (now Mexico City) and imprisoning and eventually killing the Aztec emperor Montezuma.

Spaniard Alonzo Alvarez de Piñeda explores the Gulf of Mexico from Florida to Veracruz.

1519–1521 FERDINAND MAGELLAN sails around the world. After his death in 1521 in the Philippines, the voyage is completed by Juan Sebastian del Cano, the commander of the *Vittoria*, the only remaining vessel of MAGELLAN's five-ship fleet.

1524 Italian navigator GIOVANNI DA VERRAZZANO sails along the Atlantic Coast from Cape Fear north into New York Bay.

1532–1535 Spaniard Francisco Pizarro conquers Peru, seizing control of the rich Inca empire and founding Lima, which becomes the capital of Peru.

1534 On his first voyage to the New World, Frenchman JACQUES CARTIER sights Labrador, Newfoundland, and New Brunswick, and enters the mouth of the Saint Lawrence River.

1535–1536 On his second voyage, CARTIER sails up the Saint Lawrence River.

1536 ÁLVAR NÚÑEZ CABEZA DE VACA reaches the area of the Gulf of California, after an eight-year overland journey from Texas through New Mexico, Arizona, and possibly California.

1539–1542 Spaniard HERNANDO DE SOTO leads an expedition from Florida and in 1541 crosses the Mississippi River.

1540–1542 FRANCISCO VÁSQUEZ DE CORONADO leads an army from Mexico through the American Southwest and reaches the Pueblo villages of New Mexico; his lieutenant, Garcia López de Cárdenas, sights the Grand Canyon.

1542 Juan Rodríguez Cabrillo explores the coast of California.

EARLY SETTLEMENTS AND COLONIES

1562 Jean Ribault and 140 French Huguenots (Protestants) establish a colony on Parris Island, off the coast of South Carolina, calling it Charlesfort. While Ribault is in France obtaining supplies, the other colonists are rescued from starvation by an English ship and return to France.

René de Laudonnière establishes Fort Caroline, a post near the mouth of the Saint Johns River, Florida.

1565 Spanish naval officer Pedro Menéndez de Avilés, ordered by King Philip II to found a Spanish colony in Florida, establishes the fort of Saint Augustine, which becomes the oldest permanent European city in North America.

Jean Ribault sails with reinforcements for Fort Caroline, but the fleet is wrecked in a tropical storm, leaving the survivors stranded on the coast of Florida. The undefended colonists at Fort Caroline are massacred by Spanish forces under Pedro Menéndez de Avilés, who has been dispatched by King Philip II of Spain to crush the French Huguenots. The Spanish murder most of Ribault's men as they attempt to reach Fort Caroline by land.

1567 In revenge for the Spanish destruction of Fort Caroline, French soldier Dominique de Gourgues and his men decimate San Mateo, the colony the Spanish have set up on the same spot.

1576 Englishman MARTIN FROBISHER discovers what will be called Frobisher's Bay in Canada.

BARTHOLOMEW COLUMBUS

CHRISTOPHER'S older brother, Bartholomew Columbus (1432?–1514?) was an accomplished sailor and mapmaker who unsuccessfully solicited English and French royalty for support of the voyage of discovery. Commanding three Spanish supply ships, he met his brother on Hispaniola during the latter's second voyage (1493–1496). Bartholomew stayed on, founding the city of Santo Domingo in 1496 and administering the colony until turmoil forced him back to Spain in 1500. He accompanied Christopher on his fourth voyage (1502–1504) and his nephew Diego in 1509.

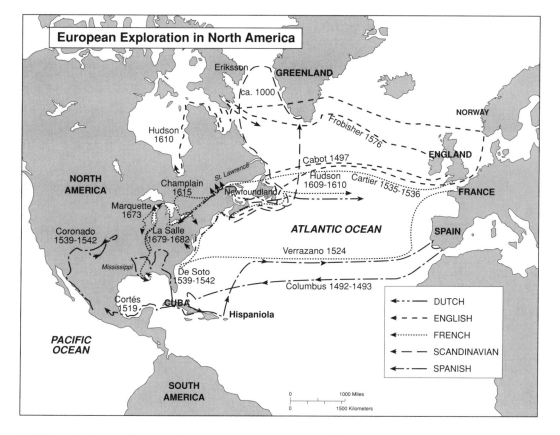

European Exploration in North America

1579 Englishman FRANCIS DRAKE reaches northern California on his voyage of circumnavigation, 1577–1580.

1585 Navigator and courtier Sir Walter Raleigh sends a group of British to found a colony on the mid-Atlantic coast of North America. They land on Roanoke Island, North Carolina, where they establish a settlement. A year later, SIR FRANCIS DRAKE, returning to England from raiding Spanish treasure ships, rescues the surviving colonists and takes them back to England.

1587 A group of colonists, organized by Raleigh, establishes a second settlement on Roanoke Island. VIRGINIA DARE, the first child of English parents to be born in America, is born here. Her fate is unknown.

1590 The first relief expedition reaching Roanoke Island finds no trace of the colony, hereafter referred to as the Lost Colony.

1596 Spanish merchant Sebastián Vizcaíno attempts unsuccessfully to colonize southern California.

1598 On his first expedition, JUAN DE OÑATE takes possession of New Mexico for Spain.

1601 On his second expedition, JUAN DE OÑATE explores what will become Oklahoma, crossing into Kansas.

1603 Frenchman SAMUEL DE CHAMPLAIN sails up the Saint Lawrence River to what is now Montreal. Over the next four years he explores the coasts of Maine, New Brunswick, and Nova Scotia.

1605 On his third expedition, JUAN DE OÑATE reaches the Colorado River and descends it to the Gulf of California.

1606 England's King James I grants a charter to the Virginia Company of London, a joint stock company, to establish colonies in America.

1607 The Virginia Company sends more than 100 colonists to the Chesapeake Bay region, where they found Jamestown, Virginia, the first permanent English settlement in North America. Capt. JOHN SMITH, Jamestown's military commander, is, according to legend, rescued from execution at the hands of the Indians by Chief Powhatan's daughter, POCAHONTAS. (Historians now believe that Smith misinterpreted a traditional Indian adoption ceremony.)

1608 SAMUEL DE CHAMPLAIN founds the French colony of Quebec in Canada.

1609 In search of a northwest passage, HENRY HUDSON sails up the New York river that now bears his name and gives the Dutch their claim to the region.

1609–1610 Only a fraction of the Jamestown colonists survive the terrible winter. Preparing to abandon the colony and return to England, their numbers are bolstered by the arrival from England of a large additional force of men, women, and livestock.

HENRY HUDSON'S LAST VOYAGE

Having already failed in three attempts to reach the Far East by sea—the previous one west across the North Atlantic—HENRY HUDSON set sail from London on April 17, 1610, aboard the bark *Discovery*. Financed by English merchants, his mission again was to find and chart the elusive northwest passage. On board were a crew of twenty and his son, John. In July, the small ship entered what is now called Hudson Strait, and by August, it reached a large inland sea, Hudson Bay. Believing it was the route he sought, Hudson continued his exploration but found no outlet. Thickening ice and damage to the hull from an unseen shoal forced the expedition ashore, where Hudson and his men endured a harsh winter with inadequate provisions. The crew was hungry, cold, and disgruntled.

With the spring thaw, Hudson ordered the *Discovery* repaired and set course to the north and west. Could he be resuming his search for the northwest passage rather than heading home? No one knows Hudson's plans for certain, but, whatever they were, he had no chance to carry them out. On the morning of June 22, 1611, mutinous crewmen captured the unsuspecting captain and, along with his son and seven loyal sailors, cast him adrift in a rowboat. They were never heard from again.

Only eight of the men aboard the *Discovery* made it back to England. Several were killed in a skirmish with Eskimos in Labrador. Six of the survivors eventually went on trial, but the verdict has been lost to history.

c. 1612 Jamestown colonist JOHN ROLFE begins the cultivation of West Indian tobacco, a less bitter variety than that grown by Virginia Indians. With some refinements the Orinoco leaf proves to be a valued cash crop.

1614 POCAHONTAS marries colonist JOHN ROLFE; soon afterward Powhatan agrees to a truce with the Jamestown colony, which lasts until 1622.

1617 After boarding a ship for her return to Jamestown following a visit to England sponsored by the London Company to encourage new settlers, POCAHONTAS dies and is buried in England.

In 1607, weary colonists landed in the Chesapeake Bay area, naming their site Jamestown after King James I. The king's laws and instructions were placed in a sealed case on board one of the ships, only to be opened when the sailors landed for settlement.

1619 The House of Burgesses, the first colonial legislature, meets in Jamestown, Virginia.

A Dutch ship transports twenty black African bound servants to Jamestown. They are probably the first African Americans in the English colonies of America.

Among the 1,200 colonists to arrive this year are a number of single women, recruited by the company to go to Virginia to become wives.

1620 After a three-month voyage on the *Mayflower*, 102 Pilgrims sponsored by the Virginia Company establish a colony at Plymouth, on Cape Cod, Massachusetts. Before landing, the Pilgrims sign the Mayflower Compact, an agreement establishing self-government.

1621 William Bradford is elected the second governor of the Plymouth Colony. He is to serve thirty-one terms between 1622 and 1656.

The Plymouth Colony negotiates a peace treaty with the Wampanoag Indians.

1623 English colonists found a settlement at Dover in what is now New Hampshire. The Dutch West India Company is founded in the Dutch Republic for trading and colonizing in the New World.

1626 The Dutch establish the colony of New Netherland, which will soon include the town of New Amsterdam (present-day New York City) at the lower tip of Manhattan, Fort Orange (present-day Albany), and Fort Nassau (present-day Gloucester, New Jersey).

Dutchman Peter Minuit gives local Indians about $24 worth of trinkets in exchange for the island of Manhattan.

Led by Roger Conant, a group of English Puritans arrive at Massachusetts Bay and attempt to create a settlement on Cape Ann. They leave and go to Naumkeag, which they rename Salem.

1630 JOHN WINTHROP and other members of the Massachusetts Bay Company found Boston, initiating what becomes known as the Great Migration to the Massachusetts Bay Colony; about 20,000 people will settle here in the next fifteen years.

1633 The Dutch build a trading post near present-day Hartford.

The New Sweden Company (or New South Company) is organized. In 1637, it is granted a charter for settlement on the Delaware River.

1634 Frenchman Jean Nicolet explores Lake Michigan and present-day Wisconsin.

Under a grant to the Catholic Calvert family, the Lords Baltimore, colonists settle Saint Mary's, Maryland. Maryland becomes the only English colony in North America with a large Catholic minority.

John Oldham and Bay Colony settlers winter at Wethersfield in present-day Connecticut.

1635 At the mouth of the Connecticut River, the English build Fort Saybrook.

1636 Dissenting minister ROGER WILLIAMS, expelled the year before from Massachusetts, founds Providence, Rhode Island, on land he purchases from Indians.

THOMAS HOOKER, another dissenting minister, leads his followers from Cambridge, Massachusetts, to Connecticut, where they found Hartford.

1638 New Haven, Connecticut, is founded by Puritans.

Swedes build Fort Christina (now Wilmington, Delaware).

Dissenter ANNE HUTCHINSON, expelled the previous year from Massachusetts, and her followers found present-day Portsmouth, Rhode Island.

1639 The Fundamental Orders, which THOMAS HOOKER helped write, is adopted by the Connecticut Colony. The orders constitute the basic law of the colony until 1662.

1642 The French found Montreal, Canada.

1647 Peter Stuyvesant arrives in New Amsterdam to assume his position as governor of New Netherland.

1648 Landowner and lawyer Margaret Brent asks for the vote in the Maryland assembly, but her request is rejected.

1649 Maryland Act for Religious Toleration is passed.

1650 The English and the Dutch agree on the respective boundaries of their North American colonies.

The Pilgrims held a Thanksgiving feast at Plymouth Colony in 1621, but it did not become an annual national holiday until Abraham Lincoln proclaimed it in 1863.

INTERIOR EXPLORATION AND THE FIGHT FOR TERRITORY

1652 Massachusetts General Court decides that Maine belongs to the Massachusetts Bay Colony.

1655 Dutch forces, led by Peter Stuyvesant, take Swedish forts on the Delaware River.

1659–1661 PIERRE RADISSON explores Lake Superior and the northern Mississippi regions.

1662 The New Haven Colony is united with Connecticut.

1663 Carolina is chartered.

1664 British forces annex New Netherland from Connecticut to Delaware. New Amsterdam is renamed New York and Fort Orange becomes Albany.
   The New Jersey Colony is founded by the British.

1666 Connecticut Puritans found Newark, New Jersey.

"Puritanism—the haunting fear that someone, somewhere, may be happy."

—H. L. MENCKEN

PURITANISM AND THE SETTLEMENT OF AMERICA

The Puritans were groups of radical Protestants within the Church of England who believed that the Reformation of the sixteenth century had not gone far enough in ridding the church of Catholic influence. Emphasizing direct religious experience and a duty to conduct civil affairs according to God's will, they broke off from the Church of England in the early seventeenth century and set forth to New England to found a holy commonwealth. Puritanism would have a profound effect on political and cultural life in the American colonies, but division and segmentation within the movement would also have lasting consequences.

The first Puritan Separatists to sail for America were the Pilgrims (many of whom had emigrated to Holland years before), who founded the Plymouth Colony in 1620. The Great Puritan Migration, under the leadership of JOHN WINTHROP and the auspices of the Massachusetts Bay Company, began ten years later. By 1640, some 20,000 Puritans had settled in the Massachusetts Bay Colony, pursuing their dream of establishing "a city on a hill"—an ideal Christian community (see p. 238).

The first major break came in 1635, when the Puritan preacher and intellectual ROGER WILLIAMS differed with the commonwealth ministry over religious freedom and was banished from the colony. With a small band of followers, Williams bought land from Indians on Narragansett Bay and established the settlement of Providence—the first in what is now Rhode Island—as a haven for religious dissenters. Among these was ANNE HUTCHINSON, who broke with the mainstream Congregationalist ministry of Puritan leader John Cotton. Contesting the orthodox view that God's will can be discovered only through the Bible, Hutchinson was excommunicated from the church and expelled from the commonwealth in 1638. The "city on a hill," however, was already divided into two hostile camps—those who demanded strict observance of scriptural law and those who believed that true godliness comes from inner experience of divine grace. The diffusion of faith, the colonial intervention of the English throne, and the advent of new religious movements diminished the political and spiritual authority of the Puritans through the course of the seventeenth and eighteenth centuries. The social and cultural effects remain powerful.

1668 The French establish a fur-trading post and a Jesuit mission at Sault Sainte Marie, on the waterway between Lakes Superior and Huron.

1672 Mail service begins between New York and Boston.

1673 Frenchmen Louis Jolliet and Jacques Marquette descend the Wisconsin River to the Mississippi. Paddling their canoes southward, they conclude that the Mississippi flows not into the Pacific but into the Gulf of Mexico.
   Dutch forces reoccupy New York.

1674 The English regain control of New York and, by treaty with the Netherlands, recognize it as British.

Celebrating Christmas was illegal in colonial Massachusetts. According to a law passed in 1660, anyone found observing the holiday was fined five shillings. Christmas did not become a major holiday in the United States until the mid-19th century.

1675–1676 King Philip's War in New England forces back the line of the English settlement and wipes out the Wampanoag tribe.

1676 Bacon's Rebellion in Virginia, sparked by the colonial government's inability to protect settlements from Indian attack, collapses when leader Nathaniel Bacon dies.

1677 Massachusetts purchases part of Maine from heirs of Spanish explorer Sir Ferdinando Gorges.

1679 New Hampshire is established as a royal colony separate from Massachusetts.

1679–1682 Frenchman René-Robert Cavelier, Sieur de La Salle, with his lieutenant, Henri de Tonti, and Louis Hennepin explore the Great Lakes. La Salle and his party reach the mouth of the Mississippi River at the Gulf of Mexico in 1682 and claim the Mississippi Valley for Louis XIV.
   The French found the first white settlement in Arkansas.

1681 England's King Charles II grants a royal charter to English Quaker William Penn for the region that becomes Pennsylvania.

1683 German Mennonites found Germantown, Pennsylvania (see p. 264).

1684 England annuls the original charter of the Massachusetts Bay Company.

1686 In an effort to restructure England's North American colonies, James II forms the Dominion of New England. Composed of New Jersey, New York, Connecticut, Rhode Island, Massachusetts, New Hampshire, and the territory of Maine, the dominion is now governed by Sir Edmund Andros, with Francis Nicholson as lieutenant governor.

1689 Armed conflict between England and France for control of eastern North America begins. Hostilities start with English and Iroquois attacking Montreal and violence between French and English traders on Hudson Bay. These conflicts are part of a bigger conflict between England and France, which is called the War of the League of Augsburg in Europe, and King William's War in North America. Warfare between the two nations will continue for nearly seventy-five years.

In the wake of the Glorious Revolution, German-born anti-Catholic merchant JACOB LEISLER seizes New York in the name of William and Mary of England and appoints himself governor.

1690 French troops join with Algonquin warriors to attack and burn settlements in New York, New Hampshire, and Maine.

A Massachusetts fleet captures the strategic French harbor at Port Royal, Nova Scotia. A year later, the French recapture it.

1691 English troops gain New York. JACOB LEISLER, convicted of treason, is hanged.

A new royal charter is issued to Massachusetts, incorporating Maine and Plymouth.

1692 Twenty-seven people are tried for witchcraft in Salem, Massachusetts, after being accused by a group of teenaged girls; twenty are executed.

1696 French forces defend Quebec against English–Iroquois attacks.

1697 King William's War ends. The Treaty of Ryswick restores territories to prewar status.

1699 Pierre Le Moyne, Sieur d'Iberville, founds Old Biloxi (now Ocean Springs, Mississippi), the first European settlement in French Louisiana, and explores the Mississippi delta.

1701 Led by Antoine de la Mothe Cadillac, French colonists build a fort at Detroit. The French establish trading posts and forts in Michigan and Illinois.

1702 Queen Anne's War, the second North American colonial war between France and England, begins. The English burn Saint Augustine, Florida.

This is the traditional date for the founding of Vincennes, the first permanent European colony in Indiana, established by French colonists at a site on the Wabash River long known to fur traders; the site is fortified in 1732.

1704 The *News-Letter*, the first newspaper in the colonies, begins publication in Boston.

French and Indians raid Deerfield, Massachusetts, massacre 50 colonists, then take more than 100 others hostage.

English colonial forces are unable to capture Port Royal, Nova Scotia.

No women were burned at the stake after the Salem Witch Trials of 1692. Nineteen were hanged and one was pressed to death by stones.

1707 English forces again fail to seize Port Royal.

1710 English and colonial forces finally seize Port Royal, renaming it Annapolis Royal.

1711 British colonials fail to take Montreal and Quebec.

1711–1713 In Carolina, Tuscarora Indians massacre more than 150 settlers. War ensues. Using a divide-and-conquer strategy, Carolina settlers ally with other tribes against the Tuscaroras. More than 300 Tuscarora warriors are killed near the Neuse River. The war ends disastrously for the tribe, whose survivors flee north, where they join the Iroquois Confederation.

1713 The Peace of Utrecht ends Queen Anne's War.

1715–1716 Enraged by the colonists' treatment of the Tuscaroras, the Yamasee Indians stage an uprising in South Carolina. More than 200 settlers are killed before the colonists, aided by the Cherokees, defeat the Yamasees, driving them into Georgia and Florida. There the Yamasees ally with the Spanish against the English.

1716 To defend themselves against a possible French threat from Louisiana, the Spanish establish missions in Texas.

1717 In France, Scottish financier John Law, having gained a monopoly of trading rights in Louisiana, forms the Mississippi Company.

1718 French colonists found New Orleans, Louisiana.
    San Antonio, Texas, is founded by Spanish Franciscans and established as a Spanish military post and mission.

1720 Although John Law's Mississippi scheme collapses due to

ATLANTIC BOUNTY: FISHING AND COLONIAL LIFE

During the sixteenth and seventeenth centuries, the abundant fisheries of the western Atlantic provided the major source of England's New World wealth and a vital source of nutrition for the colonists. Vast shoals of cod off the coast of New England, the most populous region of colonial America, provided an economic mainstay from the early days of settlement. The first recorded colonial fishing expedition, led by Capt. JOHN SMITH from Virginia in 1614, yielded 60,000 fish from the Maine coast in one month. Pilgrim families arriving after 1620 feasted on lobsters, many of which weighed twenty-five pounds and were so plentiful that small children could snatch them out of the water. Discovery of the sperm whale and its many uses in the late seventeenth century gave rise to a flourishing whaling industry, centered in Nantucket, Massachusetts. The growth of colonial fishing by 1740 was reflected in the more than 1,000 boats sailing out of New England alone. By the end of the eighteenth century, Yankee whalers had depleted nearby waters of the sperm whale and ventured into far-flung seas for their catch. Atlantic cod, whose population dwindled over the centuries, reached near extinction in the late 1980s as a result of excessive trawling.

overspeculation, it has successfully encouraged French settlement in the southern Mississippi Valley.

In an attempt to woo the Iroquois away from the French, William Burnet, governor of New York, expands trade with the Indians.

1724 Fort Drummer (near present-day Brattleboro), the first permanent European settlement in Vermont, is built to protect English settlers from Indians.

1729 Carolina is split into two crown colonies, North Carolina and South Carolina.

Baltimore, Maryland, is founded. It will be incorporated in 1745.

1731–1743 Frenchman Pierre Gaultier de Varennes, Sieur de La Vérendrye, and his three sons explore the Northwest as far as Saskatchewan, Canada.

1732 By an act of the English Parliament, Georgia, the last of the original thirteen colonies, is created. The colony's founder, James Oglethorpe, hopes to establish a buffer against the Spanish in Florida and the French in Lousiana and a refuge for the persecuted and the poor.

1734 John Peter Zenger, the founder of the *New York Weekly Journal*, is arrested and charged with seditious libel for his paper's attacks on William Crosby, the royal governor of New York. Tried in 1735, he is defended by Alexander Hamilton, who argues that this client had not libeled Crosby because the material printed in the paper was true. Zenger is acquitted, and his case becomes a milestone in the battle for a free press (see p. 419).

1737 English colonist William Byrd founds Richmond, Virginia.

1739 Angered by border problems, the English colonists of South Carolina and Georgia decide to go to war against the Spanish in Florida.

1740 James Oglethorpe tries and fails to capture Saint Augustine, Florida, from the Spanish.

1742 At the Battle of Bloody Marsh on Saint Simons Island, Georgia, colonists led by James Oglethorpe repulse Spanish invaders.

1743 Three years after his attempt to seize Saint Augustine, James Oglethorpe tries and fails again.

The American Philosophical Society is founded in Philadelphia. The first learned institution in the United States, the Society encourages knowledge and exploration in the sciences and humanities.

1744 The French failure to take Annapolis Royal, Nova Scotia, is the first military action of King George's War in America, the third of the French–English North American colonial wars.

The colonies imported more than 2.1 million gallons of rum in 1728. Colonists drank heavily, and British sailors received regular rations.

1745 Saratoga, New York, is burned by French and Indian forces, who also raid forts and towns in Maine.

Colonial and British forces capture Louisbourg on Cape Breton Island, Canada.

1746 The British successfully defend Cape Breton Island from the French, and rivalry between the French and the English for the upper Ohio region intensifies.

1747 The Ohio Company is created by a group of Virginians to expand settlement westward from Virginia.

1748 King George's War ends and the Treaty of Aix-la-Chapelle returns Louisbourg to France. But hostility between France and England continues.

1749 The Ohio Company receives a royal charter and an enormous land grant for the area along the forks of the Ohio River—the junction of the Monongahela and the Allegheny rivers (now Pittsburgh, Pennsylvania).

Acting first, the French send a heavily armed force to the Ohio Valley to ward off the British from the region.

TRIANGULAR TRADE

By the eighteenth century, the Atlantic was a busy place. Merchant ships transported raw materials and manufactured goods—and slaves—in a series of triangles that are known as the Triangular Trade. Its base was West Indian sugar, a staple crop so seductive and labor-intensive that it transformed Europe's taste and economy and enslaved the people of Africa. New England merchants transported raw sugar and molasses up the Atlantic coast for manufacture into rum before shipping it to Africa. Ships bound for Britain carried the raw materials (naval stores, lumber), agricultural products (tobacco, rice), and animal products (furs, fish, whale oil) that many British entrepreneurs and manufacturers assumed were the colonies' primary purpose. Manufactured goods went back to the colonies and the West Indies, and to Africa, where they were traded for human beings, who then endured the cruel Middle Passage to arrive in the West Indies as slaves.

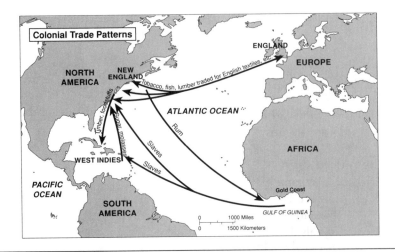

1751 The Ohio Company begins colonization of the Ohio Valley.

1752 To prevent the British from gaining control of the Ohio Valley, the French begin constructing forts south of Lake Erie to the forks of the Ohio River.

At the same time, the Iroquois and Delawares cede lands south of the Ohio to Virginia.

Thomas Bond opens the first general hospital in the colonies, in Philadelphia.

1753 Young militia officer George Washington is dispatched by Virginia's governor to effect French withdrawal from the Ohio Territory.

The Liberty Bell is hung in the newly built Pennsylvania State House, later called Independence Hall.

1754 The contest between the French and the Ohio Company for control of the Ohio Valley heats up as the French build Fort Duquesne at the forks of the Ohio. George Washington is defeated by French forces near the headwaters of the Ohio River (Great Meadows).

The Albany Congress, with representatives from seven colonies, concludes a treaty with the Iroquois and recommends BENJAMIN FRANKLIN's Plan of Union.

1755 British regulars and colonial militia led by British general Edward Braddock are ambushed and destroyed by French and Indians on the upper Ohio. Braddock is killed during the battle, and Washington assumes command. Full-scale warfare erupts after this defeat.

1756 England formally declares war on France. The conflict is called the French and Indian War in America and the Seven Years' War in Europe.

1757 Gen. Louis Joseph, Marquis de Montcalm, captures Fort Oswego, restoring control of Lake Ontario to France.

Fort William Henry on Lake George, New York, falls to French forces under General Montcalm. Many British prisoners taken during the battle are killed by Indian allies of the French.

1758 General Montcalm repels an English attack on Fort Ticonderoga, New York. The British seize two Canadian forts in French hands—Louisbourg on Cape Breton Island and Fort Frontenac on Lake Ontario. After the French burn Duquesne, Pennsylvania, the British rebuild it, renaming it Fort Pitt.

1759 British forces take Fort Niagara, New York, and the French abandon Crown Point, New York, and Fort Ticonderoga. At the Battle of the Plains of Abraham, above Quebec, Canada, the British general James Wolfe defeats General Montcalm. Both generals die in the epic battle, and Quebec falls to the British.

"The Ploughman on his Legs is higher than a Gentleman on his knees."

—BENJAMIN FRANKLIN, *POOR RICHARD'S ALMANACK,* 1758

1760 After British troops seize Montreal, the French governor of Canada surrenders the province to the British. Although Canadian resistance continues for another year, the loss of Montreal signifies the end of the French empire in America. The French surrender Detroit to the British.

1762 To prevent the Louisiana Territory from falling into British hands, France secretly cedes it to Spain in the Treaty of Fontainebleau.

LATE COLONIAL PERIOD: THE ROAD TO REVOLUTION

1763 In the Treaty of Paris, which ends the French and Indian War, France cedes to England all its territories east of the Mississippi River except for two small islands in the Saint Lawrence River, which France retains, and New Orleans, which passes to Spain. In exchange for the return of Cuba and the Philippines, Spain cedes Florida to Britain. In sum, the imperial competition for eastern North America, begun in the sixteenth century, has ended in a total English victory. France has lost all its American possessions except for the two islands mentioned above and Martinique and Guadeloupe. However, for the next three years Native American tribes wage war against the English in the Ohio–Great Lakes region, destroying all forts there, except for Forts Detroit and Pitt.

1763 The Proclamation of 1763 forbids British settlement west of the Appalachian Mountains to reserve an Indian territory and defuse tension. It also creates three new provinces: Quebec, East Florida, and West Florida.

1764 To raise money to help pay the British debt incurred in the French and Indian War, Parliament passes the Sugar Act, imposing duties on sugar, textiles, coffee, and other imports. The colonists protest this act through resolutions and boycotts.

Parliament passes the Currency Act, prohibiting the colonies from printing their own paper money.

1765 Parliament passes the Quartering Act, requiring that colonists provide food and shelter for British troops. The colonial assemblies protest the act.

Parliament passes the Stamp Act, requiring that printed documents such as newspapers, licenses, and legal documents be issued solely on special stamped paper bought from stamp collectors or distributors. Delegates sent by nine colonies to the Stamp Act Congress, in New York City, protest taxation without representation. Protest mobs riot in cities such as Boston and New York. Stamp collectors publicly resign, making it impossible for the revenue stamps to be sold.

1766 Parliament repeals the Stamp Act but passes the Declaratory Act, asserting its right to make laws governing the colonies. The colonists, celebrating the repeal of the Stamp Act, ignore the new act.

The survey by English astronomers Charles Mason and Jeremiah Dixon of the boundary between Maryland and Pennsylvania and Maryland and Delaware is completed, establishing the Mason-Dixon line. The Mason-Dixon line was often referred to as the boundary line between slave states and free states.

1767 The New York Assembly is suspended by Parliament for incompletely complying with the Quartering Act.

The Townshend Acts, imposing import duties on glass, lead, paints, and tea sent to the colonies, are passed by Parliament. Determined not to import or consume British goods, Boston and then other major ports set up nonimportation associations. The colonial assemblies protest the acts, as do the colonial newspapers.

Wealthy lawyer JOHN DICKINSON, writing as "a Farmer in Pennsylvania," acknowledges Parliament's right to regulate trade but not to tax to raise revenue.

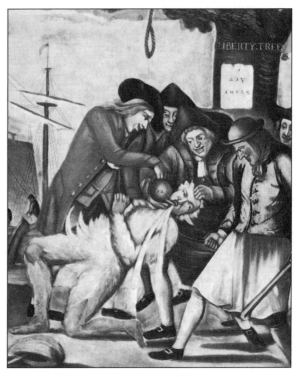

John Malcolm, the commissioner of customs in Boston, is tarred and feathered, then forced to drink tea for collecting customs duties. In this London cartoon, the Stamp Act is posted upside down on a tree in the background.

1768 In the Treaty of Hard Labor, the Cherokees cede a huge tract of land around the upper Tennessee River to British settlers. Hoping to keep English settlements away from their homeland, the Iroquois, in the Treaty of Fort Stanwix, give up their claims to the Ohio Valley.

1769 Virginia's House of Burgesses is dissolved by the colony's governor after the assembly establishes the first provincial association, which then bans goods enumerated in the Townshend Acts. Its members then meet in private. In the next few months every colony except New Hampshire establishes these nonimportation associations.

1770 Crispus Attucks, whose mother was Indian and father African American, becomes the first casualty of the Revolution when British soldiers kill five Boston colonists in what comes to be known as the Boston Massacre. The violence erupts when the troops fire on a rock-throwing mob—aroused by the quartering of 400 British troops around Boston—which attacks the offices of the customs commissioners. Parliament repeals the Townshend Acts, except for the tax on tea. Colonists respond by ending their nonimportation policy.

1772 The governor of Massachusetts announces that his salary and those of other royally appointed officials of the colony will be paid for by the Crown, making them financially independent of the colony. Leaders in Boston appoint a committee of correspondence to communicate with other towns about this challenge; SAMUEL ADAMS and other radicals assume control of the Boston committee.

THE BOSTON TEA PARTY (1773)

The colonists loved tea, but English taxes on it caused them to sharply reduce consumption, pushing the East India Company, a major importer of colonial tea, toward bankruptcy. As the company was the main agent of British power in India, Parliament tried to shore it up financially by passing the Tea Act of May 10, 1773. The new law adjusted import taxes to enable the company to undersell—at prices alluring to even the most patriotic colonist—all competitors. Four months later, the company shipped 1,700 chests of tea to selected consignees in the major colonial ports—Boston, New York, Philadelphia, and Charleston. Patriot groups were outraged, arguing that Parliament was only trying to make it easy for colonists to swallow paying an unconstitutional tax. In addition, local merchants who had not been picked saw their exclusion as an attempt by England to subvert their prosperity and independence.

Organized by colonial committees of correspondence, opposition to the Tea Act mounted.

Protests caused the consignees in every port but Boston to resign. The first tea shipped reached Boston Harbor in late November, and two others arrived shortly afterward. In mass meetings in Old South Church, colonists demanded that the tea be returned to England with the duties unpaid. On December 16, patriots meeting in the church heard that Governor Thomas Hutchinson refused their demand. At midnight, a small group of patriots (perhaps including SAMUEL ADAMS) disguised themselves as Indians and marched to the ships, boarded them, and dumped forty-five tons of tea into Boston Harbor. Other colonial cities quickly followed Boston, either dumping tea or burning it. Such actions confirmed for the British that Massachussets was the bastion of resistance to their power over the colonies. In response, in 1774 an angry Parliament passed a series of acts, called the Intolerable Acts (the colonists labeled them the Coercive Acts), designed to punish the rebellious colony.

1772, *cont.*

Rhode Islanders burn the grounded English schooner *Gaspee*, a customs warship.

The formal signing of Declaration of Independence did not take place on July 4, 1776. The Second Continental Congress adopted a final draft on that day, but the official document was not signed until August 2.

1773 In Virginia, the House of Burgesses appoints PATRICK HENRY, RICHARD HENRY LEE, and THOMAS JEFFERSON, among others, to the just formed Committee for Intercolonial Correspondence. A year later all other colonies, except conservative Pennsylvania, have formed committees. These become the main channels for sharing information about British actions affecting the colonies, building intercolonial cooperation, and shaping public opinion.

To save the East India Company from bankruptcy, Parliament passes the Tea Act, which gives the company the right to sell tea directly to the colonies, by passing an export tax but retaining an important tax on the colonies. The colonists protest the unconstitutional tax and the threat of a tea monopoly. In the most dramatic protest, the Boston Tea Party, colonists dressed as Indians dump British tea into Boston Harbor.

1774 As punishment for the Boston Tea Party, Parliament passes the Coercive Acts, which close the city's port pending restitution for the destroyed tea; put the royal governor in charge of all civil officials, virtually annulling the Massachusetts Charter; permit an official who commits a capital offense while on duty to be tried in Britain instead of the colonies; and authorize the quartering of British soldiers in private homes.

Together with the Quebec Act, which enlarges the province and gives it a centralized government that preserves the privileges of the Catholic Church, the colonists label these the Intolerable Acts.

Delegates from all the colonies except Georgia meet in Philadelphia as the First Continental Congress, where they denounce the Coercive Acts, advise the people to arm, and propose to cut off trade with Britain.

1775 In a speech against British rule, PATRICK HENRY pronounces, "Give me liberty or give me death."

Paul Revere rides at night to tell colonists that British redcoats are marching on Concord, Massachusetts, to destroy colonial arms supplies. In the first clash of the American Revolution, minutemen fight the British at Lexington and Concord.

1776 The Declaration of Independence, drafted by THOMAS JEFFERSON, is adopted by Congress and signed by the delegates.

The Original Thirteen Colonies, 1775

THE SIGNERS OF THE DECLARATION OF INDEPENDENCE

SIGNER	COLONY	SIGNER	COLONY
Adams, John	Massachusetts	Lynch, Thomas Jr.	South Carolina
Adams, Samuel	Massachusetts	McKean, Thomas	Delaware
Bartlett, Josiah	New Hampshire	Middleton, Arthur	South Carolina
Braxton, Carter	Virginia	Morris, Lewis	New York
Carroll, Charles	Maryland	Morris, Robert	Pennsylvania
Chase, Samuel	Maryland	Morton, John	Pennsylvania
Clark, Abraham	New Jersey	Nelson, Thomas Jr.	Virginia
Clymer, George	Pennsylvania	Paca, William	Maryland
Ellery, William	Rhode Island	Paine, Robert Treat	Massachesetts
Floyd, William	New York	Penn, John	North Carolina
Franklin, Benjamin	Pennsylvania	Read, George	Delaware
Gerry, Elbridge	Massachusetts	Rodney, Caesar	Delaware
Gwinnett, Button	Georgia	Ross, George	Pennsylvania
Hall, Lyman	Georgia	Rush, Benjamin	Pennsylvania
Hancock, John	Massachusetts	Rutledge, Edward	South Carolina
Harrison, Benjamin	Virginia	Sherman, Roger	Connecticut
Hart, John	New Jersey	Smith, James	Pennsylvania
Hewes, Joseph	North Carolina	Stockton, Richard	New Jersey
Heyward, Thomas Jr.	South Carolina	Stone, Thomas	Maryland
Hooper, William	North Carolina	Taylor, George	Pennsylvania
Hopkins, Stephen	Rhode Island	Thornton, Matthew	New Hampshire
Hopkinson, Francis	New Jersey	Walton, George	Georgia
Huntington, Samuel	Connecticut	Whipple, William	New Hampshire
Jefferson, Thomas	Virginia	Williams, William	Connecticut
Lee, Francis Lightfoot	Virginia	Wilson, James	Pennsylvania
Lee, Richard Henry	Virginia	Witherspoon, John	New Jersey
Lewis, Francis	New York	Wolcott, Oliver	Connecticut
Livingston, Philip	New York	Wythe, George	Virginia

In 1823, Asher Durand created this engraving based on a painting by John Trumbell, who consulted extensively
with Thomas Jefferson and John Adams to accurately depict the scene of Jefferson submitting the
Declaration of Independence to John Hancock.

THE INTRODUCTION AND SPREAD OF SLAVERY, 1441–1807

1441 African slaves are first transported to Portugal.

1518 Spain licenses Portuguese slavers.

1619 Twenty bound African servants disembark from a Dutch ship at Jamestown, Virginia. They probably are the first Africans in the English colonies of America.

1641 The Massachusetts Body of Liberties decrees that "no bond slavery" will exist in the colony, except for captives in a just war.

1661 Colonial statutes in Virginia first recognize the legal existence of slavery.

1662 In Virginia a new law makes slavery hereditary.

1663 In London, the Royal African Company, a slave-trading enterprise, is reincorporated.

1670 Virginia law enacts classifications defining slavery.
   A Massachusetts law states that the offspring of slaves can be sold into slavery.

1681 Maryland's assembly decrees that the children of a white woman and black man inherit the status of the mother.

1684 New York laws recognize slavery as a legitimate institution.

1686 By this date South Carolina statutes define slavery in the fashion in which it will be known until 1865.

1688 Quakers in Germantown, Pennsylvania, issue a protest against slavery.

1698 England ends the monopoly of the Royal African Company, allowing independent merchants to engage in the slave trade.

1699 The Spanish open Florida as a refuge for runaway slaves.

1705 Virginia enacts a comprehensive slave code.

1708 Virginia counts 12,000 slaves in a total population of 30,000.

1712 Following a slave revolt in New York City, nine whites are dead and about twenty African Americans are executed (see p. 220).

1713 The Treaty of Utrecht ending the War of the Spanish Succession gives Great Britain the monopoly on the slave trade. New England shippers thrive on the insatiable demand for slaves in Spanish America, the Caribbean, and Brazil.

1715 Virginia counts 23,000 slaves in a total population of 95,500.

1730–1750 Pennsylvania declines to allow the importation of slaves.

1731 New York restricts the number of slaves at a burial to twelve plus the grave digger and the pallbearers.

1732 Georgia is founded with the specific proviso that "no Negro slaves" be allowed in the colony. The inhabitants petition the trustees for a reversal of this policy. Slavery is finally allowed in 1750, though slaves had been hired from South Carolina on 100-year leases since 1741.

1739 In South Carolina three slave revolts leave dozens of blacks and whites dead. In one of these revolts, a group of Angolans sack the armory at Stono, killing thrity whites.

1741 In New York City thirty African Americans are executed for arson.

1756 Virginia has 120,156 slaves in a total population of 293,472.

1758 New Jersey Quakers oppose the importation and sale of slaves.

THE INTRODUCTION AND SPREAD OF SLAVERY, 1441–1807, cont.

1767 Delaware requires that a $60 bond be posted for each manumitted (released) slave.

1770 The population of the thirteen colonies is 1,688,254 whites and 459,822 blacks, almost all slaves.

1774 The Continental Congress asks that the slave trade be terminated, while THOMAS JEFFERSON calls for the abolition of slavery in "A Summary of the Rights of British America."

1775 In Philadelphia the first antislavery organization, the Pennsylvania Society for the Abolition of Slavery, is formed.

1777 Vermont becomes the first state to abolish slavery.

1807 Congress votes to terminate the international slave trade in the United States, effective January 1, 1808.

VOYAGE OF THE SLAVES

The Middle Passage—that leg of the Triangular Trade that took Africans to the West Indies as slaves—was a six- to eight-week voyage of terror. To pack as many human beings as possible into ships—called "slavers"—designed for this purpose, Africans were chained on shelves less than three feet apart. Sickness and insanity were rampant. So was death; at least one in every six Africans died. But, with an eye to potential profits, slave traders did exercise and feed their cargo. In the eighteenth century, some 600,000 Africans crossed the Atlantic this way.

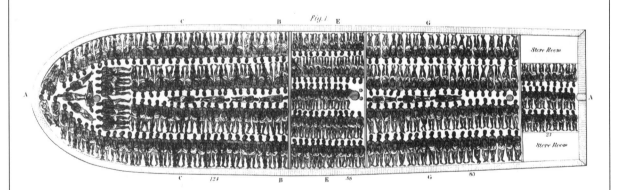

This 1808 diagram of the interior of a slave ship, drawn by artist Thomas Clarkson, illustrates how Africans were packed into "slavers" during the middle passage.

NOTABLE FIGURES IN EXPLORATION AND COLONIZATION

Adams, John (1735–1826). A Revolutionary leader and the second U.S. president, he entered politics by opposing the Stamp Act. He served as a delegate to the Continental Congress and was a member of the committee that drafted the Declaration of Independence.

Adams, Samuel (1722–1803). This Revolutionary leader wrote a protest to the Stamp Act, helped found the Non-Importation Association to repeal the Townshend Acts, and drafted the Circular Letter to the other colonies, in which he argued that the acts constituted taxation without representation. He also formed the Boston Committee of Correspondence, helped organize the Boston Tea Party, served as a delegate to the First and the Second Continental Congresses, and signed the Declaration of Independence.

Bacon, Nathaniel (1647–1676). Disobeying the orders of Virginia governor William Berkeley, Bacon led expeditions against local Indians. After Berkeley declared him a rebel, in 1676 Bacon organized a popular revolt called Bacon's Rebellion, during which Jamestown was captured and burned. In effective control of the colony, Bacon died suddenly, probably of dysentery, and the rebellion collapsed.

Balboa, Vasco Núñez de (c. 1475–1519). While crossing the Isthmus of Panama, Balboa discovered the Pacific Ocean and claimed it and the lands it touched for Spain. He was unique among the conquistadors for gaining the friendship of the Indians. Accused and found guilty in Spain of treason, Balboa was beheaded.

Boone, Daniel (1734–1820). This frontiersman traveled through the Cumberland Gap (near where Virginia, Kentucky, and Tennessee meet) and in 1775 led settlers into Kentucky, where he built a fort at present-day Boonsboro. Boone lived in Kentucky until 1799, when he moved into what is now Missouri. Many legends grew up around his exploits.

Cabeza de Vaca, Álvar Núñez (c. 1490–c. 1557). After surviving a shipwreck off the Texas coast and subsequent slavery by Native Americans, this Spanish explorer and three companions trekked overland from Texas to Mexico. It is believed that they were the first Europeans to see buffalo. Their stories about the Pueblo villages may have been the source of the tales of the legendary Seven Cities of Cíbola, fabled lands rich in gold, silver, and jewels.

Cabot, John (fl. 1461–1498). An Italian explorer in the service of England, Cabot discovered the North American coast on his first voyage. The fate of his second voyage is unknown. England based its claims to the New World on Cabot's discovery.

Cabot, Sebastian (c. 1483–1557). In the service of England, this Italian explorer searched for a northwest passage, and in 1509, he may have reached as far north as the Hudson Bay and as far south as North Carolina. Between 1526 and 1530, in the service of Spain, Cabot explored South America.

Cartier, Jacques (1491–1557). Cartier was the first explorer of the Gulf of Saint Lawrence and the discoverer of the Saint Lawrence River. The French based their claims to the Saint Lawrence Valley on his discoveries.

Champlain, Samuel de (1567–1635). This Frenchman explored the Saint Lawrence River, founded Quebec, and discovered Lake Champlain. He also sailed up the New England coast for three years (1605–1608), discovering Mount Desert Island and most of Maine's big rivers.

Columbus, Christopher (1451–1506). In the service of Ferdinand and Isabella of Spain, Columbus, an Italian, made four voyages in search of a western route to Asia. Instead of finding this route he sailed to the Caribbean and the West Indies. Columbus is credited as the first European to discover the New World. He died in poverty in Valladolid, Spain.

Coronado, Francisco Vásquez de (c. 1510–1554). Between 1540 and 1542, Coronado reached the fabled Cíbola, actually New Mexico, but found no cities of gold, although his lieutenant, Garcia López de Cárdenas, did discover the Grand Canyon. Coronado is credited with encountering the Pueblo Indians and opening the Southwest to exploration.

Cortés, Hernando (1485–1547). Cortés is known as the conquerer of Mexico. He landed on the Mexican coast in 1519 and marched to the Aztec capital at Tenochtitlán (now Mexico City). After the emperor Montezuma welcomed him as a descendant of the god Queztalcoatl, Cortés seized the ruler and used him as a figurehead. The Aztecs rebelled in 1520; Montezuma was killed, but the Spanish had to retreat from Tenochtitlán. The following year Cortés regained the capital after a three-month seige that destroyed the Aztec empire. He conquered

NOTABLE FIGURES, *cont.*

most of Mexico before returning to Spain. Cortés's triumph has been attributed to superior arms and horses, the slow response of the cumbersome Aztec bureaucracy to crisis, and his clever exploitation of the anger of native peoples who lived under Aztec domination.

Dare, Virginia (1587–?). Dare was the first child born to English parents in America. Her grandfather was the founder of the Roanoke Island colony, who left her nine days after her birth when he sailed to England for supplies. In 1591, aid for the colony finally arrived, but all traces of the settlement had disappeared.

de Soto, Hernando (c. 1500–1542). On a quest for gold, silver, and jewels, de Soto, a Spaniard, explored the American Southwest and discovered the Mississippi River, on whose banks he died. To conceal his death from the Indians, whom he had treated cruelly, de Soto was buried in the Mississippi.

Dickinson John (1732–1808). A Philadelphia lawyer, Dickinson was a member of the Stamp Act Congress and the author of the famous *Letters from a Farmer in Pennsylvania to the Inhabitants of the British Colonies* (1767–1768). In 1776, he helped draft the Articles of Confederation but, still hoping for a peaceful solution with England, voted against the Declaration of Independence.

Drake, Sir Francis (1540?–1596). The first Englishman to circumnavigate the world between 1577 and 1580, Drake sailed possibly as far north as what is now Washington. Then, deciding to cross the Pacific, he repaired his ship north of present-day San Francisco, claiming the region for Queen Elizabeth I.

Eric the Red (fl. tenth century). Seeking land west of Iceland, this Norse explorer discovered Greenland. About four years later he returned and with 500 settlers established a colony there. Although it gradually died out, other Viking settlements in Greenland survived.

Eriksson, Leif (fl. 1000). Son of Norse explorer ERIC THE RED, Eriksson is probably the discoverer of America. According to a Norse saga, Eriksson sighted the unknown land he named Vinland when he was blown off course during a voyage from Norway to Greenland.

Franklin, Benjamin (1706–1790). A Renaissance man, Franklin was a printer, writer, philosopher, scientist, and inventor as well as a Revolutionary leader and statesman. In 1727, he founded a discussion club called the Junto, which

later became the American Philosophical Society. He also helped create a library for public use, which developed into the Philadelphia Library; contributed to making that city's streets better lit; and served jointly, with William Hunter, as deputy postmaster general for the colonies from 1753 to 1774. A member of the Continental Congress (1775), he served on the committee that drafted the Declaration of Independence, which he also signed. In 1776 he was sent by Congress with two others to France to win French recognition of the new republic, which was accomplished in 1778. With John Jay and JOHN ADAMS, he negotiated peace with England in the Treaty of Paris (1783).

Frobisher, Sir Martin (1535?–1594). Englishman Frobisher made three voyages along the North American coast in search of a northwest passage. During the first voyage, he discovered Frobisher Bay in Canada, returning with an Eskimo as "proof" that he had reached China.

Hancock, John (1737–1793). The president of the Continental Congress from 1775 to 1777, Hancock, a Massachusetts businessman, was the first signer of the Declaration of Independence.

Hennepin, Louis (1640–1701?). Hannepin was a Franciscan missionary among the Iroquois before accompanying the French explorer RENÉ-ROBERT CAVELIER, SIEUR DE LA SALLE on his expedition to the Mississippi River valley. Hennepin named the Falls of Saint Anthony, later the site of Minneapolis. His lively accounts contain the first description of Niagara Falls.

Henry, Patrick (1736–1799). Henry's speeches in defense of individual liberty, which included the famous declarations "If this be treason, make the most of it" and "Give me liberty or give me death," fueled colonial Revolutionary fire. With fellow Virginians RICHARD HENRY LEE and THOMAS JEFFERSON, Henry, a lawyer and a leader of the so-called radicals, formed the Committee for Intercolonial Correspondence. Elected to the First and Second Continental Congresses (1774–1776), he later served as governor of Virginia.

Hooker, Thomas (1586–1647). Discontent with the strictness of Massachussetts Puritanism, Hooker, a minister, led many of his Cambridge congregation to found Hartford, Connecticut, where he continued as pastor to his followers until his death.

Hudson, Henry (fl. 1607–1611). Hoping to find a northwest passage for the Dutch East Indies Company,

English navigator Hudson explored in 1609 the Chesapeake Bay, the Delaware Bay, the New York Bay, and the Hudson River, laying the base for Dutch claims to this region. A year later he reached the Hudson Strait and Hudson Bay, which lay between Labrador and Greenland. This exploration enabled England to claim the entire Hudson Bay region.

Hutchinson, Anne (1591–1643). Hutchinson was convicted and exiled from the Massachusetts Bay Colony for preaching that salvation could be gained through faith rather than through obedience to the laws of church and state. Following her banishment, she and her followers moved first to Rhode Island and then to present-day Pelham Bay, New York, where Hutchinson and all but one of her family were killed by Indians.

Jefferson, Thomas (1743–1826). Before becoming the third U.S. president, Jefferson served in Virginia's House of Burgesses between 1769 and 1775. He wrote the first draft of the Declaration of Independence, presenting it on July 2, 1776, to the Continental Congress, of which he was a member. Jefferson was also one of the signers of the declaration.

Jolliet, Louis (1645–1700). With French Jesuit priest JACQUES MARQUETTE, Frenchman Jolliet discovered the upper Mississippi River and proved that a water highway existed from the Saint Lawrence to the Gulf of Mexico. In 1673 the two sailed the Mississippi to the Gulf of Mexico. Ascending the Illinois River in the same year, they came upon the site of what is now Chicago.

La Salle, René-Robert Cavelier, Sieur de (1643–1687). With his lieutenant, HENRI DE TONTI, Frenchman La Salle explored the Great Lakes in 1679, sailed to Green Bay, and continued on to the Illinois River. Two years later he descended the Mississippi to its mouth, claiming the river's valley, which he called Louisiana, for France. In 1683, he built Fort St. Louis in Illinois. Four years later he was killed by his men in a mutiny.

Lee, Richard Henry (1732–1794). As a member of Virginia's House of Burgesses from 1758 to 1775, this Revolutionary patriot defended colonial rights. With THOMAS JEFFERSON and PATRICK HENRY, he formed the Committee for Intercolonial Correspondence in 1773. A delegate to the Continental Congress from 1774 through

Anne Hutchinson's unorthodox preaching style displeased many male Puritan ministers.

1779, he moved a resolution that resulted in the Declaration of Independence, which he later signed.

Leisler, Jacob (1640–1691). Leisler and his followers ousted England's New Amsterdam agent, proclaiming loyalty to England's William and Mary. Leisler ruled the colony until 1691, when he relinquished his power to an appointed governor. He was subsequently convicted of treason and hanged.

Magellan, Ferdinand (c. 1480–1521). Looking for a route around South America to Asia, Magellan, a Portuguese, was the first to circumnavigate the globe, sailing over unknown parts of the world. After he was killed in a conflict between Philippine natives, his lieutenant, Juan Sebastian del Cano, completed the more than 50,000-mile (80,000-km) voyage in 1522. Besides conclusively proving that the earth was round, the voyage changed views of the proportions of land to water.

Marquette, Jacques (1637–1675). Marquette, a French explorer and Jesuit missionary, was appointed by Louis Frontenac, governor of New France, to accompany LOUIS JOLLIET in his search for the Mississippi River. In 1673, they descended the Mississippi and concluded that it emptied into the Gulf of Mexico. Next they ascended the river's eastern bank, entered the Illinois River, and came upon the site of present-day Chicago.

Oñate, Juan de (fl. 1595–1614). In three expeditions, Oñate, a Spaniard, explored the American Southwest from the Colorado River to Kansas. His first expedition was to New Mexico, which he claimed for Spain.

Penn, William (1644–1718). An English religious reformer and colonist, Penn received a charter for Pennsylvania from Charles II in repayment of a debt. In 1682, Penn visited his colony, where he made peace with the Indians and directed the laying out of the city of Philadelphia. Returning to Pennsylvania in 1699, he reestablished peace with the Indians and granted a liberal constitution to the colony.

Pocahontas (c. 1595–1617). Pocahontas was the favorite daughter of Algonquin chief Powhatan. Captain JOHN SMITH wrote that she had saved his life after he had been captured by Powhatan's warriors. Modern historians believe, however, that Smith may have mistaken a

NOTABLE FIGURES, *cont.*

religious rite for an execution. Pocahontas was seized by the English in 1613 as a way of making Powhatan cease hostilities against the colonists. Converted to Christianity during her captivity, she married colonist JOHN ROLFE and accompanied him to England, where she was presented to the king and queen. Pocahontas died as she was returning to the New World.

Ponce de León, Juan (c. 1460–1521). According to legend, seeking the Fountain of Youth, Ponce de León, the Spanish governor of Puerto Rico, sailed to Florida. Landing near Saint Augustine, he named the land he had first sighted on Easter Sunday "La Florida."

Radisson, Pierre Esprit (1632–1710). A French explorer and fur trader, Radisson, with his brother-in-law, Medard Chouart, set off from Canada, entered Lake Superior, and went as far west as present-day Minnesota, becoming the first Europeans to venture there, before returning with a rich bounty of furs. Their explorations and the furs they brought back led to the establishment of the Hudson Bay Company.

Rolfe, John (1585–1622). A Jamestown settler, Rolfe introduced the cultivation of West Indian Orinoco-leaf tobacco, which had a better taste than Virginian varieties. Such a valuable cash crop helped the colony to survive and became the basis for Virginia's prosperity. Rolfe married POCAHONTAS in 1614. He was probably killed by Indians.

Smith, John (c. 1580–1631). Smith, an Englishman, helped establish Jamestown, Virginia, and served on the colony's governing council. Captured by the Algonquin Indians, Smith believed that he was about to be executed but was saved by Chief Powhatan's daughter POCAHONTAS. Modern historians suggest he may have been incorrect in that he probably mistook a religious rite for an execution. Afterward Smith explored the areas around the Potomac and Rappahonnock Rivers and the Chesapeake Bay. He was the leader of Jamestown from 1608 to 1609 and is credited with helping it survive. Smith also explored the New England coast before finally returning to England, where he spent the rest of his life. He wrote several accounts of his experiences in the New World.

Tonti, Henri de (1650–1704). Selected by RENÉ-ROBERT CAVELIER, SIEUR DE LA SALLE, to be his lieutenant at Fort Niagara, Tonti built the first sailboat ever to be used on the Great Lakes. He then went ahead of La Salle to Detroit, where he established good relations with the Illinois Indians. The two men joined forces to travel down to the mouth of the Mississippi River, claiming the surrounding region for France.

Verrazzano, Giovanni da (c. 1480–1527?). An Italian navigator in the service of France, Verrazzano voyaged west seeking Asia and sailed into New York Bay in 1524.

Vespucci, Amerigo (1454–1512). An Italian navigator, Vespucci helped outfit vessels for the third and the fourth voyages of CHRISTOPHER COLUMBUS. In 1507, German mapmaker Martin Waldseemüller named the New World America after Vespucci in honor of his exploration of the mouths of the Amazon in 1499 and the Río de la Plata in 1501, as well as his exploration of the northern and southern coasts of South America.

Williams, Roger (1603?–1683). Williams, a pastor in Plymouth, Massachusetts, believed in religious toleration. When the Massachusetts General Court banished him from the colony for his criticism of the local authorities, he and his followers founded Providence, the first Rhode Island settlement. There Williams formed good relations with the local Narragansett Indians. Williams served as president of the colony for three terms, 1654–1657.

Winthrop, John (1588–1649). One of the original Salem, Massachusetts colonists, Winthrop was elected the first governor of the Massachusetts Bay Colony. He served again in 1631, 1632, 1633, 1637 to 1640, 1642 to 1644, and 1646 to 1649. Winthrop presided over the trial of ANNE HUTCHINSON, which resulted in her banishment from Massachusetts. In 1643, he helped establish the United Colonies of New England, serving as the confederation's first president. Three volumes of his journals, including *The History of New England from 1630 to 1649*, were published posthumously.

CHAPTER 3

TERRITORIAL EXPANSION

■

HIGHLIGHTS

Timeline of Territorial Expansion

WESTWARD EXPANSION BEGAN with the first movement of European settlers inland from the Atlantic coast. As colonists from Plymouth and Massachusetts Bay moved west into what would be Connecticut, and as the leaders of Massachusetts Bay annexed towns in what would be New Hampshire and Maine, they were engaging in a territorial expansion that would be repeated in a multitude of ways and places over the next three centuries. From tiny settlements hugging the Atlantic Coast, a nation grew to encompass a vast continent and far-flung islands. The perception of unlimited resources and an endless frontier shaped the national character—first at the expense of indigenous peoples, who experienced encroachment, displacement, and broken promises, and, over the centuries, at the expense of the natural environment.

TOWARD NEW HORIZONS: THE EIGHTEENTH CENTURY

1749 The Ohio Company receives a royal charter and an enormous land grant for the area along the forks of the Ohio River (where the Monongahela and Allegheny Rivers join, now Pittsburgh).

1754–1763 During the French and Indian War both France and Britain attempt to secure the west by building forts. Their forces clash repeatedly, while fierce Indian raids signify that no European claim to these lands is secure.

1763 Britain wins the French and Indian War, and by the Treaty of Paris all French claims in North America except the two small islands of Saint-Pierre and Miquelon pass to Britain. The Royal Proclamation of 1763 forbids British settlement west of the Appalachian Mountains to reserve an Indian territory and deflate tension.

1767 DANIEL BOONE makes his first trip to Kentucky.

1774 Parliament passes the Quebec Act, organizing land west of the Appalachians and south to the Ohio River into the new province of Quebec, thus violating colonial charters. Intended to win the allegiance of the French in the region, the Quebec Act violated colonial land charters and infuriated English colonists.

1776–1779 On his third voyage to the Pacific, Englishman James Cook explores the northwest coast of North America and becomes the first white person to set foot on Hawaii.

1781 The Articles of Confederation are finally ratified only when states with claims to western lands agree to give them up.

1783 By the Treaty of Paris, ending the Revolutionary War, Britain cedes its empire in North America to the new United States, retaining only Canada (which the colonists had hoped would join them in rebellion). Indian lands are considered a prize of war.

THE RECTANGULAR SURVEY

Prior to the first surveys in 1785, mandated by the Land Ordinance of that year, property lines ran along waterways, ridgetops, or meandered along tree lines, and corners were noted by distinctive trees, springs, or physical features. Over time, trees died, decayed, and disappeared; streams shifted course or dried up; and boundaries became difficult to ascertain. Title to a piece of land could be hard to verify, because the same piece of land might be described two different ways; often land had been settled before it had been surveyed. Wanting to sell the vast public domain it had acquired when the states ceded their western lands, and recognizing that clear land titles were essential to stability, Congress ordered a rectangular survey of all land in the public domain and required that land be surveyed before it could be sold.

Beginning at the point where Ohio, Pennsylvania, and Virginia (today West Virginia) meet as the Ohio River leaves Pennsylvania, the land was surveyed and divided into townships, each six miles square and consisting of thirty-six sections, each containing 640 acres or one square mile. The proceeds from the sale of one section in each township went to support public education. Every so often on the way west a correction was made to take into account the curvature of the Earth. Each section of a township was numbered in precisely the same way once the details were worked out in Ohio, and the practice continued as the survey moved west. Each township had its own unique description that could never be confused with any other township. Anyone following the legal description could find the piece of land described; ambiguity was eliminated. Surveyed townships marched westward across the continent without

respect to any physical feature, creating the pattern of straight roads and rectangular fields that remain a source of amazement today as one flies over the vast land west of the Appalachians.

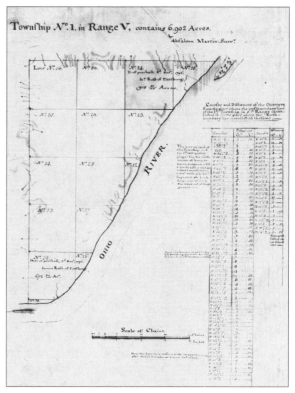

This map of Township No. 1 in Range 5 shows a section of Ohio's "Seven Ranges"—the first land surveyed under the Land Ordinance of 1785. This new system of dividing land into sections, townships, and ranges will alleviate ambiguity about the boundaries of property.

The United States, 1776-1800

Claimed by U.S. and Britain
Claimed by U.S. until 1798
To Britain
To Massachusetts
"Erie Triangle" sold to Pennsylvania 1792
St. Lawrence
VT 1791
NH 1788*
NEW YORK 1788*
MA 1788*
CT RI 1790*
1788*
INDIANA TERRITORY 1800
Mississippi
PENNSYLVANIA 1787*
NEW JERSEY 1787*
DELAWARE 1787*
TERRITORY NORTHWEST OF OHIO RIVER 1787
MARYLAND 1788*
Missouri
Ohio
VIRGINIA 1788*
DISTRICT OF COLUMBIA 1791 (FEDERAL TERRITORY)
KENTUCKY 1792
NORTH CAROLINA 1789*
To France 1800
TENNESSEE 1796
TERRITORY SOUTH OF OHIO RIVER 1790
SOUTH CAROLINA 1788*
Mississippi
GEORGIA 1788*
ATLANTIC OCEAN
To Spain
To Spain 1783 MISSISSIPPI TERR. 1798
To Spain 1783
BAHAMA IS. (To Britain)

UNITED STATES, 1800 :
STATES
TERRITORIES
TERRITORY BOUNDARY CHANGED BY FORMATION OF STATE

GULF OF MEXICO

0   400 Miles
0   600 Kilometers

* ORIGINAL THIRTEEN STATES' DATE OF RATIFICATION OF THE CONSTITUTION

1785 The Land Ordinance provides for the survey and sale of public lands.

1787 The Northwest Ordinance provides for the governance of public lands in the Old Northwest Territory, which includes the area northwest of the Ohio River and east of the Mississippi, establishing the process by which U.S. territories will qualify for statehood.

Slavery is banned in the Old Northwest Territory, establishing another precedent.

1788 The Constitution of the United States, ratified by nine states, goes into effect. It gives Congress the power to make rules and regulations for the territories of the United States and to admit new states into the Union.

The first lands surveyed under the Land Ordinance Act are made available for sale. Federal troops are brought in to maintain order.

1793 ALEXANDER MACKENZIE completes the first overland trek across North America to the Pacific Ocean.

WESTWARD HO: 1800–1890

The term "cowboy" was first used during the Revolutionary War for Tory sympathizers in upstate New York. These backwoods guerrillas used cowbells to lure patriot soldiers into ambush.

1803 The Louisiana Purchase more than doubles the size of the country. For $15 million, THOMAS JEFFERSON negotiated from the French the purchase of land between the Mississippi River and the Rocky Mountains, and the Canadian border and the Gulf of Mexico. At 827,192 square miles, this huge parcel of land includes most of today's Great Plains and is the largest single acquisition of land the United States will make.

1804–1806 In what will become the prototype for western exploratory expeditions, MERIWETHER LEWIS and WILLIAM P. CLARK, commissioned by President JEFFERSON, explore the Louisiana Purchase territory to find "the most direct and practical water communication across the continent for purposes of commerce." Jefferson's scientific curiosity makes certain that they will report on all aspects of the peoples they meet and the country through which they pass (see p. 75 and p. 384). SACAJAWEA, a Shoshone woman married to a French Canadian, is their guide and interpreter.

ROADS AND TRAILS

Early routes and trails through the frontier gave way to steamboats, canals, and the first railroads as primary means of trade in the mid-nineteenth century. These trails stretched clear across the continent—through prairies, mountains, deserts, and Indian country—to the promise of land ownership, gold, religious community, and new opportunities. Famous for the great wagon trains, these now-fabled thoroughfares also established commercial access to eastern markets for fur, beef, cattle, and other goods. By the 1870s and '80s, however, the expanding network of railroads had relegated them to history.

Bozeman Trail: Blazed in 1863–1865 by pioneer John M. Bozeman, it branched from the Oregon Trail in southeastern Wyoming and provided a clear route to the gold fields of southern Montana. It was abandoned in 1868 due to Indian resistance and the railroad.

Chisholm Trail: Extending from San Antonio, Texas, to Abilene, Kansas, it was the major cattle connection through Indian Country to rail lines east. Cut by trapper Jesse Chisholm in 1866, it carried 4 million cattle during the 1870s.

Natchez Trace: Originally an Indian trail, it ran 450 miles from Natchez, Mississippi, to Nashville, Tennessee. It became important in the early nineteenth century as a post road, settlement trail to the Old Southwest, and trade route. The advent of Mississippi River steamboats in the 1830s curtailed its use.

National Road: Also called the Cumberland Road, it was the first U.S. federal highway. Built between 1811 and 1852, it linked Cumberland, Maryland, and Vandalia, Illinois. Today it is part of U.S. Route 40.

Oregon Trail: Stretching some 2,000 miles from Independence, Missouri, to the Pacific Northwest, it was blazed by trappers, traders, and missionaries in the 1830s and carried thousands of settlers west during the "Oregon fever" of the following decade.

Overland Trail: Including several overland routes to California, it split from the Oregon Trail beyond South Pass (a route through the Rockies in Wyoming). The California Gold Rush brought a flood of traffic beginning in 1849—45,000 people in that year alone.

Santa Fe Trail: Pioneered in 1821–1822 from Independence, Missouri, to Santa Fe, New Mexico, it was the first major wagon road and overland trade route to the Far West. Its two major forks and many secondary routes served numerous merchant caravans, and commerce in both directions flourished until a rail link to Santa Fe opened in 1880.

Wilderness Road: Cleared by DANIEL BOONE and a team of axmen in 1775, it ran from eastern Virginia through the Cumberland Gap to the Kentucky River. Some 200,000 settlers traveled the road by 1800.

1805 ZEBULON PIKE leads an expedition to find the source of the Mississippi River. He does not find the source but explores the upper Mississippi Valley.

1806–1807 ZEBULON PIKE undertakes a major expedition through the Great Plains and the southern Rocky Mountains. He pronounces the high western plains "incapable of cultivation," a characterization that lasts most of the century.

1807–1810 David Thompson, a Hudson's Bay Company fur trader, crosses the Canadian Rockies, discovers the source of the Columbia, and explores the area of present-day Washington, Idaho, and Montana.

1810 United States takes over West Florida.

WESTERN LANDS: FIRST CLAIMS

Most colonial charters granted rights to land "from sea to sea." Only Pennsylvania, New Jersey, Delaware, Maryland, New Hampshire, and Rhode Island had no western lands. Britain's disregard for colonial claims angered the colonists before the Revolution, and during the Revolution states with western lands promised land bounties to veterans. Fearing domination by the large states in the new confederation, Maryland announced in 1778 that it would not ratify the Articles of Confederation until all western lands were ceded to Congress. By 1781, all states had promised to comply, and Maryland signed the Articles, completing ratification. By 1802, all western land claims were settled, becoming the public domain.

1812 Louisiana is admitted to statehood.
The Missouri Territory is established.

1814–1820 After the Creek War between Creeks and white settlers in Alabama, large land concessions are forced on the Choctaws, the Chickasaws, and the Creeks, opening more new land to white settlement in the Old Southwest.

1815–1820 Their attention no longer diverted by British threats in the War of 1812, Americans become interested in settling the west. In what is one of the most rapid migrations the nation will ever experience, large numbers of settlers move into the Old Southwest, which will become the states of Alabama and Mississippi. In one decade the population of Alabama grows sixteen times and that of Mississippi doubles. Another wave of settlers sweeps into the Northwest Territory.

1817–1818 While the federal government is negotiating with Spain to obtain parts of present-day Florida, Gen. ANDREW JACKSON, fighting the Seminoles, oversteps his order and invades the Florida Territory.

1818 The United States and Britain extend the boundary between the United States and British North America along the 49th parallel, from the Lake of the Woods, Minnesota, to the crest of the Rocky Mountains. The Oregon Country, between 42° N and 54°40' N, is occupied jointly.

1819 A national crisis and a heated public debate begin when Missouri applies to enter the Union as a slave state; abolitionists oppose this expansion of slavery.
STEPHEN HARRIMAN LONG departs on a two-year, army-supported expedition to explore and map the Great Plains. In part,

The Louisiana Purchase, 1803

the federal government plans these expeditions as a show of power to other nations occupying North American territories. He confirms PIKE's assessment of the Great Plains.

By treaty with Spain, the United States acquires Florida.

1820 The Missouri Compromise attempts to settle the pressing question of whether slavery will be extended in the new states that will be created out of the Louisiana Purchase: Missouri is admitted as a slave state, and Maine as a free state to maintain the balance of free and slave states in the Senate. Slavery is banned in the Louisiana Territory north of a 36°30' N boundary.

1821 Following Mexico's independence from Spain, the Sante Fe Trail is opened. From Independence, Missouri, to Sante Fe—over 800 miles (1,290 km) of open desert and Indian Country—the trail makes lucrative trade possible, as merchant-traders brought finished goods to Sante Fe to exchange for furs and other items.

1823 The Monroe Doctrine warns European nations that the Americas are not open to any future colonization and that any such move will be considered dangerous to the United States. In return, the United States promises to respect existing colonies and to stay out of the internal affairs of European nations (see p. 292).

1824 The fur trade in the West takes shape with the rendezvous system whereby trappers, who usually worked alone, would bring their furs down from the mountains to exchange for necessities, weapons, horses,

The American flag had fifteen stripes from 1795 (after the admission of Vermont and Kentucky into the Union) until 1818, when Congress passed a law that reverted permanently to thirteen horizontal bars.

LEWIS AND CLARK REACH THE PACIFIC

Nineteen months after launching their historic journey from St. Louis, Lewis and Clark's Corps of Discovery neared the Pacific Ocean from the Columbia River in Oregon. Their first sighting was mistaken—they were actually at Gray's Bay—but the sound of breakers was probably real, and the expedition celebrated its long-awaited arrival. WILLIAM CLARK's journal entry for November 7, 1805, records the event:

A cloudy foggy morning. Some rain. We set out early…the fog so thick we could not see across the river. Two canoes of Indians met and returned with us to their village, which is situated on the starboard side behind a cluster of marshy islands, on a narrow channel of the river…. After delaying at this village one hour and a half we set out piloted by an Indian

dressed in a sailor's dress, to the main channel…. About 14 miles below the last village and 18 miles of this day we landed at a village of the same nation…. Here we purchased a dog, some fish, wappato roots, and I purchased 2 beaver skins for the purpose of making me a robe, as the robe I have is rotten and good for nothing…. We proceeded on about 12 miles below the village under a high mountainous country on the starboard side, shore bold and rocky…. Rain continued moderately all day…. The fog cleared off just below the last village.

Great joy in camp. We are in view of the Ocean, this great Pacific Ocean which we [have] been so long anxious to see, and the roaring or noise made by waves breaking on the rocky shores (as I suppose) may be heard distinctly.

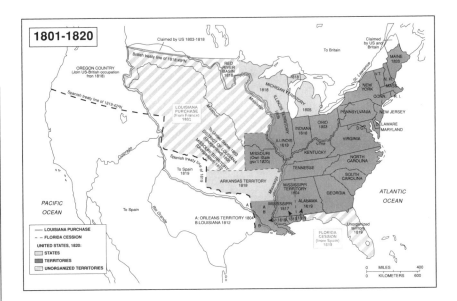

COLT AND WINCHESTER

The Colt revolving pistol—legendary six-shooter of the Old West—was invented in 1833 by Samuel Colt (1814–1862) of Hartford, Connecticut. Colt set up the Patent Fire-Arms Company to manufacture and sell the weapon, but the company failed in 1842. Five years later, when the army began ordering guns for use in the Mexican War, Colt set up a new factory and amassed a fortune. The use of interchangeable parts was an important advance in mass production.

The Winchester repeating rifle, highly prized among settlers and militia beginning in the 1860s, was produced by Oliver Fisher Winchester (1810–1880) and the New Haven Arms Company. His improvements in the quality and performance of the repeating rifle enabled the Winchester brand to dominate a growing market on the prairie.

1824, *cont.*

manufactured goods, or money brought by Indians, merchants, or fur companies. Major fur companies such as the Rocky Mountain Fur Company or the American Fur Company aided in westward expansion by exploring new routes west and laying the groundwork for permanent settlements.

1824–1826 JEDEDIAH STRONG SMITH reaches South Pass in present-day Wyoming and treks through the Rocky Mountains into the Great Basin in present-day Nevada. He then leads the first overland expedition to southern California.

1825 JAMES BRIDGER comes upon Utah's Great Salt Lake.

1827 The first volume of *Birds of America* by JOHN JAMES AUDUBON is published (see p. 384 and 386).

1830 An Indian removal policy with roots in the earlier administrations of James Monroe and John Quincy Adams finds full articulation in the Indian Removal Act, which gives the president power to move all Indians west of the Mississippi.

1832–1835 Benjamin L. E. de Bonneville takes an expedition through the Rocky Mountains to the Columbia River in the Oregon Territory.

1836 Texas declares its independence from Mexico. To put down this "rebellion," 3,000 Mexican troops massacre the 187 men defending the Alamo. Six weeks later Texans crying "Remember the Alamo" are victorious at the battle of San Jacinto.

1837 President ANDREW JACKSON recognizes the Republic of Texas on his last day in office.

John Deere invents a steel, one-piece plow and moldboard, a much-needed tool for working the heavy, rich sod and cutting through the roots of prairie grass of the Midwest and the Great Plains.

Missionaries MARCUS WHITMAN and Narcissa Prentiss Whitman move to the Oregon Territory, where they establish a mission to convert the Cayuse Indians to Christianity and to encourage them to adopt white ways. In a struggle that repeatedly will be played out in various parts of the West, the Whitmans are insensitive to the culture of the Native Americans, who in turn resist giving up their traditional ways.

A serious economic panic fuels westward migration.

1842 Led by Elijah White, the first wagon train reaches the Oregon Country, bringing about 120 settlers to live along the Pacific coast. The previous year a group led by John Bidwell abandoned its wagons at Fort Hall, in what is now Idaho. In 1843, almost 1,000 persons make the journey.

1843–1844 JOHN C. FRÉMONT maps the Oregon and the California trails, which cross Indian lands. Thousands of settlers will follow the trails west before the land boom is over. Frémont's guide is CHRISTOPHER "KIT" CARSON.

1844 Democrat JAMES K. POLK, who runs on an outspoken expansionist platform that asks for the "re-occupancy of Oregon and the re-annexation of Texas," wins the presidency.

Increasingly chauvinistic Americans in Oregon push for American occupation of the entire Oregon Country.

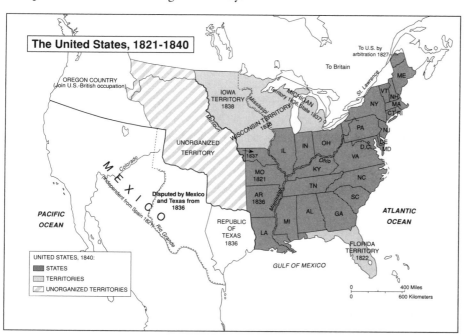

The United States, 1821-1840

WAGONS WEST: SAILING ACROSS THE PRAIRIE

*This 1866 lithograph depicts bustling F Street in Denver, Colorado, complete with prairie schooners,
stagecoaches, oxen, and horses.*

Settlers streamed west on steamboats, trains, horses, stagecoaches, and foot, but the most significant mode of transportation—the one that became the symbol of westward migration—was the prairie schooner. Named because their white-covered tops seemed to float like graceful sails through the tall prairie grass, these wagons were more properly called Conestogas, after the town in Pennsylvania where they were originally built. The Conestoga that transported people west, though, was a variation on the original wagon, with shallower sides and a flat floor.

Although they were sturdy, there was nothing comfortable about prairie schooners. They offered no heat on chilly nights, no ventilation on warm ones, no windows, and no privacy, but their great advantage was that they were big enough to hold the essential tools and household items to start over in a new land and food to make the journey. What they lacked in comfort, they made up for in reliability. Their wide, flat wheels were ideal for cutting through the prairie, whether it was drenched with spring rains or dry and hard as rock.

Prairie schooners, which were pulled by horses or oxen, traveled in wagon trains that sometimes stretched out for four or five miles. The heyday of the wagon train was the 1840s, and during the gold rush more than 12,000 wagons were counted crossing the Mississippi at just one spot. More than 300,000 people have traveled west via wagon train along the California and Oregon trails, but by the 1870s railroads were commonplace, and wagon trains had disappeared from the western landscape.

1845 Journalist John O'Sullivan coins the term "manifest destiny," which provides a rationale for the taking of western lands by any means possible; overnight it gains popularity with both politicians and the public.

Texas is admitted to the Union.

President POLK asserts U.S. title to Oregon and proposes to divide the Oregon Country along the 49th parallel. The British minister to the United States rejects the offer, whereupon Polk asserts the U.S. claim to the entire Oregon Country using the Monroe Doctrine to strengthen his argument. Preoccupied with domestic affairs, the British agree to a diplomatic solution, and under President Polk, the United States signs an agreement with Great Britain to divide the Oregon Country south of the 49th parallel.

JOHN C. FRÉMONT mounts his third major expedition, again guided by KIT CARSON, this time to California. There he joins white settlers in the Bear Flag Revolt, named for the logo on the flag. Frémont's party of well-armed men help the settlers declare their independence from Mexican rule.

1846–1848 The United States and Mexico fight the Mexican-American War, which is enormously popular with some Americans and criticized by others. When the U.S. Army reaches southern California, it discovers the region has already been claimed by the leader of the Bear Flag Revolt. When the war ends, Mexico cedes California and New Mexico—which includes present-day Arizona, Utah, and Nevada—to the United States. In return, the United States pays Mexico $15 million and assumes the claims of Texans against Mexico.

1846 Mormons begin leaving Nauvoo, Illinois, for the West. After wintering along the Missouri River they continue the journey, arriving in the valley of the Great Salt Lake in July 1847. Ultimately about 70,000 Mormons follow this overland trail on foot or in wagons.

The acquisition of the new territory once again raises the question of whether slavery will be expanded. Representative David Wilmot attempts to attach a rider, known as the Wilmot Proviso, to an appropriations bill banning slavery in any territory acquired as a result of the Mexican War. The proviso never passes Congress, but its terms are adopted by the antislavery Free-Soil Party, and its successor, the Republican Party, to further stir up the issue.

The Donner party, a group of eighty-seven people, mostly from Illinois and Iowa, headed by George and Jacob Donner, sets out in 1846 along an untested route across the Sierras. Lost and snowbound in the mountains of California, the party splits, with some heading off to look for rescuers. Before help can arrive, some of those who stay behind starve to death, and some of those who do not resort to cannibalism to stay alive. Less than half of the party remains alive by spring, when rescue parties reach them.

1847 When white settlers, ill with measles, stop to recover at the Whitmans' mission on the Walla Walla River in present-day Washington, the disease spreads among the Indians, with devastating results. The Cayuse kill MARCUS and Narcissa WHITMAN. White settlers retaliate by waging a war of extermination against the remaining Cayuse.

"My eye was caught by something shining in the bottom of the ditch."

—JAMES W. MARSHALL, recalling his discovery of gold at Sutter's mill, California, January 1848

In 1848, famed orator Daniel Webster told the Senate that the West was useless and that he could not "conceive of anything more ridiculous, absurd, and more affrontive to all sober judgment than the cry that we are profiting by the acquisition of New Mexico and California. I hold that they are not worth a dollar."

This Colorado statue pays tribute to Kit Carson's exploits as explorer, guide to Frémont, and Civil War soldier.

1847, *cont.*

Horticulturist Henderson Luelling transports about 1,000 trees and shrubs—about half survive—from Iowa to the Oregon Country; fruit remains a major agricultural product to this day.

1848 In a presidential election in which a third party, the Free-Soilers, plays a major role, Whig candidate ZACHARY TAYLOR narrowly defeats Democratic candidate Lewis Cass. Free-Soil candidate Martin Van Buren, though winning no electoral votes, splits the Democratic vote to Taylor's advantage.

Gold is discovered at a mill being built by John Augustus Sutter, born in Germany and considered a Swiss citizen. In 1839, Sutter had arrived in San Francisco and gone on to the junction of the Sacramento and American Rivers, where he founded a colony, Nueva Helvetia.

1849 San Francisco becomes the primary supply station for the gold rush, and, as a result, its population grows from 1,000 to 35,000 in two years. The population of California expands from 93,000 to 380,000 from 1850 to 1860. During this peak year of the gold rush, 50,000 "forty-niners" pass through Saint Joseph, Missouri, population 3,000.

The first of several cholera epidemics that befell westbound settlers throughout the 1850s strikes along the Platte River.

MANIFEST DESTINY

In 1776 when Thomas Paine wrote, "We have it in our power to begin the world again," Americans were already trying to figure out their place in the world order and were increasingly convinced that theirs was a special destiny. But not until the mid-nineteenth century did this thinking become a reality.

Not surprisingly, this special fate even got a name, when John L. O'Sullivan, an editor at *United States Magazine and Democratic Review*, wrote in 1845 that it was "the fulfillment of our manifest destiny to overspread the continent allotted by Providence for the free development of our yearly expanding millions." "Manifest destiny" started out as the campaign rhetoric of the Democratic Party and ended up the rallying cry of a nation.

O'Sullivan was speaking of the annexation of Texas, but once expounded, the idea encompassed the continent. Americans quickly adapted to the idea that it was their natural right to annex the Oregon Country, California, Mexican lands in the Southwest, Alaska, Hawaii, and, over and over again, the lands of Native Americans. Manifest destiny was used to justify the proposed annexation of Cuba, and it played a role in the Mexican and the Spanish-American wars. Vestiges of this idea still influence American foreign policy.

In the late nineteenth century, Darwinist ideas were appropriated by expansionists, who gave manifest destiny a boost by suggesting that Americans were the fittest nation that had ever existed. Seen in this light, it seemed only right that the United States should set its sights on the Caribbean and the Pacific as well, and indeed once the continent was secured the nation imposed its presence south into Latin America and across into the Pacific. Eventually, critics of manifest destiny saw the concept for what it was: a rationalization for colonization.

TEXAS, 1682–1845

Texas is the only state to have been an independent republic, then annexed by the United States.

Pre-1682 Apaches, Comanches, and other Indian tribes live in present-day Texas.

1682 The Spanish arrive, claiming Texas as part of Mexico. The first settlement is at Yselta, near present-day El Paso.

1718 The Spanish begin establishing missions, including San Antonio.

1744 A fort-cum-chapel named the Alamo, which means "cottonwood," is built at San Antonio.

1821 The first Anglo settlers arrive in Texas, led by Stephen F. Austin, a Missourian.

1820s Austin's settlements prosper, and by 1830 Americans in Texas outnumber Mexicans two to one.

1826–1827 In the Fredonia Rebellion, two American settlers attempt to break away from Mexico and establish "Fredonia," but, lacking Austin's support, the effort collapses at the approach of Mexican troops. The incident draws attention to the conflict of cultures in Texas and raises American interest in the area.

1829 Newly elected Mexican president Vicente Guerrero abolishes slavery in Mexico, including the province of Texas, and levies new taxes.

1830 Texans seek to exempt Texas from the antislavery decree. Mexico responds by banning any further colonization by Americans and any additional importation of slaves, and by sending troops.

1833 Stephen Austin travels to Mexico City to present American grievances and ask that Texas be a separate state. He is imprisoned.

1835 Fighting breaks out between Texans and Mexicans in Gonzales.

1836 On March 2, Texas declares its independence. But Mexican troops are already besieging the Alamo, and on March 6 the fort is overrun. Davy Crockett, Jim Bowie, and William Travis are among the 187 defenders who are killed, inspiring the battle cry "Remember the Alamo!"

Sam Houston retaliates and, at the decisive battle of San Jacinto on April 21, overcomes a larger Mexican force. Mexican president Antonio Lopez de Santa Anna is taken prisoner, and the Mexican army is routed. The Lone Star flag is raised as Texas declares itself a republic. Sam Houston becomes its first president (and serves again from 1841 to 1844).

1837 On his last day in office, President Andrew Jackson formally recognizes the Republic of Texas.

Texas petitions for annexation to the United States, but the opposition of antislavery forces embroils Texas in the slavery issue, and the Republic of Texas sets an independent course.

1842 The Mexicans invade Texas, hoping to regain the territory. A truce is negotiated the next year, as the question of the United States' annexation of Texas is reopened.

1845 Over the protests of Mexico, Texas is annexed by the United States, becoming the twenty-eighth state and the fifteenth slave state.

Mexican forces surrender to Texan rebels in December 1835, prompting Mexico's president to send in more troops and leading to the famed siege of the Alamo.

Gold is discovered at Sutter's Mill in San Francisco in 1848, heralding the rush of gold prospectors to California.

1849, *cont.*

FRANCIS PARKMAN writes *The California and Oregon Trail.*

The Department of the Interior is established, incorporating the General Land Office.

1850 The Compromise of 1850, masterminded in large part by Illinois senator STEPHEN A. DOUGLAS, but based on the work of John C. Calhoun, HENRY CLAY, and Daniel Webster, is another attempt to resolve North–South tensions over extending slavery. Under its terms, California is admitted as a free state, the borders of Texas are defined, the slave trade is ended in the District of Columbia, and the Fugitive Slave Act of 1850 is passed. Increasingly a line is drawn between the North and the South in an already sectionalized country.

Mid-1850s The gold rush is over, with the suppliers, for the most part, having gotten richer than the seekers. Its attraction has turned the United States into a continental country.

1852 Wells, Fargo & Co., a name synonymous with the West, is founded in New York City to ship "Gold Dust, Bullion, Specie, Packages, Parcels and Freight all kinds" between the two coasts.

1853 The Gadsden Purchase adds 29,670 square miles (76,895 sq km) to the western section of the country and costs the federal government $10 million, which is paid to Mexico. It comprises present-day southern Arizona and extreme southwestern New Mexico.

The invention of barbed wire, by Joseph Glidden in 1873, revolutionized life on the frontier. The fencing of the range enabled farmers to protect their crops from cattle drives and forced cowboys to become ranchers.

1854 Hoping to build a transcontinental railroad with its terminus in Chicago, the Illinois senator STEPHEN DOUGLAS proposes to divide Indian Territory, opening all areas above Oklahoma to white settlement. Rather than extend the 36°30' N boundary of the Missouri Compromise, Douglas promotes the idea of popular sovereignty as a means of determining whether slavery will be permitted in a state. The cost to the nation is enormous: Indians are robbed of their land; the Whig Party is destroyed in the ensuing national debate over slavery; northern Democrats lose two-thirds of their seats, giving control of their party to southerners; and Kansas, which Douglas himself did not believe would be a slave state, becomes a bloody battleground, suffering rioting, massacres, looting, and lynchings before the issue is settled.

Railroads now reach as far west as the Mississippi.

The city of Omaha is founded.

1855 In the struggle to control Kansas, actions so divide people that the state in effect ends up with two governments and two constitutions. The Free-

Soilers, who oppose slavery, hold forth in Topeka, while the proslavery forces operate from Pawnee and Shawnee Mission.

1856 In one shocking week in May, proslavery guerrilla forces destroy Lawrence, Kansas, an abolitionist stronghold. Abolitionist JOHN BROWN and his followers retaliate along the Pottawatomie Creek, brutally killing five proslavery persons. Open warfare continues through the summer.

1857 The Supreme Court's *Dred Scott* decision establishes that Congress has no authority to restrict slavery in the territories.

1857–1858 President James Buchanan proposes to admit Kansas as a proslavery state under the Lecompton Constitution. Congressional opposition demands a statewide referendum in which the document is overwhelmingly defeated. Kansas does not achieve statehood until 1861 (see p. 113).

1858 Denver is founded in the Kansas Territory, which will one day be the state of Colorado.

Another gold rush begins in Colorado. Miners pour into the state; their motto "Pikes Peak or bust."

1859 Oregon becomes a state.

The first telegraph message is transmitted between Washington, D.C., and San Francisco, soon putting the Pony Express—founded a year earlier and operating between Saint Joseph, Missouri, and Sacramento, California—out of business.

This Union Pacific Railroad advertisement boasts of the extremely low prices, rich soil, and mild climate of land adjacent to the railroad in Nebraska. In this instance, a copy of the Homestead Law was provided to all applicants.

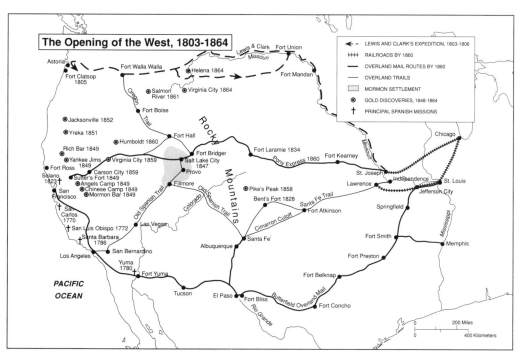

"What the Mediterranean Sea was to the Greeks, breaking the bond of custom, offering new experiences, calling out new institutions and activities, that the ever retreating West has been to the eastern United States...."

—FREDERICK JACKSON TURNER

1863 The Idaho Territory is formed out of parts of present-day Nebraska, Utah, and Washington.

A new gold rush occurs at Alder Gulch, Idaho.

1864 Montana Territory is formed out of Idaho Territory.

1867 When Alaska is purchased from Russia for $7.2 million, it is jokingly referred to as Seward's Icebox or Seward's Folly, after Secretary William H. Seward, who promoted the purchase.

The United States annexes Midway, an island in the central Pacific.

1869 The building of the transcontinental railroad is completed when the Union Pacific and Central Pacific tracks are joined together at Promontory Point, Utah.

TURNER'S FRONTIER THESIS

Historian FREDERICK JACKSON TURNER (1861–1932) believed that the opening of the West was the seminal event in American history and that it, more than any other single factor, shaped the national character and institutions. It was, he maintained, responsible for the much-touted image of Americans as individualistic, adventurous, gregarious, and democratic.

Raised on the frontier and educated at the University of Wisconsin and Johns Hopkins, where he obtained his Ph.D., Turner initially studied the then-popular view, known as the "germ thesis," which held that American customs and character were rooted in German tribalism. Eventually he rejected this idea to develop his own theory. In his charismatic speaking manner, he presented his theory in a paper entitled "The Significance of the Frontier in American History," which he read in 1893 at an American Historical Association meeting. Within ten years, Turner's view was taught in every U.S. history course and abroad as well. If it had served no other purpose, it would at least have been important for inspiring Americans to look within themselves rather than to Europe for their roots.

Turner argued that the existence of cheap or even free land in the West provided a buffer or "safety valve" for the impoverished, discontent, or rebellious who might otherwise strike out at the American establishment. The vast, unexplored territory of the American West also existed as the stomping ground for the adventurer. The rugged individual who ventured west created his world as he went, exemplifying the confident, resourceful, and strong pioneering mentality that is considered by some a lasting American trait.

American historians have long debated the Turner thesis. It has come under attack for its bias in describing the experience of white Americans and overlooking women, Native Americans, and Hispanics. Turner's Frontier thesis has also been criticized for presenting American "rugged individualism" as an entirely good thing and ignoring the reckless exploitation of resources and destruction of Native American ways of life that accompanied the pioneers west.

Other historians have built upon the Turner thesis. After the U.S. Census Bureau declared the frontier closed in 1890, Turner detailed how American history to 1890 could be considered the story of the dwindling frontier and the colonization of the West. As pioneers reached the Pacific Ocean, they began to look outside of the country's borders for new adventures. It is no wonder that the 1898 Spanish-American War, the 1899 assertion of an Open Door Policy with China, the 1903 Hay-Banau-Varilla Treaty giving the U.S. the rights to build the Panama Canal and other expansionist events come on the heels of the closing of the frontier.

Historians will continue to debate the importance of the frontier in American history, but it is safe to say that it has had a pervasive influence in defining the American spirit.

THE EXODUSTERS: AFRICAN AMERICANS IN KANSAS

In 1877 Reconstruction ended and conservative whites returned to power throughout the South. African Americans, fearing that their new freedoms might be in jeopardy, turned to the West as a haven from mounting social and political repression. Already in the years immediately after 1865 a few black colonies had been established in Kansas. Life, though hard, was an improvement over what the former slaves had known.

Railroad promoters and land speculators were ready to lure even more migrants. In 1879 alone, more than 20,000 African Americans left the South for Kansas. These migrants, known as the Exodusters, created the first, but hardly the last, significant migration of the black population.

The huge numbers of new settlers pouring into Kansas strained charitable and government resources, but some Kansans—those with racist leanings—also were not happy with this influx of African Americans. By 1880, black migration to Kansas had slowed to a trickle once again as word of difficulties in Kansas became known in the South. During the exodus, several black communities were established and still exist today. Nicodemus was named a National Historic Site in 1996.

1870s Good well-drilling machinery and windmills pull water up from aquifers on the high plains.

1879 The United States Geological Survey is established to monitor the nation's water and mineral resources, to study and evaluate the surface of the land, to collect geologic and geographic information, and to prepare topographic maps.

1890 The Bureau of the Census announces the closing of the American frontier. The United States can no longer be divided into settled and unsettled lands.

EMPIRE-BUILDING: 1890–1959

1890 Alfred Thayer Mahan publishes *The Influence of Sea Power upon History, 1660–1783*. His belief that controlling the seas enables a state to conduct an effective foreign policy influences Theodore Roosevelt, who is assistant secretary of the navy, 1897–1898.

1893 In an attempt to outmaneuver the domineering U.S. government, Hawaiian queen Liliuokalani writes a new constitution, granting herself and subsequent Hawaiian rulers additional powers. At the urging of pineapple magnate Sanford B. Dole, Marines from a U.S. warship are brought on shore as a show of power. Liliuokalani is deposed, and the United States installs a protectorate government without Hawaii's consent. President Grover Cleveland is urged to annex Hawaii but resists.

1895 A boundary dispute between Venezuela and British Guiana finds the United States giving a broad interpretation to the Monroe Doctrine when Secretary of State Richard Olney declares that the doctrine allows

In this Puck *magazine cover about America's growing involvement overseas, Theodore Roosevelt is pictured in military garb trying on a hat labeled "Imperialism."*

Despite the threat of lethal landslides and tropical diseases, workers built a railroad to aid in the excavation of 240 million cubic yards of earth in order to build the 40-mile Panama Canal.

The famous Stetson cowboy hat was the product of John Batterson Stetson, who opened a small factory in Philadelphia in 1865; by 1906, he was selling 2 million hats a year. The crown of the Stetson was big enough for ten decorative braids called "galloons"—thus the term "ten-gallon hat."

1895, *cont.*

the United States to enter into any Western Hemisphere dispute. In time passions cool when the British agree to arbitration.

1896 Congress passes a resolution in favor of Cuban rebels fighting against Spanish rule.

1898 In the first action of the Spanish-American War (declared by Spain April 24, by the United States April 25 but retroactive to April 21), the U.S. fleet sails into Manila Bay and defeats the Spanish fleet in a few hours. By mid-August, Spanish forces throughout the Philippines surrender. In Cuba the war lasts ten weeks. On August 12, an armistice goes into effect, and the Treaty of Paris is signed on December 10.

Spain grants independence to Cuba and cedes Guam and Puerto Rico to the United States. The United States pays Spain $20 million for the Philippines. What little organized opposition there is to U.S. colonialism takes shape in the form of the Anti-Imperialist League with roots in Chicago and Boston.

After fifty years of increasing economic involvement, Hawaii is annexed by joint resolution. Japan, with 25,000 nationals living there and its own ambitions for empire, had hoped to derail American plans.

1899–1901 The Anti-Imperialist League, with many respected figures among its membership, has little influence over U.S. expansionist policies.

1900 The United States annexes Samoa in the south-central Pacific Ocean.

1901 The Platt Amendment, introduced by Secretary of War Elihu Root to clarify U.S.–Cuban relations, undermines Cuba's autonomy by insisting that it provide land for U.S. bases, sign no treaty that is against U.S. interests, and permit the United States to intervene any time it becomes necessary to protect U.S. interests.

1903–1904 The United States expedites the building of the Panama Canal with what comes to be called "gunboat diplomacy." Under the Hay-Bunau-Varilla Treaty, the United States agrees to lease a six-mile strip on either side of the canal in exchange for $10 million plus annual payments of $250,000.

1917 Because they are strategically located near the Panama Canal, the United States buys the Danish West Indies, which include Saint John, Saint Thomas, Saint Croix, and about fifty smaller islands, for $25 million.

1947 The United States begins administering the Trust Territory of the Pacific Islands (the Marianas, the Carolines, and the Marshall Islands) in the west-central Pacific, thus completing the chain of way stations to Asia that it began to acquire in 1867.

1959 Alaska and Hawaii are admitted as the forty-ninth and fiftieth states, respectively.

In the last and largest of the Oklahoma land rushes, held on September 16, 1893, settlers claimed 6 million acres of land in a matter of hours.

WOMEN OF THE WEST

Although most women who migrated west with their husbands have remained anonymous figures, virtually all played an important role in building their families' new lives. To be successful a farmer or rancher needed a wife. Western women, in turn, often used this power to make their marriages more egalitarian than those of their counterparts back east. Pioneer women had many responsibilities that went far beyond simply supporting their men.

A woman's first big task was to turn whatever awaited her arrival into a home. This was no small achievement with living quarters that ranged from the dirty, leaky, mud-brick "soddy" cabins to cavelike dugouts built into the sides of hills to, at their most sophisticated, one-room, dirt-floor log cabins. Rugs were made from buffalo or cow hides, and flour sacks or greased paper were put up in windows until glass could be ordered. Trunks were converted into tables, and chairs were carved out of barrels.

Unlike the East, where there were many social constraints on women, the West offered women the opportunity to participate as much as they liked, and many women went to work alongside their husbands, plowing, planting, and harvesting.

In addition there were the jobs considered "women's work." Around the farm or ranch, women were often in charge of rearing the heifers, lambs, and other livestock; managing a flock of chickens; milking the family cow; and tending the vegetable garden and fruit trees.

Women were responsible for the family's food. They rose early to bake biscuits and churn butter, two staples of the western diet, and they learned to make do with less when the wheat crop failed and there was no flour. They did the skinning and the butchering, the salting, curing, and sausage making. They brought in the daily supply of water, which often meant a walk of a mile or two to the nearest creek before a well could be dug. Many women supplied the family's fuel, no easy task on the treeless prairie. They collected twigs, hay, cornstalks, corncobs, and buffalo chips for this purpose.

Women were also in charge of providing the family's clothing, and when they weren't consumed with other chores, they made and remade, mended, knitted, and embroidered. Where cloth was unavailable, they sheared and spun and wove as well. Without benefit of sewing machines, animal skins were turned into leather coats, hats, and shoes.

Long before women were admitted to medical schools, pioneer women were nurses, midwives, and doctors. Sometimes they even had to doctor themselves. One Kansas woman had to deliver her own baby when she was left alone, except for an infant and a four-year-old, for the day. When she realized she was in labor, she calmly drew fresh water, made sandwiches to sustain herself, put out milk for her two children, and set out clothes for the baby. At noon she gave birth to a baby, whom she cared for alone until her husband returned at sunset.

Women not only worked hard, but they worked in isolation. It was not only at such important times as childbirth that women lacked the comfort and companionship of other women, but all the time, since farms and ranches were far apart.

U.S. TERRITORIAL ACQUISITIONS

CONTINENTAL				
TERRITORY	**DATE**	**HOW ACQUIRED**	**AMOUNT OF LAND**	**PRESENT STATUS**
Original Territory	1783	Treaty with Great Britain	888,811 square miles (2,302,020 sq km)	Maine, New Hampshire, Vermont, Massachusetts, Rhode Island, Connecticut, New York, New Jersey, Pennsylvania, Maryland, West Virginia, Virginia, North Carolina, Georgia, Tennessee, Kentucky, Ohio, Michigan, Wisconsin, Illinois, Indiana, and part of Minnesota, Alabama, and Mississippi
Louisiana Purchase	1803	Purchase from France for $15 million	827,192 square miles (2,142,425 sq km)	Louisiana, Arkansas, Missouri, Nebraska, Iowa, South Dakota, North Dakota, and part of Minnesota, Montana, Colorado, Kansas, Wyoming, and Oklahoma
Florida	1819	Treaty with Spain	71,993 square miles (186,460 sq km)	Florida and part of Alabama and Mississippi
Texas	1845	Annexation; Texas Republic had won independence from Mexico in 1836	390,144 square miles (1,010,475 sq km)	Texas and part of New Mexico, Oklahoma, Colorado, and Wyoming
Oregon Cession	1846	Treaty with Great Britain	285,580 square miles (739,650 sq km)	Washington, Oregon, Idaho, and part of Montana and Wyoming
Mexican Cession	1848	Treaty with Mexico following victory in Mexican War and payment of $15 million	529,017 square miles (1,370,155 sq km)	California, Nevada, Utah, and part of Wyoming, Colorado, New Mexico, and Arizona
Gadsden Purchase	1853	Purchase from Mexico for $15 million (later reduced to $10 million)	29,640 square miles (76,767 sq km)	Part of New Mexico and Arizona

OVERSEAS				
TERRITORY	DATE	HOW ACQUIRED	AMOUNT OF LAND	PRESENT STATUS
Alaska	1867	Purchase from Russia for $7.2 million	589,757 square miles (1,527,470 sq km)	State since 1959
Midway Island	1867	Annexation	2 square miles (5 sq km)	Territory
Wake Island	1898	Annexation	3 square miles (8 sq km)	Territory
Palmyra	1898	Annexation	4 square miles (10 sq km)	Territory
Hawaii	1898	Annexation of independent kingdom	6,423 square miles (16,635 sq km)	State since 1959
Philippine Islands	1898	Treaty with Spain, following U.S. victory in Spanish-American War and payment of $20 million	115,600 square miles (299,405 sq km)	Independent since 1946
Puerto Rico	1898	Treaty with Spain, following U.S. victory in Spanish-American War	3,435 square miles (8,895 sq km)	Self-governing commonwealth
Guam	1898	Treaty with Spain following U.S. victory in Spanish-American War	206 square miles (535 sq km)	Territory
American Samoa	1900	Treaty with Germany and Great Britain, which with the United States had administered Samoa as a protectorate after 1889, and by treaty with Samoan chiefs, with whom treaties had been negotiated for the use of harbors since 1872	76 square miles (200 sq km)	Territory

TERRITORIAL EXPANSION

U.S. TERRITORIAL ACQUISITIONS, cont.

OVERSEAS				
TERRITORY	**DATE**	**HOW ACQUIRED**	**AMOUNT OF LAND**	**PRESENT STATUS**
Canal Zone	1904	Treaty with Panama (which had just broken away from Colombia and declared its independence), recognized by the United States three days later, the United States agreeing to pay $10 million and a $250,000 annual fee	553 square miles (1,430 sq km)	Full sovereignty restored to Panama on December 31, 1999
U.S. Virgin Islands	1917	Purchase from Denmark for $25 million	133 square miles (345 sq km)	Territory
Pacific Island Trust Territories (Mariannas, Carolines, Marshall Islands)	1947	Trusteeship agreement with the United Nations (former Japanese mandates)	716 square miles (1,855 sq km)	Administering authority of United Nations' trusteeship

Originally considered a waste of money by many Americans, Alaska was virtually ignored by the federal government until the discovery of gold. In the winter of 1897–1898, miners and packers carried sawmills, stoves, boats, tools, and several months' provisions over the "Golden Stairs" of the Chilcoot Pass in hopes of striking rich in the Alaskan gold fields.

THE CONSERVATION MOVEMENT, 1832–PRESENT

Land conservation and protection of the natural environment were not ideas that occurred to the first Europeans who came to North America. The land was good land, and there was plenty of it free for the taking. If land gave out, as it did when intensively farmed for tobacco, more could be cleared to the west. Little matter, either, that the continent already had inhabitants—"uncivilized" peoples with primitive weapons and no concept of land ownership. The forests, unlike any known in Europe, seemed inexhaustible; new growth would replace anything that was cut.

Not until the mid-nineteenth century did a few writers begin to raise questions about how the land, its indigenous peoples, and its wildlife were being exploited. Gradually, attitudes changed as Americans came to realize that certain farming and mining practices damaged the land, that the mighty forests were finite, and that the demands of a rapidly growing population sometimes outran water supplies, eroded the landscape, and depleted wildlife. A few farsighted individuals began stressing forest management, crop rotation, the protection of natural resources, and the preservation of historic landmarks. By the late twentieth century, it was clear that population growth and modern industry had been destroying the land, the water, and the air that early settlers took for granted. Managing the land in the public interest while respecting the rights of individual property owners, and balancing the interests of the environment with those of the economy, became critical tests of democratic government.

1832 Four sections of land are withdrawn from the public domain to protect the hot springs of Arkansas "for the future disposal of the United States."

The artist GEORGE CATLIN, traveling up the Missouri River, keeps a journal in which he proposes that large stretches of the Great Plains be turned into "a nation's Park" to preserve the buffalo, the Plains Indians, and the landscape. His writings are later published as *Letters and Notes on the Manners, Customs, and Conditions of the North American Indians* (1841).

1849–1862 The writings of Henry David Thoreau provide the intellectual foundation of the environmental movement.

1856 Frederick Law Olmsted begins the work of developing and planning New York City's Central Park, a determined effort to provide and preserve parklands for the use of city dwellers (see p. 245).

1858 The Mount Vernon Ladies' Association of the Union purchases the home of George Washington to protect it from falling into decay.

1864 The federal government transfers Yosemite Valley and the Mariposa Big Tree Grove to the state of California on the condition that these lands remain "inalienable for all time."

George Perkins Marsh publishes *Man and Nature; or, Physical Geography as Modified by Human Action.* His ringing indictment of the effect of deforestation on water quality is the beginning of the conservation movement.

1869 One-armed JOHN WESLEY POWELL leads an expedition down the Colorado River. His party is the first to pass through the Grand Canyon. His studies and observations are published in 1878 as the Report of the Lands of the Arid Region of the United States. In 1881, Powell becomes director of the Geological Survey.

1872 The world's first national park, Yellowstone, is created by act of Congress.

1877–1881 Carl Schurz serves as secretary of the interior and advocates a responsible policy of forest management and replanting.

1885 New York State establishes the Adirondack Forest Preserve, later renamed Adirondack State Park.

1891 The Forest Reserve Act authorizes the president to proclaim forest reserves out of the public domain; in 1907, these reserves are renamed national forests.

THE CONSERVATION MOVEMENT, 1832–PRESENT, cont.

1892 JOHN MUIR founds the Sierra Club, one of today's premier conservation organizations.

1893 GIFFORD PINCHOT is named chief of the Division of Forestry, later to become the United States Forest Service, in the Department of Agriculture.

1902 The Newlands Reclamation Act devises a scheme whereby public lands in arid portions of the country could be made available for sale if they were "reclaimed" by irrigation. The Bureau of Reclamation is also established.

1903 President Theodore Roosevelt signs legislation creating the National Wildlife Refuge System. Initially the system was established to protect birds whose plumage was in great demand for women's hats. Today the Fish and Wildlife Service manages more than 500 areas throughout the country where habitats for birds, marine animals, fish, and land mammals are protected.

1905 William Dutcher incorporates several state organizations into the National Audubon Society.

1906 The Antiquities Act authorizes the president to proclaim as national monuments "historic landmarks, historic and prehistoric structures, and other objects of historic or scientific interest." The first national monument is Wyoming's Devils Tower, prominently featured in the movie Close Encounters of the Third Kind. In 1978, President Jimmy Carter uses this authority to proclaim fifteen new and two expanded national monuments in Alaska that total more than 30 million acres.

1908 President Theodore Roosevelt invites a distinguished gathering of national leaders and the state governors to the White House to discuss the various conservation issues confronting the country.

1913 Hetch Hetchy Valley within Yosemite National Park is dammed to provide drinking water for San Francisco. The dispute over this use pits a specific local need against a greater national need.

1916 The National Park Service is established, with Stephen T. Mather as its first director.

1920 Visitors to forty-three units of the National Park System, consisting of 8,560,760 acres, total 1,058,455.

1921 Benton MacKaye proposes in an article that an Appalachian trail be laid out along the mountain crests from Maine to Georgia. MacKaye later becomes one of the founders of the Wilderness Society.

1926 The restoration of Colonial Williamsburg begins, financed by John D. Rockefeller Jr., at the urging of the rector of Bruton Parish Church in Williamsburg. The work of historic preservation comes of age.

Shenandoah (Virginia) and Great Smoky Mountains (Tennessee and North Carolina) National Parks are created. With Acadia National Park (Maine), created seven years earlier, these are the first national parks east of the Mississippi, and make the park system truly national.

1930 Visitors to fifty-five units of the National Park System, consisting of 10,339,507 acres, total 3,246,656.

1933 The Civilian Conservation Corps (CCC) is one of many New Deal programs to give jobs to out-of-work Americans. This small army of young men builds roads, bridges, culverts, trails, cabins, and entrance stations in various state and national parks, and lays water and sewage lines. At its peak there are 118 CCC camps in national parks and 482 camps in state parks. All told, more than 120,000 young men participate in the program.

Congress creates the Tennessee Valley Authority (TVA), an ambitious regional planning effort. Basically, the TVA is responsible for flood control, navigation on the Tennessee River and its tributaries, and the production of electricity. Over the years, it has become a model for dealing with an entire river basin in ways that go far beyond its basic environmental concerns.

1934–1937 Drought strikes the high plains of Texas, Oklahoma, Kansas, and Colorado, creating a "dust bowl" in this semi-arid region in the midst of the Great Depression.

1935 The Wilderness Society is organized, with Benton MacKaye and Robert Marshall among its founders. Marshall, an independently wealthy Forest Service employee, argues for the protection of wilderness.

1940 Visitors to the 161 units of the National Park System, consisting of 21,550,783 acres, total 16,755,251.

1949 Aldo Leopold's influential *Sand Country Almanac* is published posthumously. Leopold is one of the first modern writers to go beyond an appreciation of nature and consider human beings and all the plants and animals as part of one great whole.

1950 Visitors to the 182 units of the National Park System, consisting of 24,597,613 acres, total 33,252,589.

1956 Plans for the Echo Park Dam on the Green River inside Dinosaur National Monument in northeastern Utah are permanently scrapped, ensuring that a Hetch Hetchy situation will not be repeated.

1960 Visitors to the 187 units of the National Park System, totaling 26,193,774 acres, total 80,039,100.

1962 RACHEL CARSON publishes *Silent Spring*.

1963 The Clean Air Act becomes law with the assignment of monitoring smog, acid raid, automobile emissions, and toxic air pollutants. Initially it is administered by the Public Health Service and later by the Environmental Protection Agency (EPA).

1964 The Wilderness Act, authored by Howard Zahniser, executive secretary of the Wilderness Society, is enacted into law. It proposes to preserve into perpetuity, with the approval of Congress, those pieces of land of at least 5,000 acres that are "untrammeled by man, where man himself is a visitor who does not remain."

1970 The Environmental Protection Agency is created and begins work to monitor the nation's environmental health.
Visitors to the 281 units of the National Park System, consisting of 29,620,444 acres, total 172,004,600.

1978 The New York State Commissioner of Health decrees the Love Canal area outside Niagara Falls to be a "threat to human health and the environment." From 1942 to 1953 Hooker Chemical disposes of more than 44 million pounds of toxic wastes (sludges, solvents, ash, pesticide residue) in this area. The outcry over conditions at Love Canal leads to the establishment of the EPA's Superfund to clean up toxic waste dumps.

1979 A near meltdown in a nuclear reactor at Three Mile Island near Harrisburg, Pennsylvania, gives new fuel to those wishing to limit severely the construction of nuclear power plants.

1980 Visitors to the 333 units of the National Park System, consisting of 77,440,418 acres, total 190,185,155.

Workers clean rocks on the Alaska coastline after the Exxon Valdez *disaster.*

THE CONSERVATION MOVEMENT, 1832–PRESENT, cont.

1989 The oil tanker *Exxon Valdez* founders and spills 11.2 million gallons of crude oil into Prince William Sound in Alaska. One of the largest oil spills in North America, it damages more than 730 miles (1,175 km) of coastline.

1990 Visitors to the 357 units of the National Park System, consisting of 80,155,984 acres, total 258,682,828.

1996 President Clinton signs into law major overhauls of federal regulations pertaining to drinking water, pesticides, and fisheries.

Controlled flooding of the Colorado River in the Grand Canyon and Glen Canyon of Arizona gives the river ecosystem a fresh start. Over the next several years, the U.S. Department of the Interior opens or dismantles several major river dams built by the TVA.

2000 A total of 368 animal species are listed as endangered in the United States, up from 263 in 1990.

Visitors to the 382 units of the National Park System, consisting of 84,327,466 acres, total 285,891,275.

2001 Seeking relief from dependence on foreign energy sources, the newly installed administration of President George W. Bush proposes the opening of the Arctic National Wildlife Refuge in Alaska to drilling for oil and natural gas. Despite strong opposition by conservation groups, Congress agrees to the proposal as part sweeping energy legislation.

STATES ADMITTED TO THE UNION

STATE	DATE	STATE	DATE
1. Delaware	December 7, 1787	26. Michigan	January 26, 1837
2. Pennsylvania	December 12, 1787	27. Florida	March 3, 1845
3. New Jersey	December 18, 1787	28. Texas	December 29, 1845
4. Georgia	January 2, 1788	29. Iowa	December 28, 1846
5. Connecticut	January 9, 1788	30. Wisconsin	May 29, 1848
6. Massachusetts	February 6, 1788	31. California	September 9, 1850
7. Maryland	April 28, 1788	32. Minnesota	May 11, 1858
8. South Carolina	May 23, 1788	33. Oregon	February 14, 1859
9. New Hampshire	June 21, 1788	34. Kansas	January 29, 1861
10. Virginia	June 26, 1788	35. West Virginia	June 19, 1863
11. New York	July 26, 1788	36. Nevada	October 31, 1864
12. North Carolina	November 21, 1788	37. Nebraska	March 1, 1867
13. Rhode Island	May 29, 1790	38. Colorado	August 1, 1876
14. Vermont	March 4, 1791	39. North Dakota	November 2, 1889
15. Kentucky	June 1, 1792	40. South Dakota	November 2, 1889
16. Tennessee	June 1, 1796	41. Montana	November 8, 1889
17. Ohio	February 19, 1803	42. Washington	November 11, 1889
18. Louisiana	April 30, 1812	43. Idaho	July 3, 1890
19. Indiana	December 11, 1816	44. Wyoming	July 10, 1890
20. Mississippi	December 10, 1817	45. Utah	January 4, 1896
21. Illinois	December 3, 1818	46. Oklahoma	November 16, 1907
22. Alabama	December 14, 1819	47. New Mexico	January 6, 1912
23. Maine	March 15, 1820	48. Arizona	February 14, 1912
24. Missouri	August 10, 1821	49. Alaska	January 3, 1959
25. Arkansas	June 15, 1836	50. Hawaii	August 21, 1959

SUPREME COURT DECISIONS AFFECTING TERRITORIAL EXPANSION, 1823–1903

1823 *Johnson v. McIntosh.* In a decision that will aid white settlement of western lands, the Supreme Court rejects the validity of land titles granted to individuals by Indians.

1857 *Dred Scott v. Sandford.* In one of its most controversial decisions, the Court asserts that Dred Scott, a slave who has sued for his freedom because his owner had taken him to a free state, is not a citizen and therefore has no standing to sue in the federal courts. Moreover, slaves are classified as property, and the federal government cannot prohibit slavery in the territories, and the Missouri Compromise is overturned as unconstitutional.

1901 *Insular Cases.* The Court rules that Puerto Rico, recently annexed by the United States, is neither a foreign country nor a state with constitutional protection. Congress must decide whether the Constitution should apply to particular territories.

1903 *Lone Wolf v. Hitchcock.* The Court rejects a plea that tribal lands were taken without due process, thus putting its seal of approval on white ownership of western lands.

LEGISLATION AFFECTING TERITORIAL EXPANSION, 1785–1877

1785 Land Ordinance. This plan for developing the western lands, one of the major achievements of the Confederation government, is created in part by THOMAS JEFFERSON. The territories will be surveyed, subdivided into 36-square-mile (93-sq-km) townships, then sold.

1787 Northwest Ordinance. This act imposes federal authority in the Northwest Territory and sets forth the protocol for creating states. Initially, a governor, secretary, and three judges are appointed by Congress to govern. When the free adult male population reaches 5,000, an elected territorial legislature is formed and the territory can send a nonvoting delegate to Congress. When the adult male population reaches 60,000, a territory is eligible to apply for statehood. Although the ordinance specified that no fewer than three and no more than five states are to be carved out of the territory, present-day Ohio, Indiana, Illinois, Michigan, Wisconsin, and Minnesota were created from the Northwest Territory.

1790 Southwest Ordinance. This act organizes the Southwest Territory (which will become Tennessee) on similar principles but permits slavery.

1820 Missouri Compromise. Temporarily and awkwardly solving the problem of free versus slave states in the territories, the compromise permits Maine to enter the Union as a free state and Missouri to enter as a slave state and forbids slavery in the Louisiana Purchase north of 36°30′ latitude.

1830 Indian Removal Act. This creates an Indian Country (later known as Indian Territory) west of Missouri and Arkansas, and appropriates funds for the resettlement there of southeastern Indian tribes (Cherokees, Chickasaws, Choctaws, Creeks, and Seminoles).

1850 Compromise of 1850. This is another attempt to resolve North–South tensions over the extension of slavery. California is admitted as a free state; territorial governments for Utah and New Mexico are organized without mention of slavery; Texas borders are settled and the federal government assumes Texan debts incurred before statehood; the slave trade is forbidden in the District of Columbia; and a more stringent fugitive slave law is enacted.

1854 Kansas-Nebraska Act. This act, proposed by STEPHEN DOUGLAS, opens Kansas, in Indian Territory, to white settlement and applies Douglas's principle of popular sovereignty by permitting territorial voters to decide whether to permit slavery. Although

LEGISLATION AFFECTING TERRITORIAL EXPANSION, 1785–1877, cont.

ostensibly leaving the question open, Douglas did not believe Kansas would choose slavery—and could not have foreseen the guerrilla warfare that would break out after the act was passed.

1862 Homestead Act. This act offered any head of household (including widows and single men) 160 acres of the public domain by registering the claim, making some improvement on the land within six months, and living on it for five years.

The Morrill Act authorizes grants of land to support state schools teaching agriculture or the mechanical arts.

1871 The Indian Appropriations Act. Bolstering white settlement on Indian lands, this act terminates the treaty process between Native Americans and the federal government without tribal consent.

1873 Timber Culture Act. Designed to encourage the planting of trees and thereby improve the climate and soil on the prairie and plains, this act grants homesteaders an additional 160 acres of land for every 40 acres of trees they plant. Because settlers are not required to reside on this land, land speculators use this act (as well as the Homestead Act) to their advantage, often buying up the best land and then reselling it to settlers. Trees do not solve the dry conditions of the high plains, and the act is repealed in 1891.

1877 Desert Land Act. This permits homesteaders to buy 640 acres at $1.25 per acre, with the obligation that they irrigate the land within three years.

NOTABLE FIGURES IN TERRITORIAL EXPANSION

Audubon, John James (1785–1851). Born in Santo Domingo, Audubon began observing and studying birds on his family's estate near Philadelphia. His famous *Birds of America*, published from 1827 to 1838, reflected his studies and travels from 1810 to 1824 in the Ohio and Mississippi Valleys, where he made sketches and took specimens. His drawings and paintings, still impressive today, exemplify the scientific interest some Americans took in the country's expanding territories.

Austin, Stephen Fuller (1793–1836). Called the Father of Texas, Austin took over his father's plans to establish the first Anglo settlement in Texas. Named San Felipe de Austin, the community soon drew 8,000 white settlers. Austin was active in the Texas Revolution and later served as secretary of state in the Texas Republic.

Benton, Thomas Hart (1782–1858). As an influential

The model of the American frontiersman, Daniel Boone explored and settled areas of Kentucky in the 1760s and 1770s.

Democratic politician who represented Missouri in both the House and the Senate, he worked hard to settle the West and keep the territories free of slavery.

Blaine, James Gillespie (1830–1893). As secretary of state (1881; 1889-1892), the Maine Republican was actively involved in developing U.S. interests in Latin America, including building a canal on the isthmus between Central and South America. He also worked on Alaskan, Canadian, and Hawaiian relations and called the first Pan-American conference. Although the best-known political figure of his time—having served in both the House and the Senate—he lost his bid for the presidency in 1884.

Boone, Daniel (1734–1820). Legendary in his own time, this frontiersman mounted several expeditions into the unsettled Kentucky Territory and blazed the Wilderness Trail, which homesteaders later used to move into this region. In the 1790s, when his land titles in Kentucky proved to be invalid, he migrated to Missouri.

Bowie, James (c. 1795–1836). Inventor of the Bowie knife, which was widely used on the frontier, Bowie was one of the commanders of the Alamo and died in the battle that led to the liberation of Texas.

Bridger, James (1804–1881). A fur trader, Bridger accompanied JEDEDIAH SMITH on many of his treks and is credited with discovering the Great Salt Lake.

Brown, John (1800–1859). An abolitionist most remembered for his 1859 raid on a government arsenal at Harpers Ferry, Virginia, Brown was deeply involved in the territorial struggle in Kansas, which centered around the issue of slavery. By 1855, he controlled the Free-Soil militia in the territory, and in retaliation for the Lawrence Massacre in 1856, he and his sons are believed to have brutally murdered five settlers along the Pottawatomie Creek.

Bryan, William Jennings (1860–1925). This three-time Democratic presidential candidate (in 1896, 1900, and 1908) was known in part for his anti-imperialist efforts and for his insistence on the free coinage of silver.

Carson, Christopher "Kit" (1809–1868). Born in Kentucky and reared in Missouri, Carson traveled as a youth to the far western frontier and made it his home. He served as guide on the expeditions of JOHN C. FRÉMONT and distinguished himself as a Union general during the Civil War.

Carson, Rachel (1907–1964). A writer and marine biologist, Carson is best known for her book *Silent Spring* (1962), which demonstrated the devastating effect of agricultural chemicals and insecticides on wildlife. Eggshells full of DDT residue are incapable of supporting the weight of the mother bird during incubation and of protecting the chick until ready for hatching. With declining songbirds—only one of many manifestations—some future springtime will be silent. Her book raised a storm of protest, especially from chemical companies and agricultural interests. But independent tests confirmed her work, and many insecticides have since been banned.

Catlin, George (1796–1872). Catlin is known for his moving and dignified portraits of American Indians. He lived among the Indians in the Southeast, Old Northwest, and Great Plains. His work was published in books, the best known of which is *Letters and Notes on the Manners, Customs, and Conditions of the North American Indians* (1841).

Clark, William P. (1770–1838). An army officer, Clark was selected by his friend MERIWETHER LEWIS to lead an expedition exploring the Louisiana Purchase. His observations of nature contributed to the expedition's success, and his records of the journey rendered in his maps and journals proved invaluable. His oldest brother was George Rogers Clark, a Revolutionary War hero.

Clay, Henry (1777–1852). Serving in both the House and the Senate, Clay, known as the Great Compromiser, presided over the Missouri Compromise and the Compromise of 1850, both of which, while failing to outlaw slavery in the territories, at least served to stave off the Civil War. Clay was one of the founders of the Whig Party, and also served as John Quincy Adams's secretary of state.

Crockett, Davy (1786–1836). Crockett, a frontiersman who served in the Tennessee legislature and the U.S. House of Representatives, then went to Texas to fight in the Revolution and dies at the Alamo. He was also known for his folksy humor, and several books were written under his name, although historians are not convinced of his authorship.

Douglas, Stephen A. (1813–1861). Although best remembered for defeating Abraham Lincoln, as a Democrat Douglas played a significant role during the westward expansion in the controversy over slavery in the territories. He sponsored the Kansas-Nebraska Act, which replaced the Missouri Compromise, and promoted the idea of popular sovereignty, in which territorial settlers would decide for themselves whether to permit slavery once they joined the Union. Douglas did not foresee the bloody guerrilla war that would break out as a result of the Kansas-Nebraska Act, ruining his political future. In 1860, he and two other candidates were defeated by Abraham Lincoln in a bid for the presidency.

Frémont, John Charles (1813–1890). An American explorer and general, Frémont mapped the overland trails to Oregon and California (1843 and 1844). The first presidential candidate of the newly formed Republican Party, Frémont was defeated in 1856 by the Democratic candidate, James Buchanan.

Houston, Sam (1793–1863). A popular fighter in ANDREW JACKSON's Indian campaigns, Houston was sent to the House of Representatives by his home state of Tennessee. He was elected governor in 1827 but resigned

NOTABLE FIGURES, *cont.*

when his very short-lived first marriage dissolved. He moved to Indian Territory and lived among the Cherokees, whom he knew and revered from his childhood in Tennessee. He adopted Cherokee citizenship. Houston headed the Revolutionary Army during the Texas Revolution and became the first president of the Republic of Texas, later serving in the post a second time. He was also senator and governor, but he lost favor (and the governorship) when he opposed secession at the time of the Civil War.

Jackson, Andrew (1767–1845). Old Hickory, as this president (1829–1837) was affectionately known, was, among many other things, a great promoter of western settlement. He fought ruthlessly against Native Americans and favored their relocation, which partly explained his popularity among the Anglo settlers.

James, Jesse (1847–1882). In a land famous for its lawlessness, James might best be described as the prototypical desperado. A Confederate sympathizer during the Civil War, he joined the proslavery guerrillas led by William Quantrill but reserved most of his energy for robbing banks, trains, and stagecoaches. He and his brother Frank formed their own gang, and Jesse was killed by one of its members for the reward.

Jefferson, Thomas (1743–1826). As president, Jefferson brought about the Louisiana Purchase in 1803. During his administration both the LEWIS and CLARK expedition and the exploration of ZEBULON PIKE took place.

Lavérendryer, Pierre Gaultier de Varennes, Sieur de (1685–1749). A French Canadian, Lavérendryer began to explore the American West in 1731. He sent two of his sons to explore the lands beyond the Missouri River, which led them to the Dakotas, western Minnesota, and possibly part of Montana.

Lewis, Meriwether (1774–1809). This former army officer led an expedition, with WILLIAM CLARK, to explore the Louisiana Purchase. Lewis was President THOMAS JEFFERSON's secretary when Jefferson chose him to explore a land route to the Pacific. In 1807, he was appointed governor of the Louisiana Territory. As inept a politician as he was a brilliant explorer, he began to fall into ever deeper depressions. In 1809, he died under mysterious circumstances, now judged to have been a suicide.

Long, Stephen Harriman (1784–1864). An army engineer, he was best known for his expeditions to the upper Mississippi and, in 1820, the Rocky Mountains. Long's Peak in Colorado is named after him. Later, as a surveyor for the Baltimore and Ohio railroad route, he compiled an authoritative topographical manual.

Mackenzie, Alexander (c. 1763–1820). Scottish-born Mackenzie went to Canada as a fur trader. Eventually he became a partner in the North West Company. In 1789, he led an expedition to the Arctic Ocean, and in 1793, he guided a party across northern Canada to the Pacific, completing the first transcontinental journey north of Mexico.

Muir, John (1838–1914). Born in Scotland, Muir immigrated to the United States in 1849 and eventually settled in California. A naturalist, he traveled throughout the country, often on foot, arguing that scenic beauty was a value in itself and advocating conservation measures and the establishment of national parks.

Oakley, Annie (1860–1926). Although countless anonymous women helped to settle and build the West, figures like Oakley, whose forte was her ability to shoot a playing card in half from ninety feet, loom larger in the American imagination. Oakley, whose life was immortalized in the Broadway musical *Annie Get Your Gun*, traveled for nearly two decades with Buffalo Bill's Wild West Show.

Parkman, Francis (1823–1893). The eminent historian of his era, Parkman wrote vividly about the opening of the West in his book *The California and Oregon Trail* (1849), about his experiences living with the Sioux in *History of the Conspiracy of Pontiac* (1851), and about the struggle between the French and the British for North America in his masterful *France and England in North America* (1865–1892).

Pike, Zebulon (1779–1813). Supported by the army, Pike explored the Rocky Mountains and Spanish New Mexico in a major expedition mounted in 1806–1807. In 1810, he published *An Account of Expeditions to the Sources of the Mississippi* and *Through the Western Parts of Louisiana*.

Pinchot, Gifford (1865–1946). Pinchot, chief of the Division of Forestry in the Department of Agriculture, was the first American to have chosen forestry as a career. After schooling in France and work on George

Vanderbilt's estate in North Carolina, Pinchot promoted his belief that forests, if managed wisely, could be as profitable and enduring as any cash crop.

Polk, James K. (1795–1849). The first "dark horse" ever to win the presidency (1845), Polk campaigned on a prowestern platform. He advocated annexation of Oregon and statehood for California. Polk resolved the dispute over Oregon amicably and led the United States into the Mexican War, which resulted in the annexation of large parts of the Southwest and California.

Powell, John Wesley (1834–1902). Under the auspices of the Smithsonian Institution and the U.S. Congress, geologist-ethnologist Powell explored the West, specifically the Green and Colorado Rivers, and studied and classified many Indian languages. Powell did a great deal of work for the U.S. Bureau of Ethnology; he served as the second director of the U.S. Geological Survey.

Sacajawea (c. 1786–1812?). This Shoshone woman, who was wed to a French Canadian, acted as LEWIS and CLARK's guide and interpreter on their major 1804–1806 expedition and was the sole woman on the trip.

Smith, Jedediah Strong (1799–1831). Smith's explorations opened trails and territory for westward-bound pioneers as well as for fur trappers and land traders. In 1824, Smith traveled into Montana and north to the Canadian boundary before returning to Great Salt Lake. A year later, in his most famous trek, he journeyed into California to what is now San Diego, crossing the Colorado River and the Mojave Desert along the way. Smith was murdered by Comanches soon after setting out from St. Louis on the Santa Fe Trail.

Starr, Belle (1848–1889). Along with JESSE JAMES, Belle Starr, who was born Myra Belle Shirley, was a notorious western outlaw. She also belonged to William Quantrill's gang and during the Civil War supplied information to Confederate guerrilla forces regarding the location of Union troops. She died of gunshot wounds.

Taylor, Zachary (1784–1850). A popular general during the Mexican War, he was president only fifteen months (1849–1850) before succumbing to cholera. Taylor worked to ban slavery in the western territories and for rapid admission of California and New Mexico to statehood.

Travis, William (1809–1836). As co-commander of the Alamo, he died there during the Texas Revolution. Travis also fought in the Battle of San Antonio.

Turner, Frederick Jackson (1861–1932). Turner, a historian, originated the highly influential "frontier thesis," also called the "Turner thesis," which holds that the development of the West strengthened American democracy and nationalism as well as forging character traits that distinguished Americans from Europeans.

Whitman, Marcus (1802–1847). Accompanied by his wife, Narcissa Prentiss Whitman, Whitman went west to convert and teach the Indians in his Christian mission. The Whitmans were also energetic recruiters of other settlers. This missionizing effort failed when, seeking revenge for the epidemic of diseases spread by white settlers, the Cayuse killed the Whitmans.

CHAPTER 4

IMMIGRATION AND MINORITY LIFE

HIGHLIGHTS

Timeline of Immigration and Minority Life

FROM ITS VERY BEGINNINGS, America has been a nation of immigrants. For nearly 100 years after the Revolution, immigration went almost entirely unrestricted. Until the early nineteenth century, however, many of those who arrived from foreign shores came not of their own free will but in chains; by 1820, according to the U.S. census, approximately 17 percent of the nation's 9.6 million people were slaves. Throughout the South, slaves represented more than 30 percent of the total population until emancipation in 1863.

Voluntary immigration, by contrast, has reinvigorated American society in every generation, bringing strength in numbers and cultural diversity. Yet the arrival of foreigners has often been a source of controversy and fear among the established citizens. Could the masses of newcomers fit in without undermining American values and the American way of life? Would they take away jobs from those who had worked so hard to succeed? Many Americans today remain proud of their immigrant roots and the ethnic diversity that has defined the national character. Still, the debate over immigration remains very much alive, and minority groups continue to struggle for full acceptance and equal opportunity.

EARLY ARRIVALS

1564 French Huguenots establish Fort Caroline on the Saint Johns River in Florida.

1565 Spanish soldiers build a fort at Saint Augustine and defeat the French at Fort Caroline.

1607 English settlers found Jamestown, Virginia.

1609 The Spanish establish Santa Fe, New Mexico.

1620 Plymouth Colony on Cape Cod, Massachusetts, is founded by 102 English Pilgrims.

"THE STARVING TIME"

Governor William Bradford recounts the ordeal of the Pilgrim settlers during the winter of 1620–1621, their first at Plymouth Colony:

But that which was most sad and lamentable was, that in two or three months' time half of their company died, especially in January and February, being the depth of winter, and wanting houses and other comforts; being infected with scurvy and other diseases which this long voyage and their incommodate condition had brought upon them. So as there died some times two or three of a day in the foresaid time, that of 100 and odd persons, scarce fifty remained. And of these, in the time of most distress, there was but six or seven sound persons who to their great commendations, be it spoken, spared no pains night nor day, but with abundance of toil and hazard of their own health, fetched them wood, made them fires, dressed them meat, made their beds, washed their loathsome clothes, clothed and unclothed them. In a word, did all the homely and necessary offices for them with dainty and queasy stomachs cannot endure to hear named; and all this willingly and cheerfully, without any grudging in the least, showing herein their true love unto their friends and brethren; a rare example and worthy to be remembered.

1624 The Dutch establish New Netherland, which will soon include New Amsterdam (present-day New York City).

1628 English Puritans settle at Naumkeag, which they rename Salem, on Massachusetts Bay.

1630 John Winthrop and other members of the Massachusetts Bay Company found Boston, initiating the "Great Migration" of English Puritans to Massachusetts and Connecticut. About 20,000 Englishmen and -women will settle in New England in the next fifteen years.

1633 The Dutch build a trading post near present-day Hartford.

1634 Under a grant from Charles I to the Calvert family, the Lords Baltimore, Englishmen and -women settle Saint Mary's, which will become the colony of Maryland. The Calverts will encourage both Roman Catholic and Protestant settlement, making Maryland the only English colony in North America with a large Catholic minority.

The first slave shipment from Africa arrived on American shores in 1619—a year before the Pilgrims.

1636 Banished from Salem, dissenting minister Roger Williams founds Providence, Rhode Island.
   Puritan minister Thomas Hooker, escaping the strict religious rule of Massachusetts, founds Hartford, Connecticut.

1638 Swedish and Finnish settlers establish Fort Christina (present-day Wilmington), Delaware.
   Banished from Massachusetts for her religious beliefs, Anne Hutchinson, with her followers, founds present-day Portsmouth, Rhode Island.
   Puritans found New Haven, Connecticut.

1641 The Massachusetts Body of Liberties decrees that "no bond slavery" will exist in the colony.

1649 Maryland passes an Act for Religious Toleration, providing legal protection for Catholic settlers.

1650 Scottish royalists, taken as prisoners of war by Oliver Cromwell, are shipped to Boston.

1654 Jewish immigrants from Brazil arrive in New Amsterdam. They are not allowed to worship in public or have a synagogue.

1658 Jews arrive in Rhode Island, attracted by the colony's religious freedom.

1661 Colonial statutes in Virginia first recognize the legal existence of slavery.

1662 In Virginia a new slave law makes slavery hereditary.

1664 It is reported that eighteen different languages are spoken in New Amsterdam, where the population includes not only Dutch but Walloons, Germans, Swedes, and English and French people. British forces annex New Amsterdam and rename it New York.

1668 The French establish a fur-trading post and a Jesuit mission at Sault Sainte Marie, on the waterway between Lakes Superior and Huron.

1670 In response to moral outrage over the servitude of Christians, a Virginia law forbids slavery for blacks who converted to Christianity prior to their arrival in the colony.

English settlers found Charles Town (later Charleston) in the Carolinas.

A Massachusetts law states that the offspring of slaves can be sold into slavery.

1677 French Huguenots settle New Paltz, New York.

1680 French Huguenots settle near Charles Town, bringing their brand of aristocracy to the English settlement. They join the established Church of England and adopt the English language, strengthening English claims to the area.

1681 England's Charles II grants Quaker William Penn an immense tract of land that becomes Pennsylvania. Penn and other Quakers purchase East Jersey.

Maryland's assembly decrees that the children of a white woman and a black man inherit the status of the mother.

1682 The French establish the first white settlement in Arkansas.

Early settlers in Pennsylvania include groups of Welsh and Irish, as well as Quakers from England, the Rhineland, and the lower Palatinate.

1683 German Mennonites found Germantown, Pennsylvania.

AFRICAN ROOTS

Most slaves were seized in the interior of Africa by European and African traders and then marched to the west African coast, where they were sold to ships bound for the colonies. Some were kidnapped by slavers, some captured during local wars, or some sold into slavery for transgressing tribal laws. Among the West African peoples enslaved were the Ashantis, Bakongas, Fantis, Hausas, Ibos, Mandingos, Sekes, Wolofs, and Yorubas. The majority of the enslaved were between the ages of fifteen and thirty, with men outnumbering women about two to one.

1684 New York laws recognize slavery as a legitimate institution.

1686 Following the repeal of the Edict of Nantes, which protected their civil rights and their right to worship, French Huguenots settle in Rhode Island, Massachusetts, Maine, New York, Pennsylvania, Virginia, and South Carolina.

1688 German Quakers in Germantown declare that slavery is contrary to Christian principles.

1689 An unfavorable religious and political climate in Britain prompts increasing numbers of Scots and Scots-Irish to leave Scotland and Ireland for America.

1699 Old Biloxi (today Ocean Springs, Mississippi) is the first permanent settlement in French Louisiana.
The Spanish open Florida as a refuge for runaway slaves.

1700 English and Welsh settlers make up 80 percent of the population in the British colonies, Africans 11 percent, the Dutch 4 percent, Scots 3 percent, and other ethnic groups 2 percent. Of the African population, some 27,817 are slaves, with about 22,600 of them in the southern colonies.
French colonists build a fort at Detroit.

1705 Virginia enacts a comprehensive slave code.

1708 Virginia counts 12,000 slaves in a total population of 30,000.

1710 Germans, many from the Palatinate, begin to immigrate in large numbers, settling in North Carolina and along the Hudson River in New York.

1712 In New York City a slave revolt ends in the execution of about twenty blacks.

1714–1720 A mass exodus of Scots and Scots-Irish begins, following failed revolts in Scotland and increased rents in Ireland. Many settle in the back country from Pennsylvania south to Georgia.

1715 Virginia counts 23,000 slaves in a total population of 95,500.

1716 To defend themselves from a possible French threat in Louisiana, the Spanish begin to establish missions in Texas.

1718 French settlers found New Orleans, Louisiana.
San Antonio is founded by Spanish Franciscans.

1730–1750 Pennsylvania declines to allow the importation of slaves.

1730 In New York, Jews establish Congregation Shearith Israel and open a synagogue.

1731 New York restricts the number of slaves at a burial to twelve plus the grave digger and pallbearers.

1732 French families incorporate Vincennes on Indiana's Wabash River at a site known to fur traders and a post since 1702.

Georgia is founded with the specific proviso that "no Negro slaves" be allowed in the colony. The white inhabitants petition the trustees for a reversal of this policy. Slavery is finally allowed in 1750, though slaves have been hired from South Carolina on 100-year leases since 1741.

1739 In South Carolina a group of Angolans sack the armory at Stono, killing thirty whites. Two other slave revolts erupt in the colony and are quashed.

1741 In New York City about thirty African Americans are executed for arson.

1753 Moravians settle Wachovia, North Carolina, today part of the city of Winston-Salem.

1756 Virginia has 120,156 slaves in a population of 293,472.

1758 New Jersey Quakers oppose the importation and sale of slaves.

1763 Touro Synagogue in Newport, Rhode Island—the second synagogue in the colonies—is dedicated.

1767 Delaware requires that a £60 bond be posted for each manumitted slave.

1768 Immigrants from Minorca, Leghorn, Italy, and Greece settle New Smyrna, East Florida.

1769 Spanish Franciscans found San Diego. In the next ten years the Spanish establish a string of missions up the California coast.

1770 The population of the thirteen colonies is 1,688,254 whites and 459,822 blacks, almost all slaves.

British troops kill five colonists in the Boston Massacre; one of the victims is CRISPUS ATTUCKS, whose mother was Indian and whose father was African American.

Shackles like these (c. 1700) were used to immobilize Africans during their journey to slavery in North and South America and the Caribbean.

IMMIGRATION & MINORITY LIFE

1774 The Continental Congress calls for the end of the slave trade, while Thomas Jefferson urges the abolition of slavery in "A Summary of the Rights of British America."

1775 In Philadelphia the first antislavery society is formed.

POPULATING A NEW NATION

1776 Thomas Jefferson's proposal to abolish slavery is not included in the Declaration of Independence.
 English Shakers found a colony at Watervliet, New York.
 Spanish Franciscans establish San Francisco.

1778 Rhode Island passes an act guaranteeing freedom after the war to any slave who enlists.

1780 Pennsylvania passes a law granting the gradual emancipation of slaves.

1781 Spanish settlers found Los Angeles.

1783 Virginia legislature says that slave veterans who fought against the British in the Revolutionary War cannot be returned.

1784 Rhode Island and Connecticut follow Pennsylvania and pass gradual abolition acts.

1785 The New York Society for Promoting Manumission is founded.

1787 The Constitutional Convention agrees to the three-fifths compromise, whereby for purposes of representation and taxation five slaves are counted as the equivalent of three whites.
 The Northwest Ordinance prohibits slavery in the Northwest Territories (see p.72).

1788 The Constitution is ratified. One provision guarantees that the importation of slaves cannot be banned for twenty years. Another establishes that slaves escaping to nonslave areas will not be free but must be returned.
 In Philadelphia, Richard Allen and other African Americans establish the Free African Society, withdrawing from the Methodist Church.

1790 The first U.S. Census reveals that less than half the population is English, nearly 20 percent African, 15 percent Irish or Scottish, and 7 percent German, with the remaining composed of other ethnic groups. Of the 757,208 African Americans, 697,681 are slaves.
 Exiled by the French Revolution, French royalists settle on the Ohio River at Gallipolis in present-day Ohio.
 Quakers submit the first petition to Congress for the emancipation of slaves.

Revolution and war in Europe suppress immigration. Fewer than 300,000 newcomers arrive between 1790 and 1820.

1791 African American astronomer and mathematician Benjamin Banneker helps survey the site of the District of Columbia (see p. 384).

1793 Congress passes the first of several Fugitive Slave Acts, making it illegal to aid runaway slaves or interfere with their arrest.

1795 In Louisiana, twenty-three slaves are executed after a failed slave revolt.

1798 Congress passes the Alien and Sedition Acts, which extend the residency requirements for citizenship; authorize the president to deport aliens dangerous to the public safety; and in wartime authorize the government to arrest, jail, and remove aliens.

1800 In Virginia, after a planned slave revolt led by slave Gabriel Prosser is revealed, Prosser and at least twenty-five followers are hanged.
    According to the second U.S. Census, there are 1,002,037 African Americans in the United States, 893,602 of whom are slaves.

1803 With the Louisiana Purchase, the United States gains 43,000 people, primarily French. Only 6,000 describe themselves as Americans.

1807 Congress prohibits importation of African slaves as of January 1, 1808. This is the earliest date the Constitution will allow.

1810 The third U.S. Census counts more than 7.2 million Americans, including 1,377,808 African Americans; 1,191,362 are slaves.

1811 Near New Orleans, U.S. Army troops and state militia put down a rebellion by several hundred slaves.

1817 The American Colonization Society is founded; its goal is to resettle freed blacks in Africa. By 1860, it will have resettled about 12,000 blacks, mostly in Liberia on the west coast of Africa.

1819 Congress passes the first immigration law, ordering ship captains to prepare passenger lists in an effort to improve conditions on the Atlantic crossing and decrease mortality.
    Some 3,000 Irish contract laborers arrive to help build the Erie Canal in upper New York State.

1820s Following the conclusion of the Napoleonic Wars in Europe, immigration begins to rise. During the decade, 150,000 immigrants enter the United States, mostly from Ireland, Germany, England, and Scandinavia. Many are escaping starvation in their native lands; others are

1820s, *cont.*

attracted by the possibility of religious and political freedom or greater economic opportunity.

1820 In the Missouri Compromise, Congress agrees to admit Missouri to the Union as a slave state but declares all parts of the Louisiana Purchase territory north of 36°30' latitude, Missouri's southern boundary, forever free. Maine, too, is accepted as a free state.

1821 In West Africa, the American Colonization Society establishes Liberia as a refuge for ex-slaves.
    Benjamin Lundy founds *The Genius of Universal Emancipation,* one of the first abolitionist journals.

1822 In Charleston, South Carolina, former black slave Denmark Vesey plans a slave rebellion; the conspiracy is discovered, and Vesey and thirty-four others are hanged.

1824 The capital of Liberia is named Monrovia after President James Monroe, who supported the creation of the country. The American Colonization Society first brought freed slaves to the west African coastal nation in 1822.

1825 A small group of Scandinavians settle in western New York. Later, hundreds of thousands will come to America, many settling in the Midwest and northern plains.

1826 In Tennessee, the Nashoba community is established to train blacks for resettlement outside the United States.
    Pennsylvania passes a personal liberty law, prohibiting forceful seizure and removal of fugitive slaves.

1827 In New York City, John Russwurm and Samuel Cornish begin publishing *Freedom's Journal,* the first newspaper owned by African Americans.

1829 African American David Walker publishes *Appeal to the Colored Citizens of the World,* calling for a slave insurrection; the pamphlet is banned in the South.

1830s Six hundred thousand Europeans emigrate to the United States.

1830 The fifth United States Census counts 12.9 million Americans. The first count in Florida following its acquisition from Spain in 1819 reports 18,000 whites and 16,000 blacks, almost all slaves.
    A failed revolution in Germany results in an influx of German immigrants into the United States.

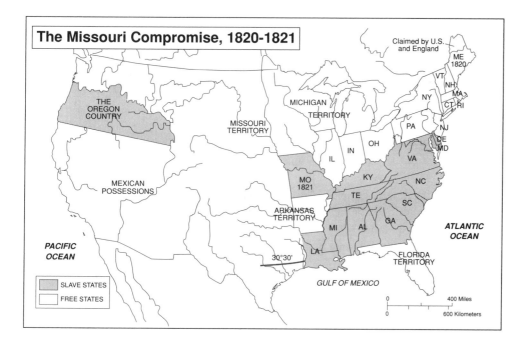

The Missouri Compromise, 1820-1821

SLAVE STATES
FREE STATES

IMMIGRATION & MINORITY LIFE

1831 In Virginia, black slave and preacher NAT TURNER leads slaves in a revolt that kills more than fifty whites; Turner is hanged for his role (see p. 221).

The New England Anti-Slavery Society is founded by white newspaper editor WILLIAM LLOYD GARRISON and others.

WILLIAM LLOYD GARRISON begins publication of his antislavery newspaper the *Liberator*.

1833 The American Anti-Slavery Society is founded by New York and New England abolitionists.

In Philadelphia, Lucretia Mott helps found the Female Anti-Slavery Society.

1834 In a New York City riot, free black churches and homes are damaged and abolitionist Lewis Tappan's home and store sacked. A riot in Philadelphia also destroys churches and homes and results in the death of one African American.

1836 Congress passes the gag rule, sponsored by southern congressman, preventing abolitionist petitions from being introduced, read, or discussed in Congress.

Lorenzo de Zavala, with other Texans, signs Texas's declaration of independence from Mexico. He will be the new republic's vice president under President Sam Houston.

1837 In Alton, Illinois, mobs murder abolitionist editor Elijah Lovejoy and destroy his printing press.

1837, *cont.*

Sisters Angelina and Sarah Grimké begin addressing small groups of women on the subject of abolition for the American Anti-Slavery Society.

The Native American Association is formed in Washington, D.C. Anti-Irish, anti-Catholic, and anti-immigrant, it testifies to a growing nativism.

1838 Frederick Bailey escapes from slavery, changing his name to FREDERICK DOUGLASS. He will be a leading writer and lecturer for the abolitionist cause.

1839 Led by Cinque, African slaves on the Spanish slave ship *L'Amistad* mutiny and sail the ship to Long Island, New York. In 1841, the Supreme Court orders the slaves freed and returned to Africa. John Quincy Adams represents the Africans before the Supreme Court.

1840 American abolitionists attend the World's Anti-Slavery Convention in London. Lucretia Mott and Elizabeth Cady Stanton are barred because they are women.

The Liberty Party, founded by abolitionists, nominates James G. Birney for president. It pushes for an end to slavery in the District of Columbia, the abolition of the interstate slave trade, and a ban on the admission of slave states to the Union.

British immigrants numbering 2,613 enter the United States, as do 39,430 Irish immigrants.

1841 Slaves being transported from Virginia to New Orleans aboard the ship *Creole* revolt and sail to the Bahamas, where they are given asylum.

1842 The Supreme Court strikes down a Pennsylvania law prohibiting fugitive slaves from being seized in that state.

In Boston, abolitionists buy captured fugitive slave George Latimore from his owner; it is the first of many such acts.

In Philadelphia, Irish Catholics riot and target African Americans.

Immigration from Scandinavia reaches its pre–Civil War peak at 1,777.

1843 Massachusetts passes a new personal liberty law that forbids state officials from catching fugitive slaves, forcing federal officials to act.

To support social service projects such as hospitals, orphanages, and homes for the elderly, American Jews found the organization B'nai B'rith.

Isabella, daughter of James and Betsy, slaves in Ulster County, New York, adopts the name SOJOURNER TRUTH and starts giving eloquent speeches around the country against slavery and for women's rights.

1844 In Philadelphia clashes erupt between native-born Americans and Irish Catholic immigrants; twenty are killed.

UNDERGROUND RAILROAD

The Underground Railroad was not a railroad; nor was it underground. It was rather an informal system for helping fugitive slaves flee to the North or Canada. It is estimated that perhaps as many as 100,000 escaped between 1800 and 1861. Quakers, one of the first groups to question slavery, often gave assistance and shelter to the runaways. Free blacks and other slaves played equally important roles in helping many individuals reach safety. The courage and ingenuity of the runaways also played a large part in the success of the enterprise. Both North and South saw the Underground Railroad's propaganda advantages: the North, especially the abolitionists, used it to publicize the horrors of slavery, whereas the South used it to prove that the North was undermining Fugitive Slave Laws, southern institutions, and a distinctive way of life.

1845 Irish potato famines spark the beginning of large-scale Irish immigration. Throughout the next decade approximately 1.5 million Irish will emigrate to the United States.

Unable to agree on the issue of slavery, the Baptist Convention breaks into northern and southern conventions and the Southern Baptist Convention is established.

1846 The Wilmot Proviso, which would ban slavery in territory captured from Mexico, is passed by the House but repeatedly defeated in the Senate.

1847 Former slave FREDERICK DOUGLASS begins publishing the *North Star;* it will become the most influential antislavery newspaper.

1848 The Free-Soil Party, which opposes slavery with the slogan "Free soil, free speech, free labor, and free men," nominates Martin Van Buren for president.

Another failed revolution in Germany, followed by a series of crop failures, sparks a great exodus to the United States. More than 1 million Germans, including future senator CARL SCHURZ, will immigrate over the next decade. Many prosperous Germans settle in the Midwest and the Mississippi Valley.

1849 California, now a U.S. possession following the Mexican War and with an influx of more than 100,000 people following the gold rush, writes a constitution prohibiting slavery and requests statehood. More than 10,000 of the new Californians are from Mexico and Latin America, and 7,000 are from Europe and Asia.

The Supreme Court declares in the *Passenger Cases* that New York and Massachusetts cannot impose a tax on each alien who enters the United States.

1850 The U.S. population is 23.2 million, including about 3.2 million slaves and 2.2 million immigrants.

The Compromise of 1850 admits California as a free state and permits residents of New Mexico and Utah Territories to decide whether they will be slave states or free. It ends the slave trade in the District of Columbia, but it also enacts a new Fugitive Slave Law compelling citizens in free states to turn in runaway slaves.

Escaped slave HARRIET TUBMAN returns south to lead her family to freedom. As a famed "conductor" on the Underground Railroad, she will rescue an estimated 300 slaves before the Civil War.

1851 Irish immigration peaks at 221,253. Most Irish settle in the seaport cities of the East.

1852 HARRIET BEECHER STOWE's antislavery novel *Uncle Tom's Cabin* is published in book form; a runaway best-seller, it increases northern antislavery sentiment.

NATIVISM

It may seem strange that nativism should develop in a nation of immigrants, in a country in which all but Indian peoples (and actually even they) have roots elsewhere. Yet almost from the very beginning some early arrivals have sought to preserve their dominion by excluding or limiting newcomers, especially those who seemed less like themselves.

In the 1830s and 1840s, as waves of German and Irish immigrants increased, nativists complained that the newcomers drank too much, that the Catholicism some of them practiced was opposed to American democratic principles, and that their willingness to work for the lowest wages was threatening the jobs and livelihoods of American workers. Immigrants were blamed for their poverty, for their lack of education, for urban crime, and for the political corruption that their presence seemed to encourage. Nativism turned political, and the American ("Know-Nothing") Party formed in upstate New York became a national party. In the 1854 midterm election, the Know-Nothings made strong showings in Massachusetts and Pennsylvania, but by 1856, the next presidential election year, the party had split over the dominating issue of slavery and was swallowed up in the vortex of civil war.

After the war nativism reemerged, this time buttressed with "scientific" evidence about racial and ethnic classifications that, for nativists, seemed to confirm the superiority of white, Anglo-Saxon, Protestant culture. This culture seemed more threatened than ever by the "new immigrants"—darker-skinned people from southern and eastern Europe and Russia, some of them Jews, who came in ever greater numbers as the century drew to a close. These newcomers, like their predecessors, crowded in city tenements, worked for low wages, and spoke languages not heard before in the United States. Again they were blamed for their poverty

and ignorance but now also for a lack of "cleanliness." They were also accused of fomenting labor unrest and of holding Socialist views that were contrary to American economics and politics.

Some old Know-Nothing proposals, such as immigration restriction, began to be passed into law. Chinese laborers, convicts, paupers, "lunatics" and "idiots," and those who might become public charges were excluded first. Later, as immigration from northern and western Europe paled beside the masses of "new immigrants," immigration laws sought to shift the balance back to the "Nordic races" through a quota system that assigned immigration slots based on the population profile of 1910, then back to 1890, before the great surge of southern and eastern Europeans peaked.

In these same years, the nativism that in northern cities targeted foreigners found expression in the South against black people, who were systematically disenfranchised and segregated. When the Ku Klux Klan revived during the 1920s, its targets encompassed all those who seemed to be threats: blacks and foreigners, Catholics and Jews.

After midcentury, with Nazi Germany pushing nativism to the extreme, the legal structures supporting a nativist outlook in the United States were dismantled. Within a year of each other, segregation and the quota system were ended by acts of Congress, and the nation embarked on an effort to make equal protection, equal opportunity, and equal access realities. It hasn't proved easy, however, and as the century came to an end, debates over new waves of immigration from Asia and Latin America, over welfare rights and public education for illegal aliens, and over English as the proposed official language were steeped again with nativist concerns, now modernized but not completely unlike those heard more than a century and a half ago.

1854 The Kansas-Nebraska Act repeals the Missouri Compromise and establishes the territories of Kansas and Nebraska according to the principles of popular sovereignty; the residents themselves will decide whether to permit slavery.

Founded in reaction to the Kansas-Nebraska Act, the Republican Party calls for the abolition of slavery.

The Massachusetts Emigrant Aid Society is established in New England to promote antislavery immigration to Kansas.

Thirteen thousand Chinese emigrate to the United States, marking the start of a mass influx (the highest number for a previous year was forty-two).

Attracted by the gold rush, many stay to help build the transcontinental railroad.

Appealing to anti-immigrant and anti-Catholic sentiment among "native" Protestants, the new American, or Know-Nothing, Party wins many local races in Massachusetts, New York, and Pennsylvania.

Castle Garden, a former theater in Manhattan's Battery—so named for the English gun batteries that were positioned there to protect the Hudson and East Rivers in the mid-1600s—is selected to become an immigrant receiving station.

1855 In Kansas, bloody clashes break out between pro- and antislavery forces for control of the government.

German immigration reaches its pre–Civil War peak, at 215,009.

1856 Proslavery groups sack Lawrence, Kansas. In response, abolitionist JOHN BROWN, his four sons, and three others murder five proslavery colonists at Pottawatomie Creek. Warfare continues between pro- and antislavery forces until federal troops restore order.

In Congress, Senator Charles Sumner makes a strong antislavery speech, criticizing, among others, Senator Andrew Butler. Representative Preston Brooks, Butler's nephew, attacks and nearly kills Sumner with a cane in the Senate.

"His argument is as thin as the homeopathic soup that was made by boiling the shadow of a pigeon that had been starved to death."

—ABRAHAM LINCOLN on Stephen A. Douglas, 1858

1857 In the *Dred Scott* decision the Supreme Court holds that African Americans are not citizens, that a slave who lives in free territory is still a slave, and that slavery cannot be prohibited from the territories.

Kansas elects an antislavery legislature, but proslavery delegates meet at Lecompton and draft a constitution that permits slavery in the territory. President James Buchanan splits the Democratic Party by accepting the Lecompton constitution.

1858 In the Lincoln-Douglas debates, ABRAHAM LINCOLN and Illinois senator Stephen A. Douglas argue the slavery issue during the campaign for the U.S. Senate. Douglas is reelected, but the debates make Lincoln a national figure.

Kansans reject the Lecompton constitution in a direct referendum, and Kansas enters the Union as a free state in 1861.

1859 Led by JOHN BROWN, twenty-two men, including five African Americans, seize the federal arsenal at Harpers Ferry, Virginia, hoping to ignite a slave rebellion. Brown is hanged for murder, treason, and insurrection; the North sees him as a martyr, the South as a traitor.

In Vicksburg, Mississippi, the Southern Commercial Convention urges repeal of state and federal laws prohibiting the importation of slaves.

In Texas, Juan Cortina leads a raid on Anglo-controlled settlements in retaliation for Anglo abuses of Mexican Americans by whites.

1860 Republican ABRAHAM LINCOLN is elected president without a single electoral vote from a slave state.

On December 20, South Carolina becomes the first southern state to secede from the Union; in the following weeks six other southern states—Florida, Alabama, Georgia, Mississippi, Louisiana, and Texas—follow suit.

1861 The Confederate States of America is established in February with Jefferson Davis and Alexander Stephens as provisional president and vice president. The Civil War begins.

1862 Congress approves the recruitment of African Americans to serve in the Union forces during the Civil War. Ultimately about 179,000 serve. More than 2,700 die on the battlefield and almost 30,000 die of wounds and disease.

EMANCIPATION AND IMMIGRATION

1863 President Lincoln issues the Emancipation Proclamation, freeing all slaves in rebelling states.

In New York City about forty people die in draft riots. The rioters, largely Irish workers too poor to hire a substitute or pay a draft commutation fee of $300, turn against African Americans. The riots are as much about economic inequity as they are about the draft. Racism and unsolved urban problems are also factors in the tensions.

Martin Van Buren, the eighth president of the United States was the first to fulfill the requirement that the president be a "natural-born citizen." Before him, they were all born British subjects.

1865 The North wins the Civil War. Reconstruction of Confederate states, begun under President LINCOLN, is taken over in December by Congress.

To provide former slaves with fuel, food, clothing, provisions, and medical and economic help, the Freedmen's Bureau is established as part of the War Department. In 1866 its scope is enlarged.

The Thirteenth Amendment, abolishing slavery, is ratified.

1865–1866 State governments in the South pass Black Codes, harsh vagrancy, apprenticeship, and civil rights laws that severely limit former slaves' freedom.

1866 The Ku Klux Klan, founded as a social club in Pulaski, Tennessee, spreads quickly and begins intimidating and terrorizing southern blacks.

Congress passes the first Civil Rights Act, giving African Americans full citizenship and equal rights under the law, thereby overturning the *Dred Scott* decision and the Black Codes.

The Freedmen's Bureau is given the power to establish courts to prosecute violators of African American civil rights.

Fearing that the Supreme Court might declare the Civil Rights Act unconstitutional, Congress passes the Fourteenth Amendment, making African Americans citizens and guaranteeing all citizens "the equal protection of the laws." The amendment will be ratified in 1868.

1869 Congress passes the Fifteenth Amendment, stating that the right of citizens to vote "shall not be denied or abridged…on account of race, color, or previous condition of servitude." The amendment will be ratified in 1870.

1870 Hiram Revels of Mississippi becomes the first African American elected to the U.S. Senate.

British immigration (excluding Irish) peaks at 103,677.

1870–1871 Congress makes the violent abuse of civil and political rights a federal crime and authorizes the use of the armed forces to subdue Klan violence. Hundreds are arrested and imprisoned or fined, causing Klan activity to decline.

1873 Slavery is ended in Puerto Rico.

1875 Congress passes a Civil Rights Act that prohibits discrimination in public places such as inns, amusement and recreation areas, and vehicles of transportation.

1877 Federal soldiers withdraw from the South, ending Reconstruction.

Following Reconstruction, thousands of African Americans begin to migrate from the rural South to Kansas and Oklahoma.

Anti-Chinese riots break out in San Francisco.

Jewish population numbers 299,087 persons, about half of 1 percent of the total U.S. population.

1878 In the El Paso "Salt War," Mexican Americans and Mexicans in Texas revolt against Anglo politicians and profiteers, accusing them of trying to seize communal salt mines. Numerous deaths and destruction of property result.

1879 President Rutherford B. Hayes vetoes a bill limiting Chinese immigration.

California's new constitution prohibits employing Chinese workers.

1880s Southern states pass "Jim Crow" laws, consigning black passengers to segregated seating in railway cars and ultimately enforcing a barrier between blacks and whites in all aspects of public life.

1880 The United States signs an agreement with China, giving the United States the right to regulate but not exclude Chinese laborers.

There are 250,000 Jews in the United States. Before 1924, some 2.5 million more will arrive from Eastern Europe and Russia. Many settle in Eastern cities, especially New York.

1882 Chinese immigration peaks at 39,579.

Congress passes, and President Chester A. Arthur signs, the Chinese

LYNCHINGS

The withdrawal of federal troops from the South in 1877 effectively ended Reconstruction and protections for African Americans. New laws and penal systems enforced many restrictions, and vigilantes often took the law into their own hands. Between 1882 and 1900, there were at least 100 lynchings a year. By 1968, more than 3,500 African Americans would be lynched, mostly in the South. The record year was 1892, when 161 African Americans were lynched.

In the 1890s, African American journalist IDA B. WELLS-BARNETT initiated a campaign to make people aware of the lynching and prevent it. She headed the Anti-Lynching Bureau of the National Afro-American Council, which proved that most lynchings were not the outcome of rape or attempted rape. Instead the victims were lynched for outspokenness, and lynching was a device used to frighten and intimidate African Americans both politically and socially.

1882, *cont.*

Exclusion Act, which bars Chinese laborers from immigrating to the United States for ten years. The ban is subsequently extended.

Scandinavian immigration peaks at 105,326. Many, taking advantage of the Homestead Act, settle in the northern Great Plains.

German immigration reaches its post–Civil War peak, at 250,630.

An Immigration Act bars entry to criminals, paupers, the insane, and other undesirables from entering the country.

In this year, 87 percent of immigrants are from northern and western Europe.

Immigrants pouring into the United States number 789,000; more than 350,000 come from Germany and England, 32,000 from Italy, and 17,000 from Russia.

1883 Touro Synagogue in Newport, Rhode Island, closed in the 1790s, is reopened to serve the many Jews now arriving from central and eastern Europe.

ELLIS ISLAND

For years New York City, the nation's largest port, served as the unofficial port of entry for immigrants. By the 1840s, as German and Irish newcomers pointed out the benefits of having an official receiving station to assist immigrants, New York State set up the Board of Commissioners of Emigration. In 1855, it opened Castle Garden, at the southern tip of Manhattan Island, where officials helped immigrants change money, buy railroad tickets, and find lodging. Critics complained, however, that the depot ruined property values and that the immigrants caused "pestilential odors." When a larger facility was sought, the U.S. government built a depot on an island in New York Harbor.

The new immigration station at Ellis Island opened on January 1, 1892. Eventually it consisted of more than thirty-five buildings on twenty-seven acres. Here newcomers underwent a medical examination and an interview with questions about their work, their destination, the amount of money they had with them, and whether they had been in prison. Later a literacy test was added. Those who could not qualify for admittance were liable to be deported.

At its peak, more than 5,000 people a day were processed at Ellis Island. More than a million entered in 1907 alone, and on its busiest day officials recorded 11,745 arrivals. In all, more than 12 million newcomers passed through Ellis Island before 1924, when new immigration restrictions were passed.

In 1954, Ellis Island was declared "surplus property," and in 1965, President Lyndon Johnson made it a national monument. After an eight-year restoration project, the Ellis Island Immigration Museum opened in 1990, displaying artifacts, photographs, and documents recording the experience of arriving in America as an immigrant.

An Italian family arrives at Ellis Island in 1905.

The Supreme Court rules the Civil Rights Act of 1875 unconstitutional, as the rights enumerated are social rather than civil and government has no jurisdiction in such matters. The provision prohibiting the exclusion of blacks from jury duty is upheld.

1885 The importation of contract laborers is prohibited.

1886 In Chicago's Haymarket Square, police try to break up a meeting of anarchists; a bomb explodes, and in the ensuing riot seven policemen are killed and many others injured. The Haymarket bombing fans nativist rage at foreign-born extremists, especially Catholics and other minority groups.

1887 The American Protective Association, an anti-immigrant, anti-Catholic organization, is founded. Its membership peaks at 2.5 million in 1896.

1889 In Chicago, Jane Addams opens Hull-House, the most famous of the settlement houses that will help immigrants adjust to life in America (see p. 251).

1890 Substantial Japanese migration begins. During the next decade at least 25,000 Japanese will enter the United States. Most are young men who work as laborers on the West Coast.

By 1890, New York City had more Italians than in Naples, more Germans than in Hamburg, and twice as many Irish as in Dublin.

IMMIGRANT COUNTRIES OF ORIGIN, 1820–1998

COUNTRY	1820–1998		1991–1998	
	NUMBER	% OF TOTAL	NUMBER	% OF TOTAL
All Countries	64,599,082	100.0%	7,605,066	100.0%
Germany	7,156,257	11.1	72,792	1.0
Mexico	5,819,966	9.0	1,931,237	25.4
Italy	5,431,454	8.4	58,346	0.8
United Kingdom	5,247,871	8.1	25,671	1.6
Ireland	4,779,998	7.4	54,865	0.7
Canada	4,453,149	6.9	157,564	2.1
USSR*	3,830,033	5.9	386,327	5.1
Austria	1,842,722	2.8	20,515	0.3
Hungary	1,675,324	2.6	14,113	0.2
Philippines	1,460,421	2.3	433,768	5.7

*After 1991, includes countries that had been constituent Soviet Republics.

"For the protection of the equality of our American citizenship and of the wages of our workingmen, against the fatal competition of low-priced labor, we demand that the immigration laws be thoroughly enforced, and so extended as to exclude from entrance to the United States those who can neither read nor write."

—REPUBLICAN PARTY PLATFORM, 1896

1890 JACOB RIIS publishes *How the Other Half Lives*, exposing the living conditions of New York's slum dwellings and immigrant neighborhoods.

1891 After three of them are acquitted, eleven Italians indicted for the murder of the New Orleans police chief are lynched by a mob.

1892 African American journalist IDA B. WELLS-BARNETT begins an antilynching crusade in a Memphis newspaper of which she is part owner.

New York Harbor's Ellis Island opens as an immigration depot; more than 12 million immigrants will pass through it by 1924.

The American Jewish Historical Society is founded to collect, preserve, exhibit, and popularize the history, accomplishment, and lives of Jews in America.

1893 The Supreme Court upholds the constitutionality of the Chinese Exclusion Act.

An agreement between the United States and Canada provides for surveillance of illegal immigrants entering into the United States through Canada's western ports.

1894 In Boston the Immigration Restriction League is founded; it suggests literacy tests be given to immigrants to keep out "undesirables."

1895 In Atlanta, at the Cotton States Exposition, BOOKER T. WASHINGTON delivers his famous "Atlanta Compromise" speech, asking African Americans to give up the struggle for civil rights and submit to segregation. Social and political equality will come from self-reliance and economic advancement, he argues.

1896 In *Plessy v. Ferguson*, the Supreme Court rules that "separate but equal" facilities for blacks and whites are constitutional. The ruling legalizes segregation.

1897 President Grover Cleveland vetoes a bill requiring that immigrants take literacy tests.

1898 With the annexation of Hawaii comes a population of 154,000: 29,000 are whites, and 125,000 are classified as "other," including native Hawaiians and Chinese and 25,000 Japanese nationals. The Chinese Exclusion Act is extended to this territory.

1900 The U.S. population is 75.9 million, including 3.6 million immigrants who have entered since 1890.

Over the next decade almost 9 million immigrants will pour into the United States from Italy, Russia, and central Europe.

1905 In Ontario, Canada, the Niagara Movement organizes at a conference of African American leaders called to protect the denial of civil rights and to oppose the conciliatory views of BOOKER T. WASHINGTON. Headed by W. E. B. DU BOIS, the organization released a "Negro Declaration of Independence" demanding full equality for black Americans.

In Chicago Robert Abbott begins publishing the *Chicago Defender;* the paper will mount a militant attack against racism.

In response to warnings of an Asian threat by politicians and the press, restrictionists, including labor leaders, establish the Asiatic Exclusion League in San Francisco.

1906 The San Francisco School Board orders that Chinese, Japanese, and Korean children attend a separate school. Whites talk of a "yellow peril."

1907 In this year, 81 percent of immigrants are from southern and eastern Europe—Poles, Russian Jews, Ukrainians, Slovaks, Hungarians, Romanians, Italians, and Greeks. For the first time, these peoples are becoming important elements in the U.S. population. These new immigrants, mostly poor and uneducated, almost always settle in cities.

1907 Theodore Roosevelt intervenes in the San Francisco School Board decision, concluding a "gentleman's agreement" that reverses the segregation decision, with Japan agreeing to stop the emigration of laborers. Japanese immigration peaks this year at 30,226.

1908 African American boxer Jack Johnson wins the world heavyweight title; his reign inspires a search for a "white hope" to depose him.

1909 The National Association for the Advancement of Colored People (NAACP) is founded to advance the rights of African Americans.

At the North Pole African American explorer Matthew Henson, a member of Adm. Robert Peary's expedition, raises the American flag.

1910 The U.S. population is 91.9 million; 8.8 million immigrants have entered since 1900, and 14.7 percent of the population is foreign born.

The Mexican Revolution begins; in the next decade the fighting will drive hundreds of thousands of Mexicans over the easily crossed border, with many settling in cities such as Tucson, El Paso, San Antonio, Laredo, and San Diego. Mexican refugees help spur the economic growth of the Southwest, particularly in agriculture, ranching, and mining.

The NAACP publishes the first issue of its journal, the *Crisis*, edited by W. E. B. DU BOIS. The National Urban League is founded by African Americans to help end racial segregation and provide community services in housing, employment, education, and social welfare.

This cartoon reads "The Chinese Must Go" and touts a washing liquid that will render the stereotypical foreign launderer unnecessary. The Chinese Exclusion Acts of 1880, the legislative embodiment of anti-Chinese fervor, were finally repealed in 1943.

1913 In California the Alien Land Law prevents Japanese from owning land in the state.

1914 Immigration reaches its all-time high, reduced in the following years by war in Europe. This year, 1,218,480 persons enter the United States. Nearly three-quarters are from southern and eastern Europe, including 283,738 from Italy, and 255,660 from Russia and the Baltic States, a flow that peaked the previous year at 291,040.

The Great Migration of blacks out of the rural South to cities in the North begins. Between 1914 and 1920, 500,000 or more blacks go north for jobs in industry and better opportunities.

1915 In Fulton County, Georgia, the Ku Klux Klan is revived.

African American scholar Carter G. Woodson establishes the Association for the Study of Negro Life and History.

Membership in the Ku Klux Klan—whose name derives from the Greek *kyklos,* for "circle" or "band"—reached more than 4 million in the 1920s.

1916 Black nationalist MARCUS GARVEY establishes the Universal Negro Improvement Association and launches the Back to Africa Movement.

LOUIS BRANDEIS becomes the first Jewish Supreme Court Justice.

1917 Despite President Woodrow Wilson's two vetoes, an immigration act is passed by Congress requiring immigrants to pass a literacy test. The act keeps out immigrants from an Asiatic barred zone but exempts refugees from religious persecution.

Puerto Ricans are granted U.S. citizenship.

In East Saint Louis, Illinois, at least 200 African Americans die in a race riot and hundreds are injured.

1919 At least twenty-five serious race riots break out in cities across the nation, including Charleston, Knoxville, Omaha, and Washington, D.C.

In Paris, W. E. B. DU BOIS organizes the first Pan-African Congress, whose goals are to promote self-determination for colonized peoples and to abolish Western imperialism.

Attempts by a handful of terrorists to murder prominent Americans result in a public outcry against foreign-born radicals, especially Italian, Jewish, or Slav immigrant industrial workers. In the ensuing "Red Scare," thousands of political and labor agitators are arrested, and hundreds of aliens, including anarchists Emma Goldman and Alexander Berkman, are deported.

THE STRUGGLE FOR ACCEPTANCE

1920s Throughout the decade the revived Ku Klux Klan expands to the North and Midwest. Besides African Americans, its new targets are immigrants, Catholics, and Jews. At its peak in the mid-1920s, it attracts 4 to 5 million members.

1920 A new California law prohibits Japanese from leasing farmland in California.

There are 3.5 million Jews in the United States. Jews constitute a quarter of New York City's population.

In many industrial cities, immigrants and their children constitute more than half the population.

1921 Congress passes the Emergency Quota Act (Dillingham Bill), which establishes a quota system as the basis of immigration policy. Only 3 percent of the people of any nationality (Mexicans and other Latin Americans exempted) who lived in the United States in 1910 may enter each year. The total maximum is 375,000. Immigration from eastern and southern Europe now slows to a trickle. Some maintain that the act is designed to keep out Jews.

After a widely reported trial, two Italian immigrants, Nicola Sacco and Bartolomeo Vanzetti, are convicted of murder during a Massachusetts shoe-factory robbery and sentenced to death. Many believe they are innocent, and protests delay their execution until 1927.

1924 Congress passes the Johnson-Reed Immigration Act, halving the maximum and limiting the annual quota from a country to 2 percent of U.S. residents of that nationality in 1890, thereby reducing further the proportion of eastern and southern Europeans admitted. Asians are also severely restricted by quotas, and the Japanese are completely excluded. The act does not limit immigration from Canada or Latin America. Family exemptions pertain only to wives and minor children of American citizens.

The Jewish population is now 4.2 million, but because of the restrictive quotas of 1924 and the Depression beginning in 1929, Jewish immigration falls sharply. Between 1933 and 1934 up to 25,000 intellectual refugees from Nazism, many of them Jews, find a haven in the United States (see p. 398).

1925 Internal scandals cause the Ku Klux Klan to lose much of its power.

African American A. PHILIP RANDOLPH organizes the Brotherhood of Sleeping Car Porters and is elected its president.

1927 The Supreme Court strikes down as unconstitutional a Texas law prohibiting African Americans from voting in the state's Democratic primary.

The Jewish population numbers 4,228,029, or 3.6 percent of all Americans.

1928 In New Mexico, OCTAVIANO LARRAZOLO becomes the first Hispanic elected to the U.S. Senate. He had been elected governor of New Mexico in 1918.

W. E. B. DuBois, editor of the National Association for the Advancement of Colored People journal Crisis, *was the first black man to receive a Ph.D. from Harvard University. The educator and activist fought for racial equality throughout his life.*

1929 The national-origins quota for immigration goes into full effect. The yearly maximum is 150,000, and from 1931 until after World War II the annual number of immigrants never exceeds 100,000.

In Texas, several Mexican American organizations unite to form the League of United Latin American Citizens (LULAC), committed to providing legal services to Mexican Americans, working for equal rights, and guaranteeing voting rights.

1931 In Detroit, Elijah Poole, later ELIJAH MUHAMMAD, joins the Temple of Islam, a black separatist sect founded by Wali Farad (W. D. Fard). In 1934, he will take over the leadership of the Black Muslims (see p. 478).

In Scottsboro, Alabama, nine young African Americans are charged with raping two white women. The convictions of the "Scottsboro boys" are reversed by the Supreme Court on procedural grounds. Following retrials, charges against five are dropped. There is widespread belief that the charges are unfounded and the boys the victims of prejudice.

1933 Nearly 16,000 Mexicans are deported, having entered the United States illegally. The campaign to deport illegal aliens, intensified by competition for jobs during the Great Depression, reduces the Mexican population in the United States by one-third during the 1930s.

Albert Einstein accepts a post at Princeton's Institute for Advanced Study. He is only the most famous of refugees from Hitler's Germany (see p. 398). Between 1935 and 1941, about 150,000 Jewish refugees are accepted by the United States.

1934 Jewish baseball star HANK GREENBERG refuses to play a game on Yom Kippur. He endured the anti-Semitism of some, but was praised by many for his decision. Poet Edgar Guest penned a poem about Greenberg that ended with: "We shall miss him on the field and shall miss him at the bat, but he's true to his religion—and I honor him for that."

1935 African American JOE LOUIS becomes world heavyweight boxing champion. Called the "Brown Bomber," Louis, who will retire undefeated in 1949, becomes a symbol of black achievement.

1938 Elected to the Pennsylvania House of Representatives, Crystal Bird Fauset becomes the first African American female to serve in a state legislature.

1939 After the Daughters of the American Revolution (DAR) bars her from performing in Washington, D.C.'s Constitution Hall, African American contralto MARIAN ANDERSON sings before 75,000 at the Lincoln Memorial. First Lady Eleanor Roosevelt resigns from the DAR in protest over their treatment of Anderson.

The United States refuses entry to 937 Jewish refugees aboard the S.S. *St. Louis* from Germany, bound for Cuba. The refugees have to return to Germany.

1940 In the South, 5 percent of blacks eligible to vote are registered.

Congress passes the Alien Registration Act, also called the Smith Act, requiring all aliens to be registered and fingerprinted. The act also provides for their deportation and makes it illegal to advocate the forceful overthrow of the American government.

1941 A. PHILIP RANDOLPH threatens a march on Washington to demand equal employment for blacks. President Franklin Roosevelt responds by issuing an executive order banning discrimination in government and defense industries. Randolph calls off the strike.

1942 President Franklin Delano Roosevelt issues an executive order to intern more than 110,000 Japanese Americans living on the West Coast, two-thirds of whom are American citizens. They are sent to camps in remote regions of Arkansas, Arizona, California, Colorado, Utah, Idaho, and Wyoming, where they are guarded by military police. Those interned lose about $400 million in property (see p. 170).

In Chicago, the Congress of Racial Equality (CORE) is founded by JAMES FARMER and others who seek to end racial discrimination and segregation through the use of nonviolence. In May, it conducts the first sit-in at the Jack Spratt restaurant.

The bracero program negotiated by Mexico and the United States offers short-term employment to Mexicans. It is extended through 1964.

1943 Chinese Exclusion Acts are repealed, and annual Chinese immigration has a quota of 105.

Close to 275 race riots break out in some fifty cities, including Detroit and New York City's Harlem.

In Los Angeles a five-day riot targets Mexican Americans in "zoot suits," or loose-fitting, flashy suits indicative of new-found economic prosperity. The clashes began in response to rumors that a group of Mexican Americans had beaten up a group of U.S. soldiers.

1944 Gunnar Myrdal, a Swedish sociologist, publishes *An American Dilemma*, an examination of the racial caste system in a democracy.

Harlem voters elect civil rights activist and minister ADAM CLAYTON POWELL to the U.S. House of Representatives, where he serves for nearly a quarter century.

1945–1951 Emergency measures allow the United States to permit entry to "displaced persons." Ultimately about 400,000 Europeans are admitted.

A line of young zoot suit-clad Hispanic men are chained together waiting to board a police bus after the 1943 "Zoot suit riots."

1947 When he is brought up from a farm club, where he has won the batting crown, to the Brooklyn Dodgers, JACKIE ROBINSON becomes the first African American major-league baseball player of the modern era.

The first issue of *Ebony* magazine is published.

Jackie Robinson was not the first black American to play major-league baseball. Moses Fleetwood Walker, a catcher, played for Toledo of the American Association in 1884.

1948 President Harry Truman signs Executive Orders ending segregation in the military and banning discrimination in the civil service.

In *Shelley v. Kraemer,* the Supreme Court declares that deed covenants preventing sales of houses to certain racial groups are not enforceable by law.

1949 William Hastie becomes the first African American federal judge.

1952 The Immigration and Nationality Act, also called the McCarran-Walter Act, is passed by Congress over the veto of President Harry Truman, who objects to the continuation of the quota system. The act removes the ban on Asian and Pacific immigration to the United States and allows spouses and minor children to enter as nonquota immigrants, but it preserves the national-origins quota system. African and Asian nations have annual quotas of 100 each. The act bans "subversives" and permits the deportation of Communist immigrants.

In the South, 28 percent of blacks eligible to vote are registered.

1953 A Refugee Relief Act permits emergency entry into the United States, outside immigration quotas, of refugees from Communist persecution. Between 1954 and 1959, more than 200,000 refugees are admitted.

CIVIL RIGHTS, REFUGEES, AND MULTICULTURALISM

1954 In a unanimous decision, the Supreme Court rules in *Brown v. Board of Education* that segregated schools are unconstitutional, and in a related ruling the next year the Court orders that desegregation must proceed with "all deliberate speed" (see p. 370).

1955 In Mississippi fourteen-year-old African American Emmett Till, visiting from Chicago, is murdered because he allegedly made suggestive remarks to a white woman. The case gets nationwide attention, especially when the two defendants receive verdicts of not guilty from an all-white jury.

In Montgomery, Alabama, ROSA PARKS is arrested for refusing to give up her bus seat to a white person. Her arrest sparks Reverend MARTIN LUTHER KING JR. and others to organize a bus boycott, which ends a year later when the Supreme Court declares bus segregation illegal.

1956 The nearly 6,000 Japanese Americans who renounced their citizenship when interned in concentration camps have their citizenship fully reinstated.

1957 Led by Martin Luther King Jr. the Prayer Pilgrimage for Freedom draws 25,000 to the Lincoln Memorial.

To join together nonviolent civil rights groups, the Southern Christian Leadership Conference (SCLC) is cofounded by Martin Luther King Jr. and Ralph Abernathy.

Central High School in Little Rock, Arkansas, is integrated, but only after President Dwight D. Eisenhower dispatches federal troops to Little Rock to protect the nine black students and ensure order.

Congress passes the first civil rights bill since Reconstruction; it establishes federal safeguards for voting rights and sets up a Civil Rights Commission.

1958 In Oklahoma City, sit-ins to desegregate lunch counters are begun by the NAACP Youth Council.

1959 After Fidel Castro comes to power, about 20,000 Cubans leave for the United States. These and later waves of Cubans settle in Florida.

1960 In Greensboro, North Carolina, African American college students stage a sit-in at an F. W. Woolworth lunch counter, leading the city to desegregate eating places a few months later. Within a year sit-ins are organized in more than 100 cities in the South and border states.

Massachusetts senator John F. Kennedy is elected president; he will be the first Catholic to hold this office.

Congress passes a Civil Rights Act authorizing federal referees to assist blacks attempting to register and vote.

The Student Nonviolent Coordinating Committee (SNCC) is formed to fight segregation through direct confrontation.

1961 The biracial Congress of Racial Equality (CORE) sends several busloads of "freedom riders" through the South to test compliance with federal laws integrating bus stations; the riders are attacked by white mobs, with order restored only after Attorney General Robert Kennedy sends in federal marshals.

The Twenty-third Amendment is ratified, permitting residents of the District of Columbia, which has a black majority, to vote in presidential elections.

1962 Attempting to organize migrant farmworkers into unions, Cesar Chavez founds the National Farm Workers Association, mainly made up of Mexican and Mexican American grape pickers in California. In 1966, it merges with an AFL-CIO affiliate to form the United Farm Workers.

James Meredith, trying to register as the first black student at the University of Mississippi, is refused entrance. A riot ensues, and federal troops are called in to restore order. Protected by federal marshals, Meredith graduates the next summer.

1962, *cont.*

An Executive Order signed by President John Kennedy places a partial ban on racial discrimination in federal housing programs.

1963 After television viewers see Birmingham, Alabama, police use water hoses and police dogs against peaceful demonstrators led by MARTIN LUTHER KING JR., there is a large public outcry against the police tactics (see p. 221).

In Mississippi, civil rights leader Medgar Evers is murdered by Byron de la Beckwith, who is finally convicted of the crime in 1994.

Addressing some 250,000 participants in the March on Washington, MARTIN LUTHER KING JR. delivers his "I Have a Dream" speech.

1964 Congress passes a Civil Rights Act, banning discrimination in education, employment, and public accommodations.

A project to register Mississippi blacks to vote becomes Freedom Summer, with schools and community centers offering legal and medical assistance. But the murder, in June, of three civil rights workers creates an atmosphere of tension and fear.

The Mississippi Freedom Democratic Party, formed in response to the Democratic Party's refusal to include black delegates, is not recognized at the Democratic National Convention.

MARTIN LUTHER KING JR. wins the Nobel Peace Prize.

The Twenty-fourth Amendment, outlawing the poll tax, is ratified.

Cassius Clay wins the heavyweight boxing title; later in the year he will convert to Islam, renaming himself MUHAMMAD ALI.

1965 A Voting Rights Act sends federal agents to register African American voters in states and districts where there was evidence that voting rights had been denied.

In February in Harlem, militant civil rights leader MALCOLM X is shot dead as he is about to make a speech. The following year three men, possible members of a rival Black Muslim sect, will be convicted of the shooting.

In Selma, Alabama, MARTIN LUTHER KING JR. starts a campaign to register black voters. After a violent confrontation King and other civil rights leaders and 4,000 peaceful demonstrators march from Selma to the state capital, Montgomery. During the campaign, three participants are killed.

In the Watts section of Los Angeles, one of the worst race riots in U.S. history leaves thirty-four dead and up to $200 million in property damage.

A new immigration act ends the national-origins quota system. The act sets a limit of 120,000 visas a year for Western Hemisphere countries and 170,000 per year for all other nations with a limit of 20,000 per nation. Relatives of U.S. citizens and those with special education and skills have preferences.

1966 EDWARD BROOKE of Massachusetts is elected to the U.S. Senate as the first African American senator to serve since Reconstruction.

"Ben, make sure you play 'Precious Lord, Take My Hand.' Play it real pretty for me."

—THE LAST WORDS OF MARTIN LUTHER KING JR., spoken to friend Ben Baruch moments before his assassination on April 4, 1968

"I HAVE A DREAM"

Perhaps even as he delivered his famous speech from the Lincoln Memorial that August afternoon in 1963, Dr. MARTIN LUTHER KING JR. knew that this was the high tide of the civil rights movement. The fire hoses and bombings of Birmingham, the killing of civil rights leader Medgar Evers, were recent, painful memories, but he couldn't have known, then, of the bombings and killings to come: four little girls in a Birmingham Sunday school, three civil rights workers in Mississippi, marchers in Selma, and then there were the riots—the burning cities in the long, hot summers of the mid-1960s, and the worst of all in the wake of his own assassination.

Martin Luther King addresses supporters at the 1963 March on Washington.

flown and walked to be there. It was an incredible gathering, and for those who were there, it bespoke an incredible sense of identity and power.

When King rose to speak, he galvanized the crowd, and ultimately the nation. Long after the riots and the killings, long after the legislation and the litigation, his words are still fresh in their challenge:

I have a dream that one day this nation will rise up and live out the true meaning of its creed: "We hold these truths to be self-evident; that all men are created equal."

I have a dream that one day on the red hills of Georgia the sons of former slaves and the sons of former slave owners will be able to sit down together at the table of brotherhood.

But on that August afternoon, after years of struggle, it must have seemed like everything was coming together instead of poised to fall apart. The march had been organized by all the great leaders: JAMES FARMER of CORE, John Lewis of SNCC, Roy Wilkins of the NAACP, Whitney Young of the National Urban League, A. PHILIP RANDOLPH, who had planned a march like this almost a quarter century ago, and King himself, head of SCLC. President John Kennedy had stated his support and had already submitted a civil rights bill to Congress.

And so many were there. As Joan Baez led the crowd in singing "We Shall Overcome," the people who joined her were famous: Nobel Peace Prize winner RALPH BUNCHE; author James Baldwin; baseball star JACKIE ROBINSON; singers and entertainers Ruby Dee, Mahalia Jackson, Odetta, Lena Horne, MARIAN ANDERSON, Harry Belafonte, Sidney Poitier, Dick Gregory, and Sammy Davis Jr. Some seventy-five members of Congress sat in a special section down front. And there were 250,000 more black and white Americans, who had driven and ridden and

I have a dream that one day even the state of Mississippi, a desert state sweltering with the heat of injustice and oppression, will be transformed into an oasis of freedom and justice.

I have dream that my four little children will one day live in a nation where they will be judged not by the color of their skin but by the content of their character.

I have a dream that one day every valley shall be exalted, every hill and mountain shall be made low, the rough places will be made plains, and the crooked places will be made straight, and the glory of the Lord shall be revealed, and all flesh shall see it together.

I have a dream today....

When we let freedom ring, when we let it ring from every village and hamlet, from every state and every city, we will be able to speed up that day when all of God's children, black men and white men, Jews and Gentiles, Protestants and Catholics, will be able to join hands and sing in the words of that old Negro spiritual: "Free at last! Free at last! Thank God Almighty, we're free at last!"

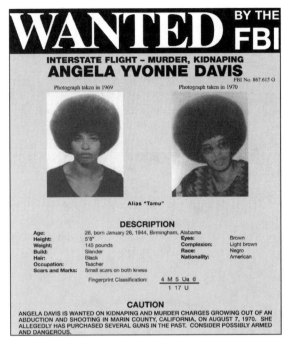

WANTED BY THE FBI

INTERSTATE FLIGHT – MURDER, KIDNAPING
ANGELA YVONNE DAVIS
FBI No. 867.615 G

Photograph taken in 1969   Photograph taken in 1970

Alias "Tamu"

DESCRIPTION

Age:	26, born January 26, 1944, Birmingham, Alabama		
Height:	5'8"	Eyes:	Brown
Weight:	145 pounds	Complexion:	Light brown
Build:	Slender	Race:	Negro
Hair:	Black	Nationality:	American
Occupation:	Teacher		
Scars and Marks:	Small scars on both knees		

Fingerprint Classification: 4 M 5 Ua 6
1 17 U

CAUTION

ANGELA DAVIS IS WANTED ON KIDNAPING AND MURDER CHARGES GROWING OUT OF AN ABDUCTION AND SHOOTING IN MARIN COUNTY, CALIFORNIA, ON AUGUST 7, 1970. SHE ALLEGEDLY HAS PURCHASED SEVERAL GUNS IN THE PAST. CONSIDER POSSIBLY ARMED AND DANGEROUS.

After a gun registered in her name was used during an attempted courtroom escape, militant black activist Angela Davis appeared on the FBI's Most Wanted List in 1970.

1966, *cont.*

Robert Weaver becomes the first African American cabinet member, heading the new Department of Housing and Urban Development.

Race riots erupt in a number of cities, including Chicago and New York.

The new leader of the Student Nonviolent Coordinating Committee (SNCC), STOKELY CARMICHAEL, advocates black power, a more militant approach to civil rights.

Huey Newton and BOBBY SEALE found the militant Black Panthers.

To celebrate African American culture, the holiday of Kwanzaa is created, based on ancient African festivals surrounding the gathering of crops that will feed the community. It runs seven days, from December 26 through January 1.

Chicano rights activist Rudolfo Gonzalez founds the Crusade for Justice to pursue social and political equality for Mexican Americans.

1967 During the "long, hot summer" race riots erupt in more than 100 American cities. The worst riots are in Detroit and Newark.

President Lyndon Johnson names THURGOOD MARSHALL, the NAACP attorney who argued the landmark *Brown v. Board of Education*, to be the first African American Supreme Court justice.

1968 The National Advisory Committee on Civil Disorders (the Kerner Commission), established by President Johnson following the race riots of 1967, issues a report stating that American is "moving toward two societies, one black, one white, separate and unequal."

On April 4 in Memphis, Tennessee, MARTIN LUTHER KING JR. is shot to death on the balcony of his motel room. James Earl Ray is arrested for the murder. Ray pleads guilty and is sentenced to ninety-nine years in prison. After the shooting, riots break out in 125 cities across the country, with forty-six deaths resulting.

Participating in the Poor People's Campaign planned by MARTIN LUTHER KING JR. before his death, African Americans led by RALPH ABERNATHY, head of the Southern Christian Leadership Conference, demonstrate in Washington, D.C., to protect racial discrimination.

Brooklyn's SHIRLEY CHISHOLM becomes the first African American woman elected to the House of Representatives.

1970s More than 4.5 million immigrants enter the United States; 1.6 million come from Asia, and 1.3 million come from Latin America and Asia.

1970 The percentage of foreign-born persons in the United States hits its century low, at 4.8 percent.

1971 In *Griggs v. Duke Power Company*, the Supreme Court declares that "objective" criteria unrelated to job skills for hiring employees are discriminatory if they put minorities at a relative disadvantage.

In a separate decision the Court upholds busing of schoolchildren where segregation had been official policy and no acceptable alternative has been suggested by local authorities.

More than 1,000 black and Latino prisoners, angered over prison conditions and a lack of educational opportunities, riot at the Attica Correctional Facility in New York; forty-two people are killed.

To fight racism, Reverend JESSE JACKSON organized People United to Save Humanity (PUSH).

In 1972, Congresswoman Shirley Chisolm became the first black woman to run for president.

1972 The Supreme Court declares that people living in segregated housing developments may sue to have them integrated.

In California black militant Angela Davis is found not guilty of murder, kidnapping, and conspiracy during a courtroom shooting in 1970.

African American congresswomen SHIRLEY CHISHOLM, a Democrat, fails in her campaign for U.S. president.

1973 Cuban-born Mercedes Cubria retires as a lieutenant colonel in the U.S. Army; the recipient of the Bronze Star and the Legion of Merit, she has had one of the most distinguished military careers of any American woman.

These orphans were among the refugees evacuated from South Vietnam before the fall of Saigon in April 1975.

Cesar Chavez, tireless in his work on behalf of migrant workers, protests the use of harmful pesticides in grapes at a New York City rally in 1986.

1975 Federal judge Arthur Garrity rules that the Boston School Committee has deliberately segregated schools by race; he suggests a plan for exchanging students in black Roxbury and white Boston, but white mob-incited violence erupts, and extra police are called to the scene to restore order.

Congress broadens the protections of the Voting Rights Act of 1965 to include Spanish-speaking Americans and other "language minorities."

Congress passes the Indochina Migration and Refugee Assistance Act, creating a program to help Cambodian and Vietnamese refugees settle in the U.S. Laotians become eligible for this program in 1976.

After the fall of Saigon, the United States accepts 130,000 Vietnamese.

1976 The Supreme Court decides that it is constitutional to order mainly white suburbs to provide low-cost public housing to minorities, even if the suburbs do not deliberately practice housing discrimination.

LOUIS FARRAKHAN splits the Black Muslims by founding the more militant Nation of Islam.

1977 The attorney general authorizes 15,000 Indochinese refugees to enter the United States on an emergency basis.

Korean immigration is significant, exceeding 30,000 per year by 1977, with one-third of new immigrants related to earlier immigrants. By this date, more than 4,500 Korean Americans operate small businesses in southern California.

More than 130 million viewers watch the TV miniseries *Roots,* based on Alex Haley's book about the African American experience; the last episode has the largest television audience to date.

1978 The Supreme Court rules that a special admissions program in a medical college favoring minority students is unconstitutional.

The federal government estimates that there are 8.2 million illegal aliens in the United States, 90 percent of Hispanic origin.

1979 The Supreme Court rules that unions may create programs designed to help African Americans be hired and gain promotions where "manifest racial imbalance" exists.

Membership in the Ku Klux Klan is once again on the rise, reaching 10,000 when it had been 8,000 in 1977.

Immigration from the Philippines is up, at 41,300 this year alone.

With the Panama Canal Act, the government allowed certain aliens who had worked with the United States on the Panama Canal or in the canal zone and their families to become permanent residents (see p. 285).

1980 In Miami fourteen people are dead as a result of riots following the acquittal of four white ex-policemen charged with beating black motorcyclist Arthur McDuffie to death.

The Supreme Court declares that Congress can impose quotas in awarding federal contracts as a way of redressing past racial discrimination.

Congress creates the first systematic plan for accepting refugees into the country, conforming to the United Nation's definition of refugee. The limit of 270,000 immigrants worldwide does not include refugees.

The United States permits more immigrants to enter from Cuba; more than 125,000 Cubans leave the country before Fidel Castro closes the port of Mariel.

The population of the United States is 228 million, including 26.5 million African Americans and 14.6 million Hispanics. In the 1980s, about 1 million illegal aliens are sent back to Mexico each year.

1981 Between 1981 and 1996, the top six countries of origin for immigrants are Mexico, the Philippines, Vietnam, China, the Dominican Republic, and India.

1982 Children in Korea, Vietnam, Laos, Cambodia, and Thailand born after 1950 and having an American father are permitted into the country as immediate relatives. Similar legislation is passed in 1987 for children of Vietnamese mothers and American fathers, allowing their immediate family to come to the United States as nonquota immigrants.

1983 In *Bob Jones University v. United States*, the Supreme Court rules that private schools practicing discrimination are ineligible for tax exemptions.

Lt. Col. Guion Bluford is the first African American in space.

JESSE JACKSON begins his campaign to win the Democratic nomination for president; despite winning several primaries, he will fail in his bid.

1986 The United States receives 601,516 immigrants; most of them come from Asia and Latin America.

Following the passage of a bill in Congress, signed into law by President Reagan in 1983, the first MARTIN LUTHER KING Day is observed as a national holiday. It is celebrated the third Monday in January.

Congress passes the Immigration Control and Reform Act (Simpson-Mazzoli Act), which allows illegal aliens who can prove they have resided continuously in the country since 1982 to remain in the country legally. The act responds to concerns over illegal aliens. Thousands, mainly from Latin America, also enter the United States illegally by crossing the Mexican border; some are refugees escaping from repressive regimes in Cuba, Central America, and Haiti. Other illegals come from Asian countries like Vietnam.

1987 Mae Carol Jemison is the first African American female selected to become an astronaut in training.

The eight episodes of the 1977 miniseries *Roots*, a fictionalized account of the genealogy of author Alex Haley, all rank among the fifty most widely viewed shows in TV history. The combined audience exceeded 130 million.

IMMIGRATION & MINORITY LIFE

Boats loaded with refugees from Haiti arrived on American shores in the early 1990s, amounting to an immigration nightmare for the United States.

1988 In his campaign to be the Democratic Party's presidential nominee, JESSE JACKSON wins millions of primary votes, but Michael Dukakis gains the nomination.

Congress enacts legislation giving Japanese Americans interned during World War II $20,000 each.

Asian Americans are estimated to number 6.5 million.

1989 In Virginia Lawrence Douglas Wilder is elected governor; taking office in 1990, he becomes the first elected African American governor since Reconstruction.

New York City elects David Dinkins as its first black mayor.

The Supreme Court invalidates a Richmond, Virginia, program requiring that 30 percent of the city's public works funds be set aside for minority-owned construction companies.

1990 The proportion of foreign-born persons in the U.S. population is on the rise, at 7.9 percent. About 14 percent of Americans speak a language other than English at home; for more than half of these people, the language is Spanish.

In an overhaul of immigration policy, total immigration levels are increased to 675,000 persons, including 480,000 family sponsored, 140,000 employment based and 55,000 considered "diversity immigrants."

From war-torn El Salvador, 80,173 immigrants enter the United States They represent over 50 percent of immigrants from Central America.

Throughout the 1990s, immigration from Jamaica remains steady, with an average of 17,500 entering each year.

1991 Unarmed black motorist Rodney King is severely beaten by Los

THE NEW IMMIGRANTS

The last decades of the twentieth century saw a radical change in the origin of U.S. immigrants. From the first settlement through World War II, the vast majority had come from Europe, escaping political upheaval and religious persecution. During the last quarter of the twentieth century, Asians and Hispanics accounted for more than three-fourths of all new arrivals. Many of the former, escaping the killing fields of Southeast Asia—especially Cambodia, Vietnam, and Laos—arrived as "boat people," facing difficulties of assimilation no less formidable than those of European predecessors. Hispanics, fleeing poverty and political turmoil throughout the Western Hemisphere, accounted for more than 40 percent of immigrants. Some time in the first decade of the twenty-first century, according to the U.S. Census Bureau, Hispanic Americans will surpass African Americans as the nation's largest minority group.

Angeles police. An amateur videotape of the incident is shown on national television, and the officers are indicted. Their acquittal the following year sparks the worst urban violence in the nation's history, with more than 50 dead and 2,000 injured in south-central Los Angeles.

Clarence Thomas becomes the second African American Supreme Court justice.

Immigrants from South Asia arrive in particularly high numbers, with 45,064 reported from India, 20,355 from Pakistan, and 10,676 from Bangladesh.

The same year as the breakup of the Soviet Union, the Immigration Naturalization Service (INS) reports that 56,980 immigrants from the region arrive in the United States, in addition to 38,661 accepted refugees.

1991–1992 Thousands of Haitian refugees, mainly fleeing political oppression, try to enter the United States by boat, but the U.S. Coast Guard starts intercepting them and returning them to Haiti.

1993 President Bill Clinton, vowing to select a cabinet that "looks like America," appoints a record number of women and minorities to cabinet posts and other top-level positions.

1995 Former football star O. J. Simpson is acquitted in the murder of his wife and an acquaintance after a trial in which race plays a major role. Most blacks applaud the verdict, while most whites disagree.

In Washington, D.C., Nation of Islam leader LOUIS FARRAKHAN leads the Million Man March to encourage black men to take responsibility for their own lives.

1996 This year alone, 163,572 Mexican immigrants come to the United States. Other major immigrant groups include 55,876 from the Philippines, 44,859 from India, 42,067 from Vietnam, and 41,728 from China. The United States also accepts 32,906 refugees from the post-Soviet states, 14,654 refugees from Bosnia-Herzegovina, 8,175 refugees from Somalia and 2,672 refugees from Iraq.

1996, *cont.*

Popular sentiment against affirmative action is reflected in the passage of California's Proposition 202, barring such programs in hiring, contracting, and education.

New federal legislation enacts a series of measures to restrict illegal immigration.

1997 The Million Woman March attracts hundreds of thousands of African American women to Philadelphia in October to promote racial unity and social activism.

1998 Racial profiling, the police practice of stopping and searching suspects on the basis of race, is thrust into the national spotlight after an April incident in which New Jersey state troopers shot into a van and wounded three men.

A black man in Jasper, Texas, is beaten, chained to the back of a pickup truck, and dragged to death. The incident leads to calls for stronger hate-crime legislation.

U.S. immigration hits a ten-year low of 660,477. More than one third of total immigration during the decade is from Asia.

1999–2000 Six-year-old Cuban refugee Elián Gonzalez, found floating off the coast of Florida after his boat sank and his mother drowned, is the object of an international custody battle between Cuban American relatives and his father in Cuba. The boy is returned to his father in June 2000, seven months after arriving in Miami.

Senator Joseph Lieberman campaigns in California on the ticket with Democratic presidential hopeful Al Gore. He is the first Jewish American to run for vice president.

2000 Democratic senator JOE LIEBERMAN, Al Gore's running mate, becomes the first Jewish American to run for vice president.

In the aftermath of the disputed national election, minority leaders in Florida and elsewhere level charges of voting irregularities and racial disenfranchisement.

As of November, according to the Census Burea, the total U.S. population is 276,059,000, of whom 226,861,000 (82.2 percent) are white and 35,470,000 (12.8 percent) are black. Hispanics, the fasting-growing group, number 32,832,000 (11.9 percent).

SUPREME COURT DECISIONS AFFECTING IMMIGRATION AND MINORITY LIFE, 1837–PRESENT

1837 *New York v. Miln.* The Court declares that state statutes requiring ship captains to supply descriptions of passengers entering the country are constitutional, a legitimate exercise of police power to promote public welfare and not a violation of the commerce clause.

1842 *Prigg v. Commonwealth of Pennsylvania.* The Court declares unconstitutional a Pennsylvania law that prohibits the seizure of fugitive slaves.

1857 *Dred Scott v. Sandford.* The Court holds that African Americans are not citizens, Congress cannot prohibit slavery in the territories, and residence in a free state does not confer freedom on African Americans. The decision hastens the start of the Civil War by sweeping aside legal barriers to the expansion of slavery and inciting the anger of northerners.

1883 *Civil Rights Cases.* The Court strikes down the Civil Rights Act of 1875, saying that "social" rights are beyond federal control, but blacks cannot be excluded from juries.

1890 *Louisville, New Orleans, and Texas Railroad v. Mississippi.* The Court upholds the constitutionality of states' attempts to segregate railway cars.

1896 *Plessy v. Ferguson.* The Court decides that if segregated railroad cars offer equal accommodations, then such segregation is not discriminatory against blacks and does not deprive them of their Fourteenth Amendment rights to equal protection under the law.

1898 *Williams v. State of Mississippi.* The Court rules that the state has a right to require voters to pass a literacy test.

1915 *Guinn v. United States.* The Court rules that the "grandfather clause," which disenfranchised most African Americans, is unconstitutional. The clause, adopted by Oklahoma and Maryland, exempted citizens from certain voter qualifications if their grandfathers had voted; obviously, this could not apply to blacks whose grandparents lived before the ratification of the Fifteenth Amendment.

1917 *Buchanan v. Warley.* The Court strikes down as unconstitutional a law that prohibits members of one race to buy, reside in, or sell property on streets where a majority of residents are of another race.

1927 *Nixon v. Herndon.* State laws prohibiting blacks from voting in primaries are held to be in violation of the Fourteenth Amendment.

1940 *Hansberry v. Lee.* The Court rules that African Americans cannot be prevented from buying homes in white neighborhoods.

1944 *Korematsu v. United States.* The Court upholds as a "military necessity" the relocation of Japanese Americans from the West Coast to detention camps.
Smith v. Allwright. The Court rules that excluding blacks from a political party on the basis of race violates the Fifteenth Amendment.

1946 *Morgan v. Commonwealth of Virginia.* The Court rules that segregation on interstate buses is unconstitutional.

1948 *Shelley v. Kraemer.* The Court rules that racially restrictive covenants in housing contracts are not enforceable.

1954 *Brown v. Board of Education of Topeka.* The Court unanimously overrules *Plessy v. Ferguson* (1896) and declares that segregated public schools violate the equal protection clause of the Fourteenth Amendment.

1960 *Gomillion v. Lightfoot.* The Supreme Court rules that the drawing of election districts so that blacks constitute a minority in all districts is a violation of the Fifteenth Amendment.

1964 *Heart of Atlanta Motel, Inc. v. United States.* The Court declares constitutional Title II of the Civil Rights Act of 1964, which outlaws private

SUPREME COURT DECISIONS AFFECTING IMMIGRATION AND MINORITY LIFE, cont.

discrimination in public accommodations. Congress has the power to bar racial discrimination in facilities that serve interstate travelers.

1966 *South Carolina v. Katzenbach.* The Court upholds the right of the federal government to intervene to protect voting rights.

1971 *Griggs v. Duke Power Co.* The Court makes its first ruling on the job-bias provisions of the Civil Rights Act of 1964, declaring that "objective" criteria, unrelated to job skills, for hiring workers are discriminatory if they result in minorities' being relatively disadvantaged.

 Swann v. Charlotte-Mecklenburg Board of Education. The Court unanimously upholds school busing for the purpose of racial balance in situations where segregation has been official policy and the school authorities have not come up with a viable alternative to busing.

1977 *United Jewish Organization of Williamsburgh, New York v. Carey.* The Court upholds the use of racial quotas in reapportioning legislative districts to comply with the Voting Rights Act of 1965.

1978 *University of California Regents v. Bakke.* The Court requires that the University of California Medical School at Davis admit white applicant Allan Bakke, who had argued that the school's minority admissions program made him a victim of "reverse discrimination."

1979 *Weber v. Kaiser Aluminum and Chemical Corporation.* The Court upholds affirmative-action programs, declaring that a job-training program that gives preference to African Americans in situations with a "manifest racial imbalance" is constitutional.

1989 *City of Richmond v. J. A. Croson.* The Court declares illegal a Richmond, Virginia, set-aside program mandating that 30 percent of the city's public works funds go to minority-owned construction firms. Such programs are legal only if they redress "identified discrimination."

1995 *Adarand Constructors v. Pena.* The Court sharply restricts federal affirmative action, ruling that programs offering special help to minorities as a remedy for past discrimination must meet a standard of "compelling government interest."

1999 *Hunt v. Cromartie.* The justices rule that congressional redistricting is not invalid simply because it diminishes minority voting power. In several recent cases, the Court refused to allow redistricting intended solely to boost minority voting power.

2000 *Reeves v. Sanderson Plumbing Products, Inc.* The Court rules that an employee does not have to prove that an employer's actions were intentionally discriminatory in order to sustain a claim of unlawful job discrimination under federal statutes.

LEGISLATION AFFECTING IMMIGRATION AND MINORITY LIFE, 1787–PRESENT

1787 Northwest Ordinance. This act, passed by the Confederate Congress, bans slavery in the Northwest Territories (see p. 72).

1793 Fugitive Slave Act. This act makes it illegal to aid runaway slaves or to interfere with their arrest.

1795 Naturalization Act. Under this act, a five-year residency is required for U.S. citizenship. Allegiance to foreign sovereigns must be renounced.

1798 Alien and Sedition Acts. The Naturalization Act raises the residency requirements for citizenship from five to fourteen years. The Alien Act gives the president the power to deport any dangerous or treasonable alien during peacetime. The Alien Enemy Act empowers the government to arrest, imprison, and banish aliens in the employ of an enemy nation during times of war. The Sedition Act, providing penalties for obstructing the government or publishing slanderous writing against it, does not apply directly to aliens.

1807 Act to Prohibit the Importation of Slaves. This act, authorized by the Constitution, prohibits the importation of African slaves as of January 1, 1808.

1820 Missouri Compromise. In this series of acts Missouri is admitted to the Union as a slave state, Maine as a free state, and slavery is forbidden in the rest of the Louisiana Purchase north of 36°30′ latitude.

1850 Compromise of 1850. In this series of acts the slave trade is prohibited in the District of Columbia, but the Fugitive Slave Law of 1793 is amended to require citizens in free states to assist in the capture of runaway slaves and makes those who aid them liable to fines and imprisonment. The territories of New Mexico and Utah are established and allowed to decide the slavery issue for themselves.

1854 Kansas-Nebraska Act. This act establishes the territories of Kansas and Nebraska and repeals the Missouri Compromise by allowing the residents of these territories to decide whether to permit slavery.

1866 Freedmen's Bureau Act. This act expands the bureau's power to include establishing courts for prosecuting violations of African American civil liberties, constructing schools, and paying teachers.
  Civil Rights Act. In this landmark act, passed over President Andrew Johnson's veto, Congress confers full citizenship on "all persons born in the United States…excluding Indians not taxed." These citizens, "without regard to any previous condition of slavery or involuntary servitude," are guaranteed the same rights to "security of person and property" as "white citizens."

1870–1871 Ku Klux Klan Acts. These acts grant the president the power to suspend habeas corpus, declare martial law, and dispatch troops to combat Klan violence and maintain order. The act also gives federal courts jurisdiction over cases involving terrorism against freed slaves.

1875 Civil Rights Act. The second Civil Rights Act recognizes that all people are equal before the law and establishes penalties for interfering with any citizen's "full and equal enjoyment" of inns, theaters, "public conveyances," and "other places of public amusement." It is declared unconstitutional in 1883.

1882 Chinese Exclusion Act. The act bars Chinese laborers from entering the United States for ten years. It will be extended until it is repealed in 1943.
  Immigration Act. This act bars entry to criminals, the insane, paupers, and persons likely to become public charges.

1917 Immigration Act. This act establishes literacy as a requirement for entry and sets up an Asiatic barred zone but exempts refugees from religious persecution.

1918, 1920 Alien Acts. The acts exclude anarchists and others advocating the overthrow of government. They authorize the government to deport any aliens who are members of revolutionary organizations.

LEGISLATION AFFECTING IMMIGRATION AND MINORITY LIFE, 1787–PRESENT, cont.

1921 Emergency Quota Act. This act establishes a national-origins quota system. Only 3 percent of the people of any nationality who lived in the United States in 1910 may enter from a country each year. The total maximum is 375,000. Mexicans and other Latin Americans are exempted.

1924 Johnson-Reed Immigration Act. This act halves the maximum and sets the annual quota of immigrants entering the United States from a country at 2 percent of U.S. residents of that nationality in 1890. Immigrants from Canada and Latin America are exempted.

1940 Alien Registration (Smith) Act. This act requires that all aliens be registered and fingerprinted and provides for deportation of aliens who belong to any organization advocating or teaching about the overthrow of the U.S. government.

1943 Chinese Act. This act repeals the Chinese Exclusion Acts, makes Chinese residents eligible for naturalization, and sets an annual Chinese immigration quota of 105.

1952 Immigration and Nationality (McCarran-Walter) Act. Spouses and minor children become nonquota immigrants under this act, but the national-origins quota system is preserved for European countries. The ban against Asian and Pacific immigration is lifted, and African and Asian nations have annual immigration quotas of 100 each. "Subversives" are barred, and the deportation of Communist immigrants is permitted.

1957 Civil Rights Act. This act protects the right to vote and establishes a Civil Rights Commission.

1964 Civil Rights Act. This prohibits discrimination in education, employment, and public accommodations on the basis of "race, color, religion, or national origin."

1965 Voting Rights Act. By this act, federal agents are empowered to register black voters in states and districts where there is evidence that voting rights

have been denied. The act is expanded in 1975 to include Spanish-speaking Americans and other "languages minorities" and to mandate bilingual elections in some circumstances.

Immigration and Nationality Act. This act ends the national-origins quota system. A limit of 120,000 visas a year for Western Hemisphere countries and 170,000 a year (with a limit of 20,000 per country) for all other nations is set. Relatives of U.S. citizens and those with special education and skills have preferences.

1968 Fair Housing Act. This act forbids discrimination in the sale or rental of housing.

1980 Refugee Act. The act raises the annual number of refugees admitted to 320,000 and provides a new definition of *refugee,* no longer limited to those fleeing Communist persecution.

1986 Immigration Reform and Control (Simpson-Mazzoli) Act. This act allows illegal aliens who can prove they have resided continuously in the country since 1982 to stay in the country legally, but criminal sanctions will be imposed on employers using undocumented workers.

1990 Immigration and Naturalization Act. By this law, 700,000 immigrants (excluding refugees) will be granted visas annually during the first three years following passage. Afterward, the yearly limit will be 675,000, of which 140,000 visas will be given to immigrants sponsored by employers with specified jobs for them to fill. In addition, 55,000 nationals of countries restricted by previous immigration acts will receive "diversity" visas.

1996 Illegal Immigration Reform and Immigrant Responsibility Act. Designed to curb illegal immigration, the law reinforces INS border patrols, tightens border checks, curtails judicial review for undocumented asylum seekers, and limits access to social benefits and public services for illegal immigrants.

NOTABLE FIGURES IN IMMIGRATION AND MINORITY LIFE

Abernathy, Ralph (1926–1990). A clergyman, Abernathy helped MARTIN LUTHER KING JR., organize and lead the civil rights movement between the 1950s and 1960s. In 1957, he and King founded the Southern Christian Leadership Conference (SCLC) to coordinate activities of civil rights groups. On King's death in 1968 he became its president and in the same year led the Poor People's Campaign, a protest against racial discrimination held in Washington, D.C.

Ali, Muhammad, formerly Cassius Clay (1942–). After first winning the title of world heavyweight champion in 1964, Clay joined the Black Muslims and changed his name to Muhammad Ali. He then refused to serve in the military, citing religious objections; he also opposed the Vietnam War. He was stripped of his title and convicted of draft evasion, but in 1970, the Supreme Court reversed the lower-court decision and upheld his draft appeal on religious grounds. His title was restored, and he went on to win the world heavyweight title again in 1974.

Anderson, Marian (1902–1993). Because of discrimination against African Americans in the United States, Anderson, a contralto, had to win fame mainly by performing in Europe during the 1930s. In 1939, she was prevented from singing in Washington, D.C.'s Constitution Hall by the Daughters of the American Revolution (DAR). The incident caused a large public outcry against the DAR, and Anderson sang instead before 75,000 people at the Lincoln Memorial. In 1955, she became the first black to perform at New York City's Metropolitan Opera. She was named alternate delegate to the United Nations in 1958 and in 1963 was awarded the President's Medal of Freedom.

Angelou, Maya (1928–). In works such as *I Know Why the Caged Bird Sings* (1970) and *All God's Children Need Traveling Shoes* (1986), poet and writer Angelou celebrated the lives of African Americans, while detailing racial, sexual, and economic struggles. Known for her wrenching autobiographical works, she delivered a poem at President Clinton's inauguration in 1993.

Antin, Mary (1881–1949). A Russian Jew who immigrated with her family in the 1890s, Antin published a series of letters she had written to her uncle about the immigrant experience, *From Plotz to Boston* (1899). She went on to write *The Promised Land* (1912) and *They Who Knock at Our Gates* (1914), an argument against a growing movement for the restriction of immigration.

Attucks, Crispus (1723?–1770). Attucks, born to an Indian mother and African American father, is remembered as one of five colonists killed by British soldiers in the Boston Massacre in the 1770s, an event leading to the American Revolution.

Baker, Ella (1903–1986). A civil rights activist, in 1938 Baker became a field secretary in the South for the National Association for the Advancement of Colored People (NAACP). She later worked in the South with the Southern Christian Leadership Conference (SCLC), where she helped students create the Student Nonviolent Coordinating Committee (SNCC). After leaving SCLC for SNCC, she remained at the center of the struggle for black voting rights in the South.

Banneker, Benjamin (1731–1806). An astronomer and mathematician, Banneker helped to survey Washington, D.C., in 1791 and defended the equality of fellow African Americans in his correspondence with Thomas Jefferson (see p. 384).

Bethune, Mary McLeod (1875–1955). An educator, Bethune founded the Daytona Normal and Industrial Institute for Negro Girls (today Bethune-Cookman College) in 1904. During the presidency of Franklin Roosevelt, Bethune was director of Negro Affairs for the National Youth Administration from 1936 to 1944. She also founded the National Council of Negro Women, serving as its first president from 1935 to 1949.

Brandeis, Louis Dembitz (1856–1941). Nominated to the Supreme Court by President Wilson 1916, Brandeis would become the first Jew on the Supreme Court. Since he supported women's rights, trade unions, a federal minimum wage, and antitrust legislation, his appointment was opposed by conservatives, anti-Semites, and some business leaders. During World War I, he served as chairman of the Provisional Committee for General Zionist Affairs. Founded in 1948 after his death, Brandeis University is named after Justice Brandeis.

Brooke, Edward (1919–). Brooke, a Republican, was elected attorney general of Massachusetts in 1962. Four years later, he was elected to Congress, becoming the first African American senator since Reconstruction.

Brown, John (1800–1859). A militant abolitionist, Brown and his five sons moved in 1855 to Kansas, where he and a small group of supporters murdered five supposed proslavery settlers along Pottawatomie Creek.

NOTABLE FIGURES, *cont.*

In 1859, he led an attack on the federal arsenal at Harpers Ferry, Virginia. In the ensuing battle with the militia, Brown was wounded and captured; later he was hanged. The raid was widely popular in the North, where some considered Brown a martyr, but enraged and terrified the South (see p. 221).

Bunche, Ralph (1904–1971). The grandson of a slave, Bunche drafted the sections of the U.N. charter on trusteeship territories. In 1948, as chief U.N. mediator in Palestine he arranged for a cease-fire between the Arabs and the Jews, for which he was awarded the 1950 Nobel Peace Prize. From 1967 to 1971 he was undersecretary-general of the United Nations, the highest rank held so far by an American.

Carmichael, Stokely, later Kwame Toure (1942–1998). Elected chairman of the Student Nonviolent Coordinating Committee (SNCC) in 1966, Carmichael championed militant civil rights activism by African Americans, coining the term "black power." His position split the SNCC, and he eventually joined the Black Panthers. Later he preached Pan-Africanism.

Carver, George Washington (1864–1943). The son of slaves, Carver, a botanist, directed the Tuskegee Institute's Department of Agriculture and Agricultural Research from 1896 to 1915. He urged southern farmers to diversify their crops by using such soil-enriching crops as peanuts, sweet potatoes, and soybeans, and developed a multitude of products and uses for these crops. In 1943 the George Washington Carver National Monument in Missouri became the first national park honoring an African American.

Chavez, Cesar (1927–1993). The son of Mexican American migrant farmworkers, Chávez founded the National Farm Workers Association in 1962. His United Farm Workers (UFW) union became part of the AFL-CIO in 1972. Chavez used nonviolent tactics such as boycotts against California's vineyard owners to gain better working conditions for migrant workers.

Chavez, Dennis (1888–1962). Chavez was the first American-born Hispanic to be elected a U. S. senator. A

Stokely Carmichael fervently advocates civil rights in a 1970 speech.

Democrat, he was appointed in 1935 to fill the seat made vacant by the death of New Mexico's Bronson Cutting. A year later Chavez was elected to that seat, which he held to his death.

Chisholm, Shirley (1924–). In 1968, Chisholm, a Brooklyn Democrat, was elected to Congress, becoming the first black woman in the House of Representatives. In 1972, she made an unsuccessful bid for president.

Chung, Connie (1946–). The youngest of ten children born to Chinese immigrants, Chung began working at CBS in 1971 and in 1993 became the first Asian American woman to coanchor a national news program. She remains one of the few Chinese Americans seen regularly on national television.

Clark, Kenneth (1914–). This psychologist's research on the negative effects of segregation on African American children influenced the 1954 landmark case *Brown v. Board of Education of Topeka*, in which the Supreme Court ruled that segregation in public schools was unconstitutional.

Delaney, Martin (1812–1885). An early black nationalist and proponent of black emigration to Africa, Delaney served as coeditor of the *North Star* with Frederick Douglass. Briefly a medical student at Harvard, he organized the National Emigration Conventions and went to Liberia to investigate sites for colonization. Later he served in the Civil War and the Freedmen's Bureau.

Douglass, Frederick, originally Frederick Bailey (1817–1895). Born a slave, Bailey escaped in 1838, settling in Massachusetts and renaming himself Frederick Douglass. In 1841, he spoke at the antislavery convention and became an agent of the Massachusetts Anti-Slavery Society. After buying his freedom with money from lecturing, Douglass settled in Rochester, New York, where, in 1847, he founded and coedited the *North Star*, an abolitionist paper. During the Civil War he helped recruit black soldiers. In 1845, he published his autobiography, *Narrative of the Life of Frederick Douglass*.

Du Bois, William Edward Burghardt (W. E. B.) (1868–1963). An educator, editor, writer, and civil rights activist, Du Bois in 1905 was one of the founders of the Niagara movement, which led, four years later, to the establishment of the National Association for the Advancement of Colored People (NAACP), which he also helped create. From 1910 to 1934, as editor of the NAACP magazine, the *Crisis*, he argued for a more militant approach to civil rights. From 1934 to 1944, Du Bois, the first black to receive a Ph.D. from Harvard, was professor of sociology at Atlanta University. Du Bois also pioneered the concept of Pan-Africanism. Among his influential writings are *The Souls of Black Folk* (1903) and *Black Reconstruction in America* (1935).

Farmer, James (1920–1999). Farmer helped found the Congress of Racial Equality (CORE) in 1942, and served as its national director from 1961 to 1966, when he organized the first "freedom rides" through the South. During the Nixon administration he was briefly assistant secretary for the Department of Health, Education, and Welfare. He later returned to teaching and lecturing and, in 1985, published his autobiography *Lay Bare the Heart*.

Farrakhan, Louis (1933–). Born Louis Walcott, Farrakhan joined the Nation of Islam in his twenties, becoming the organization's national representative after MALCOLM X's death, and then the leader of one faction of the movement. In 1995, Farrakhan organized the Million Man March in Washington, D.C., to encourage African American males to assume greater personal responsibility for their own lives, those of their family, and the community.

Fong, Hiram Leong (1907–). In 1959, Hiram Fong became the first Asian American to serve in the U.S. Senate. The son of Chinese immigrants, Fong grew up in Hawaii and attended the University of Hawaii and Harvard Law School. During his three terms as a Republican senator, he promoted relations between the United States and Pacific Rim countries, and touted the multiracial nature of Hawaiian society.

Garrison, William Lloyd (1805–1879). From 1831 to 1865 Garrison, a radical abolitionist, published *The Liberator*, one of the most influential antislavery journals. In 1833, he founded the American Anti-Slavery Society, serving as its president from 1843 to 1865. Before the Civil War, Garrison advocated northern secession from the Union. He was an early supporter of women's rights.

Garvey, Marcus (1887–1940). Jamaican-born Garvey arrived in the United States in 1916 and, urging blacks to be proud of their race and to become economically self-sufficient, initiated the Back to Africa Movement to establish a black-run nation there. Within the year, branches of his Negro Improvement Association had sprung up in the United States. In 1925, he was convicted of mail fraud; two years later President Calvin Coolidge commuted his five-year sentence, and Garvey was deported to Jamaica.

Gates, Henry Louis Jr., (1950–). The leading African American scholar of his generation, Gates has pioneered black studies in higher education, an African American perspective in literary criticism, and cultural diversity in the Western canon. The head of African American studies at Harvard since 1991, he has written such influential works as *Colored People* (1994), *The Future of the Race* (1996, with Cornel West), and *Thirteen Ways of Looking at a Black Man* (1997).

Greenberg, Hank (1911–1986). As the first Jewish baseball star, Greenberg made headlines in 1934 when he refused to play an important game that fell on Yom Kippur. He was twice awarded the American League's Most Valuable Player Award and was elected to the National Baseball Hall of Fame in 1956.

Gutierrez, José (1944–). Gutierrez founded the Mexican American Youth Organization (MAYO) and La Raza Unida (United Race) Party, which attracted Mexican Americans in the Southwest.

Harris, Patricia (1924–1985). In 1965, President Lyndon Johnson appointed Harris ambassador to Luxembourg, making her the first African American woman to achieve the rank of ambassador. Eleven years later, president-elect Jimmy Carter named Harris secretary of the Department of Housing and Urban Development, making her the first African American female cabinet member.

Hayslip, Le Ly (1949–). Le Ly Hayslip came to the United States from Vietnam in 1970 and later founded The East Meets West Foundation. She wrote two popular memoirs detailing her experiences during the Vietnam War and chronicling her attempts at assimilating to American life: *When Heaven and Earth Changed Places* (1989), and *Child of War, Woman of Peace* (1993).

Huerta, Dolores Fernandez (1930–). Huerta helped CESAR CHAVEZ to found the Farm Workers Association (later the United Farm Workers), organizing strikes and boycotts to better the lives of migrant farmworkers.

NOTABLE FIGURES, *cont.*

Hurston, Zora Neale (1903–1960). Hurston is a celebrated novelist, playwright, and autobiographer. In addition to her important novel *Their Eyes Were Watching God*, she conducted seminal work in American anthropology by traveling throughout the rural South and collecting and publishing the folklore and stories of black Americans. *Mules and Men*, published in 1935, is a collection of folklore.

Jackson, Jesse (1941–). An associate of MARTIN LUTHER KING JR., Jackson, a clergyman, was executive director from 1966 to 1971 of Operation Breadbasket, a Southern Christian Leadership Conference program to assist blacks in northern cities. In 1971, he founded Operation PUSH (People United to Save Humanity) to fight racism. Since 1981, he has headed the National Rainbow Coalition, an organization linking racial minorities, peace activists, the poor, and environmentalists. In 1984 and 1988, Jackson sought the Democratic nomination for president, the first serious presidential bids by an African American. In 1990, he was instrumental in the release of hostages from Kuwait and Iraq and, more recently, helped to secure the release of three American soldiers captured by Serbs in 1999.

Johnson, James Weldon (1871–1938). As NAACP field secretary from 1916 to 1920 and then its executive secretary from 1920 to 1930, Johnson, a writer and civil rights leader, helped make the organization into the nation's dominant civil rights unit. While in office, he mounted a legal assault on lynching and segregation, deftly using publicity and lobbying to achieve his ends. During the 1920s, Johnson was also a key member of the Harlem Renaissance, writing songs, poems, and novels. He is known for the anonymously published *Autobiography of an Ex-Colored Man* and for "Lift Every Voice and Sing," the Negro National Anthem.

King, Coretta Scott (1927–). The widow of MARTIN LUTHER KING JR., Coretta Scott King in 1970 helped found the Martin Luther King Jr. Center for Nonviolent Social Change, which she later headed, in Atlanta. She also established the Martin Luther King Jr. Library, a collection of materials on the civil rights movement.

King, Martin Luther Jr. (1929–1968). The pastor of a Montgomery, Alabama, Baptist church, King became nationally known in 1956 after he helped organize a Montgomery bus boycott, which led to integrated busing

in that city and to a Supreme Court decision declaring segregated seating unconstitutional. A believer in nonviolence, King founded the Southern Christian Leadership Conference (SCLC) in 1957 to coordinate activities of civil rights groups. In 1963, he led the great civil rights March on Washington, delivering there his famous "I Have a Dream" speech. King received the 1964 Nobel Peace Prize. In 1968, he initiated the Poor People's Campaign to fight for economic rights not obtained by civil rights gains. The campaign was cut short later that year, on April 4, when he was assassinated by white ex-convict James Earl Ray as he stood on the balcony of a Memphis, Tennessee, motel. The third Monday of January is celebrated as Martin Luther King Day in the United States.

Kingston, Maxine Hong (1940–) The daughter of Chinese immigrants, Kingston established her literary reputation in 1976 with the publication of the award-winning book *Woman Warrior: Memoirs of a Girlhood Among Ghosts*. In this book, as well as the bestselling book *China Men* (1980), she combines autobiography and fiction to explore the Chinese American experience.

Koufax, Sandy (1935–). In 1965, baseball pitcher Sandy Koufax brought the issue of Jewish sports figures to the national forefront when he refused to pitch the opening game of the 1965 World Series because it fell on Yom Kippur. Koufax is considered the best left-handed pitcher in baseball history.

Larrazolo, Octaviano (1859–1930). An important figure in New Mexico politics, Larrazolo was elected governor in 1918 and to the U.S. Senate in 1928. Throughout his life he fought for bilingual education and the rights of Hispanics.

Lazarus, Emma (1849–1887). Most famous for writing the words that adorn the base of the Statue of Liberty, Lazarus was a Jewish poet and author. She became a vocal supporter of Jewish causes in the wake of Russian pogroms in the 1880s. She wrote "The New Colossus" in 1883, but did not live to see her words added to Lady Liberty in 1888 (see p. 143).

Lieberman, Joe (1942–). A Democrat from Connecticut, Lieberman was elected to the Senate in 1988. When Democratic nominee Al Gore chose him for a running mate, Lieberman became the first Jewish American to run for the office of vice president.

Lincoln, Abraham (1809–1865). During his campaign for senator from Illinois, Lincoln debated slavery and unionism with his Democratic opponent, the incumbent Stephen Douglas. Elected president in 1860, Lincoln issued the Emancipation Proclamation three year later, declaring free all slaves in states fighting against the North. Reelected in 1864, he was assassinated while watching a play at Washington's Ford Theatre on April 14, 1865, by actor and Confederate sympathizer John Wilkes Booth.

Louis, Joe (1914–1981). In 1937, boxer Louis, nicknamed the "Brown Bomber," defeated James Braddock to win the world heavyweight championship, a title he held for a record twelve years, until his retirement in 1949. Throughout his career many African Americans looked with pride to Louis, who in their eyes symbolized black achievement.

Malamud, Bernard (1914–1986). The son of Russian Jews, Malamud grew up in Brooklyn, New York, which is often the setting for his novels and stories. With works such as *The Assistant* (1957) and *The Tenants* (1971), Malamud has earned a reputation for exploring the tough lives of Jewish immigrants with charm and compassion. Praised for his mastery of the Jewish American idiom, Malamud won the Pulitzer Prize in 1966.

Malcolm X, Muslim name el-Hajj Malik el-Shabazz, originally Malcolm Little (1925–1965). Imprisoned for robbery from 1946 to 1952, he became a Black Muslim, changing his name to Malcolm X. In 1963, Malcolm X became the organization's first national minister, preaching black separatism, racial pride, and racial achievements. In 1964, after splitting from the Muslims, he formed the Muslim Mosque, Inc. The same year he created the Organization of Afro-American Unity and converted to orthodox Islam. Before he was assassinated in Harlem, possibly by Black Muslims, he had begun to back away from his separatist views. His book, *The Autobiography of Malcolm X*, was published in 1964 and is widely read today.

Marshall, Thurgood (1908–1993). Before becoming the first African American Supreme Court justice in 1967, Marshall helped establish the NAACP's Legal Defense and Education Fund to legally challenge racial segregation. He himself argued more than thirty cases before the Supreme Court, including *Brown v. Board of Education of Topeka*, in which the Court declared unconstitutional racially segregated public schools. While a court justice he supported individual rights, affirmative action, and First Amendment freedoms.

STATUE OF LIBERTY: THE TRUE STORY

Long a symbol to travel-weary immigrants of the freedom and opportunity offered in America, the great statue on Liberty Island in New York Harbor meant other things to other people when erected in 1886. Originally called "Liberty Enlightening the World," the 151-foot-tall copper statue was a gift from the people of France, recognizing their friendship with the United States on the occasion of the American centennial in 1876. But the gift was ten years late, delayed by funding problems on both sides of the Atlantic. Designed by the French sculptor Frederic Auguste Bartholdi and engineered by Alexandre Gustave Eiffel, the statue was paid for by a lottery and special events in France. The stone-and-concrete base, designed by the noted American architect Richard Morris Hunt, was built with American money that proved slow in coming.

Commemoration of the monument on October 28, 1886, came at a time when many Americans passionately opposed and deeply feared the influx of foreigners. In the first great wave of immigration,

millions of Europeans were pouring into the country, bringing their own dreams, faiths, and political ideas. Many Americans worried that their livelihoods and most cherished values were at risk. The tenor of the times was reflected in the so-called Haymarket Riot less than six months earlier, in which a bomb exploded in the midst of policemen trying to break up a Chicago workers' rally. Rioting ensued, and eight alleged foreign radicals were blamed; those who were not hanged were later pardoned.

EMMA LAZARUS's famous sonnet "The New Colossus" was not part of the monument when it was commemorated in 1886. Only in 1903, sixteen years after her death, was the plaque inscribed with her words placed inside the pedestal:

Give me your tired, your poor,
Your huddled masses yearning to breathe free,
The wretched refuse of your teeming shore.
Send these, the homeless, tempest-tossed, to me,
I lift my lamp beside the golden door!

NOTABLE FIGURES, *cont.*

Morrison, Toni (1931–). Morrison, the 1993 Nobel Prize winner, is a novelist known for her examinations of the experiences of black women in America. Her major novels include *The Bluest Eye* (1970), *Sula* (1973), *Tar Baby* (1981), and *Beloved* (1987).

Muhammad, Elijah, originally Elijah Poole (1897–1975). After assisting Wali Farad (W. D. Fard), who founded the Nation of Islam for blacks, in Detroit, Muhammad became the movement's leader. He called for the formation of an independent, all-black nation within the United States.

Muñoz Marín, Luis (1898–1980). Having spent most of his youth in the United States, Puerto Rican-born Muñoz Marín, the son of Luis Muñoz Rivera, returned to Puerto Rico in 1926 to edit the family newspaper, *La Democracia*. In 1938, he founded the Popular Democratic Party and ten years later became Puerto Rico's first elected governor, serving until 1964. In 1952, he secured commonwealth status for Puerto Rico.

Muñoz Rivera, Luis (1859–1916). In 1889, Muñoz Rivera founded the Puerto Rican newspaper *La Democracia*, which he used to fight for greater Puerto Rican autonomy and the end of military governorship. A key figure in gaining a Spanish charter for home rule in 1897, he served for the next two years as the president of the autonomist cabinet during the U.S. occupation. Between 1910 and 1916 he served in Washington, D.C., as resident commissioner of Puerto Rico, lobbying for U.S. citizenship for Puerto Ricans, a goal achieved in 1917.

Owens, Jesse (1913–1980). In the 1936 Olympic Games held in Berlin, Owens won four gold medals in track events. His achievements refuted the Nazi myth of Aryan superiority and enraged German chancellor Adolf Hitler.

Parks, Rosa (1913–). Parks's refusal to give up her seat to a white person on a segregated bus in Montgomery, Alabama, in December 1955, sparked the bus boycott led by Martin Luther King Jr., which began the civil rights movement.

Pei, I. M. (1917–). Pei is a Chinese American architect who has designed well-known buildings all over the United States, including the Mesa International Center for Atmospheric Research in Boulder, Colorado, the East Wing of the National Gallery of Art in Washington, D.C., the John F. Kennedy Library in Boston, Massachusetts, and the Rock and Roll Hall of Fame and Museum in Cleveland, Ohio. One of the twelve naturalized Americans to receive the Medal of Liberty at the 100th anniversary of the Statue of Liberty, Pei also received the Medal of Freedom in 1990.

Powell, Adam Clayton (1908–1972). A Harlem clergyman, Powell was from 1945 to 1955 the only black congressman besides Chicago's William Dawson. In Congress, Powell was a strong voice against discrimination and segregation. In 1967, the House denied his seat in Congress on grounds of misuse of public funds. But in 1968, Powell was reelected, returning to Congress in 1969. That year the Supreme Court declared Congress had acted unconstitutionally in excluding Powell in 1967.

Powell, Colin (1937–). The son of Jamaican immigrants, Powell served two tours in Vietnam and spent four years as the chairman of the Joint Chiefs of Staff under Presidents George H. W. Bush and Bill Clinton. After being appointed by George W. Bush in 2001, he became the first African American to serve as the secretary of state. Powell also chairs America's Promise, an organization dedicated to American youth.

Randolph, Asa Philip (1889–1979). In 1925, Randolph organized the Brotherhood of Sleeping Car Porters, serving as its first president until 1968. He ensured that railway porters and maids, most of whom were African Americans, were included under the protections of the 1934 Federal Railway Labor Act, and he successfully campaigned for President Roosevelt in 1941 to sign the Executive Order banning discrimination in defense industries and federal bureaus. He led the 1963 March on Washington for jobs and freedom.

Riis, Jacob (1849–1914). This Danish-born journalist and social reformer documented life in the city slums. His powerful photographs in *How the Other Half Lives* (1890) exposed the wretched conditions of the urban immigrant.

Robeson, Paul (1898–1976). The son of a former slave, Robeson had an outstanding career as a college athlete and graduated from law school before beginning a career as an actor and concert singer. He became identified with the title role in Eugene O'Neill's play *The Emperor Jones* (1925; film, 1933). Touring the world from 1928 to 1939, Robeson returned to America convinced that the Soviet Union was a society without racial prejudice. He helped found the Progressive Party, campaigned for civil rights, and spoke up against discrimination against blacks. In 1950, the government revoked his passport, charging that he would not sign an anti-Communist oath; the passport was restored in 1958.

Robinson, Jackie Roosevelt (1919–1972). Joining the Brooklyn Dodgers in 1947, Robinson became the first African American player in modern major league baseball. Breaking baseball's "color line," Robinson was the object of open resentment by opposing players and the recipient of racial epithets and death threats from the general public. His personal dignity and success as a player eventually earned him universal respect. Robinson was named Rookie of the Year in 1947 and the National League's Most Valuable Player in 1949. He led the Dodgers to six World Series appearances in ten years and was elected to the Baseball Hall of Fame in 1962.

Rolvaag, Ole Edvart (1876–1931). A Norwegian American novelist and teacher, Rolvaag is most famous for his *Giants in the Earth* (1927), the first of a trilogy that hauntingly depicts the exhilaration and despair of making a life in a new land and becoming American.

Schurz, Carl (1826–1906).
One of the nation's most famous immigrants, Schurz was born in Germany but left after the collapse of the 1848 revolutions. A supporter of LINCOLN, he was named minister to Spain in 1861 but resigned to fight in the Civil War, rising to the rank of major general. He served in the U.S. Senate from 1869 to 1875, then was named secretary of the interior by President Rutherford B. Hayes. His wife is credited with introducing German kindergartens to the United States, the first at Watertown, Wisconsin, in 1855.

Seale, Bobby (1936–). In 1966, Seale cofounded the militant Black Panthers with Huey Newton. In 1968 he was arrested for inciting a riot during the 1968 Democratic National Convention but was tried separately from the Chicago Seven. In 1974, he resigned from the Black

Abolitionist and orator Sojourner Truth poses for a photo in 1864.

Panthers and has attempted to work within the political system, encouraging black youth to enroll in doctoral programs.

Singer, Isaac Bashevis (1904–1991). Singer left Poland in 1935 and came to the United States, where he wrote for the *Jewish Daily Forward* and published stories and novels in Yiddish. Singer describes Jewish life in Poland as well as the United States in his many important works, such *The Family Moskat* (1950) and *The Magician of Lublin* (1960). A naturalized citizen in 1943, Singer won the Pulitzer Prize in 1978.

Stowe, Harriet Beecher (1811–1896). Stowe became famous for her antislavery novel *Uncle Tom's Cabin; or Life Among the Lowly*, first serialized between 1851 and 1852 in the newspaper the *National Era* and then published in book form in 1852. A runaway best-seller (300,000 copies sold in America in a year), Stowe's sympathetic depiction of slave life strengthened antislavery sentiment in the North, thereby helping to bring about the Civil War.

Szold, Henrietta (1860–1945). The daughter of Hungarian immigrants, Szold actively helped Eastern European immigrants settle in the United States and became a Zionist leader in the United States before moving to Palestine. She organized night classes for immigrants, and she founded the Jewish Publication Society of America, and Hadassah, the Women's Zionist Organization of America.

Tan, Amy (1952–). For her 1989 semi-autobiographical novel *The Joy Luck Club*, Tan won the National Book Award. In her writing, Tan explores the lives of Chinese American women and contrasts the experiences of mothers who grew up in China to those of the daughters who grow up in America. *The Joy Luck Club*, *The Kitchen God's Wife* (1991), *The Hundred Secret Senses* (1995), and *The Bonesetter's Daughter* (2001) were all best-sellers and helped bring the experiences of Chinese Americans to a large audience.

NOTABLE FIGURES, *cont.*

Tijerina, Reies Lopez (1926–). During the 1960s, this controversial Chicano leader sought to improve the lives of poor Mexican Americans in the Southwest, organizing protests and La Alianza, an organization that focusing on restoring lands to Mexican Americans that Tijerina believed were wrongfully taken in 1848.

Truth, Sojourner (c. 1797–1883). Born a slave with the name Isabella, Truth gained freedom in 1827. In 1843, she changed her name to Sojourner Truth and became a religious missionary, nationally famous for preaching against slavery and for women's suffrage. In 1851, at the Women's Rights Convention in Akron, Ohio, she delivered her famous speech entitled "Ain't I a Woman?"

Tubman, Harriet, originally Araminta (c.1820–1913). An escaped slave, Tubman made nineteen trips into the South, leading more than 300 slaves to freedom in the North on the Underground Railroad. During the Civil War, she acted as a spy for federal forces in the South (see p. 110).

Turner, Nat (1800–1831). A charismatic slave preacher, in 1831 Turner led an uprising of about seventy-five slaves in Southampton County, Virginia, in which about fifty whites were killed. He was hanged for his role in the revolt.

Washington, Booker T. (1856–1915). Born a slave, Washington was educated at the Hampton Institute. In 1881, he became the first head of Alabama's Tuskegee Institute, founded to train African Americans for trades and professions. Washington's conservative, accommodationist views aroused the ire of civil rights activists like W. E. B. Du Bois.

Wells-Barnett, Ida B. (1862–1931). A journalist and newspaper owner in Memphis, Wells launched a crusade against lynching. Barnett helped found the National Association for the Advancement of Colored People (NAACP) and the National Association of Colored Woman. She also headed the Anti-Lynching Bureau of the National Afro-American Council.

Wiesel, Elie (1928–). Born in Romania, Wiesel came to the United States in 1956 after having suffered in a Nazi concentration camp during World War II. With books such as *And the World Remained Silent* (1956, abridged as *Night* in 1958), Wiesel provided the world with a haunting depiction of the Holocaust. Naturalized in 1963, he has taught at schools such as Boston University and the City College of New York, and has chaired the President's Commission on the Holocaust at the request of Jimmy Carter. Wiesel received the Nobel Peace Prize in 1986.

Young, Andrew (1932–). As a young minister he joined MARTIN LUTHER KING JR.'s Southern Christian Leadership Conference in 1961 and served as its executive director from 1964 to 1970; during that time he helped draft the Civil Rights Act of 1964 and the Voting Rights Act of 1965. Entering politics, he was elected to the U.S. Congress from Georgia in 1972, 1974, and 1976; served as U.S. ambassador to the United Nations from 1977 to 1979; and was mayor of Atlanta from 1982 to 1990. In 1999, he became president of the National Council of Churches.

CHAPTER 5

MILITARY HISTORY

■

HIGHLIGHTS

Timeline of U.S. Military History

FROM RAGTAG MILITIAS fighting for independence to the most powerful military force in the world, the United States has resorted to war to protect and extend its interests whenever and wherever necessary. Its costliest and most protracted conflicts have been fought on home soil, between the Union and Confederacy in the Civil War, and against the native peoples who occupied the land before colonization. As American power and prestige grew to world pre-eminence in the twentieth century, U.S. armed forces were mobilized overseas to oppose totalitarianism, to protect democratic ideals, and to promote economic interests. The balance of war powers between the president and Congress, the free expression of dissent, and, more recently, nuclear capability have operated as restraints on military action to a degree unmatched by any other nation. Yet, since the Battles of Lexington and Concord, more than a million U.S. servicemen and women have died in defense of national principles and policies. Even minorities struggling for freedom and equal rights have been willing to sacrifice their lives on the battlefield. No aspect of American history better reflects the interests and values of the nation, for better or for worse, than the wars it has fought.

REVOLUTIONARY WAR

1763–1775 Growing unease over America's colonial status is punctuated by heavier taxes, imposed by England's Parliament, which colonists argue were passed without representation; the Boston Massacre, in which five colonial protesters are killed by British soldiers; and finally the Boston Tea Party, in which colonists dressed as Indians dump tea in Boston Harbor (see p. 60).

1775 War erupts April 19 after British troops based in Boston head to Concord to destroy colonists' munitions there. Paul Revere and William Dawes embark on a late-night ride to alert the minutemen, and, at dawn, fighting breaks out at Lexington, later at Concord. Americans quickly lay siege to Boston, headquarters for the British army.

On May 10, ETHAN ALLEN and BENEDICT ARNOLD capture Fort Ticonderoga.

The Continental Army is organized, and, on June 15 GEORGE WASHINGTON is appointed its head. On June 17, the British suffer heavy losses at the Battle of Bunker Hill, which is actually fought on Breed's Hill.

Paul Revere was not the only rider to warn the colonists that British troops were advancing on Lexington and Concord on April 18, 1775. William Dawes, a cobbler, and Samuel Prescott, a doctor, rode with him that night. Revere was captured; only Dawes reached Concord.

With the British reconnoitering in Canada and the Americans afraid that they will use it as a staging ground, Continental Army brigadier general RICHARD MONTGOMERY stages a Canadian invasion. Americans fight all the way to the city of Quebec, which they surround and blockade.

1776 In March, British soldiers escape from the colonists surrounding Boston and head to Halifax, Nova Scotia, to regroup.

With the Canadian threat much diminished, the blockade of Quebec ends in May.

In June, Americans successfully hold off Gen. Sir Henry Clinton's forces along the East Coast, and the focus of the war shifts to New York, where the British hope to capture New York City and its strategic harbor.

The Continental Congress signs the Declaration of Independence on July 4.

In August, WASHINGTON loses the Battle of Long Island. The British occupy New York City, defeat Washington again at White Plains in October, and pursue his army into New Jersey but give up the chase when Washington's troops escape across the Delaware River into Pennsylvania. The Americans recross the Delaware in December and rout the British and their Hessian mercenaries at Trenton and Princeton.

The British execute NATHAN HALE as a spy.

The first year of fighting ends in a draw. Neither army has the upper hand, but both are inclined to continue fighting.

Nearly 5,000 free African Americans, many from Massachusetts and Rhode Island, fight in the Continental Army. The Cherokees and most Iroquois also fight for Britain. The colonists begin receiving support from France. Later, Spain will help the colonists as well.

1777 The British strategy to seize control of the Hudson Valley and separate New England from the rest of the colonies is thwarted at Saratoga, where John Burgoyne's army surrenders. The American victory encourages French support, realized in an alliance the next year.

In Pennsylvania, WASHINGTON falls back at Brandywine Creek, and British troops under Sir William Howe occupy Philadelphia. Washington establishes his winter camp twenty miles away at Valley Forge.

1778 In February, after two years of secretly sending aid to the Americans, the French, who now believe the Americans can win the war, formally recognize the new nation and conclude an alliance.

Sir Henry Clinton, who replaced Howe, sets out for New York but is pursued by WASHINGTON's army, which in June overtakes the British at Monmouth Court House. The British press on to New York, and Washington camps above the city.

On the frontier, George Rogers Clark seizes British outposts in Illinois country while Daniel Boone does the same in Kentucky. The British turn their attention to a southern campaign. By December, they hold most of Georgia.

Andrew Jackson was the only president to have been a prisoner of war. In 1781, he was captured by the British at Hanging Rock.

MILITARY HISTORY

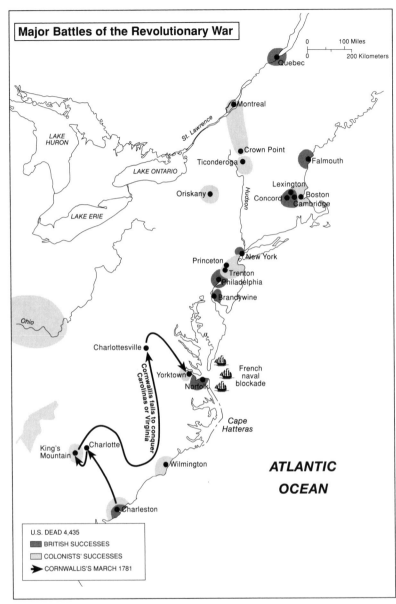

Major Battles of the Revolutionary War

0   100 Miles
0   200 Kilometers

LAKE HURON

LAKE ONTARIO

LAKE ERIE

Ohio

Quebec

Montreal

St. Lawrence

Crown Point

Ticonderoga

Falmouth

Lexington

Oriskany

Hudson

Concord   Boston
Cambridge

New York

Princeton

Trenton

Philadelphia

Brandywine

Charlottesville

Cornwallis fails to conquer Carolinas or Virginia

Yorktown

Norfolk

French naval blockade

Cape Hatteras

King's Mountain

Charlotte

Wilmington

ATLANTIC OCEAN

Charleston

U.S. DEAD 4,435
■ BRITISH SUCCESSES
□ COLONISTS' SUCCESSES
➤ CORNWALLIS'S MARCH 1781

1779 Fighting continues to be focused in the South, but repeated skirmishes along the Georgia–South Carolina border do not produce a clear victor.

Spain declares war on Britain.

In a war in which a single naval battle is a major victory, Americans are thrilled when the *Bon Homme Richard*, captained by JOHN PAUL JONES, triumphs over the HMS *Serapis* in the North Sea, in the most famous sea battle of the war.

1780 Early in the year, Gen. Sir Henry Clinton lays siege to Charleston. In the spring the Americans under the command of Maj. Gen. Benjamin Lincoln surrender to Clinton, who then heads north to deal with a French sea blockade.

In August, in the war's concluding campaign, Gen. Charles Cornwallis's forces crush an American army commanded by Gen. HORATIO GATES at Camden, South Carolina. Guerrilla fighters FRANCIS MARION and Thomas Sumter continue to plague Cornwallis. Maj. Gen. NATHANAEL GREENE replaces Gates and cleverly employs such tactics as rapid troop movement, division of his forces (an especially brave move with his lesser might), and guerrilla warfare.

1781 In January, the Americans beat the British at Cowpens, South Carolina. When Cornwallis chases one division through North Carolina, another one moves in behind him. After Cornwallis retreats, GREENE systematically knocks off every southern British outpost.

On October 19, while waiting for reinforcements from Gen. Henry Clinton in New York, a weary Cornwallis surrenders to combined French and American forces at Yorktown, Virginia.

1783 The Treaty of Paris is signed on September 3; John Quincy Adams, Benjamin Franklin, and John Jay represent the United States.

AMERICAN WARS: WHEN AND WHY

WAR	DATES	CAUSES	ENEMIES AND ALLIES
American Revolution	1775–1783	Economic (British tax colonists too heavily) and political (liberty was in the air) issues. Rising up against its mother country, the United States became the first new nation of the modern era.	Enemies: Britain Allies: France (formal alliance); Spain (declares war on Britain but does not recognize U.S. independence), and Holland
War of 1812	1812–1815	Trade, border, and maritime issues.	Enemy: Britain
Mexican War	1846–1848	Land acquisition.	Enemy: Mexico
Civil War	1861–1865	Slavery and states' rights.	The northern states (Union) vs. the southern states (Confederacy)
Spanish-American War	1898	Imperial ambitions.	Enemy: Spain
World War I (also called the Great War)	1914–1918; U.S. participation, 1917–1918	Nationalism, imperialism, anti-colonial unrest, hostile alliance systems, militarism, and an arms race.	Allies: France, Russia, Britain, Italy Enemies (Central Powers): Germany, Austria-Hungary, Ottoman Empire
World War II	1939–1945; U.S. participation, 1941–1945	Fascism, militarism, imperialism.	Allies: Britain, France, U.S.S.R. Enemies (Axis Powers): Germany, Italy, Japan
Korean War	1950–1953	First limited war of the Cold War era, played out as Korean civil war.	Allies: South Korea, United Nations Enemies: North Korea, China, with support from U.S.S.R.
Vietnam War	1964–1975	Second limited war of the Cold War era, played out as Vietnamese civil war.	Allies: South Vietnam, Australia, New Zealand Enemy: North Vietnam, supported by the U.S.S.R.
Persian Gulf War	1990–1991	Iraqi invasion of Kuwait, threat to oil shipments from the Gulf region.	Allies: United Nations Enemy: Iraq
War on Iraq	2003	Iraqi failure to comply fully with United Nations disarmament resolution, President Saddam Hussein's refusal to step down.	Allies: Britain, Spain, Australia Enemy: Iraq

INDIAN WARS

1636–1637 The Pequots are wiped out in the Pequot War, a campaign deliberately waged by the Puritans in Connecticut and parts of Massachusetts.

1675–1676 Metacom's Rebellion, also called King Philip's War. In this last major New England war, which effectively drives the Indians out of southern New England, Narragansetts, Wampanoags, and Nipmucks fight the Puritans in a battle that devastates twelve towns. The Indian effort is led by Metacom, a chief whom the English call "King Philip." The war ends when he is captured and beheaded.

1680 Pueblo Revolt. Pueblos in the Southwest rebel against the Spanish and drive them out of Santa Fe for twelve years.

1711–1713 Tuscarora War. Following a massacre by Tuscarora Indians in Carolina, white settlers ally with other tribes. After a defeat in which more than 200 Tuscarora warriors are killed, the tribe's survivors flee north, where they join the Iroquois Confederation.

1715–1716 Yamasee War. Enraged by the destruction of the Tuscaroras, Yamasees kill more than 200 South Carolina settlers before the colonists, aided by the Cherokees, defeat them. The Yamasees retreat into Georgia and Florida, where they ally with the Spanish against the English.

1763 Pontiac's Rebellion. Seeking to break the British claim on Indian lands around the Great Lakes, Ottawa Chief Pontiac organizes a confederacy of Indian forces in a series of campaigns, the largest of which occur at Fort Pitt in Pennsylvania and Fort Detroit in present-day Michigan. In response, the British issue the Proclamation of 1763, which forbids white settlement west of the Appalachians.

1774 Lord Dunmore's War. Forces led by Virginia governor John Murray, earl of Dunmore, compel the Shawnees to cede more of their land in the Ohio valley.

1790–1794 Little Turtle's War. Miami Chief Little Turtle organizes Miamis, Shawnees, and other tribes in what is now Ohio and Indiana and scuttles the forces of Josiah Harmar along the Maumee River, then defeats Arthur St. Clair along the Wabash River in Indiana. But his forces are defeated at the Battle of Fallen Timbers in Ohio.

1811 Battle of Tippecanoe. This Indian defeat in northwestern Indiana dashes Shawnee chief Tecumseh's hopes for an Indian confederacy of Old Northwest tribes.

1814 Battle of Horseshoe Bend. Creek resistance in the South is crushed by ANDREW JACKSON on the Tallapoosa River in Alabama.

1817–1818 First Seminole War. Forces led by ANDREW JACKSON capture Pensacola but fail to subdue the Seminoles in Spanish Florida.

1832 Black Hawk's War. Sacs and Foxes are crushed while defending the Mississippi River valley in present-day Illinois and Wisconsin.

1835–1842 Second Seminole War. The United States begins moving the Seminoles out of the Florida region to land west of the Mississippi. A war of resistance follows, known for its guerrilla-style fighting.

1855–1858 Third Seminole War. Remaining members of the tribe are crushed.

Pacific Coast Wars (in present-day Washington and Oregon): the Rogue River War, 1855–1856; the Yakima War, 1855–1856; and the Spokane War, 1858. These wars devastate the Native American population in the Northwest, forcing the remaining Indians onto reservations.

1865–1867 Red Cloud's War, also called the Sioux War. In this campaign, Sioux, Northern Cheyennes, and Arapahos force the U.S. Army to abandon the Bozeman Trail in Montana, the Sioux's primary buffalo range.

1874–1875 Red River War. The Kiowas, Comanches,

Cheyennes, and Arapahos mount several successful campaigns against the U.S. Army, but in a year of all-out war, mostly in northern Texas, the Indians are finally defeated and forced onto reservations.

1874 Battle at Palo Duro Canyon. Whites are victorious over the southwestern Indians in the Texas Panhandle in a battle noted for the slaughter of more than 1,000 Indian ponies.

1876–1881 Sioux War. In a struggle that spread across the plains of present-day Wyoming, Montana, South Dakota, and Nebraska, the U.S. Army fights a Plains Indian coalition composed chiefly of Sioux, Cheyennes, and Arapahos and led by Crazy Horse and Sitting Bull. In a major battle, Gen. George Armstrong Custer is defeated at Little Bighorn—Custer's Last Stand—in 1876 when an estimated 2,000 Indian warriors fells Custer's troops, numbering about 260. They army continues to harass the Indians throughout 1877, until the Indians, driven back into the Dakota Territory, sue for peace. The surrender of Sitting Bull in 1881 officially ends the conflict, although resistance movements persist for years.

1881–1886 Geronimo's Resistance. Apache leader Geronimo engages in a guerrilla war against white settlers in Arizona and New Mexico.

1890 Battle of Wounded Knee. More a massacre than a battle, the tragic events at Wounded Knee (in what is now South Dakota) unfold as the Ghost Dance sweeps the northern plains, holding out for Indians the promise that performance of the dance can make whites disappear. Jittery troopers open fire when officials try to intervene, and soon more than 200 Sioux men, women, and children are dead (see p. 29).

Known as "Buffalo Soldiers," African Americans were members of the 10th Cavalry during the Apache campaign of the 1880s.

WAR OF 1812

1812 War erupts between the United States and Great Britain over trade and border disputes, the rights of neutrals, and freedom of the seas, including maritime practices. New Englanders generally oppose the war, and Westerners support it.

Early land campaigns in Canada bring defeat to U.S. forces, who surrender Detroit and Fort Dearborn (Chicago).

A series of early sea victories creates optimism and make heroes at home, but ultimately the British strangle the East Coast with a naval blockade. Among notable U.S. sea victories are: USS *Essex* captures *Alert*, USS *Constitution* destroys *Guerrière*, USS *Wasp* seizes *Frolic*, USS *United States* defeats *Macedonia* off the Madeira Islands, USS *Constitution* beats *Java*.

1813 The United States claims victory at the Battle of Lake Erie. When the fleet of OLIVER HAZARD PERRY defeats the British fleet there, the British are forced out of the Great Lakes region, including Detroit. In retreat, the British are overtaken and further damaged at the Battle of the Thames. Indians fight alongside the British, and the great Shawnee leader Tecumseh dies in this battle.

1814 Despite these victories, the United States is nearly bankrupt and near defeat at the start of the new year, and the British, having just defeated Napoleon, can now turn their full attention toward this war. They plan a three-pronged attack that they believe will bring the Americans to their knees.

One campaign is directed at the Chesapeake Bay. The British win at the Battle of Bladensburg on August 18, and then they march on the nation's capital, burning much of it and forcing President James Madison to flee.

In the second campaign, just as 10,000 British troops are preparing to march southward from Canada and take New York City, the American fleet in September decisively wins the Battle of Lake Champlain, destroying the British fleet.

Days later, back in the Chesapeake, the Battle of Fort McHenry in Baltimore provides another pivotal American victory, inspiring Francis Scott Key to write "The Star-Spangled Banner."

Even the duke of Wellington can promise little success without control of the Great Lakes, and when British negotiators learn of the Battle of Lake Champlain, they decide not to request the territorial concessions they had hoped for, and return to the bargaining table at Ghent.

The Treaty of Ghent is signed on December 24: no land has changed hands, and neither side has gained anything from the war.

1815 The third British campaign was to take New Orleans, but the battle here—an American victory—does not take place until two weeks after the treaty is signed.

The Battle of New Orleans, in which more than 2,000 British were killed, was fought two weeks after the Treaty of Ghent had been signed, ending the War of 1812. The commanders on both sides were unaware of the peace.

MEXICAN WAR

1845 The United States annexes Texas, a move that Mexico has warned will be tantamount to an act of war because Mexico has never recognized Texas's independence. President James K. Polk sends troops, led by Gen. ZACHARY TAYLOR, to the Nueces River in Texas.

1846 Polk orders TAYLOR to advance south to the Rio Grande, which the United States claims is the southern border of Texas. Mexico maintains that the Nueces is the border, and when Mexican troops attack a reconnoitering party of Americans, Polk claims that Mexico has invaded the United States and "shed American blood upon American soil." Congress declares war.

The United States attacks in three campaigns: in northern Mexico, spearheaded by Taylor; along the Santa Fe Trail, led by Brig. Gen. STEPHEN KEARNY and set to culminate in California; and toward Mexico City, headed by Gen. WINFIELD SCOTT.

In June, even before hearing that war has broken out, Anglo settlers under Mexican rule in southern California stage the Bear Flag Revolt and declare themselves an independent republic.

KEARNY heads down the Santa Fe Trail in July. In August, his troops occupy Santa Fe.

By sea, Cdor. John Drake Sloat lands at Monterey, California. He takes San Francisco.

KEARNY heads for San Diego, which he reaches in December, to complete the occupation of California.

Taylor advances on Monterrey, Mexico, which he captures in September.

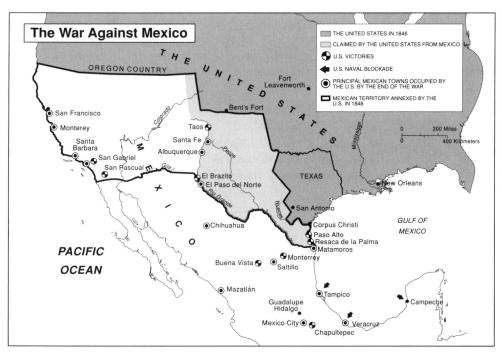

The War Against Mexico

1847 Antonio López de Santa Anna counterattacks at Buena Vista in February and is beaten. TAYLOR remains in command of a small occupying force for nine months.

SCOTT's army lands at Veracruz in March. At Cerro Gordo, Santa Anna is routed. The Americans advance toward Mexico City.

In September, Scott's men surround Mexico City. The final battle takes place on Chapultepec Hill, stormed in a savage American assault.

1848 The Treaty of Guadalupe Hidalgo, agreed to on February 2, ends the Mexican War. ULYSSES S. GRANT, WILLIAM TECUMSEH SHERMAN, GEORGE B. MCCLELLAN, GEORGE G. MEADE, ROBERT E. LEE, THOMAS J. JACKSON, Albert Sidney Johnson, James Longstreet, and many more officers who will later be enemies are colleagues in arms.

CIVIL WAR

1860 With the nation deeply divided over slavery, tariffs, and representation ABRAHAM LINCOLN's election brings the situation to crisis point. South Carolina secedes from the Union on December 20.

1861 By February 1, six other southern states—Mississippi, Florida, Alabama, Georgia, Louisiana, and Texas—secede.

The Confederate government forms in February. Its first capital is Montgomery, Alabama; after Virginia secedes on April 17, Richmond becomes its capital on May 21. The Confederacy easily raises an army of more than 100,000 men.

"It is well that war is so terrible—we should grow too fond of it."

—ROBERT E. LEE

Although the Confederates fire the first shots of the war at Fort Sumter in Charleston Harbor on April 12, antagonism has built steadily on both sides, and ABRAHAM LINCOLN may have baited the South into making the first move. Four other states—Virginia on April 17, Arkansas on May 6, Tennessee on May 7, and North Carolina on May 20—secede. The remaining slave states—Missouri, Kentucky, Maryland, and Delaware—stay with the Union despite obviously divided loyalties. The western counties of Virginia secede from Virginia and enter the Union as West Virginia in 1863.

In the First Battle of Bull Run (Manassas Junction, Virginia) in July, outnumbered Confederate forces under Gen. PIERRE G. T. BEAUREGARD beat back Union forces under Gen. Irvin McDowell. Union troops retreat to Washington, and Confederate commander THOMAS J. JACKSON earns his nickname "Stonewall."

1862 President LINCOLN orders a naval blockade of the South, but few ships are stopped in the first year.

In February, ULYSSES S. GRANT, newly promoted to brigadier general, successfully takes Forts Henry and Donelson in Tennessee, forcing a Confederate retreat toward Mississippi.

The great naval battle of the Civil War is fought in March between two ironclad ships, the Confederate *Merrimac* and the Union *Monitor*. Although the battle is a draw, it is the first time that ironclad ships have met in battle.

At the Battle of Glorieta Pass in New Mexico, Colorado volunteers keep Confederate troops out of the rest of the West.

At the Battle of Shiloh in Tennessee in April, Grant, Union commanders WILLIAM T. SHERMAN, Don Carlos Buell, and John Pope meet the forces of Confederates Albert Sidney Johnston and BEAUREGARD. The Confederates first rout Union troops, but the next day Grant routs the Confederates, who fall back exhausted. Grant, however, shaken by his losses, does not pursue the enemy. Casualties are extraordinarily high on both sides. The Union navy, headed by Adm. DAVID FARRAGUT, takes New Orleans and begins to move up the Mississippi River, cutting off Arkansas, Louisiana, and Texas from the rest of the South.

After months of preparation, Gen. GEORGE B. MCCLELLAN begins the Peninsular Campaign in Virginia. ROBERT E. LEE, a new commander of the Army of Northern Virginia, mounts a strong counterattack, and McClellan is caught off guard during the Seven Days' Battles in late June. Lee wins, but both armies suffer heavy losses.

U.S. Congress passes legislation allowing blacks to serve in the U.S. Army.

In late August, in the Second Battle of Bull Run (Manassas Junction, Virginia), the Confederates, led by Generals Lee, JACKSON and James Longstreet, force Union Gen. John Pope to retreat to Washington.

In September, at the Battle of Antietam (near Sharpsburg, Maryland), McClellan and Lee duel to a draw in the bloodiest one-day battle of the war. Although Lee's position is highly vulnerable, McClellan does not initiate battle the next day, allowing the Confederates to cross the Potomac into Virginia.

Entitled A Harvest of Death, *this photograph by Timothy H. O'Sullivan reveals the horrors of the battlefield. Warfront photography is one of the many lasting legacies of the Civil War.*

"SO COSTLY A SACRIFICE"

In the autumn of 1864, the adjutant general of Massachusetts, William Schouler, informed President LINCOLN that a widow named Lydia Bixby of Boston had lost five sons in the Civil War. When the elections of that year were over, Lincoln wrote a letter of condolence to Mrs. Bixby. Of all his writings, none express his compassion and humanity more eloquently than this letter, written in his own hand at the White House on November 21, 1864. It was later learned that three of Mrs. Bixby's sons had, in fact, survived the war.

Dear Madam,

I have been shown in the files of the War Department a statement of the Adjutant General of Massachusetts that you *are the mother of five sons who have died gloriously on the field of battle. I feel how weak and fruitless must be any word of mine which should attempt to beguile you from the grief of a loss so overwhelming. But I cannot refrain from tendering you the consolation that may be found in the thanks of the republic they died to save. I pray that our Heavenly Father may assuage the anguish of your bereavement, and leave you only the cherished memory of the loved and lost, and the solemn pride that must be yours to have laid so costly a sacrifice upon the altar of freedom.*

Yours very sincerely and respectfully,

A. Lincoln

1862, *cont.*

At the December Battle of Fredericksburg, Virginia, the Confederates gain another important victory.

More American soldiers—over 23,000—died in the two-day Battle of Shiloh (April 6–7, 1862) than in all previous U.S. wars combined, including the Civil War to that point.

1863 After the Emancipation Proclamation, effective January 1, state governments begin enrolling African Americans in the Union army; ultimately about 179,000 serve in the federal forces. More than 2,700 die on the battlefield and almost 30,000 die of wounds and disease.

In June, LEE heads to Maryland and Pennsylvania. In early July, he is stopped at Gettysburg. Beginning on July 1, the Battle of Gettysburg lasts three days and is the largest and bloodiest battle of the Civil War, claiming over 51,000 lives.

The Union army is victorious, successfully turning General Lee's forces back—a major turning point in the war. The next day, GRANT takes Vicksburg, Mississippi, which had been under siege for seven weeks.

Grant and Gen. WILLIAM T. SHERMAN seize Chattanooga, Tennessee, in November, opening the way to Atlanta and Sherman's infamous march through the South.

1864 By this time, the Union sea blockade of the East Coast from Virginia to the Gulf of Mexico is increasingly effective, halting about one-third of the ships trying to enter or exit the South.

In March, GRANT becomes supreme commander of all the Union armies. Leaving General SHERMAN in Chattanooga, he moves into northern Virginia

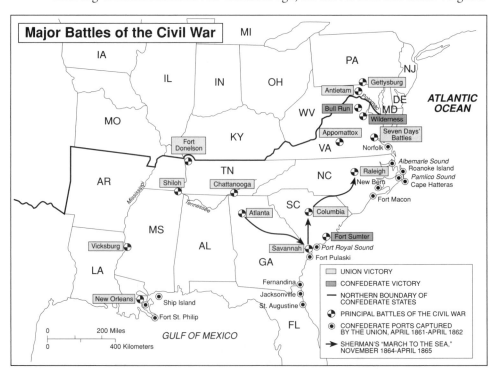

and begins to attack civilian supply lines.

In September, General Sherman marches into Atlanta.

In November, Sherman begins his march to the sea. Taking Savannah in December, he sends a telegram to LINCOLN declaring the Georgia city to be a Christmas present for the president. The march is deliberately destructive in an attempt to demoralize both the military and civilian population.

Grant continues to hammer LEE's troops in Virginia at the Battles of the Wilderness, Spotsylvania, and Cold Harbor. Lee fights well, but his troops are weary, and the hard fact is that the more populous North can continue to send reinforcements while the South cannot.

Grant surrounds Lee at Petersburg and besieges the city.

General MCCLELLAN runs for president against Lincoln, who is reelected.

1865 In April, LEE retreats. The Confederates burn Richmond behind them.

On April 9, Lee surrenders at Appomattox Court House, Virginia. GRANT is remembered for his compassion at the surrender. He immediately orders that "each officer and man will be allowed to return to his home, not to be disturbed by United States authorities." GRANT also provides 25,000 rations to Lee's starving army.

This postcard depicts the final meeting between Confederate military leaders Robert E. Lee and Thomas J. "Stonewall" Jackson. Accidentally wounded by his own men at the Battle of Chancellorsville, Jackson did not live to see Lee surrender at Appomattox.

SPANISH-AMERICAN WAR

1895–1898 The drift toward war begins when Cuba revolts against Spain's dictatorial colonial policy and the United States once again casts a longing gaze on the "Pearl of Antilles." U.S. tabloids, especially those of William Randolph Hearst, inflame public opinion by describing the unsanitary Cuban concentration camps, in which about 100,000 Cubans die. Many Americans want Cuba "rescued."

1898 On February 9, Hearst publishes an inflammatory private letter in which Dupuy de Lôme, Spanish minister to Washington, refers to President William McKinley as "weak" and a "would-be politician."

On February 15 the U.S. battleship *Maine* explodes in Havana harbor, killing 260 Americans. Although a mine is blamed, the *Maine* actually suffered an internal explosion. "Remember the *Maine* and to hell with Spain" becomes the slogan of the hour.

In April, McKinley asks for war, and Congress complies; the Teller Amendment asserts that the United States does not seek to annex Cuba.

In the Pacific, the U.S. fleet of modern, steel battleships under

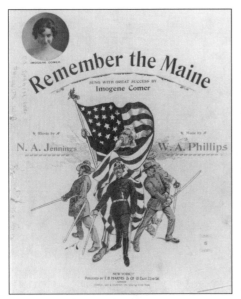

The cover of the lyrics to the song "Remember the Maine" features four soldiers depicting the North, South, East, and West with swords drawn surrounding flag-shrouded "Uncle Sam." The public outcry following the destruction of the battleship Maine *rendered war inevitable.*

"It was said in the First World War that the French fought for their country, the British fought for freedom of the seas, and the Americans fought for souvenirs."

—HARRY S TRUMAN

1898, *cont.*

Cdor. GEORGE DEWEY destroys an outdated Spanish fleet in the Manila harbor in the Philippines in May. In Cuba the Spanish fleet is blockaded in the Santiago harbor.

The Rough Riders, led by THEODORE ROOSEVELT and Leonard Wood, are victorious at San Juan Hill on July 1. Black troops make a significant contribution.

On July 3, in a battle at Santiago Bay, the Spanish fleet is destroyed.

U.S. troops seize Spanish Guam and unclaimed Wake Island, achieving a much desired foothold in the Pacific that will facilitate commercial expansion after the war.

Commodore Dewey's forces in the Philippines take the city of Manila on August 13.

The Treaty of Paris is signed on September 10. Cuba is independent. Spain cedes Puerto Rico, Guam, and the Philippines to the United States.

WORLD WAR I

1914–1918 War erupts in Europe when Archduke Franz Ferdinand, heir to the throne of Austria-Hungary, is assassinated by Gavrilo Princip, a Serbian, in Sarajevo. Austria-Hungary declares war against Serbia, and due to a set of alliances among the European nations, Russia mobilizes against Austria, Germany declares war against Russia, and France mobilizes to help Russia. The war, though centered in Europe, will gradually expand to include many of the world's nations. It will consume at least 10 million lives, 116,516 of them American. At the onset, the United States claims strict neutrality, although France has been a longtime friend. ("Forget us, God, if we forget the sacred sword of Lafayette.") President WOODROW WILSON hopes to negotiate peace.

After the Battle of the Marne, the Germans retreat but begin digging trenches in order to keep the French territory they already held. Since the Allied forces could not break through the German line, they, too, created intricate zigzag-shaped lines of trenches, protected by barbed wire. The trench lines soon stretched from the North Sea to Switzerland. While trenches had been used in warfare before, they played a much more significant role in World War I than ever before. The conditions of the trenches were terrible. Often waterlogged and muddy, and crawling with rats and lice, the trenches caused medical problems that became known as trench fever, trench nephritis, and trench foot. Between the opposing lines of trenches was "No Man's Land." Tanks, hand grenades, poison gas, and other means were used in an effort to overcome the stalemate caused by the trenches, but breakthroughs rarely occurred.

1915 On May 7, a German submarine sinks the British ship *Lusitania*, and 128 Americans are killed. The ship was carrying war materiel, and passengers were warned it might be attacked, but the unfairness of submarine warfare turns American public opinion against Germany.

1916 In March, a German submarine in the English Channel torpedoes the unarmed leisure vessel *Sussex*, injuring a few Americans. Public outrage forces Germany to promise to halt unrestricted submarine warfare.

1917 In February, hoping to bring Britain and France to their knees before the United States can enter the war, Germany unexpectedly resumes unlimited submarine warfare against all shipping headed for Britain.

In March, the United States intercepts the Zimmerman Telegram, a note proposing a Mexican-German alliance. Germany promises Mexico the return of territory in Texas, New Mexico, and Arizona taken by the United States in the Mexican War. When Congress still proves lukewarm about entering the war, WILSON responds by arming merchant marine ships.

With Wilson insisting that the "world must be made safe for democracy," on April 6, the United States declares war on Germany. Wilson calls for volunteers. Quickly, however, he and his military advisors realize that much greater numbers will be needed, and Congress passes the Selective Service Act, which requires all males between the ages of twenty-one and thirty-five to register for the draft. Ultimately the draft increases the 200,000-man army to almost 5 million.

The first American troops arrive in France in July, one month after Gen. JOHN J. PERSHING. Eventually 2 million Americans serve in France. Navy convoys help to lay 56,000 to 70,000 antisubmarine mines in the North Sea. Five U.S. battleships work with the British Grand Fleet.

In France the United States does not formally join the Allies, remaining an Associated Power and naming its army the American Expeditionary Force. Initially American troops are assigned to the sector around Verdun, France.

In December, Congress declares war on Austria-Hungary.

1918 Once Russia makes peace with Germany in March 1918, great numbers of German soldiers are moved west, and PERSHING comes under increasing pressure to integrate American forces into British and French units.

U.S. infantry in France with little or no battle experience help stem German advances at Castigny in May and Château-Thierry and Belleau Wood in June.

German losses in July and August

The uniform worn by Theodore Roosevelt at the Battle of San Juan Hill came from Brooks Brothers.

MILITARY HISTORY

On April 4, 1918, a book drive was held on the steps of the New York Public Library to gather reading material for the soldiers serving overseas.

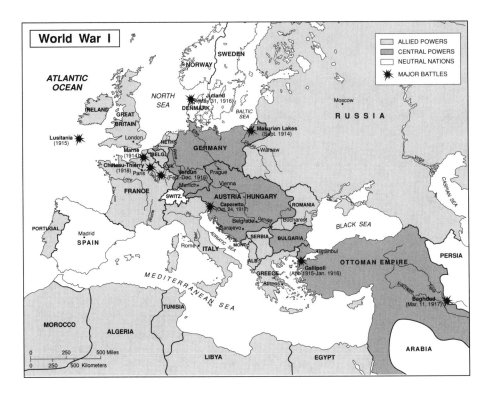

1918, *cont.*

convince German military leaders that the war cannot be won. They urge civilian leaders to consider entering into peace negotiations. A major consideration for the Germans is the apparently inexhaustible American resources.

Still an independent fighting force, U.S. troops under Pershing move on September 12 to reduce the salient at Saint-Mihiel. With Allied air support—about 1,500 planes (609 American) under the command of U.S. colonel BILLY MITCHELL—the U.S. forces are successful. Under cover of darkness, Pershing now begins moving the troops engaged at Saint-Mihiel along with fresh units to a new front: the Argonne Forest along the Meuse.

In late September, inexperience, difficult terrain, and strong German positions slow American advances. In October, Pershing renews his offensive, clearing the Argonne Forest of German forces.

On October 30, the U.S. Army pushes through the last German line, clearing the way for a major French offensive.

Germany formally surrenders, and an armistice is signed, with the cease-fire going into effect at eleven A.M. on November 11. The United States has enabled its allies to wage war more effectively by bringing them much needed replacements. Germany cedes Alsace-Lorraine to France and is effectively disarmed by the Treaty of Versailles.

THE MILITARY ESTABLISHMENT AND ITS POWERS, 1774–PRESENT

Having suffered under the British monarchy and committed to the power of "we, the people," the framers of the Constitution were careful to divide and disperse military powers. Congress was given the power to declare war, and the president was made commander in chief of the armed forces. As a result, the U.S. military establishment has been shaped and deployed to serve the sometimes competing interests of the legislative and executive branches, subject to the same checks and balances as other federal institutions. The growth and maintenance of a modern, professional fighting force has been guided simultaneously by the need for a strong national defense and a military establishment that is answerable to the public will.

1774 The First Continental Congress urges the people to arm and form their own militias.

1775 The Second Continental Congress resolves to raise six companies of riflemen, appoints a committee to establish rules for the army, and elects George Washington to be commander in chief.

1783 The Confederation Congress discharges the troops in the Continental Army, and George Washington resigns his commission.

1784 The Confederation Congress authorizes a small force that is the nucleus of the military institution that will be maintained by government under the Constitution (1789).

1789 Congress's power to "raise and support armies" is established in the Constitution.

The War Department is established, with Henry Knox named its first secretary (see p. 184).

1791 The Second Amendment accepts the idea of compulsory military service that is the legacy of the individual colonial militias.

1791–1898 Even though a small standing army of "regulars" is maintained, the United States primarily draws on volunteers and state militias throughout this period. Volunteer militias provide the primary source of manpower in the Indian Wars, the Mexican War, and the Spanish-American War. They are the basis of both the Union and the Confederate Armies during the Civil War.

1798 The Navy Department is established, with Benjamin Stoddert named its first secretary.

The U.S. Marine Corps is established under control of the secretary of the navy. Marines have participated in all U.S. wars, and their specialized training has made them experts not only in amphibious landings but in counterinsurgency and guerrilla warfare. Today they are self-sufficient units, with their own tanks, armor, artillery, and air forces.

1802 The United States Military Academy at West Point, New York, is founded to train professional army officers.

1845 The United States Naval Academy is founded at Annapolis, Maryland, to train professional naval officers.

1862 During the Civil War, the Confederacy imposes a national draft, conscripting men aged seventeen to fifty. But only 21 percent of the soldiers are draftees; most volunteer.

1863 The Union institutes a national draft, enlisting men aged twenty to forty-five years, but draftees are permitted to buy a replacement or pay a commutation fee (eliminated in 1864) of $300. Draftees constitute 2 percent of the army, and 6 percent of those fighting are substitutes.

When draft riots occur in several cities (the worst in New York City), the federal government rescinds the right to commute army service.

1876 The U.S. Coast Guard Academy is founded in New London, Connecticut.

1884 The Naval War College is established at Newport, Rhode Island.

THE MILITARY ESTABLISHMENT AND ITS POWERS, 1774–PRESENT, cont.

1900 With its new steel navy, built over the course of nearly two decades, the United States ranks third among world naval powers.

1901 The Army War College opens in Washington, D.C., designed to improve officer training as part of a general army reorganization. In 1951, the college moves to Carlisle, Pennsylvania.

1907 The Aeronautical Division of the Army Signal Corps is established and is variously renamed until amendments to the National Security Act in 1949 make the air force a military department within the new Department of Defense.

1915 The U.S. Coast Guard is established, combining the Revenue Cutter Service and the Life Saving Service.

The Selective Service System held national draft lotteries to determine if and when eligible men would enter the war. While on the air, radio announcer Stephen McCormick indicates that his draft number has been included in the lottery.

1917 Upon entering World War I, the United States initiates its first wide-scale draft; 72 percent of the army is conscripted.

1940 World War II in Europe prompts the first peacetime draft in U.S. history. Men aged twenty-one to thirty-five are conscripted for one year of service, to be served within the Western Hemisphere.

1941 In the summer, the term of service for the draftees is extended. After the United States enters World War II, all men between the ages of eighteen and thirty-eight and at one time up to age forty-five are conscripted for the duration of the war.

1943 The U.S. Merchant Marine Academy is founded in Kings Point, New York.

1945 The draft remains in existence after peace is established.

1947 The Joint Chiefs of Staff is organized to provide military advisors to the secretary of defense and the president. It consists of the chief of staff of the army and of the air force, the chief of naval operations, the commandant of the marines, and the chairman, whose job is to represent the other committee members' opinions.

The National Security Act combines the army, navy, and air force into a new Department of Defense, with James V. Forrestal as its first secretary. The act also creates the National Security Council and Central Intelligence Agency.

1948 The draft, ended in 1947, is reinstituted.

1954 The U.S. Air Force Academy is founded at Colorado Springs, Colorado.

1965 Draft quotas rise steadily during the escalation of the Vietnam War, soaring from 100,000 men in 1964 to 400,000 men in 1966. Draftees make up 16 percent of the army but constitute 88 percent of the troops in Vietnam.

1969 Under growing public pressure to end the draft, a lottery is instituted for all eighteen-year-olds.

1970 A government report on the military recommends an all-volunteer army, with a standby draft for emergencies.

1971 After the invasion of Cambodia the draft is extended for two more years only after long debate, and student deferments are eliminated. In preparation for an all-volunteer armed force, the military pay scale is increased substantially.

1973 On January 27, the day a cease-fire is reached in Vietnam, the draft ends; eighteen-year-old men are still required to register for the draft.

1975 President Gerald Ford halts compulsory draft registration.

1976 The National Defense University is established in Washington, D.C., combining the Industrial College of the Armed Forces and the National War College.

1980 President Jimmy Carter reinstitutes compulsory draft registration when the Soviets invade Afghanistan.

1986 The Joint Chiefs of Staff is reorganized to strengthen the role of its chairman, who is now the president's chief military advisor.

1988 The Department of Veterans Affairs is established, with Edward J. Derwinski named its first secretary.

1990–2000 The demise of the Soviet Union and end of the Cold War lead to cuts in the federal defense budget, in stockpiles of nuclear weapons, and in military personnel. By the year 2000, there are 1.14 million active-duty officers and enlisted men, or about half the total of 1980 and 1990.

1992 Restructuring for the post–Cold War world, the Air Force dismantles the Strategic Air Command (SAC) and establishes the Air Combat Command at Langley, Virginia.

1993 President Clinton eases a ban on gays in the military, instituting a "don't ask, don't tell" policy.

2001 In the aftermath of September 11 terrorist attacks, President George W. Bush creates the new cabinet-rank position of director, Office of Homeland Security. Without military command authority, the director is responsible for coordinating national strategy to strengthen protections against terrorist threats. Former Pennsylvania governor Tom Ridge is appointed to the position. In 2002, President Bush creates the Department of Homeland Security, which envelopes the Office of Homeland Security and many other agencies—a sweeping federal reorganization.

WORLD WAR II

1931–1935 The specter of a major war once again hangs over the world when Japan, seeking its own empire in Asia, invades Manchuria (September 1931), Hitler assumes power in Germany (January 1933), and fascism is on the rise elsewhere in Europe. Italy, led by Benito Mussolini since 1922, invades Ethiopia and declares it a colony. A plebiscite in the Saar (January 1935) results in the area's returning to Germany. Germany advances into the Rhineland (March 1936), a region demilitarized by several international agreements at the end of World War I.

1935 The Nazi government passes the Nuremberg Laws, which deprive all Jews (anyone with at least one Jewish grandparent) of citizenship and forbid marriage with Gentiles. Gradually all civil rights for Jews are rescinded.

1935–1937 Strongly isolationist, the United States passes the Neutrality Acts, which forbid U.S. companies to sell raw materials, fuel, and materiel to warring nations and tells its citizens that they travel in war zones at their own risk.

1936–1937 Germany and Italy form the Berlin-Rome Axis in October, and one month later Germany and Japan conclude a pact that is the basis for future cooperation. One year later, in November 1937, Japan and Italy sign a pact. Germany, Italy, and Japan become known as the Axis Powers.

1936–1939 Fascist forces led by Generalissimo Francisco Franco wage a civil war to overthrow Spain's center-left elected government. Germany and Italy supply Franco throughout the struggle.

1937 Japan invades China. It also sinks the *Panay*, a U.S. patrol boat in Chinese waters, but apologizes, wishing to avoid a confrontation.

In March, Germany annexes Austria.

1938 Britain and France meet with Germany in Munich in September and agree to let Hitler take over a part of Czechoslovakia called the Sudetenland, German-speaking territories bordering Germany and Austria.

Ostensibly in retaliation for the murder of a German diplomat in Paris by a Polish Jew, Jewish shops, homes, and synagogues throughout Germany are pillaged, burned, and destroyed. Because of the destroyed property and shards of glass lining the streets, the events of November 9 and 10 are referred to as *Kristallnacht* or "Night of Broken Glass." A fine of 1 billion marks is levied against the Jewish community.

1939 Germany annexes the rest of Czechoslovakia and sets up the puppet state of Slovakia. Western nations are stunned when Germany and the U.S.S.R. sign a nonaggression pact on August 23. When Germany invades Poland on September 1, hostilities break out. France and England declare war on Germany. President FRANKLIN ROOSEVELT issues a proclamation of neutrality on September 5.

In late November, Russia invades Finland.

The Declaration of Panama warns belligerents away from Western Hemisphere seas south of Canada.

1940 Germany goes on the march in northern Europe, invading Denmark and Norway in April and Holland, Belgium, Luxembourg, and France in May. British, French, and Belgian forces are surrounded at Dunkirk in northeastern France. The Nazi war machine inexplicably comes to a halt, and more than 330,000 Allied troops escape to Britain.

The Selective Service and Training Act begins to increase U.S. military ranks.

In June, France signs an armistice with Germany.

During the Battle of Britain, Germany relentlessly pounds England by air from mid-August to the end of October, but Britain does not surrender.

Germany, Italy, and Japan sign a ten-year treaty in which they pledge mutual assistance in case of attack.

In an executive order, ROOSEVELT gives Great Britain fifty World War I–vintage destroyers in return for eight U.S. naval sites on British territory.

World War II in Europe

Legend:
- ALLIED POWERS
- AXIS POWERS
- AREAS UNDER AXIS CONTROL, MAY 1941
- NEUTRAL NATIONS
- ★ MAJOR BATTLES

1941 In March, the United States institutes Lend-Lease, a program designed to aid any country whose continued existence is deemed vital to the interests of the United States. The hope is that the aid will enable these nations successfully to prosecute the war and the United States will not need to fight.

The United States agrees to defend Greenland. U.S. troops land in Iceland to take over defense of the Danish colony.

In August, ROOSEVELT and British prime minister Winston Churchill meet in the North Atlantic to formulate broad postwar aims—the Atlantic Charter (see p. 288).

Despite its nonaggression pact, Germany marches against Russia on June 22.

Roosevelt decrees an embargo on all iron and steel exports except to Western Hemisphere nations in September, having frozen all Japanese exports in July.

Roosevelt extends Lend-Lease aid to the Soviet Union.

Eager to disable the United States in the Pacific, Japan on December 7 launches a surprise attack on Pearl Harbor and destroys much of the Pacific Fleet. Casualties total 2,280 killed and 1,109 wounded. Sixty-eight civilians lose their lives. At the same time (December 8, west of the international date line), Japanese forces attack the Philippines, Guam, Midway, Hong Kong, and the Malay Peninsula.

"You can no more win a war than you can win an earthquake."

—JEANNETTE RANKIN

(see p. 288).

AFRICAN AMERICANS IN THE MILITARY

Even when they were forced to serve in segregated units under white commanders, African Americans have always responded to the country's need for soldiers and have enlisted in numbers greater than their population warrants.

Segregation was in effect throughout both world wars. Blacks and whites ate in separate messes and slept in separate barracks. Worst of all from many blacks' point of view, blacks were not permitted to serve in certain units. African American women who tried to enlist in the WAVES, for example, were turned away on the grounds that there were no black fliers for them to support. During World War II, the lines began to break down gradually (the WAVES opened to black women in 1944), and in 1948 President HARRY TRUMAN ordered complete integration of the armed forces. Here are the numbers of African Americans who served in major U.S. wars:

Revolutionary War	.5,000
Civil War	.200,000
World War I	.367,000
World War II	.1,000,000
Vietnam War	.275,000
Persian Gulf War	.104,000

1941, *cont.*

John J. Pershing was the only U.S. general to win a Pulitzer Prize. He received the award for *My Experiences in the World War* (1931).

On December 8, Congress declares war on Japan. On December 11, Germany and Italy declare war on the United States.

The United States lost valuable time needed to prepare for war, but enlisted an enormous and enthusiastic pool of laborers and the impressive production capacity of the country to prepare for the new technology available since World War I. The United States entered the war with five aircraft carriers and managed to produce 139 before its conclusion in 1945, which was only part of the transformation of the navy. The country's war industry also produced 40,000 M4 Sherman tanks, armed with a 75mm main gun, two light machine guns, and a heavy machine gun for anti-aircraft fire. The United States also made advances in developing amphibious assault vehicles, the semiautomatic rifle, submarines, planes and strategies in aviation, and, of course, nuclear weaponry.

Russia, helped by an especially harsh winter and overextended German supply lines, rallies against the Germans just in time to stop them from entering Moscow.

1942 In the Pacific the Japanese win the battles of Manila, Luzon, and the Java Sea in January and February.

In the United States Japanese Americans are forced into internment camps.

In May, the Battle of the Coral Sea, an air struggle over the east coast of Australia, provides a much-needed Allied victory in the Pacific theater.

A month later, the Allies are again victorious at Midway, in a three-day naval battle. Four Japanese aircraft carriers are sunk; the United States loses the Yorktown. The victory is assured in part by Operation Magic, in which the Allies crack the Japanese secret code and learn Japan's battle plans in advance. This victory renders Hawaii safe from further Japanese attack.

The Manhattan Project is assigned the task of building an atomic bomb. The United States and Australia mount a counteroffensive in the

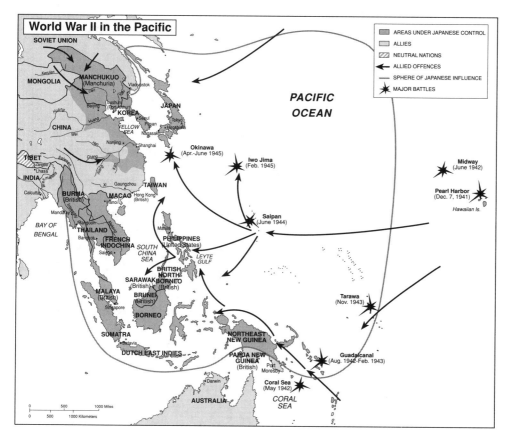

World War II in the Pacific

SOVIET UNION

MONGOLIA

MANCHUKUO (Manchuria)

Vladivostok

JAPAN

KOREA

Seoul

Pusan

Tokyo

Nagasaki Hiroshima

CHINA

YELLOW SEA

Nanjing

Shanghai

PACIFIC OCEAN

TIBET

Lhasa

INDIA

Calcutta

BAY OF BENGAL

BURMA (British)

Mandalay

Rangoon

MACAO

Guangzhou

TAIWAN

Hong Kong (British)

Hanoi

Okinawa (Apr.-June 1945)

Iwo Jima (Feb. 1945)

Midway (June 1942)

Pearl Harbor (Dec. 7, 1941)

Hawaiian Is.

THAILAND

Bangkok

FRENCH INDOCHINA

Saigon

SOUTH CHINA SEA

PHILIPPINES (United States)

Manila

Saipan (June 1944)

LEYTE GULF

BRITISH NORTH BORNEO (British)

SARAWAK (British)

BRUNEI (British)

Tarawa (Nov. 1943)

MALAYA (British)

Singapore

BORNEO

SUMATRA

Batavia

DUTCH EAST INDIES

NORTHEAST NEW GUINEA

PAPUA NEW GUINEA (British)

Port Moresby

Guadalcanal (Aug. 1942-Feb. 1943)

Darwin

Coral Sea (May 1942)

AUSTRALIA

CORAL SEA

0   500   1000 Miles

0   500   1000 Kilometers

AREAS UNDER JAPANESE CONTROL

ALLIES

NEUTRAL NATIONS

ALLIED OFFENCES

SPHERE OF JAPANESE INFLUENCE

MAJOR BATTLES

MILITARY HISTORY

Solomon Islands and Papua New Guinea. In a protracted, six-month battle, lasting until January 1943, the U.S. Marines win Guadalcanal in the Solomon Islands, gaining a strategic airstrip.

In November, during Operation Torch, Gen. DWIGHT D. EISENHOWER coordinates amphibious landings with the British in North Africa at Casablanca, Oran, and Algiers to follow up on the earlier British army victory over Erwin Rommel's forces at El Alamein, Egypt. By mid-May 1943, all Axis forces in North Africa have surrendered.

At Stalingrad, Soviet forces rally again and besiege German forces.

1943 Churchill and ROOSEVELT meet at Casablanca. They agree to seek unconditional surrender of the enemy and to launch an invasion of Italy. EISENHOWER is named supreme commander in North Africa.

German troops at Stalingrad surrender.

Allied air strikes target civilian populations in Germany to weaken morale. As in Britain in 1940, the German population becomes more unified, and war production continues at full capacity. The only lasting result is that many cultural monuments are destroyed.

In July, the Allies invade Sicily. Their victory results in the downfall of Italian dictator Benito Mussolini. The Italian mainland is invaded in September, and American and British troops begin the slow and methodical advance northward against German troops.

JAPANESE AMERICAN INTERNMENT

The Japanese immigrants who began arriving in significant numbers on the West Coast of the United States after 1890 confronted a wall of hostility toward Asians that had already led to a law specifically prohibiting Chinese immigration. The Japanese were excluded from many occupations, and when in 1906 the San Francisco School Board sought to segregate Japanese students, President THEODORE ROOSEVELT intervened to negotiate a "gentleman's agreement" whereby the children would not be segregated but Japan would agree not to permit any more laborers to emigrate to the United States. California soon passed laws prohibiting Japanese from owning or leasing farmland, and in 1924 a new federal immigration law specifically excluded Japanese as "aliens ineligible for citizenship."

Following the surprise attack on Pearl Harbor, the long-standing prejudice against people of Japanese descent reached a fever pitch. And, as the great majority were concentrated on the West Coast, where a Japanese air attack or actual invasion seemed most likely, fears of sabotage seemed to justify racial animosity. Although there were no instances of disloyalty, President FRANKLIN ROOSEVELT in February 1942 authorized the creation of military areas from which suspect persons could be excluded. A month later, more than 110,000 persons of Japanese descent (41,000 issei, or first-generation aliens, and 72,000 nisei, or second-generation U.S. citizens) were removed from the strategic military areas in California, Oregon, and Washington into detention centers in the interior.

The camps themselves were miserable—inadequate in size, sanitation, rations, and protection from the elements. The assets of the issei had been frozen, and the property the evacuees had to leave behind was sold off to opportunists or vandalized. The total was estimated at more than $400 million. In *Korematsu v. United States* (1944), the Supreme Court upheld the relocation on the grounds of national security.

Even as the evacuees lived behind barbed wire, the 442d Combat Team, an all Japanese American unit fighting in Italy and France, established an impressive military record: more casualties and more decorations than for any other unit of its size in American history. More than 25,000 Japanese Americans served in the U.S. armed forces during the war.

While German and Italian noncitizens were also designated as enemy aliens during the war, no group suffered the humiliation, loss of wages and property, and denial of civil rights that Japanese Americans endured. In 1988, the U.S. government issued a formal apology and granted $20,000 in restitution to each of the 60,000 surviving Japanese Americans who had been interned.

1944 In the Pacific theater the Battle of the Marshall Islands from November through February 1944 provides another Allied victory.

Under EISENHOWER'S command, Operation Overlord, D day, begins on June 6 with the invasion of France, the largest air and sea invasion ever mounted. Initially 176,000 soldiers and 20,000 vehicles hit the beaches of Normandy. Within a month more than 1 million troops, almost 600,000 tons of supplies, and about 2,100,000 vehicles are in Normandy. By late July, the Germans realize that the Battle of Normandy is lost and begin withdrawing east across the Seine. Paris is liberated on August 25.

In the Pacific in July, the United States wins the Mariana Islands with the Battle of the Philippine Sea consolidating those wins. Airfields are constructed on Guam and Saipan to begin the bombing of Japan.

In September, victories at Palau and Yap open the way for the invasion of the Philippines.

The Battle of Leyte Gulf in late October destroys Japanese naval support for their armed forces in the Philippines. The land battle rages from October to late February 1945.

1944–1945 The Battle of the Bulge, which lasts from December 16 to

For ten years prior to the Japanese attack on Pearl Harbor, the following question appeared on the final exam of the Japanese Naval Academy: "How would you carry out a surprise attack on Pearl Harbor?"

WORLD WAR II: THE HOME FRONT

Among the many advantages of the United States in World War II was its strong support on the home front. Ordinary citizens made material sacrifices that contributed mightily to the massive industrialization effort, making raw materials available for wartime manufacture, investing in war bonds, supporting volunteer services, and conserving goods—from oil to food—vital to success on the battlefield. Americans had supported previous war efforts, but the organized response to World War II was unprecedented. It was the greatest mobilization of the American people in the nation's history.

Even before the United States formally entered the war, the federal government had advocated "meatless Mondays" and "wheatless Wednesdays" as a means of stockpiling food. Citizens were encouraged to grow their own vegetables, and many complied. Huge rallies were held to encourage the purchase of war bonds, which increased the funds available for military buildup. Buying bonds also gave ordinary citizens a financial stake in the war effort.

In February 1942, two months after Pearl Harbor and the declaration of war, the last new commercial automobiles rolled off Detroit's assembly lines, and the factories were retooled for jeep and tank production.

Many other industrial facilities were converted to the manufacture of weapons and supplies. Steel pennies replaced copper ones to provide raw material. Gasoline was rationed, not only to save fuel but also to preserve rubber, effectively banning pleasure driving, and the speed limit, even for truckers, was reduced to thirty-five mph.

Food was also rationed. Coupons were issued for reduced amounts of coffee, flour, sugar, and milk, and people stood in line for hours to buy what little was available. People were encouraged to grow "victory gardens," and 20 million sprung up across America—only to fade just as quickly when the war ended. Metals were recycled.

Shoes were rationed to save leather. Wool was in short supply, as the soldiers needed wool socks and pants. Silk stockings became scarce when all the silk was used to make parachutes. Shorter skirts saved cloth and manufacturing time and let industry get on with the real business of making uniforms.

Americans at home learned to make do with far less and to spend more for it. The sacrifices, however, often produced a sense of community and lifted spirits among civilians, who believed their savings—large and small—helped the fighting men.

January 25, is the largest land battle of the war. Fought in cold snowy weather in the Ardennes Forest on the German-Belgian border, the battle claims approximately 81,000 American lives and 100,000 German casualties.

1945 In February, Roosevelt, Churchill, and Stalin meet at Yalta in Ukraine to be begin to plan the postwar peace. They agree to organize the United Nations.

President Franklin Roosevelt dies April 12. Harry Truman becomes president.

Germany surrenders, unconditionally, May 7. The war in Europe is over.

The last major land battles of the Pacific are won at Iwo Jima (March) and Okinawa (June).

In July, the Big Three—the United States, Britain, and the U.S.S.R.—meet at Potsdam near Berlin, Germany, to hammer out details of the peace.

In August, the United States drops leaflets warning the civilian population of Hiroshima that it will obliterate the city if Japan does not surrender immediately. On August 6, the United States drops an atomic bomb on Hiroshima. Three days later a second atomic bomb is dropped on Nagasaki. Two hundred thousand people eventually lose their lives; 100,000 die immediately. On August 14, Japan surrenders, and World War II ends.

"Look in any infantryman's eyes and you can tell how much war he has seen."

—BILL MAULDIN
CARTOON CAPTION, 1944

KOREAN WAR

1945 After the defeat of the Axis powers in World War II, the Soviets occupy Korea (previously a Japanese colony) north of the 38th parallel, and the Americans occupy the area south of that line. These arrangements had been made hastily at the end of the war and were considered temporary. In North Korea, the U.S.S.R. supports Kim Il Sung, while in South Korea, the United States supports Syngman Rhee.

1950 President HARRY TRUMAN interrupts a long weekend in Independence, Missouri, to return to the capital when North Korea invades South Korea on June 25.

On June 27, President Truman orders American forces to give South Korea air and sea support. On the same day, the U.N. Security Council unanimously calls on member states to support South Korea. The U.S.S.R. is boycotting meetings to protest the continued presence of the Nationalist Chinese and is unable to veto the resolution.

On June 30, President Truman authorizes Gen. DOUGLAS MACARTHUR to lead American ground forces into Korea.

By September 14, North Korea controls all but the southeastern corner of the peninsula.

President Truman meets with General MacArthur in October at Wake Island. MacArthur assures Truman the Chinese won't get into the war.

By mid-November, U.N. forces under MacArthur's command stage a successful counterattack that pushes the North Koreans back behind the 38th parallel, almost to the Chinese border. China issues a warning that it will fight if U.N. forces move any closer, but the U.S. public, buoyed by this victory and egged on by MacArthur himself, demands total victory.

In late November, the Chinese enter the war and mount a counteroffensive into South Korea.

1951 U.N. forces stage their final counterattack early in the year and drive the Chinese and North Koreans back to the 38th parallel.

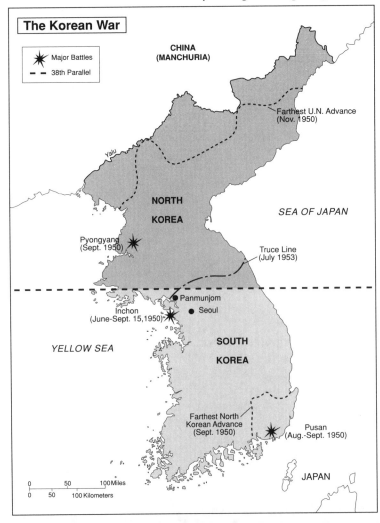

The Korean War

✴ Major Battles
– – 38th Parallel

CHINA
(MANCHURIA)

Farthest U.N. Advance
(Nov. 1950)

Yalu

NORTH
KOREA

SEA OF JAPAN

Pyongyang
(Sept. 1950)

Truce Line
(July 1953)

Panmunjom
Inchon
(June-Sept. 15, 1950)

Seoul

YELLOW SEA

SOUTH
KOREA

Farthest North
Korean Advance
(Sept. 1950)

Pusan
(Aug.-Sept. 1950)

JAPAN

0   50   100 Miles
0   50   100 Kilometers

WOMEN IN THE MILITARY

Disguised as men, operating as spies, or volunteering as field nurses, women served informally in America's wars through the nineteenth century. They were not officially enlisted in the armed forces until World War I, when 11,000 women served as nurses and in certain circumstances as naval yeomen.

World War II saw the creation of female auxiliary units: the Women's Auxiliary Army Corps, or WAACS (later WACS), and a naval corps called Women Accepted for Volunteer Emergency Service, or WAVES. There were also auxiliary services for the U.S. Air Force, Marine Corps, and Coast Guard. Although 350,000 women joined them, women still could not serve in combat positions or on active duty, nor could they attend military academies. Yet they served in war zones, enduring the same dangerous and physical hardships as combat troops. One thousand women flew planes in World War II, although not in combat. In the Korean War, they were regularly stationed in combat zones.

Although women had been generals since 1970, not until 1973 did the Department of Defense undertake a formal program to expand women's roles in the military. One big step came in 1976, when women were admitted into military professional schools. Another came in 1993, when women were allowed to serve aboard warships and fly combat missions. During the Persian Gulf War, eleven U.S. women were killed in combat and four in noncombat situations.

As the number of women in the military increases, so, too, will their roles. By late in 2000, there were a total 90,563 women serving in the U.S. Army, Navy, Marines, and Air Force, representing 6.7 percent of active-duty officers and enlistees. Women were still not required to register for the draft, and sexual harassment remained a recurring problem, but women had secured a firm place in the modern military establishment.

On April 12, President TRUMAN removes General MACARTHUR from command. MACARTHUR had tried to continue to widen the war and advocated the strategic bombing of China, while Truman sought to initiate peace talks.

Fighting continues throughout the summer, but the warring parties have reached a stalemate.

1953 Negotiations, which have been under way since June 1951, finally produce a settlement in the summer. The fighting stops where it began, along the 38th parallel. Little territory has changed hands, and little has been accomplished by this first war of containment.

VIETNAM WAR

1950–1956 Eager to preserve an anti-Communist regime in Asia, the United States supports the French colonial effort in Indochina. It gives France $2.6 billion in aid, almost as much as the French themselves pour into the region. When the French are finally defeated at the Battle of Dienbienphu, delegates from nine nations meet in Geneva. They draft the Geneva Accords, which divide Vietnam along the 17th parallel, with the north being supported by the U.S.S.R. and the south by the United States. Vietnam is supposed to be unified two years later in 1956 when nationwide elections are held, but South Vietnamese ruler Ngo Dinh Diem, with U.S. assent, refuses to hold elections because he fears Communist victory. The Diem regime is harsh, and, as a result, guerrilla forces form in North and South Vietnam. Civil war looms.

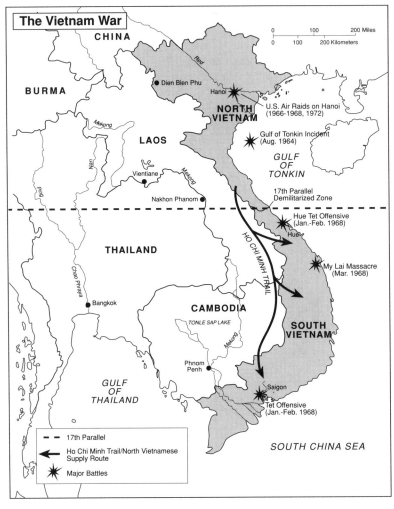

The Vietnam War

1962 U.S. troops on a training mission in Vietnam are told to fire back if fired upon. A military assistance command is set up in South Vietnam.

1963 Ngo Dinh Diem is overthrown.

1964 Alleged attacks on U.S. destroyers prompt President Lyndon Johnson to ask Congress "to join in affirming…that the United States will continue in its basic policy of assisting the free nations of the area to defend their freedom." Congress responds with the Gulf of Tonkin Resolution, which gives the president power to wage war without a formal declaration from Congress and provides the legal basis for escalation of the war.

1965 In February, South Vietnamese Communist rebels attack the U.S. military compound at Pleiku and kill eight Americans. President Johnson responds with Operation Rolling Thunder—air raids over North Vietnam.

The first war protests take place at home.
At year's end, 184,000 U.S. troops are in Vietnam.

1966 The buildup of U.S. troops continues—385,000 soldiers are now in Vietnam—as does the bombing. Hanoi and Haiphong, major cities in North Vietnam, are heavily bombed, and for the first time the United States bombs Communist strongholds in Cambodia.

1967 The war is stalemated. Heavy and continuous warfare is waged. In a pattern that will be repeated regularly, President Johnson restricts (but does not halt) the bombing so that peace talks can take place, then escalates the bombing when the talks break down.

War protesters march against the Pentagon.

1968 The war reaches a turning point with the massive North Vietnamese attack known as the Tet Offensive. In three weeks of intense fighting, the United States holds its own militarily, but morale begins to sag. The American public increasingly opposes the war, and the North Vietnamese have proven to be a far more determined enemy than the United States ever imagined. With 536,000 troops in Vietnam, U.S. manpower reaches its highest level.

The My Lai massacre takes place when U.S. troops on a search-and-destroy mission kill almost 500 South Vietnamese civilians—men, women, and children—in one village. First reported in the press in 1969, the troops involved are later charged with war crimes and tried for murder; one man, Lte. William Calley, is convicted of murder.

1969 With the United States still employing a strategy of "talk and fight," peace talks begin again. When they fail, President Richard Nixon secretly orders B-52s to bomb Communist strongholds in Cambodia.

1970 After the invasion of Cambodia, public pressure escalates to a fever pitch in the United States when Ohio National Guardsmen kill four students during a spring protest at Kent State University and two more at Jackson State in Mississippi.

American troop strength is reduced to 334,600 by year's end as a policy of Vietnamization is introduced: The war will be gradually turned over to the South Vietnamese. U.S. troops continue to fight, and the United States continues to bomb Cambodia. President Richard Nixon defends the bombing and invasion, but his power to wage war is undermined by his failure to be frank and honest with members of Congress and by their relentless questioning when military realities differ from Nixon's and Henry Kissinger's public and private statements.

Congress repeals the Gulf of Tonkin Resolution on December 31. Nixon believes this action is irrelevant.

1971 The Pentagon Papers, which reveal deeper U.S. involvement in the war than the executive branch has ever acknowledged, are published, further undermining what little congressional support is left for the war.

The United States continues to bomb North Vietnam, hoping to cut off materiel from China and the U.S.S.R. U.S. troop strength is down to 156,800. Morale among the troops that remain is low.

NATIVE AMERICANS IN THE MILITARY

Notwithstanding their deprivations, displacements, and loss of life at the hands of federal forces in the past, Native Americans fought with distinction in the major U.S. armed conflicts of the twentieth century.

WORLD WAR I
1917–1918
12,000 volunteers

WORLD WAR II
1941–1945
24,000

VIETNAM WAR
1965–1975
42,500

PERSIAN GULF WAR
1991
3,000

VIETNAM VETERANS MEMORIAL

Honoring the men and women who served in America's least popular war, the Vietnam Veterans Memorial was designed by Maya Lin, then a twenty-three-year-old Yale architecture student, as a nonpolitical monument in the spirit of communion and reconciliation. Lin's design, the winning entry in a public competition, features a 463-foot, V-shaped, black-granite wall inscribed with the names of the more than 58,000 servicemen killed or missing in Vietnam. Among the most moving monuments in the nation's capital since its dedication in 1982, it is a place where Vietnam veterans, family members, friends, and others come to pay their respects and leave tokens of remembrance. The complex also includes a seven-foot bronze statue, "The Three Servicemen," designed by Frederick Hart and dedicated in 1984; a sixty-foot bronze flagpole; and the Vietnam Women's Memorial, a four-figure bronze sculpture surrounded by eight yellowwood trees representing the eight female nurses killed in Vietnam, designed by Glenna Goodacre and dedicated in 1993.

1972 Following North Vietnam's Easter Offensive, B-52 bombers again bomb Hanoi and Haiphong. Initially the North Vietnamese are successful, and Quang Tri in South Vietnam falls under their control. After U.S. bombing and mining of North Vietnamese harbors, Quang Tri is recaptured.

After Nixon is reelected, he escalates the bombing on a massive scale. At year's end, 24,000 U.S. troops are in Vietnam.

1973 U.S. involvement in Vietnam ends with a whimper when peace accords are signed on January 27 by the United States, North Vietnam, South Vietnam, and the Provisional Revolutionary Government (the Vietcong). On the day of the peace treaty, Nixon announces an end to the draft.

1975 The North Vietnamese seize Saigon in April, as U.S. helicopters rescue about 1,100 Americans and 5,500 South Vietnamese.

PERSIAN GULF WARS

1990 Iraq invades Kuwait in August. President George H. W. Bush sends troops and air support to the region. The United Nations imposes sanctions, but Iraq continues to amass forces along Kuwait's border.

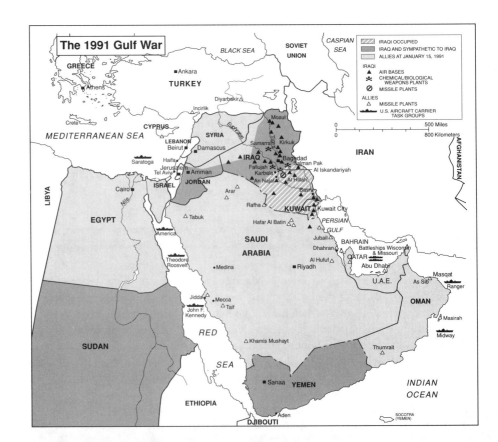

1991 After warning Iraq's Saddam Hussein to stand down, the United States initiates massive bombing on January 16. On February 24, U.S. forces invade Kuwait and in four days clear Kuwait of Iraqi forces.

2003 Citing Iraqi noncompliance with United Nations Security Council Resolution 1441, which calls for complete disclosure of chemical, biological, and nuclear weapons programs and elimination of weapons of mass destruction, the United States begins military operations in Iraq on March 19th. With the help of allies such as Great Britain, Spain and Australia, President George W. Bush aims to depose President Saddam Hussein, fully disarm the country, and aid in the creation of a democratic government. Major fighting comes to an end after six weeks.

ANTIWAR PROTEST AND PACIFISM, 1600s–PRESENT

Pacifism and antiwar protest have been closely intertwined with American military history—not surprising when one considers that the nation was founded by religious and political dissidents. Virtually every U.S. armed conflict has encountered opposition, whether religious or ideological in nature, whether pertaining to all war or the conflict in question. Conscientious objectors, who object to military service on strict religious or moral grounds, are legally recognized and may be exempt if they meet narrowly defined requirements (most notably that they object to *all* wars, not just a particular war). Protesters have sought to halt or impede the war effort whenever possible, albeit with limited success. The major exception is the Vietnam War, whose course was radically affected by strong public opposition.

Mid–1600s Setting a precedent that will prevail after the United States becomes a nation, some colonies exempt conscientious objectors—Quakers, Mennonites, Moravians, Schwenkfelders, and other pacifistic religious communities—from service in state militias.

1798 The Kentucky (written by Thomas Jefferson) and Virginia (written by James Madison) Resolutions argue that the Alien and Sedition Acts are unconstitutional because the federal government is exercising powers not delegated to it.

1799 John Fries, a Pennsylvanian, leads an armed tax revolt in opposition to the House Tax, which was a tax on homes, property, and slaves aimed at raising $2 million in the event that mounting tensions with France led to war. Although he is more opposed to taxes than to war, his action demonstrates the willingness of citizens to challenge decisions of the federal government.

1815 Disgruntled by the disruption to commerce during the long prelude to the War of 1812, and opposing the war itself, delegates from New England meet in Hartford to attest to the power of states to protect their citizens against the federal government, including protection from conscriptions not authorized by the Constitution. The convention also calls for the use of federal revenues and an interstate defense unit for repelling invasions.

1846–1848 Peace groups and some pacifist churches oppose the Mexican War. Writer Henry David Thoreau is jailed for one night for refusing to pay a tax to support the war effort. In "Civil Disobedience" he defends his actions by declaring that unjust laws should be resisted: "The only obligation which I have a right to assume is to do at any time what I think right."

1863 During the Civil War, draft riots break out in northern cities, and in New York about 110 people

ANTI-WAR PROTEST AND PACIFISM, 1600s–PRESENT, cont.

are killed. The new draft law allows draftees to buy their way out of service by paying $300, a sum only the wealthy can afford. Scholars now believe that the riots were as much about this economic inequity as about the draft. Racism and unsolved urban problems were also factors.

1864 Quakers, the country's leading religious pacifists, sponsor a successful campaign for legislation that allows alternate service. The Confederate draft originally exempts conscientious objectors on religious grounds. As the need for men grows, the exemption is repealed.

1898 The Teller Amendment to the declaration of war against Spain disavows any claims on Cuba's sovereignty.

The Anti-Imperialist League is organized in Boston to protest military action, especially in the Philippines. By 1899, it has half a million members.

1915 As Europeans are destroying one another in battlefields in France and Russia, Americans organize for peace. JANE ADDAMS helps found the Woman's Peace Party and attends the International Women's Conference at The Hague (see p. 251).

1917 Once the United States enters the war, Americans stand behind the effort, and conscientious objectors, exempt on religious grounds only, encounter considerable prejudice. Five hundred conscientious objectors are court-martialed for their beliefs, 17 are sentenced to death (none carried out), and 142 receive life sentences.

1918 Under the Alien Act, foreign-born conscientious objectors are deported without a trial. One famous conscientious objector, Alvin York, who is drafted despite his beliefs, fights heroically and receives awards such as the Medal of Honor.

Eugene V. Debs, a Socialist labor leader, is sentenced to jail for ten years for violating provisions of the Espionage Act. While in prison he receives 920,000 votes for president in the election of 1920. President Warren G. Harding releases him from prison in 1921.

1919 The Women's International League for Peace and Freedom is founded, and JANE ADDAMS is elected its president.

1940 With World War II raging in Europe, U.S. conservatives eager to stay out of the war form the America First Committee. The most famous World War II isolationist is Charles Lindbergh. Conscientious objectors are exempted from service only on religious grounds, and alternate service is mandatory. Many are imprisoned for seeking conscientious objector status. More than 400 blacks are conscientious objectors: some belong to the Nation of Islam, while others object to serving in a segregated army.

1941 A. Philip Randolph, head of the Brotherhood of Sleeping Car Porters, threatens to stage a march on Washington to demand jobs for blacks in defense industries. President FRANKLIN ROOSEVELT issues Executive Order 8802 outlawing discrimination in the defense industries.

1961 In his Farewell Address, President (and former general) DWIGHT D. EISENHOWER warns of the "unwarranted influence" of the "military-industrial complex."

1964–1975 The Vietnam War is the nation's most unpopular war. Joining in protests and antiwar agitation are pacifists, clergy, students, Old Leftists, liberals, intellectuals, civil rights leaders, feminists, and eventually even soldiers and members of Congress. There are demonstrations, protest marches, draft-card burnings, "teach-ins," and violence, including break-ins at draft boards, destruction of records, and bombings. Hundreds of cities and campuses experience unrest.

More than 50,000 conscientious objectors are believed to have left the country. Roughly 250,000 men never registered for the draft and approximately 110,000 men burned their draft cards to protest the war. The Supreme Court rules that exemptions for CO status can be based on moral and ethical grounds as well as religious grounds.

1967 Influential persons speak out against the war. The Reverend Martin Luther King Jr. describes the United States as the "greatest purveyor of violence in the world today." In the Senate, J. William Fulbright (Arkansas), Eugene McCarthy (Minnesota), Robert Kennedy (New York), George McGovern (South Dakota), George Aiken (Vermont), Edward Kennedy (Massachusetts), Frank Church (Idaho), and Mark Hatfield (Oregon) are critics of the war. So are scientist Linus Pauling, historian Arthur Schlesinger, economist John Kenneth Galbraith, and boxing champion Muhammad Ali, who is stripped of his crown for refusing induction. Pediatrician-author Benjamin Spock, Beat poet Allen Ginsberg, and folk singer Joan Baez show up regularly at protests.

In response to this escalation of antiwar activism, the CIA launches Operation Chaos, a massive effort to catalog antiwar protesters and interfere with their activities. More than 1,000 organizations and 200,000 individuals are logged in files, and CIA informants penetrate most antiwar groups.

Fifty thousand protest at the Pentagon.

1968 Between January and June, the National Student Association reports 221 demonstrations at 101 colleges and universities, involving over 40,000 students.

Nine Jesuit priests, including brothers Daniel and Philip Berrigan, enter a Selective Service office in Catonsville, Maryland, burn draft records, and then wait outside to be arrested. In a highly publicized trial, the "Catonsville Nine" all receive prison terms.

In August, outside the Democratic National Convention in Chicago, 5,000 activists stage five days of protest and at least 1,000 are clubbed by Chicago police in what some term a "police riot."

1969 Between January and June, 232 campus protests are reported.

In November, on Moratorium Day, up to 750,000 protesters in Boston, New York, Washington, and other cities stage peaceful candlelight vigils.

By year's end, draft board offices and army reserve installations are subject to repeated break-ins and vandalism.

1970 Campuses erupt in protest over the U.S. invasion of Cambodia. On May 4, at Kent State University, National Guardsmen open fire on a crowd of protesters, killing four and wounding nine. A few days later Mississippi policemen kill two and wound eleven students at Jackson State. On May 9, at the largest antiwar rally in U.S. history, several hundred thousand protesters march on

Students at Kent State flee from tear gas and gunfire when the Ohio National Guard fires at students during an antiwar demonstration.

ANTIWAR PROTEST AND PACIFISM, 1600s–PRESENT, cont.

Washington, D.C. At the University of Wisconsin an antiwar activist blows up a laboratory to protest the university's involvement in war research. The explosion kills one person and injures four. Two million students protest at 350 campuses. Many colleges close early to avoid student unrest over the war.

1971 Former Defense Department employee Daniel Ellsberg arranges for the publication of a classified analysis of U.S. involvement in Vietnam. The government sues to stop publication of the papers but loses. *The Pentagon Papers* are published in the *New York Times* and the *Washington Post* before injunctions are issued on the grounds of national security. Later in the year, the Supreme Court ruled that freedom of the press allowed for further publication of the *Pentagon Papers.*

1971 In May, antiwar protesters attempt to disrupt the federal government, and more than 10,000 are arrested in dragnet operations carried out by the Washington, D.C., police.

1974 The Boland Amendment prohibits sending military aid to the rebels (contras) fighting against the Marxist-leaning government in Nicaragua.

1977 President Jimmy Carter grants a blanket pardon to draft evaders, who can now return to the United States without fear of arrest.

THE COSTS OF WAR

WAR	LENGTH OF TIME	NUMBER SERVING	BATTLE DEATHS	OTHER DEATHS	DIRECT COST	VETERANS PAYMENTS	INTEREST	TOTAL
American Revolution	8 years	180,000–250,000	4,435	—	$100–$140 mil.	$80 mil.	$20 mil.	$220 mil.
War of 1812	2 years	286,700	2,260	—	$89 mil.	$49 mil.	$14 mil.	$152 mil.
Mexican War	3 years	79,000	1,733	11,500	$82 mil.	$64 mil.	$10 mil.	$156 mil.
Civil War:	4 years	600,000–1,500,000						
Confederacy		1,500,000	74,524	59,297	$1 bil.	—	—	—
Union		2,213,363	140,363	224,097	$2.3 bil.	$8,574 mil.	$1,200 mil.	$12,074 mil.
Spanish-American War	5 months	306,760	385	2,061	$270 mil.	$5,964	$60 mil.	$6,294 mil.
World War I	2 years	4,743,826	53,513	63,195	$32.7 bil.	$81,000 mil.	$11,000 mil.	$124,000 mil.
World War II	4 years	16,353,659	242,131	115,185	$360 bil.	$30l,000 mil.	—	—
Korean War	3 years	5,764,143	33,651	—	50 bil.	$72,000 mil.	—	—
Vietnam War	11 years	8,744,000	47,369	10,799	$140.6 bil.	$136,000 mil.	—	—
Persian Gulf War (1991)	6 weeks	500,000+	148	151	—	—		

OTHER MILITARY ACTIONS

1893 Hawaii. U.S. sailors land to protect American property, and the U.S. minister proclaims Hawaii an American protectorate.

1898 Cuba. Following the U.S. victory in the Spanish-American War, U.S. military occupation of Cuba continues until 1902.

1899 Samoa. Native conflict over royal succession triggers action by the British-German-U.S. protectorate, and U.S. and British sailors land to restore order. In a new protectorate agreement, Germany and the United States divide the island group.

The Philippines. A year after the Spanish-American War, during which the United States seized the Philippines, Filipino nationalist forces led by Emilio Aguinaldo fight a three-and-a-half-year war of liberation but are unable to defeat the United States. The Philippines remain a U.S. territory until 1946.

1900 China. The United States send troops to help put down the Boxer Rebellion and maintain the Open Door policy (see p. 282).

1903 Panama. President Roosevelt sends warships to Panama even before the province declares its independence from Colombia. Three days later the United States recognizes the Republic of Panama and begins to negotiate a treaty establishing a canal zone (see p. 285).

1906 Cuba. The military occupation of Cuba is reinstated, until 1909.

1911 Nicaragua. The United States takes over the supervision of Nicaragua's finances until 1924. Marines are not finally withdrawn until 1933.

1912 Cuba. U.S. troops intervene to put down internal unrest.

1914 Mexico. When Mexico stands on the brink of a civil war that could endanger U.S. business interests, President Woodrow Wilson sends a naval force to bombard and occupy Veracruz.

1915 Haiti. U.S. troops invade Haiti, making it a U.S. protectorate, which it will remain until 1934. U.S. fiscal control continues until 1947.

1916 Mexico. A border raid by Pancho Villa in New Mexico launches a punitive expedition under Gen. John J. Pershing that fails to capture Villa but succeeds in creating considerable ill will toward the United States among Mexicans.

Santo Domingo. Military occupation by U.S. Marines is proclaimed as necessary to stabilize the country's finances, under American protection since 1907. U.S. financial management continues until 1924.

1918 Russia. The United States sends 15,000 troops into Russia to support anti-Bolshevik forces and to counter Japanese influence in Siberia.

1954 Guatemala. When the elected progressive president of Guatemala proposes land reforms and trade unionism, changes that would threaten the considerable U.S. commercial interests there, the CIA supports the opposition and installs Col. Castillo Armas, a military leader sympathetic to U.S. interests.

1958 Lebanon. U.S. forces land to bolster the regime led by President Camille Chamoun against rioting and rebellion by opposition forces supported by the United Arab Republic.

1961 Cuba. At the Bay of Pigs, the United States backs 1,500 CIA-trained and -armed Cuban expatriates in an attempted invasion that is intended to overthrow Fidel Castro. Most of the invaders are taken prisoner.

1965 Dominican Republic. President Lyndon Johnson sends troops to end a civil war and impose a truce.

1983 Grenada. Following a military coup, U.S. troops invade to protect and evacuate American citizens and to see that the hard-line Marxist regime is deposed.

OTHER MILITARY ACTIONS, cont.

1989 Panama. The United States invades Panama in an attempt to capture Manuel Noriega, a dictator and former U.S. ally whom the United States now holds responsible for much of the drug traffic. The United Nations denounces the U.S. invasion as a "flagrant violation of international law." Noriega eludes capture and finally turns himself in.

1993 Somalia. U.S. and U.N. forces attack rebel factions and administer humanitarian aid.

1995 Bosnia. NATO, U.S., and U.N. forces attempt to secure a cease-fire in an ethnic war.

2001 Afghanistan. After September 11 terrorist attacks on the World Trade Center in New York City and the Pentagon in Washington, D.C., President George W. Bush declares war on international terrorists and any nation that harbors them. U.S. forces, with the military or diplomatic support of a coalition of countries, launch air and ground attacks on the Taliban regime of Aghanistan. The Taliban are accused of harboring Osama bin Laden and his Al Qaeda terrorist network, believed to be directly involved in the September 11 attacks.

LEGISLATION AND SUPREME COURT DECISIONS AFFECTING THE MILITARY, 1798–PRESENT

According to the Constitution, Congress has the power "to raise and support armies," "to provide and maintain a navy," and "to make rules...for the regulation of land and naval forces." Most actions concerning the armed forces listed there came by acts of Congress. A few are highlighted below.

1798 Alien and Sedition Acts. This series of four acts, passed when war against France seemed imminent, extends the period of residence required for citizenship, authorizes the president to imprison or deport enemy aliens during wartime, and provides for penalties for "writing, printing, uttering or publishing any false, scandalous, and malicious writing or writings" against the government of the United States, the Congress, or the president.

1863 Conscription Act. This draft is actually the second in U.S. history, as the Confederacy had enacted a draft a year before. It makes men between twenty and forty-five eligible for military service but provides that service can be avoided by payment of $300 or by hiring a substitute.

1917 Selective Service Act. This draft, passed the month after the United States entered World War I, makes men between the ages of twenty and thirty eligible for military service. An amendment the following year requires registration of all men between the ages of eighteen and forty-five.

Espionage Act. This act seeks to prevent treasonable and disloyal activities by providing penalties for aiding the enemy, obstructing recruitment of armed forces, or uttering, printing, writing, or publishing "any disloyal, profane, scurrilous, or abusive language about the form of government of the United States, or the Constitution of the United States, or the military or naval forces of the United States."

1918 Sedition Act. This amendment to the Espionage Act provides further penalties for disloyalty. Both acts are rigidly enforced, and freedom of speech and of the press virtually disappear.

Selective Draft Law Cases. In a landmark ruling, the Court rules that the draft is constitutional.

1919 *Schenck v. United States.* The Supreme Court upholds the Espionage Act (1917), which provided penalties for acts of disloyalty, including writing or speaking out against the draft. Justice Oliver Wendell Holmes introduces the "clear and present danger test" for limiting free speech.

Abrams v. United States. The Supreme Court upholds the Sedition Act (1918), an amendment to the Espionage Act that specified additional acts of disloyalty.

1940 Alien Registration Act (Smith Act). Passed before the United States becomes involved in World War II, this act requires the registration and fingerprinting of aliens and provides for their deportation and prohibits certain subversive activities, including advocating the overthrow of the U.S. government.

Selective Service and Training Act. This first peacetime draft in U.S. history requires the registration of all men between ages twenty-one and thirty-five. After the United States enters World War II, the draft age is lowered to eighteen and raised to thirty-eight.

1944 *Korematsu v. United States.* The Supreme Court upholds the relocation of Japanese Americans from the West Coast on the grounds of national security.

1947 The National Security Act coordinates the army, navy, and air force into a new Department of Defense and creates the National Security Council and Central Intelligence Agency.

1948 Selective Service Act. This peacetime draft, requiring registration of all males between the ages of eighteen and twenty-six, continues throughout the Cold War and the Vietnam War.

1964 Gulf of Tonkin Resolution. Passed with only two dissenting votes in the Senate, this resolution affirms that Congress "approves and supports the determination of the President, as Commander in Chief, to take all necessary measures to repel any armed attack against the forces of the United States and to prevent further aggression." Giving the president almost a free hand, the resolution is the legal basis for escalation of the Vietnam War.

1971 *New York Times v. United States (Pentagon Papers Case).* The Supreme Court rules that the government has not demonstrated sufficient cause for an injunction against publication of the *Pentagon Papers,* a Defense Department analysis of involvement in Vietnam.

1973 War Powers Resolution. Passed over President Richard Nixon's veto, this resolution limits presidential war-making power by establishing guidelines for military emergencies. The president must consult Congress before sending troops into hostilities "in every possible instance," must report to Congress during the hostilities, and, unless Congress acts to declare war, must withdraw troops within sixty days.

MILITARY HISTORY

CABINET SECRETARIES

SECRETARIES OF WAR*

SECRETARY	PRESIDENT	YEAR APPOINTED
Henry Knox	Washington	1789
Timothy Pickering	Washington	1795
James McHenry	Washington	1796
James McHenry	Adams, J.	1797
Samuel Dexter	Adams, J.	1800
Henry Dearborn	Jefferson	1801
William Eustis	Madison	1809
John Armstrong	Madison	1813
James Monroe	Madison	1814
William H. Crawford	Madison	1815
John C. Calhoun	Monroe	1817
James Barbour	Adams, J. Q.	1825
Peter B. Porter	Adams, J. Q.	1828
John H. Eaton	Jackson	1829
Lewis Cass	Jackson	1831
Benjamin F. Butler	Jackson	1837
Joel R. Poinsett	Van Buren	1837
John Bell	Harrison, W. H.	1841
John Bell	Tyler	1841
John C. Spencer	Tyler	1841
James M. Porter	Tyler	1843
William Wilkins	Tyler	1844
William L. Marcy	Polk	1845
George W. Crawford	Taylor	1849
Charles M. Conrad	Fillmore	1850
Jefferson Davis	Pierce	1853
John B. Floyd	Buchanan	1857
Joseph Holt	Buchanan	1861
Simon Cameron	Lincoln	1861
Edwin M. Stanton	Lincoln	1862
Edwin M. Stanton	Johnson, A.	1865
John M. Schofield	Johnson, A.	1868
John A. Rawlins	Grant	1869
William T. Sherman	Grant	1869
William W. Belknap	Grant	1869
Alphonso Taft	Grant	1876
James D. Cameron	Grant	1876
George W. McCrary	Hayes	1877
Alexander Ramsey	Hayes	1879
Robert T. Lincoln	Garfield	1881
Robert T. Lincoln	Arthur	1881
William C. Endicott	Cleveland	1885
Redfield Proctor	Harrison, B.	1889

*The positions of secretary of war and secretary of the navy were abolished after World War II, replaced by the new cabinet-level position of secretary of defense in 1947.

SECRETARIES OF WAR*

SECRETARY	PRESIDENT	YEAR APPOINTED
Stephen B. Elkins	Harrison, B.	1891
Daniel S. Lamont	Cleveland	1893
Russel A. Alger	McKinley	1897
Elihu Root	McKinley	1899
Elihu Root	Roosevelt, T.	1901
William H. Taft	Roosevelt, T.	1904
Luke E. Wright	Roosevelt, T.	1908
Jacob M. Dickinson	Taft	1909
Henry L. Stimson	Taft	1911
Lindley M. Garrison	Wilson	1913
Newton D. Baker	Wilson	1916
John W. Weeks	Harding	1921
John W. Weeks	Coolidge	1923
Dwight F. Davis	Coolidge	1925
James W. Good	Hoover	1929
Patrick J. Hurley	Hoover	1929
George H. Dern	Roosevelt, F. D.	1933
Harry H. Woodring	Roosevelt, F. D.	1937
Henry L. Stimson	Roosevelt, F. D.	1940
Robert P. Patterson	Truman	1945
Kenneth C. Royall	Truman	1947

SECRETARIES OF THE NAVY*

SECRETARY	PRESIDENT	YEAR APPOINTED
Benjamin Stoddert	Adams, J.	1798
Benjamin Stoddert	Jefferson	1801
Robert Smith	Jefferson	1801
Paul Hamilton	Madison	1809
William Jones	Madison	1813
Benjamin W. Crowninshield	Madison	1814
Benjamin W. Crowninshield	Monroe	1817
Smith Thompson	Monroe	1818
Samuel L. Southard	Monroe	1823
Samuel L. Southard	Adams, J. Q.	1825
John Branch	Jackson	1829
Levi Woodbury	Jackson	1831
Mahlon Dickerson	Jackson	1834
Mahlon Dickerson	Van Buren	1837
James K. Paulding	Van Buren	1838
George E. Badger	Harrison, W. H.	1841
George E. Badger	Tyler	1841

*The positions of secretary of war and secretary of the navy were abolished after World War II, replaced by the new cabinet-level position of secretary of defense in 1947.

CABINET SECRETARIES, cont.

SECRETARIES OF THE NAVY*

SECRETARY	PRESIDENT	YEAR APPOINTED
Abel P. Upshur	Tyler	1841
David Henshaw	Tyler	1843
Thomas W. Gilmer	Tyler	1844
John Y. Mason	Tyler	1844
George Bancroft	Polk	1845
John Y. Mason	Polk	1846
William B. Preston	Taylor	1849
William A. Graham	Fillmore	1850
John P. Kennedy	Fillmore	1852
James C. Dobbin	Pierce	1853
Isaac Toucey	Buchanan	1857
Gideon Welles	Lincoln	1861
Gideon Welles	Johnson, A.	1865
Adolph E. Borie	Grant	1869
George M. Robeson	Grant	1869
Richard W. Thompson	Hayes	1877
Nathan Goff Jr.	Hayes	1881
William H. Hunt	Garfield	1881
William E. Chandler	Arthur	1882
William C. Whitney	Cleveland	1885
Benjamin F. Tracey	Harrison, B.	1889
Hilary A. Herbert	Cleveland	1893
John D. Long	McKinley	1897
John D. Long	Roosevelt, T.	1901
William H. Moody	Roosevelt, T.	1902
Paul Morton	Roosevelt, T.	1904
Charles J. Bonaparte	Roosevelt, T.	1905
Victor H. Metcalf	Roosevelt, T.	1906
Truman H. Newberry	Roosevelt, T.	1908
George von L. Meyer	Taft	1909
Josephus Daniels	Wilson	1913
Edwin Denby	Harding	1921
Edwin Denby	Coolidge	1923
Curtis D. Wilbur	Coolidge	1924
Charles F. Adams	Hoover	1929
Claude A. Swanson	Roosevelt, F. D.	1933
Charles Edison	Roosevelt, F. D.	1940
Frank Knox	Roosevelt, F. D.	1940
James V. Forrestal	Roosevelt, F. D.	1944
James V. Forrestal	Truman	1945

*The positions of secretary of war and secretary of the navy were abolished after World War II, replaced by the new cabinet-level position of secretary of defense in 1947.

SECRETARIES OF DEFENSE*		
SECRETARY	PRESIDENT	YEAR APPOINTED
James V. Forrestal	Truman	1947
Louis A. Johnson	Truman	1949
George C. Marshall	Truman	1950
Robert A. Lovett	Truman	1951
Charles E. Wilson	Eisenhower	1953
Neil H. McElroy	Eisenhower	1957
Thomas S. Gates Jr.	Eisenhower	1959
Robert S. McNamara	Kennedy	1961
Robert S. McNamara	Johnson, L. B.	1963
Clark M. Clifford	Johnson, L. B.	1968
Melvin R. Laird	Nixon	1969
Donald H. Rumsfeld	Ford	1975
Harold Brown	Carter	1977
Caspar W. Weinberger	Reagan	1981
Frank C. Carlucci	Reagan	1987
Richard B. Cheney	Bush, G. H. W.	1989
Les Aspin	Clinton	1993
William J. Perry	Clinton	1994
William S. Cohen	Clinton	1997
Donald H. Rumsfeld	Bush, G. W.	2001

*The positions of secretary of war and secretary of the navy were abolished after World War II, replaced by the new cabinet-level position of secretary of defense in 1947.

MILITARY HISTORY

NOTABLE FIGURES IN U.S. MILITARY HISTORY

Abrams, Creighton (1914–1974). After fighting in World War II and Korea, General Abrams became commander of the U.S. forces in Vietnam in mid-1968. He later served as army chief of staff.

Addams, Jane (1860–1935). Known primarily as a social worker and the founder of Hull-House in Chicago, Addams was also an ardent pacifist, helping to found the Woman's Peace Party in 1915 and attending the International Women's Conference at The Hague, where she was appointed head of a commission to seek an end to World War I. At the Second Women's Peace Conference in 1919, she was elected the first president of the new Women's International League for Peace and Freedom, a post she held for the rest of her life. Her account of women's work for peace, *Peace and Bread in Time of War*, was published in 1922, and in 1931, she was a corecipient of the Nobel Peace Prize (see p. 251).

Allen, Ethan (1738–1789). During the Revolutionary War, Allen headed the Green Mountain Boys, a Vermont independent force that captured Fort Ticonderoga and fought in the Battle of Bennington. Allen was an important figure in Vermont's struggle to remain free of New York.

Arnold, Benedict (1741–1801). Remembered mostly as the most notable traitor in the Revolutionary War, Arnold fought bravely with the colonists during the American Revolution before becoming involved in a plot to turn over West Point to the British. He died in Britain.

Arnold, Henry (1886–1950). Head of the air force during World War II and one of five men after World War II who was awarded the rank of five-star general, Arnold worked to turn the air force, which was initially part of the army, into the world's best.

NOTABLE FIGURES, *cont.*

Barry, John (1745–1803). During the Revolution, Barry served in the Continental Army and fought in several major naval battles. He commanded the brig *Lexington*, which took the first British ship, the tender *Edward*, captured during the war. He went on to command several more ships and to capture two more British ships.

Beauregard, Pierre G. T. (1818–1893). As commander of Confederate forces at the start of the Civil War, General Beauregard issued the order to fire on Fort Sumter, which began the war. He was second in command at First Manassas (Battle of Bull Run).

Bradley, Omar (1893–1981). Recognized by his superiors for his planning abilities during World War II, General Bradley played a key role in North Africa and later in Sicily, and still later in the Normandy invasion. He became the first chairman of the Joint Chiefs of Staff in 1948. He supported President Harry Truman in his clash with Gen. Douglas MacArthur.

Chennault, Claire (1890–1958). A flyer in both world wars, General Chennault organized the Flying Tigers, an elite group of volunteer American fighter pilots in China, in 1941.

Clark, Mark (1896–1984). Clark commanded the Fifth Army in North Africa and Italy during World War II and was supreme commander of the U.N. forces in Korea from May 1952 to October 1953.

Cochran, Jacqueline (1910–1980). In 1953, Cochran was the first woman to break the sound barrier. During World War II, she was the first woman to fly a bomber over the Atlantic, where she worked ferrying aircraft for the British Air Transport Auxiliary. She organized the Women's Flying Training Detachment to prepare more women for work as pilots in the event of a shortage during the war. In 1943, she was appointed to direct the newly created Women's Air Force Service Pilots (WASP). A tremendous pilot, Cochran received the Distinguished Service Medal for her wartime record, won the Harmon trophy for best female pilot of the year fourteen times, and set dozens of speed records throughout her career.

Decatur, Stephen (1779–1820). A naval officer, Decatur was noted for his daring exploits in the Barbary wars and was engaged in some of the most important sea battles during the War of 1812. He was forced to surrender once while trying to fight four British ships with his one.

Dewey, George (1837–1917). Dewey commanded the naval forces that destroyed the Spanish fleet at Manila during the Spanish-American War. In 1899, he became admiral of the navy.

Early, Jubal (1816–1894). Early fought with the Confederate Army in most of the Civil War battles along the East Coast. He led a raid on Washington in July 1864 that was more dramatic than effective. After his forces were defeated by Philip Sheridan in the Shenandoah Valley, Early was relieved of his command.

Edmonds, Sarah (1841–1898). Sarah Edmonds disguised herself as a man named Frank Thompson and enlisted in the Union Army during the Civil War. During the war, she participated in the Battle of Blackburn's Ford and the First Battle of Bull Run among others. She also conducted spy missions into Confederate camps disguised as a black man and, more believably, as a woman. After contracting malaria, she deserted the army for fear of being discovered and worked as a nurse. Edmonds wrote *Nurse and Spy in the Union Army*, a fictionalized account of her time in the army, which became very popular. In 1884, Congress issued her a pension for serving in the army.

Eisenhower, Dwight David (1890–1969). Head of the Allied forces in North Africa and later supreme allied commander in Europe, Eisenhower oversaw the Normandy invasion and accepted the Germans' surrender (though he did not sign the official document). After the Second World War, he served as chief of staff and headed NATO forces in Europe in 1950. Eisenhower later became the thirty-fourth president of the United States.

Farragut, David (1801–1870). During the Civil War this southerner became one of the Union's most admired naval officers and was responsible for the capture of two strategic outposts, New Orleans and Mobile Bay.

Forrest, Nathan Bedford (1821–1877). A Confederate cavalry commander during the Civil War, Forrest carried out strategic raids that played havoc with the Union Army's supply lines.

Gates, Horatio (1728–1806). This Revolutionary War general headed the army at the Battle of Saratoga, which was the turning point in the Revolutionary War, for it ensured French support.

Grant, Ulysses S. (1822–1885). After fighting in most of the major battles of the Civil War in the west, Grant was appointed head of the Union Army. He accepted ROBERT E. LEE's surrender at Appomattox Court House. Grant later became the eighteenth president of the United States.

Gravely, Samuel (1922–). Gravely was the first African American to achieve the rank of admiral, in 1971. He served in the U.S. Navy during World War II, Korea, and Vietnam, and was commander of the Third Fleet, 1976–1978.

Greene, Nathanael (1742–1786). During the American Revolution, General Greene, a superb strategist, planned the defense of New York City, stood with WASHINGTON at the Battle of Trenton, and, though frequently defeated, weakened the British during the southern campaign that led to their defeat at Yorktown.

Hale, Nathan (1755–1776). Sent to Long Island to gather intelligence during the Revolution, Hale was captured by the British and hanged without a trial. On the gallows, he allegedly declared: "I only regret that I have but one life to lose for my country."

Halsey, William (1882–1959). A naval commander, Halsey led forces in many of the major battles in the Pacific theater during World War II and was responsible for the 1944 defeat of the Japanese fleet at Leyte Gulf.

Hobby, Oveta Culp (1905–1995). During the World War II, President ROOSEVELT appointed Hobby the director of the Women's Auxiliary Corps, which becomes the Women's Army Corps (WAC) in 1943, and she recruited nearly 100,000 women to aid the war effort. For her service, Hobby became the first woman to receive the U.S. Army Distinguished Service Award and was asked by President EISENHOWER to head the Federal Security Administration, which later became the Department of Health, Education, and Welfare. After Frances Perkins, Hobby was the second woman to hold a cabinet post in the government.

Hull, Isaac (1773–1843). In the War of 1812, Hull commanded the USS *Constitution*, also known as Old Ironsides, which defeated the British frigate *Guerrière*.

Jackson, Andrew (1767–1845). This president of the United States had a long military career that began when he was a teenager, fighting against the British in the Revolution. During the War of 1812, he defeated Creek warriors at the Battle of Horseshoe Bend and the British

in the Battle of New Orleans. His reputation as an Indian fighter increased with his incursions into Spanish Florida against the Seminoles.

Jackson, Thomas J. (Stonewall) (1824–1863). A Civil War general, Jackson headed the Confederate forces in the Shenandoah Valley. Jackson was mistakenly shot by his own men and died a few days later.

Johnson, Henry (1897–1929). Pvt. Henry Johnson, an African American, was one of the first Americans to receive France's Croix de Guerre, awarded for his valor during World War I.

Jones, John Paul (1747–1792). This professional naval officer was known for his daring ingenuity during the Revolution. He commanded the *Bon Homme Richard* in a major battle against the British ship *Serapis*. When his smaller vessel appeared to be defeated, he rallied with the cry "I have not yet begun to fight"; several hours later the *Serapis* was forced to surrender.

Kearny, Stephen (1794–1848). During the Mexican War, Kearny headed the Army of the West. As military governor of New Mexico he established the civil government. He also was active in California. He was briefly civil governor of Veracruz and Mexico City as well.

Kosciuszko, Thaddeus (1746–1817). An ardent believer in the ideas of the American Revolution, this Polish general fought valiantly alongside Americans during the Revolution. His skill in positioning artillery contributed to the victory at Saratoga.

Lafayette, Marie Joseph Paul Yves Roch Gilbert du Motier, Marquis de (1757–1834). A native Frenchman, Lafayette came to the colonies and offered his services in the American Revolution. He became a close friend of GEORGE WASHINGTON and fought at Brandywine, Valley Forge, and in the Yorktown campaign. His grave in France is covered with earth from Bunker Hill.

Lee, Henry (Lighthorse Harry) (1756–1818). Lee, who was father of Confederate general ROBERT E. LEE, was an army officer who fought daringly in the Revolution.

Lee, Robert E. (1807–1870). Head of the Army of Northern Virginia during the Civil War, Lee surrendered to General ULYSSES S. GRANT at Appomattox Court House in 1865.

NOTABLE FIGURES, *cont.*

Lincoln, Abraham (1809–1865). As president from 1861 to 1865, Lincoln was closely involved in directing the course of the Civil War, always with the goal of preserving the Union.

MacArthur, Douglas (1880–1964). One of the most controversial and brilliant officers in military history, MacArthur led a brigade during World War I, served as superintendent of West Point from 1919 to 1922, headed U.S. forces in the southwest Pacific theater during World War II and occupation forces after the war in Japan, and was U.N. commander during the Korean War. When he made public his dispute with President HARRY TRUMAN over the conduct of the war, Truman removed him from command.

Mahan, Alfred Thayer (1840–1914). This graduate of the U.S. Naval Academy, naval officer, and historian is best known for his writings on the importance of sea power, entitled *The Influence of Sea Power Upon History*, which convinced THEODORE ROOSEVELT to expand the navy and embark on overseas expansion.

Marion, Francis (c. 1732–1795). A Revolutionary War hero, Marion led guerrilla battles in South Carolina.

Marshall, George (1880–1959). A staff army officer during World War I, when he served under General PERSHING, Marshall later rose to the rank of five-star general in World War II. Marshall was an important strategist. As President HARRY TRUMAN's secretary of state, he organized the European Recovery Program, better known as the Marshall Plan, and also served briefly as secretary of defense.

McClellan, George B. (1826–1885). A Union general, McClellan commanded the Army of the Potomac during the early days of the Civil War. He was responsible for the Union victory at Antietam. In 1864, he opposed LINCOLN in the general election.

Meade, George G. (1815–1872). During the Civil War, Meade led the victorious Union forces at Gettysburg.

Mitchell, Billy (1879–1936). Having played a lead role in developing air power in World War I, Mitchell was one of the first to recognize the value of aviation in fighting wars. After the war, he pioneered tests that showed that planes were capable of sinking ships. His determination to promote air power brought him into conflict with conservative members of the military establishment. His public statements, critical of leadership in the Departments of War and Navy, led to his subsequent court-martial. He was found guilty and suspended from duty for five years. He resigned.

Montgomery, Richard (1738–1775). A Continental Army general during the Revolution, Montgomery fought in several major battles and died during an unsuccessful attempt to take Quebec.

Morgan, Daniel (1736–1802). Commanding several companies of Virginia sharpshooters during the Revolution, Morgan fought at Saratoga and Cowpens.

Murphy Audie (1924–1971). Murphy was the most decorated American soldier in World War II. He was awarded the Medal of Honor for single-handedly holding off and killing or wounding more than fifty Germans.

Nimitz, Chester (1885–1966). During World War II, Nimitz was the chief strategist of the naval war against the Japanese in the Pacific. He commanded the Pacific fleet and was present at the surrender. Nimitz became a five-star admiral.

Patton, George (1885–1945). During World War II, General Patton played a role in the invasion of North Africa, headed the Third Army forces during the invasion of Normandy, and helped stop the Germans at the Battle of the Bulge.

Perry, Oliver Hazard (1785–1819). A naval officer who fought victoriously at the Battle of Lake Erie during the War of 1812, Perry reported his triumph with the now-famous words, "We have met the enemy, and they are ours."

Pershing, John J. (1860–1948). Pershing commanded forces during the Spanish-American War and in the Philippines from 1906 to 1913. During World War I, he headed the American Expeditionary Force and was known to be expert at shaping unskilled soldiers into skilled fighters.

Pickett, George (1825–1875). A Confederate general, Pickett led an assault, known as Pickett's Charge, at the Battle of Gettysburg during the Civil War.

Powell, Colin L. (1937–). Powell was the first African American to serve as national security advisor and chairman of the Joint Chiefs of Staff. His term coincided with the Persian Gulf War. In 2001, he was named secretary of defense in the administration of George W. Bush.

Quantrill, William (1837–1865). During the Civil War, Quantrill's proslavery raiders burned, looted, and murdered their way through Union camps and communities in Kansas and Missouri, causing thousands of Union troops to be diverted from the more pressing war theater in the South. In 1863, he raided Lawrence, Kansas, killing more than 140 civilians and burning more than 200 buildings.

Rankin, Jeannette (1880–1973). A social worker who had campaigned for women's suffrage, Rankin was twice elected to the U.S. House of Representatives and has the unusual distinction of being the only member of Congress to vote against the declarations of war against Germany in both World War I and World War II.

Rickover, Hyman (1900–1986). Admiral Rickover pioneered the development of the nuclear navy, directing the construction of the world's first nuclear-powered submarine, the USS *Nautilus*, launched in 1954.

Roosevelt, Franklin Delano (1882–1945). As president during World War II, Roosevelt, who had served as assistant secretary of the navy, was intimately involved in the direction of the war, working closely with the various military leaders.

Roosevelt, Theodore (1858–1919). During the Spanish-American War, Roosevelt resigned his position as secretary of the navy, rounded up his East and West Coast friends to form the First Regiment, better known as the Rough Riders, and fought valiantly and victoriously at San Juan Hill in Cuba. Roosevelt went on to serve as the twenty-sixth president of the United States.

Scott, Winfield (1786–1866). Made a brigadier general during the War of 1812, Scott went on to serve in Seminole and Creek campaigns and as supreme commander of the U.S. Army during the Mexican War, capturing Mexico City. He was still supreme commander when the Civil War began but retired in November 1861.

Sheridan, Philip (1831–1888). An outstanding cavalry commander, Sheridan led the Union Army of the Shenandoah during the Civil War.

Sherman, William Tecumseh (1820–1891). During the Civil War, General Sherman marched Union troops through Atlanta and then to the sea, destroying everything in his path.

Spaatz, Carl (1891–1974). Spaatz commanded the strategic air bombing of Germany and Japan during World War II.

Steuben, Friedrich Wilhelm von, Baron (1730–1794). A Prussian army officer who became a general for the Americans during the Revolutionary War, Steuben was invaluable in building the Continental Army into a tough fighting force.

Stilwell, Joseph (1883–1946). As commander of U.S. troops in the China-Burma-India theater during World War II, Stilwell also served as chief of staff to China's Generalissimo Chiang Kai-shek.

Taylor, Zachary (1784–1850). Taylor fought in the War of 1812 against the Seminoles and in Black Hawk's War in 1832. President Polk dispatched him to the Texas-Mexico border, where a skirmish initiated the Mexican War. A popular hero, especially after his victory at Buena Vista, he was elected president in 1848.

Thomas, George (1816–1870). A Civil War general, Thomas is credited with saving the Union Army during the Chattanooga campaign and winning the Battle of Nashville. He headed the Army of the Cumberland.

Truman, Harry (1884–1972). Inheriting the presidency from FRANKLIN ROOSEVELT, Truman oversaw the end of World War II, made the decision to drop the world's first two atomic bombs on Japan, and negotiated the peace.

Washington, George (1732–1799). In addition to being the first president of the United States, Washington headed the Continental Army during the Revolution.

Wayne, Anthony (1745–1796). Wayne fought in the Revolution, capturing the British outpost at Stony Point, New York Later, he decisively defeated the Ohio Indians at the Battle of Fallen Timbers.

Wilson, Woodrow (1856–1924). As president from 1912 to 1919, Wilson claimed to be a great foe of imperialism, but no president meddled more in Latin America. Although much more interested in establishing a lasting peace, Wilson led the United States during World War I.

CHAPTER 6

GOVERNMENT, POLITICS, AND LAW

HIGHLIGHTS

Timeline of Government, Politics, and Law

THE EARLY YEARS OF THE AMERICAN REPUBLIC were devoted to establishing the laws and institutions of democratic government as envisioned by the founding fathers. By no means was there a consensus, and the system for which they laid the foundation has evolved in ways they may never have anticipated. Perhaps the single principle shared by the originators of American democracy and by legislators and judges over the centuries, however, is that the balance of power among the three branches and the sovereign rights of the people—however precisely defined—are the defining characteristics of the American experiment in government.

COLONIAL ERA

1619 The first colonial legislature, the House of Burgesses, meets at Jamestown, Virginia. This house, and its present-day successor, the Virginia General Assembly, is the oldest representative government in the Western Hemisphere.

1620 The Mayflower Compact, establishing self-government for the Plymouth Colony in Massachusetts, is signed aboard the *Mayflower.*

1639 The first American constitution, the Fundamental Order of Connecticut, is written by representatives of the towns of Hartford, Wethersfield, and Windsor.

1641 In an early gesture of colonial independence, the Massachusetts Bay Colony establishes its own legal code, the Body of Liberties.

1647 Rhode Island's code of laws guarantees freedom of conscience: "Otherwise than…what is herein forbidden, all men may walk as their consciences persuade them, everyone in the name of his God."

1774 With a war for independence now on the horizon, the First Continental Congress meets in Philadelphia and draws up a list of grievances to give to the king of England.

1775 The Revolutionary War begins.

"In Rivers & bad Governments, the lightest Things swim at top."

—BENJAMIN FRANKLIN, *POOR RICHARD'S ALMANACK,* 1758

1776 THOMAS JEFFERSON drafts the Declaration of Independence, which asserts the colonies' independence from England and defines the natural rights of Americans. The Continental Congress adopts it.

EARLY REPUBLIC

1776 States begin writing state constitutions. Maryland, Delaware, New Hampshire, Pennsylvania, North Carolina, and South Carolina are among the states with completed constitutions by the year's end.

Virginia adopts a Declaration of Rights written by GEORGE MASON, asserting that "all men are by nature free and independent" and outlining rights and freedoms, such as the free exercise of religion, that will eventually be written into the U.S. Constitution and the Bill of Rights.

1777 The Continental Congress adopts the Articles of Confederation, which provide for a loose union of states and a weak central government with virtually no power to tax. It goes into effect in 1781.

The Continental Congress drafts the Articles of Confederation.

1786 Virginia adopts a statute of religious freedom, written by THOMAS JEFFERSON.

1786–1787 Shays' Rebellion in Massachusetts, a tax protest, is the first internal challenge to the new nation's power.

1787 Beset by financial and diplomatic crises, Congress endorses a plan for a convention to revise the Articles of Confederation. Delegates write a new Constitution instead, one that significantly strengthens the central government. Federalists support this Constitution, while anti-Federalists oppose it.

Written by JAMES MADISON, ALEXANDER HAMILTON, and JOHN JAY, *The Federalist Papers* present a masterly interpretation and analysis of the Constitution, and argue for its ratification.

1788 The new Constitution takes effect when nine states ratify it.

1789 GEORGE WASHINGTON becomes the first president, and JOHN ADAMS the first vice president.

Congress adopts the Bill of Rights written primarily by JAMES MADISON. It will be ratified as the first ten amendments of the Constitution in 1791.

A federal judiciary is organized.

Three federal departments—State, War, and Treasury—are formed, and the office of the attorney general is established. A postmaster general is also named, under the secretary of the treasury. When Washington consults with these heads, he sets a precedent for cabinet meetings, well established by the time he leaves office.

George Washington was not the first president of the United States. That distinction belongs to John Hanson of Maryland, who was elected "President of the United States in Congress Assembled" under the Articles of the Confederation in 1781.

THE ELECTORAL COLLEGE

When the framers of the Constitution established the office of president, they hesitated to allow this powerful individual to be elected directly by the people. Instead they devised a system, known as the electoral college, whereby the president is actually elected by electors, who in turn are elected by the people. Each state has as many electors as its Senate and House members combined, and the electors usually vote as a block for the candidate who has received the greatest number of votes in the state.

This system has produced some erratic results. In 1800, THOMAS JEFFERSON and AARON BURR were tied for the electoral vote. As a consequence, the House of Representatives made the final decision, and passage of the Twelfth Amendment made sure this kind of tie would not occur again.

But there have been other problems. For example, a president with a larger popular vote majority can lose in the electoral college, as happened to Grover Cleveland in 1888. When there is no majority in the electoral college, the House of Representatives decides the outcome, with each state's delegation voting as a block. Following the election of 1824, the House awarded the presidency to John Quincy Adams, even though he had received more than 38,000 *fewer* votes than contender ANDREW JACKSON. And following the election of 1876, with disputed returns in four states, the House appointed a commission that put Rutherford B. Hayes in office, even though Samuel J. Tilden had an edge in the popular vote of more than 264,000 votes. And in the hotly contested 2000 election, a protracted series of court proceedings established Republican George W. Bush as the winner even though Democratic candidate Al Gore appeared to win the popular election by several hundred thousand votes.

Reformers maintain that the electoral college system is outdated and unfair, and that it should be abolished. This is an unlikely prospect, however, given that the constitutional amendment necessary to overturn it would require ratification by three-quarters of the states.

GOVERNMENT, POLITICS, & LAW

1790 Congress meets in Philadelphia and votes to establish a new capital on the Potomac.

1791 Although there is no national currency, Congress charters a national bank. It is responsible in part for regulating state banks.

The Bill of Rights becomes the first ten amendments to the Constitution.

1792 The Democratic-Republican Party, led by THOMAS JEFFERSON, takes shape in opposition to the Federalists. It advocates strong states' rights.

Kentucky is admitted to the Union with universal manhood suffrage for free citizens. Other states drop property qualifications in the following decades.

1793 Regional issues arise early; one such issue is solved by passage of the first Fugitive Slave Act, which makes it illegal to aid runaway slaves or to interfere with their arrest.

1794 The federal government uses force to quell the Whiskey Rebellion by frontier farmers in Pennsylvania who refuse to pay an excise tax on their whiskey.

1796 JOHN ADAMS, a Federalist, is elected president, and THOMAS JEFFERSON, a Democratic-Republican, is elected vice president.

"He is distrustful, obstinate, excessively vain, and takes no counsel from anyone."

—THOMAS JEFFERSON, SPEAKING OF JOHN ADAMS

EXECUTIVE DEPARTMENTS

The creation of executive departments—the responsibility of Congress—reflects the changing nature and concerns of the Union. The First Congress created only the State Department, the War Department, and the Treasury Department. The attorney general was a cabinet member, but the Justice Department that he heads today wasn't officially created until 1871. The following table lists the executive departments in order of their creation.

DEPARTMENT	YEAR CREATED
State	1789
War	1789
Treasury	1789
Navy	1798 (consolidated with Defense in 1947)
Interior	1849
Agriculture	1862 (raised to cabinet status in 1889)
Justice	1871 (with attorney general as head)
Commerce and Labor	1903
Commerce	1913 (originally Commerce and Labor, 1903)
Labor	1913 (originally Commerce and Labor, 1903)
Defense	1947 (consolidates War, Navy, and other military units)
Health, Education, and Welfare	1953
Housing and Urban Development	1965
Transportation	1966
Energy	1977
Education	1979 (originally Health, Education, and Welfare, 1953)
Health and Human Services	1980 (originally Health, Education, and Welfare, 1953)
Veterans Affairs	1988
Homeland Security	2002

1798 The Eleventh Amendment is ratified, in effect stating that a state cannot be sued by a citizen of another state.

With war against France seeming imminent, Congress passes the Alien and Sedition Acts, which extend the residency requirements for citizenship, authorize the president to deport aliens dangerous to the public peace or safety, and make it a crime to obstruct the execution of the national laws or to publish "any false, scandalous, or malicious writing" against the U.S. government, Congress, or the president. Targeted were newspaper editors aligned with JEFFERSON's Democratic-Republicans and supporting Revolutionary France.

The Kentucky (written by THOMAS JEFFERSON) and Virginia (written by JAMES MADISON) Resolutions argue that the Alien and Sedition Acts are unconstitutional because the federal government was exercising powers not delegated to it. A second set of Kentucky Resolutions outlines the doctrine of nullification—that states can nullify actions of the U.S. Congress.

The Department of the Navy is established. In 1947, it will be consolidated with other military units in the Department of Defense.

SECTIONALISM AND STATES' RIGHTS

1800 The seat of the federal government moves from Philadelphia to Washington, D.C.

The first election involving political parties is held, with Democratic-Republican THOMAS JEFFERSON running against Federalist JOHN ADAMS. Jefferson beats Adams, but thanks to party discipline, Jefferson receives the same number of electoral votes as the vice presidential candidate, AARON BURR.

1801 The election is forced into the House of Representatives, where thirty-six ballots are required to elect JEFFERSON.

1803 In *Marbury v. Madison*, the Supreme Court establishes its right to review the constitutionality of acts of Congress.

1804 The Twelfth Amendment, which remedies the problem of the 1800 election by providing for the separate election of president and vice president, is ratified.

THOMAS JEFFERSON is reelected president. His presidency is increasingly preoccupied with neutral rights, an embargo that hurts U.S. commerce, and increasing tensions with Britain.

This engraving entitled "Washington Giving Laws to America" boasts classical and biblical imagery. The original artist, H. Singleton, likens the country's first president to Moses presenting the Ten Commandments.

1807 AARON BURR becomes the first major public official to be tried for treason. Charged with trying to establish an independent country in the Southwest, he is acquitted.

1808 JAMES MADISON is elected president on the Democratic-Republican ticket.

Congress halts the slave trade but not slavery.

1812 JAMES MADISON is reelected president as the country is already at war against Britain.

The Second Bank of the United States is granted a charter.

1816 JAMES MONROE is elected president on the Republican ticket. The Federalist Party, in disarray, does not formally nominate a candidate. Monroe's election (he receives 183 out of 217 electoral votes in 1816 and all but 1 of the 232 possible votes in 1820) ushers in the Era of Good Feeling, a period when the country is expanding its territory and settling its boundary disputes.

1818 Connecticut abolishes ownership of property as a voter qualification.

1820 Henry Clay helped to devise and secure the passage of the Missouri Compromise, which admits Maine to the Union as a free state, Missouri as a slave state, and forbids slavery in the Louisiana Territory north of 36°30' (the southern boundary of Missouri).

President Monroe is reelected.

1824 Neither the populist war hero Andrew Jackson nor National Republican John Quincy Adams garners a majority in the electoral college, although John Calhoun is elected vice president.

1825 The presidential election is forced into the House of Representatives, and John Quincy Adams wins with the support of Henry Clay. Jackson supporters vow revenge.

1828 Andrew Jackson is elected again, this time as a disaffected Democrat, as the Democratic-Republicans now call themselves.

1829 Jackson furthers the spoils system in the federal bureaucracy, in which winners of elections reward their friends and party members with government jobs. His Kitchen Cabinet, an informal group of advisors, became some of the most powerful men in Washington and had more influence over policy than some formal cabinet members.

1830 With South Carolina angered over high tariffs and promoting the doctrine of nullification, whereby a state may choose to nullify a federal law within its borders, South Carolina senator Robert Y. Hayne and Massachusetts senator Daniel Webster debate the power of the Union. Hayne takes the states' rights position, while Webster, an eloquent orator, defends the Union: "Liberty and Union, now and forever, one and inseparable."

Former president John Quincy Adams is elected to Congress.

THE JACKSON INAUGURAL

Vowing to "turn the rascals out," the famous Indian fighter, War of 1812 general, and Tennessee senator Andrew Jackson ran a successful anticorruption campaign against incumbent John Quincy Adams of Massachusetts in the presidential election of 1828. Jackson's election marked a turning point in the politics of the young nation: Old Hickory, as admirers called him, was the first president nominated by the Democratic Party, the first chief executive from a frontier state, and, unlike his predecessors, a "self-made" man.

Perhaps nothing in his presidency more epitomized the spirit of Jacksonian populism than the events of Inauguration Day, March 4, 1829. After the swearing-in and Inaugural Address, throngs of supporters—many of whom had come from Tennessee—followed the presidential entourage back to the White House, which Jackson had declared open to the public. Inside, the halls of the White House were overrun with revelers. So large and unruly was the crowd that some people stood on chairs and tables. Invited guests were knocked down; glass and china shattered. Tubs of punch were set up on the South Lawn to lure the crowd outside, with only partial success. The new president was ushered out a back door for protection. The "people" had taken over the White House—literally.

1832 A state convention in South Carolina passes an Ordinance of Nullification, nullifying the tariff acts of 1828 and 1832.

The "Bank War" erupts when ANDREW JACKSON attempts to disband the Second National Bank by refusing to renew its charter, due to expire in 1836 (see p. 318).

Jackson began putting federal money into state banks, which became known as his "pet banks." Nicholas Biddle, the president of the Second National Bank, countered Jackson by collecting notes and canceling loans to state banks in hopes of creating a financial crisis that would prove the necessity of a strong federal bank.

Debate over the issue raged in Washington, but Jackson never returned the money to the national bank, and its charter expired in 1836.

Andrew Jackson is reelected president.

1833 Congress responds to South Carolina's Ordinance of Nullification by passing the federal government's first Force Bill, which specifies the federal government's ability to use armed force to enforce federal laws in the states. The crisis is averted when the tariff bill is rewritten to make it more acceptable to the South.

JACKSON escalates the Bank War by pulling $10 million in government funds out of the national bank and putting it in favored state banks. The head of the national bank responds by calling in commercial loans, thus causing a panic, which soon turns to recession.

1835 Recession turns to boom as state banks proliferate, the price of cotton soars, and western land speculation reaches new highs.

1836 President ANDREW JACKSON, concerned about widespread use of paper money, issues the Specie Circular, declaring that the federal government will henceforth require hard currency (gold or silver) to buy western public lands.

English banks raise interest rates and reduce credit, sending shock waves in the cotton market that initiate a six-year depression.

Martin Van Buren, a Democrat, succeeds Andrew Jackson as president.

1839 The Liberty Party forms in the North, organized in opposition to slavery.

1840 William Henry Harrison, a Whig, is elected president.

1841 When Harrison dies one month after taking office, Vice President John Tyler succeeds him (the first vice president to do so). Tyler vetoes several Whig measures, and becomes increasingly isolated from the party.

1842 Dorr's Rebellion in Rhode Island leads to a liberalization of the voting laws in that state by 1843. Prior to the rebellion, the state relied on voting rules from the original 1663 charter, leaving nearly half of the adult male population disfranchised.

Thomas Jefferson and John Adams, the only presidents to have signed the Declaration of Independence, both died on its fiftieth anniversary, July 4, 1826.

GOVERNMENT, POLITICS, & LAW

POLITICAL PARTIES

Political parties aren't written into the Constitution, and indeed some of the framers, especially JAMES MADISON, feared factionalism and parties. But Madison also recognized that "the causes of faction are...sown in the nature of man," and inevitably, even in GEORGE WASHINGTON's first term, political factions began to align around the differing positions of THOMAS JEFFERSON and ALEXANDER HAMILTON. At issue was nothing less than the nature of the Union: Hamilton hoped for a stronger, more centralized federal government than Jefferson could tolerate. Hamilton's followers became known as the Federalists and Jefferson's as the anti-Federalists or Republicans.

By the time of the War of 1812, the Federalists were torn by internal strife, and conservative Federalists in New England were so highly critical of the war that when it was successfully concluded, the party practically self-destructed. JAMES MONROE, a Republican from Virginia, had no real opposition in the elections of 1816 and 1820: hence the Era of Good Feeling.

In 1824, there were five candidates for president, each representing different sections of the Republican Party. But that contest proved decisively divisive. Running as a Democratic-Republican, ANDREW JACKSON won the popular vote, but failed to get a majority of the electoral vote. Consequently, the election was decided in the House of Representatives, which awarded the presidency to National Republican John Quincy Adams. Claiming that Adams had entered into a "corrupt bargain" to secure the presidency, Jackson's followers vowed revenge, and, in 1828, Jackson—this time running with the shortened party name of simply Democrat—beat National Republican Adams in both the popular and electoral vote. There hasn't been an uncontested presidential election since.

By 1840, Adam's National Republican Party gave way to the Whig Party, which was led by HENRY CLAY and DANIEL WEBSTER. William Henry Harrison and Zachary Taylor were elected president from the Whig Party, and, in 1856, members of the Whigs joined with various antislavery factions and became the new Republican Party, setting the stage for the familiar two-party races that have been a political tradition since the Civil War. Occasionally, a third party has mounted a serious challenge to the two parties. For a survey of third parties, see page 213.

Following the Civil War, the Republican Party consisted of factions deeply divided over the treatment of the former Confederate States. Another storm for the Republicans occurred when former president THEODORE ROOSEVELT ran again on the ticket of the Progressive Party, splitting the Republican vote and allowing Democrat WOODROW WILSON to win the election.

Since Reconstruction, the Republican Party has maintained a platform arguing that individuals, businesses, and financial interests should protect and serve many of the country's needs rather than creating a sprawling centralized government. It is interesting to trace today's Republican Party, which wants a smaller government and more power to be in the hands of the states, businesses, and individuals, to the Federalists. The Federalist Party, which favored a strong, central government, dissolved, and many of its members drifted toward the National Republican Party, which also dissolved and led to the emergence of the Whig Party, which eventually merged with others to form the Republicans.

The question of slavery in the western territories divided the Democratic Party in the period directly before the Civil War, putting northern and southern Democrats at odds and helping to secure the election of Republican ABRAHAM LINCOLN in 1860. The Democratic Party continued to defend agrarian interests and oppose high tariffs, trusts, and monopolies, attracting support from Catholics, immigrants, and many people from lower income brackets. Democrats favored reconciliation after the Civil War, which helped them to create a stronghold in the South. The twelve-year presidency of FRANKLIN D. ROOSEVELT restructured the party a bit, expanding public service projects and social programming to combat the effects of the Great Depression.

Today the Democratic Party is considered the party of a large government that advocates providing extensive services to Americans, such as education, health care, and social programs, aid for the underprivileged, and protection for civil and individual rights. Ironically, the party can trace its roots through the Democratic-Republicans to the Republicans to the anti-Federalists, who believed that government should be weak and decentralized.

1844 James K. Polk, a Democrat, becomes the first dark-horse candidate ever to win the presidency. He settles the Oregon question and fights the Mexican War, encouraging expansionism.

1846 David Wilmot of Pennsylvania proposes that no territory acquired from Mexico as a result of war shall be open to slavery. Passed by the House but defeated by the Senate, the Wilmot Proviso exacerbates the growing bitterness between the North and South.

1846–1847 The Free-Soil Party forms, an alliance of antislavery northern Democrats, so-called Conscience Whigs, and old Liberty Party members. In 1848, the Free-Soilers run Martin Van Buren for president.

1848 Zachary Taylor, a Whig, is elected president. A national hero from the Mexican War, he supports the expansion of the nation and the admission of California as a free state.

1849 The Department of the Interior is created to act as custodian of the nation's natural resources and manage land sale and Indian affairs (see p. 37, 91).

1850 When President Zachary Taylor dies, Vice President Millard Fillmore becomes president.

Congress engages in acrimonious debate over slavery and finally passes the Compromise of 1850, in which California is admitted as a free state and Utah and New Mexico residents are permitted to decide the slavery issue in their territories. The slave trade is abolished in the District of Columbia; a more stringent Fugitive Slave Law is enacted; and questions concerning the Texas boundary and debt are resolved. In this debate three men who have dominated U.S. politics for decades are heard for the last time: JOHN C. CALHOUN (who died shortly after the passage of the compromise), HENRY CLAY (who passed away in 1852), and DANIEL WEBSTER (who left the Senate to serve as secretary of state and also died in 1852).

1852 Franklin Pierce, a compromise candidate in the deeply divided Democratic Party, defeats the Whig candidate but does not fare well as president. His one accomplishment is to sign the Gadsden Purchase, buying what is now southern New Mexico and Arizona from Mexico, but he also signs the Kansas-Nebraska Act, which leaves the issue of slavery up to settlers of various territories. This angers northerners and leads to a bloody civil war in Kansas. Although opposed to slavery, Pierce also opposes the civil war in Kansas. His party denies him the nomination a second time.

1854 The Republican Party, with a staunch antislavery platform, is founded in opposition to the Kansas-Nebraska Act.

1856 James Buchanan, a Democrat, is elected president. His administration reels from crisis to crisis, lacking the strength or wisdom to avert civil war.

President Zachary Taylor never voted, belonged to a political party, or took interest in politics until running for president at the age of sixty-two.

1857 In the *Dred Scott* decision, the Supreme Court holds that blacks are not citizens and overrules the Missouri Compromise on grounds that Congress has no right to make any laws prohibiting slavery in the territories.

1858 The seven Lincoln-Douglas debates during a campaign for the Senate focus still more attention on the issue of slavery. Stephen Douglas, a brilliant debater, supports popular sovereignty. LINCOLN takes the position that slavery is morally wrong and that the federal government should decide the slavery question in the territories. Douglas wins reelection to the U.S. Senate by the Illinois state legislature. (At the time, all senators are elected by state legislature.)

VICE PRESIDENTIAL SUCCESSION

When John Tyler took the oath of office as vice president on April 6, 1841, no one knew quite what would happen. President William Henry Harrison, dead exactly a month after his inauguration, had just become the first president to die in office. Would the vice president be the president, or just the acting president?

Tyler did assume the title of president, of course, and since then eight vice presidents have followed suit. In all, they are:

President	Year	Reason
John Tyler	1841	Death of William Henry Harrison
Millard Fillmore	1850	Death of Zachary Taylor
Andrew Johnson	1865	Assassination of Abraham Lincoln
Chester A. Arthur	1881	Assassination of James A. Garfield
Theodore Roosevelt	1901	Assassination of William McKinley
Calvin Coolidge	1923	Death of Warren G. Harding
Harry S. Truman	1945	Death of Franklin D. Roosevelt
Lyndon Johnson	1963	Assassination of John F. Kennedy
Gerald R. Ford	1974	Resignation of Richard M. Nixon, whose vice president, Spiro T. Agnew, also resigned

Other vice presidents have been elected president in their own right. Aside from those who succeeded to the presidency and were then reelected (THEODORE ROOSEVELT, CALVIN COOLIDGE, HARRY TRUMAN, and LYNDON JOHNSON), a few vice presidents have managed to use their office as the road to the White House.

Vice President	Serving Under	Became President
John Adams	George Washington	1797
Thomas Jefferson	John Adams	1801
Martin Van Buren	Andrew Jackson	1837
Richard M. Nixon	Dwight Eisenhower	1969
George H. W. Bush	Ronald Reagan	1989

1859 Abolitionist John Brown captures the federal arsenal at Harpers Ferry, intending to incite a slave revolt. Although Brown is hanged for treason, he is venerated as a martyr by many in the North.

1860 In a vote that severely divides the nation into pro- and antislavery camps, ABRAHAM LINCOLN, a Republican, is elected president. The Civil War follows.

1861 The Civil War begins when South Carolina soldiers fire on Union-held Fort Sumter in Charleston Harbor.

CIVIL WAR AND RECONSTRUCTION

1862 Slavery is abolished in the nation's capital.

1863 The Emancipation Proclamation is issued, freeing slaves in areas in rebellion.
LINCOLN delivers the Gettysburg Address.

1864 LINCOLN wins reelection, largely because after four years of fighting, the tide has begun to turn in favor of the North.

1865 President LINCOLN is assassinated at Ford's Theatre, and Andrew Johnson becomes president. His presidency is largely occupied with Reconstruction, which wins him many enemies in Congress.
The Thirteenth Amendment, abolishing slavery, is ratified.

1866 In an attempt to put some backbone into the Thirteenth Amendment, Congress passes the first Civil Rights Act, which decrees that all persons born in the United States (except Native Americans, who are not taxed) are citizens. When President Andrew Johnson vetoes the bill, Congress overrides the veto. Congress also passes the Fourteenth Amendment.

1867 Congress passes a series of Reconstruction Acts initiating military rule of the former Confederate States, except Tennessee. When President Johnson realizes that his secretary of war, Edwin Stanton, is feeding information to the opposition, Johnson fires him—in violation of the newly passed Tenure of Office Act, which prohibits the president from firing high-ranking officials without Senate approval.

1868 The House of Representatives impeaches President Andrew Johnson for defying the Tenure of Office Act. He is tried in the Senate and acquitted by only one vote.
The Fourteenth Amendment, granting citizenship to former slaves, is ratified by the states.
Ulysses S. Grant, a Republican, is elected president.

"We did not conceive it possible that even Mr. Lincoln would produce a paper so slipshod, so loose-jointed, so puerile, not alone in literary construction, but in its ideals, its sentiments, its grasp. He has outdone himself."

—*CHICAGO TIMES* EDITORIAL ON THE GETTYSBURG ADDRESS

1869 The temperance movement goes political when the Prohibition Party is founded in Chicago.

1870 The Fifteenth Amendment, guaranteeing that the right to vote cannot be denied on account of race, color, or previous condition of servitude, is ratified.

The Ku Klux Klan Acts (1870, 1871) place congressional elections under federal control, and the militia is used to enforce the voting rights of blacks.

1871 President Ulysses S. Grant, in an attempt to clean up the spoils system, institutes civil service reforms.

The Department of Justice is established, with the attorney general named its head.

1872 President Grant ushers an amnesty bill for southerners through Congress.

Women's rights activist Victoria Woodhull is the first woman presidential candidate, running on the People's Party ticket with Frederick Douglass as her running mate.

President Grant is reelected.

1873 In the *Slaughterhouse Cases,* the Supreme Court rules that the Fourteenth Amendment only protects the national rights of citizens, not the rights conferred—or withheld—by the states.

1875 A second major Civil Rights Act gives equal rights to African Americans in public accommodations and on jury duty. It is ruled unconstitutional in 1883.

1876 A crisis is precipitated when Samuel J. Tilden, a Democrat, wins the popular vote but not the electoral vote, as the returns in four states are disputed.

1877 An electoral commission gives Rutherford B. Hayes the electoral college majority by assigning all the disputed votes to him.

President Hayes orders federal troops withdrawn from the South.

INDUSTRIALISM AND POST-RECONSTRUCTION POLITICS

1878 The American Bar Association is established.

1880 James Garfield, a Republican, is elected president.

LINCOLN AND PRESIDENTIAL POWER

Not the least of ABRAHAM LINCOLN's enduring political legacy is the war-making power he brought to the office of president. The advent of his administration and the Civil War in 1861 brought a level of executive authority not previously known and in some respects beyond that contemplated by the Constitution. With the outbreak of civil war and the very life of the nation in peril, Lincoln took several steps based on a radical interpretation of Article II, section 2, of the Constitution, which invests the president as commander in chief of the military. With Congress out of session, he called up 75,000 men and waged war for twelve weeks. He unilaterally suspended the writ of habeas corpus, imposed a blockade on southern ports, and allocated Treasury funds to the conduct of war—all steps normally requiring congressional approval. In these measures as others throughout the conflict, Lincoln's strategy was to act first and ask Congress later, if at all. His constitutional authority, he claimed, was based on presidential "war powers" implied by the duty "to take care that the laws be faithfully executed" (Article II, section 3).

The powers of the American president have risen and fallen throughout the nation's history, but, due in large part to Lincoln, several commanders in chief have felt justified in committing troops to combat without congressional approval—as in Korea and Vietnam.

1881 President James Garfield is assassinated in a railroad station in Washington, D.C., and Vice President Chester A. Arthur succeeds him. Arthur's administration is marked by civil service reform and agrarian discontent.

1883 The Supreme Court finds most of the Civil Rights Act of 1875 to be unconstitutional; only the provision that black men may serve on juries survives. In reality, African Americans and other minorities and women neither serve on juries nor vote.

Congress passes the Pendleton Act, which establishes a Civil Service Commission to administer a merit-based civil service.

1884 Grover Cleveland, a Democrat, is elected president with a mandate to clean up machine politics.

1886 A Presidential Succession Act is passed, stipulating that cabinet members, in the order of the creation of their offices, will succeed to the presidency if both the president and vice president die or are removed or unable to serve. The order of succession is revised again in 1947.

1887 The Electoral Count Act authorizes states to certify their own electoral votes, thus avoiding the possibility of another disputed national election like the Tilden-Hayes contest.

1888 Benjamin Harrison, a Republican, is elected president with fewer popular votes but more electoral votes than Democrat Grover Cleveland.

The Bureau of Labor is made the Department of Labor, but, in 1903, it is reorganized as the Department of Commerce and Labor.

The first racially mixed federal jury was impaneled in 1865 for the treason trial of Confederate president Jefferson Davis. The trial never took place, and Jefferson was later set free.

1891 Congress passes the Circuit Courts of Appeals Act, giving the Supreme Court the right to review all cases.

1892 President Grover Cleveland is reelected, becoming the first president to serve two nonconsecutive terms. His second administration is plagued by a money crisis and a deepening depression.

1893 Colorado becomes the first state to enact women's suffrage, but Wyoming Territory has permitted women to vote since 1869 and Utah Territory since 1870 (see pp. 223–224).

1894 Congress passes the first graduated federal income tax.

1895 The Supreme Court, in *Pollock v. Farmers' Loan and Trust Company*, finds the federal income tax unconstitutional.

1896 The Supreme Court in *Plessy v. Ferguson* rules that separate-but-equal facilities in railway facilities, and by implication in education and

AFTER THE WHITE HOUSE

What else is there after you've been president? Many former presidents have simply retired, but a few have gone on to have surprising careers. John Quincy Adams, disappointed in losing his bid for reelection in 1828, was approached by a Massachusetts delegation who asked him to run for Congress. He agreed and, in 1830, was elected to the House of Representatives, where he served until the end of his life. In 1836, he opposed the "gag rule," which suppressed all petitions for the abolition of slavery, and, in 1844, finally succeeded in getting it rescinded. He also defended the slave mutineers of the *Amistad* before the Supreme Court. On February 21, 1848, Adams suffered a stroke and collapsed in the House of Representatives. He was carried from his seat to the Speaker's Room, where he lay until he died two days later.

Andrew Johnson was the only other president to serve in Congress after his term of office. He ran for the House of Representatives in 1872, but lost. In 1875, he was elected to the Senate, perhaps relishing a return to the very institution that had given him so much trouble when he was president.

THEODORE ROOSEVELT had picked William Howard Taft to be his successor, but once Taft was in office, Roosevelt could hardly stand not to be there himself. He ran against Taft in 1912, splitting the Republican

Party and spoiling his former friend's chances for reelection. In 1921, President Warren G. Harding appointed Taft to the Supreme Court, as chief justice. Former presidents Martin Van Buren and Millard Fillmore had also accepted third-party nominations for president, but ran with less success.

Herbert Hoover was another president who would have liked to continue. Hardly retired after 1933, he again took up the relief work that had first made him famous. After World War II, he conducted a study of food and economic conditions in defeated Germany for President TRUMAN and chaired a commission to study reorganization of the executive branch. President Eisenhower asked him to direct a similar effort. Hoover may have lost the presidency but certainly not the respect of those who held it.

More recently Jimmy Carter has pursued, out of office, the themes of his presidency: international peace through missions to Panama, North Korea, and Haiti, and social justice through Habitat for Humanity. For his efforts to resolve conflicts, promote democracy, and advance human rights, Carter received the 2002 Nobel Peace Prize.

What about First Ladies? In 2000, Hillary Clinton became the first former First Lady elected to the U.S. Senate.

GOVERNMENT, POLITICS, & LAW

all public accommodations, are acceptable for blacks, thus legitimizing segregation.

William McKinley, a Republican, is elected president. His administration reluctantly goes ahead with the short-lived Spanish-American War, passes the highest tariff in U.S. history, and initiates the Open Door policy with China.

1898 Labor leader Eugene V. Debs helps to organize the Social Democratic Party, later renamed the Socialist Party.

EMERGING WORLD POWER

1901 President William McKinley is shot by anarchist Leon Czolgosz on September 6. Eight days later, McKinley dies, and Vice President THEODORE ROOSEVELT becomes president. An energetic Progressive, he initiates forty-four lawsuits to break up trusts and champions such social reforms as the Food and Drug Act. Through the force of his personality and his seemingly inexhaustible energy, Roosevelt expands the powers of the presidency. Through a series of forays into the foreign arena, he helps to establish the United States as a world power.

1903 The Department of Commerce and Labor is established.

1904 President THEODORE ROOSEVELT is overwhelmingly reelected. In a statement that he will come to regret, he promises not to run again.

1908 William Howard Taft, a Republican, is elected president. Groomed by ROOSEVELT to be his successor, Taft begins ninety antitrust actions and continues to press for the dissolution of the Standard Oil Trust. Nevertheless, he alienates Progressives by supporting high tariffs and by becoming embroiled in a public lands controversy that pits him against Forest Service chief Gifford Pinchot.

The Bureau of Investigation is established with Stanley Finch at the helm. J. Edgar Hoover becomes director in 1924 and over time, with the cooperation of Congress, greatly expands the bureau's duties and jurisdiction. It is renamed the Federal Bureau of Investigation in 1935.

1911 Wisconsin senator Robert M. La Follette helps found the National Progressive Republican League, which seeks to deprive President William Howard Taft of the Republican nomination in 1912.

This election day cover of Leslie's *magazine paints a favorable portrait of an energetic and fashionable suffragette. Antisuffragette publications often portrayed them as overly emotional, unable to exercise power, or as neglectful mothers.*

1911, *cont.*

Congress submits an amendment providing for direct election of senators to the states. The House has passed such legislation in 1893, 1894, 1898, 1900, and 1902. The Senate had neither enacted nor defeated the legislation.

1912 Angry at Taft, THEODORE ROOSEVELT organizes the Bull Moose Party and runs against his protégé but succeeds only in splitting the vote. WOODROW WILSON, a Democrat, wins the presidency. Wilson initially works to keep the United States out of World War I but then leads the nation into the war in 1917. Throughout the war he works to establish the League of Nations, a forerunner to the United Nations.

1913 The Sixteenth Amendment, giving Congress the power to impose federal income taxes, is ratified.

The Seventeenth Amendment, providing for the direct election of senators, is ratified.

The Department of Commerce and Labor is split into two departments.

1915 The House of Representatives restricts its membership to 435 to keep it from getting even more unwieldy.

1916 President WOODROW WILSON is reelected.

1917 The United States enters World War I.

Women picket in front of the White House for the right to vote.

Even though women cannot yet vote, Montana's JEANNETTE RANKIN takes her seat in the House of Representatives, to which she was elected the previous fall.

1918 For his opposition to the government's prosecution of citizens charged with sedition, Socialist Party leader Eugene V. Debs is sentenced to ten years in prison under the Espionage Act. He will eventually receive a presidential pardon in 1921. While in prison, Debs is the Socialist Party candidate for U.S. president. He receives almost 1 million votes.

World War I ends.

1919 The Eighteenth Amendment, enacting Prohibition, is ratified.

The Supreme Court holds that in wartime rights and privileges that would have been considered normal in peacetime may be curtailed when a "clear and present danger" exists.

The Communist Party of America is founded, but it never becomes an important force in American politics.

Using the authority of the 1918 Alien Act, which permits the government to deport any alien who is, or has been, a member of a revolutionary organization, the Justice Department deports hundreds of aliens, among them anarchists Emma Goldman and Alexander Berkman.

1920 The Nineteenth Amendment is ratified, giving women the right to vote.

Republican Warren Harding is elected president. He pledges to return the nation to "normalcy" after the chaos of the war.

The American Civil Liberties Union (ACLU) is founded by Jane Addams, FELIX FRANKFURTER, Helen Keller, Judah Magnus, and Norman Thomas.

1921 Former president Taft becomes chief justice of the Supreme Court, the only person ever to hold both positions.

1923 President Warren Harding dies unexpectedly just as the Teapot Dome oil scandal is about to break. Calvin Coolidge assumes the presidency.

1924 The Progressive Party runs Senator Bob La Follette for president. President Coolidge is elected. Coolidge, who is laissez-faire about the government's role in regulating business, presides over an economic boom, although the speculation that occurs during his administration leads to the Great Depression.

"I will tell you Folks, all Politics is Apple Sauce."

—WILL ROGERS, *THE ILLITERATE DIGEST*, 1924

1926 The Supreme Court in *Myers v. United States* supports the president's right to fire executive-branch employees, voiding the Tenure of Office Act of 1867 that was used to impeach Andrew Johnson.

1928 The Socialist Party runs Norman Thomas for president. Herbert Hoover, a Republican, is elected.

1929 The stock market crashes, plunging the nation into the Great Depression.

Convinced of the fundamental strength of the economy and that the deepening depression will run its course, Hoover keeps government intervention to a minimum. In foreign relations, he arranges for a one-year moratorium on the nation's World War I loans.

1932 FRANKLIN ROOSEVELT, a Democrat, is elected president.

Hattie Wyatt Caraway of Arkansas is the first woman elected to the Senate.

1933 In the first few months of his term, ROOSEVELT introduces a package of economic and social legislation designed to end the Great Depression; it becomes known as the New Deal.

The Twentieth Amendment, changing the induction dates for Congress, president, and vice president, is ratified. As a result, Congress will now convene on January 3 and new presidents will be inaugurated on January 20, rather than on March 4, thus shortening the "lame duck" period, or the time between the election and inauguration.

The Twenty-first Amendment, repealing Prohibition, is ratified.

Roosevelt appoints FRANCES PERKINS, the first woman to sit in a president's cabinet, to the post of secretary of labor.

GOVERNMENT, POLITICS, & LAW

FDR'S COURT-PACKING SCHEME

As he began his second term in January 1937, President Franklin Roosevelt was angry at the Supreme Court. In several of its decisions, he felt, the Court had interfered with New Deal programs and had stood in the way of much-needed economic reform. Within weeks of his second inauguration—and just two days after entertaining the justices at a White House dinner—Roosevelt announced a shocking plan to "reform" the High Court.

The judiciary was overworked, the president claimed, and something had to be done. For every justice who refused to retire within six months of his seventieth birthday, according to his plan, the president would be allowed to appoint a new one, up to a maximum of six. As it happened, a total of six Supreme Court justices were already over the age of seventy. Thus, Roosevelt would be allowed to appoint six reform-minded jurists to the Court and gain support for his programs.

In one of his most famous Fireside Chats, Roosevelt pointed out that Congress has the right to expand the Supreme Court and indeed had done so in the past. But most members of Congress, including many in his own party, as well as the public, saw right through his scheme. It was hotly debated for months but never really had a chance. Congress voted down the plan in midsummer.

As fate would have it, President Roosevelt made no fewer than seven appointments to the Supreme Court during his term of office.

1936 Franklin Roosevelt is reelected.

1938 The House of Representatives establishes a committee to investigate "un-American activities." In 1945, it is renamed the House Committee on Un-American Activities. Its task is to investigate Socialists, Communists, and other individuals and organizations deemed un-American.

1940 The Alien Registration Act, also known as the Smith Act, requires all aliens to register with the government and be fingerprinted, and makes it illegal to advocate the overthrow of the federal government.

While World War II rages in Europe, Franklin Roosevelt wins an unprecedented third term.

1941 After African Americans press the issue, President Roosevelt issues an Executive Order creating the Fair Employment Practices Committee and barring war manufacturers from racial discrimination in hiring workers.

The United States enters World War II.

1944 President Franklin Roosevelt is reelected for a fourth term.

Congress passes the first GI Bill of Rights, which provides benefits for veterans.

1945 Franklin Roosevelt dies, and Harry Truman becomes president. His administration will oversee the conclusion of the war, the development of the Marshall Plan, and the establishment of NATO.

POSTWAR ERA

1946 The Atomic Energy Commission is formed to monitor and control all research on atomic energy.

1947 The Presidential Succession Act establishes the speaker of the house as next in line for the presidency following the vice president, followed by the president pro tempore of the Senate and then the cabinet members according to the date on which each cabinet department was established.

1948 President HARRY TRUMAN, a Democrat, is reelected president.

1950 Senator Joseph McCarthy accuses State Department employees and many members of the American literary, film, and theatrical communities of being members of the Communist Party. His accusations cast a shadow in which no one wishes to stand.

1951 The Twenty-second Amendment is ratified, limiting the president's service to two terms.

In New York, a federal judge finds husband and wife Julius and Ethel Rosenberg and their friend Morton Sobell guilty of selling atomic secrets to the Soviet Union; after three stays of execution, the couple is executed in 1953. Sobell is sentenced to thirty years in prison. The controversy over this case continues, with some people arguing that the Rosenbergs were victims of the anti-Communist hysteria of the time.

1952 Dwight David Eisenhower, a World War II leader, president of Columbia University, and a Republican, is elected president. A dedicated moderate, Eisenhower takes a laissez-faire approach to the economy, and only when pressed, sends the military to enforce civil rights for blacks in the South.

1954 Congress censures Senator Joseph McCarthy for behavior during hearings conducted by his subcommittee on Investigations of the Senate Committee on Governmental Operations.

1956 Eisenhower is reelected president.

1957 Under the Civil Rights Act, the first legislation on the rights of minorities to be passed since the Reconstruction, the Civil Rights Commission is set up and the Civil Rights Division in the Justice Department is established to investigate cases in which people are prevented from voting.

Senator Joseph McCarthy delivers one of his signature rants during the 1954 investigation into communism in the Army.

1960 JOHN F. KENNEDY, a Democrat, is elected president. Although he is most interested in domestic affairs, Kennedy is forced to attend to foreign policy for much of his presidency.

He initiates the space exploration program, establishes the Peace Corps, stands up to the Soviets in Berlin, and organizes the Alliance for Progress to provide aid to Latin America. He is a strong voice for civil rights just as civic unrest is growing over this issue. His most notable foreign-affairs disaster is the Bay of Pigs invasion of Cuba. At the same time, one of his greatest successes also involves Cuba: the Cuban Missile Crisis, in which he forces the Soviets to remove their missiles from the island nation.

1961 The Twenty-third Amendment, granting voting rights in presidential elections to citizens residing in the District of Columbia, is ratified.

The Peace Corps is established.

1963 President KENNEDY is assassinated, and LYNDON JOHNSON becomes president. The Warren Commission finds that there was no conspiracy to assassinate Kennedy and that Lee Harvey Oswald was the sole assassin. The report is greeted skeptically by many.

Congress passes the first Clean Air Act (see p. 93).

"Being president is like being a jackass in a hailstorm. There's nothing to do but stand there and take it."

—LYNDON B. JOHNSON

1964 LYNDON JOHNSON, a southern Democrat, is elected president. Vowing to win the "war on poverty," Johnson works with Congress to develop a network of social programs more expansive than any since FRANKLIN ROOSEVELT's New Deal. Johnson also works to guarantee civil rights for minorities. Despite his unprecedented efforts at home, his administration is weakened by his inability to extricate the United States from the increasingly unpopular Vietnam War, and Johnson does not run for a second term.

Congress passes a powerful Civil Rights Act (see p. 138, 228).

The Twenty-fourth Amendment prohibits poll taxes.

The Wilderness Act becomes law (see p. 93).

1965 The Voting Rights Act makes the federal government responsible for ensuring that all citizens are allowed to vote (see p. 138).

The Department of Housing and Urban Development is created.

Medicare, which pays health-care expenses of senior citizens, is enacted.

1966 The National Organization for Women (NOW) is formed to push for greater political power and civil rights for women.

The Department of Transportation is established.

1967 THURGOOD MARSHALL becomes the first black Supreme Court justice.

Edward Brooke of Massachusetts becomes the first black senator since Reconstruction.

In re Gault is handed down by the Supreme Court. In this landmark ruling for youth, the Court finds that juveniles have the same constitutional rights as adults in legal proceedings.

THIRD PARTIES

Third parties in the American political system are possible but not likely. The high point may have been in 1912, when THEODORE ROOSEVELT, disgusted with the conservatism of his hand-picked successor, William Howard Taft, bolted from the Republican Party to form his own Progressive party, better known as the Bull Moose. He attracted 27 percent of the popular vote and eighty-eight electoral votes, putting Democrat WOODROW WILSON in the White House.

Before the Civil War, the most significant third parties were the Free-Soil Party, which in 1848 nominated ex-president Martin Van Buren and got 10 percent of the vote; and the American (or Know-Nothing) Party, which in 1856 ran ex-president Millard Fillmore and got 22 percent. On the brink of civil war, there were four serious contenders. In addition to ABRAHAM LINCOLN, the Republican, and Stephen A. Douglas, the Democrat, there was John C. Breckinridge, a southern Democrat, and John Bell of the Constitutional Union Party, which attempted to unite the remnants of the Whig and American Parties. But the nation seemed beyond a political solution, and when Abraham Lincoln won the presidency without a single electoral vote from a southern state, secession and civil war were inevitable.

Late in the nineteenth century, James B. Weaver's People's (or Populist) Party made a strong showing in 1892, attracting 9 percent of the popular vote, but, in 1896, the Democrats co-opted the Populists' message and candidate, WILLIAM JENNINGS BRYAN.

In the 1912 election, beside Roosevelt's spectacular showing with the Bull Moose Party, Eugene V. Debs, running on the Socialist Party ticket, got 6 percent of the vote. In 1924, Robert La Follette, running as a Progressive Party candidate (not the same party as Roosevelt's) got 17 percent. In 1948, Strom Thurmond, leading a group of southern Democrats who found HARRY TRUMAN too strong on civil rights, got 2 percent of the vote with his States' Rights Party, or Dixiecrats. Henry A. Wallace, running on yet another Progressive Party ticket, also got 2 percent. In 1968, George C. Wallace, another southerner who balked at his party's civil rights stand, ran as an American Independent and picked up 14 percent of the vote. John Anderson, in 1980, ran as an independent and got 7 percent. Finally, in one of the strongest showings ever, Ross Perot, running for an organization called United We Stand, America, that he said was not a political party, garnered 19 percent of the vote. In 1996, he formed the Reform Party but got less than 10 percent. Ralph Nader, the candidate for the Green Party, won nearly 3 percent of the vote in the hotly contested 2000 election.

Third parties have not done very well in national elections. Their chief successes have been in pushing issues onto the national agenda and getting major parties to adopt them as their own. The major parties, ever jealous of their priority, know that's one sure way to make a third party go away.

GOVERNMENT, POLITICS, & LAW

The Twenty-fifth Amendment is ratified, providing for the disability, death, or removal of the president.

1968 In a campaign marked by violence and unrest, Senator Robert Kennedy, a presidential candidate and the brother of President JOHN KENNEDY, is assassinated hours after a California-primary victory.

Even after protesters disrupt the televised Democratic National Convention, revealing the deep divisions within the Democratic Party, RICHARD NIXON, a Republican, has a difficult time getting elected. Alabama governor George Wallace mounts a creditable third-party effort. Hubert Humphrey does much better than anyone expects; less than 1 percentage point divides the two when all votes are counted. Nixon, like JOHNSON, will spend much of his term in office mired in the Vietnam War. His accomplishments are in foreign affairs; he establishes relations with China

1968, *cont.*

and détente with the Soviet Union. Domestically, he creates the Office of Management and Budget, an oversight agency for the federal budget.

SHIRLEY CHISHOLM is the first black woman elected to Congress.

The Kerner Commission cites widespread racial discrimination as the cause of racial unrest and riots in the 1960s.

1969 The Chicago Seven trial takes place as the leaders of the protest at the Democratic National Convention (Abbie Hoffman, Jerry Rubin, David Dellinger, Rennie Davis, Tom Hayden, John Froines, Lee Weiner, and Bobby Seale) are tried on charges of conspiracy to riot. They will be found not guilty, although five are convicted of lesser charges.

1970 The Environmental Protection Agency is established.

Congress passes the Occupational Safety and Health Act (OSHA).

1971 The Twenty-sixth Amendment lowers the voting age to eighteen.

1972 President RICHARD NIXON is reelected, but a burglary at Democratic National Headquarters, staged by persons representing the Republican Party, ultimately mars his victory; this affair and its subsequent cover-up, known as the Watergate scandal, eventually bring down his presidency.

The Supreme Court declares capital punishment unconstitutional, a decision that will be reversed in 1976.

The Equal Rights Amendment, banning discrimination on the basis of gender, is submitted to the states (see p. 224).

1973 President NIXON signs the Endangered Species Act, more wide-ranging than its 1966 predecessor.

Passed over President Nixon's veto, the War Powers Resolution limits presidential war-making power by establishing guidelines for military emergencies.

Charged with tax evasion, Vice President Spiro Agnew resigns and is replaced by Gerald Ford, the first person ever to hold his office without being elected.

In *Roe v. Wade*, the Supreme Court rules that women have a legal right to obtain abortions.

The Watergate hearings begin.

1974 The Budget and Impoundment Control Act strengthens the role of Congress in budget making.

When asked to turn over tape recordings that could implicate him in the Watergate crime, President NIXON claims executive immunity, but the Supreme Court finds that his privilege is not unlimited, as he claims. The House Judiciary Committee institutes impeachment proceedings against

President Nixon, who then becomes the first person to resign the presidency. Gerald Ford, a Republican, assumes the office. One of his first acts is to pardon Nixon. Ford is mostly a caretaker president, although he vetoes sixty-six bills in fewer than two years in office. Twelve of the vetoes are overridden.

1975 Several top advisors to former President RICHARD NIXON are found guilty in the Watergate trial.

Two unsuccessful attempts are made to assassinate President Gerald Ford.

1976 Jimmy Carter, a Democrat, is elected president. He makes human rights part of American foreign policy and pardons approximately 10,000 draft evaders from the Vietnam War. Although Carter negotiates the first important breakthrough in Middle East peace, this one-term president's administration is plagued by foreign policy problems and a troubled economy.

The Supreme Court reverses itself and rules that the death penalty is legal.

Jimmy Carter was the first American president born in a hospital.

1977 The Department of Energy, a cabinet-level post, is created, partly in response to concerns over fuel resources.

1978 The Supreme Court decides that reverse discrimination is illegal.

1979 The Department of Education is established.

Iranian Islamic militants seize the U.S. embassy in Tehran and hold fifty-two embassy employees hostage for 444 days. The humiliation contributes to Carter's defeat in the 1980 election.

1980 Republican Ronald Reagan is elected president. At sixty-nine, he is the oldest president when elected. Reagan presides over some of the largest tax cuts in U.S. history as well as the biggest buildup of the deficit, but neither this nor a scandal in which some of his top aides are found guilty of trading arms for hostages tarnishes the personal popularity of this president. Reagan wins passage of a major tax-reform bill. He survives an assassination attempt, though seriously wounded.

1981 SANDRA DAY O'CONNOR becomes the first woman Supreme Court justice.

President Ronald Reagan appoints conservatives who oppose quotas to the Civil Rights Commission and stirs up a controversy that nearly leads to the commission's demise. Congress renews its mandate in 1983, with the added provision that members have fixed terms.

1982 Three-fourths of the states having failed to ratify it even with an extended deadline, the proposed Equal Rights Amendment dies.

1984 Ronald Reagan is reelected.

SUPREME COURT JUSTICES OF THE UNITED STATES

JUSTICE	TERM	JUSTICE	TERM
John Jay*	1789–1795	John M. Harlan	1877–1911
John Blair	1789–1796	Stanley Matthews	1881–1889
William Cushing	1789–1810	William B. Woods	1881–1887
John Rutledge	1789–1791	Samuel Blatchford	1882–1893
James Wilson	1789–1798	Horace Gray	1881–1902
James Iredell	1790–1799	Melville W. Fuller*	1888–1910
Thomas Johnson	1791–1793	Lucius Q. C. Lamar	1888–1893
William Paterson	1793–1806	David J. Brewer	1890–1910
John Rutledge*	1795	Henry B. Brown	1891–1906
(Congress rejected his appointment as chief justice)		George Shiras Jr.	1892–1903
Oliver Ellsworth*	1796–1799	Howell E. Jackson	1893–1895
Samuel Chase	1796–1811	Edward D. White	1894–1910
Bushrod Washington	1798–1829	Rufus W. Peckham	1896–1909
Alfred Moore	1799–1804	Joseph McKenna	1898–1925
John Marshall*	1801–1835	Oliver W. Holmes Jr.	1902–1932
William Johnson	1804–1834	William R. Day	1903–1922
Henry Brockholst Livingston	1806–1823	William H. Moody	1906–1910
Thomas Todd	1807–1826	Edward D. White*	1910–1921
Joseph Story	1811–1845	Charles E. Hughes	1910–1916
Gabriel Duvall	1812–1835	Horace H. Lurton	1910–1914
Smith Thompson	1823–1843	Joseph R. Lamar	1911–1916
Robert Trimble	1826–1828	Willis Van Devanter	1911–1937
John McLean	1829–1861	Mahlon Pitney	1912–1922
Henry Baldwin	1830–1844	James C. McReynolds	1914–1941
James M. Wayne	1835–1867	Louis D. Brandeis	1916–1939
Roger B. Taney*	1836–1864	John H. Clarke	1916–1922
Philip P. Barbour	1836–1841	William H. Taft*	1921–1930
John Catron	1837–1865	Pierce Butler	1922–1939
John McKinley	1837–1852	George Sutherland	1922–1938
Peter V. Daniel	1841–1860	Edward T. Sanford	1923–1930
Samuel Nelson	1845–1872	Harlan F. Stone	1925–1941
Levi Woodbury	1845–1851	Charles E. Hughes*	1930–1941
Robert C. Grier	1846–1870	Owen J. Roberts	1930–1945
Benjamin R. Curtis	1851–1857	Benjamin N. Cardozo	1932–1938
John A. Campbell	1853–1861	Hugo L. Black	1937–1971
Nathan Clifford	1858–1881	Stanley F. Reed	1938–1957
David Davis	1862–1877	William O. Douglas	1939–1975
Samuel F. Miller	1862–1890	Felix Frankfurter	1939–1962
Noah H. Swayne	1862–1881	Frank Murphy	1940–1949
Stephen J. Field	1863–1897	Harlan F. Stone*	1941–1946
Salmon P. Chase*	1964–1873	James F. Byrnes	1941–1942
Joseph P. Bradley	1870–1892	Robert H. Jackson	1941–1954
William Strong	1870–1880	Wiley B. Rutledge	1943–1949
Ward Hunt	1873–1882	Harold H. Burton	1945–1958
Morrison R. Waite*	1874–1888	Fred M. Vinson*	1946–1953

JUSTICE	TERM	JUSTICE	TERM
Tom C. Clark	1949–1967	Harry A. Blackmun	1970–1994
Sherman Minton	1949–1956	Lewis F. Powell Jr.	1971–1987
Earl Warren*	1953–1969	William H. Rehnquist*	1971–
John Marshall Harlan	1955–1971	John Paul Stevens III	1975–
William J. Brennan Jr.	1956–1990	Sandra Day O'Connor	1981–
Charles E. Whittaker	1957–1962	Antonin Scalia	1986–
Potter Stewart	1958–1981	Anthony Kennedy	1988–
Arthur J. Goldberg	1962–1965	David H. Souter	1990–
Byron R. White	1962–1993	Clarence Thomas	1991–
Abe Fortas	1965–1969	Ruth Bader Ginsburg	1993–
Thurgood Marshall	1967–1991	Stephen G. Breyer	1994–
Warren E. Burger*	1969–1986		

*Chief justice

Timeline, *cont.*

1988 George H. W. Bush, a Republican, is elected president. His administration is beset by an ailing economy after the boom of the early 1980s comes to an abrupt end. Unable to jump-start the economy, Bush is also seen by many Americans as uncaring on domestic issues. Despite this, his popularity does not plummet—largely due to the apparent success of the war against Iraq—until the very end of his presidency.

1992 Bill Clinton, a Democrat, is elected president, defeating incumbent George Bush. A notable feature of the campaign is the candidacy of Ross Perot, who wins 19 percent of the popular vote but no electoral votes. This is an achievement second only to THEODORE ROOSEVELT's in 1912. Plagued by an uncooperative Congress, Clinton manages to bring down the deficit a small amount each year, largely by increasing taxes and cutting spending. He creates Americorps, a national service program, but fails to achieve major national health-care reform.

The Twenty-seventh Amendment, prohibiting Congress from raising its own pay within a session, is ratified—after 203 years! It was first proposed in 1789 as part of a package that became the Bill of Rights, ratified by only six of the thirteen original states, then practically forgotten until revived in 1982 by a student at the University of Texas.

1994 Newt Gingrich becomes an unusually powerful Speaker of the House following a Republican landslide in the congressional elections.

1995–1996 The White House and the Republican-dominated Congress reach an impasse over the fiscal year 1996 budget. President Clinton refuses to agree to Republican cuts; the Republican leadership also refuses to negotiate, and the government shuts down for three weeks. Clinton's stand boosts his approval rating at the Republicans' expense.

1996 President Clinton is reelected.

1998 Democratic successes in national midterm elections reduce the Republican majority in Congress and force Speaker Newt Gingrich to resign.

1999 President Clinton is acquitted on two articles of impeachment stemming from the Lewinsky affair, ending a thirty-seven-day trial but not the eighteen-month national preoccupation with the scandal.

2000 In the closest and most controversial presidential election in U.S. history, Republican George W. Bush is declared the winner over incumbent Democratic Vice President Al Gore after a protracted series of proceedings in Florida state and federal courts. The major point of contention is the counting of ballots in Florida, whose electoral votes are decisive but whose popular vote is eyelash close. The issue is finally resolved by the U.S. Supreme Court.

Vermont becomes the first state to sanction gay marriage, or "civil union."

2001 The 107th Congress takes up the issue of campaign finance reform, made prominent in the 2000 Republican primary campaign by Senator John McCain of Arizona. Tax cuts, a centerpiece of the Bush campaign, and how to allocate the budget surplus are other items high on the legislative agenda. The 107th Congress also enacts major tax cuts, a centerpiece of the Bush campaign.

Vermont senator Jim Jeffords causes an uproar when he switches affiliations from Republican to Independent, giving the Democrats control of the Senate.

2002 The Department of Homeland Security is created with Tom Ridge as its head.

TEN SCANDALS IN AMERICAN POLITICS

Political corruption is nothing new, predating the country itself. Colonial governors were involved in land, customs, and military scams. In contemporary times, only the administration of FRANKLIN ROOSEVELT, JOHN KENNEDY, and LYNDON JOHNSON have been, relatively speaking, among the most scandal-free.

1797–1798 XYZ Affair. The new nation encountered a foreign affairs scandal when President JOHN ADAMS sent three prominent envoys to France, with a mandate to establish trade and amity between the two nations. The envoys were told by French agents (later designated in documents X, Y, and Z) that they would need to pay bribes to achieve their ends. The American envoys refused. When word of the requested bribe became public knowledge in the United States, Americans were scandalized and the trade talks collapsed. "Millions for defense, not one cent for tribute!" was the slogan that helped galvanize anti-French feeling.

1807 AARON BURR's Trial. Burr, brilliant but bristly, seemed to annoy everyone. His career in politics appeared to be over after he killed political foe ALEXANDER HAMILTON in a duel. But when Burr became involved in a scheme to carve an independent nation out of the American Southwest, President THOMAS JEFFERSON, another political foe, ordered him arrested for treason. Burr's trial was a highly partisan event, although Burr was eventually acquitted.

1871 Tammany Hall. The quintessential political machine, Tammany Hall won elections for New York City Democrats by paying voters and then rewarding them with jobs. Boss William Marcy Tweed was arrested in 1871 and eventually imprisoned for graft. Although the Tweed Ring was gone, Tammany survived until the 1940s when Mayor Fiorello La Guardia's attack finally ended its power (see p. 260).

1872–1873 Crédit Mobilier scandal. Ulysses Grant's administration was wracked with major and minor corruption scandals. The worst revolved around an attempt to divert into public officials' hands funds for building the Union Pacific Railroad. A dummy company called Crédit Mobilier was created to hold the funds, in the form of stocks, for high-level Republicans and other government officials. The scandal ended the political career of Vice President Schuyler Colfax and led to the reprimand of two congressmen.

1923–1924 Teapot Dome Affair. Warren G. Harding's presidency was also plagued by scandal and corruption, the worst being the last. Secretary of the Interior Albert Fall accepted a $100,000 interest-free loan and additional "loans" for oil-leasing rights to a site called Teapot Dome. Convicted of bribery, Fall paid a fine and spent a year in jail. Harding died unexpectedly just as the scandal was breaking.

1972–1974 Watergate Scandal. The granddaddy of all political scandals, this affair toppled the presidency of RICHARD NIXON, who was the only U.S. president ever to resign. It began when some low-level political operatives in the employ of the Committee to Re-elect the President (CREEP) burglarized the Democratic National Committee's headquarters. What started as an attempt to sabotage the Democratic challengers soon led to an illegal cover-up. Nixon resigned the presidency the day after the House Judiciary Committee voted three articles of impeachment.

1980 Abscam scandal. Under Jimmy Carter's presidency, members of Congress were caught in a sting operation. FBI agents posing as sheiks offered bribes in exchange for introducing legislation. Six representatives and one senator were found guilty of bribery.

1986–1988 Iran-Contra Affair. President Ronald Reagan's National Security Council undertook a series of covert operations in which they sold arms to Iran in hopes that hostages held by pro-Iranian forces in Lebanon would be released. Profits from the arms sales were diverted, in defiance of Congress, to contra forces in Nicaragua, seeking to topple a Marxist Sandinista government (see p. 300).

1991 Keating Five. Charles H. Keating, a wealthy banker, had asked five senators, all of whom had received large campaign contributions from him, to

TEN SCANDALS, cont.

convince federal regulators not to examine his savings and loan, which eventually failed. The affair highlighted the connection between money and influence in Congress.

1998–1999 Lewinsky Affair. President Bill Clinton, accused of lying under oath to federal prosecutors that he did not have sexual relations with young White House intern Monica Lewinsky, was acquitted on two articles of impeachment in February 1999. The glare of public scrutiny and disillusionment of White House staff, however, proved damaging to his administration and likely to its legacy.

California artist Robbie Conal created this poster critical of President Reagan after the Iran-Contra scandal broke.

POLITICAL PROTEST AND DISSENT, 1712–PRESENT

Not surprisingly for a nation born out of revolution, Americans have resorted to organized civil disobedience—and rebellion—when they have felt abused by the government. In the early days of the nation, the reason was usually taxes, but since the turn of the century most protest has centered around the struggle for individual rights.

1712 Slave Uprising. About two dozen armed slaves march through lower Manhattan, killing at least nine whites, mostly women and children, before they are apprehended. About twenty of the rebels are sentenced to die and indeed are tortured to death, thus setting a precedent for punishment of slave revolts.

1786–1787 Shays' Rebellion. Led by Revolutionary War veteran Daniel Shays, farmers in Massachusetts protest high taxes and strict foreclosure laws. The rebellion triggers protests by farmers in other states and fuels public sentiment that a stronger central government is needed, which in turn leads to the convening of the Constitutional Convention in 1787.

1794 The Whiskey Rebellion. In the first test of the new government's power, Pennsylvania farmers are subdued with armed power when they protest a liquor tax.

1799 Fries's Rebellion. Among the militia who put down the Whiskey Rebellion is John Fries, who now finds himself on the other side when he leads Pennsylvania farmers in revolt against tax assessors. Later found guilty of treason and sentenced to die, his sentence is pardoned by President JOHN ADAMS.

1800 Gabriel's Rebellion. In one of several planned slave uprisings that don't happen but nevertheless have great psychological impact on slaveowners and slaves, Gabriel Prosser, an abolitionist preacher, makes plans to march on Richmond, Virginia. A storm on the night of the gathering washes out the roads and scatters his armed cohorts, but slaveowners who hear of the plan punish and restrict their slaves anyway.

1831 Nat Turner's Rebellion. Of the hundreds of slave rebellions, this is the one that most frightens whites and constricts the lives of slaves. In a region of small farms in southeastern Virginia, a band of five slaves, which soon expands to eighty, is led by Nat Turner in a march through the countryside, killing sixty whites before they are finally stopped by the militia. To the utter terror of slaveowners, Turner himself remains at large for several weeks, but eventually he and about twenty of his followers are caught and executed. Most slave uprisings, like this one, take place not on plantations, where slaves are strictly guarded, but in towns and on small farms, where slaves are less constrained physically.

1848 Seneca Falls Convention. Organized by Lucretia Mott and ELIZABETH CADY STANTON, the convention, held in Seneca Falls, New York, in July, was the first major event in the struggle for women's rights. Participants drafted a Declaration of Sentiments, modeled after the Declaration of Independence, calling for equal rights for women in education, property, employment, and voting.

1859 Harpers Ferry. John Brown, a white abolitionist active in Kansas border wars who is determined to keep slavery out of the state, gathers followers and moves to Harpers Ferry, Virginia, where his band seizes a government arsenal. His intention is to incite a slave rebellion and establish a slave sanctuary and stronghold that will end slavery in the South, but local militia and federal troops stop him. In a nation increasingly divided over slavery, Brown's rebellion is a pivotal event. He is a martyred hero to abolitionists.

1863 Civil War Draft Riots. The worst of these take place in New York City, where Irish and other new immigrants protest the fact that wealthy draftees can buy their way out of military service. Their rage is misdirected at blacks, and at least forty people, mostly African Americans, die in the riot.

1913 Woman Suffrage Parade. Suffragists Alice Paul, Lucy Burns, and others organized a "Woman Suffrage Parade." Over 5,000 marchers arrived in Washington, D.C., the day before WOODROW WILSON's inauguration. The event, marked by a great deal of pageantry and some violence, helped draw national attention to the suffrage movement.

1932 Bonus March. At the height of the Great Depression, World War I veterans descended on Washington seeking payment of a cash bonus promised them at the end of the war. By July, 25,000 protesters were camped out in makeshift lodgings in a "Hooverville" on the Anacostia River. When the Senate vetoed the Patman Bonus Bill, nearly 20,000 veterans marched on Pennsylvania Avenue. At the end of the month, Gen. Douglas MacArthur moved in on the protesters, chasing them out of the city. At the end of the ordeal, four people were dead and the Anacostia camp was burned to the ground, contributing to the negative public opinion of President Hoover. After congressional debate in the ROOSEVELT administration, the veterans were awarded $2.5 billion.

1955–1956 Montgomery Boycott. Following Rosa Park's arrest for refusing to give up her seat to a white person on a city bus, the blacks of Montgomery, Alabama, boycott city buses for more than a year. The boycott produces a Supreme Court ruling outlawing segregation on buses and catapults Reverend Martin Luther King Jr. into the leadership of the emerging civil rights movement.

1961 Freedom Riders Protest. An interracial group of protesters organized by the Congress of Racial Equality (CORE) rides buses throughout the South attempting to test the desegregation of bus station rest rooms, waiting rooms, and restaurants. A mob attacks the buses in Alabama. The first bus is set on fire, and those who flee it are beaten—all in full view of television cameras covering the story (see p. 125).

1963 Birmingham Protest. Martin Luther King Jr. and the Southern Christian Leadership Conference (SCLC) plan to desegregate Birmingham, Alabama, department stores. Violence erupts as the number of protesters swells. Bombs are set off at SCLC headquarters and in a black church, where four little girls die. Thousands are arrested, including King, who writes

POLITICAL PROTEST AND DISSENT, 1712–PRESENT, cont.

his eloquent Letter from Birmingham Jail, outlining the justification for direct action (see p. 127).

1964 Freedom Summer. White college students converge on Mississippi to work with local blacks to mount a voter registration drive. Two white students, Michael Schwerner and Andrew Goodman, and one local black youth, James Chaney, are beaten to death. Their bodies are not found for six weeks.

1964–1973 Vietnam War Protests. Opposition to the increasingly unpopular war gives rise to protests, teach-ins, bombings, break-ins, and destruction of draft records. In 1967, 50,000 protesters descend on the Pentagon. Two years later, the "Catonsville Nine" burn draft records in Maryland and antiwar activists gather on college campuses nationwide. A 1969 protest at Kent State University in Ohio leaves four students dead, and, in May of the same year, several hundred thousand protesters march on Washington.

1965 Selma Protests. Selma, Alabama, is targeted by Martin Luther King Jr.'s organization for voter registration. Protesters and police clash, and the ensuing publicity draws attention to the need for a national voting rights act, which is soon passed.

1968 Chicago Police Riot. Thousands of youthful antiwar activists converge on the Democratic National Convention in Chicago, chanting, "The whole world is watching"—and indeed it is, for the first time, thanks to satellite television. Mayor Richard Daley orders 22,000 armed police officers, the National Guard, and federal troops to deal with the protesters, and at least 1,000 are clubbed in what is termed a police riot. Seven antiwar leaders, known as the Chicago Seven, are tried on conspiracy and other charges, and five are found guilty of lesser charges. Black Panther Bobby Seale is tried separately.

1969 The Stonewall Riot. Protesting police raids and harassment, gay people take to the streets in anger in Greenwich Village, New York, and the gay rights movement is born.

1999 In a scene reminiscent of the 1960s, thousands of angry demonstrators, including union members, environmentalists, and other interest groups, take to the streets of Seattle in late November to protest the annual World Trade Organization (WTO) summit and the global trading policies of the United States and other members. Police use tear gas to disperse the protesters, and violence breaks out.

This 1979 poster announces events celebrating the tenth anniversary of the Stonewall Riot.

WOMEN AND POLITICS, 1776–PRESENT

1776 ABIGAIL ADAMS appeals to her husband, JOHN ADAMS, and his colleagues in the Continental Congress to "Remember the Ladies" and consider granting women some rights in the new code of laws.

The New Jersey Constitution grants the right to vote to "all free inhabitants," thus enfranchising women until 1807, when a new state constitution restricts suffrage to males.

1848 The Women's Rights Convention, the first public meeting to advocate for women's rights, is held in Seneca Falls, New York. Led by ELIZABETH CADY STANTON and Lucretia Mott, participants issue a "Declaration of Sentiments" denouncing tyranny of men and demanding equal rights for women under the law and in public and private life. A series of similar meetings follow.

1864 Anna Elizabeth Dickson, who addresses the House of Representatives on abolition and women's rights, is considered the first woman to speak before Congress.

1869 SUSAN B. ANTHONY and ELIZABETH CADY STANTON found the National Woman Suffrage Association, whose goal is to obtain the vote for women.

The Wyoming Territory grants women the right to vote.

1872 Victoria Woodhull is the first woman to run for president.

1878 A constitutional amendment to grant women the right to vote is introduced in Congress.

1890 Two rival suffrage organizations, the National Woman Suffrage Association and the American Woman Suffrage Association, unite to form the National American Woman Suffrage Association.

1912 When she is appointed director of the Children's Bureau, Julia Clifford Lathrop becomes the first woman to head a federal agency.

1916 The National Woman's Party is founded with the purpose of obtaining the vote for women.

1917 JEANNETTE RANKIN, a Montana Republican, becomes the first woman elected to the House of Representatives.

1920 The Nineteenth Amendment passes, granting women the right to vote.

The League of Women Voters is organized to educate women about politics and promote the status and rights of women.

1923 An Equal Rights Amendment is first introduced in Congress.

1924 Nellie Ross is elected governor of Wyoming, and Miriam ("Ma") Ferguson is elected in Texas, the first women to serve as state chief executives.

1929 Appointed to the U.S. Customs Court by President Coolidge, Genevieve Cline is the first woman to serve as a federal judge.

1932 Hattie Wyatt Caraway, a Democrat from Arkansas, is the first woman elected to the Senate.

1933 Secretary of Labor FRANCES PERKINS becomes the first woman appointed to a cabinet position.

1940 Elected to serve out her husband's term, Margaret Chase Smith of Maine serves in and is reelected to the House and is elected to the Senate in 1948, the first woman to serve in both chambers.

1945 ELEANOR ROOSEVELT becomes the first former first lady to be appointed to a public position when she assumes the post of U.N. delegate.

1966 The National Organization for Women, the first powerful women's group to advocate for women's legal rights since the nineteenth century, is organized. Betty Friedan, author of *The Feminine Mystique* (1963), a book that changed women's consciousness about their personal and political status, is a founder and the first president.

GOVERNMENT, POLITICS, & LAW

WOMEN AND POLITICS, 1776–PRESENT, cont.

1972 The Equal Rights Amendment is approved by Congress, although it must still be ratified by the states. Leaders of the women's movement, such as Betty Friedan and Gloria Steinem, work hard to ensure the ratification of the Equal Rights Amendment and continue to advocate for equality on other fronts as well. In 1982, the amendment is three states short of the ratification requirements and fails. It will be unsuccessfully reintroduced in Congress in the same year.

1979 Patricia Roberts Harris becomes the first woman ever to hold two cabinet posts. She is appointed to Housing and Urban Development in 1977 and in 1979 heads Health, Education, and Welfare.

1981 SANDRA DAY O'CONNOR is the first woman Supreme Court justice.

1982 The Equal Rights Amendment fails to achieve ratification.

1984 New York Democrat GERALDINE FERRARO is the first woman ever nominated by a major political party to run for vice president.

1993 Newly inaugurated president Bill Clinton appoints his wife, lawyer Hillary Rodham Clinton, to head his task force on national health care.

Carol Moseley Braun, an Illinois Democrat, becomes the first black woman to serve as a U.S. senator. She serves one term and then loses her bid for reelection in 1998.

1997 Madeleine Albright is appointed secretary of state by President Bill Clinton. She is the first woman to hold that office.

1999 ELIZABETH DOLE becomes the first woman to conduct a serious campaign for the U.S. presidency, seeking the Republican Party nomination. She withdraws from the race in October after mixed success.

Feminist writer Betty Freidan, First Lady Rosalynn Carter, and former first lady Betty Ford are among the women campaigning for the Equal Rights Amendment in Houston, Texas, in 1977.

WELFARE OF CHILDREN, 1886–PRESENT

During the colonial era and for many years afterward, as in most parts of the world, children were permitted to work, if not on the family farm or in the shop, then as apprentices. Gradually, however, the United States joined other progressive nations in outlawing child labor and turned its attention to child welfare (see p. 324).

1886 The Knights of Labor, at the height of its membership and power, advocates the abolition of child labor.

1904 The National Child Labor Committee is organized to eliminate child labor.

1912 The Children's Bureau is established in the Labor Department to monitor and enforce child labor laws, issue reports, and promote the protection of children.

1916 Congress passes the Child Labor Act, also known as the Keating-Owen Act, which bars any company involved in interstate commerce from employing a child under age fourteen.

Renowned photographer Lewis Hine captured the plight of child laborers in his work.

1918 In *Hammer v. Dagenhart,* the Supreme Court rules that the Keating-Owen Act is unconstitutional.

1924 Congress passes a constitutional amendment making child labor illegal, but it fails to be ratified by the states.

1935 Title V of the Social Security Act provides the nation's first maternal and child health services, including Aid to Families with Dependent Children.

1938 The Fair Labor Standards Act prohibits manufacturing and mining businesses involved in interstate commerce from employing anyone under age sixteen.

1941 The Supreme Court upholds the constitutionality of the Fair Labor Standards Act.

1949 The Fair Labor Standards Act is amended to cover more industries.

1950 With only twenty-six states having ratified the 1924 constitutional amendment to outlaw child labor (thirty-six are needed), the bill is dropped.

1964 Head Start, primarily an educational program for disadvantaged preschool children, provides some emergency health and social services.

1965 The Elementary and Secondary School Act provides aid to schools based on the number of poor children.

The Medicaid program, enacted under a new extensive federal welfare law, provides medical services to indigent children and is later expanded to include preventive health services.

1972 The Special Supplemental Food Program for Women, Infants, and Children (WIC) is the first major support for mothers and children. It grows out of nutrition programs and does not exist initially as a separate program.

1990s Because of mounting budget deficits, Congress debates cuts in programs that may affect women and children.

1998 Federal legislation provides states with $48 billion over ten years to broaden efforts to provide children with health insurance. Children are believed to make up about 25 percent of the nation's 40 million uninsured.

1999 The U.S. Supreme Court requires public schools to accommodate the nonmedical needs of disabled schoolchildren at public expense.

GOVERNMENT, POLITICS, & LAW

PRESIDENTS AND VICE PRESIDENTS OF THE UNITED STATES

PRESIDENT	TERM	BIRTH AND DEATH	PARTY	VICE PRESIDENT
1. George Washington	1789–1793 1793–1797	1732–1799	F	John Adams
2. John Adams	1797–1801	1735–1826	F	Thomas Jefferson
3. Thomas Jefferson	1801–1805 1805–1809	1743–1826	D-R	Aaron Burr George Clinton
4. James Madison	1809–1813 1813–1817	1751–1836	D-R	George Clinton Elbridge Gerry
5. James Monroe	1817–1821 1821–1825	1758–1831	D-R	Daniel D. Tompkins
6. John Quincy Adams	1825–1829	1767–1848	D-R	John C. Calhoun
7. Andrew Jackson	1829–1833 1833–1837	1767–1845	D-R	John C. Calhoun Martin Van Buren
8. Martin Van Buren	1837–1841	1782–1862	D	Richard M. Johnson
9. William Henry Harrison	3/4–4/4 1841	1773–1841	W	John Tyler
10. John Tyler	1841–1845	1790–1862	W	—
11. James K. Polk	1845–1849	1795–1864	D	George M. Dallas
12. Zachary Taylor	1849–1850 1784–1850	W Millard Fillmore		
13. Millard Fillmore	1850–1853	1800–1874	W	—
14. Franklin Pierce	1853–1857	1804–1869	D	William R. King
15. James Buchanan	1857–1861	1791–1868	D	John C. Breckinridge
16. Abraham Lincoln	1861–1865 3/4–4/15 1865	1809–1865	R	Hannibal Hamlin Andrew Johnson
17. Andrew Johnson	1865–1869	1808–1875	NU	—
18. Ulysses S. Grant	1869–1873 1873–1877	1822–1885	R	Schuyler Colfax Henry Wilson

PRESIDENT	TERM	BIRTH AND DEATH	PARTY	VICE PRESIDENT
19. Rutherford B. Hayes	1877–1881	1822–1893	R	William A. Wheeler
20. James Garfield	3/4–9/19 1881	1831–1881	R	Chester A. Arthur
21. Chester A. Arthur	1881–1885	1829–1886	R	—
22. Grover Cleveland	1885–1889	1837–1908	D	Thomas A. Hendricks
23. Benjamin Harrison	1889–1893	1833–1901	R	Levi P. Morton
24. Grover Cleveland	1893–1897	1837–1908	D	Adlai E. Stevenson
25. William McKinley	1897–1901 3/4–9/14 1901	1843–1901	R	Garret A. Hobart Theodore Roosevelt
26. Theodore Roosevelt	1901–1905 1905–1909	1858–1919	R	— Charles W. Fairbanks
27. William H. Taft	1909–1913	1857–1930	R	James S. Sherman
28. Woodrow Wilson	1913–1917 1917–1921	1856–1924	D	Thomas R. Marshall
29. Warren G. Harding	1921–1923	1865–1923	R	Calvin Coolidge
30. Calvin Coolidge	1923–1925 1925–1929	1872–1933	R	— Charles G. Dawes
31. Herbert C. Hoover	1929–1933	1874–1964	R	Charles Curtis
32. Franklin D. Roosevelt	1933–1936 1936–1941 1941–1945 1/20–4/12 1945	1882–1945	D	John N. Garner Henry A. Wallace Harry S. Truman
33. Harry S. Truman	1945–1949 1949–1953	1884–1972	D	— Alben W. Barkley
34. Dwight D. Eisenhower	1953–1961	1890–1969	R	Richard M. Nixon
35. John F. Kennedy	1961–1963	1917–1963	D	Lyndon B. Johnson

GOVERNMENT, POLITICS, & LAW

PRESIDENTS AND VICE PRESIDENTS OF THE UNITED STATES, cont.

PRESIDENT	TERM	BIRTH AND DEATH	PARTY	VICE PRESIDENT
36. Lyndon B. Johnson	1963–1965 1965–1969	1908–1973	D	— Hubert H. Humphrey
37. Richard M. Nixon	1969–1973 1973–1974	1913–1994	R	Spiro T. Agnew Gerald R. Ford
38. Gerald R. Ford	1974–1977	1913–	R	Nelson A. Rockefeller
39. James (Jimmy) Earl Carter, Jr.	1977–1981	1924–	D	Walter F. Mondale
40. Ronald Reagan	1981–1985 1985–1989	1911–	R	George H. W. Bush
41. George H. W. Bush	1989–1993	1924–	R	J. Danforth (Dan) Quayle
42. William (Bill) Clinton	1993–1997 1997–2001	1946–	D	Albert (Al) Gore
43. George W. Bush	2001–	1946–	R	Richard (Dick) Cheney

F=Federalist; D-R=Democratic-Republican; D=Democrat; W=Whig; R=Republican; NU=National Union party; a coalition of Republicans and War Democrats (Andrew Johnson was a Democrat)

LEGISLATION AFFECTING INDIVIDUAL AND COLLECTIVE RIGHTS, 1866–PRESENT

1866 Civil Rights Act. This initial civil rights act grants the rights of citizenship to all persons born in the United States, and is specifically intended to cover former slaves. Native Americans are excluded.

1875 Civil Rights Act. This is the first act to address the issue of equality on a broader scale, by ordering that public places and accommodations be open to all. In 1883, the Supreme Court rules this legislation unconstitutional.

1957 Civil Rights Act. This first important piece of civil rights legislation since Reconstruction signals renewed government interest in protecting the rights of minorities. The most important element of the act is the establishment of the Civil Rights Commission. Although intended to be temporary, the commission has survived to the present day.

1964 Civil Rights Act. The most comprehensive piece of legislation on civil rights, this act prohibits discrimination in public places, in public spending or government contracts, and in employment. The latter clause is enforced by the Equal Employment Opportunity Commission (EEOC), which is also created by the act.

1965 Voting Rights Act. The right to vote is enforced by the federal government, which is also given the right to review state voting laws. Literacy tests as a requisite to voting are banned.

1967 Age Discrimination in Employment Act. This act prohibits job discrimination against employees aged forty to sixty-five. An amendment in 1986 eliminates mandatory retirement.

1968 Fair Housing Act. The act prohibits discrimination in sales and rentals on the basis of race, color, religion, or national origin.

1988 Civil Rights Restoration Act. This act counters a Supreme Court decision by affirming that antibias provisions apply to an entire institution even if only one department in it is receiving federal funds.

1991 Americans with Disabilities Act. This act prohibits discrimination based on disability in employment, public accommodation, and public services and requires that facilities be made accessible to people with disabilities.
Civil Rights Act. This act strengthens civil rights enforcement by countering the specifics of nine Supreme Court decisions.

SUPREME COURT DECISIONS AFFECTING GOVERNMENT, POLITICS, AND LAW, 1803–PRESENT

1803 *Marbury v. Madison.* The Supreme Court establishes the right to review the constitutionality of acts of Congress.

1810 *Fletcher v. Peck.* The Court, for the first time, overturns a state law violating the Constitution. In this case an act of the Georgia legislature is held to impair "the obligation of contracts."

1816 *Martin v. Hunter's Lessee.* The Supreme Court establishes the right of the federal judiciary to review state court decisions involving constitutional issues.

1819 *McCulloch v. Maryland.* The Supreme Court, in deciding that the federal government has a right to charter a national bank, establishes that the federal government has implied powers beyond those expressly stated in the Constitution. The case greatly enhances the power of the federal government to do what is "necessary and proper" to run the country.
Dartmouth College v. Woodward. The Court rules that a charter issued to a private corporation is a contract protected by the Constitution.

1842 *Prigg v. Pennsylvania.* The Court rules that state laws obstructing the capture and return of slaves are unconstitutional.

1857 *Dred Scott v. Sandford.* The Court declares that Congress cannot prohibit slavery in the territories and that African Americans are not citizens and have no legal standing. The Court also rules that the federal government cannot deprive a person of his property, including slaves.

1883 *Civil Rights Cases.* The Court strikes down the Civil Rights Act of 1875, saying that "social rights" are beyond federal control but blacks cannot be excluded from juries.

1896 *Plessy v. Ferguson.* The Supreme Court accepts the principle of "separate but equal" facilities for blacks and whites in public transportation and by implication other public facilities and education, thus instituting an era of legal segregation that will last until 1954.

1919 *Schenck v. United States.* In its first major First Amendment decision, the Court sustains the Espionage Act and finds that free speech can be constrained if the words used "present a clear and present danger."

1925 *Gitlow v. New York.* The Court decides that states cannot interfere with free speech any more than the federal government can. This decision also establishes that the Fourteenth Amendment, guaranteeing all citizens the right of due process, extends to state as well as federal actions.

SUPREME COURT DECISIONS AFFECTING GOVERNMENT, POLITICS, & LAW, 1803–present, cont.

1951 *Dennis et al v. United States.* The Supreme Court upholds the Smith Act of 1940, which made it a crime to advocate the overthrow of the government by force.

1957 *Yates v. United States.* The Court modifies its earlier ruling in *Dennis et al v. United States* to protect free speech advocating the overthrow of the government in the abstract so long as it is not connected to any actions.

1961 *Mapp v. Ohio.* In the first of several decisions extending the rights of those accused of crimes, the Court finds that evidence obtained through illegal search and seizure is inadmissible in court.

1962 *Baker v. Carr.* The Court rules that arbitrarily drawn federal districts violate constitutional rights and voters have the right to challenge reapportionment. This overturns an earlier decision that found such issues to be political rather than constitutional.

1963 *Gideon v. Wainwright.* The Supreme Court decides that free legal counseling must be provided to indigent persons accused of felonies.

1964 *Griswold v. Connecticut.* The Court rules that a ban on the use of contraceptives and on medical advice concerning them is unconstitutional and reinforces the notion of privacy as a constitutional right.

1966 *Miranda v. Arizona.* The Court decides that before those accused of a crime can be interviewed by the police, they must be informed of their rights, which include the right to remain silent, the fact that anything they say can be used against them, and the right to counsel.

1973 *Roe v. Wade.* The Court rules that the right to privacy protects a woman's decision whether to bear a child. State laws that make abortion a crime are overturned.

1975 *Goss v. Lopez.* The Court finds that suspended students are entitled to notice and a hearing before any disciplinary action can be taken against them.

1978 *University of California Regents v. Bakke.* The Court declares that affirmative-action programs with required racial quotas are unconstitutional, thus undermining one of the major strategies that has been used for several decades to equalize opportunity.

1986 *Bowers v. Hardwick.* In upholding a Georgia law prohibiting sodomy that was enforced only against same-sex couples, the Court declines to extend to same-sex couples the same rights of privacy extended to heterosexual couples.

1992 *R.A.V. v. St. Paul.* The Court upholds the right to "symbolic speech," including burning crosses.

1996 *United States v. Virginia.* In a highly publicized ruling, the Court holds that the exclusion of women from the Virginia Military Institute violates the constitutional guarantee of equal protection and orders the school to end single-sex admissions.

1998 *Clinton v. New York.* The Court strikes down the Line Item Veto Act of 1996, which gave the president the power to cancel specific appropriation items in bills he had already signed into law.

In a series of four cases, the Court issues guidelines on sexual harassment, a form of gender discrimination prohibited under Title VII of the Civil Rights Act of 1964.

2000 *Dickerson v. United States.* The Court reaffirms the Miranda decision.

NOTABLE FIGURES IN GOVERNMENT, POLITICS, AND LAW

Adams, Abigail (1744–1818). The wife of the second U.S. president, JOHN ADAMS, Adams is best remembered for admonishing her husband and his fellow delegates at the Constitutional Congress in 1776 to "Remember the Ladies" when they wrote laws for the new nation.

Adams, John (1735–1826). The second U.S. president and a signer of the Declaration of Independence, Adams also helped negotiate the peace with Britain and served as a minister to that country. His son, John Quincy Adams, was the sixth president.

Anthony, Susan B. (1820–1906). A feminist reformer, Anthony cofounded, along with ELIZABETH CADY STANTON, the National Woman Suffrage Association, the first major organization to work in behalf of women's right to vote. She is also the first woman to be depicted on a U.S. coin, the Susan B. Anthony silver dollar.

Black, Hugo L. (1886–1971). As a Supreme Court justice, Black was a strong advocate of unfettered civil liberties, free speech, and the Fourteenth Amendment, which guarantees due process to all persons.

Brandeis, Louis Dembitz (1856–1941). A Supreme Court justice, Brandeis was the first person to use statistics, demographics, and other sociological factors, in addition to the traditional legal analysis, to shape legal arguments, and his strategy became the model for what is known as the Brandeis brief. He showed a remarkable understanding of industrialization and its effects on the law and helped to shape business law. He was an advocate of judicial liberalism and social reform.

Bryan, William Jennings (1860–1925). This Democratic party leader and three-time presidential candidate served as secretary of state under WOODROW WILSON and resigned rather than abandon his isolationist policy in the face of World War I. Bryan supported women's suffrage and women's rights but, as a religious fundamentalist, increasingly opposed the evolution theory, eventually serving on the prosecution team in the Scopes Monkey trial (see p. 367).

Burr, Aaron (1756–1836). One of the more irascible persons ever to cross the American political landscape, Burr was a New York attorney general, a senator, and vice president under THOMAS JEFFERSON. An ongoing political feud with ALEXANDER HAMILTON led to a duel and Hamilton's death. The incident ended Burr's political career. When he became involved in a scheme to carve a new nation out of the American Southwest, he was arrested for treason, but acquitted in 1807.

Calhoun, John C. (1782–1850). With HENRY CLAY, DANIEL WEBSTER, and ANDREW JACKSON, Calhoun was one of the powerful political figures of his time. A secretary of war, vice president, senator from South Carolina, secretary of state, and political theorist, he defended the institution of slavery, promoted nullification, and predicted the demise of the Union if the slave states were not permanently protected.

Cardozo, Benjamin N. (1870–1938). Known as a lawyer's lawyer, Cardozo worked in contract and commercial law before becoming a judge. He sat on the supreme court of New York, the court of appeals in New York, which he single-handedly turned into one of the great courts of its era, and finally on the U.S. Supreme Court. His most famous opinions emanated from the court of appeals, since he served on the Supreme Court for only six years before he died.

Catt, Carrie Chapman (1859–1947). As president of the National American Woman Suffrage Association (NAWSA) from 1900 to 1904 and then from 1915 to 1920, Catt, a superb strategist and organizer, helped gain the vote for women in 1920. She also helped organize the League of Women Voters.

Chisholm, Shirley (1924–). The first black woman elected to Congress (in 1968), Chisholm was an advocate for minority and women's rights and the urban poor. She retired from Congress in 1982, and in 1984 organized the National Political Congress of Black Women.

Clay, Henry (1777–1852). For more than forty years, Clay, a Kentuckian and the leader of the Whig Party, was a dominant force in American politics. He served as secretary of state, was Speaker of the House of Representatives, and then became the most powerful member of the Senate during his time. A Nationalist, Clay was called "the Great Compromiser" for his role in bringing about the Missouri Compromise of 1820, the Tariff Compromise of 1833, and the Compromise of 1850.

Darrow, Clarence (1857–1938). One of the greatest lawyers of his time, Darrow achieved notoriety in a series of sensational first-degree murder trials. He is famous for his defense of John Scopes, who was charged with violating a Tennessee law against teaching evolution in

NOTABLE FIGURES, *cont.*

public schools. The so-called "Monkey trial" in 1925 pitted Darrow against William Jennings Bryan, who had joined the prosecution. His examination of Bryan was intended to show how literal interpretation of the Bible revealed scientific ignorance (see p. 367).

Dole, Elizabeth (1936–). The wife of longtime senator Robert Dole, she mounted the first serious campaign for the U.S. presidency by a woman, seeking the Republican Party nomination in 1999. Though unsuccessful, her effort catalyzed the women's political movement at the national level. She previously had served as president of the Red Cross (1991–1999), secretary of labor (1989–1990), and secretary of transportation (1983–1987).

Douglas, William O. (1898–1980). As a Supreme Court justice from 1939 to 1975, Douglas had the longest tenure of any Supreme Court justice and also wrote more opinions—and dissents—than any other justice in history. Douglas's judicial philosophy was to keep government "off the backs of the people," and to achieve this he wrote many opinions defending free speech, especially during the protest era of the late 1960s and early 1970s.

Ferraro, Geraldine (1935–). A New York Democratic congresswoman, in 1984 she was the first woman ever nominated by a major political party to run as vice president.

Frankfurter, Felix (1882–1965). This law professor and Supreme Court justice was appointed by Franklin Roosevelt and was one of the great legal defenders of the New Deal legislation and civil liberties. Born in Austria, he was also the only naturalized citizen ever to sit on the Supreme Court. He helped found the American Civil Liberties Union (ACLU) in 1920.

Hamilton, Alexander (1755–1804). An aide to George Washington during the Revolution, Hamilton was a delegate to the Constitutional Convention and a strong advocate of the new Constitution, defending it in *The Federalist Papers*. As the first secretary of the treasury, he advocated a strong central government. Hamilton was killed by Aaron Burr in a duel.

Harris, Patricia Roberts (1924–1985). After an early career devoted to civil rights activism, in 1965, Harris became the first African American woman appointed to the rank of ambassador, when President Lyndon Johnson sent her to Luxembourg. In 1976, President Jimmy Carter named her the first female African American secretary of housing and urban development.

Holmes, Oliver Wendell (1841–1935). A Civil War veteran and Massachusetts judge before sitting on the Supreme Court, Holmes was most influential in shaping what is known as a "loose" interpretation of the Constitution. He believed the law should keep pace with social change and was reluctant to dismantle what he considered to be good social legislation, especially minimum wage and maximum hours laws. He enunciated the "clear and present danger doctrine" for interpreting free speech.

Hughes, Charles Evans (1862–1948). This former governor of New York was also chief justice of the Supreme Court, secretary of state, a Republican presidential candidate, and a World Court judge. Hughes wrote several landmark opinions involving the free press and free speech.

Jackson, Andrew (1767–1845). A military hero before he ran for president, Jackson had a popular appeal among westerners, farmers, workingmen, and artisans. He attacked privilege, especially the U.S. Bank, introduced the spoils system to the federal bureaucracy, and preferred his Kitchen Cabinet, an informal group of friends and advisors, to the official elite.

Jay, John (1745–1829). With Hamilton and Madison, Jay wrote *The Federalist Papers*. This delegate

Alexander Hamilton was important in shaping early American politics.

to the first Continental Congress made his mark negotiating the truce at the end of the Revolutionary War and was an effective diplomat. GEORGE WASHINGTON persuaded him to become the first chief justice of the Supreme Court, a post he later resigned because he thought it would be an ineffective vehicle of government.

Jefferson, Thomas (1743–1826). Jefferson was the author of the Declaration of Independence, minister to France, secretary of state under WASHINGTON, vice president under ADAMS, and the third president of the United States. He advocated a limited federal government. Jefferson was a scientist, an architect, the author of Virginia's statute of religious freedom, and founder of the University of Virginia.

Johnson, Lyndon Baines (1908–1973). A powerful leader in the Senate, Johnson was JOHN F. KENNEDY's vice president, becoming president following Kennedy's assassination, and then elected in 1964. Although the war in Vietnam overshadowed his accomplishments, this Democratic president pushed hard to forge a federal program of economic and social welfare, collectively known as the Great Society, that would end poverty. A Texan, he pushed the Civil Rights Act of 1964 and the Voting Rights Act of 1965 through Congress.

Jordan, Barbara (1936–1995). Best known for her eloquent speeches, this stateswoman was the first black law student at Boston University, the first and only black legislator in the Texas senate, and served in Congress for six years. A defender of the poor, Jordan was often consulted by presidents on civil rights issues. She was the first black and first woman to give the keynote speech at the Democratic National Convention.

Kennedy, John F. (1917–1963). A charismatic Democrat whose presidency ended with his assassination in 1963, Kennedy is remembered for his contribution to civil rights, for starting the Peace Corps, and for facing down the Soviets during the Cuban Missile Crisis.

Lincoln, Abraham (1809–1865). The sixteenth president of the United States, Lincoln was elected president on the Republican ticket, then led the nation through the Civil War. He is known as the Great Emancipator, for signing the Emancipation Proclamation that freed the slaves. A fine writer and rhetorician, he is also remembered for his speeches, especially the Gettysburg Address and the Second Inaugural Address.

Madison, James (1751–1836). Known as the Father of the Constitution, Madison brought a scholarly voice to the Constitutional Convention of 1787. With ALEXANDER HAMILTON and JOHN JAY, he coauthored *The Federalist Papers*. He also worked to add the Bill of Rights to the Constitution. As the fourth president, he oversaw the War of 1812.

Marshall, John (1755–1835). During his thirty-four years as chief justice of the United States, Marshall took over a foundering Court and turned it into a respected institution. In his most famous ruling, *Marbury v. Madison*, he invoked the right of the Court to review state and federal laws. In addition, he served as a diplomat, congressman, and secretary of state.

Marshall, Thurgood (1908–1993). A Supreme Court justice and a civil rights lawyer, Marshall helped to lay out the strategy for *Brown v. Board of Education*, the Supreme Court decision that desegregated schools. The first black Supreme Court justice, he was one of the most egalitarian persons ever to sit on the Court.

Mason, George (1725–1792). He wrote the Virginia Declaration of Rights in 1776, a brilliant document that helped to establish individual rights. It formed the basis of many state constitutions and, as the Bill of Rights, was later incorporated into the U.S. Constitution.

Monroe, James (1785–1831). The fifth U.S. president, he was also governor of Virginia, secretary of state, and secretary of war. In 1823, he issued the Monroe Doctrine, a cornerstone of U.S. foreign policy that warned European nations not to interfere in political affairs in the Western Hemisphere.

Nixon, Richard M. (1913–1994). A congressman, senator, and vice president, Nixon was also the only president ever to resign, facing certain impeachment for obstructing justice and abusing presidential authority. His administration's successes included opening diplomatic relations with China and extricating the nation from Vietnam.

O'Connor, Sandra Day (1930–). As the first woman to sit on the Supreme Court, O'Connor has been considered a swing vote in cases involving gender discrimination and sexual harassment. She is a centrist.

Perkins, Frances (1882–1965). The first woman to serve in a president's cabinet, Perkins was secretary of labor under FRANKLIN ROOSEVELT. She fought for many lasting pieces of legislation, such as unemployment insurance, child labor laws, and public works.

NOTABLE FIGURES, *cont.*

Rankin, Jeannette (1880–1973). The first woman ever elected to Congress (1917), Rankin was a pacifist and voted against entry into World War I. She returned to Congress in 1941, where she cast the only vote against entry into World War II. An advocate of women's rights, Rankin's last official antiwar gesture was to lead the Jeannette Rankin Brigade in the 1968 March on Washington to oppose the Vietnam War.

Rehnquist, William (1924–). Present chief justice of the United States, Rhenquist was named to the Court by President NIXON. An advocate of law and order, he has guided the Court toward a conservative orientation.

Roosevelt, Franklin Delano (1882–1945). As thirty-second president of the United States, Roosevelt, a Democrat, guided the country through the Great Depression. His primary vehicle was the New Deal, a package of social and political programs that restored economic health to the nation. He served as president during World War II and was the only president elected to four terms.

Roosevelt, Theodore (1858–1919). When he took over the presidency after McKinley's assassination in 1901, Roosevelt was at forty-three the youngest person ever to hold the office. An active reformer, he was known as a trust-buster and a proponent of conservation. Dissatisfied with the conservatism of his successor William Howard Taft, Roosevelt formed the Progressive (Bull Moose) Party in 1912, splitting the vote of his party and ensuring the election of WOODROW WILSON.

Roosevelt, Eleanor (1884–1962). One of the most influential First Ladies in history, Eleanor Roosevelt served as FDR's "ears and eyes" as she traveled around the country. She was a strong supporter of civil rights, women's issues, and programs for the poor. After her husband's death, she was delegate to the United Nations.

Stanton, Elizabeth Cady (1815–1902). Along with Lucretia Mott, Stanton was one of the organizers of the 1848 Seneca Falls Women's Rights Convention, the first public meeting ever held to advocate women's rights. A leader in the women's suffrage movement, she cofounded, with SUSAN B. ANTHONY, the National Woman Suffrage Association. As lecturer, she spoke around the country, advocating not only voting rights for women but full legal and social equality.

Truman, Harry (1884–1972). This Democratic president is remembered for authorizing the use of the atomic bomb on Japan in order to end World War II, instituting the Marshall Plan to rebuild Europe, and sponsoring the Fair Deal and civil rights legislation.

Warren, Earl (1891–1974). Like JOHN MARSHALL, Warren was one of two or three Supreme Court justices whose name personifies an era. The Warren Court will be remembered for such decisions as *Brown v. Board of Education*, which reversed the "separate but equal doctrine" and ordered that public schools be desegregated; *Gideon v. Wainwright*, which established that poor persons were entitled to free legal counsel; and *Miranda v. Arizona*, which expanded and protected the rights of crime suspects. During the late 1950s and early 1960s, under the guidance of this chief justice, the Court became known for its liberal interpretation of the Constitution and for taking on social and racial issues.

Washington, George (1732–1799). Commander of the Continental Army and the first president of the United States, Washington was elected to a second term as president but refused a third. He was one of the architects of the present federal system of government and set precedents for the presidency that have endured.

Webster, Daniel (1782–1852). The highest-paid lawyer of his time, Webster, also known for his skill as an orator and his defense of the Constitution, won several significant, precedent-setting cases before the Marshall Court. Originally a supporter of states' rights, he later became a unionist. As a secretary of state and senator, he was a leading political figure of his time.

Willard, Frances (1839–1898). One of the most famous women of the nineteenth century, Willard is best remembered for her temperance work. She organized the Women's Christian Temperance Union and worked with women's suffrage activists to combine the two causes.

Wilson, Woodrow (1856–1924). As president during World War I, Wilson was an advocate for world peace and a supporter of the League of Nations, the forerunner to the present-day United Nations.

CHAPTER 7

A RURAL TO AN URBAN NATION

■

HIGHLIGHTS

Timeline of Rural and Urban Life

THE UNITED STATES EVOLVED FROM a nation of farms at the beginning of the nineteenth century to a nation of cities by the beginning of the twentieth. In 1820, a mere 7 percent of the population were city dwellers. By 1860, the figure had risen to 20 percent, and, by 1920, the balance had shifted: 51 percent of Americans lived in urban areas. This shift from predominantly rural to urban living was essentially completed by the 1970s, and more recent shifts in population reflect migration within the urban system itself—from one city to another, from city to suburbs, or from suburbs to city.

Many factors contributed to the urbanization of America. The number and size of cities increased as the new nation expanded westward. Cash crops spurred the growth of market towns and port cities. Advances in transportation sped the movement of goods. Industrialization drew rural youth to manufacturing towns. City populations grew dramatically with the influx of foreign immigrants.

During and after World War I, the migration of rural southern blacks to the industrial North caused a major population shift, institutionalizing the urban ghetto and inner-city life. In the decades after World War II, large manufacturers closed down or left the "rust belt" of the Northeast and Midwest. Older cities went into decline, and the population shifted toward the Sunbelt. With the spread of the suburbs, then the "exurbs," cities with distinctive boundaries and identities gradually gave way to the sprawling megalopolises that define much of the contemporary American landscape.

FOUNDINGS

1524 Italian navigator Giovanni da Verrazzano sails into New York Harbor. A rugged forested island in the harbor will later be called Manhattan.

1564 French Huguenots build Fort Caroline near the mouth of the Saint Johns River.

1565 Saint Augustine, Florida, is founded by Spanish conquistador Pedro Menéndez de Avilés 32 miles (52 km) south of Fort Caroline. It becomes the first American city. Menéndez de Avilés routs the French Huguenot Fort Caroline, slaughtering the entire male population.

1607 The Virginia Company sends more than 100 colonists to Virginia, where they found Jamestown.

1609 Henry Hudson sails up the river in New York that eventually will bear his name.

Sante Fe is founded by the Spanish, on the site of ancient Pueblo Indian ruins.

1614 The coast of Manhattan is mapped by Dutch navigator Adriaen Block.

1620 The Pilgrims establish Plymouth.

1626 PETER MINUIT buys Manhattan Island from chiefs of the Canarsie tribe for 60 guilders (the fabled $24) worth of gadgets and trinkets. Dutch settlers build thirty houses and call their settlement New Amsterdam.

1628 English Puritans settle at Naumkeag, which they rename Salem, on Massachusetts Bay.

1630 Under their leader, John Winthrop, members of the Massachusetts Bay Company establish "a city on a hill," named Boston in 1633 after a town in Lincolnshire, England.

The Mission or Chapel of San Miguel is the oldest church in Santa Fe, New Mexico, and among the oldest churches in the nation. It was partially destroyed in the Pueblo Revolt of 1680 and has been rebuilt and restored several times.

1630, *cont.*

A thatched cottage with a wooden chimney burns down in Boston. Authorities require that thatched houses not have wooden chimneys in what may be the first "building code" in the New World.

1631 One year after its founding, Boston begins its long association with the sea and shipbuilding when *Blessing of the Bay* is launched.

1634 Under a grant to the Catholic Calvert family, the Lords Baltimore settle Saint Mary's, Maryland, on the Chesapeake Bay.

1635 English settlers build Fort Saybrook at the mouth of the Connecticut River.

1636 Providence, Rhode Island, is founded by dissenting minister Roger Williams, who has been banished from Massachusetts.

Thomas Hooker, another dissenting minister, founds Hartford, Connecticut.

1638 Puritans establish New Haven, Connecticut.

Swedish colonists establish Fort Christina, now Wilmington, Delaware.

John Wheelwright, a Puritan clergyman who publicly defends the views of his sister-in-law Anne Hutchinson, is banished from Massachusetts Bay and establishes Exeter, in what will eventually be New Hampshire. When Massachusetts claims authority over Exeter and nearby towns, he moves to Wells, Maine.

"A CITY ON A HILL"

In 1630, somewhere in the middle of the Atlantic Ocean, John Winthrop delivered a sermon, "A Model of Christian Charity," to the Puritans aboard the *Arabella* who had selected him as governor of their enterprise. He exhorted his shipmates, who would soon establish a new community in a new land, to put their ideals of harmony and Christian charity into practice. We must enter into a covenant, he explained, "to do justly, to love mercy, to walk humbly with our God. For this end, we must be knit together in this work as one man. We must entertain each other in brotherly affection, we must be willing to abridge ourselves of our superfluities, for the supply of others' necessities. We must uphold a familiar commerce together in all meekness, gentleness, patience and liberality. We must delight in each other, make others' conditions our own, rejoice together, mourn together, labour and suffer together, always having

before our eyes our commission and community in the work, our community as members of the same body. So shall we keep the unity of the spirit in the bond of peace." If we do these things, Winthrop promised, then God will be among us. "He shall make us a praise and glory that men shall say of succeeding plantations, 'the lord make it like that of New England.' For we must consider that we shall be as a city upon a hill. The eyes of all peoples are upon us…We shall be made a story and a by-word through the world."

While Winthrop's "city on a hill"—soon to be named Boston—did not turn out the way he had hoped, his vision would be repeated again and again in the New World, in hundreds of new communities founded by groups of like-minded people who sought to carve from wilderness a community that would realize an ideal.

1640 Dutch colonists in New Amsterdam settle Hoboken, across the Hudson River, in what is now New Jersey.

1653 Fearing hostile Indian attacks as well as assaults by the British, New Amsterdam colonists construct a defensive wall across lower Manhattan. Extending from the North (Hudson) River to the East River, it gives Wall Street its name.

1658 Dutch settlers in New Amsterdam move north on Manhattan Island to found Nieuw Haarlem, today Harlem.

1664 New Amsterdam becomes New York as the English take the town and rename it after the king's brother, the duke of York.

1666 Connecticut Puritans found Newark, New Jersey.

1668 The French establish a fur-trading post and Jesuit mission at Sault Sainte Marie, on the waterway between Lakes Superior and Huron.

THE FIRST URBAN PLANNING

Those who settled America had an unusual opportunity—to plan, from scratch, the towns they would settle. Colonists from Spain, France, the Netherlands, and England arrived in the New World with many ideas of what their new communities should look like.

The Spanish built missions—adobe and stone churches surrounded by fields, vineyards, and orchards that the Indians would farm, converted to the Christian, peaceful, and servile life that the Spanish envisioned for them. The French built fur-trading posts and small farming towns—with a manor house for the lord and a church surrounded by fields that the *habitants* would farm—resembling those of northern France. The Dutch built a farming village, with narrow, crooked streets, on the tip of Manhattan Island. The Bowery (in Dutch, *bouwerie*, meaning "farm"), the street that gave the area its name, once went to the farm of Governor PETER STUYVESANT. The English in Virginia built forts. It was in New England that urban planning, in this country, first began.

In New England, individuals owned houses on individual lots that were clustered around a public common, owned by the whole community. On the main street around the common stood the church, and probably the minister's house and a school. The community was actually a corporation, organized through the church, in which all families held shares. Each individual holder had a house, kitchen garden, barn, orchard, and a strip of land on the outskirts for cultivation. Additional jointly owned land was used for pasturage and as a woodlot.

When the new nation sited a new capital on the banks of the Potomac, planners had an opportunity to plan a new city on a grand scale. George Washington selected Maj. Pierre Charles L'Enfant—artist, draftsman, and Revolutionary War soldier—to create the design. Thomas Jefferson sent him plans of a dozen European cities, and L'Enfant himself studied the plans of Annapolis, Savannah, Williamsburg, Philadelphia, and New York.

L'Enfant's final plan seemed to combine them all: a geometric grid with diagonal avenues that were to allow for wide vistas and create rectangles, squares, triangles, and even circles for public purposes, parks and gardens, statues and fountains. While today trees and traffic sometimes obscure the "reciprocity of sight" L'Enfant so desired, Washington remains a beautiful city, with a low profile and a green complexion that is unlike any capital city in the world.

1670 British settlers found Charles Town (later Charleston) in the Carolinas.

1679 Most of Boston is destroyed in a fire; its wooden buildings are densely packed.

1682 William Penn founds Philadelphia. The city is designed by Thomas Holme and other members of the Society of Friends (Quakers) with a grid pattern in a successful effort at town planning.

Norfolk, in Virginia, is established. Its excellent natural harbor will be an important port and eventually a naval headquarters.

Members of French explorer René-Robert-Cavalier, Sieur de La Salle's expedition establish Arkansas Post.

1683 German Mennonites found Germantown, Pennsylvania.

1694 The capital of Maryland is moved from Saint Mary's to Annapolis.

1699 Pierre Le Moyne, Sieur d'Iberville, founds Old Biloxi (now Ocean Springs, Mississippi), the first European settlement in French Louisiana.

Middle Plantation, on the peninsula between the James and York Rivers in Virginia, is laid out and named Williamsburg, the new capital of the colony.

1701 The French establish a fort on the Detroit River that will become the city of Detroit.

1710 Swiss and German immigrants settle New Bern, North Carolina. It will later be an early colonial capital.

1713 Boston begins grading streets so that water drains to the side.

1718 New Orleans is founded by Jean-Baptiste Le Mayne, sieur de Bienville. Near the mouth of the Mississippi, it will become one of the most important port cities in the country.

1729 Baltimore is founded, and its excellent harbor soon makes it an important shipping center.

1733 Savannah, founded by James Oglethorpe, is laid out on a grid pattern with wide streets and many parks.

1751 Philadelphia becomes the first city to have a police force.

1754 Pittsburgh has its roots in the establishment of Fort Duquesne. The French erect the fort where the Allegheny River meets the Monongahela, forming the Ohio River. Four years later the British capture the fort and rename it Fort Pitt. A village surrounding the fort is settled in 1760.

Philadelphia's Christ Church is completed, and its 200-foot steeple makes it the tallest structure in North American.

1763 Pierre Laclède selects the site of St. Louis, near the junction of the Mississippi and Missouri Rivers, for a fur-trading post.

1765 Philadelphia's population reaches 25,000. New York's is 12,500, up from 5,000 in 1700.

1766 Irish soldiers in the British army stage New York City's first Saint Patrick's Day parade.

1776 San Francisco begins with the settlement of Yerba Buena as a Spanish mission.

1781 Spanish settlers found Los Angeles, which they call El Pueblo de Nuestra Señora la Reina de los Angeles de Porciuncula ("The Town of Our Lady the Queen of the Angels of Porciuncula").

1788 Cincinnati is founded, named in 1790. This Ohio River city will be an important shipping and trade center.

The Ohio Company founds Marietta, on the Ohio River.

1789 New York City is the capital of the United States when George Washington is inaugurated as the first president on April 30 at Federal Hall.

A customs house is opened in New York, which soon becomes the new nation's major port of entry.

1790 The first ten-year census of the United States is taken; there are only twenty-four urban places—areas with 2,500 people or more. Philadelphia is the largest city, with New York second. Ten years later New York moves into first place, a position it has not relinquished.

The site for the new national capital is selected on the banks of the Potomac River. Maryland and Virginia each cede sections to establish a federal district of 100 square miles (260 sq km). In 1847, the underutilized portion south of the Potomac is retroceded to Virginia.

GROWTH AND INFRASTRUCTURE

1793 A yellow fever epidemic in Philadelphia causes 4,000 deaths and the city to be evacuated. Many cities suffer from epidemics caused by poor sanitary conditions: no municipal water supplies, outdoor privies, and no organized public garbage removal.

1798 Benjamin Latrobe designs a public water supply system for Philadelphia, the first in the United States. It is hoped that a plentiful, dependable supply of clean water will help combat disease.

1800 Washington, D.C., becomes the U.S. capital; the city has 3,210 residents, of whom 623 are slaves.

1801 Boston's board of health begins to improve the city's hygiene, ordering vaccinations against smallpox; it also regulates burials and imposes quarantines.

Philadelphia completes a city water system, but customers have to pay for the service, so it benefits only the richest citizens.

New York's Common Council creates a commissioner of police who coordinates the work of city marshals and the city watch.

1803 Fort Dearborn is built by U.S. troops on Lake Michigan; it will later become Chicago.

1810 New Orleans has a population of 17,242; Pittsburgh has 4,768; Cincinnati has 2,540; Louisville 1,357; Savannah 5,215; and Richmond 9,735.

1811 New York institutes a grid pattern to mark off future streets and avenues.

1814 During the War of 1812, the British occupy Washington, D.C., and burn its public buildings.

1818 Boston establishes public elementary schools.

1820s–1830s The earlier notion of the city as a harmonious community breaks down. Rapid growth, immigration, and industrialization create pressures that eventually explode in a series of riots, often against the two poorest urban groups: Catholics (mainly Irish) and free blacks.

Cities become divided along class lines. The rich and poor segregate in separate neighborhoods. Some areas become slums, marked by poverty and foreign-born populations.

New York City responds to the worries of prosperous citizens by expanding on the old colonial system of city watchmen, adding to the informal force of constables and marshals. The federal militia is called out to handle riots.

More than half of city dwellers live in four cities: New York, Baltimore, Philadelphia, and Boston.

1820 Only 6 percent of Americans live in cities.

New York City's population is now almost 152,056. Pittsburgh has a population of 7,248.

1822 The Boston Associates begin to build a factory at the junction of the Concord and Merrimack Rivers, renaming the settlement Lowell in memory of Francis Cabot Lowell, who had improved on British models for a spinning machine and a power loom. When the factory opens the next year, it employs young girls from New England farm families, who live in dormitories provided by the company. Lowell is the first designed manufacturing city.

1825 The Erie Canal opens, bolstering the economy of New York City; commerce is facilitated between the rapidly developing interior of the country and the city's flourishing financial center. The port of New York, already the busiest on the eastern seaboard, becomes the Atlantic port for the Midwest. The opening of the canal also sparks the economies of Buffalo, Rochester, Cleveland, Columbus, Detroit, Chicago, and Syracuse.

1827 The Baltimore and Ohio Railroad is chartered on February 28 to connect Baltimore to the West and thus position Baltimore in direct competition with New York (and the Erie Canal) for trade with the Midwest.

1829 New York City's first public transportation is provided by a horse-drawn bus, or omnibus. Philadelphia and Boston follow suit in the 1830s.

Boston opens the first modern hotel, Tremont House. A prototype of modern hostelries, it sets new standards. Unlike earlier inns, where strangers were forced to share rooms and even beds, each guest has a private room. The basement held eight water closets for the 170 rooms.

1831 New York's Gramercy Farm is transformed into Gramercy Park, the first of New York's planned neighborhoods. Only the wealthy people who purchase surrounding lots have keys to the park, where they can enjoy walkways and carriageways.

1832 New York City's first horse-drawn streetcar is put into service. Streetcars make trips cheaper, easier, and safer.

1833 In Boston, the top 4 percent enjoy 59 percent of the city's wealth. In most cities, the rich and poor lead mainly separate lives, with the rich joining elite churches and voluntary associations with restricted membership.

1835 A major fire destroys about 700 buildings in New York near Hanover Square and Pearl Street.

Omnibuses, horse-drawn coaches operating on fixed routes, operate in Boston, Brooklyn, New Orleans, New York, Philadelphia, and Washington. Fares range from 6 to 12 cents.

1837 Buildings and paved streets occupy only one-sixth of Manhattan; the rest of the land is still farmed.

A depression hits the cities hard. In New York, unemployment leaves most laborers without work.

Atlanta is founded as Terminus, the end of the rail line. It will become a major rail junction and shipping center.

"The more I observed Washington, the more frequently I visited it, and the more people I interviewed there, the more I understood how prophetic L'Enfant was when he laid it out as a city that goes around in circles."

—JOHN MASON BROWN

Artist J. W. Hill's watercolor drawing shows the Erie Canal less than a decade after its 1825 completion.

1840 The Mississippi steamboat trade makes New Orleans prosper; by the 1850s, its port will overtake New York in volume of shipping as half the country's exports move through it.

The population of New York City is now 391,114, but the U.S. population is still 90 percent rural.

1842 New York City pipes water from the Croton watershed to a reservoir on Fifth Avenue at the current site of the New York Public Library. Voters approved the scheme in 1837.

1845 New York City has a permanent, professional police force. In 1853, those members of the police force who had objected to uniforms as "undemocratic" agree to wear them.

Lemuel Shattuck and John H. Griscom report on urban conditions in *Sanitary Conditions of the Laboring Population of New York*. This report and others like it prompt social reformers to become involved in urban planning and in public works, including sewage treatment and disposal, adequate clean water supplies, public safety, and recreational areas.

1846 William Gregg re-creates a New England mill village in Graniteville, South Carolina, including homes for 300 employees.

1847 Salt Lake City is founded by Mormon leader Brigham Young.

1850 The first prefabricated cast-iron-and-glass buildings are constructed in Manhattan. Designed by James Bogardus, these "curtain wall" buildings will soon be erected in other U.S. cities including Philadelphia and St. Louis.

The population of New York exceeds 700,000. About 140,000 New Yorkers are foreign born, mostly Irish. Irish immigrants coming at midcentury settle in eastern cities; German immigrants settle in the Midwest.

One in seven Americans is a city dweller. Ten U.S. cities have populations of more than 50,000.

1852 ELISHA OTIS invents the safety elevator, which will eventually permit construction of the high-rise buildings that will transform American cities.

1853 The Children's Aid Society raises consciousness about the plight of homeless urban children.

1855 Philadelphia's Fairmont Park, the largest park within a city in the country, is established.

More than three-quarters of New York City's workforce is foreign born (Irish and German).

1856 The value of real estate in Chicago's central business district has increased 6,000 percent over its value in 1846.

The first Boston street railway begins with a single horsecar between Cambridge and Boston. Street railways differ from omnibuses in that they operate over rails laid in the street. Omnibuses differ little from coaches.

The land for New York City's Central Park is acquired. Since 1853, the city commissioners have been buying the land from Fifty-ninth Street to 106th Street between Fifth and Eighth Avenues. In 1858, the design by FREDERICK LAW OLMSTED and Calvert Vaux is chosen from the entries in a public competition.

1857 Virginia City, Nevada, becomes a boom town when the Comstock Lode of gold is discovered nearby. Within a few years, it has a population of 6,000. By 1880, 11,000 people live here. In 1990, the county in which Virginia City is located contains 2,705 people.

The world's first passenger elevator begins operating in the Haughwout Department store in New York City.

1858 Denver is incorporated. The city lies at the junction of the South Platte River and Cherry Creek.

Although not officially completed for many years, New York City's Central Park opens to the public. Although intended for the working classes, the 840 acres of reclaimed urban space is too far north—and too far from public transportation—to be used by anyone but the rich. It will become the model for future urban and suburban parks.

R. H. Macy Company opens in New York City.

1860 One in ten southerners lives in a city, one in three northeasterners, and one in seven midwesterners. Slavery, however, remains a rural institution, with less than 10 percent of the population of the ten largest southern cities bening slaves.

1860–1900 The expansion of the nation's railroads as well as the improvements in seagoing vessels will not only accelerate the export of agricultural produce but will also cause major population expansion and shifts as immigrants populate U.S. cities, the interior, and the plains. Some cities are founded as railroad junctions and centers.

1860s WILLIAM MARCY TWEED, whose name becomes synonymous with political corruption, dominates New York City politics.

1860 Twenty percent of the country's population lives in cities, which are defined as having 2,500 or more inhabitants. New York is the largest city, with 1,174,779 residents, 20 percent of them Irish-born immigrants.

One-fourth of all cities use private water companies. Service is worse in poor neighborhoods.

In Milwaukee, the great majority of the German population lives in German neighborhoods.

Some 330,000 free blacks live in the North; most of them are in cities. There, they compete with native-born poor whites and immigrants for work as domestic servants and laborers. Philadelphia has the largest African American population of 22,000.

1861–1865 The Civil War causes northern industry to boom. In the South, Richmond, Atlanta, and Columbia, South Carolina, are destroyed. But after the war, southern cities grow faster than those in any other part of the country.

Nearly a half-million pigs passed through the streets of Cincinnati every year during the 1860s. With more than fifty slaughterhouses, the city was known as the "Porkopolis" of the Midwest.

1864 A gold rush leads to the founding of Butte, Montana. The city is planned in 1867 and incorporated in 1879. When copper is discovered about 1880, the Anaconda Copper Mining Company and Butte flourish together.

1868 In an Iowa case, the Dillon Rule—the principle that local governments are creations of state governments, with their powers and responsibilities defined by the state—is formulated.

1869 Abilene, Kansas, the railhead and shipping point for cattle driven up from Texas along the Chisholm Trail, is incorporated. The two Kansas Cities (in Kansas and Missouri) also boom as markets, shipping points, and processing and packaging centers for newly opening cattle and agricultural frontiers.

A. T. Stewart, owner of New York's largest department store, A. T. Stewart & Company, starts a planned middle-income community in Garden City, Long Island.

New York City's first apartment house, the Rutherford-Stuyvesant on East Eighteenth Street, is built.

1870 The first U.S. elevated railroad opens in New York City; a section for demonstration purposes had opened two years earlier.

THE PUBLIC LIBRARY

One of the great cultural legacies of urban America in the late nineteenth century was the public library system. The nation's oldest library, at Harvard College, was founded in 1638 by John Harvard. The first subscription library in America, the Library Company of Philadelphia, was launched in 1731 by BENJAMIN FRANKLIN; membership dues were used to purchase books, which could be borrowed for free by subscribers. The public library movement originated in Boston in the mid-1850s. Mandated by state legislation and supported by taxes, the Boston Public Library was established in 1854 as an agency of continuing adult education. Early public libraries were seen as vital to American democracy, promoting patriotism, civic duty, and a commitment to solving society's problems through moral suasion.

By 1875, more than 250 public libraries had been founded in U.S. cities and towns. With construction grants by the industrialist Andrew Carnegie and other benefactors, the public libraries of New York, Boston, Philadelphia, and Chicago soon grew to prominence. By the early 1900s, branch libraries and country or regional systems had become widespread. The free public library was an important educational and economic vehicle for immigrants, minorities, and other disadvantaged classes seeking upward mobility. As community libraries became commonplace, they also began serving the public's demand for recreational reading, cultural events, and popular media. Today, there are approximately 10,000 public libraries (plus branches) in the United States.

RURAL TO AN URBAN NATION

Dr J.S.Billings,
Director New York Public Library.

Dear Mr Billings,

Our conferences upon the needs of Greater New York for Branch Libraries to reach the masses of the people in every district have convinced me of the wisdom of your plans.

Sixty-five branches strike one at first as a large order, but as other cities have found one necessary for every sixty or seventy thousand of population the number is not excessive.

You estimate the average cost of these libraries at, say, $80,000 each, being $5,200,000 for all. If New York will furnish sites for these Branches for the special benefit of the masses of the people, as it has done for the Central Library, and also agree in satisfactory form to provide for their main-
-tenance as built, I should esteem it a rare privilege to be permitted to furnish the money as needed for the buildings, say $5,200,000. Sixty-five libraries at one stroke probably breaks the record, but this is the day of big operations. *and*

New York is soon to be the Very truly yours,

biggest of cities,   Andrew Carnegie

In this 1901 letter to the Director of the New York Public Library, Andrew Carnegie presents $5,200,000 for the creation of sixty-five branch libraries.

1870, *cont.*

The population of Kansas City climbs from 4,418 to more than 32,000 in just ten years.

Chicago also experiences a major growth spurt. Its population, 29,963 in the late 1850s, has soared to 298,977.

The story that Mrs. O'Leary's cow started the Great Chicago Fire of 1871 by knocking over a lantern was made up by a newspaper reporter. The real cause of the fire is unknown.

1871 Rumored to have been started by Mrs. O'Leary's cow kicking over a lantern in a barn, the Chicago fire burns out of control for almost three days, beginning October 8, destroying 4 square miles (10 sq km) of the city. At least 250 people are believed to have died in Chicago. Ironically, a greater loss of human life occurs simultaneously in forest fires in Wisconsin.

Birmingham, incorporated this year, is soon on its way to being an iron and steel center, the "Pittsburgh of the South."

1872 Dallas, a small Texas town, is linked by rail to eastern markets. By 1880, its population has more than tripled.

Boston now extends outward from its civic center for a distance of 2.5 miles (4 km)—a direct result of the new horsecar transportation, which allows people to live farther than walking distance from their places of work. However, an explosion results in a fire that destroys the most prosperous part of the city.

1873 San Francisco's cable cars begin to run; the underground cable system is the world's first.

1874 Boston annexes Charlestown, home of the Boston naval shipyard.

1875 FREDERICK LAW OLMSTED begins working on the foundations of the Boston public park system.

1876 The Southern Pacific Railroad arrives in Los Angeles, and the Sante Fe arrives in 1885.

The nation marks its first 100 years with the Centennial Exposition in Philadelphia.

1877 In New York City, the Museum of Natural History opens.

Gastonia, North Carolina, one of the new textile towns in the South, is incorporated. During the next two decades, textile mills in the Piedmont region of the Carolinas and Georgia, near cotton, energy, and cheap labor, surpass New England in production. Greenville, Spartanburg, Macon, and Columbus are only the biggest of these thriving mill towns. Small company towns spring up throughout rural areas.

1879 Cleveland begins to use carbon-arc street lamps.

1880 New York City lights a strip of Broadway—Fourteenth to Twenty-sixth Streets—with carbon-arc lamps.

San Francisco's population reaches 233,959.

Los Angeles's population grows from about 11,000 to more than 50,000 by the end of the decade.

On the Lower East Side of New York, housing conditions are among the worst in the world.

1880–1890 During this period even stable older cities such as Boston experience tremendous population flux. Boston's population swells to more than 448,000 from just under 363,000. In the same decade, New York and Chicago each grow by 600,000.

1882 Parts of New York City are lit by electricity; soon Manhattan will be entirely supplied with electric power. An 1884 law requires that wire be placed underground, a job not completed until 1905.

1882 Cable cars begin operating in Chicago.

1883 The Brooklyn Bridge opens. Designed by JOHN A. ROEBLING, who dies before it is completed, the span links Manhattan and Brooklyn. It is completed by his son, Washington A. Roebling.

IN THE SHADOW OF SKYSCRAPERS

1883 William Le Baron Jenney designs the first true skyscraper, the Home Insurance Building in Chicago. Its steel framework means that buildings no longer have to rely on heavy, thick, solid masonry.

1886 The Statue of Liberty, a gift to the United States from France, is dedicated in New York Harbor.

A sand garden for children, an import from Berlin, Germany, is established in Boston.

An electric street railway begins operating in Baltimore over a 3-mile (5-km) line. It draws its power from an electrified third rail.

1888 New York City's first skyscraper, the Tower Building, is constructed at 50 Broadway.

The first electric trolley starts running in the city of Richmond, Virginia. The system covers more than 12 miles (19 km). Electric trolleys will be operating in 200 other American cities by around 1889.

1889 Boston, with one of the largest horse-drawn street railways, begins electrifying its system. Within six years, almost the entire system is electric.

The world's first electric elevators are installed in a New York office building by Otis Brothers.

JANE ADDAMS opens Hull-House, the most famous settlement house in the country, in Chicago.

1890 *How the Other Half Lives* by JACOB RIIS is published. This book exposes the living conditions in the slums of New York and gives impetus to urban reform movements.

The population of Los Angeles is now 50,395. New York counts 2,507,414. More than 700 people per acre are packed into Lower East Side tenements measuring 25 by 100 feet and five stories high.

1891 The Bronx becomes home to the New York Botanical Garden.

1893 The World's Columbian Exposition is celebrated in Chicago. FREDERICK LAW OLMSTED and DANIEL BURNHAM's "White City," a model of urban planning, demonstrates everything that city planners have worked toward over the years. The fairground boasts white buildings reflected in blue water and electric lights.

Louisville, Kentucky, builds fieldhouses where city children can play in bad weather.

1894 Manhattan's tenement district has 986.4 people per square acre, the highest population density in the world.

1898 The first U.S. subway begins operation in Boston.

1900 Street railways total more than 20,000 miles.

The turn of the century still finds a majority of Americans—60 percent—living in rural areas.

The effects of immigration and urbanization are evident. In the Northeast, two-thirds of the population is urban, and 23 percent is foreign-born. An additional 28 percent has at least one foreign-born parent. In New York City in 1910, 40 percent of the 4.8 million residents are foreign-born. An additional 38 percent have at least one foreign-born parent.

The population of New York City is forty-three times greater than in the year 1800.

Electric trolleys have transformed Boston into a metropolis, encompassing thirty-one towns in a 10-mile (16-km) radius and more than 1 million residents.

Work begins on the construction of the New York subway.

A hurricane and tidal wave destroy Galveston, Texas. When the mayor and aldermen prove unable to cope with the emergency, businessmen propose a new form of city government by a board of commissioners.

One in six southerners lives in an urban place.

1901 In Washington, D.C., the McMillan Commission plan to update L'Enfant's vision for the city receives federal government approval.

Streetcars and elevators in New York City are now run by electricity, though horsecars still travel Fifth Avenue.

1902 The Flatiron Building is finished in New York City. At twenty stories high, the steel-frame structure is a wonder of urban architecture and quickly becomes a tourist mecca.

Lincoln Steffen's series *The Shame of the Cities* exposes corruption in urban politics. It is published in book form in 1904.

1904 The first New York City subway opens on October 27, and passengers pay a nickel. Eventually the New York subway system will become the largest in the United States.

Fire guts downtown Baltimore.

THE SETTLEMENT HOUSE MOVEMENT

When JANE ADDAMS and her college classmate Ellen Gates Starr opened the doors at Hull-House, on Chicago's West Side, in 1889, they were not initiating an original institution. The idea of the settlement—a house in a slum where university-trained people would "settle" to help relieve poverty—had originated in London. The first settlement house in the United States was established by Stanton Coit on New York's Lower East Side in 1886. But Addam's Hull-House would become the most famous.

Hull-House, modeled on London's Toynbee Hall, which Addams had visited in 1887–1888, quickly became a center of community life. Here the impoverished working people of the Halsted Street neighborhood, many of them immigrants, could find help and friendship. The women of Hull-House helped secure support for deserted wives and insurance for bewildered widows. They served as an information and interpretation bureau between individuals who needed help and city bureaucracies. At Hull-House there was a working girls' home, a day nursery, a labor museum, a boys' club, a social science club, a little theater, and reading parties. In addition to tutorials, there were classes in sewing, mending, and embroidering, in Shakespeare, mathematics, physics, and electricity.

The Henry Street settlement house in New York City grew out of Lillian Wald's visiting nursing service, which provided nursing care of the sick in their homes—mostly tenements in New York's immigrant neighborhoods. Combating ignorance and poverty daily, both Hull-House and Henry Street moved into the forefront of social reform, then political reform movements. Settlement house women did statistical studies, wrote reports, and campaigned for housing reform and child labor laws. Lillian Wald lobbied for the U.S. Children's Bureau, established in 1912. Jane Addams founded the Woman's Peace Party in 1915 and the Women's International League for Peace and Freedom in 1919. Settlement house women went on to careers in government, industry, and academic life. They were the first social workers, and their impact on the profession continues to be felt today.

Settlement houses, too, are still alive in the shelters for abused women and the homeless, in the free medical clinics and community centers that even today seek to ease the immigrant's transition to American life and to alleviate the problems of urban poverty with soup, services, and kindness.

When she died in 1935, founder of Hull-House Jane Addams left an impressive legacy of social and political reform, and efforts for international peace.

The utter devastation of San Francisco after the 1906 earthquake and subsequent fire can be seen in this view of Powell Street, taken the day of the disaster.

"And this is good old Boston
The home of the bean and the cod,
Where the Lowells talk to the Cabots,
And the Cabots talk only to God."

—JOHN COLLINS BOSSIDY, TOAST, 1910 HOLY CROSS ALUMNI DINNER

1905 Cleveland developers Oris and Mantis Van Sweringen purchase land, which had belonged to a Shaker congregation, to build a model suburban complex. After completion of a rail line, subsidized in part by the Sweringens, from Cleveland to the new community, Shaker Heights blossoms into one of America's premier upper-middle-class suburbs.

1906 A devastating earthquake strikes San Francisco on April 18. Severed and broken gas lines spark a fire that destroys two-thirds of the city and results in a property loss of more than $400 million. At least 2,300 people are killed as the fire blazes out of control for three days; there is little water to fight the fire, since the city's water mains have cracked in the quake. It is the worst earthquake ever to hit a U.S. city.

1907 New York City replaces its Fifth Avenue horsecars, the last in use in the city, with motorbuses.

1908 Union Station, a Beaux Arts masterpiece designed by DANIEL H. BURNHAM, consolidates rail lines at the foot of Capitol Hill in Washington, D.C.

1909 Chicago architect DANIEL BURNHAM writes *Plan of Chicago*, which will spearhead a movement in Chicago and other American cities to adopt master plans for future growth. Burnham's plan is far-reaching and ambitious. The forest preserves to the west and the lakefront parks and beaches are his legacy. "Make no little plans. They have no magic to stir men's blood," Burnham writes.

1910 Congress legislates against construction by any private builder of any edifice in Washington, D.C., higher than the Capitol.

About 1 million blacks live in northern cities. By 1940, this number has grown to 2.8 million. More than half the increase is due to migration from the South, where more than three-quarters of black Americans live.

The National Urban League is founded by African Americans to help end racial segregation and provide community services in housing, employment, education, and social welfare.

1911 The Triangle Shirtwaist Factory fire in New York City kills 146 women. The tragedy underscores the terrible working conditions of urban sweatshops and prompts both unionization and reform.

1913 The 792-foot tall Woolworth Building becomes the world's tallest and largest office building when it opens.

Los Angeles becomes a boomtown at last when it is assured an adequate water supply by the opening of the Los Angeles Owens River Aqueduct. The project of superintendent and chief engineer of the Los Angeles waterworks WILLIAM MULHOLLAND, the pipeline can carry 26 million gallons of water a day from the Sierra Nevada.

Congress approves the building of a reservoir in Yosemite that will supply the city of San Francisco with water.

1914 The Great Migration of blacks out of the rural South to the cities of the North begins. Between 1914 and 1920, some 500,000 or more blacks go north for jobs in industry and better opportunities. During the 1920s, 1.5 million more go north, and the black populations of New York, Chicago, and Detroit double.

1915 New York City's Jewish population is 1.4 million, almost 30 percent of inhabitants.

Joseph Lee publishes *Play in Education*. Arguing for the constructive use of leisure, he promotes playgrounds in congested city neighborhoods.

1916 New York City passes the first U.S. urban zoning law establishing height and setback controls and separating factories from residences. In ten years, almost 600 cities will have zoning codes.

Congress passes a Federal Roads Aid Act providing for matching federal aid to states for road improvement. U.S. involvement in World War I prevents any notable activity.

1917 A new aqueduct linking the upstate Catskill Mountain watershed to New York City provides the country's largest metropolis with 250 million gallons a day of pure water.

1920s Al Capone becomes the boss of the Chicago bootleggers. Capone, who will come to dominate gambling, prostitution, and the underworld, becomes synonymous in the American mind with the bloody era of the Chicago gangster—an image of a violent urban landscape that will continue to plague the American imagination for decades to come.

Designed by Daniel Burnham, the 285-feet (87-m) tall, steel-framed, triangular Flatiron Building in New York City was completed in 1902. It is considered the city's first skyscraper.

RURAL TO AN URBAN NATION

SKYSCRAPERS: VERTICAL ARCHITECTURE

Towering structures of metal, stone, and glass, skyscrapers define the twentieth-century urban skyline. Depending on one's viewpoint, the tall buildings transform cities into sparkling places of light and architectural marvels or into canyons of gloom.

Before the 1870s, the urban cityscape lay low-slung against the horizon. Young cities were mainly conglomerations of row houses, warehouses, and shops, over which lived merchant owners or craftspeople. The tallest buildings were generally just six stories high; with plenty of land to spare there was no need to economize on lot size or to pack more tenants into a particular square footage. And the technology just didn't exist to create taller, habitable structures.

Soon, however, population growth led to overcrowding. Real estate in downtown areas became a more valuable commodity in the nation's boomtowns. By the 1870s, the stage was thus set for the rise of the skyscraper. The event that triggered the building revolution was the 1871 Great Chicago Fire, which gutted the city's downtown. Plans to rebuild were thwarted by the existing grid pattern of the city, which was now also the hub of the nation's railroads: tracks crisscrossed sections of town.

Spurred on by developers seeking to make the most use of limited and expensive downtown lots, architects set out to find ways to build the tallest buildings possible. The first ten-story building erected in the Windy City was the Montauk Building designed by DANIEL H. BURNHAM and John Wellborn Root. It was built using a cast-iron cage or frame that supported the weight of the building.

Despite the unprecedented height of the building, as much significance could be attached to its foundation, for it "floated" on the sand and clay soil of Chicago. Both the engineering developments permitted the construction of even taller buildings.

Chicago, in the aftermath of the fire that had consumed the entire central business district, was a stimulus to architects, who competed to create modern, tall, fireproof buildings. With steel structural framework and sturdier foundations, non-load-bearing building walls were free to be lighter. More windows allowed lights into the hitherto heavy stone buildings and made outside surfaces more reflective. Technological breakthroughs, such as the invention of electricity by THOMAS EDISON and OTIS's elevator, helped fuel the skyscraper revolution. Tall buildings were a new feature on the architectural horizon. Their design and construction freed architects to pursue new ideas regarding style, function, and form.

One of the great architects of the era, LOUIS SULLIVAN, in "The Tall Office Building Artistically Considered," welcomed the opportunity to build unhampered by the need to follow historical conventions and old styles.

1920s, *cont.*

Los Angeles: "nineteen suburbs in search of a metropolis."

—H. L. MENCKEN,
AMERICANA, 1925

The Harlem Renaissance is under way. For the next decade, Harlem is the "Negro Capital of the World." W. E. B. Du Bois and Marcus Garvey stimulate intellectual debate and book publishing; Ethel Waters and Duke Ellington introduce jazz; Zora Neale Hurston writes novels; and Langston Hughes writes poetry. Dance and jazz clubs make Harlem the place to be, even for wealthy whites from uptown (see p. 489, 498).

1920 The U.S. population is now 106.5 million. For the first time urban residents (51.2 percent) outnumber rural (48.8 percent). Nevertheless, one-third of all Americans still live on farms. By 1970, only one in every twenty people will be farm dwellers.

1921 Congress passes a Federal Highway Act that creates the Bureau of Public Roads and proposes a system of highways that will connect all cities of more than 50,000 inhabitants.

1922 The Country Club Plaza in Kansas City is the country's first shopping center.

1924 ROBERT MOSES, who serves on the New York State council of parks, as New York City park commissioner, and head of the New York City tunnel authority, begins building a succession of urban and suburban bridges and parkways around the New York metropolitan area. His numerous projects include the Bronx-Whitestone, Henry Hudson, Throgs Neck, Triborough, and Verrazzano Bridges, as well as the Bruckner, Brooklyn-Queens, Long Island, Major Deegan, and West Side Highways.

The first "new town" is designed by Clarence Stein and Henry Wright. Their community, Radburn, New Jersey, is planned to protect its population from urban stresses such as air and noise pollution. Though the building of Radburn will be put off, Stein eventually designs other "planned communities," such as Chatham Village on the outskirts of Pittsburgh.

1927 The Holland Tunnel opens, linking Canal Street in Manhattan with Jersey City. Until now ferryboats have been the sole means of surface transport across the Hudson River.

1929 Chicago's gang warfare erupts in the brutal Saint Valentine's Day Massacre as mobsters "rub each other out" in a massive effort to control the illegal sale of liquor during Prohibition.

Sociologists Robert and Helen Lynd publish *Middletown: A Study in Contemporary American Society;* the book, which uses anthropological field methods to examine the lives of ordinary Americans in a midwestern city (Muncie, Indiana), influences a whole generation of sociologists.

On Wall Street in New York City, the stock market crashes, and the effects are felt in every small town across America.

1930 More than 23 million automobiles are registered in a population of 123 million people. By 1970, the number of automobiles has almost quadrupled—to 89 million—while the population has increased to 203 million.

1931 The George Washington Bridge is completed and spans the Hudson River between New York City and New Jersey. At 3,500 feet it is, at the time, the world's longest suspension bridge.

When the Empire State Building opens April 30, the 102-story skyscraper, designed by the firm of Shreve, Lamb, and Harmon, is the world's tallest building.

1933–1945 New Deal legislation and policies enhance urban life through the development of federally funded public-housing programs and the use of WPA workers to build and improve schools, hospitals, parks, and other civic structures, institutions, and services.

Construction of New York's Empire State Building took only one year and forty-five days, from March 1930 to May 1931—a rate of one story every four days. Ten million bricks and 60,000 tons of steel were used.

RURAL TO AN URBAN NATION

1933 New York's Tammany Hall, long a symbol of urban political graft and corruption, is finally quashed when FIORELLO LA GUARDIA is elected mayor of the city on a reform ticket. He will be mayor for twelve years.

The federal Home Owners Loan Corporation is established to rescue homeowners from mortgage foreclosures. Ultimately it covers 1 million mortgages.

1934 The Federal Housing Administration insures home mortgages. This demonstration of support by the federal government results in lending institutions typically requiring only 10 percent of the purchase price as a down payment. Previously half the cost had been a usual payment.

1937 Greenbelt, Maryland, is incorporated. Planned and built by the federal government as a model community for families with modest incomes, it is a garden city, surrounded by a "belt" of parkland.

The Golden Gate Bridge connecting San Francisco and Marin County is completed; until 1964, its 4,200 feet make it the world's longest suspension bridge.

1938 Chicago begins construction of a subway in the Loop, the bustling downtown section of the city.

1940 New York's Puerto Rican population is 61,000; by 1960, it will have increased to 613,000.

1942 As a wartime measure, Congress passes the Emergency Price Control Act. Its provisions allow for rent control in certain areas. The next year the act is extended to cover the entire country.

PUSHING OUT: THE MODERN MEGATROPOLIS

1944 The GI Bill of Rights (officially the Servicemen's Readjustment Act) helps provide cheap home mortgages to veterans, thus promoting the postwar housing boom and the growth of the suburbs.

1945 The end of World War II and the boom that follows spark the move to the suburbs. The GI Bill and the Federal Housing Administration make buying a home more affordable for the middle- and working-class populations. Flight from the crowded urban centers begins.

1947 Using mass production technology, WILLIAM LEVITT completes the first Levittown, in Hempstead, New York. Consisting of 17,000 landscaped homes for 80,000 people, Levittown offers young American families affordable housing. Levitt builds other Levittowns during the decades that follow. His methods will be copied by builders across the country.

TEN LARGEST CITIES, 1790–2000

1790
1. Philadelphia, Pa.
2. New York, N.Y.
3. Boston, Mass.
4. Baltimore, Md.
5. Providence, R.I.
6. New Haven, Conn.
7. Richmond, Va.
8. Albany, N.Y.
9. Norfolk, Va.
10. Alexandria, Va.

1810
1. New York, N.Y.
2. Philadelphia, Pa.
3. Baltimore, Md.
4. Boston, Mass.
5. New Orleans, La.
6. Albany, N.Y.
7. Providence, R.I.
8. Richmond, Va.
9. Norfolk, Va.
10. Alexandria, Va.

1830
1. New York, N.Y.
2. Baltimore, Md.
3. Philadelphia, Pa.
4. Boston, Mass.
5. New Orleans, La.
6. Cincinnati, Ohio
7. Albany, N.Y.
8. Washington, D.C.
9. Richmond, Va.
10. Providence, R.I.

1850
1. New York, N.Y.
2. Baltimore, Md.
3. Boston, Mass.
4. Philadelphia, Pa.
5. New Orleans, La.
6. Cincinnati, Ohio
7. St. Louis, Mo.
8. Albany, N.Y.
9. Pittsburgh, Pa.
10. Buffalo, N.Y.

1870
1. New York, N.Y.
2. Philadelphia, Pa.
3. St. Louis, Mo.
4. Chicago, Ill.
5. Baltimore, Md.
6. Boston, Mass.
7. Cincinnati, Ohio
8. New Orleans, La.
9. San Francisco, Calif.
10. Buffalo, N.Y.

1890
1. New York, N.Y.
2. Chicago, Ill.
3. Philadelphia, Pa.
4. St. Louis, Mo.
5. Boston, Mass.
6. Baltimore, Md.
7. San Francisco, Calif.
8. Cincinnati, Ohio
9. New Orleans, La.
10. Pittsburgh, Pa.

1910
1. New York, N.Y.
2. Chicago, Ill.
3. Philadelphia, Pa.
4. Detroit, Mich.
5. Los Angeles, Calif.
6. Cleveland, Ohio
7. St. Louis, Mo.
8. Baltimore, Md.
9. Boston, Mass.
10. San Francisco, Calif.

1950
1. New York, N.Y.
2. Chicago, Ill.
3. Philadelphia, Pa.
4. Los Angeles, Calif.
5. Detroit, Mich.
6. Baltimore, Md.
7. Cleveland, Ohio
8. St. Louis, Mo.
9. Washington, D.C.
10. Boston, Mass.

1970
1. New York, N.Y.
2. Chicago, Ill.
3. Los Angeles, Calif.
4. Philadelphia, Pa.
5. Detroit, Mich.
6. Houston, Tex.
7. Baltimore, Md.
8. Dallas, Tex.
9. Washington, D.C.
10. Cleveland, Ohio

1990
1. New York, N.Y.
2. Los Angeles, Calif.
3. Chicago, Ill.
4. Houston, Tex.
5. Philadelphia, Pa.
6. San Diego, Calif.
7. Detroit, Mich.
8. Dallas, Tex.
9. Phoenix, Ariz.
10. San Antonio, Tex.

2000
1. New York, N.Y.
2. Los Angeles, Calif.
3. Chicago, Ill.
4. Houston, Tex.
5. Philadelphia, Pa.
6. Phoenix, Ariz.
7. San Diego, Calif.
8. Dallas, Tex.
9. San Antonio, Tex.
10. Detroit, Mich.

RURAL TO AN URBAN NATION

1949 Congress states the need to fund slum clearance and affordable housing through an alliance of private initiative and public money in the Federal Housing Act.

1950s Suburban land values skyrocket as middle-class white Americans leave deteriorating inner cities.

1956 The Interstate Highway Act funds an interstate highway system of more than 40,000 miles to connect major cities; inadvertently the law also spurs the growth of suburbs. Railroads and public transportation systems remain unsubsidized.

1959 In an attempt to halt the deterioration of the inner cities, Congress provides $650 million for slum clearance and rehabilitation.

1961 Social critic Jane Jacobs publishes *The Death and Life of American Cities*. She theorizes that cities were more livable when they were smaller and consisted of neighborhoods and that many sanitized efforts at urban renewal destroy the very soul the reforms wish to save.

Bay area voters approve a new regional transit system that will link communities on both sides of San Francisco Bay.

Hawaii institutes a comprehensive plan stating that certain areas are reserved for agriculture and conservation as well as for urban development.

1963 At its completion, New York's Pan Am Building over Grand Central Terminal is the world's largest office building.

1964 President Lyndon B. Johnson declares the "war on poverty" in the United States. He names R. Sargent Shriver head of the Office of Economic Opportunity. Shriver directs programs like the Job Corps, Head Start, the Neighborhood Youth Corps, and other community-action programs, many of which are aimed at benefiting residents of the inner city.

The Verrazzano-Narrows Bridge is completed, linking Staten Island with Brooklyn. At 4,260 feet, it is today the longest suspension bridge in the United States.

1965 A massive power failure on November 9 causes a blackout in seven states on the Eastern Seaboard. Parts of New York City, including Manhattan, do not have power until the next morning. All electric transit systems, suburban trains, streetlights, and elevators are shut down.

A race riot erupts in the Watts section of Los Angeles. During the "long hot summers" that follow, Detroit, Newark, and other cities succumb to racial violence that destroys lives and property.

The Department of Housing and Urban Development is established to administer programs providing assistance for housing and the development of the nation's communities. Robert Weaver, the first African American to serve in the cabinet, is named secretary.

URBAN RENEWAL

After World War II, patterns of urban growth slowed and shifted. Old industries moved out, choosing to locate new plants where labor and land were cheaper. The middle classes moved out, too, attracted by suburban land and lifestyles. The central cities were left with vacant factories and slum housing. Inner-city residents as a whole were poorer, more likely to be minorities or recent immigrants, and less powerful than they had been before the war. The race riots of the 1960s only hastened all these processes. With declining tax bases, the cities were in trouble. By the 1970s, New York and Cleveland were bankrupt.

One solution was urban renewal, a program of federal money for slum clearance. But the program was fraught with mixed consequences. When decayed inner-city housing was bulldozed, the business community erected successful new office towers, but the poor and the powerless who had been displaced found themselves with even fewer options than before, exacerbating the nationwide program of homelessness.

Another solution came from the private sector. Planners such as JAMES L. ROUSE and Robert Davis turned vacant factories into new marketplaces, with gourmet restaurants, specialty stores, and museums that attracted the middle classes back to the city—if not to live, at least to spend leisure time and money.

Baltimore's Harborplace and New York City's South Street Seaport were, and are, great successes. So is Boston's Faneuil Hall, and at Museum Wharf, the Children's Museum and Museum of Transportation transformed a run-down brick wharf warehouse in an industrial, largely unoccupied section of South Boston into a lively public space.

Federal money was used to support these large ventures, which came to be known as adaptive use or reuse, and on a personal scale young men and women with college degrees and mortgage money began to renovate city brownstones that had been multifamily apartments back into the luxury homes they once were. Sections of major cities were gentrified, again displacing the poor and the powerless.

Yet another solution came in the form of new towns, planned communities with their own industries, recreational centers, and community services. Reston, Virginia, and Columbia, Maryland, established in the 1960s, are both "exurbs" of Washington, D.C., and self-sufficient communities.

There is no single cure for urban decay or a way to complete urban renewal without disrupting the lives of certain residents, but it is sure that urban planners, politicians, city organizations, and private builders will continue to experiment with ways of preserving and restoring the unique character of America's cities.

1966 A model cities program, passed by Congress, encourages rehabilitation of slums and promotes metropolitan planning in "model" or demonstration cities.

1967 Carl Stokes in Cleveland and Richard Hatcher in Indianapolis are the first blacks elected mayor of major cities.

1970 There are 2.3 million blacks and Puerto Ricans in New York City.

1972 Congress earmarks $18 billion in assistance grants to municipalities to build sewage treatment plants.

1975 New York City teeters on the brink of bankruptcy until it receives a bailout loan from the federal government. The city's financial woes stem partially from a shrinking tax base as white suburban flight continues, coupled with a loss of manufacturing jobs and light industry.

New York City: "Skyscraper National Park"

—KURT VONNEGUT, *SLAPSTICK*, 1976

URBAN BOSSES AND MACHINE POLITICS

The urban boss—a powerful political figure in nineteenth- and twentieth-century city politics—helped city dwellers handle the huge changes wrought by urbanization. So goes one interpretation of the role of the boss and the political machine.

Growing numbers of immigrants—mainly German and Irish at the period when the urban political machines gained ascendance—strained the cities' infrastructure almost to the breaking point. Housing, transportation, jobs, and general crowding made city life miserable for the poor and new arrivals. New York, Chicago, and Boston bore the brunt of the influx, but even smaller cities like Cincinnati were stressed. Water supplies kept running out, and inadequate sewer systems created serious health hazards. Outside of church groups and private philanthropy, social welfare organizations barely existed during that era.

Thus the political bosses and their machines sprang up, in part to fill a niche in urban society. Operating outside the constraints of formal government, ward workers could address problems of individual families or workers for whom the official city government had no time.

Always alert to the opportunity to line their own pockets, machine politicians pursued excessive spending plans to modernize American cities. More buildings, paved roads, and lighting meant more jobs for their constituents, which eventually meant more votes, more power, and eventually more opportunities for graft. The cities evolved slowly into more modern, better-serviced places to live—while graft and corruption became synonymous with urban politics and were often accepted as just the way things had to be done. A consequence was the inevitable rise of reform candidates and movements, for voters' tolerance of graft had definite limits.

A particularly notorious example of the political boss and his machine was Tammany Hall's BOSS TWEED. Tweed and his cronies came to be known as the Tweed Ring. Tammany Hall was formed in 1789 as a benevolent group to help mayoral campaigns in New York City It became a controlling factor in that city's Democratic Party. William Marcy Tweed, who had served in the state legislature, eventually became a supervisor of municipal elections. His political circle included the city comptroller, city chamberlain, and the mayor, Abraham Hall. Tweed and his circle continued to sponsor urban improvement projects, and money paid for city projects eventually found its way into Tweed's pockets. The exorbitant costs—almost double the Alaska purchase price—of building an opulent courthouse aroused suspicions in the community, and the building that became known as the Tweed Courthouse led to Tweed's eventual downfall. Cartoonist and political reformer THOMAS NAST brutally caricatured Tweed in *Harper's Weekly*, and series in the *New York Times* exposed him.

Tweed was finally arrested in 1871 and prosecuted for not auditing contractors' bills. Though the Tweed Ring was essentially broken, Tammany Hall continued to be an active force in New York politics into the 1940s, when Mayor FIORELLO LA GUARDIA set out with the help of President Franklin D. Roosevelt to reform New York's Democratic Party.

Other urban bosses in charge of powerful political machines over the years include Mayor RICHARD J. DALEY of Chicago, C. A. Buckley of San Francisco, David L. Lawrence of Pittsburgh, THOMAS PENDERGAST in Kansas City, and Daniel P. O'Connell in Albany.

IT EXPECTS TO DO THE CARVING.

This 1901 New York Daily Tribune *cartoon likens Andrew Carnegie's $5,200,000 gift to New York City to a pie and suggests that Tammany "expects to do the carving."*

Mid-1970s Increasing numbers of homeless people, often carrying all their possessions in bundles or shopping carts, begin to be noticeable in public urban places; by the mid-1980s, the problem will reach crisis proportions.

1976 With the reopening of Boston's Quincy Market, urban developer JAMES L. ROUSE brings the idea of the urban mall to the downtowns of various cities. He designs malls for downtown Richmond, Baltimore's Harborplace, and New York City's South Street Seaport. The urban malls revitalize urban areas that had deteriorated because of shifts in demographics and business locations.

The D.C. Metro opens; it is the largest urban public works project ever undertaken as a single unified design. Costing more than $8 billion when it opens, with extensions to come, it has an 80 percent federal subsidy. In its first five years it will generate more than $1 billion in private real estate development around Metro stations, changing the pattern of urban growth.

1977 President Jimmy Carter visits the impoverished South Bronx in New York City and leaves promising aid for urban renewal. A $500 million program is enacted but takes years to be put into effect.

1980 Data from the U.S. Census shows that for the first time in the twentieth century the rural population growth almost matches that of urban areas. Rural population, however, includes outer suburban areas and small towns on the distant periphery of sprawling metropolitan areas.

New York City experiences an eleven-day transit strike. New Yorkers end up walking, biking, or sharing cabs to get to work.

Wisconsin senator Gaylord Nelson reports that between 1945 and 1980, 75 percent of government funding for transportation went to highways, while just 1 percent was put aside for public transportation. Thus urban development is sacrificed for the "American dream" of life in the suburbs.

1985 It is estimated by the federal government that between 250,000 to 300,000 people are homeless, most of them in cities.

1988 The federal government estimates that 60,000 family members are using emergency shelters for the urban homeless.

1989 California's strict air-pollution standards are adopted by a number of other states. The laws will eventually improve urban air quality in areas affected.

The U.S. Department of Education estimates that 273,000 children are homeless. The General Accounting Office puts the number at 310,000.

The worst earthquake since 1906 strikes San Francisco on October 17 in the middle of the World Series. Bridges buckle, fires blaze, and ninety people die.

FORMS OF MUNICIPAL GOVERNMENT

Modern municipal governments serve the public welfare, manage public property, and direct public institutions in officially designated cities, towns (except in New England states, New York, Minnesota, and Wisconsin), and villages. There are currently about 20,000 municipal governments in the United States, which fall into three common categories. (Township governments in the states identified above take other forms.)

Mayor-council: Includes an elected mayor and an elected council or other body. The mayor serves as chief executive, usually with broad policymaking and administrative power. In some municipalities, the authority of the mayor is more circumscribed.

Council-manager: An elected council or other governing body is responsible for overall policy and appoints a manager responsible for administration. It may also designate a chairperson among its members, sometimes called a mayor.

Commission: Policymaking and administrative authority is invested in an elected board of commissioners, with each member responsible for administering one or more departments of municipal government. It may also designate a chairperson among its members, sometimes called a mayor.

1990 New York City subways have undergone a face-lift. Though fares rise once again, the trains are more efficient and without graffiti, and most of the cars are air-conditioned.

During the 1990 census, workers survey more than 39,000 locations where they know homeless persons can be found. The count turns up almost 460,000 people. The accuracy of these figures is open to debate.

The 900,000 Puerto Ricans in New York City constitute about 11 percent of the population.

Los Angeles has the largest Mexican population outside of Mexico City.

1992 Islamic terrorists successfully detonate a bomb at the World Trade Center in New York on February 26. Six people die and hundreds are injured in the blast; the terrorist group is quickly apprehended, but tensions of living and working in the crowded metropolis increase.

When an all-white jury acquits the four white policemen accused of beating Rodney King, a black man, Los Angeles erupts in a race riot that leaves fifty-two dead and up to $1 billion in destroyed property. Americans despair that so little progress has been made since the Watts riots of 1965.

1995 The Alfred P. Murrah Building in Oklahoma City is destroyed in a bomb blast shortly after nine A.M. on April 19. The explosion kills at least 167 people, including many of the children in a day-care center housed in the federal office building. Timothy McVeigh, a disgruntled ex-Marine sympathetic with right-wing militia groups that advocate few governmental controls, is tried and convicted of planting the car bomb.

1996–2000 Economic prosperity, including budget surpluses and low unemployment, stimulate urban development in many lower-income areas, a shrinking of welfare rolls, and continuing declines in violent crime. Still, inner-city poverty, often on racial lines, remains a chronic problem. The issue of "urban sprawl" comes to the fore, and a number of state legislatures approve measures to limit peripheral growth.

2000 More than 80 percent of the U.S. population—226.0 of 281.1 million—live in metropolitan areas, according to the 2000 census. Nearly one-third of Americans live in metro areas with more than 5 million people, and another 14 percent live in areas with 2 to 5 million.

2001 On September 11, commercial airlines hijacked by terrorists crash into each tower of the World Trade Center in New York City. The two giant structures burn and topple, killing nearly 3,000 people. The devastating attacks have an immediate effect on the economy of the city. At least 100,000 jobs are lost, and the cost of cleanup, reconstruction, city services, and lost business is expected to exceed $5 billion.

THE GROWTH OF AMERICA'S SUBURBS

As early as the mid-nineteenth century, more prosperous city dwellers built homes in outlying districts. The usual pattern saw the immigrant or working-class family advance up the socioeconomic ladder and abandon the old overcrowded neighborhoods.

At first families moved to more upscale areas of town, then to closer outlying districts still within the reach of public transportation, the "streetcar suburbs." But as train service improved and the automobile ceased to be a luxury item, the American dream of owning a house and having a better life fell within the reach of the middle class. Suburban growth accelerated in the 1920s, although it was slowed by the Great Depression. However, once World War II ended, several factors led to suburban growth: the GI Bill for returning war veterans, which provided easy mortgage terms for buying houses; new generous credit and mortgage policies of the Federal Housing Administration; the development of prefabricated building techniques that made housing cheaper to build; federal and local tax breaks for homeowners and mortgage holders; and finally, a pattern of federal funding for national highway transportation that facilitated travel from suburb to city.

Planned suburban communities—such as Shaker Heights outside of Cleveland, or the various Levittown developments—sprang up from coast to coast. Levittown took full advantage of prefab housing and mass production techniques, enabling families with incomes only marginally over $5,000 to purchase a house with a down payment of $100. The inexpensive houses were in pleasant, landscaped surroundings and fully equipped with the latest modern appliances.

Downtown became a place of work—a nine-to-five world. At five, the commuter retreated back home to the suburbs, which became known as bedroom communities. For the most part the only people who stayed in the cities were those too poor to leave.

Suburban communities also remain controversial in the national picture as having detached themselves from the urban areas that support them financially. Directly after the war, most suburban dwellers found work in the city, but commuters generally paid little or no taxes to the cities where they worked. Families could live far from one another and from retail and entertainment districts and rely on cars and the burgeoning highway system to shop, go to the movies, or go out to dinner. As the cost and logistics of shopping and going out in the cities becomes prohibitive for the average suburbanite, retail stores begin cropping up in suburban areas where the rents are smaller than in the city centers and the possibility of large parking lots exists. With the rise of suburban shopping centers, people begin to live and work in the suburbs, creating "edge cities" and "suburban downtowns" outside of the major urban centers. The cities are faced with the dwindling revenues to support increasing social, structural, and cultural service, while the "urbanization" of the suburbs leads them to confront the issues, such as drugs, crime, pollution, and violence, that cities have long dealt with.

AGRICULTURE AND FARM LIFE, 1612–PRESENT

Thomas Jefferson's vision of the new nation as a land of independent, yeoman farmers was reality in his day, and even as late as the end of the nineteenth century, most Americans made their livelihood in agriculture. Advances in transportation and technology in the nineteenth and twentieth centuries enabled farmers to cultivate large quantities of land with enormous productivity. Cycles of national economic boom and depression coupled with America's dependence on international markets for its massive agricultural output have affected the nature as well as the growth of agriculture. Although a very small percentage of Americans in the twenty-first century earn their livelihoods from farming, agriculture remains an important and vital part of the national economy.

> Corn is the only major food crop native to American soil. All others were introduced from abroad.

c. 1612 John Rolfe introduces the cultivation of tobacco at Jamestown, and, by 1615, it is the cash crop of the Virginia colony.

1615 The Virginia Company, which owns all the land, allows settlers to become tenants on company property.

1621 Squanto, a Patuxet Indian who had been kidnapped and lived in England for a few years, gives the Pilgrims seed corn and teaches them native planting practices. Corn, or maize, becomes a principal grain in New England; wheat and rye are also successful.

1690s German immigrant farmers settle in Pennsylvania because of the colony's promise of religious tolerance. While the English settlers girdle trees to kill them, then farm among the stumps, the Germans, with their superior farming technology—including heavy draft horses that can pull plows and weighty loads—clear their land completely and plow the soil deeply. They choose to plant wheat, and they house their livestock in barns, which they construct even before they build their own houses. The English, on the other hand, let their stock forage. The Germans prove to be highly suc-

cessful farmers and eventually bring their superior agricultural practices to Maryland, western Virginia, and other colonies.

1693 Rice cultivation is introduced in South Carolina. It is well suited to the colony's freshwater swamps and sluggish rivers near the sea, and it quickly becomes a staple crop. By 1730, South Carolina rice is called the best in the world.

1745 Indigo cultivation, introduced to South Carolina a few years earlier by Elizabeth (Eliza) Lucas Pinckney, reaches a stage of profitable production, stimulating a dye-stuffs industry. Indigo becomes one of the colony's major export crops, long before cotton, which is difficult to harvest and process until the invention of the cotton gin.

1785 The Land Ordinance provides for the survey and sale of public lands at auction in lots of 640 acres at a cash price of at least $1 per acre. Few would-be settlers have the money to take advantage of this early land act.

1786–1787 In Shays' Rebellion, Massachusetts farmers led by Revolutionary War veteran Daniel Shays protest farm and home foreclosures during the post–Revolutionary War depression.

1790 Almost all Americans live in rural areas. Some are subsistence farmers, and some are engaged in food production.

1793 Eli Whitney invents the cotton gin, and cotton production soon soars. U.S. cotton production rises from 4,000 bales in 1791 to 73,000 bales in 1800. A bale weighs about 500 pounds. Cotton's success further entrenches the slavery system in America.

1794 In the Whiskey Rebellion, frontier farmers protest an excise tax on whiskey, which is a medium of exchange in western Pennsylvania—grain is easier to transport in liquid form.

1796 Congress passes a Public Land Act authorizing the sale of U.S. government lands in minimum lots of 640 acres for $2 per acre.

1800 The Land Ordinance of 1785 is amended by a new congressional bill that permits the sale of 320-acre plots at $2 per acre with a down payment of one-fourth and the balance to be paid in three annual installments. Finally land sales pick up.

1820 Congress passes another land act providing for the sale of eighty-acre plots of public land at $1.25 an acre in cash. Farmers who have bought land under other acts are enraged, especially those in debt from earlier purchases at higher rates.

1831 Cyrus McCormick demonstrates his reaper, and the invention is patented in 1834. The reaper harvests four times faster than a man with a scythe, and wheat production expands rapidly.

1833 Edmund Ruffin founds the *Farmers' Register.* In other publications he promotes the application of marl, deeper plowing, and animal husbandry.

1837 John Deere invents a steel, one-piece plow and moldboard, which is capable of cutting through the roots of prairie grass in the Midwest and Great Plains and reduces the labor of plowing by half. Again acreage in production is expanded.

1847 Mormons begin farming in Utah, eventually creating communal farmlands with satellite villages and introducing dams and irrigation techniques to make crops grow in desert soil.

1860 The nation now has 2,044,000 farms. A farmer's work can support himself and three other people. In 1970, a farmer can support himself and forty-seven others.

1862 The Homestead Act offers 160 acres of public domain lands to any head of household who registers the claim, makes some improvement on the land within six months, and lives on it for five years. Unfortunately, much of the West is so arid that often 160 acres is not enough land for viable agriculture.

Much of the land falls into the hands of speculators.

The Morrill Act authorizes grants of land to support state schools teaching agriculture or the mechanical arts.

The Department of Agriculture is established. Its head becomes a cabinet member in 1889.

1867 The percentage of Americans working on farms has risen to more than 50 percent.

Oliver H. Kelley founds the National Grange of the Patrons of Husbandry ("grange" is an outdated name for a barn). At first apolitical, the Grange's mission is educational and social, but after the Panic of 1873, local granges become political forums. Eventually the Grange will become a force in agricultural politics, centering around issues involving equitable freight rates and taxation. The Grange also sets up cooperative stores, grain elevators, and mills.

1873 The depression that follows the panic this year forces many southern farmers, black and white, into sharecropping.

Springfield, Illinois, is the site of a farmers' convention that attacks the power of monopolies, in particular railroads, as "detrimental to the public prosperity, corrupting in their management, and dangerous to republican institutions."

1874 Several states pass so-called Granger Laws, establishing shipping rates railroads can charge. Railroads have long charged high and discriminatory rates, charging farmers more to ship crops a short distance than for the long hauls industrial shippers required.

1876 The Grange lobbies for protection from the railroads, for better schools, and for regulation of grain elevators.

1880 About 80 percent of the land in black belt states—Mississippi, Georgia, and Alabama—has been divided into family farms, and almost 75 percent of black southerners are sharecroppers.

1887 The Hatch Act provides federal funds for state agricultural experimental stations.

AGRICULTURE AND FARM LIFE, 1612–PRESENT, cont.

1889 A cycle of poverty locked in by the crop-lien system continues to spark agrarian protest as several regional Farmers' Alliances unite to form the National Farmers' Alliance and Industrial Union. A parallel organization is the National Colored Farmers' Alliance and Cooperative Union. Like the Grange, the Alliance protests large combinations of industry and banks that have the power to dictate prices and interest rates. It also establishes cooperative cotton gins, flour mills, and grain elevators.

1890 Two-thirds of all Americans still live in rural communities; just fifty years earlier 90 percent of the population were farm dwellers.

Nearly one-half of southern farmers are sharecroppers.

"Pitchfork Ben" TILLMAN, supported by the Farmers' Alliance, is elected governor of South Carolina. He promotes agricultural education and railroad regulation. In 1894, he is elected to the U.S. Senate, where he continues to champion the interests of the farmer.

1891 Tom Watson is elected to the U.S. House of Representatives, where he promotes populism and secures appropriation for rural free delivery in 1893. Experiments in rural mail delivery began in 1896, stimulating work on new roads and highways, and connecting previously isolated rural communities to more heavily populated and industrialized areas of the country.

1892 The Populist Party unites farmer and labor organizations, calling for the free coinage of silver, the abolition of national banks, government ownership of railroads, a maximum workday, and immigration restriction. Its presidential candidate, James B. Weaver, polls more than 1 million votes. The party collapses after the 1896 elec-

tion, in which the Democrats also nominate the Populist candidate, William Jennings Bryan, and steal many Populist issues.

The boll weevil appears in Texas. It annually destroys about 8 percent of the total cotton crop, resulting in a $200 to $300 million loss.

The first gasoline engine tractor makes its appearance in South Dakota. It weighs more than 9,000 pounds.

1901 About 25 to 35 percent of U.S. agricultural produce is exported. These figures fall as rapid population growth and increasing urbanization increase the need to ship food to urban centers within the United States.

1909 The Enlarged Homestead Act increases maximum permissible homesteads to 320 acres in cattle-raising areas of the West. The maximum is increased again in 1916 to 640 acres for grazing and forage land not suitable for crops unless irrigated.

1914 The Smith-Lever Act provides for agricultural extension services.

A meeting of influential men at the White House includes (left to right) industrialist Andrew Carnegie, populist leader William Jennings Bryan, railway president J. J. Hill, and labor organizer John Mitchell.

1916 Congress passes the Federal Farm Loan Act, which permits the establishment of farm loan banks as well as a Federal Farm Loan Board. This legislation eases the way for farmers to obtain credit to improve their farms with machinery and make additional land purchases.

1920–1969 Farm acreage at the beginning of this period equals 959 million acres. In 1969, farmland accounts for 1,063 million acres. From 1915 to 1945, almost 38 million acres of public and private lands are withdrawn from potential agricultural use and set aside as national forests, national parks, roadways, and urban areas.

1920s Chemical pesticides are introduced to American agriculture.

1930 Thirty million Americans, about one-quarter of the population, still live and work on farms. In 1890, 25 million, or 40 percent of the population, made farms their homes and workplaces.

1932 Farm prices this year are only 40 percent of what they were in 1929. Wheat sells for less than 38 cents per bushel; oats 16 cents per bushel, cotton a mere 6.5 cents a pound; and wool 8.6 cents a pound.

1933 The Tennessee Valley Authority is established. By controlling floods in the region and harnessing electric power, as well as through programs reclaiming land and preventing erosion, it will improve the area's agriculture.

Congress passes the Agricultural Adjustment Act, establishing an Agricultural Adjustment Administration (AAA) as part of the Department of Agriculture. The idea is to decrease the amount of land under cultivation.

The Norris Dam in Knoxville is among the many construction projects that utilized workers form the Tennessee Valley Authority.

The Commodity Credit Corporation is created by Congress within the Department of Agriculture to buy farm surpluses and to process subsidies due farmers for withholding acreage from production.

The Farm Credit Administration is created to consolidate farm-credit agencies. Nevertheless, the year sees 1 million farm families receive direct government aid.

1934 Congress legislates the Farm Mortgage Financing Act, establishing the Federal Farm Mortgage Corporation to assist farmers in refinancing their mortgages and avoiding foreclosures.

A Crop Loan Act sanctions loans to farmers to assist them in production and harvesting.

Mid–1930s Dust storms ravage the western states. A direct result of farming methods that stripped the land of vegetation, overproduction, especially during World War I, and several seasons of severe drought, these storms, with clouds of dust so thick day turns into night, trigger the great trek of migrants from the Dust Bowl. Already poverty-stricken by the Great Depression, 350,000 farmers, behind in their mortgages and with their farms near foreclosure, pick up stakes and move west by the end of the decade.

AGRICULTURE AND FARM LIFE, 1612–PRESENT, cont.

1935 Only 12.6 percent of rural America has electric service. President Franklin Roosevelt establishes the Rural Electrification Administration (REA) by Executive Order. The REA will underwrite and extend loans to rural electric cooperatives for the express purpose of bringing electrical power to rural America.

The number of farms reaches 6.812 million, and the farm population is 32.161 million. This is the high point of farming; after this year, numbers of farms and farmers decline steadily.

Direct payments of $573 million are made by the federal government to farmers who are participating in various farm programs.

1940s DDT becomes available in the United States. It is hailed as a godsend for its spectacular success in controlling insects. Only after the research of Rachel Carson and the publication of her book *The Silent Spring,* in 1962, are the perils of DDT recognized.

1945 More than 24 million people depend on the land for their livelihood.

1950 Seventy-seven percent of families living in rural America now have electricity. Six years later this figure jumps to 96 percent.

Rachel Carson testifies before the Senate on the dangers of pesticides

1950–1970 Millions of bushels of grain are stockpiled, and politicians question both the costs of storage and continued support payments to farmers. The Food for Peace program, passed in 1961, helps reduce stockpiles and storage costs. Rising demand for exports helps hold support payments down. Also during this period, factory farming is a growing trend, harming small farmers and leading to the mass rearing and slaughter of livestock.

1954 The Watershed and Flood Protection Act is passed to protect U.S. farmers from the effects of soil erosion.

1955 The National Farmers' Organization (NFO) is established by disgruntled farmers from Iowa and Missouri. They hope to initiate bargaining to support the prices of stock, grain, and milk.

1956 At the instigation of President Dwight D. Eisenhower and Secretary of Agriculture Ezra Taft Benson, Congress authorizes a new soil-bank program, encouraging farmers to refrain from planting their land to conserve the land itself and to decrease production.

1960 Only 8 percent of U.S. workers are farm laborers, down from 12 percent in 1950.

1962 Cesar Chavez organizes the National Farm Workers Association to represent and help the impoverished migrant farmworkers.

1964 U.S. farmers now number only 12.9 million.

1965 President Johnson's plans to end poverty in the United States lead to a $1.4 billion program of federal and state aid to help Appalachia, one of the poorest rural regions of the country.

1969 U.S. farms now number just 2.73 million, with a population of 10.3 million.

1970 Farm labor drops to just 5 percent of the workforce, or almost 10 million people. One U.S. farm laborer can produce enough food for forty-seven people.

1985 An $87 billion farm bill, in the midst of an agricultural depression, brings temporary stability to beleaguered farmers.

1986 Many midwestern farms suffer foreclosure in an extended agricultural depression following inflated land values and extensive borrowing.

1990 Crop support payments are frozen in an attempt to get control of the federal budget deficit.

1995 Agricultural funding is reduced by $5.8 billion from the previous fiscal year.

1996 A revolutionary farm bill aims at weaning farmers from federal subsidies and giving them opportunities for expansion. Supports are scheduled for elimination by 2002.

1998–1999 Drought conditions in the Midwest and South and severe storms in other areas reduce crops of major agricultural products. Prices for livestock and grains are depressed.

1999 The Food and Drug Administration holds its first public hearings on foods such as corn, soybeans, and tomatoes that are being genetically modified by producers.

2000–2001 U.S. consumers and meat producers fear the introduction of foot-and-mouth disease in cattle, swine, and other products imported from Europe. The Department of Agriculture institutes a series of restrictions and other protective measures to reduce the risk of contamination.

U.S. FARMS: NUMBER, ACREAGE, AND POPULATION, 1850–2000

YEAR	NUMBER (THOUSANDS)	TOTAL ACREAGE (THOUSANDS)	ACREAGE PER FARM	POPULATION (THOUSANDS)	PERCENT OF U.S. TOTAL
1850	1,449	293,561	203	n.a.	n.a.
1860	2,044	407,213	199	n.a.	n.a.
1870	2,660	407,735	153	n.a.	n.a.
1880	4,009	536,082	134	21,973	43.8
1890	4,565	623,219	137	24,771	42.3
1900	5,740	841,202	147	29,835	41.9
1910	6,366	881,431	139	32,077	34.9
1920	6,454	958,677	149	31,974	30.1
1930	6,295	990,112	157	30,529	24.9
1940	6,102	1,065,114	175	30,547	23.2
1950	5,388	1,161,420	216	23,048	15.3
1960	3,962	1,176,946	297	15,635	8.7
1970	2,954	1,102,769	373	9,712	4.8
1980	2,440	1,039,000	426	6,051	2.7
1990	2,146	987,000	460	4,801	1.9
2000	2,172	943,000	434	n.a.	n.a.

Sources: U.S. Census Bureau, Statistical Abstract of the United States, U.S. Department of Agriculture.

RURAL TO AN URBAN NATION

LEGISLATION AFFECTING CITIES AND URBAN LIFE, 1921–PRESENT

1921 Federal Highway Act. This coordinates state highway systems in an effort to create a national system. This act creates the Bureau of Public Roads. This is the first of several highway acts that will indirectly lead to the proliferation of suburbs, the decline of cities, and major population shifts among various metropolitan areas nationwide.

1933–1940 New Deal Legislation. A series of laws, including creation of the Civil Works Administration (CWA) in 1933 and the Works Progress Administration (WPA) in 1935, will enhance urban life through the development of federally funded public works programs that benefit urban areas through housing construction, street paving, school improvement, and the construction of hospitals and other civic structures, institutions, and services. The Federal Housing Administration (FHA) in 1934 insures loans for construction and improvements.

1942 Emergency Price Control Act. Enacted by the federal government to control wartime inflation, this has a twofold effect on cities. Middle-class housing remains affordable, but low rents are detrimental to new rental-housing starts.

1944 Federal Highway Act lays the foundation for the Interstate Highway System. Enacted to strengthen America's infrastructure and provide fast movements of goods and possibly troops during wartime, this legislation authorizes funding for the creation of the interstate highway system that will be a potent force in postwar suburbanization. Full-scale funding does not occur until 1956.

GI Bill of Rights (Servicemen's Readjustment Act). By making homes more affordable to war veterans, this legislation indirectly contributes to postwar flight to the suburbs.

1949 Federal Housing Act. Sponsored by Republican senator Robert Taft of Ohio, this provides funding for urban renewal through slum cleanup and the building of low-cost public housing.

1956 Interstate Highway Act. This funds a 42,500-mile (68,395-km) system of limited-access highways linking all major cities. Rail and public transportation systems remain unsubsidized.

1959 Housing Act. Congress legislates that $650 million out of this $1 billion housing bill should be spent for urban housing renewal and rehabilitation.

1998 Quality Housing and Work Responsibility Act. Congress overhauls the nation's public-housing system to reduce the concentration of poverty, protect access for the poorest families, bring more working families into subsidized units, and revive economically depressed and racially segregated projects.

SUPREME COURT DECISIONS AFFECTING CITIES AND FARMS, 1877–PRESENT

1877 *Munn v. Illinois.* The Court upholds an Illinois law establishing maximum rates for storing grains, one of the so-called Granger Laws enacted by state legislatures in the Midwest at the insistence of the Grange. The decision establishes the constitutional principle of public regulation of private business involved in serving the public interest.

1911 *United States v. Grimaud.* This states that Congress has the right to confer administrative power on the secretary of agriculture to establish rules and regulations on the use of federal lands.

1926 *Village of Euclid v. Ambler Realty Company.* The Court upholds municipal zoning ordinances and the right of communities to designate land for business, industrial, and residential purposes.

1934 *Nebbia v. New York.* The Court justifies state law in setting minimum prices in the dairy industry.

1942 *Wickard v. Filburn.* The Court upholds the Second Agricultural Adjustment Act of 1938. A farmer claimed that wheat grown but not brought to market was not subject to a penalty for over-production since it was never sold. The Court rules against the farmer and for the New Deal legislation setting planting limits.

1944 *Bowles v. Willingham.* The Court upholds the right of the OPA (Office of Price Administration) to impose rent controls.

1962 *Baker v. Carr.* The Court rules that arbitrarily drawn electoral districts violate constitutional rights, and voters have the right to challenge. Prior to this ruling, Tennessee voting districts had not been reapportioned for sixty years and therefore did not reflect the increase in urban populations. The Court's decision helped urban votes to carry the same weight as rural votes.

1964 *Wesberry v. Sanders.* The Court rules that congressional districts must adhere to the "one person, one vote" test laid down in *Gray v. Sanders.* The cycle is completed four months later in *Reynolds v. Sims* when the Court rules that both houses of state legislatures must be based on population.

Reynolds v. Sims. In a ruling that will eclipse the disproportionate power of rural areas, long over-represented in legislative districts, the Court invokes the "one person, one vote" principle to support its decision that both houses of a state legislature must be apportioned on the basis of population. As a consequence of massive redistricting throughout the fifty states, urban districts, long underrepresented, become more powerful.

1980 *City of Mobile v. Bolden.* The Court rules that election of city council members by voters at large does not violate the Fourteenth and Fifteenth Amendments.

1981 *Poletown Neighborhood Council v. Detroit.* The Court expands the power of eminent domain— the authority of government to appropriate private property for public purposes.

1984 *Hawaii Housing Authority v. Midkiff.* The Court upholds Hawaii's right to take private property for private use. The ruling gives great latitude to the condemnation power of the state.

NOTABLE FIGURES IN RURAL AND URBAN LIFE

Addams, Jane (1860–1935). A social reformer, Addams was inspired by a visit to Toynbee Hall, a London settlement house. In 1889 with the help of Ellen Gates Starr she founded Hull-House in Chicago, which became a mecca for immigrants. There Addams instituted a series of community services, running the gamut from language courses to craft training to child care. She fought for fair labor practices and for general social-welfare programs.

Astor, John Jacob (1763–1848). Astor invested money made in the fur trade in real estate, much of it in Manhattan, including a $350,000 bequest that established the Astor Library, later incorporated into the New York Public Library. At his death he was the wealthiest man in America.

Burnham, Daniel H. (1846–1912). Architect Burnham was one of the founders of the Chicago School and pioneered new skyscraper designs, including New York's Flatiron Building. He was a staunch advocate of urban planning and a founder of the "City Beautiful" movement.

Cooper, Peter (1791–1883). Born in New York City, Cooper was a typical self-made man of his era, who prospered financially through hard work in various trades and through farseeing investments in new technology—such as the laying of the first transatlantic cable. Active in civic matters he founded New York's Cooper Union in 1859 to provide the opportunity for adult education in art and technical subjects.

Daley, Richard J. (1902–1976). The Chicago-born politician was chairman of the Cook County Democratic Party, a powerful political machine. As Chicago's mayor for twenty years, he forged alliances with industry and unions enabling Chicago to have an urban renaissance while many other industrial cities were declining. The violent confrontations between police and anti-Vietnam War demonstrators at the 1968 Democratic National Convention hurt Daley's reputation nationally.

Edison, Thomas Alva (1847–1931). Edison invented and patented many devices, but it was his invention of the electric lightbulb in 1879 that revolutionized city life. Not only could dim interiors be lit without dangerous candles, oil lamps, or gaslights, but the city streets, once problems with mass generation of electrical energy were solved, became bright and safer at night, and urban life was able to continue full-swing twenty-four hours a day.

Feinstein, Dianne (1933–). Active in Democratic politics from an early age, Feinstein served as a city and county supervisor in San Francisco from 1970 to 1978. When the mayor and supervisor were shot, Feinstein was selected by the remaining supervisors to fill out the term as mayor, and she was subsequently elected in her own right, serving for ten years. In 1992, she was elected U.S. senator from California. Feinstein was reelected in 1994 and again in 2000.

Franklin, Benjamin (1706–1790). A printer, writer, scientist, and statesman, Franklin was born in Boston and moved to Philadelphia seeking his fortune as a printer and publisher of newspapers. His many projects included plans to pave, clean, light, and police the streets of colonial Philadelphia. He was instrumental in supporting the volunteer fire companies that protected American cities until well into the nineteenth century.

La Guardia, Fiorello (1882–1947). One of New York City's best-loved mayors, La Guardia served three terms (1934–1945) and was instrumental in instituting political reform (he aided in the final downfall of New York's corrupt Democratic political machine, Tammany Hall), and housing and welfare advances.

Lease, Mary Elizabeth (1853–1933). A teacher who moved to Kansas after the Civil War, Lease became an agrarian activist and leader of the grass-roots Populist movement. A flamboyant orator she is best known for urging farmers to "raise less corn and more hell."

Levitt, William J. (1907–1994). A New York–born builder and developer, Levitt gained experience with mass-produced residences during World War II building housing for the U.S. Navy. He later adapted his know-how to civilian life when he developed and built his first Levittown in Long Island, 30 miles (48 km) east of New York City.

Minuit, Peter (1580?–1638). Minuit was the first leader of New Amsterdam, later to become New York. He purchased Manhattan from the Canarsie Indians in 1626.

Moses, Robert (1889–1981). As New York City parks commissioner and the head of the city's Triborough Bridge and Tunnel authorities, Moses single-handedly and irrevocably altered the metropolitan area by supervising the building of most of its highways, constructing parks and playgrounds, and erecting bridges. He favored private over public transportation and was criticized for paving over neighborhoods with miles of highway.

Mulholland, William (1855–1935). Irish-born Mulholland was a hydraulic engineer who became the superintendent and chief engineer of the Los Angeles waterworks in 1886. He devised the plans for and oversaw the construction of the Los Angeles aqueduct that brought the city a water supply from the Sierra Nevada, 250 miles (400 km) away.

Nast, Thomas (1840–1902). A German American who migrated to New York with his family at age five, Nast pioneered the political cartoon. In 1861, he began working for *Harper's Weekly*. His caricatures attacking New York's Tweed Ring were instrumental in unseating "Boss Tweed" and shaking down Tammany Hall.

Olmsted, Frederick Law (1822–1903). A landscape architect, Olmsted, with Calvert Vaux, won a competition for the design of Central Park in New York City. They fashioned a pastoral rambling park out of what was then wilderness inhabited by squatters. He envisioned preserving natural habitats within urban areas, and, after completing work on Central Park, he went on to design major parks in Boston, Chicago, and Montreal.

Otis, Elisha Graves (1811–1861). Otis was employed as a master mechanic for a firm in Yonkers, New York, when he developed the first elevator as a way of hauling supplies and workmen from one floor of a building to another. He eventually patented his steam elevator.

Pendergast, Thomas J. (1872–1945). Pendergast created a powerful political machine in Missouri after he became head of the Kansas City Democrats in 1916. In control for twenty-five years, he gave Harry Truman his start in politics. He was indicted by the U.S. government for tax evasion and went to prison in 1939.

Riis, Jacob (1849–1914). As a police reporter for the *New York Evening Sun*, this Danish American photojournalist and social reformer documented life in the city slums. His powerful photographs exposed the wretched conditions of the urban immigrant, and his book *How the Other Half Lives* (1890) spurred then–New York police commissioner Theodore Roosevelt to support the tenement-reform movement.

Roebling, John Augustus (1806–1869). Considered the greatest American bridge builder of the nineteenth century, Roebling emigrated from his native Germany when he was twenty-five years old and settled in Pittsburgh. He constructed canals and aqueducts, and his innovative use of wire rope facilitated all his engineering endeavors. After earlier successful bridge-building ventures, he was

appointed chief engineer to oversee construction of New York's Brooklyn Bridge. He died of tetanus after being injured while working on the project.

Rouse, James L. (1914–1996). Rouse developed planned cities such as Columbia, Maryland, urban marketplaces, and shipping centers. In the 1970s, he designed the first of his "festival marketplaces" in Boston. He also helped found the Enterprise Foundation, which encouraged the building of affordable urban housing.

Stuyvesant, Peter (1610?–1672). Stuyvesant became governor of the Dutch colony of New Netherland in 1647. He was a stern leader and often argued with colonists living in New Amsterdam. Eventually the burghers of New Amsterdam won the right to municipal self-government, and Stuyvesant had to bargain with the young city on matters of taxes and defense.

Sullivan, Louis H. (1856–1924). Boston-born Sullivan was the leading exponent of the Chicago School of architecture. The main tenet of his design philosophy was "form follows function." One of the fathers of the contemporary skyscraper, Sullivan designed and realized more than 100 buildings in his career. Among his most famous are the Chicago Stock Exchange (1886–1889) and the Wainwright Building in St. Louis (1890–1891). His most famous student was Frank Lloyd Wright.

Tillman, Benjamin (1847–1918). In South Carolina, Tillman became the political leader of backcountry whites. As governor of the state (1890–1894), he promoted agricultural education and regulation of railroads. While serving as a Democratic senator (1895–1918), he allied himself with Populists and strongly opposed President Grover Cleveland. He earned the name "Pitchfork Ben" because he once threatened to stick a pitchfork into the president.

Tweed, William Marcy ("Boss") (1823–1878). Tweed was a major power in New York City's Tammany Hall Democratic organization. His corruption was eventually exposed through the efforts of reformer-cartoonist Thomas Nast. Tweed was arrested and convicted of graft and corruption. He fled to Spain, where he was extradited back to the United States. He died in prison.

Wright, Frank Lloyd (1869–1959). Wright studied civil engineering but began his career working for architect Louis Sullivan. He gained notice for his "prairie houses" with low, horizontal lines and projecting eaves. An innovative designer, Wright advocated open planning in buildings and pioneered textile-block slab construction.

CHAPTER 8

FOREIGN AFFAIRS

■

HIGHLIGHTS

Timeline of U.S. Foreign Affairs

U.S. FOREIGN AFFAIRS, according to the Constitution, are the joint responsibility of the president and Congress. The latter has the power to appropriate funds for defense, to raise and support an army and navy, to regulate foreign trade, and to declare war. The president, on the other hand, is designated as commander in chief of the armed forces and has the authority to negotiate foreign treaties (which the Senate must confirm), to appoint ambassadors (also subject to Senate confirmation), and to receive foreign emissaries. The judicial branch has the constitutional power to interpret treaties but rarely does so. In general, the president is the leader of the nation's foreign affairs, with the Department of State mandated to carry out the policies established in the Oval Office.

Several American presidents, including THEODORE ROOSEVELT and WOODROW WILSON, were foreign policy activists by nature and temperament. Others, such as John Adams and WILLIAM MCKINLEY, had foreign involvement thrust upon them. Only a few, all in the twentieth century—Wilson, FRANKLIN D. ROOSEVELT, and JOHN F. KENNEDY among them—emerged as world leaders.

THE FEDERALIST ERA: ASSERTING INDEPENDENCE

1783 The Treaty of Paris, which formally ends the Revolutionary War, is signed by Great Britain, France, and the United States. It recognizes the independence of the United States and settles issues relating to boundaries, debts, confiscated property, and fishing rights.

While the United States is primarily preoccupied with nation building, it establishes relations with France, Britain, Spain, the Netherlands, and Russia, the dominant and most important trading nations in Europe.

1789 President George Washington's first appointment is Thomas Jefferson, who becomes the new nation's first secretary of state and the highest ranking cabinet member.

1793 The French Revolution takes a violent turn and divided American opinion offers President Washington his administration's first serious foreign policy challenge. Washington issues a proclamation of neutrality, but Citizen Genêt (Edmond Charles), minister of the French Republic, tours the United States to organize American expeditions against Spain and

FOREIGN AFFAIRS

1793, *cont.*

Britain. Exasperated, Washington demands Genêt's recall, but by then the French Revolution has taken yet another turn and new French ministers arrive to arrest Genêt. Washington refuses to extradite Genêt (knowing he will be guillotined). Genêt becomes an American citizen and marries the daughter of New York governor George Clinton.

1794 Jay's Treaty, negotiated by Chief Justice JOHN JAY, is signed; the British agree to withdraw troops from the Northwest Territory in return for a renewed commitment by the United States that debts incurred before the Revolution will be paid.

1795 Pinckney's Treaty with Spain accepts the 31st parallel as the northern boundary of Spanish Florida and grants Americans free navigation of the Mississippi and the right of deposit at New Orleans. The right of deposit allowed farmers and manufacturers to unload their goods in New Orleans to be put on ocean-bound ships without paying duties.

1796 In his farewell address, President Washington argues for isolationism when he warns: "It is our true policy to steer clear of permanent alliances with any portion of the foreign world."

1798 Revelation of the XYZ Affair, a diplomatic scandal in which French agents solicit bribes from American commissioners in order to establish trade ties, angers Americans (see p. 219).

1798–1800 Tensions with France increase to the point that the period is described as an undeclared war. The Federalists impose severe restrictions on French sympathizers in the Alien and Sedition Acts. In 1800, the Treaty of Morfontaine formally releases the United States from its defensive alliance with France, and tensions subside.

1803 When President Thomas Jefferson learns that Napoleon has secretly bought the Louisiana Territory from Spain, he sends Secretary of State JAMES MONROE to France to buy as much of the land around New Orleans as he can. Surprisingly, Napoleon is in the mood to sell the entire territory. Monroe seizes the opportunity, thereby scoring the new nation's first major diplomatic coup: the size of the United States is doubled without going to war.

1807 A foreign crisis looms as warring France and England challenge U.S. neutrality and desire to trade with both nations. Both interfere with free trade, and President Thomas Jefferson signs the Embargo Act, which forbids all imports and exports. Designed to hurt the British, it hurts U.S. commerce far more.

"I think that a young State, like a young Virgin, should modestly stay at home, and wait the Application of suitors for an Alliance with her; and not run about offering her Amity to all the World; and hazarding their refusal."

—BENJAMIN FRANKLIN, LETTER, 1778

Napoleon was in the bathtub, where he sometimes met with advisors, when he decided to sell the Louisiana Territory to the United States in 1803.

WASHINGTON'S FAREWELL ADDRESS

One of the most frequently quoted speeches in American history—especially by those inclined to isolationism—George Washington's farewell address of September 17, 1796, urged the nation to pursue foreign trade but cautioned against permanent alliances with other nations. His advice was a cornerstone of U.S. foreign policy for over a century.

The great rule of conduct for us in regard to foreign nations is, in extending our commercial relations to have with them as little political connection as possible. So far as we have already formed engagements let them be fulfilled with perfect good faith.

Here let us stop.

Europe has a set of primary interests which to us have none, or a very remote, relation.... Hence it must be unwise in us to implicate ourselves in artificial ties in the ordinary vicissitudes of her politics.... Our detached and distant situation invites and enables us to pursue a different course. If we remain one people, under an efficient government, the period is not far off when we may defy material injury from external annoyance; when we may take such an attitude as will cause the neutrality we may at any time resolve upon to be scrupulously respected; when belligerent nations, under the impossibility of making acquisitions upon us, will not lightly hazard the giving us provocation; when we may choose peace or war as our interest guided by our justice may counsel.

Why quit our own to stand upon foreign ground? Why, by interweaving our destiny with that of any part of Europe, entangle our peace and prosperity in the toils of European ambition, rivalship, interest, humor, or caprice?

It is our true policy to steer clear of permanent alliances with any portion of the foreign world. So far, I mean, as we are now at liberty to do it, for let me not be understood as capable of patronizing infidelity to existing engagements.

1809 The destructive Embargo Act, which has brought U.S. trade to a standstill, is rescinded, although both Britain and France remain hostile toward the United States.

1812 The United States and Great Britain fight the War of 1812 over disputed boundaries, neutral rights, and trade relations.

1814 The Treaty of Ghent settles the War of 1812. No land has changed hands, and neither side has gained anything from the war, but it is the last that the United States and England will fight against each other.

1817 President JAMES MONROE's secretary of state, JOHN QUINCY ADAMS, arranges for the United States and Great Britain to sign the Rush-Bagot Treaty, which demilitarizes the Great Lakes, setting a precedent for the demilitarization of the U.S.-Canadian border.

1818 The Convention of 1818, signed by the United States and Great Britain, sets the northern U.S. border from the Lake of the Woods, Minnesota, to the Rocky Mountains at the 49th parallel and establishes joint custody of the Oregon Country, which both nations claim.

1819 The Adams-Onís Treaty cedes Spanish Florida to the United States. Spain cedes more readily, no doubt, when Gen. Andrew Jackson exceeds his orders to put down an Indian dispute while the treaty is being negotiated and invades Florida. The treaty also defines the border between the Louisiana Purchase and Spanish Mexico.

FOREIGN AFFAIRS

1823 When Britain proposes joint action to prevent European intervention in Latin America, President JAMES MONROE responds with the Monroe Doctrine, which declares an end to New World colonization by Europe and warns foreign powers that any intervention in the Western Hemisphere will be considered a threat to the United States (see p. 292).

1824 The capital of Liberia is named Monrovia after President JAMES MONROE, who supported the creation of the country. The American Colonization Society first brought freed slaves to the west African coastal nation in 1822.

1842 The Webster-Ashburton Treaty, whose terms are developed by Secretary of State DANIEL WEBSTER and Lord Ashburton, resolves several disputes over the border with Canada in Maine and the upper Midwest.

EXPANSION AND IMPERIALISM

1845 Mexico breaks diplomatic relations with the United States when Texas, a republic since 1836, becomes a state. In an attempt to find a peaceful solution, President JAMES POLK sends John Slidell to Mexico to buy California and New Mexico, but the mission fails and war breaks out.

1846 The Oregon Treaty, signed by the United States and Great Britain, resolves the disposition of the Oregon Country by extending the border along to the Pacific 49th parallel line.
    A border skirmish persuades the United States to go to war against Mexico.

1848 The Treaty of Guadelupe Hidalgo ends the Mexico War. Mexico recognizes the independence of Texas and cedes all of present-day California, Nevada, Utah, and portions of Wyoming, Colorado, New Mexico, and Arizona.

1853–1854 MATTHEW PERRY opens Japan to U.S. trade with two expeditions and a treaty of peace, friendship, and commerce.

1854–1855 The Ostend Manifesto, prepared by the American ministers to France, Great Britain, and Spain, declares that Cuba ought to belong to the United States and should be taken by force if Spain refuses to sell. Made public in 1855, the manifesto angers Spain and inflames northern antislavery sentiment, as Cuba would be a slave state.

1855 William Walker leads an expedition to Nicaragua, where he sets himself up as dictator. President Franklin Pierce recognizes Walker's government, but it is overthrown in 1857. Walker tries to conquer Central America again that same year. After landing in Honduras in 1860, he is executed by a Honduran firing squad.

SECRETARIES OF STATE

The Department of State was the first executive department created under the Constitution of 1787, and secretaries of state have usually enjoyed great prestige. Today, the secretary of state is the fourth in line in succession to the presidency. In the eighteenth and nineteenth centuries, many ambitious politicians saw the position as a stepping-stone to the presidency, though only Thomas Jefferson, James Madison, James Monroe, John Quincy Adams, and James Buchanan have seen these ambitions realized.

SECRETARY	PRESIDENT	YEAR APPOINTED
Thomas Jefferson	Washington	1789
Edmund Randolph	Washington	1794
Timothy Pickering	Washington	1795
Timothy Pickering	Adams, J.	1797
John Marshall	Adams, J.	1800
James Madison	Jefferson	1801
Robert Smith	Madison	1809
James Monroe	Madison	1811
John Quincy Adams	Monroe	1817
Henry Clay	Adams, J. Q.	1825
Martin Van Buren	Jackson	1829
Edward Livingston	Jackson	1831
Louis McLane	Jackson	1833
John Forsyth	Jackson	1834
John Forsyth	Van Buren	1837
Daniel Webster	Harrison, W. H.	1841
Daniel Webster	Tyler	1841
Abel P. Upshur	Tyler	1843
John C. Calhoun	Tyler	1844
John C. Calhoun	Polk	1845
James Buchanan	Polk	1845
James Buchanan	Taylor	1849
John M. Clayton	Taylor	1849
John M. Clayton	Fillmore	1850
Daniel Webster	Fillmore	1850
Edward Everett	Fillmore	1852
William L. Marcy	Pierce	1853
William L. Marcy	Buchanan	1857
Lewis Cass	Buchanan	1857
Jeremiah S. Black	Buchanan	1860
Jeremiah S. Black	Lincoln	1861
William H. Seward	Lincoln	1861
William H. Seward	Johnson, A.	1865
Elihu B. Washburne	Grant	1869
Hamilton Fish	Grant	1869
Hamilton Fish	Hayes	1877
William M. Evarts	Hayes	1877
William M. Evarts	Garfield	1881
James G. Blaine	Garfield	1881

FOREIGN AFFAIRS

SECRETARIES OF STATE, cont.

SECRETARY	PRESIDENT	YEAR APPOINTED
James G. Blaine	Arthur	1881
F. T. Frelinghuysen	Arthur	1881
F. T. Frelinghuysen	Cleveland	1885
Thomas F. Bayard	Cleveland	1885
Thomas F. Bayard	Harrison, B.	1889
James G. Blaine	Harrison, B.	1889
John W. Foster	Harrison, B.	1892
Walter Q. Gresham	Cleveland	1893
Richard Olney	Cleveland	1895
Richard Olney	McKinley	1897
John Sherman	McKinley	1897
William R. Day	McKinley	1898
John Hay	McKinley	1898
John Hay	Roosevelt, T.	1901
Elihu Root	Roosevelt, T.	1905
Robert Bacon	Roosevelt, T.	1909
Robert Bacon	Taft	1909
Philander C. Knox	Taft	1909
Philander C. Knox	Wilson	1913
William J. Bryan	Wilson	1913
Robert Lansing	Wilson	1915
Bainbridge Colby	Wilson	1920
Charles E. Hughes	Harding	1921
Charles E. Hughes	Coolidge	1923
Frank B. Kellogg	Coolidge	1925
Frank B. Kellogg	Hoover	1929
Henry L. Stimson	Hoover	1929
Cordell Hull	Roosevelt, F. D.	1933
E. R. Stettinius Jr.	Roosevelt, F. D.	1944
E. R. Stettinius Jr.	Truman	1945
James F. Byrnes	Truman	1945
George C. Marshall	Truman	1947
Dean G. Acheson	Truman	1949
John Foster Dulles	Eisenhower	1953
Christian A. Herter	Eisenhower	1959
Dean Rusk	Kennedy	1961
Dean Rusk	Johnson, L. B.	1963
William P. Rogers	Nixon	1969
Henry A. Kissinger	Nixon	1973
Henry A. Kissinger	Ford	1974
Cyrus R. Vance	Carter	1977
Edmund S. Muskie	Carter	1980
Alexander M. Haig Jr.	Reagan	1981
George P. Shultz	Reagan	1982
James A. Baker III	Bush, G. H. W.	1989

SECRETARY	PRESIDENT	YEAR APPOINTED
Lawrence S. Eagleburger	Bush, G. H. W.	1992
Warren M. Christopher	Clinton	1993
Madeleine Albright	Clinton	1997
Colin Powell	Bush, G. W.	2001

Timeline, *cont.*

1858 Suspicious of European motives because of British and French demands on China, Japan signs additional trade agreements with the United States, and the two nations exchange diplomatic representatives.

1861–1865 During the Civil War, Secretary of State WILLIAM SEWARD, ably assisted by Charles Francis Adams, the U.S. minister in London, works to make sure that neither Britain nor France recognizes the South. Despite strong antislavery leanings, both France and Britain need southern cotton.

1863 When the Confederacy orders two ironclad ships (the Laird Rams) from Britain, the Union applies diplomatic pressure to halt the sale. Ultimately the British government buys them for the Royal Navy. The Confederacy is optimistic in the war's early stages that it will win support from the powerful European nations, but the loss at Antietam brings an end to their hope.

   Napoleon III takes advantage of the war to install Austrian archduke Maximilian on the throne in Mexico. The United States protests and refuses to recognize the new government but does not push the Monroe Doctrine out of fear that France will help the South.

1865–1867 The United States uses increasing diplomatic pressure to persuade Napoleon III to end his support of Maximilian and to withdraw French troops from Mexico.

1867 The Russian minister to the United States, Baron Edouard de Stoeckl, negotiates a deal with Secretary of State WILLIAM SEWARD for the purchase of Alaska for $7.2 million. Known as "Seward's Folly" by disgruntled Republicans, the purchase is not considered a particularly valuable acquisition until the 1897 Klondike gold strike in Alaska.

1871 The Treaty of Washington settles fishing rights claims for both American and British subjects, resolves claims stemming from Confederate raiders, and refers the San Juan Islands boundary dispute to the German emperor for arbitration.

1881 Secretary of State JAMES BLAINE calls for the first hemisphere conference in a year when he meddles uninvited in three separate Latin America border disputes: Mexico and Guatemala, Costa Rica and Colombia, and Peru and Chile.

*After intervening in a
revolution to oust
Queen Lilioukalani,
the United States annexes
Hawaii in 1898.*

1889 BLAINE's plan for a Pan-American conference is finally realized as seventeen nations meet in Washington and establish the Commercial Bureau of the American Republics, renamed the Pan-American Union in 1910 and eventually succeeded by the Organization of American States.

1893 The United States displays its new nationalistic pride by hosting other nations at the world's Colombian Exposition in Chicago.

Sugar magnates, fearing loss of power when Queen Liliuokalani ascends the throne, force her to yield. The U.S. minister to Hawaii proclaims the kingdom an American protectorate.

1895 When Britain and Venezuela cannot agree on the boundary between Venezuela and British Guiana, the United States offers to arbitrate the dispute, claiming the Monroe Doctrine makes this dispute of interest to the United States. At first Britain will have nothing to do with this idea. Eventually both Britain and the United States see the benefits of cooperating, and the foundation for future work together is laid.

1898 Long a champion of independence for Cuba, the United States goes to war against Spain when the USS *Maine* blows up under mysterious circumstances in Havana harbor. The Spanish-American War comes to an end after only four months.

1899 When Spain and the United States sign the Treaty of Paris, Cuba gains its independence and the Philippines, Puerto Rico, and Guam are ceded to the United States. Filipinos, who had been expecting independence, mount a guerrilla war in protest. Armed resistance ends in mid-1902, with sporadic incidents until 1906.

Seeking some advantage in Asia, which the European nations have already carved into colonies or spheres of influence, the United States proposes an Open Door policy popularly believed to give all nations equal trading rights with China. In reality, little is accomplished. One year later, during the Boxer Rebellion, the United States makes an important addition to this doctrine proclaiming that it supports the territorial integrity of China.

1901 Again Europe is warned away from the Western Hemisphere when Vice President THEODORE ROOSEVELT says: "There is a homely adage which runs, 'Speak softly and carry a big stick; you will go far.' If the American nation will speak softly and yet build and keep at a pitch of the highest training a thoroughly efficient navy, the Monroe Doctrine will go far." THEODORE ROOSEVELT's approach to foreign affairs becomes known as the Big Stick policy.

1903 The Hay-Bunau-Varilla Treaty with Panama grants the United States the right to build and operate a canal across the Isthmus of Panama.

1904 President THEODORE ROOSEVELT issues what comes to be known as the Roosevelt Corollary to the Monroe Doctrine, which insists that the United States has a right to intervene, "however reluctantly," in Latin America internal affairs when these nations experience political or fiscal instability or flagrant wrongdoing or impotence (see p. 292).

1908 Secretary of State ELIHU ROOT reaches an agreement with Japanese ambassador Kogoro Takahira that the two nations will respect each other's possessions in the Pacific and uphold the Open Door policy in China.

1911 Despite a vow to substitute "dollars for bullets," President WILLIAM HOWARD TAFT moves a warship off Nicaragua and lands troops to collect customs so the country's debts can be paid. Most troops leave the next year, but a remnant force stays until 1925. Taft's goal of enforcing stability to protect the approaches to the canal is achieved at the expense of goodwill.

The Open Door policy is compromised when President Taft and his secretary of state, Philander Knox, insist on a U.S. role in building railroads in Manchuria, and thus alienate the Japanese. Japan and Russia, recently at war, now begin to see their common interests, and U.S.-Japanese relations begin a slow decline that will reach its nadir during World War II.

1913 President WOODROW WILSON repudiates what he views as his predecessors' imperialistic foreign policy in Latin America, though the Republican-controlled Senate frustrates a number of his attempts.

1914 War breaks out in Europe, but President WOODROW WILSON preserves U.S. neutrality.

The Panama Canal is completed (see p. 285).

Despite his vow not to interfere in other nations' domestic affairs, Wilson intervenes in Mexico, Haiti, and the Dominican Republic when their domestic problems jeopardize U.S. business interests (see p. 292).

1916 Under the Jones Act, the Philippines obtain home rule and a promise of future independence.

Theodore Roosevelt was the first president to travel abroad during his term of office—to Panama in 1906.

Reports that the U.S.S. Maine *was destroyed by a mine in a Havana port fuel pro-war sentiment and help lead to the Spanish-American War.*

ONTO THE WORLD STAGE

1917 The United States purchases the Danish Virgin Islands for $25 million.

When Germany's policy of unrestricted submarine warfare against all shipping bound for Britain results in the sinking of American ships, President WILSON asks Congress to declare war against Germany, which it does, with the overwhelming support of the nation. The United States provides much-needed reinforcements to a beleaguered England and France.

A second Jones Act grants political autonomy to Puerto Rico and grants Puerto Ricans U.S. citizenship.

1918 The arrival of U.S. troops at the front toward the end of 1917 helps to bring the war to a victorious close for Britain, France, and the United States. Russia, which had overthrown the czar the previous year and made a separate peace with Germany, is in the midst of the Bolshevik Revolution.

1919 President WOODROW WILSON, a heroic figure throughout Europe, personally leads the U.S. delegation to the Paris peace talks, which will result in the Treaty of Versailles. Wilson presses the Fourteen Points, a program for postwar stability, which includes a covenant for the League of Nations, but is otherwise unable to forge a satisfactory peace. Germany is made to pay huge war reparations. On his return home, Wilson mounts a national speaking tour trying in vain to gain support from the American people on the League of Nations. When he has a stroke in September, support for the organization fades. The Senate refuses to ratify the Treaty of Versailles.

1921 After rejecting the League of Nations, the United States invites Great Britain, Japan, France, Italy, Belgium, China, Portugal, and the Netherlands to a naval disarmament conference in Washington. A series of treaties follow, limiting the size of navies and outlawing poison gas. The territorial integrity of China is guaranteed.

THE ZIMMERMAN TELEGRAM

The spirit of isolationism and neutral posture of the United States after the outbreak of war in Europe in 1914 were reversed in large measure by one of the most notable coups in the history of diplomatic intelligence. On January 16, 1917, Germany's foreign minister Arthur Zimmerman sent a telegram to the German emissary in Mexico via the German ambassador to the United States. In the note, Zimmerman informed Mexico that Germany would begin unlimited submarine warfare in the Atlantic on February 1 and that, if the United States were to end its neutrality and enter the war, Germany would make Mexico a lucrative offer of alliance. Among the German promises were "an understanding on our part that Mexico is to reconquer the lost territory in Texas, New Mexico, and Arizona."

The telegram was intercepted and decoded by the British intelligence corps, which passed it along to the United States. President WILSON released it to the press, which published the text on March 1. Combined with increasing German submarine attacks on U.S. shipping vessels in the Atlantic, the telegram aroused public opinion against Germany, and Congress approved a resolution of war on April 16.

GUNBOAT DIPLOMACY AND THE PANAMA CANAL

No event or issue more clearly illustrates the aggressive activism of U.S. foreign policy, desire for foreign trade, and control of hemispheric affairs at the turn of the century than the creation of the Panama Canal. The nations of the world had long sought a shorter route from the Atlantic to the Pacific, and one obvious solution was to build a canal across Central America. As the United States gained power, it became determined to control this project, which would reap enormous commercial benefits to the canal's owner.

To this end the United States and Great Britain signed the Clayton-Bulwer Treaty in 1850, with both nations agreeing not to independently seek rights to such a canal. Fifty years later, in a major diplomatic coup, Secretary of State John Hay got the British to renounce their rights to the canal in the Hay-Pauncefote Treaty of 1901.

In 1891, the French had actually started a canal, but this and other attempts were thwarted by inferior equipment and disease—two challenges the United States would later conquer. Another problem was where to build the canal. In 1901, a U.S. commission had recommended Nicaragua over Panama, but American business interests that had taken over the French effort lobbied for Panama. Initially they wanted $109 million to build the canal, and not until they reduced the sum to $40 million did ROOSEVELT agree to the deal. In 1902, the commission issued a revised report, favoring the Isthmus of Panama as the site of the canal.

The next step was to obtain the land—or the rights to it—from Colombia. When Colombia's senate rejected the U.S. offer on grounds that it was insubstantial, Roosevelt resorted to gunboat diplomacy. The United States fomented insurrection in Colombia and let it be known that U.S. warships were steaming toward the region. Just as the USS *Nashville* arrived on November 3, 1903, the United States extended recognition to Panama. The new nation of Panama declared its independence from Colombia on November 6, 1903.

The Hay-Bunau-Varilla Treaty was signed November 18, 1903, Philippe Bunau-Varilla being one of the instigators of the revolt and an engineer working for the Panama Canal Company. As minister of the newly formed nation, Bunau-Varilla agreed to rent to the United States in perpetuity a 10-mile (16-km) strip of land on the isthmus for the sum of $10 million and an annual payment of $250,000.

In 1906, work on the 40-mile (64-km) lock canal began, and, in 1914, it was completed at a cost of $300 million and the lives of hundreds of people who supplied cheap local labor. In 1927, Colombia formally recognized Panama in exchange for a payment of $25 million.

In the 1960s and 1970s, riots in the Canal Zone against U.S. control and a changed foreign policy in the United States led to a renegotiation of the agreement. The Panama Canal was an issue in the 1976 presidential election, and the newly elected JIMMY CARTER agreed to an increased payment and home rule by the year 2000. On December 31, 1999, the United States formally ended its presence in the Canal Zone and turned over sovereignty to the Republic of Panama.

FOREIGN AFFAIRS

1923–1924 When France and Belgium seize Germany's industrial Ruhr district in exchange for unpaid war reparations, the United States resolves the crisis by presenting the Dawes Plan (named after Vice President Charles Dawes), resulting in a renegotiation of Germany's war debt.

1928 In the Kellogg-Briand Pact, named for Secretary of State FRANK B. KELLOGG and French foreign minister Aristide Briand, the idea is advanced that war be outlawed. The idea is promoted by Professor James Shotwell in conversations with French foreign minister Aristide Briand, who seizes upon the concept and advances it in a direct appeal to the American people. Briand's goal is an alliance between France and the United States should war break out again in Europe. Angered at Briand's political maneuver and the obligations of a bilateral pact, Kellogg counters with a proposal for a multinational pact,

"Mr. Wilson bores me with his Fourteen Points. Why, God almighty has only ten."

—GEORGES CLEMENCEAU, 1919

1928, *cont.*

which he know will be unenforceable. Eventually sixty-two nations sign it.

Shortly after winning the election, President-elect HERBERT HOOVER sets out on a goodwill tour of Latin America. Throughout his term as president, Hoover slowly but steadily shows that the United States has embarked on a

WOODROW WILSON AND THE DIPLOMACY OF PEACE

The idea that war is an unacceptable solution to national conflict has taken a long time to develop, and its roots can be traced to President WOODROW WILSON and the Fourteen Points. When hostilities broke out in Europe in 1914, President Wilson initially sought a negotiated settlement, going so far as to send advisors to Europe who would try not only to forestall war but also to plant the seeds for an organization of nations that would work to maintain world peace.

President Wilson and French leader Raymond Poincare meet to discuss world affairs.

When it became necessary, Wilson led the United States into World War I in 1917, but still he divided his energies between waging war and working on the peace that would follow. In 1918, he presented Congress and the world with the Fourteen Points, a program for a fair postwar settlement. Wilson and other progressives hoped it would form the basis for an entirely new kind of diplomacy.

The Fourteen Points announced "the principle of justice to all peoples and nationalities, and their right to live on equal terms of liberty and safety with one another whether they be weak or strong." To this end, the program sought to avoid the pitfalls—annexations of disputed lands, secret covenants, disputes over the high seas, colonial claims—that had precipitated the war.

Specific points called for open treaties among the world's nations, recognition of the rights of neutrals, freedom of the high seas, free trade among all nations, reduced armaments, self-determination for all nations, and mediation of colonial claims. The resolution of territorial disputes was outlined, and point fourteen called for the establishment of an organization of nations that would work together to ensure fairness in international relations and world peace. The Fourteen Points bolstered the Allied forces and encouraged forces within Germany that wished to rid themselves of their leadership by Kaiser Wilhelm II before seeking an armistice.

At the Paris Peace Conference that followed World War I, several of the points were rejected or rewritten, and the peace with Germany was harsher than Wilson had hoped for—though less harsh than it might have been had he not personally negotiated many of the terms. Most important, from Wilson's point of view, point fourteen was accepted, and a covenant for the League of Nations became part of the Treaty of Versailles.

The League of Nations was established in 1920. Although the United States had played a pivotal role in its establishment, hard-line Senate Republicans, led by HENRY CABOT LODGE, opposed U.S. membership, and even though Wilson appealed directly to the American public, the United States never joined. The League effectively settled several disputes during the decade that followed, but it was unable to resolve the larger issues of the 1930s, which included the worldwide depression, Japanese aggression in Asia, and the rise of Hitler in Germany. These events made World War II inevitable—ironically after World War I had reputedly been fought "to make the world safe for democracy," the League of Nations was established to ensure world peace, and the Kellogg-Briand Pact had outlawed war.

But the League of Nations had set a precedent; it had shown the world that cooperation on a large scale was possible. Even before the end of World War II, delegates from Allied nations met to organize a second league—the United Nations.

new course and is trying to be a "good neighbor," a term he coins. The Good Neighbor policy is continued by his successor, FRANKLIN D. ROOSEVELT, and is promoted actively by FDR's secretary of state, CORDELL HULL.

1931–1932 When Japan seizes Manchuria from China, setting up the puppet state of Manchukuo, Secretary of State HENRY STIMSON warns Japan that the United States condemns aggression. The Japanese ignore Stimson's statement and launch an attack in Shanghai, forcing Chinese troops out of the city. World opinion compels the Japanese to withdraw but not to abandon their designs on Asia.

1933 In reference to Latin America, Secretary of State CORDELL HULL at the Seventh International Conference of American States in Montevideo, Uruguay, agrees to a pact stating "that no state has the right to intervene in the internal or external affairs of another." This pledge to respect these nations' rights and to honor obligations toward them is a major new development in the Good Neighbor policy.

President FRANKLIN ROOSEVELT extends diplomatic recognition to the U.S.S.R.

1934 The Tydings-McDuffie Act promises the Philippines complete independence at the end of a ten-year move to self-government.

1938 When Hitler annexes Austria, many worry that another European war is inevitable. France and Great Britain agree to the dismemberment of Czechoslovakia later the same year.

1939 Germany marches into Poland, prompting France and Great Britain to declare war. Many Americans believe it is only a matter of time before the United States will join the fighting.

1940 As the war expands, President FRANKLIN ROOSEVELT keeps the United States out but takes steps to arm and otherwise aid the Allies against the Axis powers. Preparing Americans for their inevitable entry into the war, he says he is building an "arsenal of democracy."

1941 In the kind of personal diplomacy that will be a trademark of U.S.-British relations, President FRANKLIN ROOSEVELT and Prime Minister Winston Churchill meet at sea to discuss common concerns. They put forth their ideas in the Atlantic Charter. Churchill tries to persuade Roosevelt to enter the war, still to no avail, but Roosevelt pledges additional support.

Tensions grow between the United States and Japan as Japan moves into China. Worried about where Japan will stop, President Franklin Roosevelt bans the export of petroleum, petroleum products, and metals in the summer and in the fall freezes Japanese assets in the United States, making war between the two nations inevitable.

1941, *cont.*

When the Japanese bomb Pearl Harbor, home of the Pacific fleet, the United States declares war on Japan, and within days Germany has declared war on the United States.

1943 At the Casablanca Conference, Winston Churchill and FRANKLIN ROOSEVELT discuss Germany's surrender and decide that it must be unconditional.

1944 The June 6 invasion of Normandy by Allied forces presages Germany's total defeat.

Preparing for peace while war still rages, forty-four nations gather at the Bretton Woods Conference in New Hampshire to discuss financial issues. The International Monetary Fund and the International Bank for Reconstruction and Development are created.

1945 With the end of World War II in sight, the Big Three—Great Britain, the U.S.S.R., and the United States—meet at Yalta in the Crimea located in Ukraine. President ROOSEVELT is tired and ill (he will die two months later). Critics charge that he gave away too much to Joseph Stalin. Under secret agreements, the United States, France, Great Britain, and the U.S.S.R. divide Germany into four zones, each to be occupied by one of the victors. The capital city, Berlin, is divided as well, with the Soviet Union administering nearly half the city. The four occupying nations also agree to oversee free elections in all liberated nations. Some specific boundaries and territories are discussed, and the U.S.S.R. agrees to enter the war against Japan.

The United States drops two atomic bombs on Japan at Hiroshima and Nagasaki, and Japan surrenders, concluding the most devastating conflict the world has ever known.

World War II in Europe formally ends a few weeks after the death of President FRANKLIN ROOSEVELT in April. The peace settlement is hammered

THE ATLANTIC CHARTER

Like WOODROW WILSON, whose Fourteen Points had outlined peace (rather than war) aims, FRANKLIN D. ROOSEVELT set forth a series of lofty goals for peace even before the United States entered World War II. In a secret meeting in August 1941 with British prime minister Winston Churchill, on a ship in the North Atlantic, the Atlantic Charter was written. Its principles renounced territorial aggrandizement by the Allies and any changes in territories not in accord with the wishes of the people concerned. The charter also affirmed the right of all people to choose their own form of government, the right of all nations to equal access to trade and raw materials, the importance of collaborative efforts to secure economic advancement and social security, and the right of all people "to live out their lives in freedom from fear and want." Finally, the charter called for freedom of the seas (a principle of American foreign policy since France and Britain first threatened American shipping in the 1790s), the disarmament of aggressors, and "the establishment of a wider and permanent system of general security."

out by President HARRY TRUMAN, Joseph Stalin, and Winston Churchill (replaced halfway through by Clement Attlee, the new Labour prime minister) at Potsdam. Unconditional surrender is demanded of Japan.

THE POSTWAR WORLD

1946 Winston Churchill issues a prophetic warning to the world in a speech at Westminster College in Fulton, Missouri. Using the term "iron curtain" as a metaphor for the intensifying schism between Western Europe and Soviet-dominated Eastern Europe. Churchill cautioned that "an iron curtain has descended across the continent."

The Philippines are granted independence.

1946–1960 In the wake of World War II, the United States enjoys a remarkable and a rare era of bipartisan foreign policy in which both the president and Congress stand united against the Communists. The growing threat posed by the Soviet Union and communism gives birth to the Cold War, a fierce ideological and economic struggle between the United States and the U.S.S.R., marked primarily by huge arms buildups on both sides.

1947 The Truman Doctrine signals the United States' intention to offer military and economic aid to nations that resist Communist aggression.

GEORGE KENNAN, a policy director in the State Department, gives the name "containment" to the U.S. policy of fighting communism around the world. He first describes the idea in an article, signed "X," in *Foreign Affairs*.

English prime minister Winston Churchill, President Franklin D. Roosevelt, and Soviet premier Joseph Stalin confer at Yalta to devise a plan for post-war Germany.

FOREIGN AFFAIRS

1947, *cont.*

Kennan's concept will guide U.S. foreign policy throughout the Cold War.

Under the Marshall Plan, first proposed by Secretary of State GEORGE MARSHALL, the United States declares that the containment program is not aimed "against any country or doctrine but against hunger, poverty, desperation, and chaos." At a meeting of foreign ministers in Paris to work out the details, the Soviets walk out, stating that this is a thinly disguised plan to take over Europe. An initial amount of $540 million is authorized for France, Italy, and Austria, with a portion for China. During the next three years, Congress will authorize another $12.5 billion. This is the first time the United States has given significant amounts of foreign aid, and it will soon become an important foreign-relations tool.

The National Security Council is created to coordinate military and foreign policy. The council, which is to be brought into the Executive Office, thus strengthening the president's role as foreign-policy maker, will play a significant role in shaping U.S. foreign policy throughout the Cold War. President TRUMAN creates the Central Intelligence Agency (CIA) to handle foreign intelligence activities (see p. 295, 304).

1948 The Organization of American States, succeeding the Pan-American Union, is established to work with the United Nations in promoting peace, justice, hemispheric solidarity, and economic development.

In a series of meetings designed to consolidate the occupation zones of Germany, the U.S.S.R. opposes unification. The country's capital, Berlin, also divided into four occupied sectors, is located in Soviet-controlled East Germany. When Soviet forces begin a land blockade that cuts off Berlin from West Germany, the United States and Britain respond with an airlift of food and supplies to the 2.5 million citizens of West Berlin and the British, French, and American garrisons therein. At the height of the airlift, up to 8,000 tons of supplies—food and fuel mostly—are flown in daily. The blockade lasts a little less than a year, though the airlift itself continues a few more months to build up supplies.

Soldiers in the Haktong-ni area of Korea comfort one another during the 1950–1952 war.

Political theorist HANS J. MORGENTHAU publishes *Politics Among Nations,* a seminal work that seeks to redefine the concept of national interest.

1949 Immersed in the Cold War, the nations of Western Europe and the United States create the North Atlantic Treaty Organization (NATO) to provide a unified defense system in Western Europe in the face of growing Soviet power in Eastern Europe.

China institutes a Communist regime, and China-U.S. relations cool swiftly.

THE UNITED NATIONS

The need for an international organization to replace the League of Nations became increasingly clear as World War II drew to a close, and, in the spring of 1945, delegates from Allied nations met in San Francisco to draft a charter. Initially the organization was conceived as a forum through which peace-loving nations could work together to prevent aggression and promote humanitarian purposes. But shortly two former Allies—the United States and the Soviet Union—became major rivals, and many attempts to handle crises crumbled for lack of unanimity among the five permanent members of the Security Council: France, China, Britain, the Soviet Union, and the United States. Meanwhile, in the General Assembly, the United States often found itself attacked by member nations, many of which were aligned with the Soviet bloc or aggressively independent.

Since the end of the Cold War, however, the United Nations has moved with greater unity toward a more prominent peacekeeping role, and its blue-helmeted peacekeeping forces have been deployed in trouble spots such as the Persian Gulf, Cambodia, Somalia, Bosnia, and Kosovo. The United States funds more than a quarter of the organization's budget and supplies a substantial proportion of its troops.

In nonmilitary matters, the organization's record is impressive. Its related agencies have coordinated humanitarian aid, improved disease control, helped refugees, and set standards for human rights. Although agencies are located throughout the world and 189 nations are currently members, the United States continues to play a lead role. The organization's headquarters are in New York City, on a tract of land along the East River donated by John D. Rockefeller Jr.

1950 The Korean War begins when Soviet-controlled North Korea invades U.S.-controlled South Korea along the 38th parallel, the dividing line between the two nations.

1951–1953 Truce negotiations begin in Korea, marked by lengthy delays and bad faith on both sides. When a settlement is reached, it is unsatisfactory to everyone. No borders are changed; the peninsula remains divided roughly along the 38th parallel. The war has mainly served to expand the policy of containment far beyond Europe at the same time that it has made containment look like a losing proposition. It has also resulted in about 2 million casualties.

1952 Japan regains its sovereignty when a peace treaty with the United States is ratified by the Senate.

The United States successfully detonates a hydrogen bomb.

1953 The U.S.S.R. explodes a hydrogen bomb.

1954 The Soviet Union again rejects German unification, thus heightening Cold War tensions. The CIA supports rebels who wish to overthrow Guatemala's liberal leader, Jacobo Arbenz Guzmán, an advocate of land reform and trade unionism. A military leader is installed.

In response to worries about communism in Southeast Asia, the United States creates the Southeast Asian Treaty Organization (SEATO), an attempt at duplicating NATO. But this organization is much weaker and does not include India or Indonesia among its members.

DOCTRINES IN U.S. FOREIGN POLICY, 1823–PRESENT

1823 The Monroe Doctrine. Articulated by President JAMES MONROE in his Annual Message to Congress, this is the United States' first comprehensive foreign-policy statement. It asserts that the Western Hemisphere is closed to European colonization and that the United States will regard any attempt by a European power to extend its system to the Western Hemisphere as "the manifestation of an unfriendly disposition toward the United States." In return, the United States vows not to interfere in European affairs. The doctrine dominates U.S. foreign policy until the United States enters World War I in 1917, and still guides the U.S. role in this hemisphere.

1904 The Roosevelt Corollary. Widely viewed as an amendment to the Monroe Doctrine, this foreign-policy statement by President THEODORE ROOSEVELT asserts the right of the United States to intervene in affairs of Latin American nations whenever they are politically, financially, or economically so unstable as to threaten U.S. interests (see map below). Although WOODROW WILSON repudiates this doctrine in 1913 upon taking office, he does not stay out of Latin American affairs.

1920s Isolationism. This approach to foreign policy, dominant throughout the nineteenth century, enjoys a vigorous resurgence in reaction to U.S. participation in World War I. Following from President Washington's warning against entangling alliances in his farewell address, this approach seeks to avoid involvement in Europe's alliance systems and wars and often encourages high tariffs. Protected by two oceans, the United States can make isolationism a reality until the twentieth century, when new technologies in transportation and communication begin to negate the protection offered by distance alone.

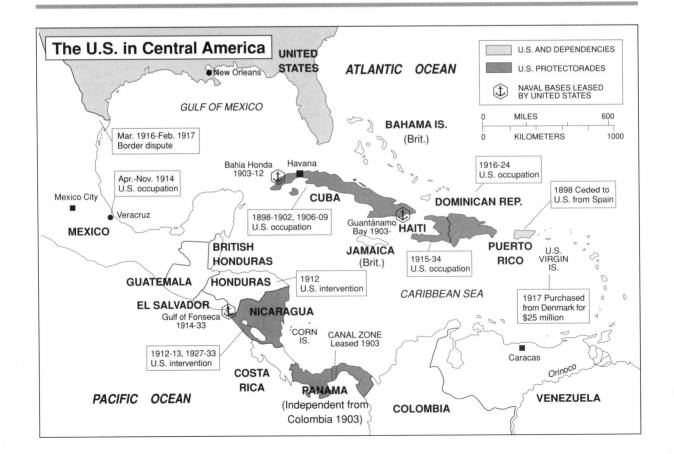

1947 The Truman Doctrine. In a message to Congress, President HARRY TRUMAN announces his intention to provide military and economic aid to free, democratic nations threatened by totalitarian regimes. The doctrine, initially advanced to build support for an aid bill for Greece and Turkey, is also useful in building support for NATO and the response to a variety of small and large crises all over the world that arise during the Cold War.

Containment. This foreign policy principle is aimed at containing communism and halting the influence of the U.S.S.R. Introduced in 1947, it is the dominant foreign and national security policy until the end of the Cold War in 1991.

1969 The Nixon Doctrine. President RICHARD NIXON attempts to reduce the United States' role as the world's policeman when he states: "America cannot—and will not—conceive all the plans, design all the programs, execute all the decisions, and undertake all the defense of nations of the world. We will help where it makes a difference in our national interest and is considered in our interest."

1979 The Carter Doctrine. In the face of U.S.S.R. encroachments in Afghanistan and the Middle East, President JIMMY CARTER declares that the United States will actively protect its interests in the Middle East.

1980 The Reagan Doctrine. President RONALD REAGAN declares that the United States has a right—indeed an obligation—to intervene anywhere in the world where there is political insurrection, and thus combat the "evil empire" of the U.S.S.R.

1990s Post-Cold War Interventionism. With the demise of the Soviet Union and Communist bloc, presidents Bill Clinton and George H. W. Bush send U.S. troops to far-flung trouble spots—such as Nicaragua, Kuwait, Bosnia, Haiti, Somalia, and Kosovo—in support of national interests, democratic principles, and humanitarian concern. An integral part of this undeclared policy is the marshaling of support from Western allies and the United Nations.

2001 Anti-Terrorism. The September 11 attacks in New York and Washington by radical Muslim fundamentalists lead to an abrupt and radical redirection of U.S. foreign policy. President George W. Bush declares that the nations of the world henceforth will be divided between those that support U.S. antiterrorist efforts and those that do not. The military, economic, and intelligence campaign against terrorism becomes the centerpiece of U.S. foreign policy.

Children surround a U.S. marine patrolling the streets of Mogadishu, Somalia, where troops attempt to provide aid from the famine and violence ravaging the country.

FOREIGN AFFAIRS

Timeline, *cont.*

1956 During President EISENHOWER's second term, Secretary of State JOHN FOSTER DULLES takes a new hard line toward the U.S.S.R. Bolstered by the United States' successful test of a new hydrogen bomb and equally worried about the U.S.S.R.'s subsequent successful test, Dulles employs an aggressively anti-Communist foreign policy. The policy of ensuring massive U.S. retaliation to a first strike requires an unprecedented peacetime buildup of arms. Despite the tough posturing, the United States does nothing to support anti-Communist rebels in Hungary in 1956. The short-lived rebellion is brutally suppressed by the U.S.S.R.

When Israel, France, and Britain attack Egypt, which has recently nationalized the Suez Canal and flirted with China and the U.S.S.R., EISENHOWER is furious. Hopes for an Arab and Israeli compromise are dashed, and Eisenhower and Dulles believe a major war is narrowly averted.

In a Cold War attempt to contain Soviet communism in Southeast Asia, the United States enters a decade of escalating involvement in Vietnam, in what will be the nation's longest war and one of its most costly in terms of human life and military spending.

Two years after the French are defeated in Vietnam, the United States supports the election of the staunchly anti-Communist dictator Ngo Dinh Diem in South Vietnam and funnels over $1 billion in aid between 1955 and 1961. American military presence in Vietnam escalates, culminating in the 1964 Gulf of Tonkin Resolution, giving the president power to initiate bombing raids in Vietnam.

The new Soviet leader, Nikita Khrushchev, at the Twentieth Party Congress severely criticizes the tactics of Joseph Stalin, who died in 1953. Though a secret speech to party leaders only, details leak out and eventually herald in a period of détente or decreased tensions with United States.

1959 In Cuba, Fidel Castro stages a successful coup against the right-wing government of Fulgencio Batista. He accepts aid from the U.S.S.R. and announces that he will export his revolution throughout Central America.

1960 Summit diplomacy, promoted by Soviet leader Nikita Khrushchev, collapses when the U.S.S.R. shoots down an American U-2 spy plane. The United States at first denies that these are spy planes, claiming instead that this is a weather plane gone off course. But the U.S.S.R. has the pilot, who bailed out. A few days later, at the long-planned summit meeting in Paris, Khrushchev demands that EISENHOWER stop the spy flights, apologize, and punish those behind the idea. Eisenhower refuses, and Khrushchev stalks out.

1961 The U.S.S.R. closes the border between East and West Berlin and builds the Berlin Wall to halt the exodus from East Germany.

In his farewell address, President EISENHOWER, who has developed reservations about the arms buildup he presided over, warns against the overwhelming power of the military-industrial complex.

The term "Cold War" was coined in a speech by Bernard Baruch before the Senate War Investigating Committee on October 24, 1948: "Although the war is over," he said, "we are in the midst of a cold war which is getting warmer."

NATIONAL SECURITY COUNCIL

Although President Franklin Roosevelt relied heavily on his own counsel during World War II, after that war it was formally recognized that planning and coordinating the nation's foreign policy had become a more complex task than any one person could reasonably be expected to handle. As a result, the National Security Council (NSC) was formed in 1947.

The council's job is to advise the president on affairs of national security, taking into account the military, domestic, and foreign resources for carrying out policy. The NSC, as it is familiarly known, is part of the executive branch of government. Its members are the president, the vice president, and the secretaries of state and defense, backed by an ever-expanding staff of policy experts. Advisers to the NSC include the attorney general, the joint chiefs of staff, and the head of the Central Intelligence Agency. The position of special assistant for national security affairs, or national security adviser to the president, was established in 1953 during the Eisenhower administration. The role and level of responsibility attached to that position, and the NSC it heads, have varied according to the preferences of each president.

NATIONAL SECURITY ADVISERS		
ADVISER	PRESIDENT	YEAR APPOINTED
Robert Cutler	Eisenhower	1953
Dillon Anderson	Eisenhower	1956
Robert Cutler	Eisenhower	1957
Gordon Gray	Eisenhower	1958
McGeorge Bundy	Kennedy, Johnson	1961
Walt Rostow	Johnson	1966
Henry Kissinger	Nixon	1969
Brent Scowcroft	Ford	1975
Zbigniew Brzezinski	Carter	1977
Richard Allen	Reagan	1981
William Clark	Reagan	1982
Robert McFarlane	Reagan	1983
John Poindexter	Reagan	1985
Frank Carlucci	Reagan	1986
Colin Powell	Reagan	1987
Brent Scrowcroft	Bush, G. H. W.	1989
Anthony Lake	Clinton	1993
Samuel Berger	Clinton	1997
Condoleezza Rice	Bush, G. W.	2001

FOREIGN AFFAIRS

On April 17, about 2000 CIA-trained Cuban exiles land at Cuba's Bay of Pigs. Believing that they have the full support of the United States and that they will foment widespread revolution, the anti-Castro rebels are defeated in three days. Although initiated during the Eisenhower administration, President JOHN KENNEDY assumed responsibility for the debacle and the negative criticism that came with it. In 1962, Castro accepted $53 million in food and medicine (raised through private donations) in exchange for 1,113 prisoners from the Bay of Pigs invasion.

Seeking nonmilitary means to forge relations with Latin America, newly elected President Kennedy creates the Alliance for Progress, an aid

1961, *cont.*

program for the economic development of Latin American nations. His good intentions are undermined when the CIA-sponsored Bay of Pigs invasion of Cuba is made public. Under President John Kennedy and his defense secretary, Robert McNamara, a policy of flexible response replaces the concept of brinkmanship or massive retaliation. Realizing the pitfalls of Eisenhower's policy of nuclear buildup as a deterrent, they invested in nonnuclear military options to deal with threats from and situations abroad.

1962 The Cuban Missile Crisis occurs when the Soviet Union secretly begins building missile-launching sites in Cuba. President KENNEDY demands removal of the missiles and imposes a naval blockade of Cuba. Since a blockade in international law is an act of war, the administration calls it a quarantine. At the last moment Soviet freighters turn back from delivering supplies to Cuba and Khrushchev promises to remove the missiles. The United States offers to remove obsolete missiles in Turkey. Cuba releases the prisoners from the Bay of Pigs invasion.

President Kennedy and Soviet premier Nikita Khrushchev meet at the Vienna Summit in 1961.

1963 The United States, the U.S.S.R., and Great Britain sign a Limited Nuclear Test-Ban Treaty, barring all above-ground tests of nuclear weapons. The modest defense buildup instituted by President EISENHOWER increases slightly under President KENNEDY.

1964 Congress sanctions the Vietnam War by passing the Gulf of Tonkin Resolution, which gives the president broad power to commit troops to Vietnam. Later, when it is revealed that Congress was given false information about the war, both Congress and the public become increasingly skeptical about the conduct of U.S. foreign policy. Presidents Lyndon Johnson and RICHARD NIXON suffer from a credibility gap, which in turn spurs on the already considerable opposition to the Vietnam War.

Late 1960s Opposition to U.S. involvement in Vietnam increases as various members of Congress of both parties announce their opposition to the war. Senator WILLIAM FULBRIGHT, chairman of the Senate Foreign Relations Committee, describes U.S. foreign policy during this era as an "arrogance of power." He becomes a harsh critic of the war.

1968 The Nuclear Non-Proliferation Treaty is signed by 115 nations, including the United States. The nuclear nations agree not to transfer nuclear power,

Cold War Europe

NATO COUNTRIES
WARSAW PACT COUNTRIES
NEUTRAL COUNTRIES

and nonnuclear signers agree not to build or develop it. Eventually 140 nations sign the treaty.

1969 The Nixon Doctrine signals a new direction in American foreign policy when President RICHARD NIXON states that the United States will consider its vital interests first rather than trying to solve the problems of other nations.

Strategic Arms Limitation Talks (SALT) begin between the United States and the U.S.S.R.

1970s A period of détente, marked by an easing of military and diplomatic strain, dominates U.S. relations with the Soviet Union. Nevertheless, Soviet meddling in Eastern Europe and the Middle East continues to challenge the United States.

The foreign policies of RICHARD NIXON reflect a turning away from the staunch anticommunism of his early career, emphasizing rapprochement with the Soviet Union and China. Spearheaded by Secretary of State HENRY KISSINGER, many of his dealings with foreign leaders are conducted in secrecy, removed from public and congressional scrutiny. To protect U.S. strategic and business interests, the Nixon administration supports the anti-Democratic and ill-fated shah of Iran, Ferdinand Marcos of the Philippines, and the white minority government of South Africa.

"There are few ironclad rules of diplomacy, but to one there is no exception. When an official reports that talks were useful, it can be safely concluded that nothing was accomplished."

—JOHN KENNETH GALBRAITH "THE AMERICAN AMBASSADOR," 1956

FOREIGN AFFAIRS

1971 "Ping-Pong diplomacy" begins when the Chinese welcome a U.S. table-tennis team and signal a willingness to open up Sino-U.S. relations. HENRY KISSINGER travels secretly to China to pave the way for a state visit by President RICHARD NIXON.

The Pentagon Papers affair erupts when former Defense Department aide Daniel Ellsberg leaks incriminating materials regarding the federal government's involvement in Vietnam to the *New York Times*. The Nixon administration takes its case to the Supreme Court, where it loses.

1972 President RICHARD NIXON travels to China in what is widely considered to be the foreign-relations coup of his presidency. It is a breakthrough in Chinese-American relations, and advantageous to U.S. foreign relations as well, serving to separate the world's two Communist powers from each other. When the U.S.S.R. expresses anxiety over the new alliance, President Nixon agrees to sell the Soviets $1 billion in U.S. wheat.

The Senate approves the SALT I Treaty.

1973 In the wake of the Yom Kippur War between Israel and allies Egypt and Syria, Arab leaders are frustrated by Israel's success. Believing that success is largely due to U.S. aid, the Arab nations declare an embargo on shipments of oil to the United States and other Western nations and Japan. The embargo lasts from October until March.

In a CIA covert operation, the United States abets a Chilean coup in order to get rid of the duly elected Socialist government of Salvador Allende. Allende is subsequently murdered by the junta that replaces him. The United States welcomes the dictatorship of Gen. Augusto Pinochet.

The United States and the North Vietnamese sign the Paris Peace Agreement, ending the direct involvement of U.S. ground forces throughout Indochina and calling for the release of any American prisoners of war.

> U.S. foreign aid, including outlays for economic, humanitarian, and military assistance, represents less than 1 percent of the total federal budget.

U.S. FOREIGN AID, 1946–1999

YEARS	TOTAL ECONOMIC AND MILITARY AID	ECONOMIC AID*	MILITARY AID
	(MILLIONS OF DOLLARS)		
1946–1952	41,661	31,116	10,545
1953–1961	43,355	24,052	19,304
1962–1969	50,254	33,392	16,862
1970–1974	21,743	10,652	11,091
1975–1979	43,971	28,160	15,811
1980–1984	62,295	40,648	21,647
1985–1989	77,835	51,434	26,401
1990–1994	92,045	69,973	22,073
1995–1999	71,597	52,680	18,917
2000–2001	31,749	22,487	9,262

Source: U.S. Agency for International Development.

Egyptian president Anwar el-Sadat, President Jimmy Carter, and Israeli prime minister Menachem Begin meet at the White House to sign the historic peace treaty ending the long war between Egypt and Israel.

1975 Saigon falls to North Vietnamese forces.

1976 Under President JIMMY CARTER, the United States weighs humanitarian concerns in executing its foreign policy. Repressive nations are pressured to grant their citizens freedom or risk losing U.S. support.

1977 The Panama Canal Treaty promises to transfer the canal back to Panama by the year 2000.

1978 The Nuclear Non-Proliferation Act sets controls on the export of nuclear technology to other nations.

1979 America and Iran become opponents when religious conservatives oust the shah, a longtime U.S. friend. In the aftermath of the revolution, Iran takes fifty-three American diplomats hostage and holds them for 444 days.

In a first step toward Middle Eastern peace, Egypt and Israel sign the Camp David Peace Accords, named for the Maryland presidential retreat where they were negotiated.

1980 In what will prove to be a major blow to the CARTER administration, a mission to rescue the Iranian hostages fails.

President Carter requests that ratification of SALT II Treaty be delayed after the Soviet Union invades Afghanistan.

1982 When its debt soars to $81 billion, Mexico twice devalues the peso, then negotiates with the International Monetary Fund for a rescheduling of payments. Other Latin American nations also have difficulty repaying U.S. loans, thus shifting the focus of foreign policy from arms to fiscal matters.

1982, *cont.*

Signaling Congress's concern about human rights in Latin American internal affairs, Edward Boland, chairman of the House Intelligence Committee, introduces an amendment bearing his name that prohibits any U.S. funding of contra forces who are waging a guerrilla war against the elected leftist Sandinistas.

1985 Mikhail Gorbachev comes to power in the U.S.S.R. As General Secretary of the Communist Party until 1991 and president of the U.S.S.R. from 1990 to 1991, he introduces the concept of "glasnost," openness, and meets REAGAN in Geneva. Tensions between the superpowers begin to relax.

1986 The Iran-Contra scandal erupts, followed by the Tower Commission investigation. During President RONALD REAGAN's first administration, the National Security Council, in defiance of the Boland Amendment, mounts a covert operation to provide aid to contra forces fighting in Nicaragua. To fund the aid, the United States secretly sells arms to Iran with the hope that hostages held by pro-Iranian groups in Lebanon will then be freed. Profits from the arms sales go directly to the contras trying to overthrow the Marxist Sandinista government in Nicaragua. The Tower Commission that subsequently investigates the Iran-Contra affair finds the president "disengaged" from foreign policy (see p. 219).

President Ronald Reagan disregards the SALT II Treaty when the limit on nuclear weapons is exceeded. Reagan states that the treaty was not ratified and that the Soviets also had not observed its limits.

In Reykjavík, Iceland, Gorbachev proposes to Reagan a 50 percent reduction in all strategic nuclear weapons. The two leaders cannot resolve differences over the Strategic Defense Initiative (SDI). Nevertheless, great strides are made.

1987 Gorbachev and REAGAN meet in Washington and sign an agreement limiting medium-range nuclear arms.

1989 In June, Poland holds elections in which the Communist Party loses power. In August, Hungary dismantles its closed border with Austria, and allows thousands of East Germans to leave the Soviet bloc via Hungary. In November, East German officials, pressured by hundreds of thousands of protesters in Leipzig and Berlin, open the wall. In December, the Velvet Revolution takes place in Czechoslovakia, and playwright Vaclav Havel, a former political prisoner, is elected president. In Romania and Bulgaria, new governments replace Communist regimes. The Cold War is coming to an end.

The United States invades Panama to oust President Manuel Noriega, previously a U.S. friend and now viewed as too permissive about drug traffic.

1990 Germany is reunited after forty-five years.

The Persian Gulf War breaks out when Iraq invades Kuwait. Within days, the United States has organized a multinational force to compel Iraq to withdraw.

1991 President George H. W. Bush and Mikhail Gorbachev sign the Strategic Arms Reduction Treaty.

Despite tremendous international pressure on the Iraqis to withdraw from Kuwait, they refuse to do so. On January 16 (due to the time difference, it was already January 17 in Iraq), U.S.-led coalition forces launch air strikes in Iraq. On February 23, allied ground forces attack, and, on February 27, President Bush orders a cease-fire.

1993 Congress ratifies the North Atlantic Free Trade Agreement (NAFTA) with Mexico and Canada. It is an attempt to form a free-trade zone similar to those formed by other groups of nations around the world.

As part of post-Cold War interventionist policy, U.S. and U.N. forces attack rebels in Somalia and provide humanitarian aid.

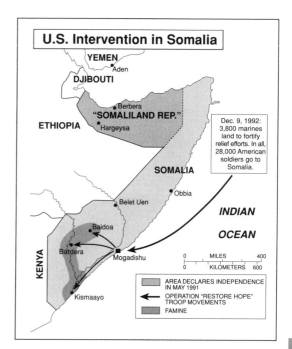

U.S. Intervention in Somalia

Dec. 9, 1992: 3,800 marines land to fortify relief efforts. In all, 28,000 American soldiers go to Somalia.

AREA DECLARES INDEPENDENCE IN MAY 1991

OPERATION "RESTORE HOPE" TROOP MOVEMENTS

FAMINE

1994 In one of the most important spy cases in U.S. history, authorities arrest CIA agent Aldrich Ames on charges of supplying the Soviets with information for more than a decade. The case seriously compromises the credibility of U.S. intelligence.

In what will prove to be indicative of the kind of foreign-policy problem it will encounter in the post-Cold War era, the United States uses the military to provide economic aid, in the form of a food-and-medicine airlift, to Rwanda, which is mired in a civil war. Troops are also dispatched to Haiti, under U.N. auspices, to oust a repressive military regime.

Central Intelligence Agency officer Aldrich Ames and his wife, Rosario, plead guilty to spying for Russia and the former Soviet Union.

1995 Mexico devalues the peso, seriously undermining U.S. investments there.

A major foreign-policy dilemma for Bill Clinton's presidency is the continued fighting in the Balkans as Bosnian Serbs wage a war of "ethnic cleansing" against Muslims and Croats, in hopes of creating a new ethnically homogenous nation. The United States commits troops as part of an international force sent to monitor the Dayton peace accords of November 1995.

1999 As part of a NATO peacekeeping effort, the United States dispatches air and ground forces to the Yugoslav province of Kosovo, where the Albanian majority faces ethnic cleansing at the hands of Serbian police and militia.

1999–2000 In a diplomatic standoff with the Cuban government, six-year-old Cuban refugee Elián Gonzalez, found floating off the coast of Florida after his boat sank and his mother drowned, remains with Cuban American relatives in the United States for seven months before being returned to his father in Cuba in June 2000.

2000 The United States grants full-partner trading status to China.

2001 In the aftermath of September 11 terrorist attacks on the World Trade Center in New York and the Pentagon in Washington, President George W. Bush declares war on international terrorism and any foreign government that supports it or gives haven to those who practice it. The administration enlists military support from several Western allies, most notably Great Britain, and diplomatic or moral support from many nations throughout the world.

Robert Hanssen, a twenty-five-year employee of the Federal Bureau of Investigation, pleads guilty to delivering classified information to Russia and the former Soviet Union.

2003 After receiving conflicting reports from Iraqi officials, United Nations weapons inspectors, and U.S. and British intelligence sources, the United States and Britain attempt to convince members of the U.N. Security Council to authorize military action against Iraq for failure to disarm as required in U.N. Security Council Resolution 1441. Deep rifts develop between the allied American and British administrations and governments throughout the world, most notably France and Germany, who advocate further weapons inspections. In March, after giving Iraq's President Saddam Hussein and his sons forty-eight hours to leave the country, the United States begins "Operation Iraqi Freedom" without U.N. approval.

MAJOR U.S. TREATIES, 1783–PRESENT

Treaties—formal agreements between nations—are negotiated by the president and his representatives in the Department of State and, to be implemented, must be ratified by a two-thirds majority in the Senate.

YEAR	TREATY	SIGNATORIES	RESULT
1783	Paris	Britain, France, United States	Formally ends the Revolutionary War
1794	Jay's	Britain, United States	Settles lingering issues related to the Revolution
1795	Pinckney's	Spain, United States	Sets border of Spanish Florida and opens Mississippi River to U.S. trade
1814	Ghent	Britain, United States	Ends the War of 1812
1817	Rush-Bagot	Britain, United States	Disarms the U.S.-Canadian border
1818	Convention	Britain, United States	Settles U.S.-Canadian border to the Pacific and agrees to joint occupation of Oregon Country
1819	Adams-Onís	Spain, United States	Spain cedes Florida
1842	Webster-Ashburton	Britain, United States	Settles U.S.-Canadian border in Maine and upper Midwest
1846	Oregon	Britain, United States	Divides Oregon Country between Canada and the United States
1848	Guadelupe Hidalgo	Mexico, United States	Ends the Mexican War
1871	Washington	Britain, United States	Resolves several issues
1899	Paris	Spain, United States	Ends the Spanish-American War
1903	Hay-Bunau-Varilla	Panama, United States	Grants the United States the right to lease the land it needs to built the Panama Canal
1919	Versailles	Allies, Germany; the United States never ratifies	Ends World War I; includes the League of Nations
1922–1930	Naval Disarmament Treaties	Allies	Set limits on navies
1928	Kellogg-Briand	15 nations at first; ultimately 62	Bans war

MAJOR U.S. TREATIES, 1783–PRESENT, cont.

YEAR	TREATY	SIGNATORIES	RESULT
1949	North Atlantic Treaty Organization (NATO) Belgium, Britain,	Canada, Denmark, France, Iceland, Italy, Luxembourg, the Netherlands, Norway, Portugal, United States, and later Greece, Turkey, and West Germany	Mutual defense pact
1954	South East Asian Treaty Organization (SEATO)	Australia, Britain, France, New Zealand, Pakistan, the Philippines, Thailand, United States	Mutual defense pact
1977	Panama Canal		United States agrees to transfer ownership of the Panama Canal Zone back to Panama
1992–1994	North American Fair Trade Agreement (NAFTA)	Canada, Mexico, United States	Trade barriers on goods and services to be lifted over fifteen years, beginning in 1994

THE CIA

The Central Intelligence Agency (CIA), an outgrowth of the Office of Strategic Services created in World War II, was established in 1947 under the same act that created the National Security Council. Its purpose is to gather, coordinate, and analyze the information necessary to conduct foreign policy and protect U.S. interests abroad. Its director often confers with the cabinet and the National Security Council.

While the Cold War seemed tailor-made for the CIA's services, it also provided an atmosphere in which the agency often undertook covert activities so that the U.S. government could deny any official involvement.

In the 1950s, the CIA, headed by director Allen Dulles, expanded its operations enormously. Agents all over the world cast a wide net, infiltrating cultural institutions, undermining organizations, spying on writers and other intellectuals as well as on students at American universities and church leaders. The CIA maintained its own radio stations and news-service organizations and financed several journals. It mounted covert military operations in Asia, Africa, and Latin America. It worked with France to maintain the colonial regime in Indochina. In 1953, when the premier of Iran was on the verge of nationalizing the oil industry, it deposed him and put the U.S.-friendly but at times despotic Muhammad Reza Shah Pahlavi on the throne.

The most notorious CIA intervention occurred in Guatemala, which since 1944 had struggled to become a democracy. In 1951, the liberal-spirited new president Jacobo Arbenz Guzmán encouraged trade unions and pursued land reform, appropriating uncultivated land owned by the United Fruit Company. The company complained to the State Department, charging that Arbenz was a Communist. In 1954, the CIA secretly effected a coup by a right-wing military leader who initiated a crackdown that led to years of guerrilla warfare.

Fear that the CIA had exceeded its mandate became a campaign issue in the mid-1970s, and investigations by Congress and a presidential commission revealed that the CIA had attempted to assassinate several foreign leaders, including Fidel Castro of Cuba who had been engaged in a secret war in Laos, supported antigovernment forces in Chile, and conducted extensive surveillance of U.S. citizens. The Senate established a permanent committee to oversee CIA activities, but, in the late 1980s, new congressional investigations uncovered CIA involvement in the Iran-Contra affair. The agency was further undermined in 1994 when a career officer, Aldrich Ames, was found to have been spying for the U.S.S.R. for nearly a decade. In 1996, a bipartisan commission recommended that the CIA focus its efforts on terrorism, narcotics trafficking, weapons proliferation, and organized crime.

NUCLEAR DISARMAMENT, 1945–PRESENT

1945 The United States drops two atomic bombs on Japan, one at Hiroshima and another at Nagasaki.

1946 In its first session, the U.N. General Assembly establishes a commission to study international control of atomic energy. The Soviet-U.S. split in the Security Council makes progress impossible.

1952 The United States explodes a hydrogen bomb.

1953 The Soviet Union explodes a hydrogen bomb. Disarmament talks are revived under the auspices of the United Nations. The United States and its allies propose on-site inspections of nuclear installations, while the U.S.S.R. calls for a total ban of nuclear weapons, with specific controls to be settled at later talks.

1958 The United States, Great Britain, and the U.S.S.R. institute talks on a nuclear-test ban.

1963 The Limited Nuclear Test Ban Treaty is signed by ninety-nine nations, banning nuclear weapons tests in the atmosphere, underwater, and outer space; only underground testing is permitted.

1967 The United States, the U.S.S.R., and fifty-seven other nations sign a treaty banning the use of nuclear weapons in outer space and establishing principles for the peaceful exploration of space.

1968 The Nuclear Non-Proliferation Treaty, ultimately signed by 140 nations, among them the United States, the U.S.S.R., and Great Britain, aims to prevent the further spread of nuclear weapons, to foster peaceful uses of atomic energy, and to encourage negotiations to end the nuclear arms race.

1969 Strategic Arms Limitation Talks (SALT) between the United States and the U.S.S.R. begin.

1972 The United States and the U.S.S.R. sign the SALT I Treaty, which limits antiballistic weapons and offensive nuclear weapons and imposes a five-year freeze on the building of new nuclear weapons.

1974 The United States and the U.S.S.R. sign a Threshold Test Ban Treaty, which limits the size of underground testing to weapons no larger than 150 kilotons.

1977 Although SALT I has expired, the United States and the U.S.S.R. agree to abide by its terms. Strategic Arms Limitations Talks II are under way.

1979 SALT II is signed in Vienna by the United States and the U.S.S.R. in June. It sets specific limits on long-range bombers and the number of nuclear weapons each nation can develop. Congress never ratifies SALT II, but both countries say they will abide by it.

1982 The United States and the U.S.S.R. begin the Strategic Arms Reduction Talks (START).

1987 President RONALD REAGAN and Soviet leader Mikhail Gorbachev sign the Intermediate-Range Nuclear Forces (INF) Treaty, which limits intermediate-range nuclear forces.

1991 The START Treaty, which further reduces nuclear arsenals, is signed by President George H. W. Bush and Mikhail Gorbachev. With the Soviet Union crumbling as a world power in the aftermath of liberalization and internal turmoil, President Bush announces the elimination of the majority of U.S. tactical nuclear arms and orders the U.S. military off alert status for the first time in decades. Bush calls for continued reduction in ballistic missiles. Soviet nuclear weapons fall into the hands of four of the new republics formed from the old Soviet Union. All but Ukraine pledge to abide by existing treaties.

1993 The United States and Russia sign a START II Treaty calling for a two-thirds reduction of nuclear weapons. North Korea withdraws from the Nuclear Non-Proliferation Treaty.

1994 Under START I Treaty modifications, the schedule for eliminating nuclear weapons is accelerated. Ukraine, which has held out on signing the 1993 treaty, signs.

NUCLEAR DISARMAMENT, 1945–PRESENT, cont.

1998 SALT II is stalled in the Russian parliament (Duma), where it encounters opposition. The U.S. Senate had voted to ratify the treaty in 1996.

1999 Even with the fate of SALT II uncertain, the United States and Russia begin talks on a SALT III agreement.

The U.S. Senate rejects ratification of the U.N. Comprehensive Test Ban Treaty (CTBT), which would have prohibited all nuclear weapons testing.

2000 The Duma (Russian parliament) approves SALT II, paving the way for new rounds of talks and prospective further cuts in SALT III.

The United Nations hosts a monthlong conference to review the 1968 Nuclear Non-Proliferation Treaty. The 187 signatory nations approve an agreement that includes a pledge by the five declared nuclear states (United States, Russia, China, France, and Great Britain) to work toward the elimination of their nuclear arsenals.

2001 President George W. Bush proposes long-term development of a space-based missile defense system, declaring "obsolete" the 1972 ABM Treaty banning such weapons. European allies, China, and other nations express concern. In November, Bush agrees with Russian president Vladimir Putin to reduce arsenals of long-range missiles to levels Putin had urged—between 1,500 and 2,200.

IMPORTANT LEGISLATION AND SUPREME COURT DECISIONS AFFECTING FOREIGN AFFAIRS, 1807–PRESENT

1807 Embargo Act. The first important act of U.S. foreign policy, this legislation forbids trade with foreign nations. Designed to force Britain and France to recognize the rights of neutral traders, it ends up hurting American business far more. It is rescinded in 1809.

1924 Rogers Act. This combines the diplomatic service and consular service into the Foreign Service, a professional diplomatic corps in which promotion is based on merit. At the highest diplomatic levels appointments are still political.

1935–1937 Neutrality Acts. This series of acts, which prohibits U.S. shipments of arms to belligerents and U.S. citizens from traveling on hostile ships, is an attempt to keep the United States out of conflicts in Europe that presage World War II.

1936 *United States v. Curtiss-Wright Export Corporation.* This decision affirms the president's "exclusive power…in the field of international relations." When Congress issues a joint resolution permitting the president to forbid the sale of arms to other nations, Curtiss-Wright sues on grounds of constraint of trade. The Supreme Court upholds the resolution, thus confirming that Congress may delegate foreign policy matters to the president.

1939 Neutrality Act. A new Neutrality Act, following the outbreak of war in Europe, authorizes the shipment of arms to belligerents.

1941 Lend-Lease Act. This enables the United States to furnish war supplies to Britain and other allies whose defense is defined as vital to U.S. interests.

1947 National Security Act. In addition to combining the armed forces into one organization, this act authorizes the establishment of the Central Intelligence Agency, which will coordinate the nation's intelligence-gathering activities. It also creates the National Security Council, which will become a major force in shaping U.S. foreign policy.

1962 *Baker v. Carr.* Although addressing legislative reapportionment, majority and dissenting opinions debated the role of the Court in foreign policy issues.

1971 *The New York Times v. United States.* The Supreme Court overrules the injunction of a lower court and permits the publication of *The Pentagon Papers,* a classified study of U.S. involvement in Vietnam that had been leaked to the *Times* by former Defense Department aide Daniel Ellsberg.

NOTABLE FIGURES IN U.S. FOREIGN AFFAIRS

Abbott, Grace (1878–1939). Nebraska native, resident of Chicago's Hull-House, and friend of Jane Addams and Florence Kelley, Abbott served in an unofficial capacity as the U.S. representative to the League of Nations Advisory Committee on Traffic in Women and Children. She was one of the planners of the Social Security Act.

Acheson, Dean (1893–1971). As secretary of state under TRUMAN and adviser to presidents KENNEDY, Johnson, and NIXON, Acheson was a shaper of post–World War II foreign policy. He worked on the Marshall Plan, fought for giving aid to Greece and Turkey, played a role in the establishment of NATO, and also secured U.N. support for U.S. intervention in Korea. Critics charged that his policies led to the Communist takeover of China and the start of the Korean War. An early supporter of the war in Vietnam, he nevertheless advised President Johnson in 1968 that he should find a way to end U.S. involvement in Vietnam.

Adams, John Quincy (1767–1848). The sixth U.S. president, he was son of President John Adams and Abigail Adams. He helped to write the treaty that ended the War of 1812, as well as the Monroe Doctrine, the latter accomplished while serving as secretary of state under President JAMES MONROE. He negotiated the cession of Florida from Spain.

Albright, Madeleine (1937–). A naturalized American citizen born in Czechoslovakia, Albright was named the U.S. permanent representative to the United Nations by President Bill Clinton in 1993. In 1997, President Clinton appointed her as secretary of state; she was the first woman to hold this prestigious position.

Anderson, Eugenie Moore (1909–1997). President HARRY TRUMAN appointed Anderson ambassador to Denmark in 1953. She was the first woman to hold the rank of ambassador. President JOHN F. KENNEDY appointed her envoy to Bulgaria. She also served in an appointed position at the United Nations.

Baker, James (1930–). As secretary of state under President Bush, Baker rallied support for U.S. military action in the Persian Gulf War, presided over a major Middle East peace conference, and helped to negotiate several arms-reduction treaties with the U.S.S.R.

Blaine, James Gillespie (1830–1893). Blaine served as secretary of state under three presidents: Garfield, Arthur, and Benjamin Harrison. He helped to improve U.S.–Latin American relations by convening the Pan-American Congress and working for reciprocal trade agreements; he also advocated the annexation of Hawaii.

Bunche, Ralph Johnson (1904–1971). Bunche was the first African American to rise to a high position in the State Department. Bunche's major contribution was at the United Nations, where his work on the U.N. Special Commission on Palestine earned him a Nobel Peace Prize in 1950.

Carter, Jimmy (1924–). Carter's one-term presidency (1977–1981) was as marred by foreign-policy problems as it was brightened by his considerable achievements in this area. His diplomacy led to the signing of the Camp David Peace Accords in 1979 between Anwar Sadat of Egypt and Menachem Begin of Israel (see p. 299). He signed the SALT II Treaty, although it was never ratified by the Senate. He was able to get ratification of the Panama Canal treaty. His administration was also plagued by fallout from the Iranian Revolution and the subsequent seizure of the U.S. embassy. Fifty-two U.S. diplomats were held hostage 444 days; they were released a few hours after Carter left office. Carter received the 2002 Nobel Peace Prize.

Dulles, John Foster (1888–1959). Dulles was a leader in the bipartisan foreign policy that emerged after World War II. He was also an internationalist who worked hard to establish the United Nations and served as U.S. representative. During the 1952 presidential campaign, however, he turned against his earlier ideas and became a staunch supporter of containment.

Eisenhower, Dwight David (1890–1969). As president from 1953 to 1961, Eisenhower fulfilled his campaign promise to end the Korean War. He worked to advance the policy of containment of the U.S.S.R., which had been started under TRUMAN, at the same time that he sought to assuage Cold War tensions. A former general and hero of World War II, Eisenhower believed that a strong military was vital to peace. At the same time, he warned Americans in his farewell address to beware the power of the military-industrial complex, which could endanger liberties and democratic processes.

Fish, Hamilton (1808–1893). As President Grant's secretary of state, Fish negotiated the Treaty of Washington in 1871, which ended disputes with Great Britain over the Confederate raiders. He also negotiated a commercial treaty with Hawaii and settled American claims in Cuba with Spain.

FOREIGN AFFAIRS

NOTABLE FIGURES, *cont.*

Fulbright, William (1905–1995). As chairman of the Senate Foreign Relations Committee from 1959 until 1974, Fulbright was a strong voice in American foreign policy and an outspoken critic of foreign intervention, especially in Vietnam. His Fulbright Act (1946) continues to sponsor exchanges of students and teachers between the United States and foreign countries.

Harriman, Averell (1891–1986). In addition to serving under Presidents FRANKLIN D. ROOSEVELT, TRUMAN, KENNEDY, Johnson, and CARTER in positions ranging from ambassador, Lend-Lease coordinator, secretary of commerce, assistant secretary of state, under secretary of state, and chief negotiator for the Nuclear Test Ban Treaty, Harriman was a negotiator at the Vietnam peace talks. He was also governor of New York from 1955 to 1959.

Harris, Patricia Roberts (1924–1985). In addition to being the first African American woman to hold a cabinet post (Housing and Urban Development, 1977), Harris also became one of the first black diplomats when she was appointed ambassador to Luxembourg.

Hay, John Milton (1838–1905). In addition to being President Lincoln's private secretary, Hay served as secretary of state under Presidents MCKINLEY and THEODORE ROOSEVELT. He originated the Open Door policy in China and negotiated the Hay-Pauncefote Treaty, in which Great Britain renounced its interest in building the Panama Canal.

Hoover, Herbert (1874–1964). A mining engineer by profession, Hoover chaired a commission that supplied food and clothing to civilians in war-torn areas of Belgium and France between 1915 and 1919. Following World War I, he was made chairman of the European Relief and Reconstruction Commission, coordinating relief operations through Europe. He also directed an organization that fed millions in Revolutionary Russia during the famine of 1921 to 1923. His reputation for support of humanitarian aid and his excellent skills in organization were part of his appeal as a presidential candidate. His inaction in the face of the stock market crash and Great Depression, however, prevented his reelection. Following World War II, he coordinated relief efforts in Europe.

House, Edward (1858–1938). An important and close adviser to President WILSON, he sought to prevent war in Europe and negotiate peace after World War I broke out. Accompanying Wilson to Paris after the war, House helped to draft the Versailles Peace Treaty and the Covenant of the League of Nations.

Hull, Cordell (1871–1955). As FDR's secretary of state, Hull was a true internationalist. He supported U.S. membership in the League of Nations and played a dominant role in the establishment of the United Nations, work that led to his being awarded the Nobel Peace Prize in 1945. Ironically, Hull was shuffled aside during World War II, since ROOSEVELT preferred to direct his own war policy, but he continued his work in the international arena by continuing the Good Neighbor policy with Latin America.

Jay, John (1745–1829). Jay helped negotiate the Treaty of Paris, which ended the Revolutionary War. Sent to Britain in 1794, he also negotiated Jay's Treaty, which resolved issues derived from the Revolution. He also served as chief justice of the Supreme Court and governor of New York.

Kellogg, Frank B. (1856–1937). A Republican senator and Calvin Coolidge's secretary of state, Kellogg is known for the Kellogg-Briand Pact, in which sixty-two nations renounced war. He also improved relations with Latin America. He won the 1929 Nobel Peace Prize.

Kennan, George (1904–). A diplomat and historian, Kennan set out the principles of containment policy that dominated U.S.-Societ foreign policy in the post–World War II era and throughout the Cold War. He was a Foreign Service officer in Europe's hot spots before and during World War II and was ambassador to the U.S.S.R. until the Soviets demanded his removal. He wrote, among other books. *American Diplomacy 1900–1950* (1951), his memoirs, and a study of Soviet-U.S. relations that won a Pulitzer Prize.

Kennedy, John F. (1917–1963). As president, Kennedy presided over several foreign-affairs crises, most notably the failed Bay of Pigs invasion and the Cuban Missile Crisis. He escalated the Vietnam War, established the Peace Corps, and developed the Alliance for Progress, which gave economic aid to Latin America.

Kissinger, Henry (1923–). This German-born statesman-scholar served Presidents NIXON and Ford during a tumultuous era in international relations. As secretary of state, he played a major role in formulating foreign policy, negotiating the end of the Vietnam War, a cease-fire in the 1973 Arab-Israeli war, and the reestablishment of relations, after a break of several decades, with China. A recipient of the Nobel Peace Prize, he is the author of several books on foreign policy.

Lodge, Henry Cabot (1850–1924). A powerful senator, as chairman of the Senate Foreign Relations Committee he opposed U.S. membership in the League of Nations and worked hard to ensure the United States did not sign the Treaty of Versailles after World War I.

Lodge, Henry Cabot Jr. (1902–1985). Grandson of HENRY CABOT LODGE, and like his grandfather a senator from Massachusetts, he became ambassador to the United Nations as well as to South Vietnam and West Germany. It was as a chief negotiator in the Vietnam peace talks that he put his stamp on American foreign policy.

Marshall, George (1880–1959). After building a stellar military career that spanned both world wars, Marshall served as TRUMAN's secretary of state. His greatest achievement was organizing the program of postwar aid to European allies that bears his name and led to his being awarded the Nobel Peace Prize in 1953.

McGillivray, Alexander (1759–1793). This half-Scot, half-Cree statesman worked on behalf of his Indian nation, serving as a British agent during the Revolution and later signing a treaty with Spain to supply him with arms, which he then used to fight the new U.S. government. In 1790, he negotiated a treaty in which the Crees acknowledged U.S. sovereignty over some Cree lands and agreed to keep the peace.

McKinley, William (1843–1901). McKinley's presidency (1897–1901) was dominated by foreign affairs: the Spanish-American War; the annexation of Hawaii and the Philippines; and the Open Door policy for China, which advanced American interests and commerce by promoting unrestricted trade.

Monroe, James (1758–1831). Monroe was the fifth U.S. president. After the Revolution, he undertook important diplomatic missions to establish the new nation's ties to France, England, and Spain. As envoy to France under Jefferson, he negotiated the Louisiana Purchase. Later, as Madison's secretary of state, he negotiated boundary settlements with Canada, and, as president, oversaw the acquisition of Florida from Spain. He is best remembered for the 1823 Monroe Doctrine, the nation's first major foreign-policy statement, which warned European nations away from involvement in the Western Hemisphere.

Morgenthau, Hans J. (1904–1980). This German American political scientist wrote a seminal work on foreign policy, entitled *Politics Among Nations: The Struggle for Power and Peace* (1948), which redefined the concept of national interest by asserting that nations should act only where there is a realistic national interest, not merely out of ideological motivation.

Nixon, Richard M. (1913–1994). From 1969 to 1974, Nixon was an active foreign-policy president who promulgated the Nixon Doctrine, which rewrote the role of America in world affairs by stating that the United States would no longer be the world's policeman. He also opened relations with China and presided over détente, a relaxing of tensions with the U.S.S.R.

Perry, Matthew (1794–1858). A U.S. naval officer, Perry undertook two important missions to Japan in 1853 and 1854 that opened Japan to trade.

Pinckney, Thomas (1750–1828). Pinckney negotiated the Treaty of San Lorenzo, better known by his name, which established commercial relations with Spain and opened the Mississippi River to navigation.

Polk, James K. (1795–1849). Elected to the presidency on an expansionist platform, Polk resolved the Oregon Question with Britain and went to war against Mexico, thus securing for the United States much of the West.

Reagan, Ronald (1911–). Foreign policy during his presidency (1981–1989) involved taking a tough stand against Communist expansion, especially in Central America, which he backed with the largest peacetime defense buildup in U.S. history. Reagan also presided over negotiations to reduce arms that produced a major arms-reduction treaty with the U.S.S.R.

Rohde, Ruth Bryan Owen (1885–1954). The daughter of William Jennings Bryan, Owens was named ambassador to Denmark in 1933, making her the first woman ever appointed to represent the United States in a foreign country.

Roosevelt, Eleanor (1884–1962). As diplomat and First Lady, Roosevelt traveled widely throughout the country and the world during the presidency of her husband, FRANKLIN ROOSEVELT. After his death, President TRUMAN appointed her delegate to the United Nations, where she became chairman of the Human Rights Commission.

NOTABLE FIGURES, *cont.*

Roosevelt, Franklin Delano (1882–1945). As president from 1933 to 1945, in addition to leading the nation out of the Great Depression, Roosevelt also mobilized and led the United States during World War II. He gradually moved the nation toward war through the Lend-Lease program, which aided European allies by providing them with arms to fight Germany. Roosevelt had hoped to play a role in shaping the postwar peace, but he died shortly after the Yalta Conference in 1945. He coined the name United Nations and actively supported its establishment.

Roosevelt, Theodore (1858–1919). A transitional president who moved the United States onto a larger world stage, Roosevelt conducted foreign policy with a bold hand. He signed the treaties granting the United States the right to build the Panama Canal and also set forth the Roosevelt Corollary to the Monroe Doctrine, which justified U.S. intervention in Latin America. He helped to bring about an end to the Russo-Japanese War, for which he won the Nobel Peace Prize in 1906.

Root, Elihu (1845–1937). As secretary of state under THEODORE ROOSEVELT, Root was an internationalist who worked to improve U.S.-Latin American relations, and concluded an agreement with Japan in support of the Open Door policy for China. He negotiated a series of treaties with European nations that encouraged arbitration, for which he was awarded the Nobel Peace Prize in 1912. Later, he supported U.S. entry into the League of Nations and helped establish the World Court at The Hague.

Seward, William Henry (1801–1872). As Lincoln's secretary of state, he helped keep Britain and France from recognizing the Confederacy, and continuing in the position, under Johnson negotiated the purchase of Alaska, known at the time as "Seward's Folly."

Stettinius, Edward (1900–1949). As secretary of state under FRANKLIN ROOSEVELT, he helped to establish the United Nations and served as its first U.S. delegate.

Stimson, Henry (1867–1950). Serving as President HOOVER's secretary of state, Stimson led delegations to disarmament conferences. His Stimson Doctrine asserted that the acquisition of territories by force would not be recognized. Stimson also served as secretary of war under TAFT, FDR, and TRUMAN; he was the first American to serve in the cabinets of four presidents.

Taft, William Howard (1857–1930). As a president expanding upon the foreign policy of his predecessor, THEODORE ROOSEVELT, Taft refocused its emphasis to "dollar diplomacy"—promoting business investment and increased trade as a means of gaining political influence.

Truman, Harry (1884–1972). As president, Truman administered the country's most massive foreign-aid bill, the Marshall Plan, which helped to rebuild a war-torn Western Europe in the face of Soviet aggression. He also worked to establish NATO, which rearmed Europe and provided for its joint defense. He made the decision to use the atomic bomb against Japan during World War II.

Tyler, John (1790–1862). In 1841, Tyler became the first vice president to step into the presidency. He presided over the signing of the Webster-Ashburton Treaty, which settled a land dispute between the United States and Canada, as well as the annexation of Texas.

Vandenberg, Arthur (1884–1951). As a senator, Vandenberg was a staunch isolationist until the attack on Pearl Harbor, after which he became a major figure in the war effort and, in its aftermath, a staunch supporter of the United Nations and NATO.

Webster, Daniel (1782–1852). As congressman, senator, and secretary of state, Webster, who was also a great orator, was an important force in the pre–Civil War years. He presided over the Webster-Ashburton Treaty in 1842, which settled boundaries between the United States and Canada.

Wilson, Woodrow (1856–1924). One of the few presidents to have an academic background, Wilson was a major force in U.S. foreign policy. An internationalist and idealist, he refuted the foreign policies of his predecessors and supported the Mexicans during their 1910 revolution, although he eventually intervened, like his predecessors, to protect U.S. interests in Mexico. Attributing the outbreak of war in Europe in 1914 to imperialism, he tried unsuccessfully to mediate a settlement before leading the United States into the war against Germany in 1917. At the war's end, Wilson led the U.S. peace delegation in Paris, where he included in the treaty a covenant establishing the League of Nations. One of his greatest disappointments was his inability, due partly to his ill health and partly to a popular disenchantment with Europe and its wars, to persuade Americans to join the world peace organization.

CHAPTER 9

ECONOMY, BUSINESS, AND LABOR

■

HIGHLIGHTS

Timeline of Economy, Business, and Labor

AMERICA HAS BEEN THE SITE of extensive commercial activity for thousands of years. Before contact with Europeans, numerous Native nations conducted trade throughout North America, utilizing a widespread network of trade routes that criss-crossed the continent. Initial European settlement was sponsored by transatlantic trading interests. The fledgling republic eschewed foreign political entanglements but vigorously pursued and fiercely protected trade with foreign partners. Fueled by ample natural resources and the entrepreneurial spirit with which it became identified, the United States played an increasingly influential role in the world marketplace. Technological inventions and the hard work of the laboring class spurred the Industrial Revolution in all its phases, and, since the beginning of the twentieth century, the nation has been one of the world's industrial giants and economic superpowers.

THE PRE-COLUMBIAN ERA

5000 B.C. Native Americans begin cultivating squash in what is now Illinois. Other crops soon follow.

700 Corn and beans, crops developed in Meso-America, are now being farmed in the American Southwest because complex trading networks have brought these products to the region. Corn will soon join other crops and innumerable resources in diffusing throughout the continent via trade.

1004 Thorvald Erikson and Thorfinn Karlseffin establish Viking settlements in Labrador, and Newfoundland, Canada. They initiate the first transatlantic trade, exchanging dairy products with Native Americans for various food and clothing items.

1300s Native peoples in the Northeast begin to use wampum as a form of currency exchange.

1460s British fishermen begin harvesting off the coast of eastern Canada.

1492 Substantial transatlantic trade begins after the arrival Christopher Columbus. The Eastern Hemisphere diet and lifestyle are radically transformed by the introduction of numerous products from the Americas, including potatoes, tomatoes, peanuts, yams, squash, corn, chili peppers, numerous beans, oranges and other citrus, turkeys, chocolate, coffee, and tobacco.

THE COLONIAL ERA

1607 The British settlement at Jamestown is sponsored by a group of London investors.

1608 Manufacturing begins at Jamestown, where a glass factory is set up a year after the settlement is established.

Quebec is founded by Samuel de Champlain as a fur-trading center. Fish and fur drive French exploration and settlement in North America. They are less significant factors in British America, but still provide occupations for many and fortunes for a few.

c. 1612 John Rolfe introduces the cultivation of tobacco at Jamestown, and, by 1615, it is the cash crop of the Virginia colony, bringing profits to the London investors who sponsored Jamestown.

1621 Squanto, a Pawtuxet Indian who had been kidnapped and lived in England for a few years, gives the Pilgrims seed corn and teaches them native planting practices. Corn, or maize, becomes a principal grain in New England; wheat and rye are also successful.

1643 The first ironworks in the colonies opens in Lynn, Massachusetts, northeast of Boston. In 1654, the colonies' first fire engine is made here. Lynn will continue to be an important manufacturing center for more than two centuries.

1651 Parliament passes the first of the navigation acts. It requires that all colonial products bound for England be carried in English-owned ships.

1693 Rice cultivation is introduced in South Carolina. It is well suited to the colony's freshwater swamps and sluggish rivers near the sea, and it quickly becomes a staple crop. By 1730, South Carolina rice is called the best in the world.

1705 Copper ore is discovered near Simsbury, Connecticut, and a small enterprise develops around the deposits. English law discourages this development, and most ore is shipped to England for smelting.

1712 Nantucket fishermen capture a sperm whale, and the superiority of its oil sparks the whaling industry.

1721 The Board of Trade reports that commerce with the colonies totals almost £2.4 million (£1.5 million in colonial products and £0.9 million in English products).

ECONOMY, BUSINESS, & LABOR

1733 New England's iron industry has six furnaces and nineteen forges.

1740 Caspar Wistar's glass manufactory in Salem County, West Jersey, begins operations.

1742 Benjamin Franklin invents the Franklin stove, an improvement in efficiency and safety over fireplaces.

1745 Indigo cultivation, introduced to South Carolina a few years earlier by Elizabeth (Eliza) Lucas Pinckney, reaches a stage of profitable production, stimulating a dye-stuffs industry. Indigo becomes one of the colony's major export crops, long before cotton, which is difficult to process until the invention of the cotton gin.

1750s The colonial shipbuilding industry thrives; by 1760, one-third of Britain's ships are built in the colonies.

Worldwide increases in wheat prices encourage farmers in Virginia to turn away from tobacco, and wheat becomes the most dynamic element in the Virginia economy, especially in the Northern Neck and Great Valley.

1750 Parliament passes the Iron Act, which prohibits colonists from manufacturing iron products and restricts them to supplying raw iron to England, where manufacturing can be done. Many colonial finishing companies are thus forced out of business.

BRITISH MERCANTILISM

If colonial industry and commerce did not always thrive, there was a reason: England did not want them to. According to the theory of mercantilism, colonies existed for the benefit of the mother country and were primarily intended to supply raw materials, not compete in their manufacture. Seeking to increase its own exports, Britain enacted a series of Navigation Laws starting in 1651 that eventually destroyed the commerce of Holland, its chief rival. First all raw materials bound for England had to be carried in English-owned ships. Later certain "enumerated articles"—including colonial sugar, tobacco, cotton, and indigo—could be shipped only to England, where they were reexported at great profits to English merchants.

The effect of these regulations not only devastated Holland and other colonial powers, it also limited American trade and enterprise. Through a series of additional acts, Parliament further suppressed colonial industries that might unfavorably compete with industries at home. The Hat Act of 1732, for example,

sought to enhance the prosperity of London felt makers by prohibiting Americans from exporting hats from one colony to another and by placing various limitations on apprenticeships in the hat trades.

Still, until political tensions between Britain and the colonies in North America intensified, many restrictions were only loosely enforced. Despite the Molasses Act of 1733, New England imported great quantities of West Indian sugar for manufacture into rum. But when, after the French and Indian War, the colonists were taxed to support both British troops and British enterprise, they claimed that their rights as Englishmen were being violated. The tax on tea was only the last in a series of laws designed to manipulate American products and markets in favor of Britain, but it proved to be the last straw. Rather than pay reduced prices, even with a tax, to support a British monopoly, colonists in Boston and elsewhere dumped the tea they loved into harbors and burned tea ships, setting in motion a drive toward independence that was as much economic as political.

1755 The first whaler is outfitted at New Bedford, Massachusetts. For the next century New Bedford will be the greatest whaling port in the world.

1760 Jared Eliot publishes *Essay upon Field Husbandry in New England*, the first major treatise that describes modified farming techniques for the colonies.

Merchants in Lynn, Massachusetts, organize the shoe industry that will make this industrial center famous.

1763 Henry William Stiegel, a German immigrant, brings glassworkers from England to his factory in Manheim, Pennsylvania.

1764 Rhode Island imports 14,000 barrels of molasses, which will be made into rum and shipped to Africa, where it will be exchanged for Africans, who will be taken to the West Indies and sold as slaves.

1765 The first chocolate factory opens at Milton Lower Mills, near Dorchester, Massachusetts. Chocolate is one of the colonies' most popular beverages.

The New England fishing industry, with 665 ships and 10,000 men, harvests a "crop" worth nearly £2 million.

1768 The New York City Chamber of Commerce is organized by merchants.

1769 Silversmith Abel Buell casts the first American type fonts.

1770 Three thousand tons of masts are shipped from the colonies to England.

The Makah Indians, shown here at Neah Bay, Washington, based their culture on the dangerous task of hunting whales. Whale products were used to make everything from oil and candles to women's corsets and horse whips. Whaling for food and other materials dates to prehistoric times and the early American whaling industry, especially in New Bedford, Massachusetts, boomed until the discovery of petroleum in the 1850s.

ECONOMY, BUSINESS, & LABOR

1772 Philadelphia leads Boston, New York, and Charleston in overseas trade.

1775 The colonies supply close to 15 percent of the world's iron.

THE FEDERAL ERA

1781 ROBERT MORRIS is appointed superintendent of finance. He is largely responsible for stabilizing the new nation's finances by chartering the Bank of North America, obtaining loans from Holland and France to back a new paper currency, and meeting interest payments on the war debt.

1784–1786 Wartime inflation, a flood of British goods following the Treaty of Paris, war debts, and a shortage of gold and silver coin send the new nation into its first depression.

c. 1784 Oliver Evans installs an automatic flour mill in Wilmington, Delaware, with a number of grain-handling machines he has patented.

1785 Based on a decimal plan formulated by THOMAS JEFFERSON, the Continental Congress makes the dollar the official currency.

1787 Robert Gray sails to Oregon and eventually, in 1790, to Canton, where he exchanges sea otter skins for Chinese goods, introducing some Boston merchants to the lucrative China trade.

The new U.S. Constitution authorizes Congress to impose and collect taxes, to borrow money, to regulate interstate commerce, to coin money, to establish post offices and post roads, and to enact patent legislation. Clearly the new, stronger federal government will play a significant role in promoting and protecting commerce and industry.

1790 Slater's mill, built by Samuel Slater in Pawtucket, Rhode Island, begins spinning cotton. Slater, who arrived from England in 1789 having memorized the construction of textile machinery that the British hoped to keep secret, makes improvements that will successfully mechanize cotton carding and spinning—creating a textile industry for New England and a new market for southern cotton.

1791 Supported by Federalists and opposed by Jeffersonians, the first Bank of the United States is chartered by the federal government.

An excise tax is imposed on distilled liquor.

ALEXANDER HAMILTON, secretary of the treasury, issues his Report on Manufactures, outlining a program of tariffs to encourage domestic industry.

1792 The Mint of the United States in Philadelphia begins coining silver and gold.

1793 ELI WHITNEY invents the cotton gin, which makes cotton a cash crop, initiates a vast expansion of the textile industry, and entrenches the slave system in the South.

1794 Cordwainers, or rope makers, in Philadelphia organize an early labor union.

1798 A direct federal property tax is levied in anticipation of war with France.

1802 The first brass-rolling mill, Abel Porter and Company, opens in Waterbury, Connecticut.

Two shipments of Spanish merino sheep set a "merino mania" in motion that greatly stimulates the wool industry, especially during the Embargo of 1807 and the War of 1812 that follow.

1807 Attempting to force warring Britain and France to stop interfering in neutral trade and shipping, Congress passes the Embargo Act, forbidding almost all foreign commerce. The embargo is repealed in 1809, but trade with Britain remains banned.

Robert Fulton launches the *Clermont* on the Hudson River, the first commercially successful steamboat.

Eli Terry and Seth Thomas begin their Connecticut clockworks concern, the first to mass-produce clocks with interchangeable parts.

Cotton is the number one export. With the exception of 1809, 1815, and the four Civil War years, cotton continues as the leading U.S. export into the 1890s.

1811 The charter of the first Bank of the United States is allowed to expire, as it is opposed by entrepreneurs and agrarian interests.

1812 William Monroe begins to manufacture lead pencils.

1814 In Waltham, Massachusetts, the Boston Associates open the first mechanized factory for producing cotton fabric, combining spinning and weaving. New England mill production quickly rises, and the region will be the leading center for cotton-textile manufacturing for the next thirty years.

1816 The Second Bank of the United States is chartered for twenty years, this time with the support of the Jeffersonians, thus establishing a central banking system that will regulate state banking and help to stabilize the economy.

The Tariff of 1816, the first protective tariff, is passed, imposing 25 percent import duties on woolens, textiles, and iron.

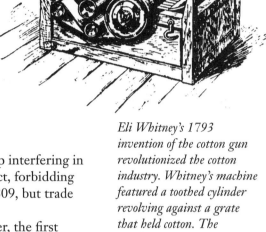

Eli Whitney's 1793 invention of the cotton gun revolutionized the cotton industry. Whitney's machine featured a toothed cylinder revolving against a grate that held cotton. The revolving cylinder caught the cotton fibers and separated them from the seeds.

ECONOMY, BUSINESS, & LABOR

1817 The New York Stock Exchange is established.

1818 Duties on iron products, cotton, and woolens are raised.

1819 A bank panic occurs following inflation, speculation in western lands, and contraction of credit, and a six-year depression sets in.

1822 The Boston Associates begin to build a factory at the junction of the Concord and Merrimack rivers, renaming the settlement Lowell in memory of Francis Cabot Lowell, who had improved on British models for a spinning machine and power loom. When the factory opens the next year, it employs young girls from New England farm families, who live in dormitories provided by the company. Lowell is the first designed manufacturing city.

The South is called "Dixie" because the most common currency in the region during the antebellum period was money issued by the Bank of New Orleans, which used French. A $10 bill was a "dix" note, more commonly known as a "Dixie" note.

1824 The Franklin Institute opens in Philadelphia, "for the promotion of the mechanic arts."

The tariff is raised again, increasing duties on lead, iron, glass, hemp, and cotton.

1825 The first patent for canning is issued to Ezra Dragget.

The Erie Canal opens, connecting Buffalo, New York, to Albany, New York, thereby linking New York City to the Great Lakes via the Hudson River. As a result, New York becomes the nation's commercial center and the upper Midwest replaces the Mississippi Valley as the country's primary supplier of foodstuffs.

1828 In the Tariff of Abominations, duties are raised to their highest levels yet. Southerners protest, and John C. Calhoun writes a treatise justifying the doctrine of nullification (see p. 198). The divergent economic interests of the nation are becoming increasingly clear.

1830 President Andrew Jackson vetoes the Maysville Road Bill, saying that the federal government ought not to support an internal improvement entirely within one state.

Peter Cooper operates *Tom Thumb*, the first commercially viable steam locomotive.

1832 South Carolina refuses to collect high federal tariffs and nullifies the tariffs of 1828 and 1832.

President Andrew Jackson creates a banking crisis by refusing to renew the charter of the Second National Bank and then transferring government funds from it to state banks. The head of the national bank responds by calling in commercial loans, causing a panic that precipitates a recession.

1833 President Jackson threatens to use federal forces to collect the tariff but also proposes a reduced tariff bill that pacifies the South.

1836 President Jackson, concerned about widespread use of paper money, issues the Specie Circular, declaring that the federal government will henceforth require hard currency for the purchase of western public lands. When, the next year, British banks call in their American loans, a six-year depression sets in.

The federal government establishes U.S. Patent Office.

1837 John Deere invents the steel plow, capable of breaking prairie sod.

1839 Inventor Charles Goodyear discovers vulcanized rubber.

1840 Samuel Cunard, a Canadian, begins the first steamship line between Britain and the United States.

1843 Congress authorizes $30,000 to build a 40-mile (64-km) telegraph line between Baltimore and Washington, D.C.

1844 Samuel Morse sends the first long-distance telegraph message ("What hath God wrought!") from Washington, D.C., to Baltimore.

1846 The Walker Tariff Act, a moderate protective tariff, lowers import duties and expands the list of duty-free goods.

Elias Howe patents the lock-stitch sewing machine.

1847 CYRUS MCCORMICK opens his reaper factory in Chicago.

1848 The first chewing gum is manufactured in Bangor, Maine.

1849 The Pacific Railroad Company becomes the first chartered railroad to operate west of the Mississippi.

1851 Isaac Singer patents an improved sewing machine and organizes I. M. Singer and Company. He continues to patent improvements, and with the help of savvy advertising, this company soon leads the industry.

Isaac Singer did *not* receive the first U.S. patent for a sewing machine. Elias Howe, who had been granted a patent five years earlier in 1846, successfully sued Singer for producing a device similar to his. Singer was forced to pay $15,000, but his machine dominated the market.

ECONOMY, BUSINESS, & LABOR

THE RISE OF INDUSTRY

1851 Western Union Company, an amalgamation of small telegraph firms, is founded.

1852 Elisha Otis invents a safety device to prevent the fall of the elevator should the hoisting mechanism fail. The first passenger elevator is installed in 1857 in the five-story china shop, E. V. Haughwout & Company located on Broadway in New York City.

1853 The New York Central Railroad is created when ten smaller railroads consolidate.

1853, *cont.*

"Money is like manure.
You have to spread it
around or it smells."
—J. PAUL GETTY

The Baltimore & Ohio opens its rail line connecting the East Coast to Chicago.

1857 A short but sharp depression grips the nation as the financial markets experience their first wave of panic selling.

1858 The first message is conveyed by transatlantic cable. When it ceases working, Cyrus Field funds a project that lays a new cable in 1866.

1859 The first oil well is drilled at Titusville, Pennsylvania.

The Great Atlantic and Pacific Tea Company is founded; it will later become the A&P, one of the first great chain stores.

1860 Macy's department store opens in New York City.

1861 There are some 30,000 miles (48,280 km) of railroad track in the country, almost three-quarters in the North.

The first oil refinery is set up in Pittsburgh.

The first transcontinental telegraph message is sent between San Francisco and Washington, D.C.

The first federal income tax—3 percent—is enacted, but only on annual incomes exceeding $800. Intended to help finance the Civil War, the tax affected only the rich. Congress will abolish the tax in 1872.

1861–1865 The North and the South struggle to fund the Civil War; inflation soars.

1862 The Morrill Land-Grant College Act funds the establishment of colleges that will promote agricultural and industrial development.

The Legal Tender Act empowers the federal government to print paper money, called "greenbacks."

The first Pacific Railway Act authorizes the building of the first transcontinental railway, the Union Pacific. A second act, in 1864, authorizes the Central Pacific.

The Internal Revenue Service is established.

1863 Ebenezer Butterick manufacturers the first commercially produced paper dress patterns.

The National Bank Act prohibits state banks from printing paper money.

1864 The Pennsylvania Railroad begins using steel for its rails.

George Pullman invents the railway sleeping car that will carry his name.

The Bessemer process of steel manufacturing is introduced in Troy, New York.

TARIFFS AND TRADE

Because all tariffs—duties on imported goods—benefit some and penalize others, the tariff has always been a hot political issue and a significant influence on the American economy. ALEXANDER HAMILTON was only the first to argue that high tariffs would benefit American industry—protecting manufacturing jobs, encouraging fledgling industries, and providing profits for entrepreneurs.

Hamilton's program was gradually enacted in the early years of the republic, as the first tariff passed by the First Congress, designed primarily to raise revenue, was replaced following the War of 1812 by protectionist tariffs, designed to protect native industries. The tariffs of 1816, 1818, and 1824 steadily increased duties on wool and cotton cloth in support of the new textile industries of New England. They also taxed iron manufactures, lead, glass, and hemp. Eventually New England commercial and shipping interests objected, but the most vocal protests came from the South following the tariff of 1828—the Tariff of Abominations—which set the highest rates yet, approaching half the value of some items. A new tariff in 1832, followed by the Compromise Tariff of 1833, expanded the list of duty-free items and provided for a gradual reduction of duties, thus pacifying the South Carolinians who had threatened to refuse to collect these duties and asserted that a state had the right to nullify an unacceptable federal law.

The crisis was averted, but the tariff issue had highlighted the divergent economies of the North and South that would eventually lead to civil war.

In short, the North had a young manufacturing economy complemented by the extraction of food stuffs, lumber, and other domestically consumed resources. High tariffs therefore benefited the North by protecting manufacturers from competition with European imports. As industry grew, the North manufactured more and imported less. The South was not developing a manufacturing sector, but relied on the export of raw materials like cotton, and was hurt by the tariffs that raised prices on goods that needed to be imported. In 1861, facing a wartime economy and in the absence of any representation from the South, Congress enacted the Morrill Tariff, which raised duties. The trend continued during the period of Republican domination after the war. The Dingley Tariff, passed in 1897, raised duties to the all-time high of 57 percent.

By this time American industries hardly needed protection, and the Payne-Aldrich Tariff (1909) and Underwood Tariff (1913) lowered duties. At the same time, the new income tax was about to replace import duties as the chief revenue source for the federal government. Although post–World War I tariffs were high, reflecting the isolationism that dominated the American outlook, the general trend throughout the twentieth century has been toward free trade. As early as 1934, the Trade Agreements Act authorized the president, without congressional action, to enter into agreements with other nations for specific reductions, and following World War II the General Agreement on Tariffs and Trade (GATT) granted concessions among the twenty-eight participating nations.

Initially a political football in contests between states and sections, the tariff became primarily a foreign-policy issue, with boycotts and most-favored nation status used as leverage to compel, for example, the Union of South Africa and the People's Republic of China to end human rights violations, the Union of Soviet Socialist Republics to permit the emigration of Soviet Jews, and Japan to open its markets to U.S. exports. Most recently, however, the North American Free Trade Agreement (1993), whereby the United States, Canada, and Mexico eliminated most tariffs on goods imported from one another, again raised regional and economic sector animosities. Organized labor feared that U.S. jobs would be eliminated as companies "moved south" to take advantage of cheaper labor in Mexico. In April 2001, President George W. Bush joined with thirty-three Western Hemisphere leaders in an agreement to pursue the world's largest free-trade zone, intending to slash tariffs and remove other trade barriers in an estimated $15 trillion international market. The leaders agreed to negotiate the final Free Trade Area of the Americas (FTAA) pact—which would require U.S. congressional approval—by January 2005, for implementation at the end of that year.

Today, in a world where the economy is increasingly global, where multinational corporations compete in international markets, tariff issues are likely to be increasingly complex and less capable of being directed by domestic or foreign policy goals.

1864, *cont.*

Congress authorizes the minting of 2-cent coins that are the first to bear the phrase: "In God We Trust," which does not become mandatory on all coins and currency until 1955.

1865 About $450 million in greenbacks are in circulation.

The Chicago Stockyards, which will become the world's largest meat-processing facility, opens in Chicago.

1866 Coinage of the first 5-cent piece made from nickel is authorized. Ten years earlier a 1-cent piece made with nickel has been introduced.

The National Labor Union (NLU) is founded in Baltimore. It is the first nationwide union to represent skilled and unskilled workers.

1867 Farmers in the Midwest and South begin organizing Granges: local cooperatives concerned with the economics, politics, and technology of farming. The Grange movement is the forerunner of the Populist movement (see p. 265).

George Pullman organizes the Pullman Palace Car Company.

The cash register—a vital instrument in the rise of American capitalism—was patented by James Ritty in 1879.

Late 1860s A huge economic boom is fueled by the end of the Civil War in 1865. Manufacturing soars, with the expansion of railroads leading the way.

1868 Congress enacts an eight-hour day for laborers and mechanics employed on federal projects.

1869 The world's first transcontinental railroad is completed when the last spike is hammered into place at Promontory Point in Utah Territory, joining the Union Pacific and the Central Pacific.

Wall Street experiences its first Black Friday when financier JAY GOULD and others try to corner the market on gold and fail.

The Knights of Labor trade union is formed in Philadelphia. After the collapse of the National Labor Union in 1872, the Knights of Labor emerge as the leading labor union in the United States.

JOHN D. ROCKEFELLER combines several smaller oil companies to found Standard Oil Company of Ohio.

1871 LUTHER BURBANK experiments with plant hybrids; his Burbank potato achieves immediate success.

1872 Montgomery Ward, the first mail-order company, begins operations in Chicago.

1873 The Coinage Act puts the United States on the gold standard. Silverites call it the "Crime of '73."

Iron ore shipments from the Lake Superior region exceed 1 million tons, most bound for Pittsburgh, where Bethlehem Steel opens in this boom year.

The failure of the banking house of JAY COOKE and Company sends the nation into a five-year depression.

ANDREW CARNEGIE begins concentrating on steel manufacturing, acquiring firms that will be consolidated into the Carnegie Steel Company and turning Pittsburgh into a major center for steel production. Carnegie will reap enormous profits and give most of it ($350 million) away.

1874 Railroads are charging farmers high rates for short-distance shipments but lower rates for long-haul industrial shippers. Several states pass so-called Granger laws, establishing maximum shipping rates railroads can charge (see p. 265).

1876 Alexander Graham Bell demonstrates the telephone.

1877 The Bell Telephone Company is organized.

The Socialist Labor Party is founded in New York City, largely by German immigrants influenced by Karl Marx.

1878 The first U.S. copper refinery to use gaseous fuel operates in Ansonia, Connecticut.

1879 FRANK W. WOOLWORTH opens the first successful "five and dime" store in Lancaster, Pennsylvania. Goods sell for a fixed price—a nickel or a dime.

Thomas Edison invents the lightbulb (see p. 393).

1880 George Pullman builds his railway car factory outside Chicago, eventually establishing a model industrial community with homes for workers and supervisors.

U.S. copper production totals 30,000 tons. The industry is centered in Michigan's Upper Peninsula.

1882 JOHN D. ROCKEFELLER founds the Standard Oil Trust, the first megacorporation organized as a trust.

1883 Thomas Edison discovers that an incandescent lamp can be used as a valve to admit negative but not positive electricity—the so-called Edison effect. He sees no practical application, but it is later the basis of the vacuum tube in radiotelephony (see p. 393).

1884 Inventor Nikola Tesla arrives in the United States from Budapest. In the next years he will work in Edison and Westinghouse labs on applications for the principle of the rotating electromagnet field, with contributions to lighting, transmission, telephony, and telegraphy.

"I have not failed. I've just found 10,000 ways that don't work."
—THOMAS ALVA EDISON

ECONOMY, BUSINESS, & LABOR

CHILD LABOR

When Slater's mill operated in the 1790s with a "workforce" of children, no one objected. Children had always worked on the family farm, and if the family engaged in domestic industry such as piecework for clothing manufacturers, children carded wool and spun. Farm boys were sometimes hired out to neighbors, and by age fourteen many were apprenticed.

The early textile mills of New England found young people suitable to the work. The machines needed only monitoring, and the work was not heavy. Girls put empty bobbins on the machines and took them off when they were full. Boys carried bobbin boxes where they were needed. The famous "Lowell girls" of a later generation were older, but the machinery was also more complex. Although all these young people worked long hours—sunup to sundown—so did most children of the farming and laboring classes of New England.

Factory owners were not inattentive to the welfare of the children in their care. Samuel Slater set up a Sunday school to teach reading and writing, and at Lowell the girls were housed in company boardinghouses where their leisure and morals were carefully supervised. As early as 1813, Connecticut required manufacturing establishments to provide for the education of child operatives, and, in the next decades, Massachusetts took the lead in compulsory education for children and the limitation of their work hours.

But when, following the Civil War, the textile industry moved south, child labor took on a more sinister cast. Cheap, nonunion labor was the reason for building mills in the Carolina Piedmont, and these new factories relied on the labor of women and children. In 1880, 6 percent of American children between the ages of ten and fifteen were employed (not including agriculture). In 1900, one-quarter of southern mill operatives were children under fifteen, and half of these were below the age of twelve.

The Knights of Labor had advocated that child labor be prohibited, and later unions recognized that, as children could not be unionized, only legislation could protect them. In the early years of the twentieth century, progressives made the abolition of child labor a pillar of their reform program. Seeking to publicize abuses, the National Child Labor Committee sent photographer Lewis Hine throughout the South to record the faces and sad fortunes of children who worked in the region's cotton mills, mines, and canneries. By 1920, most states had laws that forbade the employment of children under fourteen and set an eight-hour day for workers under sixteen. Compulsory education laws also limited the availability of children for factory work.

But when the federal government sought to enact a nationwide ban on child labor, the Supreme Court struck it down as an unconstitutional interference in local labor conditions. Progressives countered with a constitutional amendment, which was sent to the states in 1924 but never ratified. Not until the Fair Labor Standards Act of 1938 was the employment of children under sixteen prohibited in manufacturing and mining.

1885 American Telephone & Telegraph (AT&T) is formed.

1886 Police fire into a crowd of striking workers at the McCormick factory in Chicago, killing four. When anarchists organize a protest rally in Haymarket Square, a bomb explodes, killing seven policemen, and more workers are killed in the confusion that follows. Eight anarchists are later executed for conspiracy. The episode discredits labor and heightens nativist fears of immigrants and radicals. Although not directly involved, the Knights of Labor rapidly loses members.

The Westinghouse Electric Company is incorporated.

Representing only skilled workers, the American Federation of Labor (AFL) forms.

1887 The Interstate Commerce Commission is established to regulate interstate transportation, especially the railroads. It is a prototype for independent regulatory commissions (see Chapter 12).

1888 The R. W. Sears Watch Company issues its first catalog featuring only watches and jewelry. RICHARD SEARS and Alvah T. Roebuck rename the company Sears, Roebuck and Company and introduce their first large catalog in 1886.

1889 I. M. Singer and Company manufactures the first electric sewing machine.

Otis Brothers installs an electric elevator in a New York City office building.

Several regional Farmers' Alliances unite to form the National Farmers' Alliance and Industrial Union. A parallel organization is the National Farmers' Alliance and Cooperative Union (see p. 265).

1890 A tobacco trust—the American Tobacco Company—is formed.

The Silver Purchase Act has the effect of increasing the currency in operation and weakening the federal gold reserves. It is repealed following the panic of 1893.

The Sherman Anti-Trust Act is the federal government's first attempt to break up the monopolies that now control American business, commerce, and industry.

1892 Boll weevils enter the United States in Texas. They annually destroy about 8 percent of the total cotton crop, resulting in a $200 to $300 million loss.

General Electric Company opens a corporate research and development division.

Private Pinkerton militia are called in to break a strike by steelworkers at ANDREW CARNEGIE's steel plant in Homestead, Pennsylvania, and seven strikers are killed.

1893 Another panic sends the nation into a four-year depression.

1894 HENRY DEMAREST LLOYD, a muckraking journalist, publishes his influential antitrust book, *Wealth Against Commonwealth.*

When an American Railway Union strike at the Pullman factory outside of Chicago threatens to disrupt train travel across the nation, a federal court issues an injunction forbidding this interference with interstate commerce. Union leader EUGENE V. DEBS ignores the injunction and is arrested and jailed. Federal troops break up the strike, but not before thirteen workers are dead and fifty wounded. Railroad workers in twenty-six more states protest, with additional violence and death.

Labeled "The Gospel According to St. John," this cartoon depicts John D. Rockefeller crushing the little people beneath his "Standard Oil Mill Stone" while handing a Bible to an African child. The cartoon highlights the contradiction between the ruthless business practices and the philanthropy of the wealthiest industrialists.

ECONOMY, BUSINESS, & LABOR

MILLIONAIRES: AN ALL-AMERICAN ACHEIVEMENT

Only in America is it acceptable to wear a T-shirt that announces: "The one who has the most when he dies wins." Americans' fascination with wealth, spurred by the optimistic belief that anyone with enough energy can amass a lot of money, has led to speculation involving the number of millionaires in the nation—only these days we are more likely to count billionaires instead. There was a time, though, when the number of millionaires felt like a measure of the nation's progress.

Consider, for example, that in 1840 the still relatively new nation boasted 40 millionaires. By 1880, the number had more than doubled to 100. Only twelve years later, it had increased tenfold, to produce an amazing 4,000 millionaires, and in another fifteen years had increased tenfold a second time, for a count of 40,000—at which point millionaires became too commonplace to count.

1894, *cont.*

The first national minimum wage in the world was established by New Zealand in 1894.

Wheat prices bottom out, causing reverse immigration as prairie schooners head back east with the words "In God we trusted, in Kansas we busted" painted on their sides. But during the 1890s, new strains of wheat promote recovery. Turkey, a hard, red, winter wheat first introduced by German Mennonites in 1873, is planted throughout the southern plains. Other red, spring wheats are favored on the northern plains. In the 1930s through the 1960s, other varieties are introduced. In the twentieth century competition for the export market comes from Canada, Australia, and Argentina.

1897 The Klondike gold rush begins. Between 1885 and 1929, more than $175 million in gold is taken out of Alaska (see p. 90).

1898 The National Consumers' League, the first major watchdog group to oversee consumers' rights, is founded. It fights for labeling laws and criticizes workplace conditions.

Muckraker journalist Ida B. Tarbell's exposé *A History of Standard Oil* first appeared as a serial in *McClure's* magazine. Her vilification of Standard Oil founder John D. Rockefeller was so effective that he began sleeping with a loaded pistol under his pillow for fear of would-be assassins.

1899 The Olds Motor Works is formed in Detroit. Its plant uses interchangeable parts, preparing the way for mass production.

1900 The Currency Act formally puts the United States on a gold standard.

Although the value of exported cotton has continued to rise since the days when it was "king," it now constitutes only 17 percent of exports.

The United States is first in the world in productivity. In the early twentieth century it manufactures one-third of the world's goods. It is also first in iron and steel production.

BIG BUSINESS AND THE GREAT DEPRESSION

1901 J. P. Morgan forms U.S. Steel by merging several other steel companies, including Andrew Carnegie's Carnegie Steel Company; it becomes the first billion-dollar corporation.

The discovery of oil at the Spindletop field spurs Texas industry and marks the beginning of the decline of ranching and farming in the state.

King C. Gillette organizes the Gillette Safety Razor Company. In 1903, he sells 51 razors and 168 blades. One year later he sells 90,000 razors and 12,400,000 blades.

1903 MAGGIE LENA WALKER, an African American, becomes the first woman bank president.

HENRY FORD founds the Ford Motor Company in Detroit.

The Department of Commerce and Labor is created as a cabinet-level post. In 1913, it is divided into two cabinet-level departments.

1904 IDA TARBELL publishes her two-volume, muckraking *History of the Standard Oil Company*. It had been published serially in *McClure's* magazine one year earlier.

1905 The first Rotary Club, a civic organization for business and professional people, is organized by Paul P. Harris in Chicago.

1906 The agency later known as the Food and Drug Administration is established under the Pure Food and Drug Act, and the Meat Inspection Act sets standards. Both acts are strongly influenced by the revelations of corruption and disregard for safety and cleanliness from the pages of Upton Sinclair's novel *The Jungle*.

1908 FORD introduces the Model T car, which costs $850. More than 15 million are sold in the next twenty years.

The Supreme Court rules that the Sherman Anti-Trust Act applies to labor unions.

In *Muller v. Oregon*, the Supreme Court upholds a law that limits the work hours of women. Louis D. Brandeis represents Oregon and submits what comes to be known as a "Brandeis Brief," marshaling statistical and sociological evidence to bolster the state's case.

1909 Congress enacts the Payne-Aldrich Tariff, which lowers tariffs on imported goods almost 20 percent.

The National Conservation Commission makes the first systematic count of the nation's natural resources.

1911 Under the Sherman Anti-Trust Act, the Supreme Court orders Standard Oil and American Tobacco to restructure.

1913 The Sixteenth Amendment permits an income tax.

The Ford Motor Company perfects mass production technique, introducing the modern assembly line in Highland Park, Michigan. It produces 800 Model Ts per day.

The popular understanding of Horatio Alger stories—that initiative and hard work lead from rags to riches—is inaccurate. Most of Alger's young heroes achieve success after meeting rich businessmen who give them one big chance, or by some other stroke of luck. Alger himself was said to despise the ethic of "rugged individualism."

Standard Oil, the main target of Theodore Roosevelt's trust-busting crusade, contributed $100,000 to his 1904 election campaign. The money was never returned.

ECONOMY, BUSINESS, & LABOR

TRUSTS

The merger mania of the 1980s was nothing compared to the first burst of trust fever at the end of the nineteenth century. When the states relaxed their incorporation laws, individuals such as JOHN D. ROCKEFELLER and J. P. MORGAN were able to establish large monopolistic corporations that came to be known as trusts.

John D. Rockefeller was the first industrialist to overwhelm the competition—by means both legal and illegal—and thus corner the market on petroleum with Standard Oil. His corporate counsel soon devised a new method of trust management, whereby stockholders in competing enterprises would turn over control of their companies to a board of directors that would manage them to maximize their benefit. Thus, the modern industrial megacorporation was born.

Other industries quickly followed suit: By 1890, there was a whiskey trust, a sugar trust, a tin-can trust, and a tobacco trust. J. P. Morgan managed to orchestrate mergers to form International Harvester and reorganized a number of railroads. His greatest triumph was in forming U.S. Steel, the nation's first billion-dollar corporation and, at the time, the largest in the world.

It seemed only a matter of time until a money trust formed, and indeed three large investment companies—Morgan, the National Bank of New York, and the National City Bank of New York—merged, putting control of what had previously been 112 separate financial organizations into the hands of a few directors.

Trust fever soon turned to antitrust fever, though, when muckraking journalists IDA TARBELL and HENRY DEMAREST LLOYD took on the big businesses in a series of well-documented books and articles, creating a public outrage that forced the federal government to take action.

Basically there are three ways in which governments can deal with monopolies. They can break them up, regulate them, or, in a method favored in Europe and little liked in the United States, convert them to public ownership. After 1890, the Sherman Anti-Trust Act could be used to break up the trusts, and regulation was accomplished through the establishment of government oversight agencies, such as the Interstate Commerce Commission.

The Sherman Anti-Trust Act proved relatively weak, however, partly for its ambiguity, somewhat rectified by the Clayton Anti-Trust Act of 1914. Ironically, one of the first applications of the Sherman Anti-Trust Act, which outlawed combinations "in restraint of trade," was against labor unions! In 1902, when the hatters' union launched a nationwide boycott against a nonunion manufacturer in Danbury, Connecticut, the company sued the union as an unlawful combination in restraint of trade, and the Supreme Court agreed. The Clayton Act, as a consequence, specified that antitrust law was not applicable to unions.

Antitrust laws did, however, force the breakup or restructuring of Swift and Company, Standard Oil, and American Tobacco, and suits were successfully brought against General Electric and Westinghouse for price-fixing, but not until 1982 was AT&T forced to break up.

Although the United States has more antitrust laws than any other nation, like most other nations it has been unable to stop the march of corporate progress. The ownership of many industries is heavily concentrated in the hands of a few persons, and, in the late 1980s, many American corporations became or were bought by international corporations.

1913, *cont.*

Daylight savings time was put into effect during World War I to cut energy consumption during the summer hours.

The Federal Reserve System replaces the Independent Treasury System. It creates twelve Reserve Banks and a Federal Reserve Board to direct the nation's credit and monetary affairs.

Congress divides the Department of Commerce and Labor into two separate cabinet-level departments.

1914 The Federal Trade Commission is established to maintain competition in the U.S. economy but prevent monopolies and unfair or deceptive trade practices.

The Clayton Anti-Trust Act strengthens the Sherman Anti-Trust Act by outlawing specific practices. It also forbids the use of antitrust law against labor organizations and the use of the injunction against labor.

At a time when the average autoworker receives $2.15 per day, HENRY FORD raises wages to $5 per day and cuts the workday from nine to eight hours.

1915 Alexander Graham Bell places the first transcontinental telephone call, from New York to San Francisco.

1916 The Ford plant assembly line in Detroit rolls off its one-millionth car; it is producing 2,000 cars per day.

The Federal Farm Loan Act makes credit available to farmers.

Congress passes the Owen-Keating Child Labor Law, which prohibits the interstate shipping of materials produced by child labor. It is ruled unconstitutional in 1918 (see p. 324).

1917 To ensure that the railroads operate smoothly during World War I, President Woodrow Wilson orders the federal government to run them, which it does for twenty-six months.

1919 The Radio Corporation of America (RCA) is formed.

The "Red Scare" tarnishes the reputation of labor, as labor radicalism is associated with socialism, communism, and left-wing political agitation by immigrants and aliens, many of whom are deported (see p. 120).

1920 The Transportation Act returns control of the railroads to the owners.

KDKA, America's first commercial radio station, begins broadcasting from Pittsburgh, Pennsylvania.

Union membership totals 19.7 million, but only 28 percent of the workforce.

1924 A Child Labor Amendment giving Congress jurisdiction to "limit, regulate and prohibit the labor of persons under 18 years of age" passes Congress and is sent to the states but fails to be ratified (see p. 324).

1926 RCA, AT&T, and the British General Post Office hold the first transatlantic radiotelephone conversation between New York City and London.

RCA organizes the National Broadcasting Company (NBC) as the first radio network.

1927 The Columbia Broadcasting Company (CBS) is organized to compete with NBC.

The first television transmission from New York City to Washington, D.C., is accomplished by AT&T.

1928 Ford Motor Company assembly lines produce the fifteen-millionth—and last—Model T.

Clarence Birdseye accidentally discovered the frozen-foods process while ice-fishing in Labrador in 1912. Twelve years later he began marketing his first packaged frozen-food product—fish.

The Texas oil magnate H. L. Hunt, who became one of the richest men in America, acquired his first oil well in a poker game in 1921.

ECONOMY, BUSINESS, & LABOR

1928, *cont.*

Clarence Birdseye applies his quick-freeze process to poultry, fish, and shellfish. In a few years, frozen foods revolutionize American eating habits.

"The man who builds a factory builds a temple."
—PRESIDENT
    CALVIN COOLIDGE

1929 The Agricultural Marketing Act establishes the Federal Farm Board, to promote marketing of farm products through cooperatives. Its programs failed to deal with price fluctuations; it ceased to exist in 1933.

In October, the stock market crashes, and the Great Depression begins. Within just four years, national income drops by almost 50 percent and unemployment reaches 12.8 million, amounting to one-quarter of the civilian workforce. Bank closures number 659 in 1929; 1,352 in 1930; 2,294 in 1931; and 1,456 in 1932. Deposits in these banks total more than $3.5 billion.

1930 The Hawley-Smoot Act raises tariffs to an all-time high, with the result that international trade drops substantially. The American economy, at this time however, is quite self-sufficient. The year before the enactment of the tariff, imports amount to only 5 percent of national income (see p. 321).

The worst bank failure to date occurs when the Bank of the United States in New York City collapses. With more than 400,000 depositors—many recent immigrants—the effect is devastating.

1932 The Norris-La Guardia Anti-Injunction Act forbids the use of injunction in the majority of labor disputes.

To aid those left jobless by the Great Depression, Wisconsin passes the first law establishing state-supported unemployment insurance.

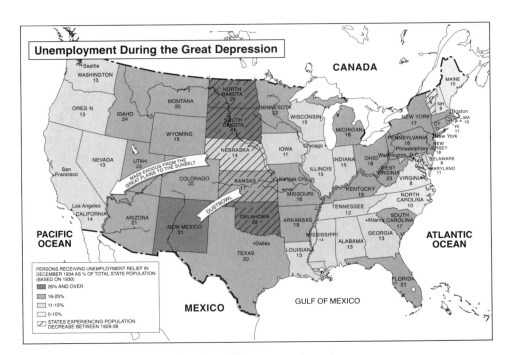

Unemployment During the Great Depression

PERSONS RECEIVING UNEMPLOYMENT RELIEF IN DECEMBER 1934 AS % OF TOTAL STATE POPULATION (BASED ON 1930)
- 26% AND OVER
- 16-25%
- 11-15%
- 0-10%
- STATES EXPERIENCING POPULATION DECREASE BETWEEN 1929-39

1933 Within 100 days of his inauguration, Franklin D. Roosevelt ushers through Congress a series of legislation intended to ease the effects of the Great Depression. The Securities Act helps provide information about the stock market. The Emergency Banking Act provides for temporary insurance for depositors. The Federal Deposit Insurance Corporation becomes permanent in 1935. Relief measures, such as the Civilian Conservation Corps, the Agricultural Adjustment Administration, and the Federal Emergency Relief Administration are created. Funding is secured for the Tennessee Valley Authority, a project for flood control as well as massive rural electrification. The Emergency Farm Mortgage Act and the Home Owners' Loan Corporation provide help to farmers and homeowners.

"When more and more people are thrown out of work, unemployment results."
—PRESIDENT
  CALVIN COOLIDGE

In one of his first acts, Roosevelt declares a bank holiday, closing all banks from March 6 to March 12. In the first few days after the bank holiday, about three-quarters of the banks are declared sound and reopened. Public confidence is restored.

Congress passes the Glass-Steagall Act, which requires banks to have deposit insurance and prohibits them from owning brokerages; it effectively separates commercial and investment banking.

When Roosevelt issues an executive order that banks cannot exchange money for gold, he in effect takes the United States off the gold standard (see p. 332).

Intended to spur economic growth and battle unemployment, the National Industrial Recovery Act states that codes of fair practice will be drawn up for different industries.

1934 The Securities and Exchange Commission is established to regulate securities trading.

The Federal Communications Commission is established to regulate communication.

The Federal Farm Mortgage Corporation is created to help farmers refinance their debt.

The Trade Agreements Act enables the president to negotiate trade agreements with individual nations. By 1941, twenty-two agreements have been negotiated and signed. The overall effect lowers tariffs and stimulates American exports.

1935 The Rural Electrification Administration is created to bring electrical power to rural areas.

The Social Security Act establishes a federal pension for retirees.

The Revenue Security Act of 1935 (Wealth Tax Act) increases taxes on incomes above $50,000 and on corporations with incomes of more than $50,000 and profits greater than 10 percent.

Pan American airlines begins transpacific air service.

In *Schechter Poultry Corp. v. United States*, the Supreme Court finds the National Industrial Recovery Act unconstitutional for allowing the executive branch to perform legislative duties.

THE GOLD STANDARD

One of the major problems confronting any nation is establishing and maintaining the value and stability of its money. From the date of its founding the United States proved to be no exception. Colonial America, for example, forbidden to mint its own coins or to import British money, traded largely in commodities. Foreign coins, especially ones from Spain, circulated freely. The initial coinage of the government under the Constitution was based on both gold and silver at a fixed ratio that tended to overvalue silver. By the late nineteenth century, this inherent tension came to have political overtones in the struggle between agrarian and industrial interests. Finally,

in 1900, gold became the official standard. Not until the Great Depression did President FRANKLIN D. ROOSEVELT, using his executive powers under the Emergency Banking Act, prohibit banks from paying in gold or from exporting gold, a gesture that, in effect, took the country off the gold standard. By the 1950s, the dollar, in addition to other methods of payment such as the "paper gold" issued by the International Monetary Fund, had replaced gold as the international unit of exchange.

President Richard Nixon officially ended the nation's tie to gold on August 15, 1971. Henceforth, gold would be traded on the free market like any other commodity.

1935, *cont.*

A new labor union, the Committee for Industrial Organizations has great success organizing steelworkers.

"I don't know much about being a millionaire, but I'll bet I'd be darling at it."
—DOROTHY PARKER

1936 The Robinson-Patman Act encourages competition and discourages monopolies by making it illegal for businesses to collude on prices.

1938 The Revenue Act reduces taxes on large corporations and raises taxes on small businesses, thus establishing a pattern that will persist for decades.

The Civil Aeronautics Board is created to oversee civil air transport.

Du Pont manufactures the first nylon product, a toothbrush. Wallace Carothers and a team of Du Pont scientists have been working on nylon for a decade. Nylon will be used in clothing and a host of other products. Nylon stockings go on the market in 1940.

1939 Regularly scheduled commercial television broadcasts begin.

1942 After the attack on Pearl Harbor, industry gears up for World War II. Government spending puts a complete end to the Depression. Unemployment virtually disappears, and by war's end 17 million jobs have been created. Industrial production increases 96 percent. Between 1941 and 1943, more than 5 million women enter the workforce, and in manufacturing hourly wages rise from 49 cents in 1940 to 79 cents in 1945, a 61 percent increase.

ECONOMIC SUPERPOWER

1945 World War II ends, and the United States enters a postwar economic boom.

1946 The Council of Economic Advisers is formed to shape domestic policy on employment.

1947 The United States produces 60 percent of the world's steel.

1950 Diners Club becomes the first comprehensive credit card.

1952 To prevent a steel strike that could cripple the nation's businesses, President Harry Truman seizes the steel mills. The Supreme Court rules the seizure unconstitutional.

1953 The first commercial color broadcast on television heralds a new market, but not until 1968 will color sets outsell black-and-white ones.

General Motors becomes the first corporation to report earnings of $1 billion annually. Six million cars roll off the assembly lines in Detroit each year.

1956 The Soil Bank is established to pay farmers not to plant certain crops in order to decrease production and to conserve the soil.

The Federal Highway Act authorizes a system of interstate highways that will make interstate commerce easier and cheaper (see p. 441).

1957 Electricity is produced by a nuclear reactor on an experimental basis in Shippingport, Pennsylvania.

1958 Pan American Airways introduces transatlantic jet travel.

1962 In the face of growing foreign competition, the Trade Expansion Act gives the president increased powers to cut tariffs.

Following the launch of *Telstar,* live intercontinental telecasts begin.

1963 The Office of the Special Representative for Trade Negotiations is established. In 1980, it becomes the Office of the U.S. Trade Representative.

1964 President LYNDON JOHNSON's "war on poverty" raises millions of poor Americans out of poverty. It is the single biggest expansion of social services since the New Deal, and the first to take place in a period of prosperity.

The Economic Opportunity Act provides funds for the Job Corps, VISTA, and other special programs for the poor and for youth.

1968 Automobiles built after this date must comply with the first government-mandated standards to improve car safety, including specific requirements regarding seat belts, rear-view mirrors, and tire dimensions.

To fund the Vietnam War, President LYNDON JOHNSON requests a personal income tax surcharge of 10 percent.

In the largest merger to date in U.S. history, the New York Central and Pennsylvania Railroads form one company.

Cesar Chavez, heading the United Farm Workers, launches a boycott of table grapes that wins widespread support. In 1970, grape workers get contracts from California growers.

"The world is very different now. For man holds in his mortal hands the power to abolish all forms of human poverty, and all forms of human life."
—PRESIDENT JOHN F. KENNEDY

ECONOMY, BUSINESS, & LABOR

1969 The Food and Drug Administration bans the sale of artificial sweeteners called cyclamates.

1970s Even though real earnings have doubled since 1930, the nation experiences "stagflation," stagnant earnings combined with inflation, which reaches 13.5 percent by the end of the decade.

1970 Congress establishes the Environmental Protection Agency, which will, among other activities, regulate businesses' interactions with the environment.

When the National Air Quality Control Act calls for a 90 percent reduction in auto pollutants, the auto industry claims it cannot afford to meet these standards.

Postal workers walk out in a wildcat strike, the largest public-employee strike in the country's history.

1971 To slow down spiraling inflation, President Richard Nixon imposes a ninety-day freeze on wages and prices and severs the dollar's tie to gold, which means the dollar will not float on the world currency market. To slow inflation, Nixon uses wage and price controls until 1973.

Amtrak, a quasi-governmental corporation, is created by Congress to operate many of the nation's remaining passenger trains.

1972 Out of fears for public health, the government bans the use of DDT, a common pesticide.

The Consumer Product Safety Commission is established.

Following a 1970 act of Congress, cigarette advertising is banned on radio and television.

1973 The Arab oil embargo by the Organization of Petroleum Exporting Countries (OPEC) sends petroleum product prices soaring and leaves Americans waiting on gas lines (see p. 298).

1974 The oil embargo ends.

Regulations for the labeling of food and household goods go into effect.

Tony Boyle, president of the United Mine Workers, is convicted of the murder of rival Joseph A. Yablonski and his wife and daughter.

1975 In a pattern that will repeat in other state and local governments during the next two decades, New York City declares itself to be near bankruptcy and must take stringent measures, including the cutting of basic services, to restore its financial standing. It also receives a bailout loan from the federal government.

Long the world leader in steel production, the United States now produces only 16 percent of the world's steel.

When seven major northeastern railroads stand on the brink of bankruptcy, the Consolidated Rail Corporation, or Conrail, is formed, with a federal subsidy, to save them.

1977 Imports exceed exports by $29.2 billion, creating the largest trade deficit in U.S. history. This, however, is only the beginning of a chronic trade imbalance that mushrooms to well over $100 billion each year throughout the mid 1980s and into the 1990s.

The Trans-Alaska pipeline from Prudhoe Bay to Prince William Sound begins operations. It is bitterly opposed by conservationists.

The Department of Energy is created.

1978 In a move to "deregulate" industry, the Civil Aeronautics Board is scheduled for phaseout. The trucking industry is also deregulated.

Californians initiate tax revolt by adopting Proposition 13, a constitutional amendment cutting local property taxes by more than 50 percent.

1978–1980 Inflation soars to a record-setting 10 to 13.5 percent.

1980 The Crude Oil Windfall Profit Tax Act and Energy Security Act are imposed to promote energy conservation and development of alternative fuels and domestic sources of fuel.

Congress authorizes loan guarantees of more than $1.5 billion to prevent Chrysler, the third largest automobile manufacturer, from going under.

The United States produces one-fifth of the world's automobiles; in 1960, it had produced nearly half.

1981 In the first major revision of the tax code in decades, President RONALD REAGAN cuts corporate and personal taxes. Domestic spending is severely cut at the same time that the military budget nearly doubles. Supply-side economics, which advocates a tax cut and reduced government spending to fix an ailing economy, replaces Keynesian economics, which has prevailed since the New Deal and favors government spending to stimulate the economy.

When air traffic controllers strike, President Reagan refuses to recognize their right to do so and replaces them, thus destroying their union.

"A recession is when your neighbor loses his job. A depression is when you lose yours."
—PRESIDENT RONALD REAGAN

1982 The country sinks into a recession, and unemployment reaches 9.5 percent, the highest since before World War II.

After a lengthy antitrust lawsuit, American Telephone & Telegraph (AT&T) is forced to break up into regional companies.

1983 The nation begins to recover, but unemployment drops only slowly; the stock market makes modest gains.

1985 The United States becomes a debtor nation. In 1986, it will be the world's number one debtor nation, with a debt of $220 billion.

1987 The stock market crashes, but federal protections and regulations initiated in the New Deal, plus an infusion from the Federal Reserve, keep the economy stable (see p. 209).

ECONOMY, BUSINESS, & LABOR

1989 A savings-and-loan scandal involving the abuse and misuse of bank funds, is scheduled for a bailout by Congress, costing taxpayers $180 billion.

1990 The country sinks into a recession that will soon prove to be worldwide. Union membership stands at 16.7 million, 16 percent of the workforce.

1993 The North American Free Trade Agreement establishes Canada, Mexico, and the United States as a free-trade zone in which most goods and services are sold without tariffs.

"Our Age of Anxiety is, in great part, the result of trying to do today's jobs with yesterday's tools."
—MARSHALL McLUHAN

1995 Republicans take over Congress and vow to cut spending even more and eradicate the deficit by the year 2000.
The Interstate Commerce Commission, the nation's first regulatory agency, is abolished.

1995–1996 The White House and the Republican-dominated Congress reach an impasse over the fiscal year 1996 budget that shuts the government down for weeks. In a compromise measure, a plan is enacted for eliminating the federal debt by the year 2002.

1998 The federal government achieves a budget surplus, the first since 1960, of $69.2 billion.

2000 A federal district court judge, Thomas Penfield Jackson, finds the computer software giant Microsoft in wide violation of the nation's antitrust laws and orders that it be broken into two companies, an order that is later reversed.

2000–2001 After more than eight years of growth, the longest period of sustained economic expansion in the nation's history, the U.S. economy begins to slow. An actual recession (technically defined as two consecutive quarters of decline) fails to materialize, but growth remains flat and the stock market drops dramatically. The situation is worsened by the impact on transportation, tourism, and other business sectors of the September 11 terrorist attacks.

2001 Keeping a campaign promise, President George W. Bush seeks tax cuts totaling $1.6 trillion over ten years. Congress finally agrees to $1.35 trillion over ten years. The plan comes amid ongoing debate as how best to spend federal budget surpluses.

2002 The giant energy company Enron collapses amid allegations of financial impropriety. The largest bankruptcy case in U.S. corporate history, the Enron case sparks a congressional investigation.

THE NATIONAL DEBT

The deficit, which is the amount the government spends beyond what it takes in during a fiscal year, is either good or bad, depending upon which group of economists one chooses to listen to. One school maintains that a deficit weakens the economy while another believes deficit spending serves as an important economic stimulus. In any event, the accumulated deficit plus interest—or national debt—grew and shrank regularly until the mid-twentieth century, when it began to skyrocket. By the latter part of the 1990s, however, bolstered by several years of rapid economic growth and low interest rates, the federal government achieved its first budget surpluses in four decades. As a result, politicians and economists began forecasting a complete elimination of the debt—a condition not enjoyed since the 1860s—within two decades, but that prospect dimmed in the face of a major economic slowdown and deep, long-term tax cuts enacted in 2001.

THE DEBT

YEAR	TOTAL NATIONAL DEBT ($)	PER CAPITA NATIONAL DEBT ($)
1791	75,463,000	—
1800	82,976,000	—
1810	53,173,000	—
1820	91,016,000	—
1830	48,565,000	—
1840	3,573,000	—
1850	63,454,000	—
1860	64,844,000	2.06
1870	2,436,453,000	61.06
1880	2,090,909,000	41.60
1890	1,122,397,000	17.80
1900	1,263,417,000	16.60
1910	1,146,940,000	12.41
1920	24,299,321,000	228.23
1930	16,185,310,000	131.51
1940	42,967,531,000	325.25
1950	257,357,352,000	1,696.67
1960	290,200,000,000	1,606.23
1970	389,200,000,000	1,898.05
1980	939,200,000,000	4,133.35
1985	1,945,900,000,000	8,178.66
1990	3,233,300,000,000	12,960.99
1995	4,974,000,000,000	18,926.72
1996	5,224,800,000,000	19,699.20
1997	5,413,100,000,000	20,214.46
1998	5,526,200,000,000	20,448.62
1999	5,656,300,000,000	20,742.60
2000	5,674,200,000,000	20,660.95
2001	5,807,500,000,000	20,354.38
2002	6,228,200,000,000	21,598.17

ECONOMY, BUSINESS, & LABOR

PANICS, DEPRESSIONS, AND RECESSIONS, 1784–PRESENT

1784–1786 The new nation's first depression results from a shortage of currency and the war debt.

1819 A panic is precipitated by wild speculation in western lands, followed by a sharp contraction of credit, led by the Second Bank of the United States. A six-year depression ensues.

1832 When President Andrew Jackson refuses to renew the charter of the Second Bank of the United States and transfers government funds to state banks, Nicholas Biddle, head of the national bank, calls in commercial loans. A panic and recession follow. Eight hundred banks close, and the banking system collapses. One-third of manual laborers are out of work in New York City alone. Nationwide, unemployment reaches 10 percent.

1836 President Jackson precipitates another banking crisis by issuing the Specie Circular, declaring that the federal government will henceforth require hard currency for purchase of western public lands.

1837–1843 In response, English banks raise interest rates and reduce credit, sending shock waves through the cotton market that initiate a six-year depression.

1857–1858 This brief panic is notable for the role that telecommunications plays. When a branch of the Ohio Life Insurance and Trust Company fails, news that would formerly have taken weeks to crisscross the nation, its impact diminishing with time, is known within hours, thanks to the telegraph. The news induces one of the first waves of panic selling in the stock market. The underlying cause of the recession is a downturn in agricultural exports brought on by the end of the Crimean War in Europe, as well as overspeculation in railroads and real estate.

A 1930s businessman is reduced to selling apples for a living.

1873–1878 A major depression begins, precipitated by the failure of Jay Cooke and Company, which financed the Northern Pacific Railroad. Business topple, and the New York Stock Exchange closes for ten days. Before the depression is over, 100 banks and 18,000 businesses will fail.

1893–1897 A series of railroad bankruptcies causes banks to call in their loans. In all, 150 banks, 200 railroads, and 15,000 small businesses succumb. Unemployment reaches 25 percent, and in New York City alone 20,000 are homeless. The depression lasts four years.

1929–1941 The Great Depression is set off by a stock market crash. In 1932 alone, 12.8 million people will have suffered unemployment and, in 1930 and 1931, 2,300 banks fail. Unemployment during the Depression reaches 25 percent, with another 25 percent considered underemployed.

1957–1958 In a short period of slow growth, this recession causes a 0.8 percent drop in the nation's gross national product (GNP) and causes 6.8 percent unemployment.

1973–1975 The GNP drops 1.3 percent, and unemployment rises to 8.3 percent.

1981–1982 The GNP drops only 2.5 percent, but unemployment soars to 9.5 percent, the highest since before World War II. A decade of stagnant growth follows. The Midwest is hit hard.

1990–1992 A worldwide recession occurs. In the United States it is regional, hitting the Northeast two years before the West Coast and leaving the usually hard-hit industrial Midwest virtually untouched.

2001–2003 After more than eight years of growth, the longest period of sustained economic expansion in the nation's history, the U.S. economy begins to slow. An actual recession (technically defined as two consecutive quarters of decline) fails to materialize. The stock market, which had yielded hefty returns since at least 1995, plummets; technology stocks, particularly in the Internet industry, are especially hard hit.

THE RISE AND FALL OF LABOR, 1741–PRESENT

The rise of the factory system changed human relationships and work patterns. The paternalistic family work system of the farm, replicated in the apprenticeship system, disappeared as men and women left their homes and household shops to work in noisy factories at repetitive tasks under the sharp eye of a supervisor whose goal was increased production and higher profits for the factory owner—the capitalist. It did not take laborers long to realize that only their numbers gave them power and to band together to demand better working conditions and more pay. Factory owners—quite naturally—sought to suppress such unions, and the story of labor is a story of the long struggle for the right to organize and to assert some measure of control over the terms and conditions of work.

1741 Journeymen caulkers in Boston combine in agreement not to accept notes for wages.

1768 An organized strike takes place when New York tailors protest a cut in wages.

1791 Slater's mill in Pawtucket, Rhode Island, employs nine operatives—seven boys and two girls—all between the ages of seven and twelve.

1794 Shoemakers in Philadelphia form the Federal Society of Journeymen Cordwainers, an early trade union that survives a strike in 1799.

The Typographical Society of New York promotes higher wages, shorter hours, better working conditions, and benefits for illness.

1824 Women organize a strike in a Pawtucket, Rhode Island, textile mill.

1828 Workers in Philadelphia join together to seek political redress for some of their grievances.

They promote a ten-hour workday, which becomes a chief aim for labor for the next two decades. By 1860, though not standard, the ten-hour day is widely accepted.

1833 When nine craft organizations in New York City join to form the General Trades Union, craft groups in other cities quickly follow suit. These workingmen's parties initiate a wave of strikes that sweep the nation and eradicate whatever bond previously existed between apprentices and journeymen and their masters.

1834 Local organizations of the General Trades Union form the National Trades Union, whose purpose is less to achieve workers' benefits than to overturn the wage system that has arisen along with factories.

Women at the Lowell mills "turn out" to protest a wage cut. They do the same in 1836, again in vain, but these are the largest strikes in the country to date.

1837 The National Trades Union movement collapses under the weight of this year's financial panic.

1840 President Martin Van Buren gives labor at least a token victory when he signs an Executive Order establishing a ten-hour workday for certain federal government employees.

1842 In Massachusetts, child labor is limited to ten hours a day for children under the age of twelve.

1845 In response to unionizing by men, women who work in the Lowell textile mills found the New England Female Labor Reform Association, which argues forcefully for a ten-hour workday.

THE RISE AND FALL OF LABOR, 1741–PRESENT, cont.

1847 New Hampshire is the first state to pass legislation limiting the workday to ten hours.

1852 The National Typographical Union is founded, combining locals in the United States. It is an early, and long-lived, national craft union.

1860 Ten thousand workers in the Massachusetts shoe industry stage a six-week walkout.

1866 The National Labor Union is founded in Baltimore. In contrast to the labor organizations formed by specific craftspeople, who promote their own interests, its focus is general labor reform, that is, worker ownership of factories and opposition to the wage system.

1869 Philadelphia garment cutters found the Knights of Labor. This early union includes skilled and nonskilled workers and welcomes women and blacks. It calls for an eight-hour day. Membership peaks in 1886 at almost 1 million.

The Coalition of Labor Union Women (CLUW) is formed when members of fifty-eight unions band together to advocate the rights of women workers, both in their existing trade unions and in the workplace.

After an unsuccessful attempt to integrate the National Labor Union, black leaders organize the Colored National Labor Union. Headquartered in Washington, D.C., it is the first national labor organization for blacks.

1877 The Great Railroad Strike occurs when workers on the Baltimore & Ohio in Martinsburg, West Virginia, stage a local strike that soon spreads across the country. For the first time, federal troops are used to quell a strike. Although more than 100 strikers are killed, this strike, the first nationwide work stoppage, gives labor a sense of its power.

Excluded by most labor unions, women formed their own.

1882 The first Labor Day is celebrated. Congress makes it a legal annual holiday in 1894.

1884 The new federal Bureau of Labor begins to compile labor statistics.

1886 The American Federation of Labor (AFL) forms to represent skilled workers, organized by craft. More disciplined than the Knights of Labor, which it supersedes, it excludes women, blacks, and immigrants, and works specifically for its members rather than for general labor reform. As it gains strength, it closes the labor-reform unions out of the negotiating process. SAMUEL GOMPERS is the influential first president.

1892 When silver miners in Coeur d'Alene, Idaho, refuse a wage cut, owners stage a lockout and bring in strikebreakers. Violence erupts, and federal troops are dispatched to the area.

1893 The Western Federation of Miners, a large and militant union, is organized.

1897 The American Federation of Labor has a half million members.

1901 The Socialist Party of America is formed as a coalition of several leftist groups.

1902 In Pennsylvania 150,000 United Mine Workers, led by John Mitchell, strike for five and one-half months, demanding a 20 percent increase in wages and an eight-hour workday. Under pressure from President Theodore Roosevelt to arbitrate, they settle for a 10 percent increase and no change in the workday.

Maryland becomes the first state to enact workmen's compensation.

Members of the Women's Trade Union League march through New York City's Washington Square Park in 1904 with signs exhorting women to unite and organize to fight for fair treatment.

1904 The AFL claims 1.7 million members.

The National Child Labor Committee is organized to promote legislation ending child labor.

1905 In an attempt to take the labor movement into a more inclusive and radical direction, workers in Chicago, with support from the Socialist Party, found the Industrial Workers of the World (IWW), which briefly becomes a force among unskilled workers and immigrant laborers.

1909–1910 The militant "Uprising of the 20,000," a New York City shirtwaist workers' strike, brings previously unorganized, unskilled workers into unions.

1911 The Triangle Shirtwaist Factory fire in New York City kills 146 women workers. The tragedy underscores the terrible working conditions of urban sweatshops. Building codes, labor reform, and the International Ladies Garment Workers Union are all taken more seriously.

1912 During its brief heyday, the Industrial Workers of the World (known as the Wobblies) turns a walkout of textile workers in Lawrence, Massachusetts, into the famous "Bread and Roses" strike and forces union recognition.

1913 A six-month silk workers' strike in Paterson, New Jersey, inspires a benefit at Madison Square Garden in which the strike's most dramatic moments are reenacted.

1914 In Ludlow, Colorado, a mining town dominated by the Colorado Fuel and Iron Company, the United Mine Workers strike for better safety, higher wages, and union recognition. When the state militia and private guards fire on the strikers,

THE RISE AND FALL OF LABOR, 1741–PRESENT, cont.

fourteen persons, including eleven children, are killed. The Ludlow massacre arouses widespread protest against management policies.

1919 When Boston police go out on strike, Massachusetts governor Calvin Coolidge becomes famous for asserting, "There is no right to strike against the public safety by anybody, anywhere, anytime."

1919–1920 Steelworkers in midwestern steel towns strike unsuccessfully to force management to recognize their union. In Gary, Indiana, a violent riot leaves eighteen dead.

1920 The AFL claims 4 million members.

1929 Only 30 percent of the industrial labor force works more than fifty-four hours a week.

1932 FRANKLIN D. ROOSEVELT and the Democratic Party earns the support—and votes—of labor.

1933 President ROOSEVELT, in recognition of the growing power of labor, appoints FRANCES PERKINS as the first female head of the Department of Labor. She is an active supporter of workers and unions.

1935 The Wagner Act establishes the right of workers to join unions and bargain collectively. It also creates the National Labor Relations Board to oversee collective bargaining.
   The AFL claims 2.5 million members.
   Advocating the organization of workers by industry rather than craft, John L. Lewis and the United Mine Workers found the Committee for Industrial Organization to concentrate on organizing workers in mass-production industries such as rubber, cars, and steel. It is later expelled from the AFL and becomes the Congress of Industrial Organizations (CIO).

1936 The Walsh-Healy Act sets a minimum wage for workers at companies that hold government contracts. It also mandates an eight-hour day and forty-hour week, and bans child and convict labor.

1936–1937 Autoworkers initiate a sit-down strike at the General Motors plant in Flint, Michigan. When GM recognizes the United Auto Workers (UAW) union, the stage is set for huge growth in the UAW and other mass-production industry unions.

1938 The Fair Labor Standards Act mandates a minimum wage and forty-hour week and forbids child labor in any business engaged in interstate commerce.
   The CIO claims 4 million members.

1941–1945 To support the war effort, unions are encouraged to sign no-strike pledges, and many do. Yet more strikes occur in this four-year period than in any other in American history.

1943 John L. Lewis and the United Mine Workers stage a walkout that resists government efforts to end it.

1945 Together the AFL and CIO claim 14.8 million members, or more than one-third of the nonagricultural workforce—an all-time high.

1946 The Employment Act establishes maximum employment as a government responsibility.

1947 The Taft-Hartley Act overrules many of the prolabor elements of the Wagner Act (1935).

1952 To prevent a steel strike that could cripple the nation's businesses, President Harry Truman seizes the steel mills. The Supreme Court decides the seizure is unconstitutional, and the seven-week strike that follows puts 600,000 unionized steelworkers and 1.4 million workers in industries dependent on steel out of work.

1955 The American Federation of Labor and the Congress of Industrial Organizations merge to form the AFL-CIO.

1957 The federal government investigates racketeering in labor unions and finds Dave Beck, the head of the Teamsters Union and vice president of the AFL-CIO, guilty of misuse of funds. Teamsters vice president Jimmy Hoffa is also charged. Several unions are expelled from the AFL-CIO.

1959 A four-month steel strike ends only when a federal court invokes the Taft-Hartley Act and orders workers to return to their jobs.

1963 To combat discriminating wage scales, the Equal Pay Act mandates equal pay for equal work for industries engaged in interstate commerce.

1964 Although traditionally discriminatory toward minorities and women, labor unions endorse civil rights legislation.

Jimmy Hoffa, head of the Teamsters, is convicted of jury tampering and fraudulent use of union funds; he receives a thirteen-year prison sentence. President Richard Nixon commutes his sentence. Shortly after he is released, he vanishes from Detroit.

1970 Workers' wages have tripled since 1945.

The Brotherhood of Sleeping Car Porters, the first black-controlled trade union, celebrate their fiftieth anniversary in 1975.

1973 Cesar Chavez's United Farm Workers becomes a member of the AFL-CIO.

1975 In the first strike by physicians, doctors in New York and Chicago protest working conditions and long hours.

1978 President Jimmy Carter halts a coal miners' strike, citing the national interest.

1981 President RONALD REAGAN, instituting strong antilabor policies, orders striking air traffic controllers to return to work or face dismissal. More than 11,000 are dismissed, and the union is decertified.

1984 For the first time, the AFL-CIO endorses a presidential candidate—Democrat Walter Mondale.

1992 Women represent 45 percent of the civilian labor force.

1993 Organized labor unsuccessfully opposes the North American Free Trade Agreement, fearing loss of U.S. jobs to cheaper labor in Mexico.

1994 Major-league baseball players go on strike in August and the rest of the season is canceled. The players object to owners' salary caps. This longest work stoppage in professional sports ends in April 1995.

1998–1999 The U.S. labor movement shows new strength, as unions aggressively add members and stage a number of successful job actions. Despite increases in overall membership, however, the percentage of unionized workers in the labor force falls below 14 percent—less than half the percentage in the 1950s.

2000 The nation's unemployment rate drops to 4.1 percent, its lowest level in more than thirty years.

ECONOMY, BUSINESS, & LABOR

THE MINIMUM WAGE

The national lower limit on wages was established by the Fair Labor Standards Act of June 1938, a prominent bill in President FRANKLIN ROOSEVELT's second New Deal, intended to prevent competitive wage cutting during the Great Depression. With the shift to a war economy, however, market forces yielded natural wage hikes, and the federal minimum of 30 cents in the early 1940s became largely irrelevant. Congress raised the level to 40 cents at the war's conclusion in 1945 and 75 cents in 1949—followed by numerous increases in the decades since.

The 1938 law originally applied only to enterprises that conducted or influenced interstate commerce. Thus, numerous professions were excluded from the bill's provisions, including farm laborers, domestic servants, and numerous government employees among others. The act established a minimum hourly wage of 25 cents; mandated at least time-and-a-half overtime pay for labor over forty-four hours per week (beginning in 1941 and reduced to forty hours per week beginning in 1944); and outlawed child labor under sixteen years of age (with exceptions) and hazardous labor under eighteen years of age. In 1961, the provisions were extended to employees in large retail and service enterprises including local transit, construction, and gas stations. In 1966, government employees were added. Farmworkers were also included at this time, but under a different scale until 1978.

As a matter of economic and social policy, the federal minimum wage remains a contentious political issue. Many conservative economists, such as supply-side theorists and Libertarians, believe that it increases inflation and unemployment. Supporters, including many liberal economists and Keynesian theorists, maintain that it adjusts wages for inflation (instead of affecting it directly), does not affect unemployment, and strengthens the economy by providing more disposable income for the lower classes. The United States Supreme Court upheld the constitutionality of the Fair Labor Standards Act in *United States v. Darby Lumber Company* (1941).

EFFECTIVE DATE	ALL WORKERS COVERED	NON-FARMWORKERS	FARMWORKERS
Oct. 24, 1938	0.25		
Oct. 24, 1939	0.30		
Oct. 24, 1945	0.40		
Jan. 25, 1950	0.75		
Mar. 1, 1956	1.00		
Sept. 3, 1961	1.15		
Sept. 3, 1963	1.25		
Feb. 1, 1967		1.40	1.00
Feb. 1, 1968		1.60	1.15
Feb. 1, 1969		1.60	1.30
Feb. 1, 1970		1.60	1.45
Feb. 1, 1971		1.60	1.60
Feb. 1, 1974		2.00	1.60
Jan. 1, 1975		2.10	1.80
Jan. 1, 1976		2.30	2.00
Jan. 1, 1977		2.30	2.20
Jan. 1, 1978	2.65		
Jan. 1, 1979	2.90		
Jan. 1, 1980	3.10		
Jan. 1, 1981	3.35		
Apr. 1, 1990	3.80		
Apr. 1, 1991	4.25		
Oct. 1, 1996	4.75		
Sept. 1, 1997	5.15		

LEGISLATION AFFECTING THE ECONOMY, BUSINESS, AND LABOR, 1791–PRESENT

1791 Bank Act. The Bank of the United States is chartered for twenty years. It will serve as the government's fiscal agent and depository for federal funds.

1807 Embargo Act. This act forbids almost all foreign commerce. It is repealed in 1809.

1816 Bank Act. The charter of the Bank of the United States having expired, a second bank is chartered, again for twenty years.

1840 Independent Treasury Act. This act, repealed in 1841 but passed again in 1846, orders public funds to be deposited in the Treasury building and in subtreasuries in various cities. It serves as the basis for the U.S. fiscal system until 1913.

1862 Legal Tender Act. This act empowers the federal government to print paper money.

1863 National Bank Act. This act prohibits state banks from printing paper money.

1873 Coinage Act. This act, which omits provision for coining silver dollars, demonetizes silver and puts the United States on the gold standard.

1875 Resumption Act. This act sets January 1, 1879, as the date for redemption of greenbacks in specie. But in 1878, gold reserves are so high that Congress agrees to allow the $347 million in outstanding greenbacks to remain in circulation.

1878 Bland-Allison Act. This act provides for the freer coinage of silver, requiring the U.S. government to purchase between $2 and $4 million of silver bullion to be coined into silver dollars.

1882 Chinese Exclusion Act. In reaction to an influx of cheap Chinese labor, this act denies Chinese laborers entry to the United States for ten years and is the first major attempt to regulate the immigrant labor force (see Chapter 4).

1887 Interstate Commerce Act. This act prohibits discriminatory rates and practices by railroads and establishes the first regulatory commission, the Interstate Commerce Commission.

1890 Silver Purchase Act. This compromise act requires the U.S. government to double its purchase of silver and adds to the amount of money in circulation.

Sherman Anti-Trust Act. This first federal attempt to regulate monopolies is ambiguous. It states that combinations "in restraint of trade" are illegal, and is actually used against labor unions as well as trusts.

1898 Erdman Act. This act provides for the voluntary mediation of labor disputes, but it is rarely used in the next decade. Its provision prohibiting railroads from requiring that employees promise not to join a union is overturned by the Supreme Court.

1900 Currency Act. This formally puts the United States on a gold standard.

1906 Pure Food and Drug Act. This act prohibits the sale of impure food and drugs and requires that food labels include contents; it also creates what is later called the Food and Drug Administration to oversee enforcement of the law.

Meat Inspection Act. This mandates improvements in the sanitary conditions at meat-packing plants and their enforcement through federal inspection.

1909 Income Tax Amendment. Congress passes this constitutional amendment, which authorizes a federal tax on incomes. It is ratified by the states and goes into effect as the Sixteenth Amendment in 1913.

1913 Federal Reserve Act. This act restructures the nation's banking and currency system and creates the Federal Reserve Board to direct the nation's credit and monetary affairs.

ECONOMY, BUSINESS, & LABOR

LEGISLATION AFFECTING THE ECONOMY, BUSINESS, AND LABOR, 1791–PRESENT, cont.

1914 Clayton Anti-Trust Act. This act strengthens the Sherman Anti-Trust Act and exempts labor organizations from antitrust laws.

Federal Trade Commission Act. This act establishes this independent agency charged with maintaining a competitive economic environment through preventing monopolies and unfair trade practices.

1916 Federal Farm Loan Act. This act makes credit available to farmers via a system of Farm Loan Banks.

Adamson Act. This act established the eight-hour workday for railroads operating in interstate commerce.

1926 Railway Labor Act. Amended later to include all forms of transportation, this law protects the collective-bargaining rights of railroad employees. A 1934 amendment establishes the National Railroad Adjustment Board to arbitrate employee-employer grievances.

1929 Agricultural Marketing Act. This establishes the Federal Farm Board, whose purpose is to encourage and promote marketing of farm products through cooperatives.

1932 The Norris-La Guardia Anti-Injunction Act. This act forbids the use of injunction in the majority of labor disputes.

1933 National Industrial Recovery Act. This act aims at preventing the contraction of business and reducing unemployment to end the Depression.

Emergency Banking Act. This stabilizes the banks during the Depression and provides the basis for the Federal Deposit Insurance Corporation, which becomes permanent in 1935.

The Farm Credit Act. This act protects farmers against foreclosures.

1934 Securities Exchange Act. This establishes the Securities and Exchange Commission to regulate securities trading and stock exchanges.

Federal Communications Act. This establishes the Federal Communications Commission to regulate the communication industry.

Reciprocal Trade Act. This gives the president the power to negotiate trade agreements with individual countries.

1935 Social Security Act. This establishes a federal pension for retirees, to be funded with a payroll tax.

Wagner Act (National Labor Relations Act). This act recognizes labor's right to organize and to bargain collectively; it also creates the National Labor Relations Board to oversee collective bargaining.

1936 Robinson-Patman Act. By making it illegal for businesses to collude on prices, this act encourages competition and discourages monopolies.

Walsh-Healy Act. This sets a minimum wage for workers at companies holding government contracts.

1938 Fair Labor Standards Act. This act mandates a minimum wage and forty-hour week and forbids child labor in any business engaged in interstate commerce.

Revenue Act. This act reduces taxes on large corporations and raises them on small businesses.

1946 Employment Act. This creates the Council of Economic Advisers to advise the executive branch and establishes the policy that maintaining employment, production, and purchasing power is a role of government.

1947 Taft-Hartley Act. Passed over President Harry Truman's veto, this act, also called the Labor-Management Relations Act, revises the Wagner Act by outlawing the unfair practices of unions as well as management. It forbids closed shops, jurisdictional strikes, secondary boycotts, and political contributions by unions (overturned by the Supreme Court). Most important, it grants the president the power to delay by eighty days a strike that threatens the national interest. It also requires union leaders to swear under oath that they are not members of the Communist Party.

1956 Agricultural Act. This establishes the Soil Bank, a program under which farmers are paid not to grow certain crops, in order to decrease production and to conserve soil.

1959 Landrum-Griffin Act, also known as the Labor-Management Reporting and Disclosure Act. Enacted after an extensive congressional investigation into labor racketeering, this law attempts to outlaw corrupt practices by unions and employers.

1962 Trade Expansion Act. This act gives the president increased powers to cut tariffs to promote world trade.

1963 Equal Pay Act. This act requires equal pay for equal work in industries engaged in interstate commerce.

1964 Civil Rights Act. Title VII forbids employers and unions to discriminate on the basis of race, color, religion, national origin, and sex.
   Economic Opportunity Act. This act funds the Job Corps and special programs for the poor and for youth.

1967 Fair Packaging and Labeling Act. The first important law to set standards for the advertising industry and for the packaging of consumer goods, this act results from pressure by the consumer movement.

1970 Air Quality Control Act. Calling for a 90 percent reduction in auto pollutants by 1975, this act is first passed in 1967 but is given real teeth in 1970.

1975 Energy Policy Conservation Act. A result of a major oil shortage, this act attempts to conserve and allocate energy resources.

1981 Economic Recovery Tax Act. This first significant rewriting of tax law in several decades reduces corporate and personal income taxes dramatically.

1985 Gramm-Rudman Act. To control the federal deficit, this act mandates across-the-board spending cuts if deficit-reduction goals are not met.

1993 Family Leave Act. This act permits workers in companies of fifty or more employees to have up to twelve weeks a year unpaid leave for family and medical purposes.

1996 Welfare Reform Act. The federal guarantee of cash assistance to low-income mothers and children is ended. Recipients are required to work within two years of receiving benefits, and states are given authority—and grants—to run their own programs.

1997 Balanced Budget Act. Also know as the budget reconciliation bill, this legislation features the most sweeping changes in the Medicare and Medicaid programs since their inception in 1965. A new program institutes the largest-ever increase in children's health insurance coverage.

1998 IRS Restructuring and Reform Act. This legislation revamps the Internal Revenue Service and expands taxpayers' rights and protections in dealings with the agency.

1999 Financial Services Modernization Act. Overhauling the nation's financial system, this law repeals the Glass-Steagall Act of 1933 and allows banks, securities firms, and insurance firms to affiliate and expand into one another's businesses.

2002 Terrorism Risk Insurance Act. After the collapse of the World Trade Center towers, which generated over $40 billion in claims, many insurers stopped offering coverage for acts of terrorism. This bill requires insurers to offer terrorism coverage, but provides a safety net by assuring that the federal government will pay for the majority of losses.

SUPREME COURT DECISIONS AFFECTING THE ECONOMY, BUSINESS, AND LABOR, 1810–PRESENT

1810 *Fletcher v. Peck.* In this first decision invalidating a state law as unconstitutional, the Court says a state cannot impair the obligation of contracts.

1819 *Dartmouth College v. Woodward.* In a major boost to commercial interests, the Court rules that a charter to a private corporation is a contract, and, again, states cannot interfere with contracts.

McCulloch v. Maryland. In ruling that the federal government has a right to charter a national bank and that states may not tax a national bank, the Supreme Court greatly expands the scope of federal power.

1824 *Gibbons v. Ogden.* In the first of what will be a series of decisions on interstate commerce, the Court declares that states cannot grant monopolies that restrain interstate commerce and that the power of Congress to regulate interstate commerce is supreme.

1937 *Charles River Bridge v. Warren Bridge.* The Court rules that any ambiguities in the chartered rights of corporations should be resolved in favor of broader public interests, again undercutting the power of monopolies.

1877 *Munn v. Illinois.* The Court upholds an Illinois law establishing maximum rates for storing grains, one of the so-called Granger laws enacted by state legislatures in the Midwest at the insistence of the Grange. The decision establishes the constitutional principle of public regulation of private business involved in serving the public interest.

1895 *United States v. E. C. Knight Company.* The Court rules that the Sherman Anti-Trust Act does not apply to the sugar trust, even though it refines more than 90 percent of the sugar sold in the country.

Pollock v. Farmers' Loan and Trust Company. The Court strikes down a general income tax law, setting the stage for a constitutional amendment that will make income taxes legal.

In re Debs. The Court upholds the validity of the injunction ordering Eugene V. Debs and others to halt the 1894 Pullman strike. A lower court had upheld the injunction on the basis of the Sherman Anti-Trust Act, but the Supreme Court upholds it on the grounds of national sovereignty and federal authority to remove obstructions to interstate commerce and the transportation of the mails.

1904 *Northern Securities v. United States.* In an important antitrust decision, the Court decides that stock transactions like those J. P. Morgan is using to form a railroad merger are an illegal restraint of interstate commerce.

1905 *Swift and Company v. United States.* In a case involving meatpackers who combined to fix prices on sales in the Chicago stockyards, the Court rules that Congress can regulate local commerce that is part of an interstate current of commerce. The ruling establishes the "stream of commerce" doctrine, explaining that the meatpackers in the stockyards are the middle link of an interstate transaction, with cattle shipped from out of state and packed meat shipped to other states for sale.

Lochner v. New York. The Court overturns a New York law seeking to regulate the hours of workers by holding that it interferes with the right of free contract. Oliver Wendell Holmes writes a famous dissent in which he argues that the Constitution "is not intended to embody a particular economic theory" and that "the word 'liberty' is perverted when it is held to prevent the natural outcome of a dominant opinion."

1908 *Adair v. United States.* The Court rules that a law prohibiting railroads from requiring that workers promise not to join a union is unconstitutional.

Danbury Hatters' Case. The Court rules that a labor union's boycott of an industry restricts trade; in other words, the Sherman Anti-Trust Act applies to labor unions.

Muller v. Oregon. The Court for the first time upholds a law that limits work hours, in this case of women.

1917 *Bunting v. Oregon.* This decision overturns *Lochner* and extends *Muller* by declaring that the government does have the power to regulate work hours.

1918 *Hammer v. Dagenhart.* The Court strikes down the Keating-Owen Child Labor Law, which prohibits shipment in interstate commerce of goods produced by child laborers, thus setting the stage for a constitutional amendment outlawing child labor (which failed to ratify).

1923 *Adkins v. Children's Hospital.* The Court strikes down an act of Congress setting minimum wages for women and children workers in the District of Columbia, again interpreting this law as price fixing and in violation of the freedom of contract.

1935 *Schechter Poultry Corporation v. United States.* The Court finds the 1933 National Industrial Recovery Act unconstitutional.

1937 *NLRB v. Jones & Laughlin Steel Corporation.* The Court upholds the Wagner Act (National Labor Relations Act), finding that the federal government has the power to regulate intrastate matters that affect interstate commerce.
   West Coast Hotel Company v. Parrish. The Court upholds the minimum-wage law for women and children, overturning *Adkins* (1923).

1941 *United States v. Darby Lumber Company.* The Court overturns Hammer, ruling that Congress has the authority to prohibit shipment in interstate commerce of goods manufactured in violation of federal minimum wage and maximum hours standards.

1952 *Youngstown Sheet and Tube Company v. Sawyer.* Following President Harry Truman's seizure of the steel industry to prevent a threatened strike during the Korean War, the Court rules that the president does not have the authority to make such a seizure.

1971 *Griggs v. Duke Power Company.* The Court rules even neutral employment practices may constitute discrimination if they have a discriminatory impact.

1975 *Goldfarb v. Virginia State Bar.* The Court states that antitrust laws apply to lawyers, specifically that bar associations adopting minimum fee schedules are in violation of price-fixing provisions.

1979 *United Steelworkers of America v. Weber.* Despite *Bakke,* which undermined the use of quotas, the Court upholds racial quotas in the workplace and states that employers may be required to reserve a specified percentage of jobs for protected workers but only for a limited period of time. The number must be tied to past discrimination and must not overly tread on the rights of nonprotected groups (see p. 136).

1986 *Sheet Metal Workers Local 28 v. EEOC.* The Court rules that courts may order unions to use quotas to overcome past discrimination.
   Meritor Savings Bank v. Vinson. The Court finds that sexual harassment in the workplace, either creating a hostile work environment or leading to loss of employment, may constitute discrimination.

1989 *Wards Cove Packing Company v. Antonio.* The Court states that statistical imbalances in race or gender in the workplace are not in themselves proof of discrimination and that plaintiffs must prove that neutral employment practices have a discriminating effect.

1996 *NLRB v. Town and Country Electric.* The justices rule that federal labor law protects union organizers who take employment at a company for the purpose of organizing workers there.

2000 *Reeves v. Sanderson Plumbing Products Inc.* The Court rules that an employee does not have to prove that an employer's actions were intentionally discriminatory in order to sustain a claim of unlawful job discrimination under federal statutes.

ECONOMY, BUSINESS, & LABOR

NOTABLE FIGURES IN ECONOMY, BUSINESS, AND LABOR

Ash, Mary Kay (1918–2001). Founder of a largest direct-sale cosmetics company in the country, this entrepreneur lived by the motto: "God first, family second, career third" and wanted to create a business environment where women could thrive. In 1963, after working in sales for twenty-five years, she started Mary Kay Cosmetics. What began with an investment of her $5,000 savings grew to a company of over 800,000 independent consultants in thirty-seven countries on five continents by 2000.

Astor, John Jacob (1763–1848). One of the country's first business magnates, Astor began as a fur trader but made his fortune in real estate. Born in poverty in Germany, he was considered the richest man in America at the time of his death.

Ayer, Harriet (1849–1903). The first woman to make a fortune selling cosmetics, Ayer associated herself with Madame Recamier, a famous beauty of the Napoleonic era, and claimed to have a special beauty cream that had been discovered in Paris.

Borlaug, Norman (1914–). An agronomist, Borlaug attempted to reduce world hunger through agriculture; his efforts led to his being awarded the Nobel Peace Prize in 1970.

Brady, James B. (1856–1917). Popularly known as Diamond Jim for the large jewels he liked to wear and for his flamboyant manner of living, Brady earned his money selling railroad supplies and later won fame as a philanthropist.

Burbank, Luther (1849–1926). Burbank single-handedly raised plant breeding to a science. He developed many new varieties of plants, among them the Burbank potato and the Shasta daisy. He was the author of *How Plants Are Trained to Work for Man* (1921) and coauthor of *Harvest Years* (1927) and *Partners of Nature* (1939).

Carnegie, Andrew (1835–1919). This financier-entrepreneur started out as a bobbin boy and telegraph messenger, then honed his managerial skills with the Pennsylvania Railroad before turning to steel manufacturing. Eventually he sold his steel company to J. P. MORGAN. He used his money to fund more than 2,800 libraries and other philanthropies across the country.

Carver, George Washington (1864?–1943). As director of agricultural research at Tuskegee Institute, Carver, an African American, devised hundreds of uses for peanuts, soybeans, and sweet potatoes, as well as working on soil improvement and crop diversification.

Chavez, Cesar (1927–1993). The son of Mexican American migrant farmworkers, Chavez founded the National Farm Workers Association in 1972. His United Farm Workers (UFW) became a member of the AFL-CIO in 1972. Chavez used nonviolent tactics such as boycotts to gain better working conditions for migrant workers.

Commons, John (1862–1945). An economist and social reformer, Commons taught at the University of Wisconsin, where he founded the field of industrial relations. Commons played a significant role in shaping the New Deal legislation. Before turning his attention to federal legislation, he helped to write much of Wisconsin's progressive reform legislation on such issues as worker's compensation and public utility regulation. These laws were the prototypes followed by other states and the federal government.

Cooke, Jay (1821–1905). A financier and investment banker, Cooke helped to fund the Civil War for the North by mass-marketing federal bonds to individual Americans, thus pioneering the idea of paper wealth and also creating the first advertising campaign that relied on appeals to people's patriotism.

Debs, Eugene V. (1855–1926). A strong leader and advocate of labor unions, pacifist, and founder of the Socialist Party in the United States, Debs was the party's five-time candidate for president. Considered by many to be a martyr to the cause of labor, he was jailed briefly during the 1894 Pullman strike for ignoring an injunction and again from 1918 to 1921 for espionage.

Disney, Walt (1901–1966). A filmmaker and animation pioneer, Disney created one of the first great entertainment empires devoted to providing "family" entertainment (see p. 517).

Eastman, George (1854–1932). Eastman, who invented many of the elements that turned photography into a modern science, founded the Eastman Kodak Company in 1892. Like CARNEGIE, he gave most of his money away before he died.

Firestone, Harvey (1868–1938). Firestone manufactured the first rubber tires and in 1900 founded Firestone Tire & Rubber Company, one of the largest tire manufacturers in the United States.

Fisher, Irving (1867–1947). An economist, Fisher pioneered the idea of a "compensated dollar" and contributed to the development of index numbers, standard figures against which certain economic factors, such as inflation and the cost of living, are measured and then used to trigger increases in wages and Social Security.

Flynn, Elizabeth Gurley (1890–1964). Known as "the Rebel Girl," Flynn became an organizer for the International Workers of the World in 1907 and was a founding member of the American Civil Liberties Union. She joined the Communist Party in 1937 and wrote a column in the *Daily Worker* for twenty-six years. Flynn spent two years in jail under the Smith Act.

Ford, Henry (1863–1906). Ford founded Ford Motor Company and was among the first to use the assembly-line method of manufacturing, which in turn enabled him to turn out an inexpensive car, the Model T. A staunch opponent of labor unions, Ford shocked the country by offering wages far above average to his factory workers.

Friedman, Milton (1912–). The foremost modern proponent of conservative, free-market economic policy, Friedman was awarded the Nobel Prize for Economics in 1976. An opponent of Keynesian economic theory, he argued against government control through tax and spending policies, and emphasized the importance of gradual, regular increases in the money supply by a central bank. A professor at the University of Chicago from 1946 to 1982, Friedman is recognized for his profound impact on U.S. economic policy in the postwar era.

Gates, Bill (1955–). As cofounder (with Paul Allen) and chairman of Microsoft, the first computer software company, Gates was at the forefront of the U.S. technology boom of the 1980s and 1990s. Creating the DOS and Windows operating systems for personal computers, his company came to dominate the software industry, leading to a Justice Department antitrust suit and, in 1999, an adverse ruling in federal court. A billionaire several times over, Gates was counted as the richest man in the world until a decline in company stock in 2000 to 2001.

George, Henry (1839–1897). This economist's thinking influenced tax legislation in many countries. As the leader of the single-tax movement, he proposed to levy a single tax on land, whose unearned gains he viewed as being the dividing line between rich and poor. The tax would then be used to operate governments. He elaborated on this theory in his book *Progress and Poverty* (1879).

Gleason, Kate (1865–1933). Gleason became the first woman to head a national bank when she filled in for the bank president after he enlisted in the service during World War I. She served until 1919, and pioneered the large-scale development of low-cost housing.

"The labor of a human being is not a commodity or article of commerce. You can't weigh the soul of a man with a bar of pig iron."
—SAMUEL GOMPERS

Gompers, Samuel (1850–1924). A cigar maker, Gompers was one of the founders of the American Federation of Labor and its longtime president. Gompers opposed labor-reform groups such as the Knights of Labor and also opposed what he considered Socialist elements in the labor movement. His success lay in his focus on more wages and shorter hours.

Gould, Jay (1836–1892). Gould made his fortune in railroad speculation and at one time controlled the New York elevated, most of the railroads in the Southwest, and Western Union Telegraph Company. He later controlled the Erie Railroad and then the Union Pacific. Gould was feared for his stock manipulations and despotic management methods.

Green, Hetty (1834–1916). After inheriting $10 million from her wealthy mercantile family, Green traded her way into a $100 million fortune and was widely held to be the richest woman of her time.

Hamilton, Alexander (1755–1804). Among the many accomplishments of this politician and economic theorist, Hamilton was the first secretary of the treasury, serving under George Washington. Hamilton devised the U.S. fiscal program, supporting tariffs and excise taxes as a means of raising money for the new federal government. He advocated a financially strong federal government, while his opponents, led by Thomas Jefferson, wanted to leave the financing of the government to state and local branches. He was killed by rival Aaron Burr in a duel.

ECONOMY, BUSINESS, & LABOR

NOTABLE FIGURES, *cont.*

Hearst, William Randolph (1863–1951). Hearst, who built the first great publishing empire, at one time owned eighteen national magazines and twenty-eight major newspapers including the *New York Evening Journal, Chicago Examiner,* and *Los Angeles Examiner.* His primary goal was to sell a lot of newspapers, and to that end he sold them for a penny, thus undercutting the competition. He virtually invented tabloid journalism, which made use of oversize, outrageous headlines, shocking photographs, and sensational reportage.

Hughes, Howard (1905–1976). The wealth of this tycoon came from the Hughes Tool Company, which he inherited from his father. Interested in aviation, he founded Hughes Aircraft Company and served as head of TWA airlines. He also produced movies, the most prominent was *The Front Page.* Toward the end of his life, he became the country's most famous recluse.

Huerta, Dolores (1930–). Probably the most prominent Mexican American woman in the labor movement, Huerta founded the National Farm Workers Association (later renamed United Farm Workers) with Cesar Chavez in 1962. The foremost contract negotiator for the union and a major force in the 1968 to 1970 grape boycott, she became the first vice president of the union and has continued to agitate for labor, social, and civil rights issues.

Hunt, H. L. (1889–1974). This Texas oil magnate once amassed enough silver to manipulate the entire U.S. market. Once one of the richest people in the United States, he held ultraconservative political views.

Jefferson, Thomas (1743–1826). The third U.S. president, Jefferson was one of the leaders of the debate over the federal government's role in the country's finances; he preferred that fiscal power reside with state and local governments. His more specific contribution to the country's economic development was to devise the decimal system that is the basis for the U.S. currency system.

Johnson, Lyndon Baines (1908–1973). Under the banner of the Great Society, Johnson as president declared the "war on poverty" and followed through with a series of social and economic programs that significantly raised the standard of living for millions of Americans. His programs included Medicare, Medicaid, and Head Start.

Jones, Mary Harris ("Mother") (1837–1930). A prominent figure in the labor movement, "Mother" Jones helped found both the Social Democratic Party and the Industrial Workers of the World. She gained fame as an effective speaker during the Great Railroad Strike of 1877 and the Haymarket riots in 1886, after which she concentrated her efforts on organizing miners in the coal fields of West Virginia. At the age of eighty-three she was convicted of conspiracy and sentenced to twenty years in prison, but the sentence was commuted in time for her to be present at the Ludlow massacre and to lobby President Wilson on the miners' behalf. After World War I, she continued as a union agitator and organizer and lived until her death in 1930.

Kelley, Florence (1859–1932). As an associate of Jane Addams at Hull-House and a proponent of labor reform, Kelley went on to head the National Consumers' League, shaping it into an effective lobbying organization that played a seminal role in passing protective legislation for women and children. She helped develop the strategy behind the successful defense in *Muller v. Oregon,* a case involving the work hours of women.

Kroc, Raymond A. (1902–1984). The father of the contemporary fast-food industry, Kroc built McDonald's from a small hamburger joint in California into an international franchise giant and universally recognized brand. His implementation of production-line automation and efficiency revolutionized food service in the United States and launched a cultural phenomenon. Kroc opened his first McDonald's restaurant in Des Plaines, Illinois, in 1955. The company went public in 1965, and Kroc retired three years later.

Laughlin, James (1850–1933). An economist, Laughlin played an important role in devising the centralized Federal Reserve System.

Lloyd, Henry Demarest (1847–1903). Along with IDA TARBELL, Lloyd, a financial reporter at the *Chicago Tribune,* exposed the evils of monopolistic corporations. He wrote *Wealth Against Commonwealth* (1894), an exposé of big business.

McCormick, Cyrus (1809–1884). In 1931, McCormick devised a mechanical reaper to lighten the workload on his father's farm. He perfected his horsedrawn reaper until 1834 when he demonstrated and patented the machine. Although there was a rival reaper, he built the more successful business, pioneering in areas such as repair and spare parts and installment buying. After his death, his firm merged with International Harvester to form the United States' largest farm-machinery manufacturer.

McWhinney, Madeline (1922–). McWhinney was the first president of the Women's Bank, chartered in 1975 and intended to counteract the prejudice women encountered in the world of finance. She later became the first woman to be named an assistant vice president in the Federal Reserve System.

Morgan, John Pierpont (1837–1913). Along with JOHN D. ROCKEFELLER, Morgan was one of the business entrepreneurs who earned the title "robber baron" in the late 1890s for his organization of trusts. Morgan was involved in railroad reorganization and the mergers that formed International Harvester. He also engineered the consolidation of U.S. Steel, the country's first billion-dollar corporation.

Morgenthau, Henry (1891–1967). As secretary of the treasury from 1934 to 1945, Morgenthau supervised the sale of the U.S. bonds that largely financed World War II and later worked to establish the World Bank and International Monetary Fund.

Morris, Robert (1734–1806). Although Morris, a colonial merchant, initially voted against independence, he became known as the "financier of the Revolution," for the role he played in raising funds for the war and in organizing the finances of the new nation. After being appointed superintendent of finances, he worked to establish a national mint and a federal banking system.

Perkins, Frances (1822–1945). Perkins worked to eradicate child labor and to establish unemployment insurance and wrote much of the prolabor legislation in New York State under governors Al Smith and FRANKLIN ROOSEVELT. Roosevelt appointed her secretary of labor, and in that role she was responsible for much of the New Deal labor legislation.

Perot, H. Ross (1903–). A self-made billionaire, Perot brought his enterprising spirit and no-nonsense Texas values to the national political arena in the 1990s. He founded Electronic Data Systems in 1962 and developed it into a major computer company before selling out to General Motors for $2.5 billion in 1984. Running for president of the United States as an independent in 1992, he earned 19 percent of the popular vote. He established United We Stand to promote his policy agenda and founded the Reform Party for his 1996 presidential bid (see p. 213).

Peterson, Esther (1906–1997). As a labor organizer, Peterson worked for the American Federation of Teachers, the Amalgamated Clothing Workers of America, and the International Ladies Garment Workers' Union before serving as the legislative representative of the AFL-CIO. Peterson held government appointments under the Kennedy, JOHNSON, Carter, and Clinton administrations. In 1981, she received the Presidential Medal of freedom, the highest civilian award in the U.S.

Powderly, Terence V. (1849–1924). A labor leader and reformer, Powderly was president of the Machinists and Blacksmiths National Union when he joined the Knights of Labor, which he led from 1879 to 1893. His program addressed labor reform generally, calling for worker-run factories, producers' and consumers' cooperatives, the regulation of trusts, the abolition of child labor, and an eight-hour day.

Reagan, Ronald (1911–). During his presidency (1981–1989), Reagan reversed the activist fiscal policies of ROOSEVELT and JOHNSON, advocating reduced federal spending on social and educational programs and increased spending on the military. Despite supporting a balanced budget, he presided over the biggest peacetime buildup of U.S. debt in history and also sponsored a major rewriting of the federal income tax law.

Rockefeller, John D. (1839–1937). As the founder of the Standard Oil trust, Rockefeller forged a new form of business organization, the horizontal corporation, whose goal was to control a single product—in his case, oil. At the time of his retirement in 1911, Rockefeller had a fortune estimated at $1 billion, much of which he gave to philanthropic enterprises.

Roosevelt, Franklin Delano (1882–1845). Elected to the presidency at the depth of the Great Depression, Roosevelt presided over major economic reforms, such as the National Recovery Administration and the Public Works Administration, that were intended to stabilize the nation's economy and restore it to health. He also instituted Social Security, the federal old-age pension, and the Federal Deposit Insurance Corporation (FDIC), which insures bank accounts.

Sears, Richard W. (1863–1914). Founder of Sears and Roebuck Company, pioneer of the mail order and retail businesses. While working on a railroad line in Minnesota, Sears began selling watches on his route. After founding the R. W. Sears Watch Company in 1886, he moved to Chicago and paired up with Alvah C. Roebuck, forming Sears, Roebuck and Company, which established a

ECONOMY, BUSINESS, & LABOR

NOTABLE FIGURES, *cont.*

thriving mail order company that allowed farmers to buy goods out of catalogs rather than at pricey local stores. He opened his first retail store in 1925 and in 2000, Sears boasted 863 major stores in mall locations.

Siebert, Muriel (1932–). After receiving a degree from Western Reserve University in Cleveland, Siebert moved to New York City. She worked as a Wall Street researcher and stock analyst before organizing her own stock brokerage firm in 1967. That same year, she paid $445,000 to buy a seat on the New York Stock Exchange, becoming the first woman to work alongside the 1,365 men who owned seats on the NYSE in 1967. Twenty years later, she and other businesswomen founded the National Women's Forum.

Tarbell, Ida B. (1857–1944). Along with HENRY DEMAREST LLOYD, Tarbell waged journalistic war on the trusts of the late nineteenth century. Her *History of the Standard Oil Company* (1904) resulted in federal action against the company. Lloyd and Tarbell were among the first journalists known as muckrakers.

Townsend, Francis (1867–1960). During the heart of the Great Depression, Townsend, a physician, proposed that the federal government establish an old-age pension. His idea was to give all retirees $200 a month in scrip out of funds raised by a federal sales tax. He popularized the idea enough to pave the way for the Social Security Act to be passed in 1935.

Vanderbilt, Cornelius (1794–1877). This industrial magnate and financier made his initial money in a steamship line and went on to make even more in railroads. Along with a handful of other industrial barons, like GOULD and CARNEGIE, he was able to amass a nearly unheard-of fortune.

Veblen, Thorstein (1857–1929). Veblen merged economic and sociological theory, most successfully in his book *The Theory of the Leisure Class* (1899), in which he coined the term "conspicuous consumption." Veblen was also interested in the conflict between technology, which he felt sought only efficiency and reduced costs, and commerce, or "business," whose primary goal was profit maximization.

Walker, Madame C. J. (Sarah Breedlove) (1867–1919). The first black female to become a millionaire, Walker was the daughter of ex-slaves. Orphaned at seven and widowed at twenty, she created a hair-care regimen and cosmetics line for black women and built the Walker Manufacturing Company from scratch. The character of a true rags to riches story, Walker founded beauty schools around the country and became a well-known philanthropist, donating to the NAACP, the YMCA, the Tuskegee Institute, and other black charities and causes.

Walker, Maggie Lena (1867–1934). Founder and president of the St. Luke Penny Savings Bank, Walker in 1903 was the first woman to be president of any U.S. bank. When her bank merged with several other African American banks to form the Consolidated Bank and Trust Company, she became chairman of the board, a position she held until her death.

Walton, Sam (1918–1992). The founder of Wal-Mart, Walton pioneered the development of superstores, huge "general" stores that provided an unprecedented array of goods at low cost.

Wanamaker, John (1838–1922). The founder of the Philadelphia department store bearing his name, Wanamaker was a pioneer in department-store management, especially in the area of customer service.

Ward, Aaron Montgomery (1844–1913). In 1872, Ward founded the first American mail-order company, which bears his name, and pioneered the mass sales of low-priced goods.

Westinghouse, George (1846–1914). Westinghouse invented the air brake and automatic signal devices and introduced the high-tension, alternating-current system of electricity. His company was organized to manufacture the latter two devices. Westinghouse owned 400 patents.

Whitney, Eli (1765–1825). An inventor, Whitney is best known for the cotton gin, which quickly and mechanically separated the cotton fiber from the seed. Whitney also produced the first rifles with interchangeable, standardized parts.

Woolworth, Frank W. (1852–1919). This innovative merchandiser created the "five and dime" store chain, which he expanded and internationalized. At one time there were more than 1,000 Woolworth stores in existence. In 1913, he built what was then the world's tallest building, in Manhattan.

CHAPTER 10

EDUCATION

■

HIGHLIGHTS

Timeline of Education in America

WITHIN A HUNDRED YEARS of its founding, the United States had established one of the world's great public-education systems. Maintaining the highest educational standards, however, has been one of the nation's great and enduring challenges. Not the least of the special circumstances in the U.S. system is the division of responsibility between individual states and the federal government. Administration of the schools themselves is generally a local matter, delegated to states, counties, and regional boards. Broad oversight and special funding are left to the federal government, whose precise role varies considerably with the ideology of the current presidential administration and Congress. The United States remains one of the few modern industrialized nations that does not have an established national curriculum.

THE COLONIAL ERA

Until 1769, class rankings at Harvard College were based on family status rather than academic performance. Sons of wealthy, high-society families were placed at the top of the list and enjoyed special privileges.

1635–1636 Boston Latin School is established by the Reverend John Cotton. This grammar school for boys between the ages of nine and fifteen is supported by the town of Boston.

1636 Harvard College is founded with a grant from the Massachusetts General Court and a bequest (1638) from John Harvard. Intended to train Puritan ministers, it grew to be a premier institute of higher learning.

1647 Massachusetts Bay Colony requires towns of more than 100 families to establish grammar schools (for boys only).

1689 By this date, Connecticut, Plymouth, and New Hampshire also require grammar schools.

1690 *The New England Primer,* first published in the 1680s becomes the most widely used reader in the colonies.

1693 The College of William and Mary in what is now Williamsburg, Virginia, becomes the second institution of higher learning in the colonies.

1700 New England has the highest literacy rate in the colonies.

Chartered by King William III and Queen Mary II in 1693, the College of William and Mary is the second college founded in the colonies and the only U.S. college with a royal charter. Presidents George Washington, Thomas Jefferson, James Monroe, and John Tyler all took classes at William and Mary.

1701 Yale College is chartered. Originally called the Collegiate School and run out of the home of its first rector in Killingworth, Connecticut, it moves to New Haven in 1716 and is renamed for benefactor Elihu Yale in 1718.

1746 The College of New Jersey is chartered at Princeton by New Light Presbyterians. It is renamed Princeton in 1896.

1776 Phi Beta Kappa, the honorary society for academic achievement, is founded at the College of William and Mary, originally as a social club.

THE FEDERALIST ERA

1782 Quakers organize the Philadelphia African School.
St. Mary's Church in Philadelphia opens the first Catholic school.

1783 NOAH WEBSTER publishes the *American Spelling Book*, standardizing American spelling as distinct from British usage. It sells millions of copies and is widely used in schoolrooms for decades.

1787 The Young Ladies Academy in Philadelphia opens. A prototype for female academies, it seeks to train the wives and mothers of the new republic to be better household managers, and to prepare their sons for citizenship.

1789 The University of North Carolina is chartered. In 1795, it is the first state university to begin instruction.

1792 Sarah Pierce opens a school for girls in her home in Litchfield, Connecticut. A quarter century later, the Litchfield Female Academy is drawing students from all over the Northeast.

EDUCATION

PAROCHIAL AND PRIVATE EDUCATION

When the huge wave of immigrants arriving in the late 1800s found the public schools too "American," meaning too Protestant, for their tastes, they pressured the Roman Catholic Church to institute a system of parochial schools. The U.S. Catholic Church, having long enjoyed the protection that freedom of religion brought, established the schools only reluctantly and made sure to fold a heavy dose of patriotism into the curriculum.

Today, Roman Catholics are not the only denomination to sponsor their own schools. Nearly every Protestant denomination supports some schools, although in recent years many mainstream denominational schools have closed while many new fundamentalist schools have opened. Jewish parochial education, especially among the very religious, has also experienced a renaissance since World War II.

No other religion, though, has established the large nationwide network of parochial schools that the Catholic Church has.

Nearly half of all private schools in the United States are Catholic. Enrollment in Catholic schools peaked in 1964, with 5.6 million children, and steadily fell off from there. By 1990, attendance had fallen to 2.5 million, climbing slightly again by the year 2000 to 2.65 million (see also Chapter 13).

Some parochial schools and a fair number of private schools were founded in the wake of *Brown v. Board of Education of Topeka* (1954) and its order, a year later, that public schools be integrated with "all deliberate speed." In recent years vouchers that parents could use as money to help pay tuition in the school of their choice—public, private, or parochial—have been proposed as part of the school reform debate.

1807 Washington, D.C., founds its first school for blacks.

1809 ELIZABETH ANN SETON founds the first free Catholic school in America in Emmitsburg, Maryland.

1817 THOMAS HOPKINS GALLAUDET and Laurent Clerc found the American School for the Deaf in West Hartford, Connecticut, the first school for the deaf in the nation.

1818 Boston establishes public elementary schools.

1819 EMMA WILLARD tries and fails to get New York State to fund higher education for women, largely as a means of training teachers.

1821 EMMA WILLARD opens the Troy Seminary in Troy, New York. Intended to be a step up from the academies, seminaries offer more advanced education, although their primary purpose is still to train women as teachers.

The first high school in the United States is established in Boston.

1822 Philadelphia organizes its first public school for blacks.

1823 CATHARINE BEECHER, an important proponent of women's education, opens the Hartford Seminary in Connecticut.

1824 The first public high school for girls opens in Worcester, Massachusetts. Across the country, more will follow Massachusetts's example.

Dartmouth College, founded in 1754, admits its first black students.

The Franklin Institute is founded in Philadelphia by Samuel Vaughan Merrick and William H. Keating. Intended to promote the "mechanic arts," the school was a tribute to Benjamin Franklin and his attention to science and invention.

1826 The lyceum movement, promoting adult education and self-improvement, is initiated when Josiah Holbrook establishes a lyceum in Millbury, Massachusetts. In 1831, the National American Lyceum is established, and, within a few years, there are town lyceums in fifteen states.

1827 Massachusetts becomes the first state to use taxes to support public education.

Every town with a population of 500 or more families is required to have a high school.

1829 The first American encyclopedia, *Encyclopaedia Americana*, begins publication.

1833 Oberlin College in Ohio opens the first coeducational college. A center of abolition, it also, after 1835, admits black students.

Prudence Crandall converts her girl's school in Canterbury, Connecticut, into a school for black girls, despite a law restricting the education of black children. She is arrested, and although the verdict against her is reversed by a higher court, harassment and violence force her to close the school.

1836 The first *McGuffey's Readers*, a series of textbooks designed to promote moral improvement and patriotism, are published; they will sell an estimated 122 million copies and influence generations of elementary schoolchildren.

1837 MARY LYON, an important advocate of women's education, opens Mount Holyoke Female Seminary, in South Hadley, Massachusetts, which will become the prestigious Mount Holyoke College.

HORACE MANN initiates school reform as the first secretary of the newly established Massachusetts Board of Education. He works to lengthen the school year, increase the number of public high schools, raise teachers' salaries, improve teacher training, and centralize authority. Believing that children learn best in nurturing environments, he also seeks to end the harsh punishments inherited from Puritan schoolrooms.

1838 HENRY BARNARD appointed secretary of the Connecticut Board of School Commissioners, initiates similar reforms in Connecticut schools.

1839 HORACE MANN establishes the first state normal school, or teacher-training school, in Lexington, Massachusetts.

EDUCATION

1848 At the Seneca Falls Convention, the first public meeting in the United States held to advocate women's rights, women protest that they have not been permitted to obtain an equal education.

1850 Young unmarried women predominate as teachers in grammar schools; most have been trained in seminary schools established by women.

1851 The society of Jesuits founds the first college in California on the site of Santa Clara de Asis mission. Now known as Santa Clara University, the school did not accept women until 1961.

1852 Massachusetts becomes the first state to enact compulsory school attendance laws.

1855 The first kindergarten opens as a special school for German-speaking children of German immigrants in Watertown, Wisconsin. Catering to upper-middle-class families, it is based on the program organized by Friedrich Froebel in Germany in 1837.

Boston public schools are integrated.

Early kindergarten programs were available to wealthy families. They quickly became tools for teaching immigrant children, as seen in this drawing of the public kindergarten in the North-End Industrial Home in Boston.

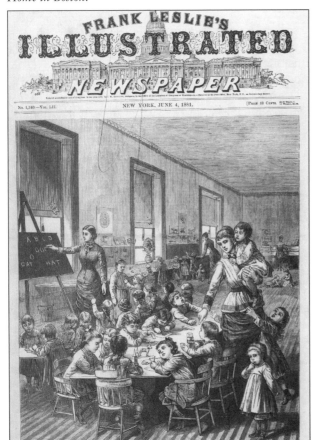

1856 Berea College is founded in Berea, Kentucky, as a one-room district school. In 1869, it becomes a college offering black and white students the opportunity to work to pay for their education. In 1904, Kentucky law prohibits integration, and, subsequently, Berea has to comply.

In Wilberforce, Ohio, the African Methodist Episcopal Church opens a coeducational college that offers academic training to African Americans.

1857 Congress incorporates the Columbia Institution for the Instruction of the Deaf and Dumb and the Blind, under the direction of Edward Miner Gallaudet. Located in Washington, D.C., it is the predecessor of Gallaudet University.

1860 On the brink of the Civil War, more than 90 percent of the southern black population is illiterate, mostly because it is illegal to educate African Americans. Free blacks attempt to educate themselves and their children through small, informally organized schools.

The first formally organized kindergarten for English-speaking children in the United States is opened in Boston. Started by Elizabeth Peabody, it is for the children of upper-middle-class families.

MCGUFFEY'S READERS

The most influential textbooks in the nation's history, *McGuffey's Eclectic Readers* sold more than 120 million copies from their initial publication in 1836 through the 1920s. Edited by William Holmes McGuffey, a professor of languages, college president, and founder of the common-school movement in Ohio, the six-volume series was designed to teach reading and grammar through maxims, fables, and literary excerpts of increasing difficulty and complexity. The official school textbook in as many as thirty-seven states after the Civil War, *McGuffey's Readers* established the norm of academic advancement. Rather than proceed from one grade level to another, students would work at their own pace in completing a volume of *McGuffey's* and then move on to the next. By the sixth volume, students could read selections from Franklin, Jefferson, Byron, Tennyson, Shakespeare, and the Bible.

Promoting a moral education as well as reading and language skills, the content of *McGuffey's Readers* emphasized the values of industry, honesty, citizenship, and right versus wrong. A consistently reinforced message was that good deeds yield material rewards. The young chimney sweep who refused to steal was invited to live in a rich lady's house; the lazy schoolboy became a beggar. By advancing the rules of democratic capitalism, the books exerted a powerful social influence during the rise of industrialism and the age of immigration. As educational philosophy in the twentieth century began to place a greater priority on individual development and specialization of study, *McGuffey's* gave way to more academically oriented texts from a variety of publishers. With minor alterations, however, the original *McGuffey's Readers* still find use in certain parochial schools today.

1861 Vassar is chartered as a women's college. It opens in 1865 in Poughkeepsie, New York.

The first Ph.D. in the United States is awarded at Yale University.

The American Missionary Association organizes the first school for free blacks in the South at Fortress Monroe, Virginia. In 1868, it becomes Hampton Institute.

1862 The Morrill Land-Grant Act sets aside public lands for support of state colleges emphasizing agricultural and mechanical subjects. Later, they will also emphasize technology. Among the many land-grant schools established under this act are the state universities of Kansas and Michigan and the Universities of Minnesota, Wisconsin, Missouri, and Vermont. Most land grants were used to expand already existing schools.

INDUSTRIAL AMERICA AND THE EARLY TWENTIETH CENTURY

1865 The American Missionary Association founds Atlanta University for black students. In 1988, historic Atlanta University merged with Clark College to become Clark Atlantic University.

1866 Fisk University in Nashville is founded by the American Missionary Association for black students.

1867 HENRY BARNARD is appointed the first U.S. commissioner of education, heading a new federal agency that would oversee the gathering of educational statistics and the dissemination of information about U.S. education. Barnard

WOMEN'S EDUCATION

Women's education, intimately tied to the restricted status of women, long put women in a double bind: they recognized that education was the means to increased autonomy and higher status, but because of their restricted lives, few educational opportunities were open to them.

In colonial America, most girls were taught at home, and their "education" consisted largely of domestic skills. In New England many girls learned to read as well, as Bible reading was deemed necessary for salvation. Toward the end of the colonial era the daughters of the wealthy attended schools that taught a few academic subjects but emphasized female accomplishments such as music, art, and fancy needlework. Following the Revolution new female academies trained women to be the mothers of the songs of the republic, upon whose enlightened citizenship the new country was thought to depend. Accomplishments were still stressed, but academic subjects increased, and in the early nineteenth century leading educators such as EMMA WILLARD and CATHARINE BEECHER promoted girls' education at private seminaries. Increasing numbers of girls, especially in New England, attended public grammar schools.

At the same time, teaching as a profession became increasingly open and attractive to women, and many female seminaries specialized in training teachers. By the time of the Civil War, women predominated in teaching and were looking to enter other professions as well, especially as increasing numbers of schools of higher education were open to women.

Following the Civil War, the new black colleges established by the Freedmen's Bureau and missionary societies were largely open to women.

Many all-male colleges opened women's affiliates, and by 1900 women constituted at least a quarter of all college students. On the high school level, girls actually outnumbered boys.

The growing predominance and assertiveness of women in education produced something of a backlash, as critics, enamored of the new Freudian psychology, pointed out that college women were less likely to marry and would bear fewer children than non-college-educated women. Did education make women unfit for their roles as wives and mothers?

In the early decades of the twentieth century, while the number of women attending college continued to increase, the percentage of women who enrolled in college, as opposed to the percentage of men, decreased, and fewer women, proportionally, received Ph.D.s than in 1900. This trend did not reverse until the late 1960s, with the resurgence of feminism, the introduction of women's studies programs, the opening to women of previously all-male schools, and federal laws prohibiting discrimination on the basis of sex. Since 1974, women college students have outnumbered men.

In the 1990s, with 19 percent of women college-educated and 59 percent in the workforce, the old debate was renewed again, with a new—and old—focus: the care of children. With women no longer "at home," were children in day-care centers and unsupervised after school at risk? Was "supermom"—the bright, professional woman who was a success at work and in the evenings spent "quality time" with her children—a fraud? Did the new empowerment—the sense that women could do it all— come with a new set of demands that put women once again in the double bind?

Interested in keeping her students fit, Catharine Beecher introduced calisthenics at the Hartford Female Seminary in Connecticut (founded 1823).

1867, *cont.*

compares the U.S. and European systems and prepares many reports.

Howard University is founded by Oliver O. Howard, former union general and head of the Freedmen's Bureau, to educate the newly emancipated slaves. It is a coeducational, integrated college. In 1868, it opens a medical school and a law school. It becomes one of the first schools to admit women to medical training.

Morehouse, another prominent black college, is established in Atlanta.

1868 The University of California is created in the merger of the College of California (founded in 1863 as Contra Costa academy with a curriculum based on that of Harvard and Yale) and the Agricultural, Mining, and Mechanic Arts College (established in 1866 on 46,000 acres of land as part of the Morrill Land Grant Act of 1862).

Iowa State University opens. Originally chartered by the state legislature in 1858 as the Iowa Agricultural College and Model Farm, it was the first to accept the terms of the Morrill Land-Grant Act in 1862.

1869 With the help of the Freedmen's Bureau, the federal agency created to serve the needs of former slaves after the Civil War, 3,000 schools are established, attended by more than 150,000 African American students. Over half of the 3,300 teachers in these schools are black. The bureau also assists in the founding of several black colleges, including Hampton, Fisk, and Tougaloo.

1870 Across the country, colleges number 563, and women make up 21 percent of college enrollees.

1873–1874 The Chautauqua movement, whose goal is adult education, begins in Lake Chautauqua, New York. Thousands of people soon sign up for the correspondence courses, and the traveling circuit of lectures proves even more popular.

1873 St. Louis opens the first public kindergarten, with the St. Louis Board of Education taking responsibility for establishing kindergarten programs in poorer neighborhoods. An endorsement from the National Education Association encourages school systems all over the United States to implement similar programs, and the idea quickly grows in popularity.

Bellevue Hospital in New York City establishes a school of nursing.

1875 Smith and Wellesley are founded in Massachusetts as women's colleges.

1876 Johns Hopkins University establishes the prototype graduate-school curriculum, which is quickly taken up by other colleges and universities and is still the model of graduate education today.

VOCATIONAL EDUCATION

Teaching the trades in a formal school setting is relatively new. During the eighteenth century, young boys learning to be artisans worked as apprentices to master craftsmen in a structure that was maintained by guild regulations and by law. But the rise of the industry "deskilled" many trades, and, as the apprenticeship system declined, concerns for the schooling of workers rose. By the end of the nineteenth century, manual training schools and vocational course offerings in high schools were integrating vocational education in public schools, and, in the twentieth century vocational training began to receive federal funding. Today this branch of education encompasses not only the traditional trades but new skills in technology and computer fields.

1877 The Women's Educational and Industrial Union opens in Boston; it is devoted to the education of working-class women.

1879 The Carlisle School in Pennsylvania is established for Native American children. Like other nonreservation schools, it seeks to "Americanize" its students.

1881 BOOKER T. WASHINGTON founds the Tuskegee Institute in Alabama to provide practical education for black males and to train teachers.

Spelman College, which will become a prestigious school for black women, is founded in Atlanta, Georgia.

1884 As part of a nationwide trend to educate boys for the trades, the Chicago Manual Training School opens. Other cities will soon establish public vocational high schools.

1885 Quakers found Bryn Mawr as a women's college, modeled on a curriculum plan developed at Johns Hopkins. It becomes one of the first women's colleges to offer graduate degrees.

Late 1880s Literacy tests begin to be used to keep African Americans from voting.

1889 Barnard College is founded as an affiliate of Columbia University.

1890 The University of Chicago is founded by the American Baptist Education Society and John D. Rockefeller. The first president, William Rainey Harper, initiates a policy whereby classes run year-round and students graduate whenever they complete.

Four percent of young people ages fourteen to seventeen are enrolled in school.

Forty percent of colleges and universities are coeducational.

1894 Radcliffe affiliates with Harvard.

1895 W. E. B. DU BOIS becomes the first African American to earn a Ph.D. from Harvard.

1896 GEORGE WASHINGTON CARVER becomes director of agricultural research at the Tuskegee Institute, where he will build his reputation as a prestigious botanist–inventor.

The Lewis Institute of Chicago is established, becoming the first private junior college in the country. After a merger in 1940, it is now part of the Illinois Institute of Technology.

1899 Educator and philosopher JOHN DEWEY publishes *The School and Society* where he stresses the importance of "learning by doing." Along with

Booker T. Washington's famed Tuskegee Institute featured a rural extension program to foster practical education for students who could not travel to campus. Teacher training was a priority at Tuskegee, as students were also encouraged to set up classes throughout the rural South after graduating.

Francis Wayland Parker, Dewey advocated progressive education whereby schools would be geared to the interests and abilities of children.

1900 There are 6,000 public high schools in the United States, up from 160 in 1870. More than 4,000 kindergartens and similar programs serve children ages three to seven. There are more than 100 coeducational black colleges and universities.

Corporate leaders like Andrew Carnegie and John D. Rockefeller have begun to make large donations to universities.

1901 The nation's first public junior college, Joliet Junior College, opens in Joliet, Illinois.

The first College Entrance Examination Board examinations are given.

1904 MARY McLEOD BETHUNE, a prominent educator, founds the Daytona Normal and Industrial School in Daytona, Florida, to educate young black girls for a life more fulfilling than domestic service. The grammar school grows rapidly, first into a high school and then a four-year accredited college—Bethune-Cookman College.

1910 Colleges number nearly 1,000, but only 3 percent of the college-age population attends them. Women constitute 40 percent of enrollment.

When a Caregie Foundation report by Abraham Flexner reveals that American medical schools are grossly inadequate compared to the great institutions of Europe, reforms in standards, organization, and curriculums are initiated.

In 1910, the average teacher in a rural school was a 25-year old native-born woman. She would make a salary of approximately $500 a year.

EDUCATION

During the 1920s and 1930s, according to a national survey, only 56 percent of U.S. public school students graduated from high school.

1916 The Bureau of Education reports that southern states spend an average of $10.32 for white students and $2.89 for black children.

JOHN DEWEY publishes *Democracy and Education*, an examination of democratic ideas and their application to the enterprise of education.

1918 Every state has a compulsory education requirement.

1920s Nursery schools are established. One of the earliest is the Ruggles Street Nursery in Boston.

1920 Thirty-two percent of young people aged fourteen to seventeen are enrolled in high school.

DEMOCRACY AND EDUCATION

JOHN DEWEY's work in the fields of psychology and child development led him to consider the purposes of education and the role of schools in a democratic society. When he published *Democracy and Education* in 1916, his theories were already well known. Education, Dewey said, should be a process whereby the child learns to solve problems effectively, thus enhancing the adult's capacity to improve not only his or her own life but, more important, society itself. Schools should serve society, and in *Democracy and Education* Dewey examined the democratic values that schools should promote. Although his statement of the relationship between democracy and education was new, especially for its application of the emerging discipline of psychology, the connection itself was as old as the republic. Schools in America had long been expected to prepare young people for citizenship, to transmit democratic values, even to solve America's problems. When, in the late nineteenth century, nativists worried that the "new immigrants" from southern and eastern Europe might not be easily assimilated into American culture, they called on the schools to accomplish "Americanization." Schooling would also "Americanize" Indian peoples and teach former slaves how they could fit into a society as free persons. Schools would teach not only the "Three Rs" but also hygiene and etiquette, agriculture to rural children, and in the cities the mechanical and industrial skills that working-class children would need in their occupations. Schools would teach the virtues of democratic government, the importance of law and

order, and a sense of individual worth.

In retrospect it seems no accident that, in the middle of the twentieth century, schools became the focal point of the struggle for equal rights. *Brown v. Board of Education of Topeka* (1954), ruling school segregation unconstitutional, made schools the testing ground and catalyst for the most significant restructuring of racial and socail relations the country had yet experienced.

Today we still ask a lot of our schools. American schools are expected to be the great equalizers, the means by which every child gets a chance. In addition to all the academic subjects, schools teach socially acceptable behavior. Student governments train students for leadership; sports programs emphasize sportsmanship and physical fitness; music and art classes transmit culture and inspire creativity. Schools teach nutrition, health, sex education, and to say no to drugs. Schools screen students, identify physical and psychological difficulties, and give assistance. Schools promote multiculturalism and self-esteem.

Dewey believed that schools should not be just a training for life but the experience of life, builders of knowledge and builders of character. Debates in the 1990s over values education, functional literacy and cultural illiteracy, declining test scores, and comparisons with other industrial nations in which the United States does poorly are shaped by our notions of the many roles of the school in a democracy and still grounded in Dewey's assumptions that schools should be the means whereby society itself is improved.

1921 The Association of Collegiate Alumnae becomes the American Association of University Women.

1925 The Scopes Monkey trial rivets the nation. Several southern school districts, pressured by religious fundamentalists, have outlawed the teaching of evolution. When John T. Scopes, a teacher in Dayton, Tennessee, breaks the law to teach it, he is arrested. The trial is broadcast nationally over the radio. Scopes is found guilty, but the state statutes outlawing the teaching of evolution, though they remain on the books, are rarely enforced. The state statutes are not repealed, but no more lawsuits are brought over this issue for decades.

1930 Forty-seven percent of young people aged fourteen to seventeen are enrolled in high school.

1932 Howard University in Washington, D.C., starts the *Journal of Negro Education*.

1935 A survey of elementary and secondary schools in ten southern states finds that public school systems in the South spend an average of $49 on each white child, compared to $17 on each black one.

1942 The General Equivalency Diploma (GED) program is established.

John T. Scopes, the defendant in the 1925 Monkey trial, had answered an ad placed in a Tennessee newspaper by the ACLU for a teacher willing to teach evolution in a public school.

THE MODERN ERA

1944 The GI Bill provides educational stipends for World War II veterans to attend vocational schools or colleges. By 1956, nearly 10 million veterans take advantage of these stipends, pushing university enrollments to all-time highs and changing the elitist character of higher education.

The United Negro College Fund is founded to support black institutions of higher learning.

1946 The Fulbright program establishes educational exchanges and fellowships for Americans studying and teaching abroad.

1947 The federal Office for Education launches a "Zeal for Democracy" campaign, designed to help teachers promote democratic values in the classroom and demonstrate, through education, the superiority of democracy over communism. It is implemented nationwide.

Early 1950s In the midst of the "Red Scare" generated by the Cold War, colleges and universities are special targets of those who fear that Communists may be attempting a takeover. As a result, many teachers are fired, perhaps as many as 600 in colleges, universities, and public schools. Across the country, a chilling effect is felt on free speech on campuses.

EDUCATION

1950 There are 2.6 million students enrolled in higher education. Women, who constituted 40 percent of all college graduates in 1940, are only 25 percent of this year's graduating class. The drop in enrollment can be attributed to the influx of male veterans attending college, which reduced women's access to school and to the many women who left school to marry or reunite with husbands after the war.

The University of North Carolina admits its first black students.

1953 The Department of Health, Education, and Welfare is established, with Oveta Culp Hobby named its first secretary.

1954 In *Brown v. Board of Education* the Supreme Court orders American public schools desegregated. A quarter century of turmoil follows, as racial tensions in American society are played out in the schools. Some schools and school systems in the South close down altogether rather than integrate.

Elizabeth Eckford, one of the nine black students who integrated Central High School in Little Rock, Arkansas, is taunted by protestors in September 1957. President Eisenhower federalized the state's National Guard and sent roughly 1,000 members of the U.S. Army to ensure the safety of the "Little Rock Nine."

1957 The U.S.S.R. launches the Sputnik satellite, and the impact is felt in education, where new emphasis is placed on science.

Central High School in Little Rock, Arkansas, is integrated, but only after President Dwight Eisenhower sends federal troops to protect black students and ensure order.

1958 Ten thousand black students march on Washington, D.C., in support of integrated education. Arkansas governor Orval Faubus closes the Little Rock schools rather than continue integration.

1959 Following a Supreme Court ruling, the Little Rock schools open again, integrated in accordance with federal requirements.

1960s Innovative school reforms include "new math," emphasizing abstract concepts rather than memory work; the "open classroom," with physical and pedagogical flexibility; and team teaching.

1962 James Meredith, an African American veteran, attempts to register for classes at the University of Mississippi, and Governor Ross Barnett personally blocks his way in defiance of a federal court order. President John F. Kennedy mobilizes the Mississippi National Guard to protect Meredith from an angry mob of several thousand. After a night of

LITERACY IN AMERICA

American colonists were more literate as a group than the population they left behind. During the 1700s when Europe's literacy rate hovered at 30 to 40 percent, half of the male colonists could read, as could a quarter of the women. Literacy tended to be highest in the New England colonies, undoubtedly because Puritans put great store in education and reading the Bible. Eighty-five percent of the men and 50 percent of the women there were literate.

Thanks largely to public schooling, by 1870, only 20 percent of Americans were illiterate, and at the turn of the century that figure was reduced to slightly over 10 percent. The rate of illiteracy continued to drop throughout the twentieth century, from 6 percent in 1920 to an effective illiteracy rate of 1 percent in 1969.

At the very point at which it would have been easy to declare that the United States suffered no illiteracy, educators realized that the ability to read meant more than being able to make out letters on a page. In an increasingly technological world, functional literacy, that is, the ability not only to read words but to use them in cultural contexts, including the workplace, would be increasingly important. Throughout the 1970s until the present day, concern has grown over the number of Americans who read but not well enough to hold down one of the 80 percent of all new jobs that now require more than a high school education. Forty percent of U.S. high school graduates cannot read at a ninth-grade level, and more than 20 million Americans cannot read at a fourth-grade level. It has been estimated that functional illiteracy costs the United States $200 billion a year.

Numerous programs have been launched to improve American literacy, but in an age of dwindling funds for education, solutions to this problem seem increasingly scarce.

violence, in which two persons are killed and more than 160 federal marshals are wounded, President Kennedy sends 5,000 National Guardsmen to Mississippi. Meredith is guarded for a year, until he graduates.

1963 When Alabama governor George Wallace makes his famous "stand in the schoolhouse door" and personally blocks the admission of black students to the University of Alabama, President John F. Kennedy sends Attorney General Nicholas Katzenbach and federal officials to confront him. Wallace backs down.

1964 Perhaps in reaction to the conflict in the public schools over desegregation, Catholic school enrollment reaches an all-time high of 5.6 million students.

1965 President LYNDON JOHNSON starts the Job Corps to give vocational training to poor urban youth, and Head Start, a preschool program for urban youth.

1966 The U.S. Office of Education reports that one-quarter of black students attend schools with white students

1967–1970 Student protests against the Vietnam War escalate each year, peaking in May 1970 following the killing of four students at Kent State University by the Ohio National Guard. Two million students at 350 campuses demonstrate, and many colleges close early.

BROWN V. BOARD OF EDUCATION

In December 1952, when Thurgood Marshall argued the *Brown* case before the Supreme Court, he had been preparing for this moment for years. The National Association for the Advancement of Colored People (NAACP) had first developed its legal strategy in the early 1930s. The "separate-but-equal" doctrine, ruled constitutional by the Court in an 1896 decision, could be chipped away, NAACP lawyers believed, through attacks on violation of "equal protection of the laws" in schools. Southern states with segregated systems did not have law schools, medical schools, or other graduate school programs for blacks, and that's where the attack would begin.

In 1935, Marshall argued before a Maryland judge that Donald Murray, denied admission to the University of

George E. C. Haynes, Thurgood Marshall, and James Nabrit celebrate their victory on the steps of the Supreme Court in 1954.

Maryland's all-white law school, should not be sent by the state to an out-of-state law school. The solution, said Marshall, was a violation of the Constitution's guarantee of equal treatment under the law. The Maryland judge agreed and ordered the University of Maryland law school to admit Murray.

Other successes followed. In *Missouri ex rel Gaines v. Canada* (1938), the Supreme Court ordered the University of Missouri School of Law to admit Lloyd Lionel Gaines (Missouri had proposed building a law school on a black campus instead). In *Sweatt v. Painter* (1950), the Court declared that the basement rooms the University of Texas said it would set up for Herman Sweatt did not constitute a law school comparable to the law school for whites. The Court said in *McLaurin v. Oklahoma State Board of Regents* that sixty-eight-year-old doctoral candidate John McLaurin, ordered by the University of Oklahoma to sit at a desk surrounded by a railing labeled "reserved for colored," was not getting an equal education either.

But when Marshall argued the case of Linda Brown, the seven-year-old daughter of a minister in Topeka, Kansas, who had to travel twenty-one blocks to an all-

black school although there was an all-white school just four blocks from her home, he did not concentrate on facilities. The facilities in Topeka, even the plaintiffs agreed, were substantially equal. The case turned on the inequality far deeper. Marshall pointed to evidence from a series of studies conducted by psychologists Kenneth Clark and Mamie Phipps Clark, who had attempted to determine the mind-set of black children in New York City, Washington, D.C., and the South. Using white and black dolls and asking the children to describe their reaction to them, the Clarks reported that black children in the South had internalized a sense of inferiority. Of sixteen children tested in Clarendon County, ten said they liked the white doll better. Nine said the white doll looked "nice" while eleven said the black doll looked "bad." When asked which doll was most like them, many of these children became emotionally upset as they pointed to the doll they had rejected.

Using this evidence, the NAACP argued that segregation itself imposed serious social and psychological handicaps on black children and even retarded their education and mental development. Because education, said the lawyers, encompasses the full development of children as human beings, segregated education could never be fair even if facilities were equal and excellent.

The Court agreed. When it handed down its historic decision on May 17, 1954, Chief Justice Earl Warren, who spoke for a unanimous court, declared: "We conclude that in the field of public education the doctrine of 'separate but equal' has no place. Separate educational facilities are inherently unequal." With that decision the legal framework supporting segregation crumbled altogether, setting in motion a tense and monumental shift in America's race relations that would be played out for decades in the nation's public schools.

1967–1970, *cont.*

During the same period, militant blacks, galvanized by the Black Power movement, demand minority scholarships and black studies programs. Demands are "nonnegotiable."

1967 Federal funds for education are increasing dramatically, from $5.4 million in 1963 to $12.2 million this year.

1968 The Supreme Court orders all the public schools in the country to draw up desegregation plans.

Berkeley, California, buses students to schools out of their neighborhoods to achieve racial balance.

Teachers' striking in New York City cite racial discrimination in hiring, wages, and facilities as major complaints.

The Children's Television Workshop is incorporated. Its *Sesame Street*, a pioneering model for children's television, premieres on Public Broadcasting Service (PBS) in 1969.

1969 Vassar College begins admitting male students. It is the first all-women's college to become coeducational.

A student strike at San Francisco State University that closes down the school ends with the administration's agreeing to fund a black studies program.

Princeton admits women. Within the next few years, many traditionally male colleges open their doors to women.

1970 Colleges are expanding dramatically to handle the baby boomers, enlarging their campuses, building new ones, and planning extension schools.

There are 7.5 million students enrolled in higher education.

The number of women in college is up, 48 percent of the college population.

1971 President Richard Nixon signs a $5 billion appropriation for the Office of Education, the largest to date. He also asks for an increase in funds for guaranteed loans for college students and a larger proportion of low-interest bank loans for students from low-income families.

The Supreme Court rules that busing is an appropriate means of achieving racial balance. Bitterly opposed for destroying neighborhood schools, busing becomes a hot political issue.

The Ford Foundation creates a $100 million six-year scholarship program to aid private black colleges.

1972 President Richard Nixon orders a one-year moratorium on school busing, and Congress agrees.

1974 Parochial school enrollment sinks to 3.3 million.

AVERAGE ANNUAL EXPENDITURE, PER STUDENT, 1910–1999*

1900	$20
1910	.33
1920	.64
1930	.108
1940	.105
1950	.260
1960	.471
1970	.955
1980	.2,491
1990	.2,491
1999	.7,960

* For school year ending in year shown. Source: National Education Association.

AVERAGE TEACHER SALARIES, 1900–1999 *

1900	$325
1910	.485
1920	.1,430
1940	.1,441
1950	.3,010
1960	.6,175
1970	.8,840
1980	.16,715
1990	.32,723
1999	.42,459

* For school year ending in year shown. Source: National Education Association.

"Education is what you must acquire without any interference from your schooling."
—MARK TWAIN

"The schools ain't what they used to be and never was."
—WILL ROGERS

1975 About 150 women's studies programs have been established. By 1980, as many as 30,000 women's studies courses will be offered at colleges and universities.

Legislation barring discrimination by sex in college admissions, classes, financial aid, and athletics goes into effect.

A major clash breaks out in Boston over school busing when a federally mandated school busing program is instituted, but by the end of the 1970s there is little remaining controversy over busing because there are so few busing programs.

1978 The Supreme Court rules that racial quotas in admission programs are illegal.

1979 The Department of Education is established, with Shirley Hufstedler as its first secretary.

1980 The U.S. Civil Rights Commission reports that nearly half of all minority schoolchildren attend "racially isolated" schools.

Housing patterns, particularly "white flight" to the suburbs, perpetuate the pattern of "minority majority" schools.

The new U.S. Department of Education publishes *A Nation at Risk*, which argues that American education is in crisis and calls for reform.

1984 College enrollment peaks at 1,662,000. Black enrollment, which has been rising, constitutes more than 10 percent of college enrollment.

1990 College expenses reach a record high; an Ivy League education costs $20,000 a year.

Of the school-age population, ages five to seventeen, 91 percent are enrolled in school.

1991 The home schooling movement is growing with more than 300,000 students being educated at home, not for religious reasons.

1993 Goals 2000, a new federal effort at educational reform, is supported by a series of new laws strengthening Head Start, creating programs to support college tuition, and otherwise promoting education through the setting of national goals.

1996 As public school enrollment hits an all-time high, it is estimated that the nation will need 6,000 more schools and 190,000 additional teachers by the year 2006.

The average annual cost (tuition and fees) of attending a private college in the United States increased *fivefold* in the twenty years from 1980 ($3,225) to 2000 ($16,332). For a public college, the average cost climbed from $738 to $3,510.

HOME SCHOOLING

Among the various alternatives to conventional public education today—under increasing criticism for inadequate facilities, elimination of extracurricular activities, racial and class inequities, and declining student performance on standardized tests—the fastest-growing is home schooling. The total number of children receiving their instruction at home, estimated at 12,500 in the mid-1970s, grew to nearly 2 million by the year 2000. The revival in home schooling was fueled in part by members of the 1960s counterculture who reached parental age and in large part by parents seeking to educate their children in religious values not taught in public schools. Today, however, the movement represents a wide variety of interests and concerns, not the least of which are crime, drugs, and the perceived quality of education in public schools.

Home schooling is legal in all fifty states, and about forty have established formal guidelines and requirements; only a handful, however, require the home instructor to have a high school diploma. Home-schooled children have shown consistently higher results on standardized tests than their public school counterparts. Whether this is a function of the learning environment, more one-on-one instruction, or merely the motivation and educational values among families who choose to follow that course is not known. Critics of home schooling point to the lack of contact with other students and the inherent impediments to socialization.

EDUCATION

1997 Under legislation passed in recent years by twenty-five states, more than 500 charter schools—publicly funded, autonomous institutions chartered by a state agency or local school board—are in operation. With financial support from the Clinton administration, the movement claims 1,000 schools by the end of the decade.

"In large states public education will always be mediocre, for the same reason that in large kitchens the cooking is always bad."
—FRIEDRICH NIETZSCHE

1998–1999 A series of fatal shootings at public middle schools and high schools throughout the country culminates in the death of fourteen students and a teacher at Columbine High School in Littleton, Colorado, at the hands of two teenagers. The continuing series of incidents leads to widespread consciousness-raising programs and new calls for gun control.

1999 The historically all-women Radcliffe College, one of the "Seven Sisters," merges with Harvard University, becoming the Radcliffe Institute for Advanced Study at Harvard.

1999–2000 The issue of school vouchers—whether federal money should be made available to parents to send their children to private schools—rises to prominence, especially during the 2000 presidential campaign. President-elect George W. Bush vows to pursue a voucher system in some form.

SPECIAL EDUCATION

The United States has been a leader in the development of special education, which involves providing specialized schooling for learning and physically disabled students. Thanks to the Handicapped Children's Act of 1975, many special programs have been set up for special-needs students, and more than 5.5 million students now receive some form of special education in the public schools. Unlike routine education, which is managed almost entirely by the states, standards for special education are mandated by the federal government, which also provides funds to research, institute, and carry out the programs.

Under the Handicapped Children's Act, public schools must educate special-needs children in the least restrictive environment. As a result, 90 percent of all special education now takes place in the regular classroom, and most special-education students attend special classes for only part of the day.

Federal funds provide for 15,000 specialized-education instructors, but students also have benefited from such technological aids as computers that convert text from written to spoken form for blind children and special wires in classrooms that relay information to hearing-impaired students who wear hearing aids. Federal funds have made classrooms, physical-education facilities, and school buses accessible to children in wheelchairs.

LEGISLATION AFFECTING EDUCATION, 1785–PRESENT

1785 Land Ordinance. This legislation, passed by the Confederation Congress to provide for the survey and sale of public lands, reserves one lot in every township for "the maintenance of public schools."

1786 Northwest Ordinance. This legislation, passed by the Confederation Congress to establish the process whereby U.S. territories will qualify for statehood, declares: "Religion, morality, and knowledge, being necessary to good government and the happiness of mankind, schools and the means of education shall forever be encouraged."

1862 Morill Land-Grant Act. This act sets aside public lands for endowing agricultural colleges that would also offer classes in home economics and engineering. Eventually more than seventy land-grant colleges are established.

1866 Supplementary Freedmen's Bureau Act. Set up to help recently emancipated slaves after the Civil War, the Freedman's Bureau helps establish nearly 3,000 schools and contributes to the founding of black colleges

1887 Dawes Severalty Act. This act provides funds to create boarding schools for Native American children, designed as much to assimilate as to educate them.

1917 Smith-Hughes Act. This act establishes federal grants to support agricultural home economics, vocational, and business education in public high schools.

1944 Servicemen's Readjustment Act. More popularly called the GI Bill, this mandates substantial educational stipends for returning World War II veterans to attend vocational schools or colleges.

1958 National Defense Education Act. This act provides funds to strengthen science, math, and modern language education and creates a federal low-interest student loan program.

1963 Vocational Education Act. This act provides federal funds for industrial education, and the field grows. Various amendments extend vocational education to adults, handicapped persons, and disadvantaged students.

1964 Civil Rights Act. This act prohibits discrimination on the basis of race, color, or national origin in federally assisted programs. As many schools and colleges receive federal money, it helps assure equal educational opportunity and provides the framework for affirmative action programs. By 1966, more than half of the school districts in seventeen states are in compliance with federal regulations.

Equal Opportunity Act. This act creates Head Start, an educational program for preschool disadvantaged children; the Job Corps, which provides educational programs and vocational training for young people; and work-study programs that support the part-time employment of students from low-income families in institutions of higher education.

1965 Elementary and Secondary School Act. This act provides aid to elementary and secondary schools.

Higher Education Act. This act provides funds for scholarships for college undergraduates.

1975 Handicapped Children's Act. This act prohibits the segregation of handicapped children and requires all classrooms to be accessible.

1978 The Tribally Controlled Community College Act is passed to spur the establishment of colleges on or near Indian reservations. This act passes ten years after the first tribally owned college is established as a result of the Navajo Community College Act (1968).

1998 Congress and the president enact a series of measures that allocate $1.2 billion to hire new teachers, authorize new teacher-training programs, reduce interest on loans to college students to the lowest level in seventeen years, and increase grants to needy students.

EDUCATION

SUPREME COURT DECISIONS AFFECTING EDUCATION, 1819–PRESENT

1819 *Dartmouth College v. Woodward.* The Court rules that the New Hampshire legislature cannot amend Dartmouth's charter to make it a public institution. The case establishes the important principle that a charter is a contract.

1889 *Cumming v. Richmond County Board of Education.* In an early decision in support of the Jim Crow laws, the Court sanctions segregated public schools and by logical extension inherently unequal facilities.

1930 *Cochran v. Louisiana State Board of Education.* Public school boards can supply secular textbooks to parochial schools. The Court holds that supplying schoolbooks to all children benefited the state. The plaintiff had brought the suit under the due process clause of the Fourteenth Amendment.

1938 *Missouri ex rel. Gaines v. Canada.* The Court rules that the University of Missouri Law School must either admit blacks or build a separate and equal facility for them.

1940 *Alston v. School Board of the City of Norfolk.* Black teachers and white teachers, according to this decision, are entitled to equal pay.
   Minersville School District v. Gobitis. The Court rules that flag saluting in public schools can be compulsory even for Jehovah's Witnesses, whose faith forbids them to worship graven images.

1943 *West Virginia State Board of Education v. Barnette.* The Court reverses the decision in the Gobitis case, saying that an individual cannot be forced to salute the flag against his or her will.

1947 *Everson v. Board of Education.* State reimbursement of money spent on busing to parochial schools does not constitute an infringement of the First Amendment.

1948 *McCollum v. Board of Education.* In a case where students were released from regular classes to attend religious ones taught in the private schools by private school teachers, the Court found that public schools and public monies could not be used to teach religion, nor can religion be promoted in the public schools.

1950 *McLaurin v. Oklahoma State Regents.* The Court agrees that equal physical facilities do not guarantee equality and overrides regulations that force a black law student to live and eat separately from whites.
   Sweatt v. Painter. The Court rules that provisions made by the University of Texas Law School for a black student are unequal.

1952 *Zorach v. Clauson.* The Court reaffirms its 1948 ruling, reiterating that public schools cannot teach religion, but validates the right of students to receive religious education, off school property, during the school day.

1954 *Brown v. Board of Education of Topeka.* In a landmark ruling, the Court unanimously overrules the separate but equal doctrine established by *Plessy v. Ferguson* (1856) and states: "We conclude that in the field of education the doctrine of 'separate but equal' has no place. Separate educational facilities are inherently unequal."

1962 *Engel v. Vitale.* The Court outlaws prayer in public schools as a violation of the separation of church and state.

1963 *Abington Township v. Schempp.* The Court outlaws Bible readings of the Lord's Prayer in public schools.

1971 *Swann v. Charlotte-Mecklenburg Board of Education.* The Court validates busing as a tool for desegregating the schools and achieving racial balance.
   Cleveland Board of Education v. LaFleur. The Court holds that mandatory maternity leave policies are unconstitutional.

1972 *Wisconsin v. Yoder.* The Court rules that, despite compulsory education laws, Old Order Amish children cannot be required to attend school after the eighth grade. Parents assert that high schools engender values contrary to Amish beliefs.

1973 *Keyes v. School District #1, Denver.* The Court strikes down a lower court's order to achieve racial balance in schools by busing black children from a city jurisdiction to suburban schools.

1974 *Milliken v. Bradley.* The Court backtracks on busing, saying that inner-city schools (mostly black) and suburban districts (mostly white) do not have to engage in interdistrict busing to achieve racial balance.

1978 *University of California Regents v. Bakke.* The Court deals a blow to educational affirmative action programs by ruling that quotas, such as the one Allan Bakke claimed kept him out of the medical school, are "reverse discrimination" and therefore illegal.

1980 *Stone v. Graham.* The Court strikes down a Kentucky law requiring the posting of the Ten Commandments in public school classrooms.

1985 *Wallace v. Jaffree.* The Court rules that Alabama's "moment of silence" in school classrooms is a violation of the First Amendment because the legislature had clearly provided for the moment to encourage prayer.

1987 *Edwards v. Aguillard.* The Court rules that the Louisiana statute requiring schools that teach evolution must also teach "creation science" is a violation of the First Amendment.

1988 *Hazelwood School District v. Kohlmeier.* The Court rules that school officials may censor the publications of a high school journalism class.

1992 *Lee v. Weisman.* The Court holds that officially sanctioned prayer at graduation ceremonies in public schools violates the establishment clause of the First Amendment.

1996 *United States v. Virginia.* The exclusion of women from the Virginia Military Institute is held to violate the constitutional guarantee of "equal protection," and VMI is ordered to begin accepting women as cadets.

1997 *Agostini v. Felton.* The Court reverses a 1985 ruling and holds that public school teachers may conduct federally funded remedial classes at parochial schools.

1998–1999 *Gebser v. Lago Vista Independent School District and Davis v. Monroe County.* The Court rules that school districts may be held liable for the sexual harassment of a student by a teacher or by another student.

1999 *Cedar Rapids Community School District v. Garret F.* The Court holds that public schools must accommodate, at public expense, the needs of disabled schoolchildren if those needs are non-medical in nature.

2000 *Santa Fe Independent School District v. Doe.* The justices rule that a school system is constitutionally barred from permitting students to lead a prayer before a high school football game.

Atheist Madalyn E. Murray and her sons William and Garth stand on the steps of the Supreme Court in 1963. A litigant in the Supreme Court case Murray v. Curlett, *Murray's case was decided along with* Abington Township v. Schempp.

NOTABLE FIGURES IN AMERICAN EDUCATION

Adler, Felix (1851–1933). An educator and founder of the Ethical Culture Society, or the ethical movement, Adler was a child-welfare activist who promoted free kindergartens and vocational-training schools. He was an early adherent of progressive education.

Barnard, Henry (1811–1900). Barnard worked to promote public school education in Connecticut through improved supervision of grammar schools. He later performed similar services in Rhode Island and Wisconsin, and, in 1867, he was appointed the first U.S. Commissioner of Education. He published the *Journal of Education* for twenty-five years.

Beecher, Catharine (1800–1878). A champion of women as grammar school teachers, Beecher argued that women were naturally more nurturing and thus better suited to teaching. Beecher founded the Hartford Academy in 1823. In the 1840s, she campaigned to send women west to teach.

Bethune, Mary McLeod (1875–1955). The seventeenth child of former slaves, Bethune became an early advocate of education for black women. After being educated at the Moody Bible Institute in Chicago, Bethune taught in a series of mission schools before founding the Daytona Normal and Industrial Institute (now Bethune-Cookman College) for black girls. She helped found the National Association of Colored Women's Clubs and the National Council of Negro Women and served as a minority-affairs advisor to President Franklin Roosevelt.

Carver, George Washington (c. 1861–1943). Born a slave, Carver received a B.A. and M.A. from Iowa State College. Starting in 1896, he headed Tuskegee Institute's agriculture department, where he built one of the nation's first productive agricultural laboratories and promoted soil improvement and crop diversification, discovering many uses for the peanut, sweet potato, and soybean. As an educator, he is best remembered for his "school on wheels," a mobile classroom dedicated to teaching poor southern farmers how to work their land more productively.

Dewey, John (1859–1952). An educational theorist and psychologist, Dewey was the author of *The School and Society* (1899) and *Democracy and Education* (1916). Influenced by G. STANLEY HALL, his teacher at Johns Hopkins, he developed and promoted progressive education, a system of teaching in which children are nurtured and rewarded instead of disciplined and punished, and in which emphasis is placed on creative thinking, experimentation, and practice. His philosophy of education continues to influence schools today. Dewey also believed schools should foster democracy and community spirit.

Du Bois, W. E. B. (1868–1963). An educator, social reformer, and African American leader, Du Bois was the first African American to be awarded a Ph.D. from Harvard. By urging the formation of a black politically oriented leadership elite, he stood in stark contrast to BOOKER T. WASHINGTON, who believed blacks should focus on learning trades and stay out of political skirmishes. Du Bois constantly promoted the cause of higher education for blacks. He taught history and education at Atlanta University and wrote many scholarly books about black culture, most notably *The Souls of Black Folk* (1903), *The Suppression of the African Slave Trade to the United States of America, 1638–1870* (1896), and *Black Reconstruction in America* (1935). In 1909, he cofounded the Niagara movement and the National Negro Committee, the predecessor to the National Association for the Advancement of Colored People (NAACP).

Galarza, Ernesto (1905–1984). An education and labor activist and professor, Galarza was one of the few Mexican Americans to successfully navigate the American school system to his advantage. Although he could just as easily have excelled as a scholar, he spent his life trying to help his fellow Mexican Americans. From 1936 to 1947, he worked with the Pan-American Union on education issues, and in later years he organized farmworkers and sought to improve public education in California. He spoke out against segregation, insensitive teachers, and overcrowding in barrio schools.

Gallaudet, Thomas Hopkins (1787–1851). A pioneer in education for the hearing impaired, Gallaudet founded the first U.S. school for the deaf in Hartford. His youngest son, Edward Miner Gallaudet (1837–1917), founded the school for the hearing impaired that is now Gallaudet University, in Washington, D.C.

Gesell, Arnold (1880–1961). A psychologist who specialized in child development, Gesell garnered a lay as well as a professional audience for his ideas and helped to change the way Americans view child rearing, largely by teaching them how children think at various stages of their development. He elucidated his views in a series of books that include *The First Five Years of Life* (1940) and

The Child from Five to Ten (1946), which to this day are widely read by teachers and parents alike.

Hall, G. Stanley (1844–1924). A founder of developmental psychology, Hall established at Johns Hopkins University, one of the first psychology laboratories in the United States. He was also one of the first persons to apply psychology to education. In his books *The Contents of Children's Minds* (1883) and *Adolescence* (1904), he wrote about the thoughts of children. He was the founder and first president of the American Psychological Association and the first president of Clark University.

Johnson, Lyndon Baines (1908–1973). As president from 1963 to 1969, Johnson, moved by his own experience teaching minority children, pushed Congress to increase funding for education. He began Head Start, a highly successful program for disadvantaged children. "Somehow you never forget what poverty and hatred can do when you see its scars on the hopeful face of a young child," he told Congress. "I want to be the president who educated young children." Johnson was the first of several presidents who tried to move public education from state control onto the national agenda.

Lyon, Mary (1797–1849). Primarily interested in advancing higher education for women, Lyon founded Mount Holyoke Female Seminary in 1837, the first U.S. college for women. As principal, she developed an academic program that emphasized service to others.

Mann, Horace (1796–1859). Along with JOHN DEWEY, Mann is one of two towering figures in American education. Studying law, Mann fought for tax-supported, nonsectarian public education. As an elected official (member of the Massachusetts House, 1877–1833, and the Massachusetts Senate, 1833–1837), he worked for compulsory education, which would also help to eradicate child labor. Mann supported the establishment of public high schools, the education of women (including their training as teachers), and the abolition of corporal punishment in schools. He also advocated breaking schools down into classes by age groups and paying extra attention to the youngest learners. He was appointed secretary of the first board of education in the country and left politics to work on it. A staunch believer in educating people for democracy, he wrote: "The scientific or literary well-being of a community is to be estimated not so much by its possessing a few men of great knowledge, as its having many men of competent knowledge."

Rush, Benjamin (1746–1813). In addition to being an innovative physician, Rush was an early advocate of women's education, and, in 1787, he founded one of the first schools for women, the Young Ladies Academy in Philadelphia.

Seton, Elizabeth Ann (1774–1821). A convert to Roman Catholicism, Seton established a school for Catholic children. She is also the first U.S.-born saint, having been canonized in 1974, and founded the first American religious order for women, the Sisters of Charity of St. Joseph.

Skinner, B. F. (1904–1990). A psychologist, Skinner helped to develop and popularize behaviorism, which holds that people are known to respond to various external stimuli in ways that can aid learning. Out of this came programmed learning, a system of study in which students get immediate feedback (the reward). Skinner wrote many books, including *The Behavior of Organisms* (1938), *Walden Two* (1948), and *About Behaviorism* (1974).

Terman, Lewis (1877–1956). A psychologist who pioneered educational testing, Terman introduced and refined the Binet Intelligence Test (later the Stanford-Binet); it would later become the leading intelligence test for American children. Terman invented the term "intelligence quotient," or IQ. In his book *Genetic Studies of Genius* (1925–1930), he traced the careers of 1,500 unusually bright children.

Thomas, Martha Carey (1857–1935). An activist for educational equality, Thomas was one of the founders of Bryn Mawr College for women in 1885, and, in 1894, she became its president. She led a movement to admit women to Johns Hopkins University, where her father was a trustee but she was banned from classes. She was the author of *The Higher Education of Women* (1900).

Thorndike, Edward (1874–1949). As the theoretical link among psychologists William James and B. F. SKINNER, Thorndike studied the measurement of mental accomplishment, especially the way that reward could function as an aid to learning. From 1922 to 1940, he directed the psychology division of the Institue of Educational Research at Columbia's Teachers College. He was the author of many books, including *Educational Psychology* (1903), and *Mental and Social Measurements* (1904).

NOTABLE FIGURES, *cont.*

Washington, Booker T. (1856–1959). A firm believer in education, even when segregated, this African American leader urged blacks to work in the trades. He founded Tuskegee Institute, a small black trade school that by the time of his departure was highly respected and trained students in more than thirty-five trades. In addition to writing his autobiography, *Up from Slavery* (1901), Washington served as adviser to presidents Theodore Roosevelt and William Taft.

Watson, John B. (1878–1958). Along with B. F. SKINNER, Watson, a psychologist, popularized behaviorism and studied its effect on the educational process. He used children to explore his principles of behavior modification. A firm believer that environment is the determining factor in development, Watson put forth his ideas in *Behavior: An Introduction to Comparative Psychology* (1914) and *Psychology from the Standpoint of a Behaviorist* (1919), among other works.

Webster, Noah (1758–1843). Webster wrote many early textbooks, including the first American dictionary. In 1783, he published the *American Spelling Book*. More popularly known as the "blue-backed speller," it sold millions of copies over its unusually long life. Webster also was a founder of Amherst College.

Willard, Emma (1787–1870). Willard campaigned for equal educational opportunities for women, and in her own school, the Troy Seminary, founded in 1821, she introduced such subjects as hitherto "masculine" mathematics and philosophy. Willard published history textbooks and lobbied the state of New York unsuccessfully to fund higher education for women. Like many of the early female educators, she trained hundreds of teachers.

CHAPTER 11

SCIENCE AND MEDICINE

■

HIGHLIGHTS

Timeline of Science and Medicine

EARLY SETTLERS OF NORTH AMERICA had a whole new world of plants, animals, and landforms to explore and classify, and small scientific communities began to be formed as early as the seventeenth century. With independence came a burst of scientific energy, as new societies, museums, laboratories, and journals propelled the nation to the forefront of technological innovation. In pure science and research, however, the United States lagged behind Europe until the early part of the twentieth century, when Americans began achieving major breakthroughs. By the 1940s, the United States had become preeminent in both theoretical and applied science, with Americans winning the most Nobel Prizes in the scientific and medical disciplines. At the beginning of the twenty-first century, as throughout the nation's history, the interdependence of pure science and technology has accelerated the advancement of both. Progress in medical science has successfully combated diseases that once struck fear in the population at large and has greatly extended the life expectancy, but it has also raised a new set of complex moral issues.

Developments in American transportation and communication technologies are discussed in Chapter 12.

BEGINNINGS: SEVENTEENTH AND EIGHTEENTH CENTURIES

1683 Boston clergyman Increase Mather and other Boston gentlemen establish the Philosophical Society, "for conference upon improvements in philosophy and additions to the stores of natural history."

1721 Boston physician Zabdiel Boylston experiments with inoculation to combat a smallpox epidemic introduced from the West Indies; all but 6 of his 247 patients survive.

1730 Thomas Godfrey invents the reflecting quadrant, a device used for sea navigation.

1730–1747 Mark Catesby publishes his two-volumed *Natural History* of Carolina, Georgia, Florida, and the Bahama Islands, one of the earliest books to describe the flora and fauna of the British colonies.

1735 First medical society in the colonies founded in Boston.

1742 BENJAMIN FRANKLIN invents the Franklin stove, or Pennsylvania fireplace; it provides more heat while burning less fuel than other fireplaces.

1743 The American Philosophical Society is founded in Philadelphia, with BENJAMIN FRANKLIN as its first secretary.

1752 BENJAMIN FRANKLIN performs his famous kite experiment, showing that lightning is a form of electricity. Franklin also invents the lightning rod, a metal conductor that prevents houses from being struck by lightning.

Thomas Bond open the first general hospital in the colonies in Philadelphia. The hospital also cares for mental patients.

1753 Mathematician, astronomer, and surveyor Benjamin Banneker fashions a wooden striking clock that keeps time accurately for more than fifty years.

1762 William Shippen Jr. begins giving anatomy lessons in Philadelphia.

1765 The College and Academy of Philadelphia opens the first medical school in the colonies, which becomes the College of Physicians and Surgeons.

JOHN BARTRAM is appointed botanist to the king. In his travels throughout the colonies he will catalogue the flora and fauna of North America.

1767 Medical instruction is inaugurated at King's College (Columbia University) in New York.

1773 The Eastern Asylum opens in Williamsburg, Virginia, to care exclusively for the mentally ill.

1775 John Lorimer develops the first dipping needle compass.

1780 The American Academy of Arts and Sciences is founded in Boston.

1783 Medical Institution of Harvard opens for classes.

1784 BENJAMIN FRANKLIN invents bifocal spectacles.

1786 Physician BENJAMIN RUSH opens the first free dispensary in the United States.

1790 The first federal patent is issued to Samuel Hopkins of Vermont for a manufacturing process for pot and pearl ash. Jacob Perkins of Massachusetts gets a patent for cutting and heading nails in a single operation.

American painter Benjamin West's created the dramatic Benjamin Franklin Drawing Electricity from the Sky *around 1816, celebrating Franklin's 1752 discovery.*

BENJAMIN BANNEKER (1731–1806)

Banneker, the son of a former slave, was largely self-taught, although for several winters when he was a child he attended school. At the age of twenty-one, Banneker became famous for devising a striking wooden clock using a borrowed pocket watch as a model. The clock kept accurate time for more than fifty years. Using borrowed books, Banneker studied astronomy, mathematics (he later taught himself calculus and spherical trigonometry), and surveying. His gifts as a surveyor were so noticeable that he was selected to assist Andrew Ellicott in surveying the site of the nation's new capital, Washington, D.C. Throughout most of the 1790s, he published almanacs containing scientific data and observations.

In 1792, Banneker sent an almanac to Thomas Jefferson, enclosing a letter protesting the low esteem in which African Americans were held and affirming "that one universal Father…hath made us all of one flesh…that He hath afforded us all the same sensations and endowed us all with the same faculties and that however variable we may be in society or religion, however diversified in situation or color, we are all of the same family and stand in the same relation to Him." Jefferson responded with warm thanks and a wish that the "degraded condition" of African Americans be ended and "a good system commenced for raising the condition both of their body and mind to what it ought to be."

1794 Charles Willson Peale, portrait painter, naturalist, and inventor, moves his gallery into the hall of the American Philosophical Society. Along with paintings and portraits, Peale displayed taxidermy animals and the reconstructed skeleton of a mastadon he had unearthed.

MEDICAL REMEDIES IN THE EARLY 1800S:
For asthma—½ oz. senna, ½ oz. flour of sulphur, 2 drams ginger, ½ dram pounded saffron, and mix with 4 oz. honey. For consumption—take 2 fresh eggs, beat in 3 tbsps. of rosewater, mix in ½ pt. of fresh milk, and sweeten with syrup of capillaire and grated nutmeg.

1803–1806 President Thomas Jefferson commissions Capt. Meriwether Lewis and Lt. William Clark to explore the Louisiana Purchase territory and the lands westward to the Pacific. Besides mapping the most accessible routes through the Rockies, the two are also asked to collect data on the region's natural resources, geography, wildlife, and climate. The expedition seeks the headwaters of the Missouri River and any connection with the Columbia. By spring of 1805, the party reaches the Pacific Ocean. They recross the Rockies and return to St. Louis in September 1806, with much of the scientific data Jefferson requested (see p. 75).

1804 Ornithologist JOHN JAMES AUDUBON does the first banding studies on wild American birds. Also known as ringing, banding helps to track the migratory patterns of birds and helps scientists learn about the life spans, reproductive cycles, and health of birds.

DISCOVERIES AND INVENTIONS: NINETEENTH CENTURY

1809 In the first operation of its kind recorded in the United States, Kentucky doctor Ephraim McDowell successfully removes an ovarian tumor.

1812 The *New England Medical Review and Journal*, now the *New England Journal of Medicine*, begins publication.

1818 BENJAMIN SILLIMAN, first professor of chemistry and natural history at

FOUNDING FATHERS, MEN OF SCIENCE

Conceived in the Age of Enlightenment and embodying the democratic principles espoused by Locke, Hobbes, Rousseau, and other European thinkers of the seventeenth and eighteenth centuries, the new American republic was the product of an intellectual revolution sweeping the Western world. Committed to the pursuit of reason and secularism, the Enlightenment was both a cause and product of the rise of modern science. The birth of a democratic nation thus coincided with the emergence of a rationalist approach to the natural and life sciences. Among those who secured the independence of the United States were several men whose interests and achievements lay equally in the pursuit of scientific knowledge. Foremost among these were BENJAMIN FRANKLIN, Thomas Jefferson, and BENJAMIN RUSH.

As a scientist and inventor, Franklin is best known for his proof that lightning is a form of electricity and for his inventions of the lightning rod, Franklin stove, and bifocal lenses. The founder in 1743 of the American Philosophical Society for Promoting Useful Knowledge, the oldest learned society in the United States, he is also credited with formulating a new theory of heat absorption, measuring the Gulf Stream, tracking storm paths, and designing ships.

President, diplomat, lawyer, drafter of the Declaration of Independence, architect, musician, and founder of the University of Virginia, Jefferson was also a passionate and lifelong man of science. As a young man in Albermarle County, Virginia, he kept detailed records of the plants, animals, and landforms he encountered, leading ultimately to the publication of his landmark work of natural history, *Notes on the State of Virginia* (1785). His enlistment of Lewis and Clark to explore the Louisiana Territory came with instructions to keep a full and precise log of fauna, flora, and the natural landscape. Jefferson's home at Monticello was filled with practical devices of his own design, and his garden was a place of meticulous botanical study.

Rush, a signer of the Declaration of Independence in 1776, ratifier of the Constitution in 1789, and treasurer of the U.S. Mint from 1797, was a physician by training. A pioneer in the field of military hygiene and the treatment of the insane, he is credited with writing the first American textbooks on chemistry and mental illness. He was also an outspoken advocate for better education for women and the abolition of slavery and capital punishment.

Yale, founds the *American Journal of Science and Arts*, which he edits until 1846.

1822 Physician William Beaumont, while employed by the U.S. Army, begins groundbreaking investigations into the nature of human gastric juices.

1829 Physicist Joseph Henry improves the electromagnet to make it practical for use.

1831 Chemist Samuel Guthrie invents chloroform, which will be used throughout the world as an anesthetic.

1836 Inventor SAMUEL COLT receives a patent for his invention of the revolver (see p. 76).

1840 Dentists Horace Hayden and Chapin Harris establish the world's first dental school, the Baltimore College of Dental Surgery.

1842 Physician CRAWFORD LONG removes a cyst from the neck of a patient using ether as anesthesia. The operation is the first recorded use of general anesthesia during surgery, although Long did not announce his achievementuntil after William T. Morton's 1846 public demonstration.

Patent leather, invented in 1829, is the only product named after the U.S. Patent Office.

SCIENCE & MEDICINE

1842, *cont.*

DOROTHEA DIX submitted a report to the Massachusetts legislature detailing the cruel treatment of the insane in jails and almhouses and calling for the separation of the criminal and the insane. Her advocacy leads to the establishment of state-supported hospitals for the insane in many states.

1844 The Association of Medical Superintendents of American Institutions for the Insane (today the American Psychiatric Association) is founded.

1845 The periodical *Scientific American* begins publication.

1846 Congress establishes the Smithsonian Institution at Washington, D.C., with a bequest from the late British scientist and philanthropist James Smithson. Physicist Joseph Henry is named first secretary and director.

Inventor Elias Howe patents the lock-stitch sewing machine.

William T. Morton demonstrates the use of ether during surgery at Massachusetts General Hospital. Henry J. Bigelow publishes an account of Morton's work in the *Boston Medical and Surgical Journal*, hastening the widespread use of anesthesia.

The American Association for the Advancement of Science (AAAS) is established in Philadelphia.

1847 Physician Nathan Davis founds the American Medical Association (AMA).

Astronomer Maria Mitchell discovers a comet and determines its orbit.

1848 Astronomer George Bond discovers Saturn's eighth moon.

Maria Mitchell is the first woman elected to the American Academy of Arts and Sciences.

1849 ELIZABETH BLACKWELL is the first American women to receive an M.D. degree; it is awarded by Geneva Medical College in Syracuse, New York.

Walter Hunt devises the modern safety pin.

1850 Astronomers William and George Bond discover the Crepe Ring of Saturn.

1851 Inventor Isaac Singer patents a continuous-stitch sewing machine.

1854 Inventors Horace Smith and Daniel Wesson devise a new type of repeating device for pistols and rifles.

John James Audubon's seminal The Birds of North America, *published between 1827 and 1838, contains 435 life-sized drawings, like this one of the ivory-billed woodpecker.*

MARIA MITCHELL (1818–1889)

Maria Mitchell was introduced to science early by her father. As a young girl, she helped him chart the stars. At the age of twelve, she observed an eclipse, which deeply impressed her. But if Maria Mitchell wanted to become a scientist, nineteenth-century America offered women virtually no opportunities. So Mitchell opened her own school in 1835, before assuming a year later the position of librarian of the Nantucket Atheneum. In October 1847, appropriating the telescope her father had installed on the roof of the bank where he was employed, she discovered a new comet. This extraordinary feat brought her international recognition. In 1848, she became the first woman member of the American Academy of Arts and Sciences. (For nearly 100 years no other woman was elected.) In 1857, a group of women gave her a five-inch telescope, which she used to study sunspots, nebulae, and planets. Taking daily photographs of the sun, she made numerous discoveries about sunspots. In 1865, she became professor of astronomy at the newly founded women's college, Vassar. A feminist, Mitchell helped establish the Association for the Advancement of Women in 1873.

1857 ELIZABETH BLACKWELL opens the New York Infirmary for Women and Children; the new hospital will be staffed only by female doctors.

Charles Darwin outlines his theory of evolution to Harvard botanist Asa Gray, who will later write a favorable review of *Origin of Species* (1859) for the *American Journal of Science* and a series of articles popularizing Darwin's theories for the *Atlantic Monthly*.

1858 In San Francisco, Dr. Elias Samuel Cooper establishes the Medical Department of the University of the Pacific, the first medical school on the West Coast. It will become the medical department of Stanford University in 1908.

1859 Naturalist JEAN LOUIS AGASSIZ establishes the Museum of Comparative Zoology at Harvard.

1860 Astronomer Alvan Clark discovers that Sirius is a double star.

1861 The U.S. Sanitary Commission is set up by Simon Cameron, the secretary of war, to provide food, shelter, and medical care to soldiers and veterans, education about sanitary practices to prevent the spread of disease, and deliveries of supplies to soldiers during the Civil War.

1862 Inventor RICHARD GATLING patents his rapid-fire Gatling gun, the predecessor of the machine gun.

CLARA BARTON volunteers as a nurse for the Union Army, serving at the Battle of Cedar Mountain. At Second Bull Run, she distributes coffee, crackers, and supplies to the wounded.

1865 Linus Yale Jr. invents the pin-tumbler cylinder lock.

Massachusetts Institute of Technology is founded in Boston. It will move to Cambridge, Massachusetts, in 1916 and will eventually become known for stellar facilities, including special laboratories for artificial intelligence, spectroscopy, and space, cancer, and nuclear research.

British naturalist Charles Darwin and his theories about evolution inspired great controversy and had profound effects on social, political, religious, and scientific thought.

1869 The first state board of health is established in Massachusetts.

1870 J. W. Hyatt invents celluloid.
Othniel Marsh, first professor of paleontology in the United States, leads a bone-hunting expedition for Yale. This and later expeditions for the U.S. Geological Survey yield 500 new species, including the type of dinosaur, the pterodactyl, that Marsh is the first to identify.

1871 Horticulturist LUTHER BURBANK begins to experiment with plant breeding and hybrids.

1872 *Popular Science* magazine begins publication.
Robert Chesebrough patents Vaseline (petroleum jelly).

1873 Florence Nightingale's nurses' training program is implemented at Bellevue Hospital in New York City.

1874 Ophthalmologist Samuel Theobald and others found the Baltimore Eye and Ear Dispensary. Eight years later, he founds the Baltimore Eye, Ear, and Throat Charity Hospital, with which he is associated for the remainder of his life. Theobald becomes the fist professor of ophthalmology at Johns Hopkins University in 1925.
Kansas doctor Andrew Still pioneers osteopathy, a therapeutic system based on the premise that restoring or preserving health can be accomplished by manipulating the skeleton and muscles.
Inventors Robert Johnson and George Seabury develop improved surgical dressings made of adhesive and medicated plaster with a rubber base.

1875 Inventor George Green patents an electric dental drill.

1876 Physicist JOSIAH WILLARD GIBBS publishes a paper on thermodynamics that will become the foundation of physical chemistry. Gibbs, unlike most American scientists who are experimenters, was the outstanding theoretician produced by the United States in the nineteenth century.
Physicist Henry Rowland uncovers the magnetic effect of electric convection.
Alexander Graham Bell patents the telephone.

1877 Astronomer Asaph Hall discovers two moons of Mars.

1878 Bellevue Hospital in New York City inaugurates the first American pathology laboratory, created by physician William Welch.

1879 Ira Remsen and Constantin Fahlberg, at Johns Hopkins University in Baltimore, formulate the sugar substitute saccharine.
The Archaeological Institute of America is founded.
Inventor THOMAS EDISON devises the incandescent electric lamp.

CLARA BARTON AND THE AMERICAN RED CROSS

In April 1861, CLARA BARTON, a clerk in the U.S. Patent Office, welcomed the Massachusetts Sixth Regiment to Washington. The boys were from her hometown, and she knew some of them. She saw immediately what they lacked: towels, handkerchiefs, serving utensils, thread, needles, preserved fruits, blankets, candles—all basic necessities that the army seemed unable to supply. After a year of devoting herself to soliciting supplies, she volunteered as a nurse, and on the battlefield she saw how truly unprepared the Union Army was to cope with the slaughter of war. "I saw many things that I did not wish to see and I pray God I may never see again," she told a friend. The wounded whose needs she attended to called her "the Angel of the Battlefield."

After the war, on a "rest cure" in Europe during the Franco-Prussian War, Barton participated in relief efforts organized by the International Red Cross, an organization that gave aid to war victims and provided medical supplies and services at the front. When she returned to the United States, she was determined to found an American branch. In 1881, she formed the American Association of the Red Cross, and a year later the U.S. Senate ratified the Geneva Convention for the Amelioration of the Condition of the Wounded and Sick of Armies in the Field. Under its terms, the neutrality and safety of medical personnel and civilian volunteers, as well as the humane treatment of the wounded, were guaranteed.

Under Barton's leadership, the domestic program of the Red Cross provided peacetime relief during forest fires, epidemics, and earthquakes. Its work following the Johnstown, Pennsylvania, flood in 1889 won national recognition. Overseas, the Red Cross sent money and supplies to victims of religious wars in Turkey and Armenia, and during the Spanish-American War it made sure that trained nurses, doctors, and supplies were on hand in Cuba.

Although her last years as head of the American Red Cross were marked by controversy and criticism of her active leadership style, Barton left a legacy of volunteer nursing, female humanitarianism, and organized aid for the care of victims of war and disaster that would give comfort and hope to millions.

1880 George Eastman patents a dry place photographic process.

Telephone inventor Alexander Graham Bell along with his father-in-law founds the magazine *Science*.

1881 Physicist ALBERT MICHELSON invents the interferometer, a device that measures distance by the length of light waves.

The American Society of Mechanical Engineers is founded.

George Sternberg, a U.S. Army bacteriologist, isolates the pneumococcus bacterium that is responsible for pneumonia. Sternberg's announcement of his discovery comes almost simultaneously with Louis Pasteur's statement of the same information.

The American Association of the Red Cross is founded by CLARA BARTON.

> Thomas Edison often failed to imagine a future for his inventions. Around 1880, he told his assistant that the phonograph "is not of any commercial value."

1882 Nikola Tesla's discovery of the rotating electromagnetic field will lead to devices using alternating current.

1884 Physician Edward Trudeau, who advocates sanatoriums for the treatment of tuberculosis patients, establishes one at Saranac Lake, New York.

Surgeon William Halsted begins to administer cocaine as a local anesthetic.

1885 In Davenport, Iowa, physician William Grant performs the first successful appendectomy in the United States.

SCIENCE & MEDICINE

1885, *cont.*

"I mean to put a potato into a pill box, a pumpkin into a tablespoon, the biggest sort of watermelon into a saucer… The Turks made acres of roses into attar of roses. I intend to make attar of everything."
—GAIL BORDEN, INVENTOR OF CONDENSED MILK

Engineer William Stanley invents the electric transformer.

Alvan Clark and his sons build the Lick Observatory on Mount Hamilton, California, and help propel American astronomy into the front ranks.

1887 Physicists Albert Michelsen and EDWARD MORLEY show that there is no absolute motion of Earth relative to an ether, an experiment that paves the way for the development of EINSTEIN's theory of relativity.

The National Geographic Society is founded. Nine months later, the first issue of *National Geographic* magazine is published.

1888 John Loud invents the ballpoint pen.

Inventor WILLIAM BURROUGHS develops the first commercially successful recording adding machine.

Chemist Herbert Dow devises a new method for the effective production of bromine. Dow's work with brines led to the creation of the Dow Chemical Company in 1897.

1889 Biophysicist Jacques Loeb pioneers artificial parthenogenesis or reproduction in which an egg develops without fertilization.

1891 Herman Frasch begins work on an economical process for the extraction of sulphur from underground deposits.

Astronomer James Keeler proves that Saturn's rings are composed of tiny meteor particles.

Nikola Tesla invents the Tesla coil, which produces high-frequency, high-voltage electric current; it will later be used in radios and televisions.

Jesse Reno devises the escalator.

President Rutherford B. Hayes used a telephone in 1876 to call Philadelphia from Washington and commented, "That's an amazing invention, but who would ever want to use one of them?"

Philanthropist Amos Throop founds Throop University, which will later become the California Institute of Technology (Caltech). With distinguished scientists such as astronomer George Ellery Hale, chemist Arthur Noyes, and physicist ROBERT A. MILLIKAN on the board of trustees, Caltech becomes a major force in the scientific community.

1892 Pathologist Theobald Smith discovers that ticks spread Texas cattle fever; this paves the way for the discovery of how diseases like malaria, typhus, and Lyme disease are spread.

Physician Andrew Still founds the American School of Osteopathy.

George Eastman incorporates Eastman Kodak Company and develops daylight loading film cartridge and processing. Late in life, he will give his fortune away, establishing, among other donations, the Eastman School of Medicine and Dentistry at the University of Rochester.

1893 ALBERT MICHELSON measures a distance of one meter, based on the wavelength of cadmium light; in 1925, it is universally accepted.

Geologist Thomas Chambers establishes the *Journal of Geology.*

Daniel Williams, a Chicago surgeon, performs the world's first open-heart surgery.

Johns Hopkins University opens its medical school and affiliated hospital in Baltimore, Maryland. Unlike previous medical programs, which were often no different than trade schools, Hopkins was revolutionary in creating an up-to-date curriculum based on the scientific method.

1895 Chemist EDWARD MORLEY determines the weight of oxygen.

Daniel Palmer establishes chiropractics; by 1930, there are 16,000 practitioners.

King Gillette invents the safety razor.

1897 Wisconsin's Yerkes Observatory installs a refracting telescope with a forty-inch lens.

1898 Physicist WALLACE SABINE devises a reverberation equation that will form the basis of the science of architectural acoustics.

MODERN MEDICINE AND THE ATOMIC AGE: 1900–1949

1900 Chemist Charles Palmer devises a new process for producing gasoline from petroleum.

1901 Industrialist John D. Rockefeller founds the Rockefeller Institute for Medical Research in New York City. It is the first organization to focus on improving health by researching the fundamental causes of disease.

Headed by army doctor WALTER REED, an Army Commission identifies the *Aedes aegypti* mosquito as the transmitter of the yellow-fever virus.

Adrenaline becomes the first hormone to be isolated and purified, in the research of chemist Jokichi Takamine, at the Johns Hopkins Medical School.

The National Bureau of Standards is established to develop measurements and standards, and to encourage technological research.

1902 Arthur Little receives a patent for his rayon-production process.

Engineer WILLIS CARRIER invents air-conditioning.

Eugene Opie proves that diabetes results from the destruction of parts of pancreatic tissue called the islets of Langerhans.

Chemists Albert Barnes and Herman Hille discover an antiseptic that, marketed as Argyrol, will protect newborns from blindness.

Geneticist WALTER SUTTON proves that chromosomes come in pairs and carry the units of inheritance; his work becomes the basis for the chromosomal theory of heredity.

1904 Astronomer Charles Perrine detects the sixth moon of Jupiter and will discover the seventh the next year.

In 1898, the Bayer pharmaceutical company marketed heroin as a treatment for bad coughs. Other dangerous substances sold as pharmaceuticals in the late 1800s included cocaine for throat ailments and baby syrups laced with morphine.

1904, *cont.*

The Mount Wilson Observatory is founded by George Ellery Hale on a mountain in Pasadena, California. It will become one of the foremost astronomical research centers in the world.

1905 The legality of compulsory vaccination laws is upheld by the Supreme Court.

Clarence McClung discovers that females have XX chromosomes and males, XY. Nettie Maria Stevens and Edmund Wilson also publish important work on sex determination in chromosomes.

1906 Pathologist Howard Ricketts isolates the cattle tick as the carrier of Rocky Mountain spotted fever.

1907 Zoologist Ross Harrison develops the first successful animal-tissue cultures.

Scientist Bertram Boltwood finds that the age of rocks containing uranium can be determined by measuring the ratio of uranium to lead.

1909 Chemist Leo Baekeland produces Bakelite, the first thermosetting plastic.

Geneticist Thomas Hunt Morgan proposes a new, innovative theory of the gene. His classic *The Physical Basis of Heredity* is published in 1919.

Chemist Phoebus Levene discovers that nucleic acid is of two kinds (RNA and DNA).

1910 Physician James Herrick is the first to diagnose sickle-cell anemia.

1911 Physicist Robert Millikan measures an electron's electric charge.

1912 James Herrick, in a written report that is the first diagnosis of a heart attack in a living patient, demonstrates that heart attacks are not always fatal.

Biochemists Elmer McCollum and Marguerite Davis isolate vitamin A.

William and Charles Mayo, brothers and physicians, build their own medical center in Rochester, Minnesota; the Mayo Clinic becomes one of the world's biggest medical centers.

1913 Biologist Alfred Sturtevant finds that genes line up in a row on chromosomes and pioneers chromosome mapping.

William Coolidge devises the modern X-ray tube.

The American Cancer Society is founded. Originally called the American Society for the Control of Cancer, the organization sought to educate the public about cancer, a disease rarely openly discussed at the time.

Pediatrician Béla Schick devises the Schick test to determine diphtheria immunity.

John B. Watson introduces behaviorism in psychology.

THOMAS ALVA EDISON (1847–1931)

In some ways, THOMAS ALVA EDISON typifies the self-made man and the Yankee inventor who specialized in practical applications for science. Born in 1847 to a family of declining fortunes in a small Ohio town, he overcame the adversities of limited schooling and hearing loss to become an American hero, the "Wizard of Menlo Park," whose incandescent lamp transformed the patterns of daily life around the world.

Edison knew how to work hard, and he knew how to organize others to do so, too. His laboratory in Menlo Park, New Jersey, was an "invention factory," and Edison's staff included mechanics who could take his endless questioning as well as his demands on their time. Under pressure to eliminate the "bugs" in one of his stock printer devices to fill a big order, he told his assistants, "I've locked the door and you'll have to stay here until this job is completed. Well, let's find the bugs." It took sixty straight hours.

Edison knew how to make the most of his inventions, too. He wasn't the first to dream of an incandescent lamp. Inventors had been working on the idea for years. The problem was to find the right material—a filament that would glow, and not burn up, when a current of electricity was passed through it. Edison pressed his assistants and Francis Upton, a theoretical mathematician who worked with Edison for more than a year. When the team found that carbonized thread cotton burned for forty hours, Edison staged a demonstration. On New Year's Eve, 1879, he invited the public to Menlo Park, illuminated with 150 bulbs. Then he set about, as he put it, making "electric light so cheap that only the rich will be able to burn candles."

In 1887, Edison built a new laboratory in West Orange, New Jersey, with brick buildings that housed precision machinery and a library holding 10,000 books. There was a music room, a darkroom, and a stockroom. A picket fence and guards kept interlopers out. Edison was less often in the lab than at his desk directing a staff of fifty or so. In his lifetime, the Edison labs boasted more than a thousand patents, most of which served useful and practical purposes.

While Edison's inventive genius clearly contributed to technology and human comfort, his genius for organization may have been equally important. Although he was the inspiration—the wizard—his team structure and regimen for orchestrating the work of mechanics, technicians, and theoreticians would become standard practice in the complex industrial research laboratories of the next century.

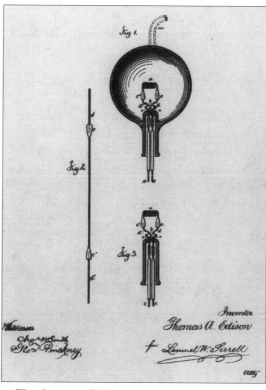

This drawing of Edison's electric lamp accompanied his patent application. He received patent no. 223,898 on January 27, 1880.

SCIENCE & MEDICINE

1914 Biochemist EDWARD KENDALL isolates the thyroid hormone thyroxine.

The Corning Glass Company creates Pyrex glass. Used primarily in cookware, it can sustain high temperatures.

1916 The National Research Council (NRC) is founded by the United States National Academy of Sciences.

1916, *cont.*

Some 20 million Americans took sick in the influenza pandemic of 1918–1919, and about 500,000 died. Worldwide the "Spanish flu" took an estimated 21.6 million lives; about *1 billion* people were affected.

Elmer McCollum isolates vitamin B.

MARGARET SANGER opens the first birth-control clinic in the United States, in Brooklyn.

1918–1919 A worldwide influenza epidemic reaches the United States, killing half a million people.

1919 Photography pioneer George Eastman founds the Eastman School of Medicine and Dentistry at the University of Rochester.

1920 Robert H. Goddard demonstrates the lifting power of rockets.

Physician KARL MENNINGER establishes the Menninger Clinic in Topeka, Kansas. The clinic will pioneer a "total-environment" approach that will change the methods for treatment of mental illness.

1922 Elmer McCollum isolates vitamin D in cod-liver oil and discovers its effectiveness in combating rickets.

1923 Physicist Peter Debye provides a mathematical description of electrolysis.

Harry Steenbock of the University of Wisconsin proposes that exposing foods to ultraviolet light can turn them into sources of vitamin D.

ROBERT MILLIKAN receives the Nobel Prize for his experiments that prove ALBERT EINSTEIN's work and theories on the photoelectric effect.

Jacob Schick invents the electric razor; he obtains a patent in 1928.

Researchers George and Gladys Dick, husband and wife, identify the streptococcus responsible for scarlet fever and devise a serum for the disease.

American Red Cross workers delivered food and supplies to families like this one during the devastating influenza epidemic of 1918 and 1919.

1925 Chemist JULIUS NIEUWLAND pioneers synthetic rubber.

Physician Thomas Cooley describes a type of anemia that will take his name; Cooley's anemia is a hereditary blood disease with no cure.

1926 Geneticist HERMANN MULLER discovers that mutations can be produced by X rays.

Biochemist James Sumner shows that enzymes are proteins.

1927 Harvard professor Philip Drinker creates the "iron lung," a device for mechanical artificial respiration.

BEHAVIORISM

Psychology had a long gestation—first in philosophy and then in physiology. In the nineteenth century German and French scientists established psychology as a separate scientific discipline and, especially after Freud, Europeans seemed to dominate the field. But it was an American, WILLIAM JAMES, who first applied to Charles Darwin's theory of natural selection to consciousness, and another American, John B. Watson, who gave psychology a new direction. The recipient of the University of Chicago's first Ph.D. in psychology for a dissertation entitled "Animal Education: The Psychical Development of the White Rat," Watson was professor and director of the psychological laboratory at Johns Hopkins when he delivered an important address at Columbia University in 1913. "Psychology as the Behaviorist Views It" became a manifesto of a new, behaviorist approach to psychology that would be highly influential for half a century.

"Psychology as the behaviorist views it is a purely objective experimental branch of natural science," proclaimed Watson. "Its theoretical goal is the prediction and control of behavior." Concerned largely with external and sensory stimuli and behavioral reaction or physiological response, behaviorists sought to explain animal and human behavior through objective observation and in measurable terms. Applying this approach to the study of learning in rats, B. F. Skinner at Harvard concluded that learning is a series of patterned responses to stimuli and rewards.

From these theories emerged therapeutic approaches focused on behavior modification. Through conditioning, clients are desensitized to anxieties and fears or, through exposure to a system of rewards and punishments, engineered to change their reactions.

1929 The first Blue Cross nonprofit health insurance association is founded in Dallas, Texas.

Astronomer EDWIN HUBBLE establishes that the universe is expanding.

1930 In Flagstaff, Arizona, Lowell Observatory astronomers led by Clyde Tombaugh discover the planet Pluto.

The Adler Planetarium, the first in the United States, opens in Chicago.

Inventor Clarence Birdseye receives a patent for freezing as a way of preserving food.

1931 Physicist HAROLD UREY and two colleagues discover heavy water (deuterium oxide), leading to the production of atomic energy.

Astronomer Karl Jansky discovers that radio waves come from space, paving the way for the science of radio astronomy.

Physicist ERNEST LAWRENCE constructs the world's first effective cyclotron; his success will speed the development of atomic knowledge.

The Food and Drug Administration is established, charged with protecting the health of the nation against impure and unsafe foods, drugs, cosmetics, and other potential hazards.

1932 Biochemist Charles King isolates vitamin C.

Physicist Carl Anderson discovers the neutron, the antiparticle of the electron.

1933 ALBERT EINSTEIN accepts a post at Princeton's Institute for Advanced Study. The Nazi government will shortly confiscate his property and revoke his German citizenship because he is Jewish.

1934 Biochemist Robert Williams isolates a substance in rice husks that prevents the deficiency disease beriberi.

1935 Du Pont chemist WALLACE CAROTHERS invents nylon.

Biochemist Wendell Stanley isolates the first crystalline virus.

Biochemists HERBERT EVANS and Oliver and Gladys Emerson isolate vitamin E.

Vitamin K is isolated by Danish biochemist Henrik Dam and American biochemist EDWARD DOISY.

Seismologist Charles Richter establishes a scale, known as the Richter scale, to measure the intensity of earthquakes.

"Science is a wonderful thing if one does not have to earn one's living at it."
—ALBERT EINSTEIN

1936 Researchers H. Houston Merritt and Tracy Putnam produce Dilantin, a drug that can be used to treat epilepsy and irregular heartbeats.

Robert Williams names his synthesized vitamin B1 compound thiamine.

1937 Physicist ISIDOR RABI develops a new method for studying the spectra of atoms in the radio-frequency range. His work will be used to create nuclear magnetic resonance (NMR), the predecessor of the diagnostic MRI test.

Carl Anderson discovers the muon, now known as a subatomic particle, with more mass than the electron.

The first radio telescope in the world is constructed by astronomer Grote Reber.

The first blood bank is opened in Chicago.

Congress funds a National Cancer Institute to sponsor research into the disease.

1938 Du Pont researcher Roy Plunkett produces the plastic Teflon.

The March of Dimes organization for research into poliomyelitis (polio) is founded. Originally called the National Foundation for Infantile Paralysis, founded by President Franklin D. Roosevelt, the name was changed to that of a successful fund-raising scheme, the March of Dimes, which invited the public to send dimes to the White House.

1939 John Dunning's cyclotron at Columbia University is the first in America to split an atom; the reaction emits gamma rays, and ALBERT EINSTEIN suggests in a letter to President Roosevelt that reactions of this kind could lead to the generation of "vast amounts of power" and also to the "construction of bombs."

Chemist LINUS PAULING publishes his theory of the chemical bond by which it is possible to construct accurate models for some anomalous molecules. *The Nature of Chemical Bonds* is still highly regarded.

1940 A research team at Columbia University separates the uranium-235 isotope from the more plentiful uranium-238 isotope using a gaseous diffusion process devised by physicist John Dunning and his colleagues; this newly isolated isotope will be the source of atomic energy.

Physicist EDWIN MCMILLAN discovers a radioactive element heavier than uranium, which he names neptunium. The following year, along with GLENN SEABORG, he will discover an even heavier element, to be named plutonium, which is suspected of having a greater energy yield than uranium.

Biologists MAX DELBRÜCK, Alfred Hershey, and SALVADOR LURIA found the field of molecular biology with their discoveries about bacterial and viral reproduction.

Biochemist Martin David Kamen discovers the carbon-14 isotope.

Engineers at RCA publicly test an electron microscope.

Immunologist KARL LANDSTEINER discovers the Rh factor in blood.

1941 Physicist Vannevar Bush is the head of the new Office of Scientific Research and Development set up by President Franklin Roosevelt.

Microbiologist SELMAN WAKSMAN coins the term "antibiotic."

To protect scientists and their results from the World War II bombing of England, a major research project on penicillin moved from Oxford University to the United States. Australian scientist Howard Florey and German Ernst Chain discovered ways to mass produce the drug (which was discovered by Alexander Fleming in England in 1929) as an antibiotic.

1942 Chemist Louis Fieser produces napalm for the U.S. Army.

Physicist ENRICO FERMI and others invent the nuclear reactor.

THE MANHATTAN PROJECT

In 1939, ALBERT EINSTEIN and other famous physicists, concerned that German scientists might build an atomic bomb, began campaigning to persuade President Franklin Roosevelt to beat Germany to the punch. Realizing that the bomb might hold the key to victory in World War II, Roosevelt established a small research project on atomic fission. The project soon expanded to include research teams at various universities such as Princeton, California, Columbia, and Chicago.

In 1942, the researchers found that a chain reaction in uranium produced atomic fission. The discovery by physicist ERNEST LAWRENCE that a common uranium isotope, U-238, could be changed into a new fissionable element, plutonium, made building a bomb practicable. When informed of this development, Roosevelt approved the creation of a section of the army, with the code name the Manhattan District, to oversee the project. Late in 1942, physicists Arthur Compton, ENRICO FERMI, and colleagues produced the first small uranium chain reaction under the bleachers of Stagg Field at the University of Chicago.

Now the focus turned to producing an actual bomb. Plutonium was produced in Hanford, Washington, uranium at Oak Ridge, Tennessee. In Los Alamos, New Mexico, a new laboratory, directed by physicist J. ROBERT OPPENHEIMER, was organized to build the bomb. During the next three years more than $2 billion in federal money was spent on research and to produce the components of the bomb.

On July 16, 1945, the atom bomb was successfully tested at Alamogordo, New Mexico. Observers were thunderstruck at the sight of the first mushroom cloud created above the explosion. On August 6 an atom bomb was dropped by order of President Harry Truman from the B-29 bomber *Enola Gay* on Hiroshima, Japan. The bomb destroyed the city, killing almost 80,000 people. Three days afterward, a second bomb was dropped on another Japanese city, Nagasaki, killing 40,000. (With burns and radiation poisoning, the death toll from the bombs would reach 200,000.) The Japanese surrendered five days later. World War II had ended, and the nuclear age had begun.

SCIENCE & MEDICINE

QUANTUM PHYSICS AND REFUGEE SCIENTISTS

Throughout the nineteenth century, American science had a bent for the practical. While Americans excelled in technology and in scientific work that was useful and profitable, basic research was neglected and unappreciated. JOSIAH WILLARD GIBBS, a professor of mathematical physics at Yale who was publishing a series of papers on thermodynamics, for example, was not paid a salary until he was on the verge of taking a post at Johns Hopkins.

Between 1910 and 1920, leaders in American physics, aware of the ferment in theoretical physics—particularly quantum mechanics—in Europe, made a concerted effort to interest American students in the subject. Particularly after World War I, some believed that the national interest depended on it. Between 1920 and 1930, degrees in physics nearly tripled. Funds from the Rockefeller fortune supported research programs. Lecture series brought Europe's most distinguished physicists to the United States. Harvard, Berkeley, Chicago, Princeton, and the California Institute of Technology emerged as thriving centers for the study of quantum theory.

Young Americans often went to Germany to study with leaders in the field, but in the 1920s, frequently young European physicists, particularly Jews blocked by faculty quotas, found positions in American universities attractive. Many left Europe for the greater opportunities life in American offered. Paul Epstein of Munich was one of the first, taking a position at Caltech in 1921. Others who came in the 1920s included John von Neumann, Fritz Zwicky, and Eugene Wigner.

After the rise of fascism in the 1930s and the enforcement of Hitler's racial laws, Jewish scientists were dismissed from German universities. Escape from Europe became a stronger push than the pull of American research opportunities, which were considerable. Among the refugees were Hans Bethe, EDWARD TELLER, ALBERT EINSTEIN, ENRICO FERMI, and Leo Szilard, whose effect on American physics and America itself cannot be overestimated. After World War II, Szilard joked that he, Fermi, and other physicists should receive the Nobel Peace Prize for not having conducted the uranium experiments that would have allowed Hitler to conquer the world.

1942, *cont.*

Physician George Nicholas Papanicolaou's "Pap" test for cervical cancer is accepted by the medical profession.

Chemist Russell Marker makes oral contraceptives possible with his discovery that the wild Mexican barbasco plant is a cheap source of the hormone progesterone.

1944 Chemists William Doering and Robert Woodward synthesize quinine. A well-known ingredient of drinks called tonics, quinine has also been used to reduce fever and pain and in the treatment of malaria.

Surgeon Alfred Blalock performs the first operation to save a "blue baby." He helps to develop the Blalock-Taussig shunt for pediatric patients with heart abnormalities that keep healthy blood flow from reaching a newborn's lungs and make the baby turn blue.

SELMAN WAKSMAN produces the antibiotic streptomycin, which will be used against tuberculosis. This disease, known as consumption during the nineteenth century, becomes curable.

Researchers Oswald Avery, Colin MacLeod, and Maclyn McCarty demonstrate that deoxyribonucleic acid (DNA) is the blueprint of heredity, determining the way an organism develops.

1945 In New Mexico, a government-funded team of scientists led by physicist J. ROBERT OPPENHEIMER explodes the first atomic bomb.

Melvin Calvin uses the carbon-14 isotope to study photosynthesis, successfully tracing the route of carbon through a plant during photosynthesis.

Grand Rapids, Michigan, is the first American community to experiment with the fluoridation of its drinking water.

1946 Congress establishes the Atomic Energy Commission.

Scientists Felix Bloch and Edward Purcell discover nuclear magnetic resonance (NMR), for which they will earn the 1952 Nobel Prize. The diagnostic tool MRI will be invented based on their NMR.

1947 EDWARD TATUM and JOSHUA LEDERBERG find that sexual reproduction occurs in bacteria.

Chemist WILLARD LIBBY finds that all organic materials contain some carbon-14 atoms, which decay at a constant rate, a discovery that paves the way for the carbon-dating of archaeological evidence.

Chloromycetin, developed by Parke-Davis chemists, is used to treat typhus patients, marking the first use of a "broad-spectrum" antibiotic.

1948 Physicists Richard Feynman and Julian Schwinger propose a new quantum theory of electrodynamics.

Biochemists EDWARD KENDALL and Philip Hench synthesize the adrenal hormone cortisone and find that it is an effective treatment for arthritis.

The anti–motion-sickness properties of the drug dymenhydrinate (marketed as Dramamine) are accidentally discovered by Johns Hopkins physicians who had thought that they were working with an antiallergy drug.

Astronomers GEORGE GAMOW, Ralph Alpher, and Robert Herman devise the big bang theory of the origin of the universe.

Zoologist Alfred Kinsey publishes *Sexual Behavior in the Human Male*; based on his interviews with 18,500 American men, it suggests that many acts thought to be perverse are, in fact, normal because they occur so commonly.

John Bardeen, Walter Brattain, and William Shockley invent the transistor.

Built by George Ellery Hale, the Hale Telescope is unveiled on Palomar Mountain in California. At 200 inches in diameter and weighing 20 tons, it is the largest telescope on earth until 1975.

1949 Researchers at the Merck laboratory synthesize the adrenocorticotropic hormone ACTH; it will be used later in treating AIDS.

THE CUTTING EDGE: 1950–PRESENT

1950 Du Pont introduces the synthetic fiber Orlon.

The U.S. Atomic Energy Commission constructs the first nuclear reactor for power production.

The National Science Foundation is established to support basic research and education.

"Thirty seconds after the explosion came, first the air blast pressing hard against people and things, to be followed almost immediately by the strong, sustained awesome roar which warned of doomsday and made us feel that we puny things were blasphemous to dare tamper with the forces heretofore reserved to The Almighty."
—THOMAS FARRELL, official report on the first atomic bomb test, Alamogordo, New Mexico, July 16, 1945

SCIENCE & MEDICINE

1951 Project Matterhorn is launched at Princeton University to explore nuclear fusion. In 1961, it will become the Princeton Plasma Physics Laboratory.

1952 Chemist H. Herbert Fox develops isoniazid, a drug to combat tuberculosis.

Scientist Eugene Aserinsky finds that sleep with rapid eye movement (REM) is a distinct stage of sleep, which is later discovered to be associated with dreams.

A government team of scientists, led by physicist EDWARD TELLER, develops the first hydrogen bomb.

1953 American researcher JAMES WATSON, English collaborator Francis Crick, and their assistants identify the basic double-helix structure of DNA and its self-duplicating process; the discovery begins a new era in the study of genetics.

Congress passes legislation to establish a cabinet-level Department of Health, Education and Welfare. Oveta Culp Hobby is named the first secretary.

Surgeon John Gibbon employs a heart-lung machine he has invented to perform successful open-heart surgery.

Researchers at New York's Sloan-Kettering Institute of Cancer Research provide early evidence of the link between tobacco products and cancer.

1954 Microbiologist JONAS SALK's polio vaccine is tested in mass trials. Pronounced safe the next year, it is distributed in a mass immunization program that will virtually wipe out the disease.

Physician Clarence Lillehei builds pumps that can maintain circulation during open-heart surgery.

The first successful kidney transplant in the world is performed by a Harvard surgery team.

Researchers William Masters and Virginia Johnson begin their revolutionary investigations into the physiology of human sexual response; in 1966, they will publish *Human Sexual Response*, based on observations of 382 women and 312 men in more than 10,000 cycles of sexual arousal.

A study of nearly 200,000 American men done by researchers Edward Hammond and Daniel Horn strongly suggests that smoking is hazardous to health.

Gregory Pincus and John Rock develop the first oral contraceptive pill.

1955 Biochemist Severo Ochoa is the first to synthesize RNA (ribonucleic acid).

Researchers discover that reserpine is effective in the treatment of schizophrenia and other mental disorders.

Physicists Owen Chamberlain and EMILIO SEGRÈ discover antiprotons.

Physicists Clyde Cowan Jr. and Frederick Reines discover the neutrino, a subatomic particle with no mass or charge.

1957 Biochemist Arthur Kornberg and his colleagues at Stanford University devise a method for synthesizing a biologically inactive form of DNA.

1958 Astronomer James Van Allen discovers radiation belts, now known as the Van Allen belts, surrounding Earth in space.

The National Aeronautics and Space Administration is established to conduct research and space exploration.

1959 Researchers William Stein, Stanford Moore, and their assistants code a complete amino-acid sequence of the biologically important enzyme ribonuclease.

1960 Laser technology is perfected by Theodore Maiman, who builds upon the earlier efforts of other scientists, such as R. Gordon Gould, Charles Townes, and Arthur Schawlow.

Kenneth Norris and John Prescott prove that dolphins use echolocation, or dolphin sonar, to locate objects in the water.

1961 Physician Frances Kelsey of the Food and Drug Administration blocks the marketing in the United States of thalidomide, a sleep-inducing drug that causes serious birth defects.

Scientist Marshall Nirenberg reads one of the "letters" of the genetic code.

Physicist Murray Gell-Mann and others develop a method of classifying subatomic particles.

NASA astronaut Alan B. Shepard Jr. is the first person to fly into space aboard the Mercury capsule.

1962 Physician JOHN ENDERS devises the first effective measles vaccine.

Biologist RACHEL CARSON's *Silent Spring*, an attack on pesticides, launches the environmental movement.

John Glenn Jr. is the first U.S. astronaut to orbit Earth. In the *Friendship* 7, he completed three orbits.

1963 Astronomer Maarten Schmidt is the first to identify a quasar.

The first liver transplant is performed by surgeon Thomas Starzl.

1964 The surgeon general issues a report that concretely connects cigarette smoking to lung cancer.

Murray Gell-Mann identifies quarks, components of heavy subatomic particles, like protons and neutrons.

Surgeon James Hardy performs the first transplant of an animal heart into a human.

Congress passes the Medicare Act, establishing the first government-run program to provide health insurance for citizens aged sixty-five and over.

1965 Congress legislates that all cigarette packaging be labeled with health warnings.

LINUS PAULING (1901–1994)

It would be hard to find a twentieth-century equivalent of BENJAMIN FRANKLIN—printer, inventor, scientist, statesman—but LINUS PAULING comes close. Pauling, born in Oregon in 1901, received his Ph.D. in chemistry from the California Institute of Technology and taught and directed laboratories there for a large part of his career. His contributions are many and notable: application of the quantum theory to calculations of molecular structure; development of a theory of resonance to explain certain bonds in organic chemicals; determination of the molecular structure of antitoxins, amino acids, and proteins; production of synthetic antibodies. In 1954, he was awarded the Nobel Prize for discovering the forces holding proteins and molecules together, thus laying the groundwork for later descriptions of the structure of DNA.

But Pauling was not always to be found in his lab. In the early 1970s, he stirred controversy for his advocacy of mass doses of vitamin C as preventing cancer and the common cold. He also took a great interest in public affairs and was especially active in the movement for nuclear disarmament. In 1957, he organized an international test-ban petition eventually signed by 11,000 scientists in forty-nine countries. The nest year, he wrote *No More War*, a compelling case for international peace. He was also an outspoken critic of the Vietnam War, continuously urging scientists to join their voices in protest. In 1963, he became one of the few recipients of two Nobel Prizes, his second a peace prize for his work on world disarmament.

Renowned scientist Linus Pauling and others march in front of the White House in April 1962, protesting the resumption of U.S. atmospheric nuclear testing.

1965, *cont.*

Astronomers Arno Penzias and Robert Wilson find radios waves produced by the big bang.

Gemini 4 astronaut Edward H. White Jr. conducts the first spacewalk.

1966 Researchers Paul Parkman and Harry Myer devise a rubella (German measles) vaccine.

Heart surgeon MICHAEL DEBAKEY implants the first artificial heart in a human.

1967 New York surgeon Adrian Kantrowitz attempts the first American transplant of a human heart, but his patient does not survive beyond a few hours.

Arthur Kornberg and coworkers synthesize biologically active DNA.

1968 Allan Cormack, working independently of England's Godfrey

Hounsfield, coinvents the CAT scanner.

Apollo 8 is the first manned mission to orbit the moon.

1969 On July 20, *Apollo* astronaut Neil Armstrong becomes the first person to walk on the moon, uttering the historic words "one small step for man, one giant leap for mankind." During this mission, Armstrong and Edwin "Buzz" Aldrin take photographs and rock and soil samples, and astronaut Mike Collins orbits the moon in the command module.

The manufacturing of most biological and chemical weapons is prohibited by President Richard Nixon.

Biochemist Jonathan Beckwith and coworkers are the first to isolate a single gene.

Surgeon Denton Cooley implants the first artificial heart for temporary use in a human.

1969 Following the signing of the Nuclear Nonproliferation Treaty, President Richard Nixon orders stockpiles of bacteriological weapons destroyed and renounces the use of chemical weapons except for defense.

1970 Biochemist Hamilton Smith finds a restriction enzyme that splits certain DNA strands at specific sites.

Microbiologist David Baltimore discovers "reverse transcriptase," a viral enzyme capable of reversing the usual DNA-to-RNA transcription, a key development in genetic engineering.

Har Khorana and coworkers produce the first artificial gene.

1970 The National Oceanic and Atmospheric Administration is established to explore and chart the global ocean and its living resources; to monitor and predict weather conditions and issue warnings; and to assess environmental modification.

1971 Choh Hao Li synthesizes somatropin, a growth hormone that is produced naturally by the pituitary gland.

The Food and Drug Administration tells doctors to stop prescribing diethylstilbestrol (DES) to ease morning sickness in pregnant women because evidence suggests that the drug predisposes their daughters to reproductive tract cancers.

Legislation providing $1.6 billion per year for cancer research is approved by Congress.

1972 The surgeon general issues a report warning that the health of nonsmokers is endangered by secondhand smoke.

Researcher Raymond Damadian devises the magnetic resonance imaging (MRI) scanner; it will be used to detect abnormalities inside the body.

1973 In the first example of genetic engineering, Stanley Cohen and Herbert Boyer put a specific gene into bacterium. Their research will make

Dr. Linus Pauling is the only man to win two Nobel Prizes in different categories. In 1954, he won the Nobel in chemistry and in 1962 he won the Nobel Peace Prize.

1973, *cont.*

the creation of synthetic human insulin possible in 1978.

Skylab 1 is launched. It's the first U.S. orbital workshop or space station.

Developed by Allan Cormack and Godfrey Hounsfield, the CAT scanner (computerized axial tomography) is introduced. It can create a three-dimensional image of internal structures in the body and is therefore helpful in diagnosis.

1974 Physician Henry Heimlich demonstrates the Heimlich maneuver, which will become the standard emergency treatment for choking victims.

In Ethiopia, U.S. anthropologist Donald Johanson and coworkers discover the nearly complete skeleton of *Australopithecus afarensis*, an early relative of humans.

1975 Lyme disease is identified in Lyme, Connecticut, and is found to be carried by ticks that live on animals in wooded areas, primarily in the Northeast.

Together with the Soviet Union, the United States successfully completed the first international human spaceflight, the Apollo-Soyuz Test Project. The Apollo and Soyuz space crews were launched from their respective countries, and they met in space to conduct two days of experiments. The prográm was more a symbol of the détente between the United States and the Soviet Union and a demonstration of cooperation between the superpowers than an important scientific mission.

1976 The National Institutes of Health suggest regulating some kinds of genetic testing to avoid the creation of dangerous new organisms.

Har Khorana announces that he and his colleagues have successfully synthesized a bacterial gene, analine-transfer RNA, and inserted it into a living cell, where it has functioned successfully.

Based on the work of F. Sherwood Rowland and Mario Molina, the National Academy of Sciences announces that the use of chlorofluorocarbons (CFCs), found in aerosol sprays, some packing materials, and air conditioners, can deplete the ozone layer. Further research will lead to a ban on the industrial production of CFCs in 1996.

At the Salk Institute for Biological Studies in California, scientist Rudolph Jaenisch injects human DNA into mouse eggs. The genetic material will be passed onto the "transgenic" mice, and scientists hope to study human diseases in them.

1977 The bacterium that causes Legionnaire's disease is identified.

Using techniques from the recent developments in genetic engineering, American scientists successfully produce insulin from bacteria.

Congress creates the U.S. Department of Energy. James R. Schlesinger is named the first secretary.

Scientists aboard the NASA-operated Kuiper Airborne Observatory, an aircraft equipped with a telescope, and capable of research projects, discover the nine rings of Uranus.

1979 The Department of Health, Education and Welfare is redesignated the Department of Health and Human Services.

The Three Mile Island nuclear reactor near Harrisburg, Pennsylvania, has a partial meltdown. It is the worst nuclear disaster in American history.

1980 In *Diamond v. Chakrabarty*, the Supreme Court upholds the patent for a genetically engineered microorganism that breaks down crude oil. Developed by General Electric, the microbe is intended for use in oil cleanups.

Physicist LUIS WALTER ALVAREZ develops the theory that dinosaurs became extinct because of the impact of a large meteorite or comet on Earth.

Researcher Martin Cline and coworkers transfer a functioning gene from one mouse to another.

1981 The first space shuttle, *Columbia*, manned by astronauts John W. Young and Robert L. Crippen successfully demonstrates the Space Transportation System (STS-1). The first manned reusable spacecraft, *Columbia* used both liquid- and solid-propellant rocket engines. Two years later, Sally Ride will become the country's first female astronaut in space aboard the *Challenger* (STS-7). The space shuttle *Challenger* (STS-8), also launched in 1983, will carry Guion S. Bluford, the first black American astronaut.

THE FEDERAL GOVERNMENT AND HEALTH CARE

Beginning in 1964 with the passage of Medicare, the U.S. government began to assume direct responsibility for the health care of Americans ages sixty-five and older. The next year Medicaid was instituted to provide medical aid to the poor. These programs, as well as veterans hospitals, now cover millions of Americans.

But these were not the first U.S. government programs to address the health and medical needs of America's citizens. In 1798, partly to encourage young men to join the merchant marine despite risks encountered in the Atlantic from warring Britain and France, Congress authorized the establishment of marine hospitals. From this beginning grew the U.S. Public Health Service, which today collects vital statistics on the health of Americans, manages health services for Indians and Alaska natives, and oversees the National Library of Medicine and the Food and Drug Administration.

Government responsibility for the purity of food and drugs manufactured and sold in the United States stems partly from the outrage following Upton Sinclair's *The Jungle* (1906), which exposed practices in the Chicago stockyards. The Pure Food and Drug Act and the Meat Inspection Act, both passed that same year, forbade adulteration and enforced sanitary regulations in the meatpacking industry. Today the Food and Drug Administration conducts research and develops standards with regard to food, drugs, and cosmetics.

Other federal units include the Centers for Disease Control, which administers programs for the prevention of communicable diseases, and the National Institutes of Health, which conducts and supports biomedical research into the causes, prevention, and cure of diseases. In fact, the federal government, through its programs supporting research, regulating drugs, promoting maternal and child welfare services, giving grants for the construction of hospitals and research facilities, and underwriting some costs of training for doctors, nurses, and other medical personnel, has a role in all health-care policies and issues with a public dimension.

SCIENCE & MEDICINE

The Hubble Space Telescope is named after astronomer Edwin Hubble, pictured here with the Schmidt telescope in 1949. Hubble is best known for confirming that the universe is expanding.

1982 The first total replacement of a human heart with an artificial one is performed at the Utah Medical Center in Salt Lake City, by surgeon William DeVries.

1983 Andrew W. Murray and Jack W. Szostak create the first artificial chromosome using yeast.

1984 American and French researchers isolate the first AIDS-inducing viruses.

A surgery team performs the first successful operation on a fetus.

1985 Construction begins in Hawaii on the world's largest telescope, the Keck, whose mirror will have a diameter of 33 feet (10 m).

1986 The space shuttle *Challenger* (STS-51L) explodes shortly after take-off from Kennedy Space Center, killing all seven astronauts onboard. A defining moment for Americans, as millions watched it on television, the *Challenger* disaster led to a comprehensive review of the space program.

The FDA-approved hepatitis B vaccine is the first accepted genetically engineered vaccine.

1987 AZT, a drug designed for the treatment of AIDS victims, is approved by the FDA.

The FDA approves Lovastatin, a drug that lowers the cholesterol level.

The National Aeronautics and Space Administration determines that the continents are drifting in patterns predicted by the theory of plate tectonics.

The first American tests of genetically engineered tobacco and tomato crops begin.

1988 JAMES WATSON founds the Human Genome Project to create a gene map illustrating the chemical composition, location, and function of all human genes. It will be completed in 2000.

A patent is issued to Harvard Medical School for a genetically engineered mouse. This is the first patent issued for a vertebrate.

1990 The Hubble Space Telescope goes into orbit. Equipped with cameras, spectographs, and a photometer, it allows scientists to see much clearer images of the universe than any telescope on the ground.

National Institutes of Health researchers put a foreign gene into a human for the first time.

1992 Astrophysicist George Smoot supports the big bang theory of the creation of the universe; using microwave and satellite technology, he has located the exact places where galaxies began to form.

1993 The Clinton administration unveils a plan to reform medical care in the United States by introducing "managed competition" among insurers, but it is defeated by vigorous opposition from many sides.

1994 Data collected by the repaired Hubble Space Telescope leads astronomers to question the age, size, and origin of the universe.

A team of U.S. scientists reports it has isolated and cloned a gene in mice that causes obesity when it malfunctions; this mouse gene has a counterpart in humans.

1995 President Clinton authorizes Food and Drug Administration regulations intended to curb tobacco use by teenagers.

American astronaut Norman Thagard boards the Russian space station *Mir*, in space since 1986.

1996 The National Aeronautics and Space Administration reports that a meteorite from Mars reveals signs of ancient microscopic life.

1997 President Clinton bans the use of federal money for human cloning endeavors after Scottish scientists create Dolly, the first cloned sheep.

The unmanned *Mars Pathfinder* lands softly on the Red Planet; a roving robotic explorer gathers data and transmits startling photographs of the Martian landscape.

Deaths from AIDS in the United States decline by 47 percent from 1996, but new HIV infections continue to increase by approximately 40,000 annually.

1998 More than fifty mice are cloned from adult cells at the University of Hawaii.

Viagra, the first pill for male impotence, is introduced.

2000 Two research teams, one government-funded and the other private, announce the completion of efforts to decode the sequence of chemical letters in the human genome.

2001 Several confirmed cases of anthrax, a potentially fatal bacterial disease, and the discovery of infectious spores in powder mailed to government officials, media offices, and other locations raise fears of widespread biological terrorism. As law enforcement officials investigate the source, public health agencies work to refine diagnostic procedures, organize testing and vaccination, and educate medical practitioners.

The life expectancy of Americans in 1876 was about forty. In the year 2000 it was about seventy-seven.

"The cloning of humans is on most of the lists of things to worry about from Science, along with behavior control, genetic engineering, transplanted heads, computer poetry, and the unrestricted growth of plastic flowers."
—LEWIS THOMAS

SCIENCE & MEDICINE

2002 Scientists in Texas clone the first cat.

2003 After a sixteen-day research mission orbiting Earth, the space shuttle *Columbia* breaks up forty miles (64 km) from its landing site. The crew of seven astronauts, including Ilan Ramon, the first Israeli in space, perish.

2003 Allegations surface that Chinese officials are covering up the outbreak of an extremely contagious, pneumonia-like disease. By the end of May, the virus, Sever Acute Respiratory Syndrome (SARS) kills 750 people and infects over 8,000 in more than 15 countries. The United States takes great precautions to keep SARS from spreading as it has in China, Taiwan, and Canada.

RESEARCH AND DEVELOPMENT

Basic scientific research and the development of technologies based on that research represent a fundamental investment in the future well-being of the nation and the quality of life of its people. These are the efforts of scientists and engineers to conceive the theories, investigate the principles, and build the systems that ensure progress in national defense, space exploration, health care, the energy supply, transportation, agriculture, and basic understandings of science and medicine. In the latter decades of the twentieth century, the United States realized increases in R&D spending that were unprecedented in its history and unparalleled in the world community. The nation's total investment in R&D—from the federal government, private industry, colleges and universities, nonprofit organizations, and state government—increased *eighteenfold* from $13.7 billion in 1960 to $247.0 billion in 1999. By far the greatest contribution has come from the private sector, whose R&D spending rose from $4.5 billion to $169.3 billion over that period. As a percentage of the gross domestic product, the 2.7 percent R&D investment in the United States is higher than for any other major industrial nation (Japan, Britain, Germany, France, etc.). Moreover, reversing a trend of the Cold War era, the vast majority of U.S. R&D investment—more than 80 percent—is now used for nondefense and nonspace objectives.

TOTAL		SOURCE OF FUNDING			OBJECTIVE (%)		
YEAR	R&D	FED. GOVT.	INDUSTRY	OTHER	DEFENSE	SPACE	OTHER
1960	$13,711	$8,915	$4,516	$280	53%	3%	44%
1970	26,271	14,984	10,449	838	30	14	56
1980	63,332	30,035	30,940	2,357	24	5	71
1990	152,039	61,668	83,382	6,989	25	4	70
1999	247,000	65,853	169,312	11,835	14	3	83

Note: Figures in millions. Source: National Science Foundation.

IMPORTANT LEGISLATION AND SUPREME COURT DECISIONS AFFECTING SCIENCE AND MEDICINE, 1789–PRESENT

1789 U.S. Constitution. This founding document gives Congress the power "to promote the Progress of Science and the useful arts by securing for limited Times to Authors and Inventors the exclusive Right to their respective Writings and discoveries." In its first session (1790), Congress passed a patent law.

1906 Pure Food and Drug Act. This act defines food adulteration and forbids the manufacture, sale, or transportation of adulterated food and drugs involved in interstate commerce. A Meat Inspection Act, passed the same year, enforces sanitary regulations in the meatpacking industry.

1921 The Sheppard–Towner Act. This establishes the first federally funded health-care program, granting the states matching funds to set up prenatal and child health-care centers.

1938 Food, Drug, and Cosmetic Act. This act expands the scope of the Pure Food and Drug Act, prohibiting the misbranding of products and providing for factory inspections.

1944 Public Health Service Act. This act consolidates and revises all legislation relating to the Public Health Service.

1964 The Medicare Act. This establishes the first federally controlled health insurance program for Americans aged sixty-five or over. The next year, Congress attaches Medicaid, a national health insurance program for low-income Americans, to the Social Security Amendments.

1973 *Roe v. Wade.* The Court rules that the right to privacy protects a woman's decision whether to bear a child. State laws that make abortion a crime are overturned.

1974 The National Research Act. Congress establishes guidelines for research on humans.

1976 The Toxic Substances Control Act. This act prohibits the marketing of new chemical compounds before their impact on the environment is tested.

1980 *Diamond v. Chakrabarty.* The Court rules that manufactured biological products can be patented.

1990 *Cruzan v. Director, Missouri Department of Health.* The Court acknowledges an individual's right to die by refusing life-sustaining treatment.

1997 Food and Drug Administration Modernization Act. A series of measures to reform the FDA and reduce the amount of time required to approve prescription drugs and medical devices.
   Vacco v. Quill and *Washington v. Glucksberg.* The justices rule that states have the constitutional authority to ban assisted suicide for the terminally ill.

AMERICAN NOBEL PRIZES IN THE SCIENCES

CHEMISTRY

1914 Theodore Richards
1932 Irving Langmuir
1934 Harold Urey
1946 James Sumner
     John Northrop
     Wendell Stanley
1949 William Giauque
1951 Edwin McMillan
     Glenn Seaborg
1954 Linus Pauling
1955 Vincent du Vigneaud
1960 Willard Libby
1961 Melvin Calvin
1965 Robert Woodward
1966 Robert Mulliken
1968 Lars Onsager
1972 Christian Anfinsen
     Stanford Moore
     William Stein
1974 Paul Flory
1976 William Lipscomb
1979 Herbert Brown
1980 Paul Berg
     Walter Gilbert
     Roald Hoffmann
1983 Henry Taube
1984 Robert Merrifield
1985 Herbert Hauptman
     Jerome Karle
1986 Dudley Herschbach
     Yuan Lee
1987 Donald Cram
     Charles Pedersen
1989 Sidney Altman
     Thomas Cech
1990 Elias James Corey
1992 Rudolph A. Marcus
1993 Kary B. Mullis
1994 George A. Olah
1995 F. Sherwood Rowland
     Mario Molina
1996 Richard E. Smalley
     Robert F. Curl Jr.
1997 Paul D. Boyer

1998 Walter Kohn
     John A. Pople
1999 Ahmed H. Zewail
2000 Alan J. Heeger
     Alan G. MacDiarmid
2001 William S. Knowles
     K. Barry Sharpless
2002 John B. Fenn

PHYSICS

1907 Albert Michelson
1923 Robert Millikan
1927 Arthur Compton
1937 Clinton Davisson
1939 Ernest Lawrence
1943 Otto Stern
1944 Isidor Rabi
1946 Percy Bridgman
     Felix Bloch
     Edward Purcell
     Willis Lamb
     Polykarp Kusch
1956 William Shockley
     John Bardeen
     Walter Brattain
1959 Emilio Segrè
     Owen Chamberlain
1960 Donald Glaser
1961 Robert Hofstadter
1963 Eugene Wigner
     Maria Goeppert-Mayer
1964 Charles Townes
1965 Julian Schwinger
     Richard Feynman
1967 Hans Bethe
1968 Luis W. Alvarez
1969 Murray Gell-Mann
1972 John Bardeen
     Leon Cooper
     Robert Schrieffer
1973 Leo Esaki
     Ivar Giaever
1975 James Rainwater
1976 Burton Richter
     Samuel Ting

1977 Philip Anderson
     John Van Vleck
1978 Arno Penzias
     Robert Wilson
1979 Sheldon Glashow
     Steven Weinberg
1980 James Cronin
     Val Fitch
1981 Nicolaas Bloembergen
     Arthur Schawlow
1982 Kenneth Wilson
1983 Subrahmanyan
     Chandrasekhar
     William Fowler
1988 Leon Lederman
     Melvin Schwartz
1989 Hans Dehmelt
     Norman Ramsey
1990 Jerome Friedman
     Henry Kendall
1993 Joseph H. Taylor Jr.
     Russell A. Hulse
1995 Martin L. Perl
     Frederick Reines
1996 David M. Lee
     Robert C. Richardson
     Douglas S. Osheroff
1997 Steven Chu
     William D. Phillips
1998 Robert B. Laughlin
     Horst L. Störmer
     Daniel C. Tsui
2000 Jack S. Kilby
     Herbert Kroemer
2001 Eric A. Cornell
     Carl E. Wieman
2003 Raymond Davis Jr.
     Riccardo Giacconi

PHYSIOLOGY OR MEDICINE

1933 Thomas Morgan
1934 George Whipple
     George Minot
     William Murphy
1943 Edward Doisy

1944	Joseph Erlanger	
	Herbert Gasser	
1946	Hermann Muller	
1947	Carl Cori	
	Gerty Cori	
1950	Edward Kendall	
	Philip Hench	
1952	Selman Waksman	
1953	Fritz Lipmann	
1954	John Enders	
	Thomas Weller	
	Frederick Robbins	
1956	André Cournand	
	Dickinson Richards	
1958	George Beadle	
	Edward Tatum	
	Joshua Lederberg	
1959	Severo Ochoa	
	Arthur Kornberg	
1961	Georg von Békésy	
1962	James Watson	
1964	Konrad Bloch	
1966	Peyton Rous	
	Charles Huggins	
	Haldan Hartline	
	George Wald	
1968	Robert Holley	
	Har Khorana	
	Marshall Nirenberg	
1969	Max Delbrück	
	Alfred Hershey	
	Salvador Luria	
1971	Earl Sutherland Jr.	
1972	Gerald Edelman	
	Rodney Porter	
1974	George Palade	
1975	David Baltimore	
	Renato Dulbecco	
	Howard Temin	
1976	Baruch Blumberg	
	Carleton Gajdusek	
	Roger Guillemin	
	Andrew Schally	
	Rosalyn Yalow	
1978	Werner Arber	
	Daniel Nathans	
	Hamilton Smith	
1979	Allan Cormack	
1980	Baruj Benacerraf	
	George Snell	
1981	Roger Sperry	
	David Hubel	
1983	Barbara McClintock	
1985	Michael Brown	
	Joseph Goldstein	
1986	Stanley Cohen	
	Rita Levi-Montalcini	
1987	Susumu Tonegawa	
1988	Gertrude Elion	
	George Hitchings	
	J. Michael Bishop	
	Harold Varmus	
1990	Joseph E. Murray	
	E. Donnall Thomas	
1992	Edmond H. Fischer	
	Edwin G. Krebs	
1993	Phillip A. Sharp	
1994	Alfred G. Gilman	
	Martin Rodbell	
1995	Edward B. Lewis	
	Eric F. Wieschaus	
1997	Stanley B. Prusiner	
1998	Robert F. Furchgott	
	Louis J. Ignarro	
	Ferid Murad	
2000	Paul Greengard	
	Eric Kandel	
2001	Leland H. Hartwell	
2002	H. Robert Horvitz	

NOTABLE FIGURES IN SCIENCE AND MEDICINE

Agassiz, Jean Louis (1807–1873). Agassiz was professor of natural history at Harvard between 1847 and 1873. In 1859, his collections formed the basis for the Harvard Museum of Comparative Zoology.

Alvarez, Luis Walter (1911–1988). A physicist, Alvarez led the atomic-bomb project team at Los Alamos, New Mexico. He also won the 1968 Nobel Prize in physics for employing bubble chambers to find subatomic particles. With his son Walter, Alvarez expounded the theory that some 65 million years ago a large meteorite or comet hit the Earth, with its impact causing the extinction of dinosaurs and other species.

Audubon, John James (1785–1851). Ornithologist Audubon made the first American bird–banding experiments, starting in 1804. His drawings of birds, based on firsthand observation, appeared in his *Birds of America*, which was published in parts between 1827 and 1838.

Baekeland, Leo (1863–1944). In 1909, Baekeland invented Bakelite, the first thermosetting plastic. From 1893 to 1899, he successfully worked on producing the first commercial photographic paper.

Barton, Clara (1821–1912). Barton, a nurse, solicited and distributed supplies during the Civil War and aided the wounded on the battlefield. Between 1870 and 1871, she helped the International Red Cross in Europe during the Franco-Prussian War. After establishing the American Red Cross in 1881, Barton served as its first president until 1904.

Bartram, John (1699–1777). A botanist, Bartram created the first botanical garden in America at his home

SCIENCE & MEDICINE

NOTABLE FIGURES, *cont.*

along the Schuylkill River near Philadelphia. He journeyed throughout the Alleghenies and Catskills, and as far south as the Carolinas and Florida, in search of new plants, often accompanied by his son William, who published Travels in 1791. John Bartram was also a keen observer of Indian life.

Blackwell, Elizabeth (1821–1910). Blackwell became the first American woman doctor after she graduated from New York State's Medical College in 1849. In 1853, she cofounded a private dispensary in New York, which later became the New York Infirmary for Poor Women and Children. This was later expanded to include the Women's Medical College to train doctors, the first such institution. In 1869, Blackwell moved to England, where she helped found the London School of Medicine for Women.

Burbank, Luther (1849–1926). A horticulturist, Burbank developed more than 800 new varieties of plants and flowers, including superior varieties of lilies, roses, corn, squash, potatoes, and the Shasta daisy.

Burroughs, William (1855–1898). Working as a bank clerk in Auburn, New York, and St. Louis, Missouri, prompted Burroughs to develop a device that would correctly add numbers and help accountants and bookkeepers. He invented the recording adding machine in 1888. He improved the machine in 1893, and, by the time of his death, more than 1,000 adding machines had been sold.

Cannon, Annie (1863–1941). A staff member at the Harvard College Observatory between 1896 and 1940, Cannon discovered 300 variable stars and 5 novae and catalogued more than 225,000 stellar spectra for the Henry Draper Catalogue, published from 1918 to 1924.

Carothers, Wallace (1896–1937). Carothers was the director of organic chemical research for the Du Pont Company from 1928 until his death. While there, he invented nylon, but the patent was issued to Du Pont after his death in 1937. Carothers also helped to develop the first commercially successful synthetic rubber.

Carrier, Willis (1876–1950). Only one year after graduating from Cornell University, Carrier had installed his first air-conditioning unit in Brooklyn. Throughout his career, he invented air-conditioning, the dehumidifier, and centrifugal refrigeration. Along with several other engineers, he founded the Carrier Engineering Corporation in 1915.

Carson, Rachel (1907–1964). Carson, a biologist, wrote three popular books of meticulous observation of sea life: *Under the Sea Wind* (1941), *The Sea Around Us* (1951), and *The Edge of the Sea* (1954). But her most famous book, generally acknowledged to have ushered in the modern environmental revolution, is *Silent Spring* (1962), an attack on the use of insecticides.

Carver, George Washington (1864–1943). Carver, an agricultural chemist, produced more than 300 derivatives from peanuts and 118 from sweet potatoes. The son of slaves, he encouraged southern farmers to plant soil-enriching crops like soybeans and peanuts rather than soil-destroying crops like cotton.

Colt, Samuel (1814–1862). Colt invented the revolver, for which he received a patent in 1836. His pistol became so popular that the name Colt is synonymous with the revolver (see p. 76).

Coolidge, William (1873–1975). A physical chemist, Coolidge did his research for General Electric beginning in 1905. In 1910, he invented the modern tungsten-filament electric light. He also invented a new tube (called the Coolidge tube) for X-ray production (1913), portable X-ray units, high-powered X rays for treating cancer, and, with Irving Langmuir, the first submarine-detecting device.

Cushing, Harvey (1869–1939). As a neurosurgeon, Cushing introduced major advances in diagnostic and surgical technique. He was also a distinguished teacher and author of medical works.

DeBakey, Michael (1908–). As head of surgery at Houston's Baylor College of Medicine, DeBakey performed the first successful carotid endarterectomy in 1953. He developed an "assisting" heart and did early work on heart transplants.

Delbrück, Max (1906–1981). While at Vanderbilt University in Tennessee and California Institute of Technology, German-born biologist Delbrück did ground breaking research on bacteriophages that furthered knowledge about DNA. Along with SALVADOR LURIA and Alfred Hershey, he was awarded the 1969 Nobel Prize for physiology or medicine.

Dix, Dorothea (1802–1887). A social reformer, Dix exposed the cruelty of incarcerating the insane and mentally ill in county jails and state penitentiaries, which she visited throughout Massachusetts before presenting her famous report to the Massachusetts legislature in 1842. Her work led to the founding of state hospitals for the insane in many states. During the Civil War, she served as superintendent of women nurses for the Union forces.

Doisy, Edward (1893–1986). A biochemist, Doisy isolated the female sex hormones estrone (1929) and estradiol (1936). He also determined the chemical nature of vitamin K (1939) and isolated K2, a variant form. He shared the 1943 Nobel Prize in physiology or medicine with Henrik Dam.

Draper, Charles (1901–1987). An aeronautical engineer, Draper is known as the father of inertial guidance. He invented gyroscope-stabilized gunsights, which helped antiaircraft guns and aerial bombs hit their targets during World War II and subsequent wars. Draper also developed the guidance technology for marine and air navigation for guided missiles.

Edison, Thomas Alva (1847–1931). Edison patented more than a thousand inventions. Some of the most significant were the incandescent electric lamp, the phonograph, the electric valve, the alkaline storage battery, and an improved movie projector. He also developed the world's first central electric light-power station. His Edison General Electric Company became the General Electric Company in 1892.

Einstein, Albert (1879–1955). In 1939, a year before he became an American citizen, German-born Einstein revolutionized the study of physics when he formulated the theory of relativity. Fleeing Nazi Germany, he settled in the United States and was among a group of distinguished scientists who urged development of the atomic bomb. Horrified by the two bombs dropped on the Japanese cities of Hiroshima and Nagasaki in 1945, Einstein later became a leading figure in the movement to control nuclear weapons. He won the 1921 Nobel Prize in physics for his discovery of the law of the photoelectric effect.

Enders, John (1897–1985). A virologist, Enders helped discover a measles vaccine. He shared the 1954 Nobel Prize for physiology or medicine with Frederick Robbins and T. H. Weller for their work cultivating polio viruses in tissue culture.

Evans, Herbert (1882–1971). Anatomist Evans, with Oliver and Gladys Emerson, isolated vitamin E in 1935.

Fermi, Enrico (1901–1954). Italian-born physicist Fermi is known as one of the founders of the nuclear age. He won the 1938 Nobel Prize for physics for his discovery of neutron-induced nuclear reactions (1934–1937), and after traveling to Stockholm to receive the prize, he continued to the United States because his wife was Jewish and they sought to escape Fascist Italy. In 1942, he directed the first controlled nuclear chain reaction. Fermi also worked on the atomic-bomb project at Los Alamos, New Mexico. The element fermium is named after him, and the prestigious Fermi Award for physics is given in his honor.

Franklin, Benjamin (1706–1790). Inventor, scientist, statesman, and philosopher, Franklin founded the Junto (1727), a discussion club that became the American Philosophical Society (1743). Among his inventions were the Franklin stove, bifocal glasses, and the lightning rod. Around 1746, he began experimenting with electricity. His famous kite experiment occurred in 1752.

Gamow, George (1904–1968). Physicist Gamow devised the theory of radioactive decay in 1928. Born in Russia, Gamow came to the United States in 1934, where he worked with EDWARD TELLER on theories of beta decay. In 1948, he proposed the big bang theory of the origin of the universe.

Gatling, Richard (1818–1903). The son of an inventor, Gatling gained a reputation for his inventions as a young man. After studying medicine, he invented a rapid-fire gun, which he patented in 1862; it was the precursor of the modern machine gun.

Gibbs, Josiah Willard (1839–1903). Gibbs's work while he was a professor of mathematical physics at Yale became the basis for the science of quantum mechanics.

Gorgas, William (1854–1920). An army officer and doctor, Gorgas was chief sanitary officer in Cuba, from 1898 to 1902. By using measures to destroy mosquitos, he effected the virtual end to yellow fever in Havana. As chief sanitary officer of the Panama Canal Commission between 1904 and 1913, he applied the same tactics, thereby making the canal's completion possible.

Hubble, Edwin (1889–1953). Astronomer Hubble showed that some nebulae are independent galaxies, discovered the "red shift" of light, and proved that all galaxies beyond the Milky Way are receding from ours and therefore the universe is expanding.

NOTABLE FIGURES, *cont.*

James, William (1842–1910). The brother of writer Henry James, William James was a psychologist and a philosopher. His classic book *The Principles of Psychology* (1980), examines the relationship among thought, experience, and action.

Kendall, Edward (1886–1972). Kendall headed the biochemistry section of Minnesota's Mayo Clinic, where he isolated the steroid hormone cortisone and, with Philip Hench, used it successfully to treat rheumatoid arthritis (1948). Kendall and Hench shared the 1950 Nobel Prize for physiology or medicine for their work with Switzerland's Tadeus Reichstein.

Landsteiner, Karl (1868–1943). An Austrian-born immunologist and pathologist, Landsteiner discovered the A, B, and O human blood types (1901), created the ABO system of blood typing, discovered the M and N blood groups (1927), and, with Alexander Weiner, discovered the the Rhesus factor (1940). He received the 1930 Nobel Prize for physiology or medicine.

Lawrence, Ernest (1901–1958). A physicist, Lawrence invented the cyclotron, produced radioactive isotopes, and used radioactivity to investigate medical and biological problems. He taught at the University of California, and he won the 1939 Nobel Prize for physics.

Lederberg, Joshua (1925–). With George Beadle and EDWARD TATUM, Lederberg proved that sexual recombination occurs in bacteria via processes that cause the exchange of genetic material. The three geneticists shared the 1958 Nobel Prize in physiology or medicine for their work.

Levene, Phoebus (1869–1940). A chemist, Levene did pioneering work on nucleic acids. He determined the formation of nucleotides and the way they combine in chains. He also isolated the sugar ribose (1909) and discovered 2-deoxyribose (1929).

Libby, Willard (1908–1980). A chemist, Libby devised the carbon-14 dating technique of objects in the 1940s. He received the 1960 Nobel Prize for chemistry for this work.

Long, Crawford (1815–1878). Long was the first surgeon to use ether as an anesthetic, beginning in 1842.

Luria, Salvador (1912–1991). With MAX DELBRÜCK, Italian-born microbiologist Luria researched bacteriophages, creating a fluctuation test and finding evidence that spontaneous mutations cause phage-resistant bacteria.

McClintock, Barbara (1901–1992). McClintock, a geneticist studying the cells of successive generations of growing corn, discovered that genes are not permanently arranged on the chromosome but sometimes "jump," or move around, possibly changing inheritance. For years McClintock's discovery was either ignored or ridiculed by other scientists. But in 1983, she won the Nobel Prize for physiology or medicine for her research into the mechanisms of genetic inheritance.

McClung, Clarence (1870–1946). McClung explored his hypothesis that sex is determined by the chromosomes.

McMillan, Edwin (1907–1991). Physicist McMillan, with Philip Abelson, discovered neptunium, element 93, and with GLENN SEABORG and others he discovered plutonium. During World War II, McMillan helped the navy develop radar and sonar, before joining the Manhattan Project for the development of the atomic bomb at Los Alamos, New Mexico.

Mead, Margaret (1901–1978). An anthropologist, Mead lived among the peoples of the Pacific Islands to study how cultures differ and how this difference affects personality development. Her most famous book, *Coming of Age in Somoa* (1928), compares the lives of Somoan adolescents with those of their peers in Western societies.

Menninger, Karl (1893–1990). Menninger was one of the first American doctors to be psychoanalytically trained. In Topeka, Kansas, he founded a psychiatric clinic (1920), and a foundation (1941), where psychiatrists received psychiatric training.

Michelson, Albert (1852–1931). A German-born physicist, Michelson devised a way of accurately measuring the speed at which light travels; invented an inferometer for determining distances via the length of light waves (1881); measured one meter in relation to the wavelength of cadmium light; performed an experiment (1887) with EDWARD MORLEY that, by demonstrating that the Earth has no absolute motion relative to an ether, paved the way for the theory of relativity. Michelson won the 1907 Nobel Prize for physics.

Millikan, Robert A. (1868–1953). A physicist, Millikan measured the electron's charge and did important work on the photoelectric effect. He received the 1923 Nobel Prize for physics.

Morgan, Thomas Hunt (1866–1945). Beginning in 1909, Morgan studied heredity in *Drosophila* fruit flies. He established that genes exist for specific traits located at specific sites on chromosomes. For this discovery, he was awarded the 1933 Nobel Prize for physiology or medicine.

Morley, Edward (1838–1923). A chemist and physicist, Morley is most known for his work with ALBERT MICHELSON on the ether-drift experiment (1887), which led to EINSTEIN's theory of relativity.

Muller, Hermann (1890–1967). A geneticist, Muller won the 1946 Nobel Prize for physiology or medicine for his work on the artificial transmutation of genes, using X rays, produced first in 1926.

Nieuwland, Julius (1878–1936). A chemist and Catholic priest, Nieuwland did pioneering work in the synthesizing of rubber.

Oppenheimer, J. Robert (1904–1967). Oppenheimer headed the team of scientists working on the Manhattan Project in Los Alamos, New Mexico, to develop the atomic bomb. Oppenheimer also was the director of the Institute for Advanced Study at Princeton University. He strongly opposed the development of the hydrogen bomb.

Pauling, Linus (1901–1994). A chemist, Pauling was one of the first to apply the quantum theory to calculating molecular structures. He devised the idea of resonance to explain covalent bonds in certain organic compounds. He also determined the three-dimensional structures of numerous amino acids, proteins, and antitoxins. For his work he won the 1954 Nobel Prize for chemistry. He also was awarded the 1962 Nobel Peace Prize for his work in favor of nuclear disarmament.

Rabi, Isidor (1898–1988). Born in Austria, Rabi came to the United States as a young boy and was educated at Cornell and Columbia Universities before spending two years in Europe working with such renowned scientists as Niels Bohr, Werner Heisenberg, Otto Stern, and Wolfgang Pauli. In 1937, Rabi invented a method for registering the magnetic properties of atomic nuclei. This discovery led to the laser, maser, atomic clock, and nuclear-resonance magnetic imaging. Rabi won the 1944 Nobel Prize for physics.

Reed, Walter (1851–1902). Reed, a surgeon, headed the U.S. Army commission sent to Cuba in 1900 to find the cause and transmission mode of yellow fever. The commission's 1901 report proved that the mosquito *Aedes aegypti* transmitted the disease. The disease was then virtually eradicated by destroying the insects. Washington, D.C.'s Walter Reed Hospital is named after him.

Rush, Benjamin (1745–1813). Rush, a physician, founded the first free dispensary in the United States (1786) and wrote the first American chemistry textbook (1770) and the first psychiatric treatise in the United States (1812).

Sabin, Albert (1906–1993). Born in Bialystock, Poland, Sabin came to the United States in 1921, graduated from New York University in 1928, received his medical degree from the university's medical school in 1931, and conducted much of his research at the University of Cincinatti. In the late 1950s, Sabin, a physician and medical researcher, developed an attenuated-virus oral polio vaccine.

Sabin, Florence (1871–1953). Sabin focused on human embryology, contributing to scientific knowledge of the histology of the brain and the development of the lymphatic system. Sabin was the first female professor at Johns Hopkins Medical School, the first female president of the American Association of Anatomists, and the first woman elected to be a member of the National Academy of Science.

Sabine, Wallace (1868–1919). Sabine created the science of architectural acoustics. He also founded and was the dean of Harvard's Graduate School of Applied Science (1906–1915). In his honor, the unit of sound-absorbing power is called the sabin.

Salk, Jonas (1914–1995). A physician and micro-biologist, Salk was known for his development, in 1952, of the Salk vaccine against polio.

Sanger, Margaret (1883–1966). As a public health nurse, Sanger clearly saw the need for family limitation, especially in the face of poverty and the frequent death of women from self-induced abortions. She advocated birth control, a term she coined, and opened the first birth control clinic in the United States. In 1921, she founded the Birth Control League, now Planned Parenthood. By the 1930s, her once scandalous notions had gained wide public acceptance.

NOTABLE FIGURES, *cont.*

Seaborg, Glenn (1912–1999). Seaborg codiscovered the elements americium, berkelium, californium, curium, einsteinium, fermium, mendelevium, nobelium, and plutonium. He shared the 1951 Nobel Prize in chemistry with EDWIN MCMILLAN. During World War II he worked on the development of the atomic bomb.

Segrè, Emilio (1905–1989). Segrè worked with ENRICO FERMI on neutron experiments that helped establish nuclear physics. With Fermi, he detected slow neutrons (1935). He also developed technetium, the first artificially made element. In 1940, he discovered astatine and plutonium with GLENN SEABORG (1941). He shared with Owen Chamberlain the 1959 Nobel Prize for their discovery of antiproton.

Silliman, Benjamin (1779–1864). Professor of chemistry and natural history at Yale for half a century, Silliman studied petroleum products and made discoveries regarding carbon, hydrofluoric acid, and bromine, but his greatest contributions were as a teacher and popular lecturer on scientific subjects. He founded the *American Journal of Science and Arts* and the National Academy of Sciences and was the first president of the Association of American Geologists, precursor to the American Association for the Advancement of Science.

Steinmetz, Charles (1865–1923). An electrical engineer, Steinmetz patented more than 200 improvements in electrical apparatuses. He derived the law of hysteresis and worked on the theory and calculation of alternating currents.

Sturtevant, Alfred (1891–1970). Sturtevant was the first scientist to map genes on chromosomes (1913).

Sutton, Walter (1877–1916). A geneticist, Sutton demonstrated that chromosomes carry units of inheritance and exist in distinct pairs (1902–1903). His work formed the basis for the chromosomal theory of heredity.

Tatum, Edward (1909–1975). With George Beadle and JOSHUA LEDERBERG, Tatum discovered that genes transmit hereditary characters by controlling specific chemical reactions. Along with his coresearchers, he received the 1958 Nobel Prize for physiology or medicine.

Teller, Edward (1908–1993). Teller, a Hungarian-born physicist, worked on the atomic bomb during World War II. He was one of the key figures in the development of the hydrogen bomb (1952).

Temin, Howard (1934–1994). Temin, an oncologist, proved that a cancerous sarcoma virus translates its RNA into DNA, which then reinstructs the reproductive activity of the cell, changing it to a cancer cell. He also identified reverse transcriptase as the viral enzyme that synthesizes the DNA containing the information in viral RNA. Temin's discovery, also independently made by David Baltimore, helped to identify the AIDS virus and aided genetic engineering. Temin shared the 1975 Nobel Prize for physiology or medicine with Renato Dulbecco and Baltimore.

Urey, Harold (1893–1981). For his discovery of deuterium, or heavy water, in 1931, chemist Urey was awarded the 1934 Noble Prize for chemistry. He also worked on the development of the atomic bomb.

Waksman, Selman (1888–1973). In 1944, Waksman, a Russian-born biochemist, discovered the antibiotic streptomycin, which became widely used in the treatment of tuberculosis. For this discovery he won the 1952 Nobel Prize for physiology or medicine.

Watson, James (1928–). While a graduate student at England's Cambridge University in 1953, Watson, a biologist, codiscovered with Francis Crick the molecular structure of deoxyribonucleic acid (DNA). For this discovery they received the 1962 Nobel Prize in physiology or medicine.

CHAPTER 12

TRANSPORTATION AND COMMUNICATION

HIGHLIGHTS

Timeline of Transportation and Communication

THROUGHOUT THE NATION'S HISTORY, the American way of life has been shaped by a never-ending revolution in the fields of transportation and communication. Pamphlets and broadsides distributed throughout the colonies helped spur the spirit of revolution. During western expansion, technologies that connected far-flung people and communities stimulated commercial enterprise and helped establish a national identity. By boat, stagecoach, railroad, the automobile, and modern aviation, the American people have been on the move for more than two centuries, connected by the mail, telegraph, telephone, and modern digital technologies. From the printing press to movies, television, and the Internet, the communications media have had a profound effect on the cultural, political, and intellectual life of the nation. At the forefront of satellite technology, space exploration, and global digital networking, the United States has pushed the boundaries of its ongoing revolution to every corner of the planet and beyond.

CANALS, STEAMBOATS, AND BIRTH OF THE PRESS

1639 At Harvard College in Cambridge, Massachusetts, the first colonial printing press is used.

1685 Maps of the Middle English colonies and Virginia are printed.

1690 The first newspaper in America, the Boston news sheet, *Publick Occurrences Both Foreign and Domestic,* appears just once

1693 William Bradford sets up a printing press in New York City.

1704 The *Boston News-Letter* becomes the first regularly published American newspaper.

1730 BENJAMIN FRANKLIN buys the *Pennsylvania Gazette* from Samuel Keimer.

1732 BENJAMIN FRANKLIN publishes the *Philadelphia Zeitung*, the first foreign-language newspaper in the English colonies.

1734 New York printer John Peter Zenger is arrested for libel; the charges against him are based on his legal responsibility for articles written mostly by others but appearing in his newspaper, the *New York Weekly Journal*.

1735 John Peter Zenger is acquitted of libel; the verdict helps establish freedom of the press in America.

1741 The first two magazines published in the colonies are the *American Magazine* and *Benjamin Franklin's General Magazine*, both published in Philadelphia. These two forerunners of later periodicals are regional and expensive.

1756 A major stagecoach line operates between Philadelphia and New York City.

1764 In Hartford the *Connecticut Courant*, a weekly, begins publication.

1773 Regular mounted mail service is established between Boston and New York.

1784 Abel Buell engraves and prints the first map of the United States; it shows the boundaries established by the Treaty of Paris (1783), which formally recognized the new nation.

1785 Regular stagecoach routes between New York, Boston, and Philadelphia are established.

1787 Having obtained from New Jersey, Pennsylvania, New York, Delaware, and Virginia exclusive rights to build and operate steamboats on their waterways, inventor John Fitch launches the first American steamboat on the Delaware River.

James Rumsey's jet-propelled steamboat, demonstrated on the Potomac in Maryland, shoots a stream of water through its stern.

"The most truthful part of a newspaper is the advertisements."
—THOMAS JEFFERSON

TRANSPORTATION

THE TRIAL OF JOHN PETER ZENGER

John Peter Zenger was a successful printer in New York City. In 1733, he began printing the *New York Weekly Journal*, which attacked the politics of another paper, the government-controlled *New York Gazette*. Although Zenger himself did not write the articles attacking the administration of Governor William Cosby, he was legally responsible for them and was arrested on libel charges in 1734. In his famous trial that took place in 1735, Zenger was defended by Andrew Hamilton of Philadelphia, who sought to establish truth as a defense in libel cases. Hamilton's arguments proved persuasive, and Zenger was acquitted. The Zenger case laid the foundation for freedom of the press in America.

In 1810, taking the 35-mile (57-km) trip from Boston to Plymouth via stagecoach cost $2.50. The 53-mile (85-km) trek from Boston to Sandwich, Massachusetts was $3.63.

1789 The first American road map is published by Christopher Colles.

1792 The Essex Merrimac Bridge, a covered timber truss construction, is built in Massachusetts by Timothy Palmer.

Work is begun on South Carolina's Santee Canal, to be completed in 1800.

1794 Construction begins on Massachusetts Middlesex Canal, which is completed in 1803.

1795 ROBERT FULTON patents the first power shovel, to be used in digging canals.

A 62-mile (100-km) stretch of road is opened for traffic between Philadelphia and Lancaster, Pennsylvania, heralding a new interest in planning and building roads. This first engineered turnpike is a toll road.

1796 James Finley builds the first American suspension bridge, across Jacob's Creek in Westmoreland, Pennsylvania.

Congress approves the construction of a road from present-day Wheeling, West Virginia, to present-day Maysville, Kentucky. Called Zane's Trace, it will become one of the routes most traveled by settlers going west.

1800 The *Nautilus*, a hand-operated submarine, is invented by ROBERT FULTON, but he fails to interest any government in it.

Semaphore, or visual signaling, communications are established on "telegraph hills" between Martha's Vineyard, Massachusetts, and Boston.

1801 The *New York Evening Post*, founded by Alexander Hamilton, begins publication.

1802 A screw-driven steamboat is invented by JOHN STEVENS. This is the first powered screw applied to ship propulsion.

1804 JOHN STEVENS crosses New York's Hudson River in a twin-screw steamboat.

1807 ROBERT FULTON's 150-long steamboat, the *Clermont*, steams from Albany to New York City and back on the Hudson River. Although not the first steamboat, the *Clermont* is the first one built economically enough to make this mode of transportation commercially viable.

1808 JOHN STEVENS invents the *Phoenix*, a steamboat powered by a low-pressure engine.

1809 The *Phoenix* becomes the world's first seagoing steamboat as it travels from New York to Philadelphia.

1811 The SS *New Orleans*, the first steamboat traveling down the Mississippi River, leaves Pittsburgh and reaches New Orleans. Subsequently, it begins a regular run between New Orleans and Natchez, Mississippi.

One popular form of overland travel for settlers is the Contestoga wagon; about 60 feet (18 m) long with a curved boatlike bottom to keep goods from shifting and broad wheels to keep from getting stuck in the mud, it is drawn by four to six horses. Decorated with bells that can be used to signal other wagons, the wagons are topped with hempen, homespun, or canvas coverings.

The *Weekly Register*, an early attempt at a news magazine, begins publication in Baltimore, Maryland. Founded by Hezekiah Niles, it will publish for four decades.

1814 The USS *Fulton*, the first steam warship, is launched by ROBERT FULTON.

1815 The *North American Review* begins publication in Boston, originally highlighting British culture and literature. It will move to New York City in the late 1870s and eventually lose the British flavor.

The National or Cumberland Road, which is to become a widely used route for westward-bound settlers, is begun at Cumberland, Maryland (see p. 71).

1817 Construction on the Erie Canal begins. This project has been promoted chiefly by New York governor DE WITT CLINTON to connect New York City with the Great Lakes via the Hudson River and a 364-mile (586-km) canal from Albany to Buffalo. Building the 40-foot-wide, 4-foot-deep canal with 83 locks and more than 300 bridges will be a great technological challenge.

1818 The Black Ball Line establishes the first regularly scheduled clipper ship service from New York to Liverpool, England. These sailing ships carry packets of mail along with cargo and passengers. Known for their speed and grace, clipper ships became the preferred vessel for commerce until being replaced by the steamship by the 1870s and 1880s. The average transatlantic voyage takes thirty days.

1820 Daniel Treadwell invents the horse-powered printing press.

1821 The *Saturday Evening Post* is first published as a four-page newspaper with no illustrations. Restructured in 1839 and converted to a journal in 1898, the *Post* boasted a circulation of 90,000 by 1855 and 2 million by 1908.

TRANSPORTATION

1822 The first steamboat voyage from New York to New Orleans is completed by the SS *Robert Fulton*.

1823 The first macadam, or paved, road opens in Maryland. Known as the Boonsborough Turnpike Road, it links the towns of Hagerstown and Boonsboro.

1825 The Erie Canal is completed in only eight years; the first boat to use the canal, the *Seneca Chief*, is launched at Buffalo and speeds at 4 miles (6 km) per hour toward New York City. The canal will be a phenomenal success, providing an easy passage for westbound settlers and for commercial goods moving from the East to the Ohio and Mississippi Valleys. Soon nearly every state will build canals, with most promoting east-west links.

JOHN STEVENS builds the first American steam locomotive, the *Action*.

1826 Connecticut inventor Samuel Morey patents an internal combustion engine.

The first railroads are constructed; powered by horses, sails, or cables, they are used to transport such items as coal or granite for short distances.

1827 Isaac Adams invents the Adams press, which will become the standard in the printing industry for the next half century.

1829 The *Encyclopaedia Americana*, the first American encyclopedia, is published in Philadelphia.

The newspaper, the *Philadelphia Inquirer* starts out as the *Pennsylvania Inquirer*.

Joseph Henry builds the first electric motor.

William Burt invents an early prototype of the typewriter.

1830 The first passenger line, the Baltimore & Ohio Railroad, opens with 13 miles (21 km) of track connecting the Baltimore Harbor to what is now Ellicott City, Maryland.

Best Friend of Charleston, the first American-built commercial locomotive, is designed by Horatio Allen and run on a track in Honesdale, Pennsylvania.

Peter Cooper builds *Tom Thumb*, the first commercially viable steam locomotive, but it races against a horse and loses because of an engine breakdown.

The daily newspaper the *Boston Transcript* begins publication; it will survive until 1940.

Godey's Lady's Book, the first periodical for women, begins publication. It features light fiction, poetry, and essays and keeps women updated on current fashions.

1831 After buying a horse-powered English locomotive called the *John Bull*, Robert Stevens establishes America's first steam railway service in New Jersey. He also invents the inverted-T rail, a flanged railroad track.

1832 The *Ann McKim*, the first American sailing clipper ship, is launched in Baltimore, Maryland.

In New York City, the New York & Harlem Railroad begins operating the first streetcar in the world. Built by John Mason, the horse-drawn car runs along part of Fourth Avenue.

1833 The *New York Sun*, the city's first successful penny daily paper, is launched.

1834 Zachariah Allen invents an automatic steam-engine cutoff valve.

Thomas Davenport invents a primitive electric motor, which he uses the following year to power the first electric locomotive.

1835 In Brownsville, Pennsylvania, America's first cast-iron bridge is constructed over Dunlap Creek.

The *New York Herald*, a one-cent daily, is first printed. The newspaper, started by editor JAMES BENNETT, will pioneer in publishing financial reports, crime stories, and society news and in using the telegraph and European correspondents.

1836 The *Philadelphia Public Ledger*, a penny daily, is founded.

1837 SAMUEL MORSE patents the Morse code for use with the telegraph and demonstrates his invention.

The *Baltimore Sun*, a penny daily, begins publication.
The *New Orleans Picayune* is established.

1839 Charles Goodyear makes rubber resistant to heat and cold through the process of vulcanization.

1840 In Ohio, the *Toledo Blade* starts publication.

1841 HORACE GREELEY establishes the *New York Tribune*, a daily that becomes very influential in molding the thought of northerners before the Civil War.

1842 The *Pittsburgh Post-Gazette* begins publication.

1843 SAMUEL MORSE receives federal money to build a telegraph line between Baltimore and Washington, D.C.

1844 After construction of the first telegraph line is completed, MORSE sends the first telegraph message, "What hath God wrought!" from Washington, D.C., to Baltimore.

1845 A weekly scandal sheet, the *Police Gazette*, is founded.

Samuel Morse's telegraph, which transmits messages by electricity, and his accompanying system of dots and dashes, later known as the International Morse Code, revolutionized the spread of information. Before that, most information traveled only as fast as the person or horse carrying it.

1846 The *Pittsburgh Dispatch* and the *Boston Herald* begin publication.

1847 Industrialist Richard Hoe invents the rotary press and web press; these inventions make possible the development of mass-circulation daily newspapers.

The *Chicago Tribune* begins publication, as does the *Philadelphia Evening Bulletin*.

1848 The New York News Agency is founded; it will change its name to the Associated Press in 1856.

In the 1840s and '50s, Americans built roads by laying wood planks side by side so mud would not splash on carriages and wagons. More than 7,000 miles of plank roads were constructed over a fifteen-year period.

1849 In Minnesota Territory, the *St. Paul Pioneer* is first published.

The Pacific Railroad Company, the first charted railway west of the Mississippi, begins laying track; the first section opens in 1852.

George Corliss patents a four-valve steamship engine, a vast improvement over the one-valve model.

1850 Using stagecoaches, the first overland mail delivery west of the Missouri River begins from Independence, Missouri, to Salt Lake City, Utah.

In New York, *Harper's Monthly*, which becomes a respected journal of opinion, fiction, and essays, begins publication.

The Portland *Oregonian* is founded.

Congress makes the first federal land grants to promote railroads.

1851 The *New York Times* publishes its first issue.

1852 A passenger elevator is designed by ELISHA OTIS. The following year, Otis invents a safety device to stop a car from plunging if the cable breaks.

Work on the Baltimore & Ohio Railroad is completed to the Ohio River, and it begins operating from Baltimore to Wheeling, West Virginia. Because of the railroad, Chicago is now connected by rail to the East.

1853 The New York Central Railroad, formed by joining ten small railroads, links New York City and Buffalo, New York.

1855 At Niagara Falls, New York, a railroad suspension bridge is constructed; a year later it is crossed by a train for the first time.

Frank Leslie's Illustrated Newspaper, the most successful early illustrated periodical, is founded in New York City.

1856 The Western Union Company is founded.

A printing telegraph is patented by David Hughes.

1857 *Atlantic Monthly* magazine founded by Francis H. Underwood and Moses Dresser Phillips begins publication. It is a monthly journal featuring literature, literary criticism, and political commentary.

1858 Financier Cyrus Field builds the first undersea telegraph cable between America and Europe.

Stagecoach service with mail delivery begins between San Francisco and St. Louis, Missouri.

1859 The first passenger elevator in an American hotel is installed in New York City's Fifth Avenue Hotel.

The *Rocky Mountain News* is the first paper to be published in the soon-to-be Montana Territory.

1860s Sylvester Roper develops a steam-powered vehicle.

1860 The Pony Express begins speedy overland mail service from St. Joseph, Missouri, to Sacramento, California.

1861 There are 31,000 miles (49,900 km) of railroad track in the United States.

ELISHA OTIS patents the steam elevator, which will become the basis of the Otis elevator business.

Telegraph wires link New York to San Francisco, making immediate bicoastal communication possible.

1862 John Ericsson launches the *Monitor*, an ironclad steam warship—a wooden ship covered by metal plates and featuring a revolving turret.

Congress passes the Pacific Railroad Act, granting the Union Pacific and Central Pacific railways vast lands from Omaha, Nebraska, to Sacramento, California, on which to build the first transcontinental railroad.

1864 Steel rails are used on the Pennsylvania Railroad.

GEORGE PULLMAN builds the first comfortable railroad sleeping car. The Pullman car has a folding upper berth and extendible seat cushions to create a lower berth.

1865 William Bullock improves the rotary press, which can now cut sheets as they are printed. Both Hoe's web press and Bullock's rotary press make the circulation of daily newspapers significantly easier.

The *San Francisco Chronicle* begins as the *San Francisco Dramatic Chronicle*. The *Nation*, a liberal weekly magazine, is founded in New York City by a group of abolitionists with Edwin Godkin as the first editor.

1866 The first refrigerated railroad car in America is constructed in Detroit.

Henry House invents a twelve-horsepower steam car.

The first truly functional transatlantic cable is completed.

1867 Alfred Beach invents a pneumatic passenger subway system. To avoid the crooked politics of New York's Boss Tweed, Beach secretly constructed

1867, *cont.*

a 312-foot-long tube roughly 21 feet below Broadway. His 1870 unveiling of the tunnel was a success, but politics and the 1873 financial panic derailed his plan to extend the subway. In 1912, workers unearthed the forgotten tunnel and incorporated it into their construction of the Broadway subway line.

In New York City, the first elevated railroad is established, running from downtown Manhattan to Thirtieth Street.

1868 GEORGE WESTINGHOUSE invents railroad air brakes.
CHRISTOPHER SHOLES invents the typewriter.
The *Atlanta Constitution* begins publication.

1869 The transcontinental railroad is completed. The last, and golden, spike is planted by former California governor Leland Stanford at Promontory Summit, Utah. A telegraph operator signals the completion to a waiting nation.

Cyrus Field builds a successful telegraph cable between France and Massachusetts.

1870 The first asphalt-paved road in the United States is created in Newark, New Jersey, by Belgian chemist Edward J. DeSmedt.

1871 An improved rotary press prints both sides of a page simultaneously.

1872 Motion-picture pioneer EADWEARD MUYBRIDGE invents the zoopraxiscope, which, by reproducing moving pictures on a screen, is a forerunner of the movie projector.

In Chicago the first mail-order house, Montgomery Ward & Company, is established.
The Boston *Daily Globe* begins publication.

1873 The first penny postcards are issued.
Free mail delivery is provided in cities with a population of 20,000 or more.
St. Nicholas Magazine, a children's magazine, begins publication.
Andrew Hallidie invents cable cars to traverse San Francisco's hills.

1874 In San Francisco THOMAS EDISON develops a telegraph system enabling four messages to be sent simultaneously over one wire.

1876 Scottish American ALEXANDER GRAHAM BELL patents the telephone. The first words transmitted over the telephone wire are to his assistant: "Mr. Watson, come here. I want you." Bell's invention signals America's rise to international leadership in industrial technology.

1877 Emile Berliner invents a microphone for the telephone.

The first Bell telephone is bought.

Charles Glidden organizes the world's first telephone exchange in Lowell, Massachusetts.

The first intercity telephone communication is between Chicago and Milwaukee and between Salem, Massachusetts, and Boston. Boston has the first telephone switchboard.

In Newark, New Jersey, electrical engineer Edward Weston sets up an electric streetlight.

The *Washington Post* is founded by Stilson Hutchins as a "Democratic daily journal."

The Great Railway Strike interrupts transportation across the country. Considered the most violent labor strike at the time, the strike began with workers in West Virginia halting trains to protest wage cuts and spread throughout the country. In one altercation in Pittsburgh, property damage was vast and twenty people were left dead.

1878 Augustus Pope manufactures the first bicycles in America.

THOMAS EDISON demonstrates the phonograph. On a tinfoil-wrapped cylinder, he records "Mary Had a Little Lamb."

1879 GEORGE SELDEN applies for a patent on a gasoline motor-driven vehicle.

1880 GEORGE EASTMAN markets a process for making photographic dry plates, which do not have to be exposed and developed immediately.

THE PONY EXPRESS

In 1859, railroads delivered mail in the eastern United States and as far west as Missouri. There, wagon trains and stagecoaches took over, journeying twenty-two days across the continent. This situation improved dramatically in 1860 with the establishment of the Pony Express, which cut delivery time to California by more than half. The Pony Express rider, pouches strapped to his horse, galloped 35 to 75 miles (56 to 121 km) before passing the mail to a fresh rider at one of the 190 stations along the way. The riders became legendary for their spirit and derring-do, but the company was short-lived. Completion of a transcontinental telegraph line in the early 1860s rendered the service obsolete. In *Roughing It* (1871), Mark Twain recalls these intrepid mounted mail carriers:

The pony rider was usually a little bit of a man, brimful of spirit and endurance. No matter what time of the day or night his watch came on and no matter whether it was winter or summer, raining, snowing, hailing or sleeting, or whether his beat was a level straight road or a crazy trail over mountain crags and precipices, or whether it led through peaceful regions or regions that swarmed with Indians, he must always be ready to leap into the saddle and be off like the wind! There was no idling time for a pony rider on duty. He rode fifty miles without stopping, by daylight, moonlight, starlight, or through the blackness of darkness—just as it happened. He rode a splendid horse that was born for a racer and fed and lodged like a gentleman; kept him at his utmost speed for ten miles, and then, as he came crashing up to the station where stood two men holding fast a fresh, impatient steed, the transfer of rider and mailbag was made in the twinkling of an eye, and away flew the eager pair and were out of sight before the spectator could get hardly the ghost of a look…. The rider's dress was thin and fitted close; he wore a roundabout and a skullcap and tucked his pantaloons into his boot tops like a race rider. He carried no arms—he carried nothing that was not absolutely necessary, for even the postage on his literary freight was worth five dollars a letter….

TRANSPORTATION

1880, *cont.*

Kansas City Evening Star begins publication, focusing on local news and advocating public improvements.

1881 Frederic Ives produces the first color photograph.

1883 Canada and the United States agree on four standard time zones.

The Brooklyn Bridge, at the time the world's largest suspension bridge, is completed, stretching from Brooklyn to lower Manhattan. The designer of the bridge, John Roebling, dies during its construction.

The *Ladies' Home Journal* begins publication under the direction of Cyrus Curtis. The magazine was an elaboration of his wife Louisa's "Women and Home" column in Curtis's weekly the *Tribune and Farmer.*

JOSEPH PULITZER, the publisher of the *St. Louis Post-Dispatch*, buys the *New York World.*

THOMAS EDISON devises a trolley that runs on an electrified third rail; it is still used by the New York subway system.

1884 Lewis Waterman manufactures the first fountain pen.

OTTMAR MERGENTHALER patents the Linotype typesetting machine, which casts one line of characters at a time, greatly increasing the speed of newspaper and magazine composition.

New York and Boston are linked by telephone wires.

1885 The Dictaphone, a device for recording dictation, is invented by Charles Tainter.

The electric transformer is invented by William Stanley.

Good Housekeeping magazine is founded.

American Telephone and Telegraph (AT&T) is formed as a subsidiary of American Bell responsible for building a long-distance network. In 1892, AT&T had opened communication from New York to Chicago and, in 1915, had connected New York and San Francisco.

1887 An electrically lit train on the Pennsylvania Railroad begins service between New York and Chicago.

Congress passes the Interstate Commerce Act, which regulates commerce extending beyond state borders.

Celluloid photographic film is developed by clergyman Hannibal Goodwin.

In Richmond, Virginia, the first electric trolley line is constructed.

1888 The Pullman Car Company constructs an electric freight-hauling locomotive.

The *National Geographic* magazine offers armchair travelers a glimpse of the world.

Herman Hollerith devises the first successful computer, a punched-card tabulating machine; Hollerith's machines tabulate the results of the 1890 Census.

GEORGE EASTMAN invents the Kodak box camera, the first camera using roll film, ushering in the age of amateur photography.

1889 In New York City, Otis Brothers installs an electric elevator.

New York World reporter Nellie Bly begins an around-the-world ship voyage in an attempt to beat the record of Phineas Fogg, the hero of Jules Verne's novel *Around the World in 80 Days.* She returns home in seventy-two days, six hours, and eleven minutes, setting a record time.

THOMAS EDISON invents the kinetograph, the first sound camera.

1891 THOMAS EDISON patents his kinetoscopic camera, which takes moving pictures on a strip of film. A single viewer looking into a lighted box, which is turned by a crank, can see the film.

In Des Moines, Iowa, William Morrison builds an electrically powered car for six passengers.

MEDIA, PLANES, AND AUTOMOBILES

1892 GEORGE EASTMAN invents daylight-loading film.

1893 The Edison Laboratories builds a film studio in West Orange, New Jersey.

Franklin and Charles Duryea build the first successful gasoline car.

McClure's illustrated magazine begins publication. In 1902, *McClure's* became known for including the muckraking journalism of Ida Tarbell and Lincoln Steffens.

1894 The first movie projector publicly shows two kinetoscopic films.

1895 GEORGE SELDEN's patent for a "road engine," the first in America for a gasoline-powered car, is granted.

The Baltimore & Ohio Railroad becomes the first American company to use electric locomotives.

Connecticut's Hart Rubber Works produces the first American pneumatic, or air-filled, tires.

1896 Rural free mail delivery (RFD) begins.

In New York City, the first moving picture is shown to the public at Koster and Bial's Music Hall.

"Telephone, n. An invention of the devil which abrogates some of the advantages of making a disagreeable person keep his distance."
—AMBROSE BIERCE, *THE DEVIL'S DICTIONARY,* 1906

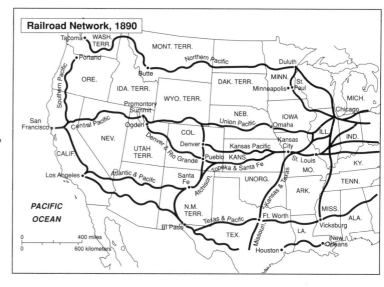

Railroad Network, 1890

TRANSPORTATION

THE GOLDEN AGE OF U.S. RAILROADS

During the fifty years following the Civil War, American railroads were the dominant mode of transportation. The railway network expanded from 35,000 (56,325 km) miles in 1865 to 254,000 (408,770 km) miles in 1916. Some factors that contributed to this expansion were:

• The completion of five transcontinental railroads from 1869 to 1894.
• Federal land grants to railroads. Between 1862 and 1872, for example, Congress granted more than 100 million acres of public lands to railroad companies and also provided them with more than $64 million in loans and tax incentives.
• Technological innovations made railway service more economical, including more powerful engines, refrigerated cars, and air brakes.
• The adoption of a standard track gauge (size of track), which allowed trunk lines (main long-distance lines) to link the many smaller systems in the Northeast and the South.
• The introduction in 1883 of four standard time zones for the nation, which permitted an orderly national scheduling system.

1896, *cont.*

Samuel Langley flies a steam-powered model plane.
HENRY FORD constructs his first successful gasoline-powered car.

1897 The *Argonaut II*, a gasoline submarine with wheels for moving on the ocean floor, is launched by Simon Lake and becomes the first submarine to travel in the open seas.

In Boston, the Boylston Street subway line begins operating; it is the first American subway.

Cyrus H. Curtis, owner of *Ladies' Home Journal*, purchases the financially troubled *Saturday Evening Post* for $1,000 and with editor George Lorimer transforms it into a magazine dedicated to middlebrow fiction and American nostalgia. The first magazine designed for the masses, it featured more than 300 Norman Rockwell paintings on its covers.

In New York City, the *Jewish Daily Forward* begins publication; it will soon become the most influential Jewish newspaper in America.

1898 The *Holland*, the first practical submarine, is powered by electricity underwater and gasoline on the surface, is launched by John Holland.

1900 The Olds Motor Works, founded the previous year by RANSOM OLDS, begins the first mass production of cars in Detroit.

Physicist REGINALD FESSENDEN uses radio waves to transmit spoken words for the first time.

Work begins on the New York City subway.

More than 1 million miles of telephone line are now strung across the United States.

In Boston, electrified trolleys replace horsecars.

1901 In Philadelphia, Otis Brothers installs what comes to be called an escalator in Gimbel's Department Store.

1902 The American Automobile Association (AAA) is founded to help members organize automobile tours and provide them with emergency road service.

1903 In Kitty Hawk, North Carolina, ORVILLE and WILBUR WRIGHT make the world's first successful sustained manned flights in a gasoline-powered aircraft. In the longest of their four flights this day, Wilbur stays in the air fifty-nine seconds, as his plane, *Flyer I*, covers 852 feet.

The Pulitzer Prizes are established by *New York World* publisher JOSEPH PULITZER.

Linking Honolulu with San Francisco, the first Pacific cable is completed.

The United States and Panama sign the Hay-Bunau-Varilla Treaty, giving the United States a renewable ninety-nine-year lease on a 10-mile (16-km) strip of land across the Isthmus of Panama in exchange for $10 million and an annual payment of $230,000. The United States wants to use this land to build a canal to make ocean travel from the Atlantic to the Pacific easier (see p. 285).

HENRY FORD founds the Ford Motor Company.

Massachusetts issues the first automobile license plates; soon all states will follow.

The Harley-Davidson motorcycle is devised by William Harley.

1905 The Long Island Railroad installs a third rail, becoming the first American railroad to have no steam locomotives running on its tracks.

The *Chicago Defender*, the first significant black newspaper, begins publication.

The first movie theater is built in Pittsburgh; it charges a nickel for admission and is called a nickelodeon.

AT&T introduces rotary dialing.

1906 Directed by the U.S. Army Corps of Engineers, construction of the Panama Canal begins. The cost of the 40-mile (64-km) canal will be over $300 million.

From a station in Brant Rock, Massachusetts, REGINALD FESSENDEN broadcasts the first radio program combining voice and music.

LEE DE FOREST, "Father of the Radio," invents a three-electrode vacuum-tube amplifier that forms the basis for the development of the radio.

1907 The first taxis, imported from Paris, arrive in New York City.

The United Press (UP) is founded to compete with the Associated Press (AP), established in 1848.

1908 HENRY FORD introduces the Model T, soon to be the most popular motor car.

The Cadillac Automobile Company is the first to use interchangeable parts in assembling cars.

The General Motors Company is founded by WILLIAM DURANT.

"Success. Four flights Thursday morning. All against twenty-one-mile wind. Started from level with engine power alone. Average speed through air thirty-one miles. Longest fifty-nine seconds. Inform press. Home Christmas."
—WILBUR AND ORVILLE WRIGHT, telegram to father from Kitty Hawk, North Carolina, December 17, 1903

TRANSPORTATION

1908, *cont.*

The University of Michigan establishes the first professional school of journalism.

Mutt and Jeff, drawn by Bud Fisher, becomes the first comic strip to appear each day with the same characters.

Glenn Curtiss makes the first official American public flight of over 1 kilometer (0.62 mi).

1909 In New York City the *Amsterdam News* begins publication; it will become America's largest secular black weekly newspaper.

THOMAS EDISON creates the Motion Pictures Patents Company to prevent unlicensed filmmaking companies from producing motion pictures.

1911 Cartoonist John Bray develops animated motion picture cartoons. All future animators will employ his "cel" system, in which each frame is composed of layers of celluloid transparencies, with only those layers showing figures in motion changing from frame to frame.

The introduction of *Photoplay*, the first fan magazine, allows Americans to keep close tabs on such adored Hollywood stars as Charlie Chaplin, Rudolph Valentino, Theda Bara, and Clara Bow.

CHARLES KETTERING's electric self-starter for cars enables engines to be started without being manually cranked.

The Keystone Company is formed by motion picture pioneer MACK SENNETT.

1912 Albert Howell invents a continuous printer that automatically copies motion pictures, making possible their mass distribution.

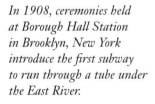

In 1908, ceremonies held at Borough Hall Station in Brooklyn, New York introduce the first subway to run through a tube under the East River.

The seaplane is invented by Grover Loening.

1913 The assembly line is introduced at the Ford Motor Company; by 1925, Ford is turning out more than 9,000 cars a day.

U.S. Parcel Post begins operating. Approximately 300 million packages have been mailed by year's end.

The Dodge Brothers, John and Horace, begin making their own cars, which are among the first U.S. automobiles with all-steel bodies.

1914 The Panama Canal, linking the Atlantic and Pacific Oceans, is completed (see p. 285).

In Cleveland, the world's first red-green traffic lights are installed.

Gulf Oil produces and then distributes the first American automobile road maps; soon free maps given away at gas stations will encourage car travel.

Charles Lawrence develops an air-cooled airplane engine that will make long-distance flight possible.

1915 The Federal Trade Commission is established to regulate interstate commerce.

Long-distance telephone service starts between San Francisco and New York.

The first transatlantic telephone communication is transmitted; it is between Virginia and Paris.

The Ford Motor Company produces its one-millionth car.

The Chevrolet Motor Company is founded by WILLIAM DURANT.

1916 LEE DE FOREST broadcasts the first radio news.

Work on a nationwide U.S. highway system is begun.

The first mechanical windshield wipers, patented by Mary Anderson in 1905, are introduced in America.

Teletype is invented by Markrun Company of Chicago; it will become operational in 1928.

1917 EDWIN ARMSTRONG invents the superheterodyne circuit, which will be the design for amplitude modulation (AM) radios.

A new barge canal replaces New York's Erie Canal, which has become obsolete because of steam power.

President Woodrow Wilson orders the federal government to take control of the railroads to ensure their smooth operation during World War I.

1918 The first U.S. airmail stamps are introduced as the post office opens airmail service; the first route is New York–Philadelphia–Washington.

Louis B. Mayer Pictures is founded.

1919 The NC-4 aircraft completes the first transatlantic flight by a heavier-than-air machine from Newfoundland to Lisbon.

TRANSPORTATION

1919, *cont.*

The Radio Corporation of America (RCA) is founded.

The first successful tabloid, the New York Daily News, starts publication.

With director D. W. Griffith, actors Mary Pickford, Charlie Chaplin, and Douglas Fairbanks found United Artists.

1920 The first regular radio broadcasts begin.

The first transcontinental airmail route is established between New York City and San Francisco.

International Telephone and Telegraph (ITT) is founded.

The Transportation Act gives control of the railroads back to their owners.

1921 The first transcontinental U.S. day-night flight is completed from North Platte, Nebraska, to New York City.

The first transcontinental airmail from New York City to San Francisco takes twenty-seven hours.

Congress passes a Federal Highway Act, coordinating state highways and standardizing U.S. road buildings.

1922 James Doolittle completes the first single-day bicoastal flight between Pablo Beach, Florida, to San Diego.

The *Reader's Digest* begins publishing monthly; pocket-sized, it features articles condensed from magazines and books.

William Stout develops the first completely metal aircraft.

The first radio commercials are aired by New York's WEAF.

1923 The Hertz Drive-Ur-Self System, which will become the world's largest rental-car company, is founded.

Warner Bros. Pictures is incorporated.

Time magazine, founded by HENRY LUCE and Briton Hadden, begins publication. Luce became the editor in chief after Hadden's sudden death in 1929.

Juan Trippe and John Hambleton buy seven surplus float planes from the navy; through mergers their venture will eventually become Pan American Airways.

VLADIMIR ZWORYKIN patents the iconoscope, an early type of television.

1924 Two U.S. Army planes complete the first round-the-world air trip, with stops.

RCA transmits photographs by radio from New York City to London; transmission time per photo is about twenty-five minutes.

The first American diesel electric locomotive begins running on New Jersey's Central Railroad.

The *New York Herald Tribune* starts publication; it will compete with the *New York Times* until the *Tribune* ends publication in 1966.

The Computing-Tabulating-Recording Company, created in 1911,

MEDIA GROWTH IN THE TWENTIETH CENTURY

YEAR	NEWSPAPER CIRCULATION (THOUSANDS)	MOVIE ADMISSIONS (MILLIONS)	TELEVISION HOUSEHOLDS (MILLIONS)	% OF U.S. HOUSEHOLDS	CABLE TV SUBSCRIBERS (MILLIONS)
1900	15,102	—	—	—	—
1920	27,791	—	—	—	—
1930	39,589	4,680	—	—	—
1940	41,132	3,900	—	—	—
1950	53,829	4,160	3.9	9.0	—
1960	58,882	2,080	45.8	87.1	.7
1970	62,108	920	58.5	95.3	3.9
1980	62,202	1,022	76.3	97.9	17.7
1990	62,324	1,189	92.1	98.2	54.9
1995	58,193	1,263	95.4	98.2	63.
2000	55,700	1,420	102.2	98.2	68.7

renames itself International Business Machines (IBM).

Metro-Goldwyn-Mayer (MGM) is formed through merger by Marcus Loew, SAMUEL GOLDWYN, and LOUIS B. MAYER.

1925 The *New Yorker* magazine begins publishing; the editor, Harold Ross, will feature the work of talented young cartoonists such as Peter Arno and James Thurber, and urbane writers such as Dorothy Parker and Robert Benchley.

The first Lockheed Vega, a single-engine transport plane, is introduced and goes on to become one of the most widely used transport planes through the early 1930s.

1926 Francis Davis patents power steering; it will be installed by commercial automakers in 1951.

Richard Byrd and Floyd Bennett make the first flight over the North Pole.

DAVID SARNOFF establishes the National Broadcasting Company (NBC).

The *National Enquirer* begins publishing; after Generoso Pope assumes control in 1952, it will emphasize sensationalism, a focus that will enable it to increase weekly circulation to more than 400 million by 1975.

ROBERT GODDARD launches the first liquid-fueled rocket.

1927 CHARLES LINDBERGH completes the first nonstop solo transatlantic flight from New York to France in the *Spirit of St. Louis*; the flight, which makes "The Lone Eagle," or "Lucky Lindy," a world hero, covers 3,600 miles (5,800 km) in thirty-three and a half hours.

Built under the Hudson River, the Holland Tunnel opens, connecting New York City with New Jersey.

The Jazz Singer, the first successful feature-length motion picture with sound, is released. Its success marks the beginning of the end for silent films (see p. 517).

TRANSPORTATION

1928 The first bicoastal bus service, the Pioneer Yelloway Bus Line, begins operating from Los Angeles to New York City.

Charles Smith and his crew make the first flight across the Pacific Ocean.

The last Model T is produced by the Ford Motor Company.

VLADIMIR ZWORYKIN receives a patent for color television.

In Schenectady, New York, the General Electric station broadcasts the world's first regularly scheduled television programs.

WILLIAM S. PALEY buys United Independent Broadcasters, changing its name one year later to the Columbia Broadcasting System (CBS).

WALT DISNEY's *Steamboat Willie*, which introduces Mickey Mouse, is the first animated cartoon with a soundtrack.

VANNEVAR BUSH builds the differential analyzer, the first computer to use electronic parts—vacuum tubes for storing values as voltages.

1929 Ford produces the first station wagon.

Glenn Curtiss designs the first mobile home.

Delta Air Lines begins operations.

The first commercially successful car radio is invented by Paul Galvin.

The first car radios are sold in America.

The first instrumented rocket is launched by ROBERT GODDARD.

Richard Byrd and his crew make the first flight over the South Pole.

1930 The first successful transcontinental glider flight, from San Diego, California, to New York City, is made by Capt. Frank M. Hawks.

Both Transcontinental and Western Air (TWA) and United Airlines are formed by mergers.

HENRY LUCE's *Fortune* magazine begins publication.

The Hays Office, a self-monitoring and enforcement organization established by the film industry in 1922, develops a strict censorship code prohibiting motion picture depictions of cohabitation and seduction, among other things.

1931 The world's largest suspension bridge, the George Washington Bridge, is completed, connecting New York City to New Jersey.

Clyde Pangborn and Hugh Herndon make the first nonstop flight across the Pacific Ocean.

1932 U.S. Route 66 opens; this 2,200-mile (3,540-km) highway links Chicago and Los Angeles.

New York City's Radio City Music Hall opens.

The first "walkie-talkie" portable two-way radio sets are invented by the U.S. Army Corps of Engineers, assisted by Motorola's Paul Galvin.

A television receiver with a cathode-ray picture tube is demonstrated by RCA.

AMELIA EARHART is the first woman to make a solo flight across the Atlantic Ocean.

The first electronic television system was designed in 1922 by a fifteen-year-old high school student named Philo T. Farnsworth. He demonstrated a functional device in 1927 and received his first patent the following year.

Paramount Pictures is formed through a merger.

1933 EDWIN ARMSTRONG perfects frequency modulation (FM) radio. The new FM radio eliminates much of the static heard on AM radio.

Wiley Post makes the first solo round-the-world flight.

The first modern airliner, the Boeing 247, begins operating.

Esquire magazine begins publishing; it will become an important arbiter of men's tastes.

The World's Fair, celebrating a century of progress, opens in Chicago.

1934 American Airlines is created by reorganizing the American Airways Company, established four years earlier.

Chrysler Motors produces the world's first curved single-piece windshield.

The new Burlington *Zephyr,* the first diesel-powered streamlined passenger train, operates between Chicago and Denver, marking the end of steam engines on American tracks.

Introduced by Chrysler, the Airflow is the first streamlined car.

Congress creates the Federal Communications Commission (FCC) to oversee the radio, telephone, and telegraph industries; radio stations must now receive their operating license from the FCC.

1935 Boeing's B-17 bomber is the first low-wing, four-engine, all-metal aircraft.

Becky Sharp, starring Miriam Hopkins, is the first full-length film shot in three-color and Technicolor.

Congress passes the Motor Carrier Act, putting the Interstate Commerce Commission in control of interstate bus and truck lines.

Statistician George Gallup founds the American Institute of Public Opinion (the Gallup poll).

Kodachrome, a film sensitive to three primary colors, is invented by Leopold Mannes and Leopold Godowsky.

1936 HENRY LUCE founds *Life* magazine, a weekly photographic news and feature publication.

Pan American Airways begins transpacific flights from San Francisco to Manila.

Douglas DC-3 transport planes are introduced; they become the most popular airplanes in history.

1937 Filled with dangerous hydrogen gas, the dirigible *Hindenburg* explodes at Lakehurst, New Jersey, killing thirty-six, including thirteen passengers.

AMELIA EARHART vanishes during a Pacific Ocean flight from New Guinea to Howland Island.

Frank Whittle constructs the first working jet engine.

The Golden Gate Bridge, spanning San Francisco Bay and linking San

TRANSPORTATION

1937, *cont.*

Francisco with Marin Country, is completed; until 1964 it is the world's longest suspension bridge.

Newsweek and *Woman's Day* magazines start publication.

WALT DISNEY's *Snow White and the Seven Dwarfs* is the first feature-length animated film.

1938 The Civil Aeronautics Board is established to regulate air transportation.

CHESTER CARLSON invents xerography. The Haloid Company, later named Xerox, purchased the rights to Carlson's invention in 1947. By the 1960s, the process will revolutionize duplication of papers, which has until now been achieved by carbon copying.

1939 IGOR SIKORSKY develops the first practical helicopter.

John Atanasoff begins developing the first electronic computer.

Pan American begins regularly scheduled transatlantic passenger flights.

New York City's La Guardia Airport opens.

New York publisher Simon & Schuster introduces the pocket book, or paperback, to U.S. readers.

1940 The first commercial plane using pressurized cabins is the Boeing 307-B.

Designed with driver safety and comfort in mind, the Pennsylvania Turnpike becomes the first modern, tunneled American superhighway.

The first Los Angeles freeway, the Arroyo Seco Parkway, opens to traffic.

PETER GOLDMARK invents the first successful color television system.

General Motors introduces the first automatic transmission in American cars.

1941 The FCC approves TV broadcasting.

The Atchinson, Topeka, and Santa Fe Railroad begins operating the first American diesel freight locomotives.

1942 Built by the Bell Aircraft Company, the first American jet airplane is flown by Robert Stanley.

1943 The American Broadcasting Company (ABC) is established by millionaire Edward Noble.

1944 Aided by a grant from IBM, Howard Aiken develops the second electronic digital computer, the Mark I Automatic Sequence Controlled Calculator, but it often breaks down.

Walter Annenberg founds *Seventeen* magazine for female teens.

1945 *Ebony* magazine, a monthly picture magazine for blacks, is started by John Johnson.

1946 Douglas Aircraft's DC-6 is introduced; it can fly 300 miles (483 km) per hour and carry up to fifty-two passengers.

A pilotless rocket missile is built by the Farey Aviation Company.

ENIAC, the first electronic computer, is developed by John Eckert and JOHN MAUCHLY.

1947 B. F. Goodrich produces the first tubeless car tires.

U.S. Air Force captain Chuck Yeager makes the first supersonic flight in a U.S. Bell X-1 rocket plane.

WILLIAM SHOCKLEY, WALTER BRATTAIN, and JOHN BARDEEN develop the transistor, which will become the essential semiconductor device used on microprocessors and other chips.

The advent of television and the mass exodus to the suburbs (where there are, at least initially, few movie theaters) leads to the decline of movies as America's favorite entertainment (see p. 263).

Community Antenna Television (CATV), a precursor of modern cable, is devised for small rural towns in Oregon, Arkansas, and Pennsylvania.

1948 In New York City, Idlewild International Airport (later Kennedy International Airport) opens; at the time it is the world's largest commercial airport.

U.S. News & World Report magazine starts weekly publication.

PETER GOLDMARK invents the 33⅓-rpm phonograph record, the first long-playing record.

EDWIN LAND invents the Polaroid Land Camera; it develops photographs inside the camera in approximately sixty seconds.

The first chess-playing computer is built at the Massachusetts Institute of Technology (MIT).

One million homes have television sets.

1949 U.S. Air Force pilots complete the first nonstop flight around the world.

The Department of Justice, charging that AT&T has monopolized the telephone industry in violation of the Sherman Anti-Trust Act of 1890, requests that AT&T break up its Western Electric division into separate companies, thereby permitting competition in telephone production and installation.

JOHN MAUCHLY and John Eckert build BINAC, the first American electronic-stored program computer.

1950 New York City's Port Authority opens and will become the world's busiest bus terminal.

The first Xerox copies are produced by the Haloid Company in Rochester, New York.

The FCC licenses CBS to make color TV broadcasts, which it begins doing a year later.

SPACE FLIGHT AND THE DIGITAL AGE

1951 The first transcontinental television broadcast is made; it's of an address by President Harry Truman in San Francisco.

JOHN MAUCHLY and John Eckert build UNIVAC I, the first commercial electronic computer; it stores data on magnetic tape. (The U.S. Census Bureau installs the first UNIVAC I.)

Wang Laboratories is established by An Wang, who hopes to product small business calculators.

1952 The passenger ship SS *United States* sets a new record, making the transatlantic crossing in three days, ten hours, and forty minutes.

The first videotape, invented by John Mullin and Wayne Johnson, is demonstrated.

CBS relies on a UNIVAC computer to predict the results of the presidential election; the computer correctly predicts a landslide victory by Republican candidate Dwight Eisenhower.

Mad comic strip, which will evolve into *Mad* magazine, presents a satirical take on life that appeals primarily to adolescents.

Bwana Devil, the first commercial three-dimensional motion picture, is released.

1953 The first IBM computer, the IBM 701, is introduced, and the first high-speed printer is linked to a computer.

TV Guide, with weekly program listings, begins publication.

Hugh Hefner begins publishing *Playboy* magazine, which features photographs of nude women as well as serious fiction.

The first operational supersonic fighter, the North American F-100 Super Sabre, is introduced.

1954 The first practical silicon transistors are introduced by Texas Instruments.

RCA produces the first American color television sets. It also produces the first video recorder. The Nautilus, the first nuclear-powered submarine, is launched at Groton, Connecticut.

The first 115-mile (185-km) section of the 559-mile (900-km) long New York State Thruway opens, linking Lowell to Rochester. Completed in 1960 and expanded in 1991, it is the longest toll superhighway in the United States.

Sports Illustrated magazine begins to publish.

1955 At Tarrytown, New York, the Tappan Zee Bridge, a cantilever span across the Hudson River, opens.

IBM introduces its first business computer, the IBM 752.

In New York City, the *Village Voice*, a liberal weekly paper, begins publication.

William F. Buckley Jr. founds the *National Review*, a biweekly journal of conservative political thought.

1956 The first nonstop transcontinental helicopter flight is made from San Diego to Washington, D.C.

The Federal Aid Highway Act allocates 90 percent of the estimated $33.5 billion needed to construct a 42,500-mile (68,395-km) network of roads connecting the nation's major urban centers.

An IBM team led by John Backus invents FORTRAN, the first computer-programming language.

late 1950s John McCarthy creates LISP, the computer language of artificial intelligence.

1957 At Mackinaw City, Michigan, the Mackinac Straits Bridge replaces the George Washington Bridge in New York as the world's longest suspension bridge to date.

New York City's last trolley car is removed from service, with motor buses substituted for streetcars in most major American cities.

1958 Pan American Airways begins transatlantic jet service days after British Overseas Airways Corporation (BOAC).

The first American-manufactured commercial jet, the Boeing 707, begins service; it can seat 211.

The National Aeronautics and Space Administration (NASA) is formed, and the first U.S. Earth satellite launched.

United Press International (UPI) is created by a merger of the United Press and the International News Service.

The Control Data Corporation introduces the first completely transistorized computer, developed by Seymour Cray.

The Ampex Corporation develops the first color video recorder.

1959 Xerox produces its first commercial copier.

Jack Kilby and ROBERT NOYCE independently invent the microchip, paving the way for miniature products and electronic wristwatches.

Launched at Camden, New Jersey, the *Savannah* is the first nuclear-powered merchant ship.

NASA chooses its first seven astronauts: Gordon Cooper Jr., Virgil "Gus" Grissom, Donald K. "Deke" Slayton, JOHN GLENN JR., M. Scott Carpenter, Walter M. Schirra Jr., and Alan B. Shepard Jr.

1960 The Digital Equipment Company develops the first minicomputer, the PDP-1.

The Bulova Accutron is the first electronic wristwatch.

Echo I, the first communications satellite, is launched.

The auto industry starts producing compact cars to better compete against foreign economy and sports cars.

EDWIN LAND invents black-and-white Polaroid film.

1961 Navy commander Alan Shepard Jr. makes the first American manned space voyage, reaching an altitude of 115 miles (185 km) in a fifteen-minute flight.

Virgil "Gus" Grissom becomes the second American in space, making a fifteen-minute flight aboard the Mercury Mission's *Liberty Bell* 7.

The IBM Selectric typewriter, with a moving-ball cluster of interchangeable type, is introduced.

1962 Marine Corps pilot JOHN GLENN is the first American to orbit the Earth, in the Mercury capsule *Friendship* 7.

Telstar, the first active communications satellite, is launched and transmits the first live transatlantic telecast.

Congress creates a private company, the Communications Satellite Corporation (COMSAT), to oversee the role of the United States in developing a worldwide system of communication satellites.

Near Washington, D.C., John Foster Dulles International Airport, the first civilian airport specifically designed to accommodate commercial jets, opens.

The Learjet is developed by William Lear.

1963 The post office inaugurates five-digit zip codes.

AT&T produces transistorized electronic Touch-Tone phones.

EDWIN LAND introduces Polaroid color film.

A satellite relays color TV for the first time.

Touch-Tone telephone service begins.

1964 The Verrazzano-Narrows Bridge between Brooklyn and Staten Island, New York, opens; it is at present the world's longest suspension bridge.

JOHN KEMENY and Thomas Kurtz invent BASIC, a computer language for beginners, which becomes the main programming language for personal-computer owners.

The Boeing 727, seating 145, is introduced.

1965 *Early Bird,* the first commercial communications satellite, is put into orbit by COMSAT.

In New York City, radio station WINS pioneers all-news programming.

Astronaut Edward White is the first American to walk in space, spending approximately twenty minutes outside the *Gemini 4* spacecraft, which is in the process of orbiting the Earth three times.

IBM introduces its first integrated circuit-based computer, the 360.

Ralph Nader publishes *Unsafe at Any Speed,* an indictment of the American auto industry for its focus on profits rather than safety; the book encourages Congress to pass new safety regulations for cars.

1966 Congress passes the Freedom of Information Act, giving greater public access to public information.

The Department of Transportation is established.

HORNET + 3

President Nixon welcomes the returning astronauts after their historic 1969 moon landing. Astronauts Neil Armstrong, Michael Collins, and Edwin "Buzz" Aldrin are confined to the Mobile Quarantine Facility while being transported from their landing site to the Manned Spacecraft Center's Lunar Receiving Laboratory.

1967 Astronauts Virgil Grissom, Edward White, and Roger Chaffee are killed when fire traps them in the capsule of the Saturn 1-B rocket while it is on the ground.

Rolling Stone magazine is founded by Jann Wenner.

Congress creates the Corporation for Public Broadcasting to increase noncommercial radio and television broadcasting.

A Commission on Obscenity and Pornography is created by Congress; it finds that pornography does not influence crime or sexual deviance.

The Federal Communications Commission orders all radio and TV cigarette commercials to warn of the possible danger in smoking.

1968 The 911 emergency phone number is inaugurated in New York City, with most large cities following suit.

The Penn Central Railroad is created by a merger between the New York Central and the Pennsylvania railroads; it is among the biggest mergers in U.S. history.

Apollo 8, the first manned space mission to orbit the moon, is launched.

Front-seat shoulder belts are now required equipment in cars.

1969 Astronaut NEIL ARMSTRONG becomes the first human to walk on the moon; as he steps onto it from the lunar module *Apollo 11*, Armstrong is joined by fellow astronaut Edwin "Buzz" Aldrin, while millions worldwide watch on television.

ARPANET, a Defense Department project to develop a communications network that will survive partial destruction, gives birth to the Internet.

TRANSPORTATION

1969, *cont.*

Cigarette advertising will be gradually eliminated from radio and television during the next three years, according to a decision announced by the National Association of Broadcasters.

Reversing a Georgia antipornography law, the Supreme Court rules that in the privacy of their own homes people may read or view films without censorship.

The computer used for guidance, navigation, and flight control on the *Apollo 11* mission to the moon had only thirty-six kilobytes of fixed memory—less than many of today's handheld electronic games for children. The astronauts carried small slide rules in the event of computer failure.

1970 Pan Am puts the first jumbo jet, the Boeing 747, into service. It is capable of carrying 490 passengers.

The Burlington Northern Inc. is created by a merger of the Chicago, Burlington, & Quincy and the Great Northern, Northern Pacific, and Chicago railroads.

The floppy disk is invented for storing computer-originated data.

Lexitron introduces the first word processor, a computer for handling written text.

The Post Office Department becomes an independent agency rather than a federal agency and is renamed the U.S. Postal Service.

Ms. magazine is founded; feminist Gloria Steinem is its first editor.

1971 Amtrak (National Railroad Passenger Corporation) assumes control of nearly all the nation's passenger railway service after being authorized by Congress to operate intercity passenger trains.

The Picturephone is introduced by Bell Telephone.

Direct telephone dialing is now possible between parts of the United States and Europe.

Texas Instruments develops the first pocket calculator.

Intel introduces the first microprocessor, several integrated circuits on a single silicon chip.

1972 *Pioneer 10*, an unmanned U.S. spacecraft, begins a nearly two-year journey past the planet Jupiter; the probe will be the first human-made object to go beyond the solar system.

Frederick Smith founds Federal Express.

The Polaroid SX system develops a color print outside the camera in front of the photographer's eyes.

1973 Intel markets the 8080 microprocessor, which becomes the central processing unit (CPU) of several microcomputers.

Cable network HBO begins broadcasting to subscribers in Wilkes-Barre, Pennsylvania.

1974 *People* magazine is first published by Time Inc.

The first personal computer, the Altair, is developed.

A nationwide speed limit of 55 mph (89 kph) is established. Intended to conserve fuel consumption during the energy crisis prompted by the 1973 oil embargo, the national limit will be repealed in 1985.

1975 In the final Apollo mission, the first United States–Soviet space link occurs 140 miles (225 km) above the Earth, as astronauts Thomas Stafford, Vance Brand, and Donald Slayton meet up with cosmonauts Valery Kubasov and Aleksei Leonov.

The Sony Corporation of America begins marketing the Betamax video cassette recorder (VCR). Two years later, RCA introduced its Video Home System (VHS), which had been created by JVC engineers in Japan. Primarily because VHS tapes could record longer than Beta, the VHS system quickly dominated the market.

1977 In West Virginia, the 1,817-foot New River Gorge Bridge is the world's longest steel arch bridge.

The Trans-Alaska oil pipeline opens.

Apple introduces the Apple II, the first assembled personal computer.

The probe *Voyager 2* is launched; it will photograph Jupiter in 1979, Saturn in 1981, Uranus in 1986, and Neptune in 1989.

1978 *Self* and *Working Woman* magazines begin publication.

The Air Transport Deregulation Act phases out federal regulation of the airlines industry.

Apple introduces the first disk drive for personal computers.

Hayes markets the first microcomputer-compatible modem.

The Panama Canal treaties cede control of the canal to Panama, through a twenty-year transition, beginning in 1979 and ending December 31, 1999, but with the canal's neutrality guaranteed (p. 285).

Cellular phones are developed at AT&T Bell labs; by 1981, they are in use nationwide.

The first spreadsheet for personal computers, which allows computers to be used for accounting functions, is developed by VisiCalc.

1979 Congress passes the Chrysler Loan Guarantee Bill, which saves the company from bankruptcy.

1980 The *Voyager I* spacecraft explores Saturn.

Atlanta's Harsfield International Airport opens.

Easing some of the restrictions imposed by the Interstate Commerce Act (1887), the Staggers Rail Act deregulates the railways in various ways, such as giving them more freedom in setting rates.

The newly created (by merger) CSX Corporation's 27,000 miles (43,450) of track make it the largest American railroad.

TED TURNER's Atlanta-based Cable News Network (CNN) starts operating.

1981 The IBM personal computer, using the Microsoft disk-operating

Ray Bradbury was the only author to have a U.S. space program site on another planet named for him. The site where *Viking 1* landed on Mars in 1976 is called Bradbury.

TRANSPORTATION

1981, *cont.*

system (MS-DOS), is introduced and soon becomes the industry standard.

The first portable computer, the Osborne 1, is developed.

The space shuttle *Columbia*, the first reusable manned spacecraft, is launched.

1982 Compaq develops the first clone of the IBM personal computer.

Compact-disc players are designed. CDs will almost entirely replace long-playing records.

In a momentous antitrust case, AT&T agrees to spin off twenty-two regional and local companies but will keep its long-distance lines, Western Electric manufacturing facilities, and Bell Laboratories research facilities.

The Boeing 767, capable of seating 211, is introduced.

The space shuttle *Columbia* makes its first commercial flight.

The color daily newspaper *USA Today* begins publication.

Eastman Kodak introduces the film disk, a flat plastic cartridge containing a film disk that turns in front of an exposure window situated behind a camera lens.

The wingspan of a Boeing 747 jumbo jet is longer than the distance of the Wright brothers' first flight.

1983 Apple's Lisa personal computer introduces pull-down menus and the mouse, a hand device that moves the cursor on the screen.

IBM builds the first hard-disk drive into its PC-XT personal computer.

Astronaut Sally Ride becomes the first woman in space.

1984 IBM introduces a one-megabyte RAM memory chip, with four times the memory of earlier chips.

The Supreme Court declares that videotape recording for home use only does not violate copyrights.

Auto-focus cameras are developed.

1985 Bell Laboratories transmits over a single optical fiber the equivalent of 300,000 simultaneous telephone conversations.

Apple's LaserWriter printer and Aldus Corporation's PageMaker make desktop publishing possible.

1986 The space shuttle *Challenger* explodes after liftoff, killing the seven astronauts aboard, including teacher Christa McAuliffe.

Experimental aircraft *Voyager* circles the Earth without refueling.

IBM's OS/2 operating system enables personal computers to run several programs at once.

1987 The federal government sells its Conrail stock to private investors.

1988 TED TURNER founds Turner Network Television (TNT). Turner's company, the Turner Broadcasting System, will go on to launch the Cartoon

Network in 1992 and Turner Classic Movies in 1994.

STEVEN JOBS introduces a "computer workstation," with an optical disk drive that stores 250 times more data than IBM and Apple floppy disks.

1989 Intel introduces the 8086 chip, which, capable of containing 1 million transistors, gives the microcomputer the power and speed of a supercomputer.

1990 The space probe *Magellan* begins orbiting Venus, sending back radar images of the surface of the planet.

1993 Intel begins shipping the Pentium chip, which contains 3.1 million transistors and doubles the processing speed of previous PC microprocessors.

1997 The planetary probe *Mars Pathfinder* lands softly on the surface of Mars and launches a robotic vehicle that collects rock samples and transmits thousands of photographs.

An IBM supercomputer known as Deep Blue defeats world chess champion Garry Kasparov, the first time a computer has beaten a top-caliber player.

1998 The space shuttle *Discovery* delivers a U.S. module for the International Space Station. The crew attaches the module and boards the new station for the first time.

2000 The "Y2K bug," purported to threaten the communications, transportation, defense, and public-service infrastructure of the developed world, proves virtually harmless.

Household penetration of personal computers in the United States exceed 50 percent. The total number of Internet users is estimated to reach 100 million.

The computer software giant Microsoft is found to be in violation of federal antitrust laws and is ordered broken up into two smaller companies.

2000 Amtrak launches the Acela, a high speed train that can travel at speeds up to 150 mph.

2001 The number of wireless telephone subscribers in the United States exceeds 100 million.

After a series of legal appeals by Microsoft, the U.S. Justice Department agrees to a compromise settlement in its antitrust case against the computer software giant. The company will not be broken up but agrees to cease all anticompetitive practices.

2003 In a setback to NASA's space program, the space shuttle *Columbia* disintegrates upon reentering the Earth's atmosphere. All seven astronauts aboard are killed in the disaster.

"The nineteen-twenties is a Pierce-Arrow driven by a man in a raccoon coat. The nineteen-thirties is a Model T with a mattress strapped to the roof, bound for California. The nineteen-forties is a black sedan, driven by a Negro chauffeur wearing a cap. The nineteen-fifties is a station wagon with a dog sticking its nose out the window, four kids in the back, and no seat belts. The nineteen-sixties is a Mustang with the top down, headed for Miami Beach, passing a pink VW mini-bus, headed for a sit-in. And the nineteen-seventies, most analysts agree, is a Pinto in a gas line."
—LOUIS MENAND
THE *NEW YORKER*,
MAY 28, 2001

TRANSPORTATION

U.S. MANNED SPACE PROGRAMS: A SUMMARY

PROJECT MERCURY

Dates: 1958–1963

Number of Manned Flights: 6

Primary Purpose: To launch a human into orbit and return him safely to Earth.

Landmarks: first American in space—Alan B. Shepard Jr., May 5, 1961; Freedom 7 first American in orbit—John Glenn Jr., February 20, 1962; *Friendship* 7

PROJECT GEMINI

Dates: 1965–1966

Number of Manned Flights: 10

Primary Purposes: To perfect space rendezvous and docking techniques for use on lunar missions and to explore the effects of extravehicular activity (EVA) in space.

Landmarks: first extravehicular activity—June 3, 1965; Edward H. White, *Gemini 4* first space rendezvous—December 15, 1965; *Gemini 6* & *Gemini 7* first space docking—March 16, 1966; *Gemini 8* and Agena target rocket.

APOLLO PROGRAM

Dates: 1968–1975

Number of Manned Flights: 15

Primary Purpose: To land humans on the surface of the moon and return them safely to Earth.

Landmarks: first manned mission to orbit the moon—December 21–27, 1968; *Apollo 8* first manned approach lunar surface—May 18–26, 1969; *Apollo 10* first manned lunar landing—July 16–24, 1969; *Apollo 11* five more lunar landings—November 1969–December 1972; *Apollo 12*, 14–17.

SPACE SHUTTLE

Dates: 1981–Present

Number of Missions: 108 (through 2001)

Number of Shuttle Craft: 5—*Columbia, Challenger, Discovery, Atlantis, Endeavour*

Primary Purpose: To build and operate a reusable, large-crew spacecraft suitable for a wide range of scientific, commercial, retrieve-and-repair, and other missions.

Landmarks: first shuttle mission—April 12–14, 1981; STS-1, *Columbia* first American woman in space—Sally Ride, June 18–24, 1983; STS-7, *Challenger* disaster—January 28, 1986, STS-51-L deployment of Hubble Space Telescope—April 24–29, 1990; STS-31, *Discovery* docking with Mir space station—June 27–July 7, 1995; STS-71, *Atlantis* delivery of assembly node for International Space Station—December 4–15, 1998; STS-88, *Endeavour Columbia* disaster—February 1, 2003; STS-107.

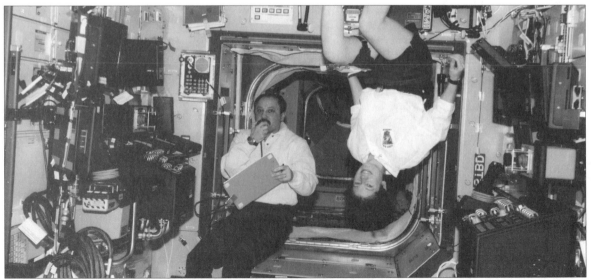

Astronaut Susan J. Helms and cosmonaut Yuri V. Usachev work aboard the U.S. Laboratory/Destiny module of the International Space Station in 2001.

LANDMARKS IN AMERICAN AVIATION, 1903–PRESENT

1903 Wilbur and Orville Wright make the first flights in a heavier-than-air machine at Kitty Hawk, North Carolina.

1908 Glenn Curtiss completes the first official American public flight of over 1 kilometer (0.62 mi).

1911 In a series of short flights, Calbraith Rodgers takes forty-nine days to make the first transcontinental flights across America—from Sheepshead Bay, New York, to Pasadena, California.

1924 Two U.S. Army planes take almost six months to make the first round-the-world flight of 26,345 miles (42,400 km).

1926 Explorers Richard Byrd and Floyd Bennett make the first flight over the North Pole.

1927 Charles Lindbergh makes the first solo nonstop-transatlantic flight. The 3,610-mile (5,810-km) journey from Garden City, New York, to Paris takes thirty-three and a half hours.

1928 Charles Smith and his crew make the first flight across the Pacific Ocean from Oakland, California, to Brisbane, Australia. They make stops at Honolulu, Hawaii, and at Fiji.

1929 Richard Byrd and his crew make the first flight over the South Pole.

1931 Clyde Pangborn and Hugh Herndon make the first nonstop flight across the Pacific Ocean—from Misawa, Japan, to Wenatchee, Washington.

1932 Amelia Earhart becomes the first woman to fly solo across the Atlantic Ocean. Starting from Harbour Grace, Newfoundland, she lands in a pasture in Wales, in fifteen hours and eighteen minutes.

1933 Wiley Post makes the first solo round-the-world flight, journeying 15,596 miles (29,100 km) in four days, nineteen hours, and thirty-six minutes.

1949 A U.S. Air Force plane makes the first nonstop round-the-world flight, traveling 23,452 miles (37,740 km) in three days, twenty-two hours, and one minute.

1986 Richard Rutan and Jeana Yeager make the first round-the-world flight without refueling, starting and ending their journey at Edwards Air Force Base, California.

1988 Clay Lacy, his crew, and thirty-six passengers fly around the world in the record time of thirty-six hours, fifty-four minutes, and fifteen seconds.

In his plane the Spirit of St. Louis, *Charles Lindbergh took off from Roosevelt Field in Long Island, New York, and landed in Le Bourget Field in Paris, France. He received a $25,000 prize from a man named Raymond Orteig for successfully becoming the first to complete a solo-nonstop, transatlantic flight.*

TRANSPORTATION

LEGISLATION AFFECTING TRANSPORTATION AND COMMUNICATION, 1798–PRESENT

1798 Alien Acts. In two acts, Congress empowers President John Adams to arrest and deport "dangerous" aliens during wartime (see p. 182).

Sedition Act. This act suppresses editorial criticism of the president and his administration (see p. 182).

1862 Pacific Railroad Act. Congress grants to the Union Pacific and the Central Pacific railroads subsidies in land and money for the construction of a transcontinental railroad.

1887 Interstate Commerce Act. Congress establishes the Interstate Commerce Commission (ICC) to regulate the railway industry, specifically to require the railroads to charge "reasonable and just" freight rates.

1903 Elkins Act. This forbids railroads to charge rates different from their published rates and holds railroad officials personally liable if rebating occurs.

1906 Hepburn Act. This authorizes the Interstate Commerce Commission (ICC) to fix railroad rates and inspect financial records.

1910 Mann-Elkins Act. Congress extends the Interstate Commerce Commission's power over railroads and also places telegraph, cable, and telephone companies under ICC control.

1920 Transportation Act. This returns the railroads to their owners after President Woodrow Wilson placed them under federal control during World War I.

1926 Air Commerce Act. For the first time Congress imposes safety regulations on aircraft, requiring registration and licensing of planes and pilots.

1934 Communications Act. This creates the Federal Communications Commission (FCC) to regulate broadcasting, basically through its power to license stations.

1940 Smith Act. Congress makes it unlawful to advocate the overthrow of the government by either force or violence.

1956 Federal Aid Highway Act. This calls for construction of a system of interstate highways covering 41,000 miles (65,980 km).

1965 Clean Air Act. Congress order the automobile industry to decrease the pollution produced by new cars.

1966 Highway Safety Act. In the first of a number of acts addressing motor-vehicle safety, Congress allows federal agencies to set mandatory safety standards for motor vehicles.

Freedom of Information Act. This act requires that federal agencies make most of their records available to the public. Nine classes of records are exempt, including documents related to national security or trade secrets.

1967 Public Broadcasting Act. Congress establishes noncommercial radio and television.

1971 Amtrak Act. This establishes Amtrak passenger service to operate nearly all American intercity passenger railway service.

1974 Privacy Act. This act requires federal agencies to give individuals any information in their files about them and to correct incorrect records.

1976 Conrail Act. Congress creates Conrail from six bankrupt railroads to provide freight service in the Northeast.

1978 Air Transport Deregulation Act. Congress virtually deregulates domestic airlines.

1980 Staggers Rail Act. This act deregulates railroads in various ways, such as permitting them increased flexibility in setting rates and greater authority to form long-term contracts with freight shippers.

Privacy Protection Act. This declares that before newspaper premises are searched, the police must obtain subpoenas.

1996 Telecommunications Act. The first major revision of federal telecommunications law in sixty-two years, this legislation lifts regulatory barriers, opening local and long-distance telephone service and cable television to new competition.

1997 Amtrak Reform and Accountability Act. This law overhauls operations of the passenger rail system and authorizes $5.1 billion in operating subsidies and capital improvements.

1998 Transportation Equity Act for the Twenty-first Century. This legislation authorizes a six-year, $218 billion program to improve highways, bridges, and rapid-transit systems.

Ocean Shipping Reform Act. This law extends economic deregulation to the U.S. international shipping industry.

2001 Aviation Security Act. This legislation gives the federal government control of airline passenger and baggage security operations.

SUPREME COURT DECISIONS AFFECTING TRANSPORTATION AND COMMUNICATION, 1824–PRESENT

1824 *Gibbons v. Odgen.* In a decision that helps prevent interstate trade wars, the Court rules that states cannot restrain interstate commerce and that the power of Congress to regulate interstate commerce does not stop at the jurisdictional lines of several states.

1876 *Munn v. Illinois.* The Illinois legislature has set maximum rates that could be charged by grain warehouses and elevators. After Ira Munn, a grain elevator operator, is sued by the state for refusing to obey the statute, he contends that the state law conflicts with the interstate commerce powers of Congress. The Court rules that because elevators and warehouses engage in local transactions, they are subject to state control. The decision triggers numerous cases in which the Court is requested to overturn state regulatory laws.

1964 *New York Times Company v. Sullivan.* The Court declares that the First Amendment protects critics of public officials, even if the charges are false.

1971 *New York Times Company v. United States.* In 1971, the *New York Times* publishes the secret *Pentagon Papers.* The Nixon administration obtains an injunction against the paper, alleging it breached national security. In an unauthorized opinion, the

Court observes that the government, in this instance, has not met "the heavy burden of showing justification" for "prior restraint" on the freedom of the press.

1973 *Miller v. California.* Communities gain greater control over pornographic films, magazines, and books. The decision also defines "contemporary community standards" as local, not national.

1976 *Nebraska Press Association v. Stuart.* The Court holds that injunctions against the press publishing information about pending criminal trials are permitted only when all other means of ensuring a fair trial prove inadequate.

1978 *Zurcher v. Stanford Daily.* The Court holds that newspaper offices may be searched by police with warrants.

1979 *Gannett v. DePasquale.* Judges may bar the press and the public from criminal proceedings.

1997 *Reno v. American Civil Liberties Union.* The Court supports freedom of speech on the Internet, striking down 1996 federal legislation intended to prevent indecent material from being seen by children.

TRANSPORTATION

NOTABLE FIGURES IN TRANSPORTATION AND COMMUNICATION

Armstrong, Edwin (1890–1954). Armstrong's electrical inventions pioneered radio. They included regenerative circuits, superheterodyne circuits, superregenerative circuits, and the frequency-modulation system of radio.

Armstrong, Neil A. (1930–). As commander of *Apollo 11*, Armstrong became the first man to walk on the moon on July 20, 1969. A combat pilot in the Korean War, he flew the X-15 rocket plane seven times before joining NASA.

Bardeen, John (1908–). With WILLIAM SHOCKLEY and WALTER BRATTAIN, Bardeen invented the transistor, for which they received the 1956 Nobel Prize in physics.

Bell, Alexander Graham (1847–1922). Bell founded a training school for teachers of the deaf in Boston in 1872. Two years later he invented a telegraph multiplexing system. In 1875, he transmitted the first intelligible words over the telephone to his assistant, Thomas Watson. Bell patented the telephone the next year. With others, he founded the Bell Telephone Company.

Bennett, James Gordon (1795–1872). Scottish-born Bennett founded the *New York Herald* in 1835, editing it until his death. He pioneered in publishing society news and Wall Street financial news, and in employing European correspondents and the telegraph.

Brattain, Walter (1902–1987). With physicists WILLIAM SHOCKLEY and JOHN BARDEEN, Brattain coinvented the transistor in 1947 at the Bell Research Laboratory.

Bush, Vannevar (1890–1974). An electrical engineer, Bush devised the differential analyzer in 1928, thereby pioneering the analogue computer.

Carlson, Chester (1906–1968). Carlson invented the electrostatic process of xerography in 1938 and patented it two years later. Xerox copies were not introduced to the public until 1958.

Clinton, De Witt (1769–1828). A two-term governor of New York (1817–1823 and 1825–1828), Clinton used the power of his office to become the chief promoter of the Erie Canal.

De Forest, Lee (1873–1961). Forest, known as "the Father of Radio," patented more than 300 inventions. Among his most important achievements are the invention of the Audion, the first grid-triode vacuum tube, which made it possible to amplify radio waves; the

introduction of the radio news broadcast; and the establishment of the first radio station.

Disney, Walter (1901–1966). Disney created animated cartoons and produced the first animated movie with sound as well as the first feature-length animated films. His animated films remain popular worldwide today.

Durant, William (1861–1947). Durant controlled the Buick Motor Car Company and subsequently founded General Motors Company and Chevrolet Motor Company (with Louis Chevrolet).

Earhart, Amelia (1897–1937). Flying from Newfoundland to Wales in 1928, Earhart became the first female to cross the Atlantic Ocean in an aircraft. In 1932, she was the first woman to fly the Atlantic solo. In 1935, Earhart achieved two solo firsts—Hawaii to the mainland and Mexico City to New York. Earhart vanished during a round-the-world flight in 1937.

Eastman, George (1854–1932). Eastman developed the process for producing photographic dry plates in 1880. Four years later he received a patent for flexible film. Eastman also invented the Kodak hand camera, daylight-loading firm, and the Brownie camera. He founded the Eastman Kodak Company in 1892.

Edison, Thomas Alva (1847–1931). Edison patented more than 1,000 inventions. Some of the most significant related to transportation and communication were the quadruplex telegraph, the mimeograph, the microphone, the phonograph, the incandescent electric lamp, and the kinetoscope, a machine for making movies.

Fessenden, Reginald (1866–1932). A radio pioneer, Fessenden devised the electrolytic detector, high-frequency alternator, and the heterodyne receiver. He also made the first radio broadcast of voice and music and patented 300 inventions.

Ford, Henry (1863–1947). Ford built his first gasoline car in 1896 and founded the Ford Motor Company seven years later. He introduced his Model T in 1908. Through the moving assembly line, which he created, Ford was able to produce more than 240,000 Model T's a year. For almost twenty years the Model T was the best-selling car; it made America into a nation on wheels.

Franklin, Benjamin (1706–1790). As well as being a statesman, scientist, and philosopher, Franklin was a printer, having apprenticed to his brother James, a

Boston printer, in 1718. On moving to Philadelphia, he published an early newspaper, the *Pennsylvania Gazette*, from 1730 to 1748.

Fulton, Robert (1765–1815). Fulton invented the submarine during the winter of 1800–1801, but no government showed interest. In 1801, minister to France Robert Livingston commissioned him to build a steamboat. Fulton returned to the United States in 1806, and the next year his steamboat, the *Clermont*, steamed from New York to Albany. Although it was not the first steamboat, it was the first of a line of commercially viable steamboats. In 1814, Fulton launched the world's first steam warship.

Gates, William, III (1955–). At the age of nineteen, Gates, along with Paul Allen, formed the Microsoft Company, which produced MS-DOS, the operating system for IBM's first personal computer. That system and other Microsoft programs such as OS/2 and Windows made Microsoft the world's largest manufacturer of microcomputer software.

Glenn, John H. Jr. (1921–). The first American to orbit the earth, aboard *Friendship* 7 on February 20, 1962, Glenn later served four terms as a U.S. senator from Ohio (1975–1999). In 1998, at age seventy-seven, he became the oldest person to travel in space as one of the seven-member crew aboard the space shuttle *Discovery*.

Goddard, Robert (1882–1945). Among Goddard's achievements in rocketry are the design and testing of the first successful liquid-fueled rocket. He also became the first person to exceed the speed of sound. Goddard received more than 200 rocketry patents.

Goldmark, Peter Carl (1906–1977). At the Columbia Broadcasting Systems laboratories, Goldmark, an engineer, invented the color television system and the 33⅓-rpm phonograph, the first long-playing record.

Goldwyn, Samuel (1882–1974). Poland-born Goldwyn founded Goldwyn Pictures in 1917, later merging with Metro Pictures to form Metro-Goldwyn-Mayer (MGM). He produced the first feature film, *The Squaw Man*, in 1913 and went on to produce many memorable films throughout the thirties, forties, and fifties.

Gould, Jay (1836–1892). A financier and speculator, Gould controlled the New York elevated, most of the southwestern railroads, and the Western Union Telegraph Company.

Graham, Katharine (1917–2001). As publisher of the *Washington Post* from 1963 to 1979, Graham became one of the most influential figures in American journalism. Under her leadership, the paper opposed the government by publishing the *Pentagon Papers*, a secret report on U.S. involvement in Vietnam in 1971, and broke the Watergate scandal in 1972. She served as president of the Washington Post Company from 1963 to 1973, and chief executive officer from 1973 to 1991. Her autobiography, *Personal History* (1997), won a Pulitzer Prize.

Greeley, Horace (1811–1872). A journalist and political leader, Greeley, with Jonas Winchester, established and edited the weekly magazine the *New Yorker* (not the current magazine of the same name) from 1834 to 1841. In 1841, he founded the *New York Tribune*, which became tremendously influential in the North, especially before the Civil War. The paper supported abolitionism, free common-school education, and various other reforms.

Harriman, Edward (1848–1909). A railroad magnate and financier, Harriman owned several railroads, including the Lake Ontario Southern Railroad and the Illinois Central. He reorganized the Union Pacific and then acquired Southern Pacific and Central Pacific, which enabled him to dominate western rail service. He later lost a hard-fought battle against JAMES HILL for control of the Northern Pacific Railroad.

Hearst, William Randolph (1863–1951). Hearst built the first great publishing empire, publishing twenty-eight major newspapers and eighteen magazines in 1935. To sell his newspapers to the mass market, he charged a penny for them and pioneered many techniques of tabloid journalism such as oversized, outrageous headlines, shocking photographs, and stories that were sometimes more sensationalistic than accurate.

Hill, James (1838–1916). With associates, Hill acquired the St. Paul and Pacific Railroad, reorganizing and extending it. He created the Northern Railway Company to merge all his lines. Hill won an epic battle against EDWARD HARRIMAN for control of the Northern Pacific.

Hughes, Howard (1905–1976). An industrialist, aviator, and motion picture producer, Hughes founded a company that made experimental planes and set many speed records.

Jobs, Steven (1955–). With Stephen Wozniak, Jobs introduced the Apple computer, launching the personal-computer revolution. Jobs created in Apple a user-friendly alternative to IBM's personal computer. After

TRANSPORTATION

NOTABLE FIGURES, *cont.*

resigning from Apple in 1985, he founded the NeXT Computer Company, which was taken over by Apple in 1996. Jobs was welcomed back to his former company, where he became chief executive officer in 1997.

Kemeny, John (1926–1992). Kemeny, with Thomas Kurtz, invented the BASIC computer language.

Kettering, Charles (1876–1958). An electrical engineer, Kettering invented the automotive electric self-starter and lighting and ignition systems for cars.

Land, Edwin (1909–1991). Land, who was mainly self-taught, invented the first Polaroid Land Camera, which developed photographs inside the camera in about sixty seconds. He also invented black-and-white Polaroid film and color film. Land received patents for more than 530 inventions.

Lindbergh, Charles (1902–1974). Lindbergh completed the first solo nonstop transatlantic flight from New York to Paris in the *Spirit of St. Louis* in 1927, becoming an instant hero.

Luce, Henry (1903–1967). Editor and publisher. With Briton Hadden, Luce founded and edited the weekly magazine *Time*. He also established the monthly *Fortune*, the weekly picture magazine *Life*, and *Sports Illustrated*.

Mauchly, John (1907–1980). A physicist and engineer, Mauchly, with John Eckert, devised the first electronic computer, the Electrical Numerical Integrator and Computer (ENIAC). They also coinvented two later models, BINAC and UNIVAC I.

Mayer, Louis B. (1885–1957). Russian-born Mayer, after having formed the largest theater chain in New England, founded Metro Pictures and Louis B. Mayer Pictures in 1918. In 1924 these merged with the Goldwyn Company to become Metro-Goldwyn-Mayer (MGM), with Mayer as vice president and general manager until 1951. Under Mayer's reign, MGM produced slick, star-studded movies, and Mayer became the most powerful magnate in Hollywood.

Mergenthaler, Ottmar (1854–1899). Mergenthaler patented the first Linotype typesetting machine in 1884; it was the first major improvement in setting type since Gutenberg's invention of moveable type in about 1440. Mergenthaler later patented improvements such as automatic justification.

Morse, Samuel (1791–1872). Morse conducted experiments on a magnetic telegraph beginning in 1832. He invented the Morse code, for which he filed a patent in 1837, to be used in a telegraph. Congress granted him $30,000 to oversee the construction of a telegraph line between Baltimore and Washington, D.C. In May 1844, Morse sent the first telegraphic message over this line: "What hath God wrought!" His invention made possible instantaneous long-distance communication.

Muybridge, Eadweard (1803–1904). Asked to use photography to prove that a running horse has four feet off the ground at one point in its stride, Muybridge went on to make photographic studies of motion. He invented the zoopraxiscope, a forerunner of the movie projector.

Noyce, Robert (1927–1990). An engineer, Noyce coinvented the integrated circuit, a system of interconnecting transistors on a single silicon microchip. The invention led to the development of pocket calculators and microcomputers. Noyce and Gordon Moore founded the Intel Corporation, which became a leading manufacturer of semiconductors.

Olds, Ransom (1864–1950). An inventor and manufacturer, Olds helped establish Detroit's Olds Motor Works. In 1901, he built 425 Oldsmobiles, beginning mass production of American cars.

Otis, Elisha (1811–1861). Otis invented the safety device that kept hoisted machinery safely in the air, making possible the first passenger elevator. Otis received a patent for a steam elevator in 1861 and established the Otis elevator business, which became the major manufacturer of passenger elevators. These, in turn, permitted the building of skyscrapers.

Paley, William S. (1901–1990). Paley bought United Independent Broadcasters Inc. in 1927, renaming it the Columbia Broadcasting System (CBS). With the coming of television, he formed CBS Television, which under his guidance became a communications giant.

Pulitzer, Joseph (1847–1911). A powerful newspaper editor and publisher, Pulitzer bought and merged the *St. Louis Dispatch* and *St. Louis Post* in 1878, generating mass circulation with sensationalist reporting and hard-hitting editorials. He purchased the *New York World* in 1833 and followed a similar formula to expand readership. At his death, he left funds that established the Columbia School of Journalism and the prizes that bear his name.

Pullman, George (1831–1897). Pullman designed the first Pullman railroad car, with a folding upper berth and a lower berth formed from seat cushions. He established the Pullman Palace Car Company in 1867 to build his cars. Pullman also designed the Pullman dining car and built the town of Pullman, near Chicago, for his workers.

Sarnoff, David (1891–1971). A radio and television pioneer, Sarnoff was the first to suggest a commercially marketed radio receiver (1915). He went on to found the National Broadcasting Company (NBC) and to create an experimental television station.

Scripps, Edward (1854–1926). With his half brother George Scripps and Milton McRae, Scripps organized the Scripps-McRae League of Newspapers in 1894 and the Scripps-McRae Press Association in 1897. He also bought Publishers' Press and merged it into the United Press.

Selden, George (1846–1922). In 1895, Selden was granted the patent for a "road engine," the first American gasoline-engine car, which he had invented in 1879.

Sennett, Mack (1880–1960). A motion picture pioneer, Sennett first worked under the director D. W. Griffith at Biograph Studios from 1910 to 1911, before leaving to form the Keystone Company, one of the early movie pictures companies in America.

Shockley, William (1910–1989). At Bell Telephone Laboratory, Shockley coinvented (with JOHN BARDEEN and WALTER BRATTAIN) the transistor, for which they won the 1956 Nobel Prize for physics. In 1954, he started his own semiconductor factory, which ignited the electronics boom and helped create "Silicon Valley," after ex-employees began their own companies.

Sholes, Christopher (1819–1890). Along with Carlos Glidden and Samuel Soulé, Sholes patented the typewriter. In 1873, after Glidden and Soulé gave up their rights to the invention, Sholes sold his to the Remington Arms Company for $12,000.

Sikorsky, Igor (1889–1972). A Russian-born aeronautical engineer and inventory, Sikorsky invented the helicopter in 1909. Four years later he designed, built, and flew the world's first successful multimotored aircraft. In 1931, Sikorsky developed the amphibian *American Clipper*, which pioneered in transoceanic commercial flights.

Stevens, John (1749–1838). Stevens built the first screw-driven steamboat; it marked the first time the powered screw was used in ship propulsion. He also designed the *Phoenix*, which steamed from New York to Philadelphia in 1809 to become the first seagoing steamboat. In 1811, Stevens started the world's first steam ferry service. In 1825, he built the first American steam locomotive.

Turner, Ted (1938–). In 1970, Turner bought an Atlanta TV station that became the WTBS "super-station" and cornerstone of his Turner Broadcasting System (TBS). TBS, in turn, launched Cable New Network (CNN), the first television network to broadcast news twenty-four hours a day. In 1995, with Turner's active support, TBS merged with Time-Warner.

Vanderbilt, Cornelius (1794–1877). Known as Commodore Vanderbilt, he established a controlling interest in a number of eastern railroads, including the New York and Harlem Railroad, the Hudson River Railroad, and the New York Central Railroad. His acquisition of the Lake Shore & Michigan Southern line extended his rail network to Chicago. Vanderbilt built New York City's Grand Central Terminal.

Warner, Harry (1881–1958). With his brothers, Samuel, Albert, and Jack, Warner established motion picture studios in Hollywood in 1918. Five years later these were incorporated into Warner Bros. Pictures.

Westinghouse, George (1846–1914). Westinghouse patented the railroad air brake in 1869 as well as automatic railroad signal devices. He founded Westinghouse Electric Company to manufacture these inventions. Interested in electric and natural gas innovation, he held more than 400 patents.

Wright, Wilbur (1867–1912) and his brother **Orville (1871–1948).** Aviation pioneers, the Wright brothers made the world's first successful flights in a motorized aircraft near Kitty Hawk, North Carolina in 1903. Orville completed the first flight, followed the same day by Wilbur, whose flight lasted fifty-nine seconds and covered 852 feet. In 1908, the Wright brothers developed the first plane for the U.S. Army.

Zworykin, Vladimir (1889–1982). In the 1920s, while working for Westinghouse, Russian-born Zworykin patented the iconoscope and the kinescope; together they became the first television system. Later, he became director of electronic development for RCA.

TRANSPORTATION

CHAPTER 13

RELIGION

HIGHLIGHTS

Timeline of Religion in America

TO ITS NATIVE PEOPLES, the North American continent was a world animated by sacred, ever-present spiritual powers (see p. 20). To many of its European settlers, the New World was a haven from religious persecution and a place to practice their chosen faiths in freedom and safety. The United States was the first modern nation founded by Protestants and the first to enforce a strict separation of church and state. Though much of the nation's history and culture have been shaped by its Protestant heritage, the United States has accepted people of all faiths and given birth to its own religious movements and churches. Never absent of intolerance and prejudice, the religious history of America reflects the diversity, tensions, and evolving beliefs of a people for whom freedom of worship itself is held sacred.

CHRISTIAN BEGINNINGS

1565 The Spanish found the city of St. Augustine in Florida; the first Catholic parish in what will be the United States is established there.
Sir Francis Drake and crew hold the first Protestant service in California.
The Church of England becomes the established church of Virginia.

1612 Pocohontas is converted to Christianity in Virginia (see p. 41).

1620 The first Pilgrims arrive in North America. Religious dissidents, they set sail from England on the *Mayflower* and are headed for Virginia, but instead they reach Plymouth, Massachusetts, where they begin a colony.

1628 Dutch colonists establish the first reformed congregation in New Amsterdam, later New York.
The first Puritans, led by John Endecott, arrive from England and settle in Salem, Massachusetts.

1630 JOHN WINTHROP founds a new community in Boston, thus beginning the Puritan Great Migration to New England (see p. 51, 238).

1634 Under charter of Charles I of England, Lord Baltimore and his sons settle Maryland, which they intend to be a refuge for persecuted Roman Catholics.

1635 The Puritan colony at Salem, Massachusetts, banishes clergyman Roger Williams, who is at odds with its union of church and state (see p. 51).

1636 Williams founds Rhode Island as a colony that will welcome religious dissidents and practice religious tolerance.

Thomas Hooker, a minister who is unhappy with the strictness of life in Massachusetts, founds Hartford, Connecticut.

Celebrating Christmas was illegal in colonial Massachusetts. According a law passed in 1660, anyone found observing the holiday was fined 5 shillings. Christmas did not become a major holiday in the United States until the mid-nineteenth century.

1637 Anne Hutchinson, a popular lay theologian, is branded a heretic for her teachings on grace and justification. In what becomes known as the Antinomian Controversy, she is accused and banished from Massachusetts Bay (see p. 51).

1639 The first Lutheran congregation in the New World is established at Fort Christiana, a Swedish colony in what is now Delaware.

1647 Rhode Island drafts the first civil code in the colonies calling for separation of church and state.

1654 The first Jewish immigrants land at New Amsterdam.

1656 Quakers arriving in Massachusetts are imprisoned and deported. When two return in 1659, they are hanged on Boston Common.

1661 Persecution of Quakers in Massachusetts is halted by Governor John Endicott on the orders of Charles II, who is a friend of William Penn.

The Massachusetts clergy adopt the Half-way Covenant, allowing the baptism of the children of those who are baptized but have not had the conversion experience necessary for full church membership.

Baptism of children is made mandatory in Virginia.

1668 The French establish a Jesuit mission at Sault Sainte Marie, Michigan.

1670 The Act of Virginia decrees that indentured servants who are not Christian must remain servants for life; it is not repealed until 1682.

1677 English Quakers settle in New Jersey.

1681 Quaker William Penn receives a charter from King Charles II of England for lands that will become Pennsylvania. He founds Philadelphia.

1683 Mennonites from Germany immigrate to America and settle near Philadelphia in Germantown. Strong advocates of a separation between church and state, Mennonites strive to live simply and are often pacifists.

1684 Francis Makemie establishes the first Presbyterian congregation in America at Snow Hill, Maryland.

1685 Louis XIV of France renounces the Edict of Nantes, thus denying religious freedom to French Protestants, or Huguenots, many of whom immigrate to the British colonies.

1687 Eusebio Kino, a Jesuit missionary, begins his work in Arizona. By his death in 1711, the mission has made 30,000 converts.

1690s Franciscans begin to build missions in Arizona.

1692 The witchcraft trials are held in Salem, Massachusetts, resulting in the execution of twenty women over the next two years.

1702 COTTON MATHER, an important Massachusetts Puritan minister, publishes *Magnalia Christi Americana*, a major history of American religious development.

1706 FRANCIS MAKEMIE establishes the Synod of Philadelphia, uniting Presbyterians of different backgrounds.

1707 Baptists organize what may be the first North American church umbrella group, the Philadelphia Baptist Association, which brings together five churches in three colonies (Pennsylvania, Delaware, and New Jersey).

1714 In King's Chapel in Boston the first pipe organ is played in an American church and is denounced by Puritans.

1719 *The Psalms of David Imitated* becomes the primary hymnal used in Protestant churches.

THE SALEM WITCH TRIALS

One of the more bizarre chapters in American history is the Salem witch trials. In Europe, people, mostly women, had been persecuted as witches for hundreds of years, and the Puritans brought a belief in witchcraft to the New World. Occasional persecutions occurred throughout the colonies, but none rivaled the witch trials in Salem, Massachusetts.

In 1692, a number of teenage girls began to behave strangely, gathering to meet and murmur incantations, suffering from minor fits, and displaying an uncanny ability to foretell the future. Initially they blamed no one for their behavior, but under pressure from the community and questioning by various clergymen, they pointed a finger at various people, mostly middle-aged women, who lived among them.

Hundreds were accused, twenty-seven were tried, and twenty were executed—nineteen by hanging, one by being pressed to death with stones. Within a few months of the initial trials, even those who believed in witchcraft began to question the procedures, specifically the mass hysteria that surrounded these events.

A new governor of the Massachusetts Bay Colony, Sir William Phipps, forbade any further trials. A new court was convened for the fifty-two people who awaited trial, and all were eventually exonerated.

Aside from mass hysteria, some historians attribute this erratic episode to social changes that were occurring within the staunchly religious community and also to class divisions within it.

RELIGION

The famous 1692 witch trials occurred in Salem Village, Massachusetts, now the town of Danvers. The accusations of several young women led to the deaths of over 20 people, left many languishing in prison awaiting trials, and fueled suspicion and growing hysteria throughout the area.

1730s–1760s The Great Awakening, the first wave of revivalism, starts in New England and soon spreads across the colonies.

1730 The first Jewish synagogue in North America is built.

1734–1735 JONATHAN EDWARDS holds a religious revival in Northampton, Massachusetts, which helps spur the Great Awakening in New England. He emphasized the Calvinist doctrine of predestination, meaning that certain people are predestined for salvation and that God alone determines who will be saved. Calvinism also stresses man's humility and complete dependence on the divine grace of God.

1735 John Wesley, the founder of Methodism in England, comes to Georgia as a missionary, where he creates the foundations of what will become the Methodist movement.

1737 JONATHAN EDWARDS publishes his *Faithful Narrative of the Surprising Work of God in the Conversion of Many Hundred Souls in Northampton*, his first widely read work, describing the extraordinary renewal that followed his preaching on justification by faith.

1740s The Great Awakening sweeps New England.

1741 Evangelical leader JONATHAN EDWARDS preaches his Great Awakening sermon, "Sinners in the Hands of an Angry God."

1743 Boston Congregationalist minister CHARLES CHAUNCY, a theological liberal, takes on the evangelicals in "Seasonable Thoughts on the State of Religion in New England," which decries the emotionalism and irrationalism of revivalist religion. The "battle of the pamphlets" begins between Chauncy and JONATHAN EDWARDS, ending only with Edwards's death in 1758.

1748 Henry Melchior Muhlenberg establishes the Pennsylvania Ministerium, the first permanent governing body for Lutherans in America.

1755 Shubael Stearns and Daniel Marshall set the stage for Baptist growth in the South when they found their Sandy Creek, North Carolina, church during the Great Awakening.

1757 The Philadelphia Quakers ban slaveholding among their members, thus initiating the religious debate over slavery.

1759 The Franciscan friar Junípero Serra establishes Mission San Diego, the first of his nine California missions.

1763 A synagogue, the oldest still standing in the United States, is built in Newport, Rhode Island. It becomes known as the Touro Synagogue after its first rabbi.

In a 1790 letter to the oldest synagogue in the United States, George Washington wrote that the government "gives to bigotry no sanction, to persecution no assistance." Located in Newport, Rhode Island, the Touro Synagogue was founded in 1658, designed by Peter Harrison, and completed in 1763.

1771 FRANCIS ASBURY, a blacksmith and Methodist minister, introduces the circuit-rider system of preaching, already practiced in England. A circuit-riding preacher can tend to thirty to forty communities rather than just one; it proves to be an invaluable way of preaching on the American frontier.

1773 The first annual conference of Methodists is held in Philadelphia.

1774 ANN LEE, an English immigrant, organizes the first American Shaker colony in upstate New York (see p. 470).

FAITH AND FREEDOM

1776 At the time of the country's founding, nine of the thirteen colonies have established religions.

1780s African Americans George Liele and David George become the first American missionaries. Liele founds churches in Jamaica, and George serves in Nova Scotia and Sierra Leone.

REVIVALISM

Four great waves of revivalism have swept the nation since the colonial era. Each of these outbreaks of evangelical religious fervor has been a reaction to a perceived apathy in the churches and the growing secularization of society; and each has at its heart an emphasis on personal conversion and the emotional aspects of religious commitment.

The first wave, called the Great Awakening, began in the 1730s and reached its peak in the early 1740s when the Anglican evangelist George Whitefield preached to thousands, and JONATHAN EDWARDS preached his most famous sermon, "Sinners in the Hands of an Angry God."

The advocates of the awakening, known as the "New Lights," were opposed by "Old Light" ministers like CHARLES CHAUNCY of Boston, who accused the revival movement of emotionalism and irrationalism. By the time of the Revolution, the first wave of revivalism was over, although Evangelicalism would remain an important part of American religious life.

The Second Great Awakening, which has been called "the most influential revival of Christianity in the history of the United States" (scholar Mark Noll) began during the late 1790s and ran its course through the 1820s. In the aftermath of the Revolution, church membership had declined to under 10 percent of the population, and in frontier regions Christian influence was almost nonexistent.

The awakening was characterized by great camp meetings, like that held at Cane Ridge, Kentucky, in 1801, where participants barked like dogs, jerked about, and danced in ecstasy, and by the efforts of circuit-riding Methodist ministers and Baptist farmer-preachers, who set up churches throughout the South and West.

The latter part of the awakening saw the beginning of the ministry of Charles G. Finney, who established many of the features of the typical revival meeting and accelerated the move away from classical Calvinist theology of the First Great Awakening to one that recognized the place of free will in salvation.

The Second Great Awakening solidified the position of evangelicals in American religious life and provided the matrix from which reform movements such as abolitionism, prohibitionism, and the women's rights movement would come.

The third wave of revivalism got under way in the 1890s, with the revival meetings of BILLY SUNDAY, a former professional baseball player who had had a conversion experience in 1886. Sunday used his pulpit to denounce Darwinism and to promote Prohibition. In 1917, he preached a revival in New York during which almost 100,000 people responded to his altar calls. The wave of revival came to an end with the publicity surrounding the Scopes Monkey trial, and antimodernist evangelicals, now known as fundamentalists, separated themselves from public and political life.

The present wave of revivalism began in the 1950s with BILLY GRAHAM, who began as a classic tent-meeting revivalist and went on to hold gigantic televised stadium revivals around the world. As his ministry evolved, Graham managed to separate his evangelical message from much of the combativeness and histrionic excess that had discredited his fundamentalist forbears. Closely associated with American leaders from Eisenhower on, Graham and the institutions that grew up around him helped to restore evangelicals as active players in American public life.

1780 The first Universalist church, emphasizing the unity of the divine, opens in Gloucester, Massachusetts.

Philadelphia Quakers vote to admit African Americans as members.

1784 John Wesley decides to allow Methodists in America to set up their own church, independent of the Church of England, although Methodists will not formally separate from the Church of England until Wesley's death in 1791. The Methodist Episcopal church is organized in Baltimore; FRANCIS ASBURY becomes its first bishop.

Samuel Seabury, a Connecticut Anglican, is consecrated a bishop by bishops of the Scottish Episcopal Church, assuring that American Anglicanism will survive the Revolution.

Boston's Anglican King's Chapel adopts an edition of *The Book of Common Prayer* without references to the doctrine of the Trinity, becoming America's first Universalist congregation.

1786 Thomas Jefferson's Bill for Establishing Religious Freedom, a prototype for the First Amendment, is passed, over the opposition of conservatives who would like established religion to continue.

1789 The Protestant Episcopal Church is officially founded in America to succeed the Church of England in the aftermath of the Revolution. *The Book of Common Prayer,* the Anglican prayer book, and the constitution and canons of the Church are adopted to suit Americans.

The First General Assembly of Presbyterians meets in America.

1790s The Second Great Awakening begins (see p. 462).

1790 John Carroll, the first Roman Catholic bishop in the United States, is installed as bishop of Baltimore.

1791 The Bill of Rights is ratified, adding ten amendments to the Constitution. The First Amendment guarantees, among other rights, freedom of religion.

1793 The first independent Methodist church for African Americans is established in Philadelphia by RICHARD ALLEN.

1794 The first Eastern Orthodox church is consecrated in North America on Kodiak Island, Alaska, by Russian monks.

1796 Black members of the John Street Methodist Church in New York, protesting discrimination, form their own congregation. It later grows into the African Methodist Episcopal Zion church.

1800 The first recorded camp meeting, a staple of revivalism, is held in Logan County, Kentucky (see p. 462).

In the Plan of Union, Presbyterians and Congregationalists on the frontier agree to unite small groups from both churches and accept the ministers of either.

At Cane Ridge, Kentucky, thousands hear the gospel from Presbyterian, Methodist, and Baptist preachers. The fervor and the unusual behavior of many in the crowds electrify the country.

Henry Ware, a liberal Congregationalist, is elected Hollis Professor of Divinity at Harvard, signaling the liberal ascendancy in Massachusetts Congregationalism.

1806 Massachusetts Congregationalists, protesting liberal trends at Harvard, found Andover Seminary to preserve Calvinist orthodoxy.

1808 The first Bible Society is established in Philadelphia by Episcopal bishop William White.

Elizabeth Bayley Seton, a young widow and convert to Catholicism, founds the Sisters of Charity of St. Joseph in Baltimore. In 1975, she becomes the first Catholic saint born in the United States.

1811 Alexander Campbell, an Irish immigrant, starts the Brush Run Church in Pennsylvania. Believing that denomination designations are not biblical, he calls for a return to a noncreedal New Testament Christianity and organizes his followers as the Disciples of Christ.

"If thinking men would have the courage to think for themselves, and to speak what they think, it would be found they do not differ in religious opinion as much as is supposed."
—THOMAS JEFFERSON, LETTER TO JOHN ADAMS

1814 The Rappites, under the leadership of George Rapp, found a utopian colony in New Harmony, Indiana (see p. 470).

1816 The African Methodist Episcopal Church becomes an independent church in Philadelphia.

With 214,235 members, there are now more Methodists in the United States than in England.

The American Bible Society is founded in New York.

1819 Unitarianism, which affirms the unity of God, is founded in Boston by WILLIAM ELLERY CHANNING (see p. 478).

1820s Shaker colonies thrive throughout New England (see p. 470).

1820 King Kamehameha II welcomes the first Christian missionaries to Hawaii.

1824 The American Sunday School Union organizes to promote Sunday schools across the country.

The Baptist General Missionary Convention becomes the first national Baptist association; it coordinates the church's active missionary program.

The Reformed Society of Israelites, a precursor of Reform Judaism, is founded in Charleston, South Carolina. Reform Jews will advocate shorter sermons using more English and will allow the mixed seating of men and women.

1825 The Owenites, organized by Robert Dale Owen, establish themselves in New Harmony, Indiana, when Owen buys the community from the Rappites (see p. 470).

1830 The Church of Jesus Christ of Latter-Day Saints (Mormons) is founded at Fayette, New York, by JOSEPH SMITH JR. A year later it establishes headquarters at Kirtland, Ohio. Mormons believe in the Trinity, the

THE ESTABLISHMENT CLAUSE

The United States is one of the few nations to try to institutionalize freedom of religion. Other countries guarantee and protect the right to practice religion freely, but no other country has expended the time and energy the United States has on maintaining what Thomas Jefferson called a "wall of separation between church and state."

The earliest bill mandating separation, which Thomas Jefferson called his proudest achievement, was a Bill for Establishing Religious Freedom introduced in 1776. It will take ten years to pass.

Jefferson was not without his reasons for believing that the new nation needed laws regarding the establishment of religion. In 1776, nine of the thirteen colonies had established religions. Massachusetts, Rhode Island, and New Hampshire supported Congregationalism and, Jefferson's bill notwithstanding, continued to do so well into the nineteenth century. In New York and the southern colonies, the Anglican faith (later Episcopalianism) was established. New York required officeholders to renounce the Pope, and even Pennsylvania, otherwise a bastion of religious freedom, required elected officials to sign an oath subscribing to their belief in the Scriptures. There were patriots, among them Patrick Henry, who wanted an official state religion to be paid for with tax moneys.

Eventually Jefferson's establishment bill (or disestablishment bill, as it might more properly have been called) was codified in the Bill of Rights, specifically in the First Amendment, which reads, in part: "Congress shall make no law respecting an establishment of religion, nor prohibiting the free exercise thereof."

In truth, though, the wall that Jefferson tried so hard to build is permeable and at times blurry, more like what James Madison described as a "line of separation between the rights of religion and civil authority." For example, churches are traditionally exempt from paying taxes, yet the taxpayers support military chaplains. Since the 1940s, the Supreme Court has regularly and continuously been called upon to settle various religious disputes: whether federal moneys can be used to bus children to parochial schools (they can), whether Nativity scenes and other religious symbols can be displayed on public property (they can), and whether the Ten Commandments can be posted in public schools (they cannot).

Perhaps the greatest accomplishment of the nation is not that it has built a wall or drawn a line between church and state but that it has displayed such an amazing amount of flexibility on the subject.

---

afterlife, marriage for eternity, and that each individual is responsible for his or her own sins. Mormons believe that the Bible is divinely inspired, but have also added new scriptures such as the Book of Mormon. Some Mormons have also advocated polygamy.

1833 The Congregational Church is disestablished in Massachusetts. A branch of Puritanism that developed in England in the 1600s, Congregationalist doctrine was highly influential in New England for many years.

1834 The California missions are secularized after Mexico wins its independence from Spain. Mexico could no longer afford the mission system and sold their land.

1836 Ralph Waldo Emerson's *Nature* is published, and the Transcendental Club meets for the first time in Boston. Transcendentalism, a philosophical and cultural movement stressing people's innate ability to discover religious truth outside the bounds of Christianity, will dominate American thought for a decade. In addition to Emerson, its champions include Henry David Thoreau, Margaret Fuller, Bronson Alcott, and, for a time, Orestes Brownson.

1838 Following the economic collapse of their Kirtland, Ohio, community, Joseph Smith and his followers flee to western Missouri, where Smith plans to build the city of Zion at Independence.

1839 John Humphrey Noyes founds the Putney Community in Vermont, a group that preaches the theory of "Bible communism" it believes existed in the early Christian Church. The Putney community featured property sharing and complex marriage, a type of polygamy, and prompted neighboring communities to chase them out of Putney (see pp. 470, 478).

Persecuted by Missourians, Joseph Smith takes his Mormon followers to Nauvoo, Illinois.

German immigrants in Perry County, Missouri, form the nucleus of what will become the Lutheran Church—Missouri Synod.

In Alaska, Russian priest John Veniaminov becomes the first Orthodox bishop to serve in the Americas.

1843 The Methodist Episcopal Church splits over the issue of slavery. The abolitionists form the Wesleyan Methodist Church.

1844 Joseph Smith, the founder of Mormonism, and his brother Hyrum are murdered by a mob at the Carthage, Illinois, jail. Brigham Young, the senior Mormon apostle, succeeds Smith as president of the church.

Orestes Brownson, after a spiritual pilgrimage that takes him from Presbyterianism through Unitarianism and Transcendentalism to his own Church of the Future, is baptized a Roman Catholic in Boston. Until his death in 1876, Brownson is America's leading Catholic journalist and lay apologist.

Splitting with their northern brethren over the issue of slavery, Baptists in the South form the Southern Baptist Convention (SBC). By the 1990s, the SBC is the largest Protestant church body in the United States.

1847 Under the leadership of Brigham Young, the Mormons migrate again, this time to the western frontier, where they found Salt Lake City, Utah, as a religious community.

Liberal Congregational theologian Horace Bushnell publishes *Christian Nature*, a precursor of Protestant modernism.

1848 John Humphrey Noyes establishes his Perfectionist Community in Oneida, New York (see p. 470).

1852 The Reorganized Church of Jesus Christ of the Latter-Day Saints is established. Rejecting the leadership of Brigham Young and such Mormon doctrines as polygamy, it is headquartered in Independence, Missouri.

1854 James Augustine Healy is ordained as the first African American Roman Catholic priest; in 1875, he will become bishop.

RELIGION AND HIGHER EDUCATION

From the seventeenth to the twentieth centuries, many of the most distinguished colleges and universities in the United States have been established by religious denominations.

YEAR	COLLEGE/UNIVERSITY	CITY, STATE	DENOMINATION
1636	Harvard University (founded as Harvard College)	Cambridge, Massachusetts	Congregational
1693	College of William and Mary	Williamsburg, Virginia	Anglican
1701	Yale University (founded as the Collegiate School)	New Haven, Connecticut	Congregational
1746	Princeton University (founded as the College of New Jersey)	Princeton, New Jersey	Presbyterian
1754	Columbia University (founded as King's College)	New York, New York	Anglican
1764	Brown University (founded as Rhode Island College)	Providence, Rhode Island	Baptist
1769	Dartmouth College	Hanover, New Hampshire	Congregational
1787	Cokesbury College	Abingdon, Maryland	Methodist
1789	Georgetown University	Washington, D.C.	Roman Catholic
1813	Colby College	Waterville, Maine	Baptist
1842	University of Notre Dame	South Bend, Indiana	Roman Catholic
1875	Brigham Young University	Provo, Utah	Mormon
1891	University of Chicago	Chicago, Illinois	Baptist
1911	Southern Methodist University	Dallas, Texas	Methodist
1963	Oral Roberts University	Tulsa, Oklahoma	Evangelical

1858 The United Presbyterian Church of North America is founded.

Isaac Hecker, a convert from Transcendentalism to Roman Catholicism, founds the Paulist Fathers.

c. 1861 The Old School Presbyterian Church splits over slavery. The proslavery forces reorganize as the Presbyterian Church in the Confederate States of America.

After recovering from a serious illness in 1866, Mary Baker Eddy founded Christian Science and began to teach the healing power of faith.

Joseph Smith, the founder of Mormonism, is believed to have had as many as fifty wives, though he publicly acknowledged only the first, Emma Hale Smith. A matter of intense political dispute in Utah, the Mormon practice of polygamy was officially discontinued in 1890.

1863 The Seventh-Day Adventist Church, which believes in the imminent second coming of Christ and considers Saturday as the Sabbath, is founded in Battle Creek, Michigan, by followers of religious leader William Miller.

President Abraham Lincoln begins the practice of annual Thanksgiving Day, "as a day of Thanksgiving and praise to our beneficent Father."

1866 MARY BAKER EDDY begins teaching the Christian Science form of faith healing.

1867 The first collection of African American spirituals, *Slave Songs of the United States*, is published.

1870s The Holiness movement sweeps through American Protestantism. Growing out of the Methodist Churches, the movement teaches the "entire santification," complete surrender to God, is possible for believers in this life.

1870 The Colored Methodist Episcopal Church is established and soon becomes the Christian Methodist Episcopal Church, South.

1872 Bible teacher Charles Russell, who will later found the Jehovah's Witnesses, announces that Christ will return in 1874 without anyone being aware of his presence.

1875 MARY BAKER EDDY publishes *Science and Health with Key to the Scriptures*, an explanation of her theology.

DWIGHT MOODY begins his American revival tour after successfully converting thousands in Britain.

The Theosophical Society, which combines occultism and spiritualism with elements of Eastern religion, is founded in New York by Helena Blavatsky and Henry S. Olcott.

1876 FELIX ADLER founds the Ethical Culture Society in New York City (see p. 478).

1879 The Supreme Court, upholding the antipolygamy law, rules that religion cannot be used as a defense against behavior that is criminal or even morally offensive to most persons (see p. 481).

MARY BAKER EDDY formally founds the Church of Christ (Scientist).

1880 The Salvation Army begins its work in the United States.

1880–1917 When pogroms threaten their existence in Russia and Eastern Europe, many Jews immigrate to the United States.

Nonkosher food is served at the banquet celebrating the first graduating class at Hebrew Union College in Cincinnati; in the aftermath, more

The Mormon Temple in Salt Lake City, Utah, completed in 1893, is the holiest place in the Mormon religion. The Tabernacle, the domed structure next to the Temple, serves as the home of the esteemed Mormon Tabernacle choir and the main social and cultural arena for the Mormon community.

traditional Jews separate themselves from the Reform movement, eventually forming Conservative Judaism.

The Third Plenary Council of Baltimore begins the intensive development of Roman Catholic parochial schools in response to the influx of Catholic immigrants and the spread of secular education.

Charles Russell founds the Zion's Watch Tower Tract Society.

The Jewish Theological Seminary, the first institution of Conservative Judaism, is founded in New York.

1890 The Mormons officially disown the practice of polygamy so that Utah can become a state, which it does in 1896.

1895 BILLY SUNDAY, an enormously popular revivalist, begins his preaching career, and a third wave of revivalism sweeps the country (see p. 462).

1897 The Rabbi Isaac Elchanan Theological Seminary is founded to train rabbis for Orthodox Jewish congregations.

1898 Gideons International is founded by traveling salesmen John Nicholson and Sam Hill in Boscobel, Wisconsin. Ten years later the Gideons will have placed twenty Bibles in hotel rooms in Montana; seventy-five years later, at their peak, they will be placing 16 million Bibles in hotel rooms every year.

1900 The Roman Catholic Church in the United States has 12 million members, and there are 6 million Methodists, 5 million Baptists, 1.5 million Lutherans, 1.5 million Presbyterians, 650,000 Episcopalians, and 1 million Jews.

RELIGION

UTOPIAN VISIONS

From the time of its discovery, the New World has held the promise of a fresh start. Blessed with an abundance of land and imposing few restraints on religion, America has been the home to many utopian communities, idealistic if impractical attempts to perfect human nature in a harmonious society.

Among the first utopian groups was the Shakers, whose founder, Mother ANN LEE, settled in Watervliet, New York, in 1774. Her followers, who believed she was the second coming of Christ, lived a celibate life in communities where the sexes were strictly separated and all property was held in common. At the height of their popularity in the 1840s, the Shakers supported nineteen communities in eight states and had about 6,000 adherents. Shaker worship, at first ecstatic, with trances, dancing, and shouting announcing the presence of the Holy Spirit, later became ritualized, with ordered singing and dancing. Although only a few Shakers survive today, the Shaker legacy survives on the simple, beautiful, and well-crafted furniture and other products they made, which today are highly prized by collectors and are often reproduced.

Central New York produced several other notable experimental communities. In 1848, the radical social reformer John Humphrey Noyes moved his community from Vermont to the town of Oneida, New York. Like the Shakers, Noyes was interested in reshaping relations between men and women, but instead of celibacy, his followers practiced a complex system of communal marriage that shocked the outside world. The Oneida Community, which numbered more than 300 at its height, was successful commercially and agriculturally but broke apart in 1881. Oneida Silver, a company Noyes founded, still survives.

The Mormons, also born in central New York, sought to be a utopian community in the early days of their existence. In planned communities like Nauvoo

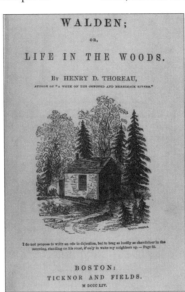

In the 1854 book Walden, *which became the benchmark of American Transcendentalism, Henry David Thoreau writes of his experiment in withdrawing from materialist urban culture and living simply on Walden Pond in Massachusetts.*

and Salt Lake City, they practiced polygamy and shared economic resources. Although they have survived and prospered as a church, their dreams of building a Western Zion were undermined by the gold rush of 1849, further weakened during the Civil War, and finally ended when polygamists were disenfranchised by Congress in 1882.

In 1842, a group of German Pietists, the Community of True Inspiration, emigrated to New York. They founded a village near Buffalo. Fleeing urban corruption, they moved to Iowa between 1855 and 1864, establishing seven villages as the Amana Society. In 1932, internal strife and outside pressure resulted in the dissolution of the community. Its assets, in the form of shares in a new corporation, were divided among the members. Now known as Amana Appliances, the corporation is best known as a manufacturer of kitchen appliances.

In 1805, another German immigrant, George Rapp, sought to build a cooperative, celibate community in Harmony in western Pennsylvania. In 1814, the community moved to New Harmony in southern Indiana. In 1824, Rapp and his followers sold the village to the industrialist Robert Owen and moved back to Pennsylvania. Owen tried to build a "Community of Equality" at New Harmony, but communal living ended in 1827. Today New Harmony's twenty-six historic buildings have been restored.

Brook Farm, a 200-acre farm in Roxbury, Massachusetts, was founded by George Ripley and seventeen others in 1841. Its visitors and members included many leading Transcendentalists, including Emerson, Thoreau, and Bronson Alcott. In 1844, Brook Farm came under the influence of the French socialist Charles Fourier. It was disbanded after a fire in 1847.

Despite their failure to survive in their communal form, these remarkable movements have left their mark on American culture.

CHURCH AND STATE

1901 The American Standard Version of the Bible is published. Based on the King James version of 1611, it will be recognized by most Protestant denominations.

The Pentecostal movement is born when students at Charles Fox Parham's Bible School in Topeka, Kansas, begin "speaking in tongues," or experiencing the gift of ecstatic speech. Parham identifies this as the primary sign of "Spirit baptism."

1906 William J. Seymour begins the Azusa Street Revival in Los Angeles, and the Pentecostal movement spreads across the country.

1907 Walter Rauschenbusch publishes *Christianity and Social Crisis*, the major work of the Social Gospel movement that seeks to apply Christ's teachings to social problems.

1908 MARY BAKER EDDY founds the *Christian Science Monitor*, a daily newspaper.

The Church of the Nazarene, the largest to grow from the Holiness movement, is formed through the union of several Holiness church bodies. The Holiness movement held that individuals are freed from their sins through conversion or justification, and are freed from the flaws that cause them to sin through the process of sanctification or salvation. People may live in corruptible bodies, but perfection is possible if believers love God with their entire heart, mind, and soul, and rely on God's forgiveness.

Thirty-three Protestant denominations with 18 million members form the Federal Council of Churches, the precursor of the National Council of Churches.

1909 C. I. Scofield publishes *The Scofield Reference Bible*, which codifies the teachings of premillennial dispensationalism, and makes a powerful impact on the nascent fundamentalist movement.

Premillennialism is the belief that Christ will return before the millennium, or the thousand-year period of peace and righteousness noted in the Bible. Dispensationalism, the most common form of premillennialism, separates history into dispensations or eras that are characterized by a change in the way God deals with humanity.

1916 Stephen Wise, a prominent Reform rabbi, organizes the American Jewish Congress to respond to pogroms in eastern Poland and lobby for liberal immigration policies.

1917–1919 World War I stimulates cooperation among churches.

The Federal Council of Churches establishes a General Wartime Commission to coordinate more than thirty denominations and

1917–1919, *cont.*

organizations and provide troops with supplies, chaplains, morale, and civilian aide. Catholic and Jewish groups also supported the war effort.

1918 Evangelist AIMEE SEMPLE MCPHERSON begins her radio broadcasts.

"Science without religion is lame, religion without science is blind."
—ALBERT EINSTEIN

1919 FATHER DIVINE organizes an evangelical communal colony in Sayville, Long Island, devoted to renunciation of personal property and racial equality.

1922 MORDECAI KAPLAN founds the Society for the Advancement of Judaism and begins to write about Judaism as a culture rather than a religion, thus laying the foundation for the Reconstructionist movement, which will seek to make Judaism more relevant to modern Jews, by retaining tradition but dispensing with any elements of the supernatural.

1923 Pentecostal preacher AIMEE SEMPLE MCPHERSON builds the Angelus Temple in Los Angeles, whose large rotating illuminated cross can be seen for fifty miles.

The Auburn Affirmation, a liberal protest against enforced orthodoxy, is signed by 1,300 Presbyterian ministers.

1926 Father Charles Coughlin, a Catholic priest in Royal Oak, Michigan, broadcasts his first radio show from Detroit. By 1930, he has turned to politics, and attracts an audience of some 40 million. During the 1930s, he becomes increasingly anti-Semitic and anti-Roosevelt. In 1942, he is silenced by the bishop of Detroit.

The Virgin Mary is the only woman to have appeared on the cover of *Time* magazine ten times.

1930s The Black Muslims begin to gain a following under ELIJAH MUHAMMAD, in Detroit, Michigan (see p. 478).

1932 REINHOLD NIEBUHR's book *Moral Man and Immoral Society* is published.

1933 DOROTHY DAY, founder of the national Catholic Worker movement, publishes the *Catholic Worker*, a newspaper that weds religious feeling to radical politics.

1939 Three branches of Methodism—the Methodist Episcopal Church; the Methodist Episcopal Church, South; and the Methodist Protestant Church—unite.

1940 In a case involving the Jehovah's Witnesses, the Supreme Court decides that the states must extend to the Jehovah's Witnesses the rights regarding religion guaranteed under the First Amendment and protect their rights as they would any other religious group.

1948 THOMAS MERTON, an ascetic Trappist monk and author, publishes *The Seven Storey Mountain*, his autobiography.

1949 Evangelical leader BILLY GRAHAM holds his first tent crusade in Los Angeles and converts some prominent Hollywood stars.

1950s The fourth (and present-day) wave of religious revivalism begins (see p. 462).

1950 Twenty-five Protestant and four Eastern Orthodox groups, with membership totaling 33 million, form the National Council of Churches.

1952 The Revised Standard Version of the Bible, based on the King James Version of 1611, is introduced.

1953 The Church of Scientology, which believes people are immortal, is founded in Washington, D.C., by L. Ron Hubbard, best-selling author of *Dianetics: The Modern Science of Mental Health*.

1954 By order of President Dwight Eisenhower, the words "under God" are added to the Pledge of Allegiance.

ORAL ROBERTS, an itinerant faith healer and evangelist, begins to broadcast his healing services on television.

1955 The Presbyterian Church becomes the first mainline Protestant denomination to approve the ordination of women.

Chosen by a group of ministers, MARTIN LUTHER KING JR. leads the Montgomery bus boycott, the first battle in the modern civil rights struggle (see p. 124).

1956 The Methodist Church, at its annual conference, becomes the first mainline Protestant denomination to ban racial segregation.

1957 MARTIN LUTHER KING JR. becomes president of the Southern Christian Leadership Conference.

The United Church of Christ is formed by the merger of the Evangelical and Reformed Church and the Congregational Christian Churches.

1960s–1970s In the wake of the changes introduced by the Second Vatican Council and the renewed condemnation of artificial contraception by Pope Paul VI, issues of sexuality increasingly come to preoccupy American Catholics.

Universalist and Unitarian Churches merge.

1962 The Supreme Court decides that mandated prayer in the public schools is unconstitutional.

RELIGIOUS BROADCASTING

The modern counterpart to nineteenth century revival meetings, religious broadcasting in the United States, grew up hand in hand with the electronic media. Regularly scheduled religious programming began with the establishment of continuous radio broadcasts in 1920. The first of the great religious media personalities was the Roman Catholic priest Charles E. Coughlin, whose broadcasts from 1926 through the 1930s drew audiences in the millions—and widespread controversy for his vehement attacks against Jews, the financial community, and the Roosevelt administration. With the rise of television in the 1950s came new formats, new personalities, and new issues. Early programming typically took the form of Sunday morning observance and

Father Charles Coughlin drew huge audiences with his controversial radio sermons, which ran from 1926 to 1940.

discussion in donated airtime. A top-rated program was the series *Life Is Worth Living*, hosted by the popular Catholic bishop Fulton J. Sheen. After a favorable ruling by the FCC in 1960, Evangelical groups began buying up airtime, giving rise by the mid-1970s to the "electronic church" ministries of ORAL ROBERTS, Jim Bakker, Pat Robertson, Jimmy Swaggert, and others. On-air requests for donations, support for conservative political causes, and personal scandal have generated criticism, but religious television programming continues to attract weekly U.S. audiences of up to 24 million. Largest among the religious media companies is Robertson's Christian Broadcasting Network (CBN), best known for its flagship program, *The 700 Club*.

1962–1965 The Second Vatican Council took place in four autumn sessions. All manner of topics were discussed from divine revelation to missionary work to Christian education. Among the most important documents issued are the Dogmatic Constitution on the Church, reemphasizing the importance of bishops, the Constitution on the Sacred Liturgy, allowing the vernacularization of and the use of some English in the liturgy to spur more lay participation, and the Pastoral Constitution on the Church in the Modern World, about the church's need to adjust to modern times. The council condemned anti-Semitism and acknowledged religious liberty, which somewhat altered the traditional relationship of the Catholic Church and other religions.

1963 MARTIN LUTHER KING JR. leads the March on Washington, a clerically inspired protest against the denial of civil rights to millions of black Americans (see p. 127).

The Supreme Court bans Bible reading in public schools.

1965 ELIJAH MUHAMMAD publishes *Message to the Black Man in America*, a religious treatise on the Nation of Islam.

Faith healer ORAL ROBERTS opens Oral Roberts University in Tulsa, Oklahoma.

1966 The International Society for Krishna Consciousness, which appeals to many American youth, is founded in New York by Swami Prabhupada, a Calcutta Hindu scholar and teacher.

The Methodist Church and the United Church of the Brethren unite to form the United Methodist Church.

1967 Presbyterians adopt their first new confession since 1647.

1970s Cults, such as the Unification Church headed by Korean reverend Sun Myung Moon, win thousands of converts, especially among the young. Moon's financial empire is vast; he publishes a conservative newspaper called the *Washington Times* and owns and operates many retail businesses. When he stages huge mass wedding ceremonies for members whose mates the church has selected, some parents protest and hire private detectives to kidnap and deprogram their "Moonie" children, whom they view as brainwashed.

1970 The entire Roman Catholic Mass is said in the vernacular.

The Supreme Court validates the right of religious organizations to remain tax-exempt.

1971 The Supreme Court rules that federal funds cannot be used to support parochial schools.

1972 Four Episcopalian bishops defy church law to ordain eleven women priests.

The first woman rabbi is ordained by the Reform branch of Judaism.

1973 The Conservative branch of Judaism permits women to be counted when forming a quorum for worship.

In the aftermath of *Roe v. Wade*, the Roman Catholic Church begins to mount organized opposition to abortion.

1974 Jim Bakker founds the Praise the Lord (PTL) ministry, which will become, ten years later, a multimillion-dollar telemedia religious organization.

1975 Pope Paul VI canonizes Elizabeth Seton, the first U.S. born-Catholic saint.

1978 Following a U.S. government investigation into allegations of abuse of congregants, followers of San Francisco clergyman Jim Jones of the People's

Heavyweight boxing champion Muhammad Ali sits onstage with leader Elijah Muhammad at the National Meeting of the Black Muslims in Chicago in 1966. Probably the most high profile convert to the Nation of Islam, Ali receives a standing ovation from the crowd.

Reverend Sun Myung Moon, leader of the Unification Church, and his wife perform a group marriage in New York City's Madison Square Garden on New Year's Day in 1982. The 2,075 participating pairs had their mates chosen by other members of the cult.

1978, *cont.*

Temple flee to Guyana, where 911 persons commit mass suicide by drinking Kool-Aid laced with cyanide.

1979 The Moral Majority is founded in Lynchburg, Virginia, by Baptist minister Jerry Falwell. It is the first Evangelical group to become politically active, advocating conservative moral and political positions.

Reaching an audience of more than 20 million, 1,400 radio stations and 30 television stations are dedicated to religious programming.

1980s After several centuries of domination by the mainstream Protestant churches, more Christians belong to Evangelical churches than to mainstream Protestant churches.

1980s–1990s Brought together in the anti-abortion Right to Life movement, Evangelical and Roman Catholic conservatives begin to cooperate more broadly in the political arena.

1983 The two branches of the Presbyterian Church (the United Presbyterian Church of North America and the Presbyterian Church of the United States), which split over slavery, merge to form the Presbyterian Church (U.S.A.).

The Supreme Court denies tax-exempt status to private religiously affiliated universities that practice racial discrimination.

1985 The Conservative branch of Judaism ordains its first woman rabbi.

1987 Televangelist Jim Bakker resigns his pulpit after confessing that he cheated on his wife with a church secretary and then used church money to buy the secretary's silence.

1988 Assembly of God televangelist Jimmy Swaggart is defrocked after he confesses to having sexual relations with a prostitute. Although ordered to stay off television for one year, he is back on the airwaves after three months.

The Reverend Jerry Falwell resigns from the Moral Majority in the wake of the scandal involving Jim and Tammy Bakker and the PTL Club.

The Lutheran Church in America, the American Lutheran Church, and the Association of Evangelical Lutheran Churches merge to form the Evangelical Lutheran Church in America.

1993 The Supreme Court invalidates a local Florida law that bans the use of animals in religious rites but still permits hunting and fishing.

1998 The Southern Baptist Convention, representing 16 million members of the denomination, issues a statement declaring that a wife should "submit herself graciously" to her husband's leadership. The declaration raises a storm of controversy within and outside the Church.

1999–2000 The Evangelical Lutheran Church in America, with 5.2 million members, and the Episcopal Church, with 2.4 million members, approve full communion. The "Called to Mission" alliance, under discussion for thirty years, may help both churches stem declines in membership.

DENOMINATION AND CHURCH AFFILIATIONS

As the twentieth century drew to a close, an estimated 168 million Americans—more than 60 percent of the population—were counted as members of a church, denomination, or organized religious group. Of these, a vast majority claimed membership in a Christian church. The U.S. Census Bureau does not collect data on religious affiliation, but estimates of church membership are compiled by the National Council of the Churches of Christ in the U.S.A. and published in the *Yearbook of American and Canadian Churches.*

CHURCH/DENOMINATION	MEMBERSHIP/AFFILIATION (MILLIONS)
All Christian Churches	151.1
Roman Catholic Church	62.3
Baptist Churches	28.4
Methodist Churches	13.2
Pentecostal Churches	11.4
Lutheran Churches	8.3
Latter-day Saints Churches	5.3
Presbyterian Churches	4.1
Orthodox (Eastern) Churches	4.0
Churches of Christ	3.5
Episcopal Church	2.4
Reformed Churches	1.9
Jehovah's Witnesses	1.0
Jewish	5.8
Muslim	3.1
Other	8.0

Note: These figures are for 1999–2000.

RELIGION

RELIGIONS FOUNDED IN AMERICA, 1819–PRESENT

Although several religions are closely identified with America—Puritanism, Shakerism, and Methodism come to mind—these were actually founded in England, and their followers settled in America to escape persecution. What follows is a list of purely indigenous American religions. Some flared only briefly before burning out, while others proved to be enduring. The religions are as idiosyncratic as Americans themselves, and if they share anything in common, it is only that each, in its own unique way, seems to speak to our national character.

1819 WILLIAM ELLERY CHANNING publishes *Unitarian Christianity.* Unitarians reject the traditional Christian doctrine of the Trinity. The American Unitarian Association is founded in Boston in 1825.

1830 The Church of Jesus Christ of Latter-Day Saints (Mormons) is founded by JOSEPH SMITH in Fayette, New York. Mormons believe in the Trinity and that every individual is responsible for his or her own sins. They believe that the Bible is divinely inspired, but have added new scriptures such as the Book of Mormon. Some Mormons have also advocated polygamy, a practice that has led to their persecution. They will eventually settle in Utah.

1839 John Humphrey Noyes founds the Putney Community in Vermont. The group hopes to duplicate the free love and communism they believe existed in early Christian communities. It moves to Oneida, New York, in 1848, but dies out within a few years.

1863 The Seventh-Day Adventist Church, which believes in the imminent second coming of Christ, is founded in Battle Creek, Michigan.

1866 MARY BAKER EDDY begins preaching the teachings of what will become the Christian Science religion, which practices faith healing. In 1879, she establishes the Church of Christ (Scientist).

1872 Jehovah's Witnesses, a millennialist group, is organized in Pittsburgh by Congregationalist minister Charles Russell.

1876 The Ethical Culture Society, or the Ethical movement, which believes that all societies share an ethical culture that is not necessarily religious in its origins, is founded by FELIX ADLER in New York City.

1930s The Black Muslims, also known as the Nation of Islam—a black nationalist group—is founded in Detroit by W. D. Fard. They adhere to some principles of Islam, such as frugality, modesty, and self-discipline. They refrain from eating pork, corn bread, catfish, or possum, which they consider to be symbols of slavery. Originally members of the Nation of Islam preached that Allah created the black people as a divine and superior race and that white people were the result of genetic manipulation by an evil scientist. However, in time they have allowed whites to join their ranks and have focused more on traditional religious beliefs and less on political goals.

1953 The Church of Scientology, an "applied religious philosophy" based on the teachings of L. Ron Hubbard in *Dianetics: The Modern Science of Mental Health* (1950), *Science of Survival* (1951), and other writings, is formally established. Scientology is known for the high profile of its many Hollywood members, such as John Travolta, Kirstie Alley, Jenna Elfman, and Tom Cruise.

1978 Cult leader Jim Jones, organizer of the People's Temple located in the California Bay Area, gathers his followers and takes them to Guyana, where 911 of them commit mass suicide when ordered to do so by Jones.

1980s After several centuries of domination by the mainstream Protestant churches, more Christians now belong to fundamentalist churches than to mainstream Protestant churches.

AFRICAN AMERICANS AND RELIGION, 1730s–PRESENT

The relationship between Christianity and African Americans is a unique and fascinating aspect of American history. At first denied the right to practice either their own African faiths or the Christianity that prevailed in America, blacks were later alternately welcomed and rejected by various Protestant denominations. In the years before the Civil War, many Protestant clergymen supported slavery from their pulpits. After the Civil War, black clergy, who had always been influential in American culture, formed their own churches, which quickly became the backbone of many black communities. During the 1950s and 1960s, these churches spearheaded the civil rights movement.

1730s The Great Awakening prompts the conversion of many blacks, most of whom are slaves (see p. 462).

1770 Blacks and whites worship together.

1780s African Americans George Liele and David George become the first American missionaries when they found churches in, respectively, Jamaica and Sierra Leone.

1794 In Philadelphia, two important and influential black churches are founded: the Bethel African Methodist Church by RICHARD ALLEN and the St. Thomas African Episcopal Church by Absalom Jones.

1800s Black churches form throughout the North. In the South, as slaveowners react to their fears about letting their slaves assemble, slaves are sometimes permitted to worship in groups and sometimes denied the right to do so.

1808 The Abyssinian Baptist Church, which will become one of the most influential houses of worship in Harlem and at times nationally, is founded. It will one day be the home pulpit of Adam Clayton Powell Sr. and, briefly, Adam Clayton Powell Jr.

1809 The first black Baptist church is founded in Philadelphia. Black Baptists will soon become one of the largest Protestant denominations.

1816 The African Methodist Episcopal Church, the first major black denomination, is established by RICHARD ALLEN.

1829 Although few African Americans have been exposed to Roman Catholicism, and thus few have converted, a black order, the Oblate Sisters of Providence, is founded.

1842 A second African American Roman Catholic order, the Holy Family Sisters, is founded.

1854 James Augustine Healy becomes the first African American ordained as a Roman Catholic priest.

1863–1865 Northern missionaries follow the Union army into the South and convert many of the newly freed slaves to Protestantism. Many blacks join white churches.

1870 The Colored Methodist Episcopal Church is founded by blacks who leave the predominantly white Methodist Church, South.

During Reconstruction, blacks are driven out of the white churches and found their own. Black denominations such as the African Methodist Episcopalian Church promote the return to Africa, but few choose to do this. Out of this movement comes, however, a commitment on the part of the black churches to build missions and seek converts in Africa.

Late 1870s The majority of blacks have withdrawn from white churches to establish their own. The primary denominations are the African Methodist Episcopalian Church and the black Baptist churches.

1875 James Augustine Healy becomes the first American Catholic black bishop and presides for twenty-five years over a diocese that includes Maine and Rhode Island.

RELIGION

AFRICAN AMERICANS AND RELIGION, 1730s–PRESENT, cont.

1890s–1920s Large numbers of southern blacks emigrate to northern cities, where many are converted to Roman Catholicism. Black enrollment in parochial schools increases.

Black sects of Islam and Judaism begin to form.

1895 The National Baptist Convention of the U.S.A. is formed by the merger of the Foreign Mission Baptist Convention of the U.S.A., the American Baptist Convention, and the Baptist National Education Convention. It is the largest of the African American churches.

1900 The African American churches that have formed in the wake of the Civil War are, and will remain, a major influence in black cultural and social life. Of 8.3 million blacks, the census shows that 2.7 are affiliated with a black church.

1906 William J. Seymour, a black preacher, leads multiracial congregations in the Azusa Street Revival in Los Angeles and thus starts the Pentecostal movement, which will become known for its members' ability to speak in tongues.

1930s–1960s From their pulpits, black clergy begin to mobilize their congregants for the civil rights movement.

1955 Baptist minister MARTIN LUTHER KING JR. organizes the Montgomery, Alabama, bus boycott, which in turn sets off the nationwide civil rights movement. An advocate of nonviolence, King will remain, until his assassination in 1968, the preeminent black civil rights leader.

1957 MARTIN LUTHER KING JR., Bayard Rustin, and black ministers form the Southern Christian Leadership Conference (SCLC), which will play a major role in coordinating the work of black churches during the civil rights movement p. 124–127).

1960s ELIJAH MUHAMMAD, the head of the Nation of Islam, calls for the creation of an all-black nation within a nation. As black militants denounce Christianity as a white religion, MALCOLM X, a charismatic Muslim leader, is able to convert many blacks to the Nation of Islam. Black Muslims, who number about 100,000, support thirty-three temples (see p. 478).

1964 MALCOLM X breaks with the Nation of Islam to found the Organization for Afro-American Unity, a splinter group of Black Muslims.

1965 MALCOLM X is assassinated at a religious rally in New York City.

1968 MARTIN LUTHER KING JR. is assassinated in Memphis, Tennessee.

1975 ELIJAH MUHAMMAD, the moving force behind the Nation of Islam, dies in Chicago.

1989 In Massachusetts, Barbara Harris, an African American, becomes the first woman bishop of the Episcopal Church.

1990 The census shows that black Baptists are the fourth-largest U.S. denomination, with 8.7 million members.

George Stallings, a dissident Roman Catholic, breaks with the church to found the African American Catholic Church.

1991 Mary Ann Coffey becomes the first black and the first woman to head the National Conference of Christians and Jews.

1995–1996 Scores of predominantly black churches throughout the South are destroyed in a wave of arson. Congress passes the Church Arson Prevention Act to make prosecutions easier and to establish loan and grant programs to rebuild burned churches.

SUPREME COURT DECISIONS AFFECTING RELIGION, 1879–PRESENT

1879 *Reynolds v. United States.* In a ruling that some would argue does not protect religious interests, the Court decides polygamy is illegal even though Mormons claim it is their religious right. The Court reasons that criminal or even morally offensible practices conducted under the auspices of religion are not protected by the First Amendment.

1940 *Cantwell v. Connecticut.* The protection of the First Amendment extends to the practices of state governments.

1948 *McCollum v. Board of Education.* In a case in which students are released from regular classes to attend religious ones taught in the public schools by public-school teachers, the Court finds that public schools and public moneys cannot be used to teach religion, nor can religion be promoted in the public schools.

1952 *Zorach v. Clauson.* The Court validates the right of students to receive religious education off public-school property during the school day.

1962 *Engel v. Vitale.* In an 8–1 decision the Court finds denominational or nondenominational prayer in schools an unacceptable breach of church-state separation.

1963 *School District of Abington v. Schempp.* The Supreme Court expands its ban on school prayer to include Bible reading.

1968 *Board of Education of Central District No. 1 v. Allen.* The Court decides that tax moneys can be used to buy textbooks in parochial schools because the benefit goes to students and not to any religion.

1970 *Walz v. Tax Commission.* The Court reaffirms the exclusion of church property from taxation.

1972 *Cruz v. Benito.* The Court rules that prisoners have a right to practice their religions while incarcerated.

1981 *Thomas v. Review Board of the Indiana Employment Security Division.* In a decision that affirms the right of the legal system to protect religious beliefs, a Seventh-Day Adventist woman who was fired for refusing to work on Saturdays is found to be entitled to unemployment benefits.

1983 *Bob Jones University v. United States.* The Court denies tax-exempt status to private schools practicing racial discrimination.

1984 *Lynch v. Donnelly.* A city is not showing a preference for one religion when it maintains a customary Christmas display of a Nativity scene on public property.

1985 *Wallace v. Jaffree.* The Court rules that Alabama's "moment of silence" in school classrooms is a violation of the First Amendment.

1987 *Edwards v. Aguillard.* The Court rules that a Louisiana statute requiring schools that teach evolution to also teach "creation science," a biblical view of the origins of the universe, is a violation of the first amendment.

1992 *Lee v. Virginia.* Officially sanctioned prayer at graduation ceremonies in public schools violates the establishment clause of the First Amendment.

1993 *Church of the Lukumi Babalu Aye v. City of Hialeah.* The Court overrules a local Florida law that bans the use of animals in religious.

1997 *Agostini v. Felton.* Perhaps signaling a new willingness to allow government aid for parochial schools, the Court reverses a pervious ruling and holds that teachers may conduct federally financed remedial classes on the grounds of parochial schools.

2000 *Santa Fe Independent School District v. Doe.* The Court holds that a school system may not permit students to conduct a prayer over the public address system before a high school football game.

NOTABLE FIGURES IN AMERICAN RELIGION

Adler, Felix (1851–1933). Adler founded the Ethical Culture Society, or the Ethical movement, which holds that an ethical culture can exist in a society independent of religious beliefs. Under Adler's direction, the Ethical Culture Society took stands on labor relations, child welfare, and better services for the poor.

Allen, Richard (1760–1831). Founder of the African Methodist Episcopal Church and a prominent African American clergyman, Allen, who was the son of slaves, organized the Free African Society, an important precursor to abolitionist and black self-reliance societies of the mid–nineteenth century. During the War of 1812, he led a group of blacks in the defense of Baltimore and probably kept the city from being burned by the British. In 1794, he founded Bethel Church, the first A.M.E. congregation; when the church was formally established, he became its first bishop. A statue of Allen, erected in Philadelphia's Fairmont Park, was the first public statue erected to honor a black American.

Asbury, Francis (1745–1816). Asbury established the Methodist Church in the United States. Following a format established by John Wesley in England, he also introduced the circuit-rider system, which proved to be a highly effective way to preach on the frontier. Circuit-rider preachers routinely attended to as many as twenty to forty congregations at a time, traveling on horseback among the communities assigned to them.

Beecher, Lyman (1775–1863). A prominent Presbyterian and Congregational preacher and founder of the American Bible Society, Beecher was a leader in several liberal nineteenth century reform movements, including abolitionism. He had thirteen children, among them Harriet Beecher Stowe, Catharine Beecher, and Henry Ward Beecher.

Blackwell, Antoinette Brown (1825–1921). After working as a teacher, Blackwell studied theology at Oberlin College. In 1853, she became the first female minister in the United States when she was ordained by the First Congregational Church in South Butler, New York. She later left the Congregational Church and became a Unitarian. Throughout her life, she was active in the fights for women's rights, temperance, the abolition of slavery, and the improvement of programs for the poor and disabled.

Cabrini, Frances Xavier (1850–1917). Born and raised in Italy, Cabrini came to the United States as a missionary in 1889. Urged by Pope Leo XIII to work with Italian immigrants in the New World, she eventually founded schools, hospitals, and orphanages and became a naturalized American citizen in 1909. Cabrini, now known as the patron saint of immigrants, became the first American to be canonized in 1946.

Channing, William Ellery (1780–1842). Founder of Unitarianism, a Protestant faith that does not accept the holiness of the Trinity, Channing also preached in favor of religious tolerance and against slavery. He was a noted author on social issues who wielded influence over the Transcendentalists, including Ralph Waldo Emerson.

Chauncy, Charles (1705–1787). A Congregational minister, he led the opposition to the Great Awakening on grounds that revivalism was too emotional and irrational.

Day, Dorothy (1897–1980). Day founded the Catholic worker movement, which merged religious devotion with radical politics. She was a pacifist. With Peter Maurin they started the *Catholic Worker* newspaper in 1933. Considered an outsider most of her life, by the time of her death Day was a significant religious leader.

Eddy, Mary Baker (1821–1910). In 1878, Eddy established the Christian Science Church, whose members believe that sickness and pain are illusions of the "mortal mind" and reject medical treatment. In 1908, she began publishing the *Christian Science Monitor*, a widely respected newspaper still published today.

Edwards, Jonathan (1703–1758). Considered by many the greatest American religious thinker, Edwards was a seminal force in the First Great Awakening. An exponent of orthodox Calvinism, he defended the role of experience and feeling in *A Treatise Concerning Religious Affections*. In 1757, he became president of the College of New Jersey, later Princeton University. In 1758, believing in the efficacy of the newly introduced smallpox inoculation, he allowed himself to be inoculated and died of the resulting complications. A multifaceted and subtle thinker and writer, he is remembered for his powerful (and uncharacteristic) sermon, "Sinners in the Hands of an Angry God."

Father Divine (1878–1965). Born George Baker, Father Divine established an Evangelical communal colony in Sayville, Long Island, from which he held forth, preaching a renunciation of personal property and racial equality, for forty-five years. He established 170 missions, or "heavens," for his largely African American followers.

Graham, Billy (1918–). A prominent and widely respected Southern Baptist minister and author, Graham took American revivalism abroad by leading highly successful international Evangelical crusades. He also used radio and television to convey his message of redemption. His books include *Peace with God* (1953), *World Aflame* (1965), and *Answers to Life's Problems* (1988).

Hutchinson, Anne (1591–1643). An influential Puritan lay leader and midwife, Hutchinson is best known for her role in the Antinomian Controversy, a theological crisis that occurred between 1636 and 1638. She argued that working hard and living a moral life did not, as most Puritans advocated, provide evidence of election. She also believed that a person could have immediate knowledge of his or her salvation. Tried and excommunicated for her beliefs, Hutchinson left the Massachusetts Bay Colony and founded Portsmouth, Rhode Island.

Kaplan, Mordecai (1881–1983). A rabbi, Kaplan originated Reconstructionist Judaism, which holds that Judaism is an evolving religion and culture, and that people, not Scripture, determine its practices. He founded the Society for Advancement of Judaism, the major Reconstructionist umbrella organization.

King, Martin Luther Jr. (1929–1968). A moving force behind the civil rights movement in the United States, the Reverend King insisted on nonviolent reform. Using his Dexter Street Baptist Church in Alabama as his base of operations, he and his followers launched the Montgomery bus boycott in 1955, which in turn led to the civil rights movement of the 1960s. He cofounded the Southern Christian Leadership Conference (SCLC) and led an important antiwar March on Washington in 1963, which culminated with his famous "I Have a Dream" speech at the Lincoln Memorial. King's death by assassination, along with that of President John F. Kennedy and his brother Robert Kennedy, deeply scarred the nation in the 1960s. He was awarded the Nobel Peace Prize in 1964 (see p. 124–127).

Lee, Ann (1736–1784). A religious mystic, Lee brought the Shaker faith to America from England and founded its first community in 1776 in Watervliet, New York. When she died, her followers were severely disappointed, since they had believed she was immortal.

Makemie, Francis (1658–1708). An Irish-born minister, Makemie established the Presbyterian Church in the United States. He preached up and down the East Coast, formed two Presbyterian churches in Maryland, and established the first presbytery in Philadelphia.

Malcolm X (1925–1965). This prominent Black Muslim leader initially demonized whites, but after visiting Mecca and learning that Islam preached equality of races, he changed his views. Malcolm X remained a staunch believer in self-help for blacks and advocated violence, only when necessary, as a form of self-defense. He is widely viewed as the father of the Black Power movement. After he broke away from ELIJAH MUHAMMAD, he was assassinated, many believe, by other Muslims.

Mather, Cotton (1663–1728). A prolific Puritan minister in the Massachusetts Bay Colony and the son of influential Puritan minister Increase Mather, he produced hundreds of sermons and at least several major books, among them *Magnalia Christi Americana* (1702), a religious history of New England, and *The Wonders of the Invisible World* (1693), a defense of the Salem witch trials. Apart from supporting the Salem trials, Mather was an enlightened man who liked to disseminate scientific information and who played an important role in introducing the smallpox vaccine to the colonies.

McPherson, Aimee Semple (1890–1944). A charismatic faith healer and radio evangelist, McPherson developed a large following composed mostly of midwesterners and southerners who had recently immigrated to southern California. She founded the International Church of Foursquare Gospel, and, in 1923, she built the Angelus Temple in Los Angeles. After a mysterious disappearance and reemergence, coupled with a claim that she was kidnapped, McPherson was tried for fraud and acquitted. She died from an overdose of sleeping medicine.

Merton, Thomas (1915–1968). A Trappist monk, Merton was also a religious theorist, scholar, author, and social critic. He was one of the first Christians to see a connection between Eastern and Western religions. Merton only gradually became interested in religion. In 1941, he entered a Trappist monastery, largely because of the order's vows of silence and solitude. Merton's autobiography, *The Seven Storey Mountain* (1948), became a best-seller.

Moody, Dwight (1837–1899). A prominent evangelist, Moody ran what may have been the first international revival campaigns, encompassing both the United States and England. Studiedly nondenominational, he converted millions in the last decades of the nineteenth century, who were then told to join the denomination of their choice. Moody founded the Moody Bible Institute as well as a theological preparatory school, both in Chicago.

NOTABLE FIGURES, *cont.*

Muhammad, Elijah (1897–1975). Under Elijah Poole, who took the name Elijah Muhammad, the Black Muslims first gained a large and significant following in Detroit. A follower of W. D. Fard, who founded the Nation of Islam, Muhammad founded the second Temple of Islam in Chicago, which became a prominent center for Black Muslim activities. When Fard mysteriously vanished at about the time the Chicago temple was founded, Muhammad became the sole leader of the religion. He published *Message to the Black Man*, a treatise on the religion, in 1964.

Niebuhr, Reinhold (1892–1971). A prominent professor of Christian ethics, theologian-philosopher Niebuhr, after many years as a Detroit pastor, spent most of his professional career at Union Theological Seminary in New York City. Early in his career he despaired about his Protestant faith's ability to maintain moral rule and became a social activist. Later he returned to his faith and tried to confront the ways in which Christianity might accommodate contemporary issues. He was the author of *Moral Man and Immoral Society* (1932), *Christianity and Power Politics* (1940), and *The Nature and Destiny of Man* (1941–1943).

Penn, William (1664–1718). Penn created the Quaker state of Pennsylvania and founded the city of Philadelphia. A convert to Quakerism as a young man, Penn was jailed in England for his beliefs. While there he wrote *No Cross, No Crown*. He advocated religious tolerance and had hoped that Pennsylvania could become a utopian community that would welcome all religions.

Roberts, Oral (1918–). One of the nation's leading faith healers and probably the first Evangelical minister to amass a large congregation via television, Roberts founded Oral Roberts University in Tulsa, Oklahoma, a conservative fundamentalist school. He briefly became controversial in 1987 when he announced that God would take his life if he didn't receive $8 million in donations. He later claimed that goal was met.

Smith, Joseph Jr. (1805–1844). Founder of the Church of Latter-Day Saints, also known as the Mormon Church, Smith began to organize the religion after undergoing a series of mystic visions, one of which included the appearance of an angel named Moroni who gave him the Book of Mormon, which Mormons today add to their Bible. In 1830, Smith established the Church of Jesus Christ of Latter-Day Saints. Almost from the beginning he and his followers were persecuted for their beliefs, especially the practice of polygamy, and forced to move, first to western Missouri, then to Illinois, where Smith was jailed for treason. When he was hauled out of jail and killed by an anti-Mormon mob, he left behind 35,000 converts.

Sunday, Billy (William Ashley) (1862–1935). A popular Evangelical preacher, Sunday employed highly dramatic (and high-pressure) tactics at his revival meetings. He began preaching in 1895 and reached the peak of his popularity during World War I. He preached in support of Prohibition and was also associated with attempts to restrict immigration. Sunday sponsored more than 300 revival meetings in all major cities and had preached to 100 million persons at the time of his death.

Williams, Roger (1603?–1638). The founder of Rhode Island and an influential colonial preacher, Williams was a religious dissenter who opposed both the Puritans and the Quakers and argued in favor of a personal God. He was an early supporter of religious tolerance and separation of church and state.

Winthrop, John (1588–1649). An influential Puritan minister and the founder of the Massachusetts Bay Colony, Winthrop was the chief persecutor of ANNE HUTCHINSON in the Antinomian crisis. Like many Puritans, he believed America could be a model of a godly society, a view he articulated in his most famous sermon, "The Model of Christian Charity" (see p. 238).

Wise, Isaac Mayer (1819–1900). Founder of the Union of American Hebrew Congregations, the Hebrew Union College, and the Central Conference of American Rabbis, Rabbi Wise was an influence on the shape and growth of Reform Judaism in the United States. Wise was an assimilationist who believed Jews should not be bound by what he viewed as archaic religious laws.

Young, Brigham (1801–1877). After inheriting the leadership of the Mormon Church from JOSEPH SMITH, Young greatly enlarged the membership, was a major force in shaping it theologically, and led the Mormon migration to their permanent settlement in Utah. He helped to found Salt Lake City and served as Utah's territorial governor.

CHAPTER 14

CULTURE AND THE ARTS

■

HIGHLIGHTS

Timeline of Culture and the Arts

LARGELY EUROPEAN IN STYLE and religious in inspiration, the art and culture of the colonies gave way to more secular and distinctively American forms of expression in the early and middle decades of the nineteenth century. The emergence of a uniquely American "voice" seemed to come first to literature, followed in subsequent decades by the visual arts, music, and dance. The arrival on U.S. shores of artists from all over the globe, the advent of new technologies and media, the growth of consumerism, and the cultivation of free expression all have contributed to the rise of the United States as an artistic mecca and major cultural influence in the world.

LITERATURE

1640 The first book printed in what is now the United States, *The Bay Psalm Book*, published this year, will print twenty-seven editions by 1750.

1650 Puritan poet ANNE BRADSTREET writes *The Tenth Muse Lately Sprang Up in America*, the first volume of poetry written in the colonies to be published.

1732 Benjamin Franklin publishes *Poor Richard's Almanack*, which becomes a perennial best-seller.

1735 Peter Zenger, founder of the *New York Weekly Journal*, is tried for seditious libel and acquitted in a seminal ruling in the development of freedom of press in the colonies (see p. 419).

1746 Jonathan Edwards delivers his sermon "Sinners in the Hand of an Angry God," perhaps his most famous (see p. 460). Essays and sermons by Puritan preachers are the primary literature of the colonies.

1773 PHILLIS WHEATLEY, an African American slave, publishes *Poems on Various Subjects*.

1776 Thomas Paine, in *Common Sense*, produces some of the finest political discourse in the colonies.

1800 The Library of Congress is established.

1817 Poet William Cullen Bryant publishes *Thanatopsis*, a reflection on death and a significant early Romantic lyric.

1820 Washington Irving's *Sketch Book* is published, with two classic American tales: "The Legend of Sleepy Hollow" and "Rip Van Winkle."

1823 The first of the *The Leatherstocking Tales*, a series of novels by James Fenimore Cooper, is published. The most popular and enduring ones are *The Last of the Mohicans* (1826) and *The Deerslayer* (1841).

1830s The first of two great flowerings of American literature begins in this decade, when writers such as Edgar Allan Poe, Herman Melville, Emily Dickinson, and the Transcendentalists Ralph Waldo Emerson, Henry David Thoreau, Nathaniel Hawthorne, and Walt Whitman produce major works.

1836 Ralph Waldo Emerson describes the principles of Transcendentalism in his book *Nature* (see p. 465).

1837 Ralph Waldo Emerson's "The American Scholar," a Phi Beta Kappa speech at Harvard, calls for a distinctly American literature.

1840 Edgar Allan Poe's *Tales of the Grotesque and Arabesque* includes "The Fall of the House of Usher" and is instrumental in the growth of the modern short story. A year later, with "The Murders in the Rue Morgue," he creates the modern detective story.

1842 Ralph Waldo Emerson begins a seminal series, called *Essays*, which is published in the literary journal *The Dial*. In them are "The Over-Soul," "Self-Reliance," and "Compensation."

1845 A classic autobiography and important primary source on slavery, *The Narrative of the Life of Frederick Douglass* is written by former slave and abolitionist Frederick Douglass (see p. 140).

1847 Henry Wadsworth Longfellow publishes the book-length poem *Evangeline*, the first of several highly romanticized American poems much loved by the reading public.

1850 Nathaniel Hawthorne publishes *The Scarlet Letter*.

1851 Herman Melville publishes *Moby Dick*, perhaps the first enduring masterpiece of American literature, chronicling Captain Ahab's obsessive pursuit of a great white whale.

1852 Harriet Beecher Stowe's *Uncle Tom's Cabin*, which depicts the evils of slavery, sells 300,000 copies in the six months after its publication.

Stephen Crane, author of the Civil War fictional masterpiece *The Red Badge of Courage* (1895), had no firsthand experience of war until years after he wrote the novel.

Walt Whitman wrote poems that were unconventional in both form and content, including those in his best-known collection Leaves of Grass, *an influential and controversial work.*

1854 HENRY DAVID THOREAU's *Walden*, a treatise on nature and self-reliance, is published (see p. 470).

1855 WALT WHITMAN anonymously publishes *Leaves of Grass;* he will continue to enlarge the collection throughout his life.

1868 Louisa May Alcott wins the hearts of the first of many generations of Americans with the publication of her book *Little Women.*

1881 HENRY JAMES's *The Portrait of a Lady* is published.

1884 MARK TWAIN publishes the book that is widely regarded as his masterpiece, *The Adventures of Huckleberry Finn.* It and *Tom Sawyer,* published in 1876, influence writers as diverse as WILLIAM FAULKNER and ERNEST HEMINGWAY.

1885 HENRY JAMES publishes one of his early realistic novels, *The Bostonians.* William Dean Howells publishes *The Rise of Silas Lapham.*

1892 Charlotte Perkins Gilman's short story "The Yellow Wallpaper" is printed in *New England Magazine.* It will become a classic of feminist writing.

1895 STEPHEN CRANE publishes his masterpiece, a searingly realistic novel about the Civil War, *The Red Badge of Courage.*

1896 *The Country of the Pointed Firs* by Sarah Orne Jewett, a collection of sketches depicting the lives of residents of a fictional village on the coast of Maine, is an important achievement in "local color" writing.

1899 Arousing a public scandal for her frank treatment of feminine sexuality, Kate Chopin publishes *The Awakening*, about Louisiana woman Edna Pontellier.

1900 Turn-of-the-century writers such as STEPHEN CRANE and THEODORE DREISER introduce a new realism to American literature as they grapple with the modern age and industrialism. Dreiser's novel *Sister Carrie*, a landmark of American realism, shocks the public and is published only in an expurgated form for decades.

1902 Jack London's masterpiece *Call of the Wild* features a dog named Buck as the protagonist.

1903 HENRY JAMES produces the first of his great psychological novels, *The Ambassadors.*

1905 EDITH WHARTON in *The House of Mirth* produces a biting psychological examination of class in America.

1907 Privately published, *The Education of Henry Adams* is an outstanding example of autobiography in which Henry Adams uses his own life to chronicle and critique the age.

1913 WILLA CATHER tries out her sparse prose style in *O Pioneers!*

1915 In *America's Coming of Age*, critic Van Wyck Brooks draws a distinction between "low-brow" and "high-brow" culture. This is both recognition of the fact that America now produces a literature that stands against the best in Europe and a bow to the popular mass culture that exists alongside it.

ROBERT FROST's acclaimed poem "The Road Not Taken" appears in *Atlantic Monthly*.

1920s America experiences its second flowering of great literature, producing novelists such as F. SCOTT FITZGERALD, ERNEST HEMINGWAY, and WILLIAM FAULKNER and poets like WALLACE STEVENS and T. S. ELIOT. Europe becomes home to many of the best American artists: Eliot eventually becomes a British subject, while Fitzgerald, Hemingway, and many other fine novelists expatriate themselves for long periods.

1920 F. SCOTT FITZGERALD's *This Side of Paradise* is an instant success.

1921 Marianne Moore, a major poet of the era, publishes *Poems*.

1922 The first of the Harlem Renaissance writers to publish is Claude McKay, who writes *Harlem Shadows*. During the 1920s, Harlem writers, poets, journalists, intellectuals, artists, and musicians, among them LANGSTON HUGHES, Jean Toomer, Countee Cullen, and ZORA NEALE HURSTON, produce an expressive literary and artistic movement rooted in black culture.

T. S. ELIOT writes *The Waste Land*, a work that changes the face of poetry with its stark modernism.

1922 SINCLAIR LEWIS's *Babbitt* satirizes middle class America. *Elmer Gantry*, which comes out five years later, focuses in fundamentalist religion and is another of Lewis's acclaimed satires.

1923 WALLACE STEVENS, one of the few American writers who never goes to Europe, publishes *Harmonium*, which contains many of his most important poems.

Harlem Renaissance novelist Jean Toomer publishes *Cane*.

e. e. cummings's first volume of poetry, *tulips and chimneys*, is published.

Ezra Pound publishes the first collection of his *Cantos;* he continues to work on this modern epic poem for the rest of his life.

1925 F. SCOTT FITZGERALD publishes *The Great Gatsby*, which many regard as his masterpiece.

1926 ERNEST HEMINGWAY publishes *The Sun Also Rises*.

Harlem Renaissance writer LANGSTON HUGHES's first collection of poems, *The Weary Blues*, establishes his reputation.

1929 ERNEST HEMINGWAY writes *A Farewell to Arms*.

WILLIAM FAULKNER, whose creative fiction illuminates the South, publishes *The Sound and the Fury*, regarded by many as his masterpiece.

1930s This decade is marked by the emergence of a new generation of writers such as John O'Hara, Nathanael West, and JOHN STEINBECK, the most enduring of the group. Their writing is marked by a grittier, more pessimistic realism than has yet been seen.

1930–1936 In the U.S.A. trilogy, which includes *The 42nd Parallel* (1930), *1919* (1932), and *Big Money* (1936), John Dos Passos employs fiction, journalistic writing, newspaper headlines, and biographical sketches to portray American life from 1900 to the Depression.

1930 Hart Crane produces *The Bridge*, an epic poem about the American experience, which employs the Brooklyn Bridge as an important metaphor.

1934 F. SCOTT FITZGERALD's last major novel, *Tender Is the Night*, is published.

Henry Miller's *Tropic of Cancer* causes an uproar for its sexual content.

1936 WILLIAM FAULKNER's novel *Absalom! Absalom!* is published.

Margaret Mitchell's only novel, *Gone with the Wind*, set in the South during the Civil War and Reconstruction, is huge hit. Mitchell will win the Pulitzer Prize, and the novel will be adapted into a film in 1939.

1937 ZORA NEALE HURSTON's *Their Eyes Were Watching God*, about a southern black woman and the men in her life, is considered an important work for its use of folklore and vernacular language.

1938 Delmore Schwartz's *In Dreams Begin Responsibilities* is published.

1939 JOHN STEINBECK produces *The Grapes of Wrath*.

1940s The important writers of this decade are NORMAN MAILER and SAUL BELLOW, who become known as Jewish writers; RICHARD WRIGHT, an African American writer; and ROBERT PENN WARREN, CARSON MCCULLERS, Eudora Welty, and William Styron, who are dubbed "southern" writers.

1940 John O'Hara published *Pal Joey*.

1946 Southern writer CARSON MCCULLERS writes her classic Member of the Wedding, and Eudora Welty publishes *Delta Wedding*.

AMERICAN NOBELISTS

The Nobel Prize for literature, which honors a body of work rather than a single book or play, has been awarded ten times to American writers.

1930 Sinclair Lewis
1936 Eugene O'Neill
1938 Pearl Buck
1949 William Faulkner
1954 Ernest Hemingway
1962 John Steinbeck
1976 Saul Bellow
1980 Czeslaw Milosz
1987 Joseph Brodsky
1993 Toni Morrison

ROBERT PENN WARREN produces his fiction masterpiece, *All the King's Men*.

1948 NORMAN MAILER becomes an overnight success with his war classic, *The Naked and the Dead*.

1950s Poetry eclipses fiction as the most important literary form, primarily because so many superb poets are writing. ROBERT FROST is the most popular and best known, but WALLACE STEVENS, Carl Sandburg, WILLIAM CARLOS WILLIAMS, Delmore Schwartz, ROBERT LOWELL, John Berryman, Elizabeth Bishop, and W. S. Merwin are also at their peaks.

1951 Novelist Kurt Vonnegut establishes his offbeat, witty style in *Piano Player*.

J. D. Salinger publishes the classic novel of adolescent alienation, *The Catcher in the Rye*.

In works such as Sister Carrie *(1900),* The Financier *(1912), and* An American Tragedy *(1925) novelist Theodore Dreiser explores naturalism, class, and culture.*

1952 Ralph Ellison publishes *Invisible Man*, about an African American man's search for identity.

1953 JAMES BALDWIN writes his masterpiece of black rage, *Go Tell It on the Mountain*.

SAUL BELLOW publishes *The Adventures of Augie March*.

Fahrenheit 451, a dystopian novel by Ray Bradbury, heralds the success of science fiction in American culture in the 1950s. Isaac Asimov and Robert Heinlein are other popular writers in the genre.

1955 Elizabeth Bishop will win the Pulitzer for her *Poems: North and South—A Cold Spring*, published this year.

Howl makes Allen Ginsberg famous as a Beat poet.

1957 Jack Kerouac publishes *On the Road*.

1959 Poet ROBERT LOWELL writes *Life Studies*.

1960 John Updike begins his series of Rabbit novels with *Rabbit, Run*.

Harper Lee's novel *To Kill a Mockingbird* recounts the story of a young girl's growing awareness of racism and hypocrisy in a small southern town. The book quickly becomes an American classic.

1961 Walker Percy, a southern writer, publishes his classic novel *The Moviegoer*.

Catch-22, Joseph Heller's black-humor novel about World War II, catches the attention of the reading public.

WHAT IS "POP CULTURE"?

We know it when we see it: best-selling books, hit movies, top-of-the-charts music, dance crazes, fashions of the day, trends in food, recreational fads, the TV shows we talk about. Popular culture is the shared interests and cultural expressions of the society in which we live. Historians tell us that popular culture was born with the arrival of "mass society" in the eighteenth century and blossomed with the Industrial Revolution of the late nineteenth century. As a matter of economics, the advent of mass-production, the clustering of people in cities, and increases in leisure time contributed to the broad sharing of tastes and entertainments. In 1915, shortly after the invention of motion pictures, the literary critic Van Wyck Brooks published *America's Coming of Age*, in which he drew a distinction between "high-brow" and "low-brow" culture. High-brow culture is original art presented for the elites in museums and concert halls and opera houses. It is created "for the ages." Low-brow culture is disseminated everywhere for the everyman. It is created for entertainment.

Yet these insights, finally, provide no definitive answers. What makes a book or movie or piece of music a "classic" rather than mere entertainment? Certainly there have been many works of creative expression that have been both popular and enduring. In the end, the distinction may not matter. The need for music and stories and fashion—call it art or call it pop—is universal. "'Tis wonderful," observed RALPH WALDO EMERSON, "how soon a piano gets into a hut on the frontier."

1962 Ken Kesey writes *One Flew Over the Cuckoo's Nest.*

1963 WILLIAM CARLOS WILLIAMS publishes *Pictures from Brueghel, and Other Poems.*

1964 ROBERT LOWELL's *For the Union Dead* is published.

1965 Poet Sylvia Plath's *Ariel* is published posthumously.

1966 Anne Sexton's poetry collection *Live or Die*, wins the Pulitzer Prize.
Novelist Truman Capote writes *In Cold Blood*, a "nonfiction novel" that creates a new literary genre, literary journalism.

"All modern American fiction comes from one book by Mark Twain called Huckleberry Finn.*"*
—ERNEST HEMINGWAY,
GREEN HILLS OF AFRICA

1967 William Styron writes what many regard as his finest work, *The Confessions of Nat Turner.*

1968 Gore Vidal's novel *Myra Breckinridge* shocks with its sexual content.

1969 Kurt Vonnegut's masterpiece, *Slaughterhouse Five*, is published.
Philip Roth's *Portnoy's Complaint* shocks with its sexual frankness.

1970 "Where Are You Going, Where Have You Been?", a short story by Joyce Carol Oates, confronts the sexuality of a teenage girl and becomes one of the writer's best-known works.

1972 Eudora Welty's *The Optimist's Daughter* is published; it will win the Pulitzer Prize.

1975 Nobelist SAUL BELLOW produces *Humboldt's Gift*.
E. L. Doctorow's novel *Ragtime* is published.

1976 Maxine Hong Kingston's autobiographical *The Women Warriors* explores the experiences of Chinese Americans.

1977 Leslie Marmon Silko's novel *Ceremony*, about a Vietnam veteran returning to his New Mexico reservation, depicts Native American culture and traditions. Silko is praised for her use of folklore, fantasy, and realism in the novel.

1978 John Cheever, known for his subtle depictions of suburban life, writes *Falconer*, a novel about prison life that may be his finest.

1982 African American novelist Alice Walker publishes *The Color Purple*.
Founded in 1979 and dedicated to preserving works of American literature, the American Library publishes its first volumes.

1985 Larry McMurtry, widely perceived as just a western writer, publishes *Lonesome Dove*, which wins the Pulitzer Prize.
With the publication of *White Noise*, acclaimed Don DeLillo begins to reach a wide readership. His other novels include *Americana* (1971), *Great Jones Street* (1973), *Underworld* (1997), and *The Body Artist* (2001).

1987 TONI MORRISON's *Beloved* confronts the legacy of slavery with the story of a woman who kills her infant daughter rather than see her enslaved. The moving work wins the Pulitzer Prize.

1992 Cormac McCarthy publishes *All the Pretty Horses*.

1993 E. Annie Proulx writes *The Shipping News*.

1994 The collected short stories of Grace Paley, one of the most accomplished writers in this form, are published.

1998 Philip Roth, best known for such previous novels as *Goodbye Columbus* (1959) and *Portnoy's Complaint* (1969), wins the Pulitzer Prize in fiction for *American Pastoral*.

U.S. POETS LAUREAATE

In 1985, Congress created the post of poet laureate. By tradition, poets laureate write commemorative poetry for special occasions of the government (or monarch), but the American poet laureate, who is appointed by the Librarian of Congress, is asked to give a lecture and a poetry reading. The American poets laureate are:

1986–87 Robert Penn Warren
1987–88 Richard Wilbur
1988–89 Howard Nemerov
1990–91 Mark Strand
1991–92 Joseph Brodsky
1992–93 Mona Van Duyn
1993–95 Rita Dove
1995–96 Robert Hass
1997–2000 Robert Pinsky
2000–01 Stanley Kunitz
2001–03 Billy Collins

MUSIC

For events in musical theater, see pages 504–505.

1600s The indigenous music in the Americas is that of the American Indian, which includes chanting and singing in a five-note scale (see p. 28). Colonists bring European music with them, much of it religious in purpose.

1731 The first public concert of secular music in the colonies is presented in a Boston home; admission is charged.

1744 The Moravian community establishes a Collegium Museum for the performance of nonreligious music such as chamber music and symphonies.

1770 William Billings publishes what is widely believed to be the first American composition, "The New England Psalm Singer."

1794 James Hewitt composes "Tammany, or the Indian Chief." Its theme is American, but its musical structure is European.

1814 Lawyer Francis Scott Key writes "The Star-Spangled Banner," after watching British ships fire on Baltimore's Fort McHenry during the War of 1812. The song becomes the nation's official anthem in 1931.

1818 Boston's Handel and Hadyn Society, founded in 1815, gives its first performance of *Messiah*.

1842 The New York Philharmonic is founded.

1865 Chicago supports an opera company in its newly built Crosby Opera House.

1878 The Central City Opera House in the Colorado mining town of the same name opens.

1881 The Boston Symphony is founded.

1883 The New York Metropolitan Opera gives its first performance, Charles Gounod's *Faust*.

1891 The Chicago Symphony is founded.

1892 The Czech composer Antonin Dvorak arrives in the United States to direct New York City's National Conservatory of Music. While in America, he writes the "New World" Symphony, also known as Symphony no. 9 in E-minor, and exhorts American composers to draw on their rich cultural heritage, including Indian and African American music. He trains several black musicians, most notably H. T. Burleigh, who goes on to arrange spirituals and other black music. EDWARD MACDOWELL, a member of this movement despite his European training, writes *Indian Suite*, completed in 1896.

1896 EDWARD MACDOWELL writes *Woodland Sketches* for piano.

1897 William Krell's *Mississippi Rag* is the first piece of ragtime music published.

1899 Pianist SCOTT JOPLIN's "Maple Leaf Rag" is an instant and huge success. Joplin helps to popularize ragtime.

1902 CHARLES IVES, a pioneer in "modern" music, writes his iconoclastic Second Symphony, but it will not be performed publicly until 1951.

1903 Victor Herbert composes *Babes in Toyland*, one of the first American operettas.

1908 Italian conductor Arturo Toscanini takes over the baton at the Metropolitan Opera, where he will reign until 1914.

1914 The American Society of Composers, Authors and Publishers is formed.
  W. C. Handy's "St. Louis Blues" is an example of the growing popularization of the blues. In the 1920s and 1930s, blues music by musicians such as Ma Rainey, Bessie Smith, and Ethel Waters will become a musical phenomenon, especially among blacks in the South.

1917 *The Livery Stable Blues* by the Original Dixieland Jazz Band is first recording of jazz music.

1918 The Boston Symphony hires its first American concertmaster.
  Blues greats Blind Lemon Jefferson and Leadbelly (Huddie Leadbetter) will play together until 1924.

1920 The first classic blues recording, Mamie Smith's *Crazy Blues*, is released.

1922 Jazz pianists Fats Waller and WILLIAM "COUNT" BASIE produce their first recordings.

1924 GEORGE GERSHWIN composes *Rhapsody in Blue*.
  AARON COPLAND composes his Symphony for Organ and Orchestra.

1926 Trumpet player LOUIS ARMSTRONG heralds a new musical style called scat with the hit "Heebie Jeebies."
  Ferdinand "Jelly Roll" Morton, the jazz pianist and composer who claimed to have invented jazz in 1902, publishes his "King Porter Stomp" one of his most famous works.

1927 EDWARD KENNEDY "DUKE" ELLINGTON, who will become an important big band composer, begins his long-term affiliation with the Cotton Club in Harlem, a jazz hot spot. Cab Calloway will become a regular three years later.
  Meade Lux Lewis's *Honky Tonk* is considered the first boogie-woogie album.

1928 Arturo Toscanini returns from Italy and assumes leadership of the New York Philharmonic and turns it into one of the world's great symphony orchestras.

"The Star-Spangled Banner," written during the War of 1812, was not officially adopted as the national anthem until 1931. Originally published as "The Defense of Fort McHenry," Francis Scott Key's lyrics had four stanzas in all.

CULTURE & THE ARTS

1928, *cont.*

George Gershwin writes *An American in Paris.*
Virgil Thomson and Gertrude Stein create an American opera, *Four Saints in Three Acts.*

1930s–1940s Blues music moves north from its roots in the Mississippi Delta and into urban areas.

1933 Foremost female jazz vocalist Billie Holiday produces her first recordings.

1934 Bandleader and jazz clarinetist Benny Goodman organizes his first band, produces recordings with Columbia Records, and plays on an NBC radio series. He will become known as the "King of Swing."

1935 George and Ira Gershwin's *Porgy and Bess,* an opera based on African American music and themes, is performed on Broadway.

1936 A book about Negro folk songs, sung by Huddie "Leadbelly" Ledbetter, makes the former chain-gang member who sings blues, African American folk, and chain-gang music, a popular performer.

1937 The NBC Symphony for the radio is created for Arturo Toscanini, one of the greatest conductors of his era.
The Count Basie Orchestra, featuring bandleader and pianist Basie, is one of the leading swing bands of the era. By the end of the decade, they will record such hits as "One O'Clock Jump" (1937) and "Jumpin' at the Woodside" (1938).

1938 Two American ballet scores are performed for the first time: Walter Piston's *The Incredible Flutist* and Aaron Copland's *Billy the Kid.*
Benny Goodman performs "Sing Sing Sing" at Carnegie Hall in New York City, signaling the growth of swing music in America.
Through a series of radio broadcasts, Glen Miller and his band become extremely popular for their swing dance hits such as "In the Mood." Unlike other jazz greats, Miller is remembered for his precise arrangements rather than his improvisational skills.
Jazz label Blue Note Records is founded.

1940 Musicians Woody Guthrie and Pete Seeger meet and help form the Almanac Singers. Guthrie and Seeger, part of a populist musical tradition coming out of the Depression, cultivate the folk music that will have a revival in the 1950s.

Early 1940s Frank Sinatra croons and makes bobby-soxers shriek and swoon with "This Love of Mine."

1942 AARON COPLAND's ballets *Rodeo* and *Lincoln Portrait* are staged.

Experimental composer JOHN CAGE creates *Imaginary Landscape No. 3*, scored for Balinese gongs, generator whine, an electric oscillator, buzzers, coil, and tin cans, among other "instruments."

Jazz singer Ella Fitzgerald begins her solo career. Her performances with the *Jazz at the Philharmonic* series will make her famous throughout the world.

Glenn Miller's album *Chattanooga Choo Choo* becomes the first gold record.

Bing Crosby sings "White Christmas" for the movie *Holiday Inn*. A classic Christmas tune, the song is the best-selling single of all time for many years. Crosby's annual Christmas special became a holiday tradition in the 1960s and 1970s.

1944 AARON COPLAND's symphony *Appalachian Spring* is first performed.

1947 WALTER PISTON writes his Pulitzer-winning Third Symphony.

1948 SAMUEL BARBER composes *Knoxville: Summer of 1915.*

1949 Birdland, a club named after jazz saxophonist CHARLIE "BIRD" PARKER, opens on Broadway in New York City. Parker is an influential and talented musician, respected for his improvisations and his musical experimentation.

Blues legend B. B. King signs his first recording contract. "Three O'Clock Blues" will catapult the singer and guitarist into the blues spotlight. Other major figures in blues music include Muddy Waters and John Lee Hooker.

1950 Spiritual singer Mahalia Jackson debuts at Carnegie Hall. She has won nationwide acclaim for performing "I Believe" and "I Can Put My Trust in Jesus."

1951 JOHN CAGE scores *Imaginary Landscape No. 4*, which consists of twelve radios randomly tuned.

Dave Brubeck forms the quartet bearing his name, and soon it becomes the most famous jazz group in the world.

1952 JOHN CAGE scores *4'33"*, his first major aleatory, or "chance," composition, which consists of a silent pianist on stage. The audience is supposed to listen to the sounds of the music hall.

1954 George Weir organizes the first American Jazz Festival in Newport, Rhode Island.

"Man, if you gotta ask you'll never know."
—LOUIS ARMSTRONG, upon being asked the definition of jazz

CULTURE & THE ARTS

UNIQUELY AMERICAN: JAZZ

Jazz, which began in the late nineteenth century, is the only uniquely American contribution to the arts. Drawing its inspiration mostly from African music and also from indigenous American music such as spirituals, work songs, blues, and field hollers, jazz originated in the South and rather quickly worked its way north and west. Some romanticists say it traveled along the rivers, but, in any event, by the 1940s, jazz,

Trumpet-player Louis Armstrong and vocalist Billie Holiday are two of jazz music's most beloved icons.

helped along by swing, was a permanent part of the American musical scene.

Jazz differs from other Western music in two important ways, first in its use of improvisation, which refers to the spontaneous creation of variations on the melody, and second, through syncopation, a stress on a normally weak note. Although all jazz shares these characteristics to a greater or lesser degree, jazz has progressed through a variety of styles, all of which are still in existence today.

The earliest jazz was Dixieland. This featured a clearly defined melody, produced by a horn, and a beat, or rhythm, supplied by piano or drums. The best of the early practitioners of Dixieland were King Oliver's Creole Jazz Band, which included such illustrious names as LOUIS ARMSTRONG and Honore Dutrey; the Wolverines, led by Bix Beiderbecke; and the New Orleans Rhythm Kings. A variation of Dixieland is ragtime, whose best-known advocate was SCOTT JOPLIN. With its distinctive style, produced mostly through marked syncopation, ragtime was spread by sheet music and piano rolls, in contrast to Dixieland, for which there typically was no written music.

Swing, which featured the big band sounds of COUNT BASIE, DUKE ELLINGTON (considered one of America's greatest composers), Glenn Miller, Tommy and Jimmy Dorsey, and BENNY GOODMAN, helped to move jazz into the mainstream and to introduce it to whites. Swing featured call-and-response playing, lots of improvisational riffs (although often of the rehearsed kind), and no written music—with the

exception of Duke Ellington, who was as much composer as bandleader.

Bebop, or bop, arose in the 1950s in reaction to swing and thus strove to be everything swing was not. Where swing was easy listening, bop was complex. Where swing was big bands, bop marked a return to the small group. Where swing emphasized melody, bop cared only about rhythm. Bop was created by such consummate musicians as Dizzy Gillespie and CHARLIE PARKER. The best bop was never particularly mainstream, since it was so sophisticated and musically complex.

Related to bop is third stream, a fusion of jazz and classical music of the kind pioneered by the Modern Jazz Quartet, and cool jazz, whose chief proponents are Miles Davis and Charlie Parker. Third stream jazz, played for the first time by academically trained musicians, adheres (on occasion) to written scores and employs such classical forms as the rondo, the fugue, and even symphonic development. Cool jazz resembles swing but without the call-and-response and the riffs. Definitely experimental, it introduced to jazz such instruments as the flute, French horn, and the baritone sax.

Jazz in the sixties sounded like the era—wailing, angry, and full of protest, and was played at its best by such artists as Ornette Coleman, Archie Shepp, and Sam Rivers. A new avant-garde jazz also emerged, featuring atonal music of the kind played by John Coltrane. The seventies and eighties saw a renaissance of jazz, with fusion performers such as Herbie Hancock and Chick Corea trying to find ways to merge jazz and rock. This was accomplished largely through the introduction of heavy drums and electronic instruments. By the late eighties and early nineties, musicians like Wynton Marsalis were bringing jazz full circle. They embarked on a new classical—or as some said, neoclassical—age of jazz. Melody reigned once more, and elegant old tunes— by the likes of Ellington, GEORGE GERSHWIN, and COLE PORTER—were once again heard.

1954, *cont.*

Radio announcer Alan Freed coins the term "rock 'n' roll."

1956 LEONARD BERNSTEIN writes the score for *Candide*.
DOUGLAS MOORE's opera *The Ballad of Baby Doe* is premiered at the Colorado Central City Opera House.
William Schuman composes *New England Triptych*.
Elvis Presley skyrockets to fame with "Hound Dog," "Love Me Tender," and "Heartbreak Hotel." He dominates rock music for the next decade.

1958 SAMUEL BARBER's opera *Vanessa* wins the Pulitzer Prize.

1959 WALTER PISTON writes *Three New England Sketches*, a suite for orchestra.
Trumpeter Miles Davis's landmark album, *Kind of Blue*, is recorded. Noted for its use of improvisation and modal jazz, it becomes a classic. Davis will receive the President's Medal of Freedom in 1966.

Early 1960s The folk music tradition cultivated by musicians such as Woody Guthrie and Pete Seeger musicians is fused with the antiestablishment atmosphere of the 1960s by Joan Baez; Bob Dylan; Peter, Paul and Mary; and others. Folk music, now featuring antiwar and antioppression protest songs, flourishes in New York City coffeehouses and at venues like the Newport Folk Festival. The folk music will begin to carry into the folk-rock genre when Bob Dylan plugs in his electric guitar at the 1965 Newport Folk Festival.

1967 The Monterey Pop Festival is the first major rock festival. Jimi Hendrix and Janis Joplin are featured performers.

1969 The Woodstock Music Festival features performers such as Joan Baez; Janis Joplin; Arlo Guthrie; Crosby, Stills, Nash & Young; the Jefferson Airplane; Joe Cocker; and Creedence Clearwater Revival. The "three days of peace and music" drew an audience of more than 450,000.

1970 Chick Korea's *Song of Singing* is an important example of atonal jazz.

1971 LEONARD BERNSTEIN composes *Mass*, a secular piece of music that is played for the first time at the opening of the John F. Kennedy Cultural Center in Washington, D.C.

1973 Keyboard player Herbie Hancock produces the album *Headhunters*, which fuses rock and jazz and becomes a bestseller. Later, Hancock is known for his experiments with electronic music.

1975 At fourteen-years-old, Wynton Marsalis plays trumpet with the New Orleans Symphony Orchestra, the beginning of his strong career.

"King of Rock 'n' Roll" Elvis Presley captured the hearts and minds of fans with his chart-topping music, charismatic personality, and unforgettable performances.

CULTURE & THE ARTS

1976 PHILIP GLASS's strikingly modern opera *Einstein on the Beach* debuts at the Metropolitan Opera House.

Known for her innovative productions, Sarah Caldwell, who founded her own opera company in Boston, becomes the first woman to conduct the Metropolitan Opera.

1980s U.S. opera houses introduce English subtitles, which are an immediate success.

1981 "Video Killed the Radio Star" by the Buggles is the prophetic first video played on MTV (Music Television). A cable network dedicated to playing music videos, MTV helped launch the careers of 1980s pop music stars like Madonna, Michael Jackson, and Prince. In 1983, MTV becomes available in such large markets as Manhattan and Los Angeles.

1983 Trumpeter Wynton Marsalis becomes the first musician to win a Grammy Award for both classical and jazz music in the same year.

1985 The Boston Pops Orchestra celebrates its 100th anniversary.

1987 Congress issues a resolution declaring jazz a national treasure.

1991 Lincoln Center for the Performing Arts in New York City adds a jazz department as its twelfth resident company. Jazz at Lincoln Center becomes the world's largest nonprofit organization devoted to promoting jazz performance, education, and preservation.

1997–1998 New concert halls open in Newark, Seattle, Houston, and Fort Worth. In addition, major renovations are completed at the Kennedy Center in Washington, San Francisco Opera, Santa Fe Opera, and Chicago Symphony Center.

THEATER

1752 Theater in the colonies begins with the arrival in Williamsburg, Virginia, of Lewis Hallam's troupe of English actors.

1770s During the Revolution, theater and other performances are discouraged.

1780s Americans establish their own playing companies. Public taste in theater runs toward melodrama, and audiences favor companies with stars' names attached to them.

1787 Typical of the melodramas so loved during the Federalist era is *The Contrast* by Royall Tyler, which is considered the first American comedy to be professionally performed.

1798 Another melodrama, William Dunlap's *Andre*, is popular.

1829 Plays like John Augustus Stone's *Metamora* introduce the stereotypes that abound in American theater, although few are as flattering as this tale of a noble American Indian. More common are images of the drunken Irishman or the savage Indian. Theater, especially minstrel shows, reinforces a stereotype of blacks as suited for menial work.

1843 The Virginia Minstrels give the first public performance of a minstrel show, which will become a popular form of theatrical entertainment. White actors in blackface sitting on an unadorned stage telling anecdotes and stories about whites' perceptions of black life and relations between blacks and whites. Later, songs and dances are added. It is the only form of entertainment based solely on American culture, but it is also the origin of one of the more painful and false stereotypes of African Americans.

1849 American actors hold their own against British stars, so much so that at the Astor Place Opera House in New York riots break out between two factions, those who admire American actor EDWIN FORREST and those who love English actor William Macready, the two leading Shakespearean actors of their day who were starring in rival productions of *Macbeth*. Twenty-two people are killed.

1852 A staged version of Harriet Beecher Stowe's influential novel *Uncle Tom's Cabin* is one of the first plays with a social conscience. Its goal is to show the evil of slavery.

1865 Americans attend burlesque, variety shows featuring coarse humor. (Only later will "burlesque" refer to strip shows.)

1880s–1910s American theater enters a golden age as hundreds of playhouses spring up all over the country. Popular works such as *Hazel Kirke* by Steele Mackay (1880) and *Girl of the Golden West* (1905) by David Belasco serve mostly as star vehicles for such performers as Maude Adams, ETHEL BARRYMORE, and JOHN DREW. Productions of serious European playwrights such as George Bernard Shaw, Henrik Ibsen, and August Strindberg encourage American playwrights to create more serious material. At the same time, a uniquely American form of entertainment, the musical, flourishes on Broadway. Many of these works are unmemorable, mostly pastiches of song and dance.

1920 EUGENE O'NEILL's drama *Beyond the Horizon* is widely hailed as the first major American tragedy. He follows this success with others: *Anna Christie* in 1921 and *Desire Under the Elms* in 1924.

1930s American actors seize upon method acting, a new, more natural acting style that is first introduced by the Russian teacher Constantin

1930s, *cont.*

Stanislavsky and is taught in the United States by LEE STRASBERG.

Many memorable comedies surfaced during the Depression as sources of relief for audiences and actors alike: Clare Booth Luce's *The Women* (1936), George S. Kaufman and Moss Hart's *You Can't Take It with You* (1936) and *The Man Who Came to Dinner* (1939), and William Saroyan's *The Time of Your Life* (1939).

1931 *Mourning Becomes Electra* by EUGENE O'NEILL opens on Broadway. A trilogy consisting of *Homecoming, The Hunted,* and *The Haunted,* it is modeled after the Greek tragedy *Oresteia* by Aeschylus.

1933 EUGENE O'NEILL's only light play, *Ah! Wilderness,* opens on Broadway.

1934 Lillian Helman's play *The Children's Hour,* about the disastrous accusation that two women who run a boarding school are lesbians, is produced.

1935 In one season, New York theatergoers can see CLIFFORD ODETS's *Waiting for Lefty* and *Awake and Sing* as well as MAXWELL ANDERSON's *Winterset,* plays that exhibit a social consciousness rarely seen in American theater. SINCLAIR LEWIS's play *It Can't Happen Here,* about possible fascism in America, is also produced.

The Federal Theater Project spurs serious theater by promoting minority theater (it funds sixteen African American companies) and staging exciting — and often controversial — new plays.

With 373 performances, LANGSTON HUGHES's play *Mulatto* becomes the longest-running play by an African American in this decade.

1938 Thornton Wilder's *Our Town* wins the Pulitzer Prize.

1939 Under attack by a group in the House of Representatives, later formalized into the House Un-American Activities Committee (see p. 210), the Federal Theater Project is closed, but not before it presents T. S. ELIOT's *Murder in the Cathedral* and an all-black cast in *Macbeth.*

1945 TENNESSEE WILLIAMS's *The Glass Menagerie* is staged.

1946 *The Iceman Cometh,* by EUGENE O'NEILL, plays on Broadway.

1947 EUGENE O'NEILL's *A Moon for the Misbegotten* is produced.

With the introduction of TENNESSEE WILLIAMS's powerful and very American play *A Streetcar Named Desire,* a new, postwar flowering of American theater gets under way.

The theatrical producer H. Harrison Frazee, also owner of the Boston Red Sox baseball team, sold Babe Ruth to the New York Yankees for $125,000 in 1920 to help finance a Broadway production of *No, No Nanette.* The 1924 show was a hit, but Boston baseball fans have never forgiven Frazee.

1949 ARTHUR MILLER's powerful *Death of a Salesman* is produced.

Late 1940s–1950s In the face of rising production costs on Broadway, many off-Broadway companies were founded both in New York and other parts of the country, including the Living Theater (founded in New York by Judith Malina and Julian Beck in 1947), the New York Shakespeare Festival (created by JOSEPH PAPP in 1954), the Arena Stage (founded in Washington, D.C., in 1950) and the Actors' Workshop (founded in San Francisco in 1952).

1953 ARTHUR MILLER's *The Crucible* receives its first production. Ostensibly about the Salem witch trials, it is actually a parable about Senator Joseph McCarthy's modern-day anti-Communist "witchhunt."

1955 *Cat on a Hot Tin Roof* by TENNESSEE WILLIAMS is staged.

1956 EUGENE O'NEILL's complex family drama *Long Day's Journey into Night* is staged.

1959 *Sweet Bird of Youth* by TENNESSEE WILLIAMS is produced.
   A less realistic, absurdist form of drama is introduced with EDWARD ALBEE's *The Zoo Story*.
   Lorraine Hansberry's riveting drama of black life, *A Raisin in the Sun*, draws large audiences.

Late 1950s–1960s Theatrical collectives, like Richard Schechner's Performance Group and Joseph Chaikin's Open Theater challenge traditional beliefs about theater, experimenting with new techniques, and questioning the relationship between performer and audience member.
   People begin converting lofts, cafés, and empty spaces into performance spaces in what is known as the Off-Off Broadway movement. Some important groups at the time include Café La Mama run by Ellen Stewart, Caffe Cino, headed by Joe Cino, and the American Place Theater and Theater Genesis.

1950 *Come Back, Little Sheba* is the first of several successful plays by WILLIAM INGE to debut in the 1950s. Noted for his works on small-town life in midwestern America, his other plays include *Picnic* (1953) for which he won the Pulitzer Prize, *Bus Stop* (1955), and *The Dark at the Top of the Stairs* (1957).

1961 TENNESSEE WILLIAMS's play *The Night of the Iguana* opens on Broadway.

1962 *Who's Afraid of Virginia Woolf?* is EDWARD ALBEE's first full-length play.

1963 Neil Simon's popular comedy *Barefoot in the Park* is followed by the Tony Award-winning *The Odd Couple* in 1965, and *The Last of the Red Hot Lovers* in 1969.

"When you are away from old Broadway you are only camping out."
—GEORGE M. COHAN

CULTURE & THE ARTS

MUSICAL THEATER, 1866–PRESENT

1866 *The Black Crook,* which opens on Broadway, is the first American musical. It would hardly be to theatergoers' taste today, but it presages the popularity of this form in America.

1881 Tony Pastor presents the first "big-time" vaudeville show in New York City. Vaudeville flourishes, making stars of such performers as GEORGE M. COHAN, Eddie Cantor, and Harry Houdini.

1903 Victor Herbert stages the first of his operettas, *Babes in Toyland.*

1904 GEORGE M. COHAN, one of the giants of American musical theater, writes, produces, and stars in his own show, *Little Johnny Jones,* introducing favorites such as "I'm a Yankee Doodle Dandy" and "Give My Regards to Broadway."

1906 Another musical starring GEORGE M. COHAN, *Forty-five Minutes from Broadway,* is a hit.

1907 Florenz Ziegfeld produces the first of his twenty-four annual *Follies,* a pastiche of vaudeville and musical theater that will be famous for its elaborate staging and chorus of beautiful women. In the 1920s, the *Follies* make an enormous star of Fanny Brice, who brings down the house with such songs as "My Man" and "Second Hand Rose."

1910 *Naughty Marietta,* another Victor Herbert operetta, successfully woos audiences.

1924 The musical *No, No Nanette,* introduces a craze for tap dancing.

1927 More sophisticated fare is presented by GEORGE and Ira GERSHWIN in *Funny Face.*

Florenz Ziegfeld's twenty-four annual Follies *were raucous revues combining visual spectacle, silly comedy, and beautiful women, like the ones featured on the cover of this 1922 song score.*

The first "modern" musical, successfully merging all the elements of song, story, and dance, is *Showboat* by JEROME KERN and OSCAR HAMMERSTEIN II.

1931 Fred and Adele Astaire make their last joint appearance on Broadway in *The Bandwagon.*
Of Thee I Sing, based on a book by George S. Kaufman with music and lyrics by GEORGE and Ira GERSHWIN, is the first musical to win the Pulitzer Prize.

1932 COLE PORTER writes the score for *The Gay Divorcee.*

1933 IRVING BERLIN's hit, *As Thousands Cheer,* leaves audiences—or rather all of America—singing "Easter Parade."

1935 GEORGE and Ira GERSHWIN's *Porgy and Bess,* a folk opera about African American life, is presented with an African American cast.

1943 *Oklahoma!* by RICHARD RODGERS and OSCAR HAMMERSTEIN, is the first musical to feature dancing that is fully integrated into the story, thanks to choreographer AGNES DE MILLE.

1949 Capitalizing on their success in *Oklahoma!* and *Carousel* (1945), RODGERS and HAMMERSTEIN present a serious story in musical format in *South Pacific.*

1951 RODGERS and HAMMERSTEIN present *The King and I.*

1956 ALAN JAY LERNER and Frederick Loewe introduce the much-loved *My Fair Lady,* based on George Bernard Shaw's *Pygmalion.*

1957 Composer LEONARD BERNSTEIN, choreographer JEROME ROBBINS, and lyricist STEPHEN SONDHEIM collaborate brilliantly on *West Side Story,* which introduces tragedy into musical theater in the form of an updated *Romeo and Juliet.*

1959 The last great RODGERS and HAMMERSTEIN musical is *The Sound of Music.*

1960 Capping out a golden age of musicals is *Camelot,* another LERNER and Loewe production.

1967 *Hair* is billed as an "American Tribal Love-Rock Musical." It moves to Broadway in 1968 as the first rock musical and the first mainstream musical to contain nudity.

1970 Composer-lyricist STEPHEN SONDHEIM introduces a more complex musical in *Company.* It is much more serious than the musicals audiences are accustomed to.

1975 *The Wiz,* a rock musical, is the first black musical produced on Broadway.

1978 *Ain't Misbehavin',* featuring music by Fats Waller, brings more sophisticated black music to Broadway audiences.

1982 *Cats,* a musical by Andrew Lloyd Webber based on poems by T. S. ELIOT, opens on Broadway. It marks the beginning of a "British invasion" on the Great White Way that continues through the 1980s and well into the 1990s.

1988 Andrew Lloyd Webber's *Phantom of the Opera,* a British import, is the year's smash hit musical.

1986 STEPHEN SONDHEIM's darkly comic *Into the Woods* delves into the world of fairy tales.

1990 *A Chorus Line* closes after 6,137 performances.

1994 The opening of *The Beauty and the Beast* brings Disney to Broadway. Another Disney production, *The Lion King* in 1997, signals a return to big-budget, large-scale blockbuster musicals.

1996 Within months of each other, two innovative musicals, *Rent* and *Bring in 'Da Noise, Bring in 'Da Funk* open on Broadway.

2000 After an eighteen-year run and a record 7,397 performances, *Cats* closes on Broadway.

2001 *The Producers,* a hit musical comedy by Mel Brooks, wins twelve Tony Awards, including best musical.

Timeline, *cont.*

1964 ARTHUR MILLER's *After the Fall* is produced.

Three of Amiri Baraka's plays are performed as part of the rising tide of black theater in the 1960s: *Dutchman, The Toilet,* and *The Slave.*

1967 SAM SHEPARD wins an Obie Award for his first play, *La Turista,* produced at the American Place Theater. Shepard worked with off-off Broadway companies such as Café La Mama and Caffe Cino, and brought his counterculture sensibilities to the forefront of theater with his plays about destructive family bonds, including *Curse of the Starving Class* (1976), Pulitzer Prize–winning *Buried Child* (1978), and *True West* (1981).

1968 Mart Crowley's play *The Boys in the Band* signaled a greater acceptance for theater with gay and lesbian themes when it ran off-Broadway for 1,001 performances.

OPENING THE THEATER DOORS

Theater, long considered, at least by the players, to be the most egalitarian art form, has nevertheless been a closed club to both women and minorities for much of its existence. The Pulitzer Prize for drama, to take but one example, has been given to women only eleven times since its inception in 1918, and even more rarely to minorities. After 1945, it was not won by a woman for twenty-eight years, a period that encompassed the rise of both the women's rights and the civil rights movements.

In 1981, dramatist Beth Henley broke the losing streak with her play *Crimes of the Heart*, which was initially produced by a regional theater. The next year, African American dramatist Charles Fuller won for his poignant play *A Soldier's Story*. Since then four women—Marsha Norman, Wendy Wasserstein, Paula Vogel, and Margaret Edson—and one black, August Wilson—have been honored with the prize. Passed over for it have been such esteemed African American playwrights as Lorraine Hansberry, who wrote *A Raisin in the Sun*, and Ntozake Shange's play, *For Colored Girls Who Have Considered Suicide/When the Rainbow Is Enuf.*

1968, *cont.*

Richard Foreman's founding of the Ontological-Hysteric Theater Company this year is one example the avant-garde theater trend that will grow and flourish in the 1970s and 1980s. The Wooster Group, founded by Spalding Gray, Joanne Akalaitis, and others in the early seventies, is another company who experiments with sound, film, and video in their quest for new theater.

1972 The Off-Off Broadway Alliance (OOBA) is formed.

1976 Ntozake Shange's play *For Colored Girls Who Have Considered Suicide/When the Rainbow Is Enuf* becomes the first black drama to play successfully on Broadway since *A Raisin in the Sun.*

1977 Playwright DAVID MAMET has his debut on Broadway, with *American Buffalo*, written two years earlier, and is immediately recognized for his facility with the rhythms of natural speech and his use of often profane street language.

1978 SAM SHEPARD's new play, *Buried Child*, is produced off-Broadway.
    The Gay Theater Alliance is formed.

1979 Lanford Wilson presents *Talley's Folley*, which will win the Pulitzer Prize.

1981 Beth Henley becomes the first woman in twenty-eight years to win the Pulitzer Prize for drama. Her play, *Crimes of the Heart*, is also noteworthy for having been produced not on Broadway but rather by the Manhattan Theater Club, a nonprofit theater company in New York City.

1982 *A Soldier's Story* by African American Charles Fuller wins the Pulitzer Prize.

1983 Marsha Norman wins the Pulitzer Prize for drama for her play *'Night, Mother.*

1984 DAVID MAMET's most important play, *Glengarry Glen Ross*, is staged. It wins the Pulitzer Prize.

1989 Wendy Wasserstein becomes the first woman to win a Tony Award for Best Play, for *The Heidi Chronicles*.

1990 African American dramatist August Wilson wins the Pulitzer Prize for *The Piano Lesson*.

1991 After several years of eclipse, EDWARD ALBEE stages a comeback with *Three Tall Women*. The play is premiered in Europe; eventually produced off-Broadway, it goes on to win the Pulitzer Prize.

1992 Robert Schenkkan's *The Kentucky Cycle* wins the Pulitzer Prize for drama, on the strength of which plans are made to mount a Broadway production the following year.

Richard Nelson, the only American dramatist whose work is regularly produced by the Royal Shakespeare Company in London, receives a Broadway production of his newest play, *Two Shakespearean Actors*, which describes the politics behind the 1849 Astor Place riot.

1993–1994 Tony Kushner's two-part drama *Angels in America* captivates Broadway audiences, earns the Pulitzer Prize for drama, and wins the Tony Award for best play two years in a row.

1995–1996 Like Kushner, Terrence McNally takes the Tony Award for best play two years in a row, with *Love! Valour! Compassion!* in 1995 and *Master Class* in 1996.

1998–1999 Two more female playwrights find success on Broadway and win Pulitzer Prizes: Paula Vogel for *How I Learned to Drive* (1998) and Margaret Edson for *Wit* (1999).

1999 A fiftieth-anniversary Broadway production of ARTHUR MILLER's *Death of a Salesman* earns four Tony Awards. A revival of EUGENE O'NEILL's 1946 classic *The Iceman Cometh* also wins acclaim.

DANCE

1835 *La Sylphide* is performed for the first time in the United States, in Philadelphia.

1846 *Giselle* makes its American debut at the Howard Atheneum in Boston.

1908 ISADORA DUNCAN, an American pioneer in modern dance who has made her name in Europe, tours to great acclaim.

1910 Anna Pavlova makes her first American appearance at the Metropolitan Opera House in *Coppélia*.

1915 Denishawn, the company of TED SHAWN and RUTH ST. DENIS, performs. Its dancers include MARTHA GRAHAM and Doris Humphrey.

1926 MARTHA GRAHAM gives her first solo performance after leaving Denishawn in 1923. It is entitled "Greenwich Village Follies."

1929 MARTHA GRAHAM, one of the pioneers of modern dance, forms her own dance troupe.

1930 Katherine Dunham begins the Ballet Negre, a black ballet company, which eventually becomes the famed Katherine Dunham Dance Company. An anthropologist and scholar, Dunham traveled extensively in the Caribbean, incorporating folk and ethnic movements into her dancing and choreography.

1934 The School of American Ballet, with GEORGE BALANCHINE at its head, is founded.

1937 The Mordkin Ballet, predecessor of the Ballet Theatre, is founded by Lucia Chase and Richard Pleasant. Along with City Ballet, it is one of two major companies performing classical ballet in the United States. It will soon be renamed the American Ballet Theatre.

1942 AGNES DE MILLE choreographs the first important American classical ballet, *Rodeo*, composed by AARON COPLAND.

1944 MARTHA GRAHAM creates the classic modern dance masterpiece *Appalachian Spring*.

1946 The New York City Ballet (originally the Ballet Society), the second major classical dance company in the United States, is founded by Russian-born GEORGE BALANCHINE, formerly of the Ballets Russes, and LINCOLN KIRSTEIN.

1947 Mexican American choreographer and dancer José Limón founds the José Limón Dance Company to foster his techniques inspired by Doris Humphrey and Charles Weidman. It will be the first company to perform at Lincoln Center in 1963.

1950 MERCE CUNNINGHAM, a seminal second-wave modern dancer, founds his own company, which will largely perform his own creations.

1954 ROBERT JOFFREY founds the Joffrey Ballet, which is devoted to performing modern classical ballet.

"I am the enemy of ballet, which I look upon as false, absurd, and outside the domain of art. I thank God that a cruel destiny did not inflict on me the career of a ballet dancer."
—ISADORA DUNCAN

1955 Paul Taylor, an innovative modern-dance choreographer, forms his own company, which performs mostly his own works.

1957 Ballet dancer-choreographer JEROME ROBBINS creates the dancing in *West Side Story*, a pivotal Broadway musical that bridges the gap between popular musical theater and classical ballet.

1958 Choreographer ALVIN AILEY founds a dance company bearing his name. It is dedicated to performing modern dance with African and African American themes.

1960 ALVIN AILEY creates his masterpiece, a modern dance called *Revelations.*

1962 Compose Robert Dunn and others secure a space at the Judson Memorial Church in New York City's Greenwich Village where dancers, choreographers, musicians, composers, and other artists can congregate. The dancers in this postmodern company, such as Trisha Brown, Lucinda Childs, and Meredith Monk, incorporated everyday movements into their dance and experimented with minimalism and nontraditional performance spaces.

1963 With *Aida*, Katherine Dunham becomes the first African American to choreograph for the Metropolitan Opera.

1965 Modern-dance choreographer TWYLA THARP, who innovates dance without music and other experimental forms, establishes her own company.

1968 The Dance Theater of Harlem, the first African American classical company, is begun by ARTHUR MITCHELL.

1969 JEROME ROBBINS creates *Dances at a Gathering*, perhaps the first major ballet with overtones of rock music. Robbins succeeds BALANCHINE at New York City Ballet in 1983 as co–ballet master with Peter Martins.

1970 The Pilobolus Dance Company is founded at Dartmouth College. They become known for their athletic form of dance, which incorporates physical feats into dance and often resembles gymnastics.

1974 The great Russian ballet dancer Mikhail Baryshnikov defects to the United States, where he dances with the American Ballet Theatre. He breaks new ground when he dances both classical and modern ballets.

1980 After working for several years in Europe and winning recognition there, choreographer MARK MORRIS establishes his own dance company, which shows off his very modern yet still classical ballets.

After defecting from the Soviet Union, Mikhail Baryshnikov spent many years with American Ballet Theatre. In 1990, he founded the modern dance company The White Oak Project with Mark Morris.

1988 TWYLA THARP becomes resident choreographer at the American Ballet Theatre and begins to expand the classical repertory to include many more modern dances.

1989 Acclaimed dancer and choreographer Judith Jamison becomes the artistic director of the Alvin Ailey American Dance Theater. In addition to a 1999 Kennedy Center Lifetime Achievement Award, she will win an Emmy for Outstanding Choreography for her work on the documentary *A Hymn for Alvin Ailey*.

1991 MARK MORRIS debuts his parody of the perennial holiday favorite *The Nutcracker*, entitled *The Hard Nut*.

1995 The Joffrey Ballet ceases to exist due to lack of funds. It will reorganize and reopen in Chicago, which many see as a sign that New York City's heyday as the ballet capital of the world has come to an end.

1996 Members of the American Ballet Theatre, the New York City Ballet, the Alvin Ailey American Dance Theater, the Royal Swedish, and others gather together to perform a tribute to choreographer and former Alvin Ailey dancer ULYSSES DOVE just days after his death from AIDS.

1997 Two touring stage shows, the enormously popular *Riverdance* and *Lord of the Dance*, ignite a surge of interest in Irish step dancing.

INFLUENTIAL AMERICAN DANCE COMPANIES

Alvin Ailey Dance Theatre, New York: African American themes

American Ballet Theatre, New York: One of the preeminent dance companies in the United States; performs classical ballet with a smattering of modern dance

Ballet Hispanico, New York: Classical ballet with a Latin edge

Trisha Brown Company, New York: Modern dance

Lucinda Childs Dance Company, New York: Innovative modern dance

Cunningham Dance Foundation, New York: Avant-garde modern dance

Dance Theater of Harlem, New York: Major African American troupe; classical ballet

Martha Graham Dance Company, New York: Classic and new modern dance

Joffrey Ballet (now defunct, formerly of New York): Mounted revivals of classic, rarely done ballets, plus new repertory

Mark Morris Dance Group, New York: Cutting-edge dancing that merges classical and modern technique

New York City Ballet, New York: Along with American Ballet Theatre, the preeminent dance company in the country. Founded by GEORGE BALANCHINE and LINCOLN KIRSTEIN, their repertory includes classical ballet (performed in the company's own inimitable style) and some modern compositions

Paul Taylor Dance Company, New York: Along with Cunningham Foundation, preeminent modern dance

Twyla Tharp, New York: Founder of various companies that dance her choreography, which is modern

1999–2000 The New York City Ballet marks its fiftieth anniversary with a landmark series of special events and 100 ballet performances over two seasons.

PAINTING AND SCULPTURE

1772 CHARLES WILLSON PEALE paints the first known portrait of George Washington.

1774 European-trained JOHN SINGLETON COPLEY leaves America for good, having achieved a reputation as a portraitist, although most of his fellow colonists prefer to have their likenesses done by the more prestigious European artists.

1781 JOHN SINGLETON COPLEY paints *The Death of Lord Chatham.*

1794 Charles Willson Peale moves his gallery into the hall of the American Philosophical Society in Philadelphia. It is one of the first American museums.

1795–1796 GILBERT STUART, another well-known portraitist, paints George Washington.

1827 JOHN JAMES AUDUBON, who has traveled throughout the United States viewing its flora and fauna, publishes his illustrations in *Birds of America* (see pp. 384, 386).

1836 Hudson River artist Thomas Cole paints *The Course of Empire.*

1840 America's first art scandal occurs when the public ridicules sculptor Horatio Greenough's *George Washington.* The statue of the first president, shown in a Roman toga, is never permanently displayed in the Rotunda of the Capitol for which it was created.

1875 Thomas Eakin's *Surgical Clinic of Professor Gross* introduced a scientific interest to the subject matter of art.

1881 Sculptor Augustus Saint-Gauden's statue of Adm. David Farragut is installed in Madison Square.

1884 Portraitist JOHN SINGER SARGENT settles in London, where he paints stunning portraits that are much sought after by the rich.

Gilbert Stuart's contemporaries sometimes referred to the artist as the "Father of American Portraiture" because he painted nearly all of the influential people of his time, including George Washington.

"A portrait is a painting with something wrong with the mouth."
—JOHN SINGER SARGENT

1890 Childe Hassam, an American impressionist, paints *Washington Arch, Spring.*

1891 MARY CASSATT, a leading American impressionist, paints *The Bath.*

1895 WINSLOW HOMER paints *The Northeaster,* one of his many fine depictions of the power of the sea. Seven years later, he produces *Early Morning After a Storm at Sea,* a painting many deem his finest.

1905 MARY CASSATT paints *Mère en enfant,* which hangs in the Louvre, one of her many studies of mothers and children.
  The Spielers, by GEORGE LUKS, defines a new subject matter that some call obscene.

1908 A group of artists gather to exhibit their paintings. They call themselves The Eight but become known as the Ashcan School. They are Arthur B. Davies, Maurice Pendergast, Ernest Lawson, William Glackens, Everett Shinn, Robert Henri, John Sloan, and GEORGE LUKS.

1912 John Sloan produces a portrait of working-class life called *McSorley's Bar.*

1913 Overnight the New York Armory Show changes the direction of American painting, creating a sensational new style known as modernism. The exhibit includes 1,250 paintings and sculptures by American and European artists and introduces the works of Marcel Duchamp, Pablo Picasso, and Wassily Kandinsky to American audiences. The first generation of modern painters includes Max Weber, MAN RAY, John Marin, and Alfred Maurer.

1914 William Glackens's *Washington Square* exemplifies a kind of social realism aligned with the Ashcan School.

1916 NORMAN ROCKWELL paints his first of more than 300 covers for the *Saturday Evening Post.* For his "vivid and affectionate portraits of our country," Rockwell is awarded the Presidential Medal of Freedom in 1977.

1922 Daniel Chester French's famous statue of Lincoln is installed in the Lincoln Memorial in Washington, D.C.

1925 MAN RAY creates *Clock Wheels,* one of the few American surrealist paintings.

1926 ALEXANDER CALDER, the preeminent sculptor of his day, exhibits one of his masterpieces, *The Circus,* a display of motorized wire sculptures.

1930 Edward Hopper paints one of his masterpieces, *Early Sunday Morning.*

GRANT WOOD paints *American Gothic*, a classic portrait of an American farmer and his wife.

1931 Stuart Davis, who belongs to the second wave of modernists, paints *House and Street*.

GEORGIA O'KEEFFE's *Cow's Skull* is a characteristic study of shape and form in a southwestern setting.

1931–1932 Ben Shahn paints a series of gouaches on the Sacco-Vanzetti trial.

1932 ALEXANDER CALDER exhibits a new art form, stabiles, which are movable, often motorized pieces of sculpture. These he follows with mobiles, delicately balanced hanging pieces that are moved by air currents.

1940 When Nazi Germany occupies France, Paris collapses as the center or the art world. Fleeing expatriates, combined with the American artists who were deeply influenced by the Armory Show, turn New York City into the new art capital of the world.

Former social realist Ben Shahn paints the melancholy solitude of the lonely city in *Willis Avenue Bridge*.

At the age of eighty Anna Mary Robertson Moses, also known as Grandma Moses, has a one-woman show in New York. An untrained farmer's wife, she wins attention for naïve painting and after World War II gains widespread popularity. In 1949, President Truman invites her to the White House.

1943 Thomas Hart Benton paints *July Hay*.

Milton Avery, an individualistic painter who produces canvases of stunning simplicity, creates *Swimmers and Sunbathers*.

1945 Sculptor ISAMU NOGUCHI completes *Kouros*. Later, he becomes better known for his integrated environmental sculptures and stone sculpture gardens.

1948 Barnett Newman makes his first stripe paintings.

Realist Andrew Wyeth produces what will become one of the world's most widely reproduced paintings, *Christina's World*.

1950 WILLEM DE KOONING paints *Excavation*, one of his most masterful abstract expressionist works.

Abstract expressionist JACKSON POLLOCK shocks the art world with his drip paintings such as *Lavender Mist*.

1954 Jasper John's flags and target images inaugurate pop art.

Milton Avery, an individualistic painter who produced canvases of stunning simplicity, creates *Green Sea*.

Grant Wood's famous evocation of midwestern rural life, the 1930 oil painting *American Gothic,* was bought for the Art Institute of Chicago for $300. Wood's sixty-two-year-old dentist, Dr. B. H. McKeeby of Cedar Rapids, Iowa, and thirty-year-old sister, Nan, posed as the farmer and his spinster daughter.

1956 Abstract expressionist FRANZ KLINE paints *Mahoning*.

ROBERT RAUSCHENBERG incorporates images and found objects into collages, such as *Gloria*.

1958 Barnett Newman, who pioneered color-field painting, begins to paint *Stations of the Cross*, which he will not finish until 1966.

1959 Color-field painters cause a stir with their brightly colored, vaguely Zen-like works of art: Kenneth Noland creates *Virginia Site*; JASPER JOHNS paints *Numbers in Color*; and FRANK STELLA paints *Jill*.

1961 Color-field painter Kenneth Noland paints *A Warm Sound in a Gray Field*.

1962 ANDY WARHOL paints one of the masterpieces of pop art, *Campbell's Soup Can*.

1963 ROY LICHTENSTEIN creates huge, comic strip–like paintings, such as *Whaam!*

1964 African American collagist ROMARE BEARDEN paints *The Prevalence of Ritual: The Baptism*.

1965 DAVID SMITH redefines contemporary sculpture with monumental steel-and-iron works that look like abstract drawings in the air. He begins his *Cubi* series.

FRANK STELLA paints *Empress of India*.

1966 LOUISE NEVELSON's *World*, a huge work, explores sculpture as environment.

1969 Pop art sculptor Claes Oldenburg's giant outdoor monument *Lipstick (Ascending) on Caterpillar* Tracks is erected at Yale. He will go on to create many ultrarealistic soft sculptures.

1975 FRANK STELLA paints *Montenegro I*.

1977 GEORGIA O'KEEFFE is awarded the Medal of Freedom by President Carter.

1981 ROMARE BEARDEN creates *Artist with Painting and Model*.

1993 The new Norman Rockwell Museum opens in Stockbridge, Massachusetts, displaying not only ROCKWELL's paintings, but his original art supplies, library, and even fan mail.

ART MOVEMENTS IN THE UNITED STATES

NAME	DATES	DESCRIPTION	EXAMPLES
Romantic	Late 1700s–early 1800s	Revolt against formalism. Main themes are man against nature, often portrayed in sentimental manner; colors light.	Copley's *Watson and The Shark*
Hudson River School	1820s–1870s	Group of landscape painters who infused vistas of New York State and the Rocky Mountains with a lofty grandeur and moral purity.	Cole's *The Oxbow* Church's *Niagara Falls*
Realism	Mid– to late 1800s	Revolt against romanticism. No sentiment or pathos in content; deeper, darker palette.	Eakins's *Gross Clinic*
Impressionism	Late 1800s	Breakthrough in painting: perspective no longer important; artist paints for sake of painting and to depict light and color.	Cassatt's *Mother and Child*
Ashcan	Pre–World War I	Urban subject matter, such as boxing, gritty city life.	Hopper's *Early Sunday Morning*
Social Realism	1920s	Reflects interest in communism, themes are intended to raise social consciousness.	Shahn's *Miners' Wives*
Regionalism	1920s	Artists whose themes consciously depict aspects of American life, such as farming or New England.	Wood's *American Gothic*
Cubism	1920s	Much more popular in Europe, this movement expands on Impressionism and predates modern art. Object is depicted from several angles at once. Analytical.	Feininger's *Blue Marine*
Surrealism	1920s–1930s	Heavily psychoanalytic; attempt to paint using subconscious.	Calder's *Lobster Trap and Fish Tail*
Abstract Expressionism	Post–World War II	Major movement of the era and the first to begin in the United States. Reaction to the chaos of the war and the post-atomic bomb era. Violent colors, frenetic gestures; no object—just color.	Pollock's *Lavender Mist*
Pop Art	Mid-1950s	London-based but uses American icons almost exclusively. Low-brow images used in art; realistic depiction.	Johns's *Three Flags*
Color field	Late 1950s	Seeks order and control that is lacking in abstract expressionism; artists often use very large canvases with vast areas of color; intense, poetic interest in color.	Frank Stella's *Empress of India*
Neoexpressionism	1970s–1980s	Figurative style in painting that conveys cultural uneasiness in purposefully clumsy forms, bold brushstrokes, and jolting colors.	Work of Julian Schnabel

THE NATIONAL ENDOWMENT FOR THE ARTS

The National Endowment for the Arts (NEA) was established by Congress in 1965. Although the nations of Western Europe have always heavily subsidized their cultural activities, this belated attempt to provide governmental support for American art and culture was the United States' first such effort, and there was little consensus that this was an appropriate government function. Despite this, the endowment managed to survive its initial three-year funding period and even proceeded to grow.

Over the years it has had its hand in nearly every aspect of American culture, from fine art to dance to theater to opera. The NEA is actively involved in educating teachers about culture. It insures fine art and cultural artifacts so they can travel to the United States from other countries, and by insuring art going the other way, it helps to carry U.S. culture abroad. It sponsors artists- and writers-in-residence programs, funds theaters and museums, aids libraries, and reaches out to youth. The endowment works with both individuals and organizations.

Other than a perpetual shortage of funds, which must be provided by a sometimes reluctant Congress, the NEA encountered no serious difficulties in its first two decades. But in the late 1980s, the conservative right began to raise objections to its existence on grounds that it was promoting art they believed should not be funded with tax dollars.

So intense was the pressure that in one case the Corcoran Galley in Washington, D.C., canceled a show of photographs by the late Robert Mapplethorpe because it contained a few examples of homoerotic themes. Senator Jesse Helms of North Carolina introduced legislation that would bar the NEA from funding "obscene" work, and Congress vowed to establish a panel that would evaluate art for obscene content. The furor died down, but the NEA remains a target of the conservative right.

In actuality, the NEA's involvement in cutting-edge projects is only a fraction of what it does. Much of its work evolves around the preservation of American folk art, crafts, and traditions. Some of its projects are as small as the collection and preservation of cowboy songs and poetry, a minor oral art that might nevertheless be entirely lost without the NEA's efforts. Other projects are more expansive, such as its efforts to preserve an entire range of Appalachian crafts.

1997 The $1 billion J. Paul Getty Center, the costliest art institution ever built in the United States, opens in Malibu, California.

A museum devoted to the works of GEORGIA O'KEEFFE opens in Santa Fe, New Mexico.

1999 The Museum of Contemporary Art opens in May in North Adams, Massachusetts. This center for visual, performing, and media arts is situated in a historic twenty-seven-building mill complex in the Berkshires originally constructed in 1872 by a cloth manufacturer. The space once housed a Massachusetts Electric Company.

2001 The Guggenheim Las Vegas opens. With its seventy-foot-high ceilings and its hangarlike feel, it is designed to show temporary exhibitions rather than house a permanent collection like most museums.

2002 The Museum of Modern Art (MoMA) opens a new exhibition space in Long Island City, Queens, in order to continue exhibiting work from its permanent collection, while the midtown Manhattan building undergoes major renovations.

THE MOVIES, 1895–PRESENT

1895 In New York City, a demonstration of the Eidoloscope is probably the first projected movie show in America.

1903 Americans attend Edwin S. Porter's silent film *The Great Train Robbery;* at twelve minutes, it's the longest film to date. It introduces the Western, a staple of American film.

1905 The first nickelodeon opens in Pittsburgh; they spread like wildfire. For a nickel, viewers watched several six- to fifteen-minute films and an occasional vaudeville act.

1908 D. W. Griffith, one of America's first great filmmakers, releases his first film, *The Adventures of Dollie.*

1912 *The Keystone Kops* debuts.

1913 The first fan magazine, *Photoplay,* is started.
    Fatty Arbuckle receives the first "pie in the face" as a Keystone Kop in *A Noise from the Deep.*

1915 D. W. Griffith makes *The Birth of a Nation,* a controversial three-hour epic about the Civil War and the Reconstruction period, and overnight feature-length films replace the shorts.

Screen idol and sex symbol Rudolph Valentino is pictured here in costume for the 1926 film The Son of the Sheik.

1916 Mary Pickford is the top box-office star.

1920s The era of the silent film is at its apex: Charlie Chaplin makes *The Kid* in 1921 and *The Gold Rush* in 1925. Genres also begin to take recognizable shapes. Buster Keaton provides humor in *Sherlock, Jr.* Ernst Lubitsch makes sophisticated comedies of manners. Among Westerns, the decade produces *The Covered Wagon* and *The Iron Horse.* Finally, epics such as Cecil B. DeMille's *The Ten Commandments* and *King of Kings* become popular.

Sports figures like Babe Ruth and Jack Dempsey are popular, as are public figures like aviator Charles Lindbergh, gangster Al Capone, and bodybuilder Charles Atlas.

1921 Rudolph Valentino becomes the first movie idol in such films as *The Sheik* and *Blood and Sand,* made in 1922.

1927 Clara Bow stars in *Wings,* the first film to win the Academy Award for Best Picture.
    Sound is introduced in *The Jazz Singer,* starring Al Jolson, who becomes an overnight sensation.

1928 Walt Disney's Mickey Mouse appears in his first cartoon, called *Steamboat Willie.* Characters such as Minnie Mouse, Donald Duck, and Pluto soon rival Mickey's popularity.

1930s This is the golden era of the studio film when stars are the driving force behind the movies. Among the better known are Greta Garbo, Marlene Dietrich, Jean Harlow, Mae West, Katharine Hepburn, Bette Davis, Cary Grant, Clark Gable, James Stewart, Gary Cooper, Jimmy Cagney, and Fred Astaire and Ginger Rogers.

1934 Frank Capra makes *It Happened One Night,* and the movie wins all four top Oscars. The first movie of the *Thin Man* series is produced.

1935 The movies feature the classic *Top Hat,* with Fred Astaire and Ginger Rogers.

1937 Walt Disney makes his first feature-length animated film, *Snow White.*

THE MOVIES, 1895–PRESENT, cont.

1939 Margaret Mitchell's best-selling novel *Gone with the Wind* becomes a wildly successful movie.

1940s The industry is dominated by a handful of male directors: Frank Capra (*It's a Wonderful Life* and *Mr. Deeds Goes to Town*), John Huston (*The Maltese Falcon* and *Treasure of the Sierra Madre*), and William Wyler (*Mrs. Miniver*).

1940 *Fantasia* is Walt Disney's second feature-length film.

Bob Hope and Bing Crosby entertain America with *Road to Singapore*, the first of several "Road to" movies including *Road to Morocco* (1942), *Road to Utopia* (1946), and *Road to Rio* (1947).

1941 Orson Welles makes *Citizen Kane*, a landmark film.

1942–1945 American movies become a propaganda tool during World War II, producing such films as those in Frank Capra's *Why We Fight* series.

1943 In the midst of the World War II, Americans go to the movies to see *Casablanca* with Humphrey Bogart and Ingrid Bergman.

1944 *National Velvet* premiers and makes Elizabeth Taylor a star.

Judy Garland, the nation's favorite chanteuse, stars in *Meet Me in St. Louis.*

1945 At the movies, people watch *Spellbound* and *A Tree Grows in Brooklyn.* They adore stars such as Ingrid Bergman, Humphrey Bogart, Joan Crawford, and Barbara Stanwyck.

1946–1953 The studio system collapses, under its own weight and under pressure from the McCarthy hearings, which devastate the Hollywood community (see 211).

1947 Americans' love affair with the movies begins to draw to a close as attendance starts a long, steady decline. Some blame it on television, but others have suggested that the migration to the suburbs (see p. 263), where there were, at least initially, no movie theaters, ended movies' heyday as an American pastime.

1952 *Singin' in the Rain,* with Gene Kelly and Debbie Reynolds, is a lavish color musical.

1954 Hollywood produces the socially conscious *On the Waterfront,* which makes Marlon Brando a star.

1961 Everyone goes to see *West Side Story,* starring Natalie Wood.

1968 Barbra Streisand, whose popularity will match that of Fanny Brice and Judy Garland, stars in *Funny Girl,* the story of Fanny Brice.

1969 *Easy Rider* with Dennis Hopper and Peter Fonda seems to embody 1960s values.

1970s American films take a hard look at American culture in such cult films as *Five Easy Pieces* (1970), *A Clockwork Orange* (1971), and *American Graffiti* (1973), but Americans also go to see the sentimental movies *Love Story* (1970) and *Rocky* (1976), which makes a star of Sylvester Stallone.

1972 Francis Ford Coppola begins his mafia trilogy with Al Pacino and Marlon Brando in *The Godfather.* Both *The Godfather* and *The Godfather: Part II* (1974) win Academy Awards. *The Godfather: Part III* is released in 1990.

1977 George Lucas's *Star Wars* is released and quickly becomes a classic, with sequels and prequels to come.

1980s *E.T.: The Extra-Terrestrial* directed by Steven Spielberg, is a popular movie.

Sequels are big in the 1980s. *Raiders of the Lost Ark* (1982), which makes Harrison Ford a star, is followed by the sequels *Indiana Jones and the Temple of Doom* (1984) and *Indiana Jones and the Last Crusade* (1989). Popular 1970s movies like

Star Wars and *Jaws* also boast sequels in the 1980s.

1984 *Sixteen Candles,* a John Hughes movie starring Molly Ringwald, is released. Other "brat pack" films include *The Breakfast Club* (1985) and *Pretty in Pink* (1986) and are indicative of the many 1980s movies that target the teen audience.

1990s Popular movies of the decade include *Jurassic Park* (1993), *Forrest Gump* (1994), *Braveheart* (1995), *The English Patient* (1996), *Titanic* (1997), *Saving Private Ryan* (1998), *Star Wars: Episode I* (1999), and *American Beauty* (1999).

1994 A growth in the independent film genre leads to major successes with movies like Quentin Tarantino's *Pulp Fiction* and Kevin Smith's *Clerks.* Todd Solondz's *Welcome to the Dollhouse* and Ethan and Joel Coen's *Fargo* come out two years later and are other good examples of movies that differ from the typical Hollywood blockbusters of the 1980s and 1990s.

1999 *The Blair Witch Project,* which is mostly improvised by three actors and shot in documentary style, using handheld cameras and digital video, is a hit at the box office. Created on a remarkably small budget and using the Internet for much of its publicity, the film earned over $140 million in the United States.

2001 *Harry Potter and the Sorcerer's Stone,* based on a book in the enormously popular children's series by English author J. K. Rowling, shatters box-office records in its debut.

TEN TOP-GROSSING MOVIES OF ALL TIME

(U.S. BOX OFFICE, AS OF JULY 2003)

1. *Titanic* (1997)	$600,743,440
2. *Star Wars* (1977)	$460,935,655
3. *E.T.: The Extra-Terrestrial* (1982)	$434,949,459
4. *Star Wars: Episode I—The Phantom Menace* (1999)	$431,065,444
5. *Spider Man* (2002)	$403,706,375
6. *Jurassic Park* (1993)	$356,763,175
7. *Lord of the Rings: The Two Towers, The* (2002)	$339,554,276
8. *Forrest Gump* (1994)	$329,452,287
9. *Lion King, The* (1994)	$328,423,001
10. *Harry Potter and the Sorcerer's Stone* (2001)	$317,557,891

PHOTOGRAPHY

1860 MATHEW BRADY photographs Abraham Lincoln. In the five years that follow, this first great American photodocumentarian will become known for his daguerreotypes depicting the horrors of the Civil War.

1873 Timothy O'Sullivan takes a magnificent photo, *Ancient Ruins in the Canyon de Chelly, New Mexico, in a Niche Fifty Feet Above the Present Canyon Bed.* Other photographers who accompany expeditions exploring the American West are J. K. Hillers and W. H. Jackson.

1890 JACOB RIIS publishes *How the Other Half Lives.* Riis's photograph such as *Bandits' Roost* exemplifies documentary photography. Unlike photojournalists who seek to capture a moment in time simply because it is there to record, documentary photographers want to capture the moment for the purpose of promoting reform.

1902 Alfred Stieglitz begins publication of *Camera Work*, a forum for the Photo-Secession movement, which rebels against "salon" photography that imitates genre painting.

1904 LEWIS HINE begins taking pictures of immigrants arriving on Ellis Island and later documents their tenement experiences and frightful work conditions in the Lower East Side of Manhattan. In 1908, the National Child Labor Committee begins paying LEWIS HINE to photograph child labor. His images of young people in factories, mines, mills, factories, canneries, and selling goods on the street help to popularize the view that child labor destroys the health, education, and future prospects of young people (see p. 225).

1908 Alfred Stieglitz and EDWARD STEICHEN open the 291 Gallery, where photography is displayed as art.

1922 In a series called *Equivalents*, Alfred Stieglitz photographs clouds, an attempt to show that photography can be as abstract as painting. Steiglitz, who is fascinated with the modern city, is also the first photographer to shoot skyscrapers as pure objects.

1923 Berenice Abbott, influenced by surrealist photographer MAN RAY, turns from sculpture to photography. She will produce a series of portraits of celebrities of the 1920s.

1927 Edward Weston merges realism and abstraction, in photographs such as *Shell*. Images like this are soon referred to as "pure" photography. In the 1930s, Weston and ANSEL ADAMS will found the f/64 Group, the name taken from the smallest lens opening, which permits great precision and detail.

Photographer Lewis Hine captured the building of the Empire State Building in New York City.

1928 MAN RAY takes *Rayograph*, an important and purely abstract photograph. Rayographs are made by placing objects directly onto photographic paper and exposing them to light. Ray experimented with many photographic techniques and was an influential Dadaist and surrealist.

1930 ANSEL ADAMS publishes *Taos Pueblo*, a book of his photographs. His goal is to make unsentimental photographs, without any manipulation.

1932 Lewis Hine published *Men at Work*, a collection of awe-inspiring photographs illustrating the construction of the Empire State Building. In contrast to his photos of child labor (see p. 225), these images celebrate the postwar American labor force.

1933 Dorothea Lange's *White Angel Breadline* exemplifies the powerful images of people, in place and time, that her camera will record.

1936 Dorothea Lange shoots the moving *Migrant Mother* in California.

1937 Margaret Bourke-White publishes *You Have Seen Their Faces*. Known for her series on the rural South during the Depression, Bourke-White also shares Steiglitz's fascination with the new city and invents a school of industrial photography, which in turn leads to commercial photography. Some of her work is sculptural in tone. This is a new kind of photojournalism, and Bourke-White is the first photographer hired for the new magazines *Fortune* and *Life*.

The New Deal's Farm Security Administration sends photographers such as Dorothea Lange across the country to document rural America, recording the farms ravaged by drought and depression and the gaunt faces of farm men and women.

1938 The Museum of Modern Art publishes *American Photography*, coinciding with its retrospective on Walker Evans.

Heroic School photographer Robert Capa, who spends his career photographing war, takes the stunning *Death of a Loyalist Soldier*.

1939 Berenice Abbott publishes *Changing New York*, a ten-year project to document the city.

1941 Walker Evans's stunning black-and-white photographs of ruran poverty accompany the text of James Agee's influential book *Let Us Now Praise Famous Men*.

1946 Robert Capa founds Magnum, an agency for photojournalists. In 1954, at age forty-one, he dies in a land mine explosion in Vietnam, where he is photographing French combat troops.

1949 Aaron Siskind produces *Water Stains on Wall*, a photo reminiscent of abstract art.

1953–1955 Edward Steichen's exhibition *The Family of Man* presents the work of 273 photographers in seventy countries.

1958 Berenice Abbott produces scientific photographs for a high school physics text.

HISTORY AND THE VISUAL ARTS

Prior to the invention of photography, the visual record of historic events and people was confined to paintings and drawings. Portrait artists such as JOHN SINGLETON COPLEY and GILBERT STUART captured the likenesses of Paul Revere, Sam Adams, George Washington, and other colonial-era figures with technical virtuosity and lifelike accuracy, however forgiving. In the early 1800s, the paintings of George Catlin and others provided a valuable and enduring ethnological record of American Indian life. The recording of historic events, however, was often more artistic than accurate. Emanuel Leutze's classic painting *Washington Crossing the Delaware* (1851) depicts an actual event—the surprise attack against the Hessians on Christmas Eve, 1776—but the image of the general clearly emphasizes heroic virtue over true life, and the details of dress, boat, and storm-tossed river are more fanciful than real. Benjamin West's famous painting of 1771, *Penn's Treaty with the Indians,* broke tradition by portraying the figures in authentic period garb rather than classical costume, but history now suggests that the meeting never took place.

The advent of photographic processes created an infallible visual record, adding a vital new dimension to the study of history. The first great photo documentation of events in the making was the work of MATHEW BRADY and the photographers who worked with him in shooting the Civil War. One of those men, Timothy O'Sullivan (see p. 157), along with William Henry Jackson, Eadweard Muybridge, and Carleton Watkins, spent the following decade bringing to light the vast, pristine landscapes of the American West. The use of the camera as a tool of social reform began in the 1880s with JACOB RIIS's shocking photos of New York City slum life, published in *How the Other Half Lives* (1890). LEWIS HINES's photos of child labor at the turn of the century (see p. 225), DOROTHEA LANGE's images of Depression-era poverty, Walker Evans's stark pictures of tenant farm life, and Margaret Bourke-White's pioneering work in photojournalism, brought contemporary issues close to home for the American people. If the motivation and inspiration of these efforts went beyond pure art, the aesthetic quality and technical virtuosity of the photos themselves helped make them icons of American culture.

1962 Minor White creates *Capital Reef, Utah,* in which natural shapes make abstract composition.

1972 The photographs of Diane Arbus are published, revealing her uncanny ability to show the sad or strange side of life.

Jerry Uelsmann revives fantasy photographs, which had a brief heyday in the 1920s. His *Untitled,* which superimposes the body of a nude woman on a landscape, is an excellent example of this genre. Similarly, W. Eugene Smith revives documentary photography with works such as *Tomoko in Her Bath,* a stunning Pietà-like image of a mother holding her daughter.

Imogen Cunningham: Photographs is published, introducing the general public to the varied styles—both classic and romantic—of photography.

1980s–1990s Diversity of style and subject matter typify contemporary photographic art. Trends range from postmodernism to experimental formalism to documentary realism. Notable photographers include Cindy Sherman, Nicholas Nixon, Robert Mapplethorpe, Roy Decarava, Nan Goldin, and Mary Ellen Mark.

ARCHITECTURE

1600s Indigenous Native American architecture includes the rubble-and-clay, flat-topped cliff dwellings of the Pueblos, such as those located at Chaco Canyon, New Mexico (c. A.D. 1300).

1636 The San Miguel Mission is built in Santa Fe, New Mexico (see p. 237).

1699 The old adobe church of San Estaban in Acoma, New Mexico, is remodeled. Its walls are sixty feet high and ten feet thick.

1700 The Mission of San Xavier del Bac is founded just south of the Indian village of Tucson. Its church, known as the White Dove of the Desert, still stands as an outstanding example of Spanish colonial architecture.

1718 The contemporary French Quarter in New Orleans recalls that the old city, below Canal Street, was founded in this year by the French.

1770 Thomas Jefferson begins building Monticello in Charlottesville, Virginia. Designed by Jefferson, it is a fine example of American classical revival.

1791 The Cibaldo in New Orleans is erected as a government building by the Spanish. Today it is the Louisiana State Museum.

1793 President George Washington accepts architect William Thornton's 1792 design of the U.S. Capitol in Washington, D.C., which follows the Palladin style of architecture popular in England throughout the eighteenth century. Construction of the Capitol and the rebuilding after being burned by the British were carried out first by architect BENJAMIN H. LATROBE and after 1818 by Boston architect CHARLES BULFINCH. Both Latrobe and Bulfinch add elements to Thornton's original design (see. p. 239).

Thomas Jefferson designed his low, red brick home Monticello with a white dome and Doric portico, echoing Andrea Palladio's Villa Rotunda in Vincenza, Italy.

1799 CHARLES BULFINCH completes the Massachusettes State House in Boston. Its neoclassic design will influence statehouses across the country.

1819 Andrew Jackson begins constructing the Hermitage House in Nashville, Tennessee. Today, open to the public, it is both a typical plantation home and an excellent example of Greek revival architecture.

1826 Construction on the U.S. Capitol is complete. CHARLES BULFINCH continues work on the decoration and landscaping until 1829 (see p. 239).

1840–1900 Victorian style prevails in domestic design, and many of the homes that line American towns and cities, both large and small, are variations of this trend.

1872 H. H. RICHARDSON begins building the Trinity Church in Boston. Romanesque in spirit, it also displays a stripped-down modernism that many people believe marks the beginning of a new era of uniquely American design.

1883 The Home Insurance Building in Chicago stirs excitement. It is the first U.S. building in which a metal skeleton rather than the walls carries the weight and therefore is a prototype for modern skyscrapers.

1885 In Chicago, H. H. RICHARDSON begins building the Marshall Field Wholesale Store (now demolished), another pioneering building that features little ornament and a new emphasis on functionality.

1886 The Auditorium in Chicago is begun by LOUIS SULLIVAN and his partner Dankmar Adler. The building is marked by its lack of ornament and wide generous arches that are the main architectural detail.

1888 Influential New York firm McKim, Mead and White begin construction of the Boston Public Library, inspired by classical and Italian Renaissance designs. Hailed as a "palace for the people," it is considered a fine example of civic art.

1890 LOUIS SULLIVAN builds the landmark Wainwright Building in St. Louis. Steel-framed and modern by virtue of its emphasis on function over form, it is nevertheless decorated with one of Sullivan's characteristic friezes.

1891 As architects begin to experiment with building skyscrapers, the Monadnock Building in Chicago, built by the firm of Burnham and Root, at sixteen stories, becomes the last tall building constructed of load-bearing walls.

1893 FRANK LLOYD WRIGHT, a disciple of SULLIVAN, begins to build "prairie" houses, an iconoclastic new form of domestic architecture. The houses are radical by virtue of their emphasis on the horizontal rather than the vertical plane. The apex of the prairie style is the Robie House in Chicago, built in 1909.

1902 DANIEL BURNHAM completes the Flatiron Building, a triangular New York landmark. It was New York's first skyscraper and one of the first buildings constructed with a steel frame (see p. 251–253).

1904 FRANK LLOYD WRIGHT designs the Larkin Soap Building in Buffalo, New York. With its central courtyard and sealed windows, it is a radical design in institutional building.

"A doctor can bury his mistakes, but an architect can only advise his clients to plant vines."
—FRANK LLOYD WRIGHT

1927 BUCKMINSTER FULLER designs the Dymaxion House, a round home with walls suspended from a central mast. One of the first prefabricated structures, the energy-efficient, self-dusting unit made primarily of aluminum would be waterproof, fireproof, inexpensive and portable. Fuller built a Dymaxion House in Wichita, Kansas, in 1946 and although the idea never caught on with the pubic, engineers and architects now hail the design as foward-thinking and innovative.

1931 The Philadelphia Savings Fund Society building, built by George Howe, exhibits one of the primary characteristics of modernism, with glass walls replacing traditional windows.

1936 FRANK LLOYD WRIGHT builds a masterpiece of modern design, a house in Pennsylvania called Falling Water. Exemplifying Wright's principle that buildings should interact with their surroundings, the structure is cantilevered, or supported, over a waterfall.

1937 LUDWIG MIES VAN DER ROHE relocates the pioneering Bauhaus School in Chicago and starts the international style in the United States.

1949 LUDWIG MIES VAN DER ROHE begins to build Nos. 845–860, two black steel, glass-walled apartment towers situated on Lake Shore Drive in Chicago. His design for the Seagram Building in New York (1958) also uses a steel frame, but employs bronze-tinted glass and bronze I-beams for a striking look.

1950 LUDWIG MIES VAN DER ROHE builds the Farnsworth House near Plano, Illinois, an elegantly simple modern building with its flat roof and glass walls.

1952 GORDON BUNSHAFT designs the first glass-walled high-rise in New York City, the spare and elegant Lever House.

1960s–1970s Architects rebel against the sparseness of modernism and begin to build in the postmodern idiom, a more ornamental style with echoes of neoclassicism. A typical postmodern building is the Sony headquarters (formerly the AT&T Building) in New York City, built by PHILIP JOHNSON.

1964 The CBS Building in New York City is completed. Designed by EERO SAARINEN, it is supported by a central core.

1968 When other architects turn to postmodernism, RICHARD NEUTRA continues to adhere to the principles of modernism with such innovative structures as the Northridge Medical Arts Building in Los Angeles.

1983 FRANK GEHRY completes the Norton House, in Venice, California. He successfully explodes the traditional rectilinear shape of most buildings to create asymmetrical buildings with great dynamism.

1980s–1990s Architecture, like painting and sculpture, diversifies into several different schools, most traditional in tone, with no one prevailing.

1990 Eighty years after construction was initially begun, the Neo-Gothic National Cathedral in Washington, D.C., is completed.

1991 ROBERT VENTURI, a founder of postmodern architecture, wins the prestigious Pritzker Prize.

1994 The American Center in Paris, designed by Californian FRANK GEHRY, wins acclaim for its eye-pleasing asymmetricality—a departure from the postmodernism of recent decades.

1998 The Ronald Reagan Building and International Trade Center in Washington, D.C., designed by James Ingo Freed, reflects a growing emphasis on context over stylistic trend.

LEGISLATION AND SUPREME COURT DECISIONS AFFECTING THE ARTS, 1789–PRESENT

1789 The Constitution gives Congress the power "to promote the Progress of Science and the useful Arts, by securing for limited Times to Authors and Investors the exclusive Rights to their respective Writings and Discoveries." In its first session (1790), Congress passes a patent law.

1832 *Wheaton v. Peters.* The Court establishes that the primary aim of copyright protection is to benefit the public, not the creator of the work.

1836 Fifty-six British authors petition Congress for copyright protection, but Congress does not intervene to stop piracy.

1846 Congress states that one copy of every copyrighted book should be sent to the Library of Congress.

1887 Bern Convention. For signatories, literary material copyrighted in one country enjoys protection in others. The United States does not sign.

1891 An international copyright law prevents pirating the works of foreign authors.

1909 The Copyright Act. The basic U.S. copyright law, this bill grants authors, publishers, and composers control over their work and, under a somewhat vague "fair use" clause, offers some protection from use of their material. Over time this law will be extended to cover prints, music, photographs, drawings, paintings, movies, sound recordings, and computer programs.

1957 *Roth v. United States.* In this first important obscenity decision, the Court rules that some materials are obscene, by virtue of lacking any redeeming social value and appealing exclusively to prurient interest, but fails to hammer out a precise definition of what constitutes obscenity.

1964 *New York Times Company v. Sullivan.* The Court protects the freedom of the press to publish information about public officials even if it is false. It becomes libelous only if published with malicious intent.

1965 The Federal Aid to the Arts Act. Provides $63 million to fund a National Endowment for the Arts and Humanities.

1973 *Miller v. California.* The Court attempts to refine the definition of obscenity, saying that a work may be banned if the average person, applying contemporary standards of the community, finds it prurient. The decision gives individual communities the power to regulate books, magazines, and movies.

1978 The Copyright Act. A further revision of previous acts brings U.S. copyright law in line with the Bern Convention. American artists now have the same international copyright protection afforded artists from other countries.

1998 National Endowment for the Arts v. Finley. The Court upholds a 1990 federal law aimed at barring government funding of arts projects considered indecent, requiring the NEA to consider "general standards of decency" in the awarding of grants (see p. 516).

NOTABLE FIGURES IN CULTURE AND THE ARTS

Adams, Ansel (1902–1984). A photographer whose work was characterized by a purist vision of the American wilderness, Adams concentrated mostly on black-and-white images of landscapes in Yosemite National Park and the American West.

Ailey, Alvin (1931–1989). A modern dancer and choreographer, Ailey formed the Alvin Ailey Dance Theatre in 1958, a primarily black modern dance troupe featuring many African American themes. Ailey's masterpiece is *Revelations* (1960).

Albee, Edward (1928–). Author of *The Zoo Story* (1959), *Who's Afraid of Virginia Woolf?* (1962), and *Three Tall Women* (1991), Albee pioneered in absurdist theater, then composed serious drama.

Anderson, Maxwell (1888–1959). A dramatist concerned with social problems, Anderson wrote *What Price Glory?* (1924), *Both Your Houses* (1933), and *Lost in the Stars* (1949).

Armstrong, Louis (1901–1971). The great trumpet and cornet soloist Louis Armstrong, also known as "Satchmo," was the most famous of all American jazz musicians. He was also a bandleader, composer, and vocalist who popularized the "scat" style of singing.

Audubon, John James (1785–1851). An illustrator–ornithologist, Audubon produced a stunningly beautiful and still unsurpassed collection of bird drawings and paintings, which were published in *Birds of America* in 1827 (see pp.384, 386).

Balanchine, George (1904–1983). Considered by many critics to be the preeminent American choreographer, Balanchine trained in Russia and danced for years with Paris's innovative Ballets Russes. He became the first director of the New York City Ballet in 1948. His dances created a new trend in world ballet, one in which ballet became simpler, streamlined, and even abstract. Among his many great ballets are *Apollo* (1928) and *Serenade* (1934). He created the original *Slaughter on Tenth Avenue* in *On Your Toes* (1963).

Baldwin, James (1924–1987). Baldwin was one of the first writers to explore black rage and racism in novels such as *Go Tell It on the Mountain* (1953) and collections of essays such as *Nobody Knows My Name* (1961), and *The Fire Next Time* (1963).

Barber, Samuel (1910–1981). This traditionalist composer wrote, among other pieces, the operas *Vanessa* (1956) and *Antony and Cleopatra* (1966), commissioned for the opening of the Metropolitan Opera in its new location at Lincoln Center.

Barrymore, Ethel (1879–1959). Part of a famous theatrical family, Barrymore made her name acting in such plays as *The Corn Is Green* and *The Second Mrs. Tanqueray*.

Barrymore, John (1882–1942). The brother of ETHEL, Barrymore is remembered for his riveting interpretation of Hamlet. He later became a matinee idol.

Basie, Count (1904–1984). The jazz pianist, bandleader, and composer William "Count" Basie was one of the earliest and most influential figures in swing music beginning in the 1930s. He wrote many of his band's most popular numbers, including "One O'clock Jump."

Bearden, Romare (1912–1988). Beardon created colorful collages such as *Artist with Painting and Model*. He also worked to support other African American artists by forming the group Spiral, whose purpose was to promote black artists, and by opening a gallery devoted to African American art.

Bellow, Saul (1915–). A Canadian-born novelist, Bellow explores in such works as *Herzog* (1964), *Mr. Sammler's Planet* (1970), and *Humboldt's Gift* (1975) the apathy of the modern world. His writing produced a new Jewish tradition in fiction. Bellow was awarded the Nobel Prize in 1976.

Berlin, Irving (1881–1989). Although unable to read or write music, Berlin became one of the most successful composers of popular song in the twentieth century. One of his first hits was "Alexander's Ragtime Band" in 1911. He wrote the music and lyrics for a number of musical compedies, including *Annie Get Your Gun* (1946) and *Call Me Madam* (1950).

Bernstein, Leonard (1918–1990). A composer and conductor, Bernstein was an overnight sensation when he substituted for Arturo Toscanini at the podium of the New York Philharmonic in 1943. He later conducted both the New York Philharmonic and the New York City Symphony Orchestra. Bernstein bridged the gap between classical and popular music with such works as *West Side*

Story (1957) and *On the Town* (1944), both Broadway musicals, in addition to his more traditional classical works, such as the symphony *Kaddish* (1963) and *Chichester Psalms* (1965).

Bradstreet, Anne (c. 1612–1672). Perhaps the most significant author to emerge from the colonial era, Bradstreet wrote several books of poetry, including *The Tenth Muse Lately Sprung Up in America* (1650) and *Several Poems.*

Brady, Mathew (1829?–1896). A pioneer of photography and accomplished portrait artist, Brady used the evolving art form to capture images of the American Civil War. His photographs usually featured full regiments posed in their formations or vast battlefields of war dead and are some of the only existing images of the Civil War.

Bulfinch, Charles (1763–1844). Bulfinch designed the Massachusetts State House, the U.S. Capitol, and Massachusetts General Hospital. He pioneered the neoclassical style that became known in the United States as Federalist.

Bunshaft, Gordon (1909–1990). Head designer at the pioneering firm of Skidmore, Owings, and Merrill, Bunshaft designed many classic modern buildings such as the Lever House in New York City (1952), the Albright-Knox Art Gallery in Buffalo, New York, and the Hirshhorn Museum in Washington, D.C.

Burnham, Daniel (1846–1912). With his partner, John Root, Burnham built many important buildings in Chicago and New York, including the Flatiron in New York City (1901), the Masonic Temple in Chicago, and Union Station in Washington, D.C. (1909). Burnham and Root did the general design for the 1893 World's Columbian Exposition in Chicago, which was largely responsible for inspiring several decades of neoclassical design in the United States.

Cage, John (1912–1992). A pioneering experimental musician and composer, Cage sought to push the definitions of music, most notably with works such as the *Imaginary Landscape* series.

Calder, Alexander (1898–1976). A rare artist who invented two new forms, the stabile and the mobile, Calder produced sculpture that was both amusing and iconoclastic.

Cassatt, Mary (1845–1926). Influenced by French painters, Cassatt was one of the few major American impressionists. Women and children were among her favorite subjects.

Cather, Willa (1876–1947). Long considered a regional novelist because she wrote about frontier life, Cather is now recognized for her attention to the craft of fiction. Her novels include *O Pioneers!* (1913), *My Ántonia* (1918), and *Death Comes for the Archbishop* (1927).

Church, Frederick Edwin (1826–1900). A member of the Hudson River School, Church was among the most celebrated American landscape painters of the nineteenth century. During his travels to upstate New York, the American West, South America, Europe, and the Far East, he painted such dramatic large-scale scenes as *Niagara Falls* (1857) and *Heart of the Andes* (1859).

Cohan, George M. (1878–1942). Cohan wrote, produced, directed, and acted in his own shows, which included *Little Johnny Jones* (1904) and *Forty-five Minutes from Broadway* (1906).

Cooper, James Fenimore (1789–1851). America's first major novelist, Cooper idealized both American life and Native Americans in such books as *The Last of the Mohicans* (1826) and *The Deerslayer* (1841).

Copland, Aaron (1900–1990). Perhaps the most "American" of the American composers, Copland is known for such ballets scores as *Rodeo* (1942) and *Billy the Kid* (1942) and the orchestral piece, *Appalachian Spring* (1944).

Copley, John Singleton (1738–1815). Copley is considered the first great American portraitist; his subjects included Samuel Adams and Paul Revere.

Crane, Stephen (1871–1900). Crane was one of the first American novelists to experiment with naturalism. He is best known for his Civil War novel, *The Red Badge of Courage* (1895).

Cunningham, Merce (1919–). This pioneering modern-dance choreographer began his career dancing with MARTHA GRAHAM but went on to develop his own unique innovations, the most famous of which was to create dances that were independent of, or incidental to, the music that accompanied them. Cunningham often worked with avant-garde composer JOHN CAGE.

NOTABLE FIGURES, *cont.*

de Kooning, Willem (1904–1997). A Dutch émigré, de Kooning was a pioneering figure in the abstract expressionist movement in American painting, exploring the human figure and natural landscapes in a variety of styles and increasing abstraction.

de Mille, Agnes (1905–1993). An innovator in classical ballet, de Mille choreographed *Rodeo*, the first major American ballet. Working in musical theater, she sought to bring many of the techniques of ballet to the modern musical theater. Her pioneering techniques can be seen in the musical *Oklahoma!* (1943). She is also remembered for the ballet *Fall River Legend* (1948).

Dickinson, Emily (1830–1886). Dickinson's unique and inventive style is revealed in the more than 1,700 poems she wrote on such topics as love, death, religion, and nature. Dickinson was a recluse, and only a handful of her poems were published in her lifetime.

Dove, Ulysses (1947–1996). Dove danced with the MERCE CUNNINGHAM company before joining the Alvin Ailey American Dance Theater in 1973 and quickly becoming a principal dancer. His choreography for ALVIN AILEY includes a memorable solo created for Judith Jamison entitled "Inside" (1980). He worked all over the world, from the American Ballet Theatre and the New York City Ballet to the Dutch National Ballet and the Groupe de Recherche Choreographique de l'Opera de Paris pieces, choreographing such pieces as "Bad Blood" (1984), "Episodes" (1987), and "Red Angels" (1994).

Dreiser, Theodore (1871–1945). Author of *Sister Carrie* (1900) and *An American Tragedy* (1925), Dreiser was a moving force behind the development of naturalism

Drew, John (1827–1862). An Irish comedian, Drew was the leading actor of his era, playing both comedy and Shakespeare.

Duncan, Isadora (1877–1927). A pioneering dancer and choreographer who rejected the restraints of classical ballet to create her own loose, free-form dances, Duncan set the stage for future and more classical modern dancers and choreographers.

Eakins, Thomas (1844–1916). A foremost portrait painter, he worked from live models and studied anatomy to produce his portraits and studies of American life.

Eliot, Thomas Stearns (T. S.) (1888–1965). One of the great modern poets, Eliot published *The Waste Land*, one of the landmarks of modernism in 1922. He became a British citizen in 1927.

Ellington, Duke (1899–1974). Ellington was a bandleader, pianist, and composer of such popular songs as "I Got It Bad and That Ain't Good" and "Don't Get Around Much Anymore." His jazz band toured the United States and Europe to great reviews.

Emerson, Ralph Waldo (1803–1832). A leader in the social and literary movement known as Transcendentalism, Emerson wrote essays entitled "Compensation" and "Reliance" and is also known for such poems as "Threnody" and "Brahma." His essays and literary connections also made him a leading figure in American literature.

Faulkner, William (1897–1962). Forging a unique fiction style, Faulkner explored the decay of traditional values in American society, invariably using the South as the setting. Considered one of a handful of truly major American writers, Faulkner is remembered for such novels as *The Sound and the Fury* (1929), whose experimental form greatly influenced other twentieth-century novelists, *Light in August* (1932), and *Intruder in the Dust* (1948). He was awarded a Nobel Prize in 1949.

Fitzgerald, F. Scott (1896–1940). Fitzgerald was the most representative fiction writer of the "Lost Generation," a period of disillusionment when American intellectuals sought solace in Paris. Writing about the dissoluteness of the period between the two world wars, Fitzgerald's best-known novels are *The Great Gatsby* (1925), *Tender Is the Night* (1934), and *The Last Tycoon* (left unfinished, but published in 1941).

Forrest, Edwin (1806–1872). Widely regarded as the first great American actor, Forrest became famous for doing Shakespeare's tragedies. His rivalry with English actor W. C. Macready was at least partly the cause of the Astor Place riot in 1849, which killed twenty-two persons.

Foster, Stephen (1826–1864). During his short life, Foster wrote a substantial number of songs that were popular in his own day and that are still sung at the end of the twentieth century. Among the best known are

"My Old Kentucky Home" (1835), "Jeannie With the Light Brown Hair" (1854), and "Beautiful Dreamer, Wake Unto Me" (1863).

Frankenthaler, Helen (1928–). One of the iconoclastic painters who does not easily fit into any school, although she is associated with the abstract expressionists and studied with JACKSON POLLOCK, Frankenthaler is known for her large, beautifully color-stained canvases.

Frost, Robert (1874–1963). One of the great American poets, who took as his subject the land, language, and people of New England, Frost published several books, most notably *A Boy's Will* (1913), *Steeple Bush* (1947), and *In the Clearing* (1962).

Fuller, R. Buckminster (1895–1983). This architect, engineer, and author is best remembered for designing the geodesic dome, a revolutionary new shape intended to provide maximum strength from a minimum amount of energy.

Gehry, Frank (1929–). Playful, dynamic, and asymmetrical, Gehry's designs eschewed the rectilinear forms of the international style and postmodernism. Winner of the 1989 Pritzker Architecture Prize, Gehry is best known for the American Center in Paris (1994), Guggenheim Bilbao Museum in Spain (1997), and Walt Disney Concert Hall in Los Angeles (2002).

Gershwin, George (1898–1937). A rare composer who bridged the gap between popular and classical music, Gershwin wrote musicals such as *Lady, Be Good!* (1924) and music that combined elements of classical and jazz such as *Rhapsody in Blue* (1924) and *An American in Paris* (1928).

Glass, Philip (1937–). This composer of modern music was influenced by IVES, and he blends traditional and untraditional tonality. He is perhaps best known for the opera *Einstein on the Beach* (1976), first performed in Paris in 1976.

Goodman, Benny (1909–1986). Known as the "King of Swing" during the 1930s and '40s, the clarinetist Benny Goodman led one of the great big bands of the era. Among the many jazz greats who played in his band were the drummer Gene Krupa and vibraphonist Lionel Hampton.

Graham, Martha (1894–1991). Martha Graham's troupe, more than any other force, made modern dance popular with American audiences. Her masterpiece is *Appalachian Spring* (1944).

Hammerstein, Oscar, II (1895–1960). A lyricist and librettist, Hammerstein was the father of modern American musicals. Hammerstein's best-remembered works are *Show Boat* (1927) and his collaborations with RICHARD RODGERS: *Oklahoma* (1943), *South Pacific* (1949), *The King and I* (1951), and *The Sound of Music* (1959).

Hawthorne, Nathaniel (1804–1864). A Transcendentalist and masterful American novelists, Hawthorne produced such memorable novels as *The Scarlet Letter* (1850) and *The House of the Seven Gables* (1851).

Hayes, Helen (1900–1993). A respected stage and screen actress for well over fifty years, Hayes won acclaim for her roles in productions of Shakespeare, TENNESSEE WILLIAMS, George Bernard Shaw, Laurence Housman, and others. She won an Academy Award for her role in the movie *Airport* (1971). In 1955, the theatrical community honored her by renaming Broadway's Fulton Theatre after her; today it is still called the Helen Hayes Theatre.

Hellman, Lillian (1905–1984). Hellman is known for her works exploring the cruel, selfish, and dark aspects of human behavior, such as *The Children's Hour* (1934), *The Little Foxes* (1939), and *Watch on the Rhine* (1941). A supporter of leftist causes, Hellman was persecuted during the McCarthy-era anti-Communist fervor in the 1950s (see p. 211).

Hemingway, Ernest (1899–1961). A figure of the Lost Generation like FITZGERALD, Hemingway lived in Paris after World War I and wrote such novels as *The Sun Also Rises* (1926), *A Farewell to Arms* (1929), *For Whom the Bell Tolls* (1940), and *The Old Man and the Sea* (1952).

Hine, Lewis (1874–1940). Hine used photography to document various societal ills, including the squalor of New York City tenements and the horrors of child labor practices. His photographs proved instrumental in the fight for stricter child labor laws (see p. 225). Some of his other well-known pieces document the works of the Tennessee Valley Authority (see p. 267) and the construction of the Empire State Building (see p. 520).

CULTURE & THE ARTS

NOTABLE FIGURES, *cont.*

Homer, Winslow (1936–1910). An American realist who eschewed Europe at a time when his most famous contemporaries were painting there, Homer created such dramatic indigenous works as *Eight Bells* (1886), *Gulf Stream* (1899), *Life Line* (1884), and *Early Morning After a Storm at Sea* (1902). He was a master watercolorist and a lithographer as well as a painter in oils.

Hughes, Langston (1902–1967). One of the most famous writers associated with the Harlem Renaissance, Hughes was a novelist and poet. His first volume of poetry was *The Weary Blues* (1926).

Hurston, Zora Neale (1903–1960). Hurston began her career as a folklorist, collecting black traditions of the American South. Her most famous novel is *Their Eyes Were Watching God* (1937).

Inge, William (1913–1973). Inge made a name for himself in the American theater by writing plays about life in small midwestern towns: *Come Back, Little Sheba* (1950), *Picnic* (1953), and *Bus Stop* (1955).

Irving, Washington (1783–1859). Irving wrote both fiction and nonfiction and is best remembered for *The Sketch Book* (1820), which contains "Rip Van Winkle" and "The Legend of Sleepy Hollow," two classic stories in American literature. Irving also wrote about the American West in *A Tour on the Prairies* (1835) and produced a biography of George Washington.

Ives, Charles (1874–1954). Although Ives is often called the grandfather of modern music, his compositions were not much played in his lifetime. His Third Symphony (1901–1904) won the Pulitzer Prize in 1947.

James, Henry (1843–1916). An American expatriate who became a British subject, James wrote novels about America, most notably contrasting the innocence of Americans to the cynicism of Europeans. His work includes *The Portrait of a Lady* (1881), *The Bostonians* (1886), and *The Golden Bowl* (1904). His complex and subtle novels were harbingers of the realistic style that would soon emerge in American literature.

Joffrey, Robert (1930–1988). As a choreographer, Joffrey created notable works like *Remembrances* (1973) and *Postcards* (1980). In 1956, he founded the Joffrey Ballet, which became known for its eclectic repertoire, drawing on classics, new works, and fusions of modern dance.

Johns, Jasper (1930–). Rebelling against the total formlessness of the abstract expressionists, Johns returned to form but still managed to shock with his huge paintings of American flags and targets. His goal was to show that any subject could—and should—be viewed as art.

Johnson, Philip (1906–). Heavily influenced by the Bauhaus school, Johnson built a well-known glass house in New Canaan, Connecticut (1949), and also worked on the Seagram Building in New York City (1958) and the New York State Theater at Lincoln Center (1962–1964). Later he joined the postmodern movement and built the AT&T Building (now the SonyHeadquarters) in New York City. In 1932, he wrote a classic text on modern architecture called *The International Style*.

Joplin, Scott (1868–1917). The son of slaves, Joplin was a jazz pianist and composer who became known as the "King of Ragtime." His sixty compositions, of which forty-one are piano rags, include the classic "Maple Leaf Rag" (1899), one of the most popular songs of its time.

Kahn, Louis (1901–1974). Widely influential as a teacher, Kahn designed the Yale University Art Gallery in New Haven, Connecticut (1953), and the Kimball Art Museum in Fort Worth, Texas.

Kern, Jerome (1885–1945). With OSCAR HAMMERSTEIN, he produced such musical hits as *Oklahoma!* (1943) and *Showboat* (1927).

Kirkland, Gelsey (1953–). Kirkland studies at the School of American Ballet and became a principal dancer at the New York City Ballet, before joining the American Ballet Theatre in 1974. She danced leading roles in *Giselle, Coppélia,* and *Don Quixote*, but is best known for her startling memoir, *Dancing on My Grave* (1986), which chronicled the physical injuries, drug abuse, and eating disorders encountered in the ballet world.

Kirstein, Lincoln (1907–1996). Kirstein was an impresario and businessman who worked with GEORGE BALANCHINE to found and direct the various ballet companies that eventually became the New York City Ballet. In addition, he helped establish the School of American Ballet.

Kline, Franz (1910–1962). This abstract expressionist painter from New York is remembered for his stark black-and-white canvases, among them *Mahoning*, painted in 1956.

Lange, Dorothea (1895–1965). Lange dedicated much of her career to photographing victims of the Great Depression, specifically migrant workers, sharecroppers, and tenant farmers in the South and West Her photograph *Migrant Mother* is a classic portrait of the 1930s.

Latrobe, Benjamin H. (1764–1820). Perhaps the first professional architect in the United States, Latrobe worked on the U.S. Capitol as well as the nation's first cathedral, the Roman Catholic Cathedral in Baltimore. Latrobe was a leader of the classic revival.

Lerner, Alan Jay (1918–1986). Collaborating with composer Frederick Loewe, Lerner wrote the book and lyrics for the hit Broadway musicals *Brigadoon* (1947), *Paint Your Wagon* (1951), *My Fair Lady* (1956), and *Camelot* (1960), and for the film *Gigi* (1958). Lerner also wrote scripts for films, including *An American in Paris* (1952).

Lewis, Sinclair (1885–1951). The first American to win the Nobel Prize for Literature, Lewis wrote a string of sharply satiric portraits of midwestern life and middle-class values, beginning with the enormously popular *Main Street* (1920) and followed by *Babbitt* (1922), *Arrowsmith* (1925), *Elmer Gantry* (1927), and *Dodsworth* (1929).

Liebowitz, Annie (1949–). A portrait photographer, Liebowitz is best known for her images of celebrities. She became famous for her photograph of John Lennon and Yoko Ono in an embrace, taken just hours before the singer's death. She is the second living photographer and first woman to have her work displayed at the National Portrait Gallery at the Smithsonian in Washington, D.C.

Lichtenstein, Roy (1923–1997). His paintings' subjects, comic strips, belie their enormous artistic sophistication. Lichtenstein is most often associated with the Pop Art movement.

Longfellow, Henry Wadsworth (1807–1882). One of the first important poets to use American subject matter, Longfellow is remembered for his narrative poems *Evangeline* (1847) and *The Song of Hiawatha* (1855).

Lowell, Robert (1917–1977). The leader of an extraordinary generation of poets, Lowell himself is known for his exploration of evil and violence and his rich, skillful, symbolic style in such works as "The Quaker Graveyard at Nantucket," "Skunk Hour," and "For the Union Dead."

Luks, George (1867–1933). A founding member of the Ashcan School, Luks was a social realist known for his spirited portraits.

MacDowell, Edward (1861–1908). A traditionalist composer who tried to use "American" themes, MacDowell wrote *Indian Suite* (1896) and *Woodland Sketches* (1896). His widow, Marian Nevins MacDowell, carried out a wish of the composer by founding the MacDowell Artists' Colony for composers, writers, and artists in Peterborough, New Hampshire.

Mailer, Norman (1923–). With the publication of his superb war novel, *The Naked and the Dead* (1948), Mailer acheived literary stardom at a young age. He went on to publish fiction and nonfiction, and pioneered the "new journalism," a blend of reportage and fiction, stunningly exemplified in his 1979 *The Executioner's Song*, for which he won his second Pulitzer Prize.

Mamet, David (1947–). This contemporary playwright is known for his crisp dialogue and strong male characters. Among his best-known plays are *American Buffalo* (1975) and *Glengarry Glen Ross* (1984).

Martin, Mary (1913–1990). The leading lady of American musical theater in the 1940s and '50s, Martin was most famous for her title role in *Peter Pan* (1954). Her first major appearance on Broadway came in *Leave It to Me* (1938), and she earned widespread acclaim in such productions as *South Pacific* (1949–1951) and *The Sound of Music* (1959).

McCullers, Carson (1917–1967). A southern writer, McCullers wrote about human despair in such novels as *The Heart Is a Lonely Hunter* (1940), *Reflections in a Golden Eye* (1941), and *The Ballad of the Sad Café* (1951).

Melville, Herman (1819–1891). Taking nothing less than good and evil as his subject, Melville wrote several novels and is best remembered for his 1851 masterpiece, *Moby Dick*.

NOTABLE FIGURES, *cont.*

Mies van der Rohe, Ludwig (1886–1969). Director of the Bauhaus in Germany from 1930 to 1933, he continued its principles in the United States in Chicago at the Illinois Institute of Design, whose campus he designed. He collaborated with PHILIP JOHNSON to build the classic Seagram Building in New York City (1958).

Miller, Arthur (1915–). One of the great playwrights of the post–World War II era, Miller wrote such modern tragedies as *Death of a Salesman* (1949), *The Crucible* (1953), and *A View from the Bridge* (1955).

Mitchell, Arthur (1934–). A dancer and choreographer, Mitchell broke away from the New York City Ballet to found the Dance Theatre of Harlem. His own choreography, of which *Rhythmetron* is among the best known, combines elements of jazz and ethnic dance with classical ballet.

Moore, Douglas (1893–1969). This composer of highly theatrical works wrote a children's opera called *The Headless Horseman* (1937) and the adult operas, *Giants in the Earth* (1951) and *The Ballad of Baby Doe* (1956).

Morris, Mark (1956–). Exemplifying perhaps the third wave of modern dance and the inevitable merging of modern and classic technique, Morris is best known for choreographing *L'Allegro* (1988) and *The Hard Nut* (1991). Unlike BALANCHINE, who demanded physical perfection of his dancers, Morris's superb dancers often have far-from-classically shaped bodies.

Morrison, Toni (1931–). This Nobelist author writes about black life in such novels as *Sula* (1973), *Tar Baby* (1981), *Beloved* (1987), and *Jazz* (1992).

Motherwell, Robert (1915–1991). One of the moving forces behind abstract expressionism, Motherwell filled large canvases with huge blocks of color.

Neutra, Richard (1892–1970). As the creator of the Northridge Medical Arts Building and the Lovell Health House in Los Angeles, he continued the functional approach in modern design.

Nevelson, Louise (1900–1988). In her sculpture, Nevelson pioneered in the use of found materials, which she incorporated into her works. She is best known for her wood box sculptures.

Noguchi, Isamu (1904–1988). Noguchi produced abstract stone sculptures that were often specifically designed for their setting, either gardens or buildings.

Odets, Clifford (1906–1963). Epitomizing the social protest school of drama, Odets wrote *Waiting for Lefty* (1935), *Awake and Sing* (1935), and *Golden Boy* (1937).

O'Keeffe, Georgia (1887–1986). A highly individualistic painter, O'Keeffe's often huge and very precise canvases are frequently magnifications of such objects as flowers or skulls. Associated with New Mexico, she also painted New York City scenes.

O'Neill, Eugene (1888–1953). A giant in American theater, O'Neill wrote such bleak and innovative psychological dramas as *Beyond the Horizon* (1920), *Anna Christie* (1921), *Desire Under the Elms* (1924), and the autobiographical *Long Day's Journey into Night* (produced in 1956). He was awarded the Nobel Prize in literature in 1936.

Page, Ruth (1899–1991). This choreographer was for years the moving force behind ballet in Chicago, where she was director-choreographer of the the Page-Stone Ballet, Chicago Opera Ballet, and the Chicago Lyric Opera's ballet company. She also ran an acclaimed ballet school. Among her best-known creations are *Frankie and Johnny* (1938) and *Billy Sunday* (1948).

Papp, Joseph (1921–1991). An influential theater producer and director for nearly four decades, Papp founded the New York Shakespeare Festival, one of the city's prominent cultural institutions, in 1954. His influential Public Theatre, a six-stage complex in lower Manhattan, opened in 1967. Among his many productions successfully mounted on Broadway were *Hair* (1967), *That Championship Season* (1972), *A Chorus Line* (1975), and *The Pirates of Penzance* (1980).

Parker, Charlie (1920–1955). The alto saxophonist Charlie "The Bird" Parker was perhaps the most influential figure in modern improvisational jazz. With trumpeter Dizzy Gillespie, heis credited with founding the bebop movement, making the first definitive recordings in 1945.

Peale, Charles Willson (1741–1827). After COPLEY, Peale was the most popular portraitist of the colonial era.

He painted George Washington, Benjamin Franklin, Thomas Jefferson, and John Adams.

Pei, I. M. (1917–). Although born in China, the American-trained architect practiced in Boston and New York. His best-known American projects include the John Hancock Tower in Boston (1973) and the East Building of the National Gallery of Art in Washington, D.C. (completed in 1977) (see p. 144).

Piston, Walter (1894–1976). This traditional composer sometimes incorporated jazz rhythms. He wrote many symphonies, concertos, and string quartets, most notably his Third Symphony (1848), for which he won a Pulitzer, and his Seventh Symphony (1961).

Poe, Edgar Allan (1809–1849). A brilliant, but erratic writer of fiction and poetry, Poe explored mystery and emotions. Some of his contributions appeared in the *Southern Literary Messenger*, which he edited. Among his best-known works are "The Murders in the Rue Morgue" (1843) and *The Raven and Other Poems* (1845).

Pollock, Jackson (1912–1956). One of the giants of abstract expressionism, Pollock dripped paint directly on the canvas, as in *Lavender Mist*. This technique gave his work unusual dynamism, so much so that it was dubbed "action" painting.

Porter, Cole (1891–1964). Porter began writing songs and musical reviews when he was an undergraduate at Yale University. He made his Broadway debut with *See America First* (1916). His mature work was notable for its wit and sophistication as exemplified in the musicals *Anything Goes* (1934) and *Kiss Me Kate* (1948).

Rauschenberg, Robert (1925–). Rauschenberg, like Johns, rebelled against the abstractionists by painting everyday figures. He created sculptures, or combines, as he called them, of everyday objects put together in shocking ways. One, called *Monogram*, consists of a lifelike model of a sheep with a tire around its middle.

Ray, Man (1890–1976). As well known for his photographs as for his other art, Man Ray was a leading figure of the artistic avant-garde in Paris during the 1920s. This American-born photographer used everyday objects as art and is credited with founding the New York City Dada group in 1917.

Richardson, Henry H. (1838–1886). Initially a Romanesque revivalist, Richardson later designed buildings that were harbingers of modernism. He is remembered for the Marshall Field Wholesale Store (demolished) and the Trinity Church in Boston (1862–1877).

Riis, Jacob (1849–1914). Riis used photography as a tool for social reform by capturing images of the poor in New York City to confront the upper classes with the harsh realities of slum life and the immigrant tenement experience. Riis is most famous for his book *How the Other Half Lives* (1890).

Robbins, Jerome (1918–1998). Dancer and choreographer Robbins attracted critical attention in 1944 when he created the ballet *Fancy Free*. He worked on many Broadway musicals, including *West Side Story* (1957) and *Fiddler on the Roof* (1964). Robbins was ballet master of the New York City Ballet with Peter Martins from 1983 to 1990.

Rockwell, Norman (1894–1978). Rockwell was only twenty-two when he produced his first cover for the *Saturday Evening Post*. His forty-seven-year association with the magazine resulted in 321 other covers, mostly depicting life in small-town America. Among his most famous pieces are *Freedom of Speech*, *Freedom to Worship*, *Freedom from Want*, and *Freedom from Fear*, inspired by President Roosevelt's 1943 speech to Congress.

Rodgers, Richard (1902–1979). The preeminent composer in American musical theater, Rodgers composed the music for dozens of musical comedies. With Lorez Hart as lyricist, he worked on *A Connecticut Yankee* (1927), *On Your Toes* (1936), and *Pal Joey* (1940). He collaborated with OSCAR HAMMERSTEIN II on such successes as *Oklahoma!* (1943), *South Pacific* (1949), *The King and I* (1951), and *The Sound of Music* (1959). He also wrote the music for the documentary film *Victory at Sea* (1952).

Rothko, Mark (1903–1970). Like Pollock and Motherwell, Rothko was one of the pioneers of abstract expressionism. His large, rectangular bands of color influenced later painters.

Saarinen, Eero (1910–1961). This inventive Finnish-born architect was a proponent of the international style. Among his best-known projects are the Gateway Arch (1965), the Trans World Airline terminal at Idlewild (now Kennedy) Airport, New York City (1962), and the Dulles National Airport outside of Washington, D.C., completed after his death.

NOTABLE FIGURES, *cont.*

Sargent, John Singer (1856–1925). Although he painted many watercolor landscapes, the largest body of Sargent's work consists of portraits of the rich. His ability to depict texture, whether in fabric or the flush of a woman's skin, is his forte.

Shawn, Ted (1891–1972). With his wife RUTH ST. DENIS, Shawn helped to forge a uniquely American form of modern dance by drawing on American and ethnic themes in his choreography. Shawn also helped to expand men's roles in dance. He and St. Denis formed their own company, Denishawn, and Shawn served as director of the dance festival at Jacob's Pillow, Massachusetts.

Shepard, Sam (1943–). The leading countercultural playwright, Shepard wrote *Curse of the Starving Class* (1977), *Buried Child* (1978), and *True West* (1980). He also acts in movies, most notably *The Right Stuff*.

Sherwood, Robert (1896–1955). This Pulitzer Prize–winning playwright wrote in several genres, producing the comedy *Reunion in Vienna* (1931) as well as the drama *The Petrified Forest* (1935).

Smith, David (1906–1965). The preeminent sculptor of his day, Smith literally made sculptures that were abstract drawings in the air. Much of his work is public and monumental.

Sondheim, Stephen (1930–). Sondheim launched his career as a lyricist by collaborating with LEONARD BERNSTEIN on *West Side Story* (1957). With Jule Styne he created *Gypsy* in 1959. On his own, he has composed more than ten musicals that have broken new ground in terms of unconventional themes and complex melodies. Sondheim won the Pultitzer Prize in 1984 for *Sunday in the Park with George*.

Sousa, John Philip (1854–1932). Renowned for his marches, Sousa led the U.S. Marine Corps band from 1880 to 1892 when he organized his own band. His works include "Semper Fidelis" (188), "The Washington Post March" (1889), and "Stars and Stripes Forever" (1897).

St. Denis, Ruth (1877–1968). Drawing on theatrical roots, St. Denis created several dances, but her more important role was the creation and expansion of interest in American modern dance at a time when it was considered a minor theatrical form.

Steichen, Edward (1879–1973). A cutting-edge photographer, Steichen was experimenting with color stills as early as 1904. He became the chief photographer of Condé Nast in 1923, and was regularly published in *Vanity Fair* and *Vogue* for fifteen years. After retiring from photography, Steichen became the curator of the MoMA. He was responsible for many important exhibitions, including *The Family of Man* (1955), which proved to be the most popular exhibition in the history of photography.

Steigletz, Alfred (1864–1946). Steigletz's work captured the changing shape of New York City and America during the first four decades of the twentieth century. He is best known for such urban photographs as *The Terminal*, as well as portraits of his wife, GEORGIA O'KEEFFE.

Stella, Frank (1936–). Considered one of the preeminent painters of his era, Stella has experimented with many styles, ranging from minimalist black works to color field canvases. In the 1970s, he created paintings that were three-dimensional. His most famous works include the *Protractor Series*, painted in the 1970s.

Steinbeck, John (1902–1968). A full-blown realist who wrote about the Great Depression and its effects on Dust Bowl farmers, Steinbeck's best-known novel is *The Grapes of Wrath* (1939). He also wrote *Tortilla Flat* (1935) and *Of Mice and Men* (1937). He won the Pulitzer and Nobel Prizes.

Stevens, Wallace (1879–1955). One of the major American poets, Stevens created brilliant physical images but was also concerned with exploring inner life, which he did eloquently in such books as *Harmonium* (1923), *Collected Poems* (1954), and *Opus Posthumous* (1957).

Strasberg, Lee (1901–1982). As an acting teacher/ director associated with the Actor's Studio in New York, Strasberg shaped several generations of actors by teaching "the Method," based on an approach created by Russian Constantin Stanislavsky.

Stravinsky, Igor (1882–1971). A native of Russia, Stravinsky came to the United States in 1939 where he remained until his death. He composed ballet music (*The Fire Bird*, 1910, and *The Rite of Spring*, 1913) and operas (*The Rake's Progress*, 1951), as well as symphonies and piano compositions.

Stuart, Gilbert (1755–1828). Along with Copley and Peale, Stuart was one of the leading portrait painters of the colonial era. He is best known for his portraits of George Washington.

Sullivan, Louis (1856–1924). Sullivan played a key role in the development of modern architecture with such buildings as the Wainwright in St. Louis (1890) and the Auditorium in Chicago (completed 1889).

Tallchief, Maria (1925–). Born to a Osage Indian father and a Scotch Irish mother, Tallchief joined the Ballet Russe de Monte Carlo as a young woman, where she met George Balanchine, to whom she was married for a short time. While dancing at the New York City Ballet, Balanchine created several memorable pieces for her, including *Orpheus* (1948), *The Firebird* (1949), and *Sylvia: Pas de Deux* (1950). With her sister Marjorie, she founded the Chicago City Ballet in 1981.

Tharp, Twyla (1941–). Tharp's choreography combines elements of classical ballet and modern dance and has been an important force in moving these often opposing forms of dance closer to one another. In the 1960s, she performed her dances in a series of companies she formed; after that, her choreography was performed by the major ballet companies. Two of her most acclaimed dances are *Deuce Comp* and *Push Comes to Shove*.

Thomson, Virgil (1896–1989). This experimental composer and critic wrote, among other pieces, *The Mother of Us All* (1947), an opera, and *The River* (1937), which featured the poems of Edward Lear. He wrote several pieces for the organ.

Thoreau, Henry David (1817–1862). A leader of the Transcendental movement, Thoreau wrote *Walden* (1854), famous for its depiction of the solitary life in harmony with nature. His essay "Civil Disobedience" influenced reformers such as Gandhi and Martin Luther King Jr.

Twain, Mark (Samuel Langhorne Clemens) (1835–1910). A novelist, newspaperman, and essayist, Twain was a satirist and a keen social observer. He is remembered for such American classics as *The Adventures of Tom Sawyer* (1876), *The Adventures of Huckleberry Finn* (1884), and *A Connecticut Yankee in King Arthur's Court* (1889).

Venturi, Robert (1925–). Rejecting the orderly functionalism of the international style, Venturi pursued a more compositional, classical approach that became central to the Postmodern movement of the 1970s and '80s. Notable buildings include the Seattle Art Museum (1991), the Sainsbury wing extension of the National Gallery in London, and an expansion of the Gill Museum in San Diego (1996). He won the Pritzker Prize, architecture's most prestigious international award, in 1991.

Warhol, Andy (1930?–1987). A leader of the Pop Art movement, Warhol created huge silk-screened canvases of popular cultural icons such as Marilyn Monroe and Mao Tse-tung. He also created iconistic paintings of such objects as Brillo boxes and Campbell's soup cans and was a talented filmmaker.

Warren, Robert Penn (1905–1989). A southern poet, novelist, and critic, Warren is best remembered for *All the King's Men* (1946), his masterful roman à clef about the despotic southern politician Huey Long. Warren also coauthored two volumes of seminal criticism, *Understanding Poetry* (1938) and *Understanding Fiction* (1943), which pioneered a new, more purely textual form of criticism. He won Pulitzers for both fiction and poetry, cofounded the *Southern Review* with Cleanth Brooks, and in 1986 became the first poet laureate in America.

West, Benjamin (1738–1820). West was the first American painter to win acclaim abroad. He settled in London in 1763, opening a school in which he taught and encouraged other American artists. In his historical paintings *The Death of General Wolfe* and *Penn's Treaty with the Indians*, he broke with tradition by depicting the figures in period dress instead of classical garb. In 1792, West became president of the Royal Academy.

Wharton, Edith (1862–1937). A chronicler of American society and the constrictions it imposed on women, Wharton wrote such novels as *The House of Mirth* (1905) and *The Age of Innocence* (1920). In an entirely different vein, she wrote *Ethan Frome* (1911), a stunning novel of sexual repression.

Wheatley, Phillis (c. 1753–1784). Brought to America as a slave, Wheatley rose above her circumstances to produce remarkable poetry, most notably in her book *Poems on Various Subjects* (1773).

NOTABLE FIGURES, *cont.*

Whistler, James (1834–1903). Working mainly in England, Whistler painted many studies of the Thames, such as *Chelsea: Nocturne in Blue and Green* (1870). He championed the idea that a painter should produce a composition that, like music, existed for its own sake, without regard for moral or didactic values. Whistler is viewed as a precursor of abstract artists.

Whitman, Walt (1819–1892). An innovative and major poet, Whitman wrote about sexuality at a time when it was still considered taboo to do so. His masterpiece is *Leaves of Grass* (1855).

Williams, Tennessee (1914–1983). Considered one of the foremost dramatists of the post–World War II era, Williams wrote plays about violence, loneliness, and anxiety. Women—especially southern women—were the great subject of this playwright, who gave women unforgettable roles in plays such as *A Streetcar Named Desire* (1947), *Sweet Bird of Youth* (1959), and *The Night of the Iguana* (1961).

Williams, William Carlos (1883–1963). One of the first and most important modern poets, Williams wrote eloquently about ordinary subjects. His work is published in *Collected Poems* (1934) and *Pictures from Brueghel* (1963). He was also a novelist and essayist.

Wood, Grant (1892–1942). In an age of modernism, Wood painted realistically, and in an age deeply influenced by European art, he was a populist, regional painter. Influenced by German and French primitivists, Wood produced stylized landscapes of the Midwest and portraits of its people.

Wright, Frank Lloyd (1869–1959). A key American architect, Wright both pioneered the modern style and developed his own unique style, as epitomized by such buildings as the Robie House (1909), Falling Water (completed 1937), and the Guggenheim Museum in New York City (completed 1959).

Wright, Richard (1908–1960). One of the most important African American fiction writers, Wright explored the pain of being black in such works as *Native Son* (1940) and *The Outsider* (1953).

ADDITIONAL SOURCES

CHAPTER 1

Andrist, Ralph K. *The Long Death: The Last Days of the Plains Indians.* New York: Macmillan, 1964; reprint 2001.

Brown, Dee. *Bury My Heart at Wounded Knee.* New York: Holt, 1970; several reprint editions.

Erdoes, Richard, and Alfonso Ortiz, eds., *American Indian Myths and Legends.* New York: Pantheon Books, 1985.

Fiedel, Stuart. *Prehistory of the Americas.* 2nd ed. New York: Columbia University Press, 1992.

Hoxie, Frederick E., ed. *Encyclopedia of North American Indians.* Boston: Houghton Mifflin, 1996.

Josephy, Alvin M. Jr. *500 Nations: An Illustrated History of North American Indians.* New York: Knopf, 1994.

———. *The Indian Heritage of America.* Rev. ed. New York: Knopf, 1991.

Marks, Paula Mitchell. *In a Barren Land: American Indian Dispossession and Survival.* New York: William Morrow, 1998.

Neihardt, John G. *Black Elk Speaks: Being the Life Story of a Holy Man of the Oglala Sioux.* Lincoln: University of Nebraska Press, 1961; reprint 2000.

Prucha, Francis Paul. *The Great Father: The United States Government and the American Indians.* 2 vols. Lincoln: University of Nebraska Press, 1984.

Sale, Kirkpatrick. *The Conquest of Paradise: Christopher Columbus and the Columbian Legacy.* New York: Knopf, 1990.

Spicer, Edward H. *Cycles of Conquest: The Impact of Spain, Mexico and the United States on the Indians of the Southwest, 1533–1960.* Tucson: University of Arizona Press, 1962; reprint 1982.

Sturtevant, William C., ed. *Handbook of North American Indians.* 20 vols. Washington, D.C.: Smithsonian Institution, 1978–2001.

Utley, Robert M. *The Indian Frontier of the American West, 1846–1890.* Albuquerque: University of New Mexico, 1984.

Waldman, Carl. *Atlas of the North American Indian.* Rev. ed. New York: Facts on File, 2000.

White, Richard. *The Middle Ground: Indian Empires and Republics in the Great Lakes Region, 1650–1815.* Cambridge, Eng.: Cambridge University Press, 1991.

In addition to these outstanding books, the Internet provides an ever-expanding source of information on the history and culture of American Indians. Compelling multimedia and historical documents can be found at the websites of the Library of Congress, National Archives, and other official institutions. Many individual tribes and nations also maintain informative and colorful sites on the Internet. The following home pages may be especially useful for general background and as starting points for in-depth research.

Bureau of Indian Affairs (www.doi.gov/bureau-indian-affairs.html): the U.S. federal agency.

National Congress of American Indians (www.ncai.org): the intertribal advocacy group.

National Museum of the American Indian (www.nmai.si.edu): part of the Smithsonian Institution and its Internet resources.

Nativeculture.com (www.nativeculture.com): a comprehensive portal site with extensive links.

CHAPTER 2

Anderson, Fred. *Crucible of War: The Seven Years' War and the Fate of Empire in British North America, 1754–1766.* New York: Vintage Books, 2000.

Bailyn, Bernard. *The Ideological Origins of the American Revolution.* Rev. ed. Cambridge: Belknap Press/Harvard University Press, 1992.

Bannon, John Francis. *The Spanish Borderlands Frontier, 1513–1821.* Albuquerque: University of New Mexico Press, 1970; reprint 1984.

Boorstin, Daniel J. *The Americans: The Colonial Experience.* New York: Random House, 1958.

Crane, Verner W. *The Southern Frontier, 1670–1732.* 1928; reprint, Westport, Conn.: Greenwood, 1977.

Crosby, Alfred. *The Columbian Exchange: Biological and Cultural Consequences of 1492.*Westport, Conn.: Greenwood, 1972.

Eccles, W. J. *The Canadian Frontier, 1534–1821.* Rev. ed. Albuquerque: University of New Mexico Press, 1983.

———. *France in America.* New York: Harper & Row. Rev. ed. East Lansing: Michigan State University Press, 1990.

Gibson, Charles. *Spain in America.* New York: Harper & Row, 1966.

Goetzmann, William. *Exploration and Empire: The Explorer and the Scientist in the Winning of the American West.* New York: Norton, 1966; reprint 1994.

Goetzmann, W., and G. Williams. *The Atlas of North American Exploration.* Upper Saddle River, N.J.: Prentice Hall, 1972; reprint 1998.

Hofstadter, Richard H. *America at 1750: A Social History.* New York: Knopf, 1971.

Morgan, Edmund S. *American Slavery, American Freedom: The Ordeal of Colonial Virginia.* New York: Norton, 1975; reprint 1995.

———. *The Birth of the Republic, 1763–1789.* 3rd ed. Chicago: University of Chicago Press, 1993.

Morgan, Edmund S., and Helen M. Morgan. *The Stamp Act Crisis: Prologue to Revolution.* New York: Macmillan, 1983; reprint 1995.

Morison, Samuel Eliot. *The European Discovery of America: The Northern Voyages, A.D. 500–1600.* New York: Oxford University Press, 1971.

———. *The European Discovery of America: The Southern Voyages, A.D. 1492–1616.* New York: Oxford University Press, 1974.

Parry, John H. *The Spanish Seaborne Empire.* New York: Knopf, 1966; reprint 1990.

Peckham, Howard H. *The Colonial Wars, 1689–1762.* Chicago: University of Chicago Press, 1964.

Quinn, David Beers. *Set Fair for Roanoke: Voyages and Colonies, 1584–1606.* Chapel Hill: University of North Carolina Press, 1985.

Tate, Thad W., and David L. Ammerman, eds. *The Chesapeake in the Seventeenth Century: Essays on Anglo-American Society and Politics.* Chapel Hill: University of North Carolina Press, 1979.

Weber, David J. *The Spanish Frontier in North America.* New Haven: Yale University Press, 1992.

The Internet offers a wealth of information, primary source documentation, and visual material about the exploration and colonization of America. Some of the more prominent sites are listed below. In many cases, link indexes provide easy access to other informative pages.

Library of Congress (www.loc.gov): includes several special exhibitions covering this period: "1492: An Ongoing Voyage," "Declaration of Independence: Drafting of the Documents," and "Religion and the Founding of the American Republic." The American Memory is a vast collection of pictures and other materials; do a word search on any topic of interest.

National Archives and Record Administration (www.nara.gov): website of the federal agency dedicated to preserving historical documents and making them accessible to the public. Find primary source materials via word search or catalogue. Explore the Rotunda Exhibition.

National Library of Canada: "Passages—A Treasure Trove of North American Exploration" (www.nlc-bnc.ca/dl/1999/passages): an extensive digitized rare book collection.

Archiving Early America (www.earlyamerica.com): includes multimedia presentations, online discussion, a digital library, and access to "The Early America Review."

Rebels With a Vision (www.rebelswithavision.com): letters, manuscripts, rare books, and other documents on the founding fathers.

Colonial Williamsburg (www.history.org): the official visitors' site.

Plymouth, Massachusetts (www.pilgrims.net): tour site and historical reference.

CHAPTER 3

Ambrose, Stephen. *Courage Undaunted: Meriwether Lewis, Thomas Jefferson, and the Opening of the American West*. New York: Simon & Schuster, 1996.

Bain, David Haward. *Empire Express: Building the First Transcontinental Railroad*. New York: Viking Press, 1999.

Billington, Ray A. *The Frontier Thesis*. Melbourne, Fla.: Krieger, 1977.

———. *Westward to the Pacific: An Overview of America's Westward Expansion*. Seattle: University of Washington Press, 1979.

Colbert, David, ed. *Eyewitness to the American West: 500 Years of Firsthand History*. New York: Penguin, 1999.

Cronon, William, George Miles, and Jay Gitlin, eds. *Under an Open Sky: Rethinking America's Western Past*. New York: Norton, 1992.

De Voto, Bernard. *The Year of Decision: 1846*. Boston: Little Brown, 1943; Rev. ed. St. Martin's Press, 2000.

———. *Across the Wide Missouri*. Boston: Houghton Mifflin, 1947; reprint 1998.

———. *The Course of Empire*. Boston: Houghton Mifflin, 1952; reprint 1998.

Farragher, John Mack. *Women and Men on the Overland Trail*, Rev. ed. New Haven: Yale University Press, 2001.

Goetzmann, William H. *The West of the Imagination*. New York: Norton, 1986.

Jeffrey, Julie Roy. *Frontier Women: Civilizing the West? 1840–1880*. Rev. ed. New York: Hill & Wang, 1998.

LaFeber, Walter. *The New Empire: An Interpretation of American Expansion, 1860–1898*. Ithaca, N.Y.: Cornell University Press, 1963; reprint 1998.

Lamar, Howard R., ed. *The New Encyclopedia of the American West*. New Haven: Yale University Press, 1998.

Limerick, Patricia N. *The Legacy of Conquest: The Unbroken Past of the American West*. New York: Norton, 1987.

Nash, Roderick. *Wilderness and the American Mind*. 3rd rev. ed. New Haven: Yale University Press, 1986.

Smith, Henry Nash. *Virgin Land: The American West as Symbol and Myth*. Cambridge: Harvard University Press, 1950; reprint 1971.

Starr, Kevin. *Americans and the California Dream, 1850–1915*. New York: Oxford University Press, 1973; reprint 1986.

Turner, Frederick Jackson. *The Frontier in American History*. New York: Henry Holt, 1920; numerous reprints.

Many informative Internet sites on U.S. territorial expansion can be located by conducting word searches on specific subjects of interest or by browsing the American History category in your index of choice. As they are for other periods and subjects, the Library of Congress (www.loc.org) and National Archives and Records Administration (www.nara.gov) are good places to start; the latter includes a special exhibit on the Louisiana Purchase. Here are other quality websites:

The Public Broadcasting System (www.pbs.org): includes comprehensive companion pages for Ken Burns's television series *The West* and other relevant documentaries.

The American West (www.AmericanWest.com): extensive content and links.

Lewis and Clark's Historic Trail (www.lewisclark.net): biographies, maps, timeline, journal excerpts, and more.

National Oregon/California Trail Center (www.oregontrailcenter.org): official web page of the travel and information office in Montpelier, Idaho.

The Alamo (www.thealamo.org): the official web page; includes detailed text, map, walking tour, visitor information, and excellent links.

CHAPTER 4

Acuna, Rodolfo. *Occupied America: A History of Chicanos*. 4th ed. Boston: Addison-Wesley, 1999.

Appiah, Kwame Anthony, and Henry Louis Gates, eds. *Africana: The Encyclopedia of the African and African American Experience*. New York: Basic Civitas Books, 1999.

Billington, Ray Allen. *The Origins of Nativism in the United States, 1800–1844*. Manchester, N.H.: Ayer, 1974.

Bodnar, John. *The Transplanted: A History of Immigrants in Urban America*. Bloomington: Indiana University Press, 1985.

Branch, Taylor. *Parting the Waters: America in the King Years, 1954–63*. New York: Simon & Schuster, 1988.

———. *Pillar of Fire: American in the King Years, 1963–65*. New York: Simon & Schuster, 1998.

Chalmers, David Mark. *Hooded Americanism: The History of the Ku Klux Klan*. 3rd ed. Durham, N.C.: Duke University Press, 1987.

Curtin, Philip D. *The Atlantic Slave Trade: A Census*. Madison: University of Wisconsin Press, 1972.

Daniels, Roger. *Coming to America: A History of Immigration and Ethnicity in American Life*. New York: HarperCollins, 1991.

De Leon, Arnoldo. *The Tejano Community, 1836–1900*. Albuquerque: University of New Mexico Press, 1985.

Fogel, Robert William. *Without Consent or Contract: The Rise and Fall of American Slavery*. New York: Norton, 1989; reprint 1994.

Franklin, John Hope, and Loren Schweninger. *Runaway Slaves: Rebels on the Plantation*. New York: Oxford University Press,1999.

Garrow, David J. *Bearing the Cross: Martin Luther King, Jr., and the Southern Christian Leadership Conference*. New York: Morrow, 1986.

Glenn, Susan A. *Daughters of the Shtetl: Life and Labor in the Immigrant Generation*. Ithaca, N.Y.: Cornell University Press, 1990.

Hale, Grace Elizabeth. *Making Whiteness: The Culture of Segregation in the South, 1890–1940*. New York: Pantheon Books, 1998.

Hampton, Henry, and Steve Fayer, ed. *Voices of Freedom: An Oral History of the Civil Rights Movement from the 1950s Through the 1980s*. New York: Bantam Books, 1990; reprint 1991.

Handlin, Oscar. *Boston's Immigrants: A Study in Acculturation*, Rev. ed. Harvard University Press, 1991.

———, ed. *Harvard Encyclopedia of American Ethnic Groups*. Cambridge: Harvard University Press, 1980.

Harding, Vincent. *There Is a River: The Black Struggle for Freedom in America*. New York: Harcourt Brace Jovanovich, 1981.

Jordan, Winthrop D. *White Over Black: American Attitudes Toward the Negro, 1550–1812*. New York: Norton, 1968; reprint 1995.

Kluger, Richard. *Simple Justice: The History of Brown v. Board of Education and Black America's Struggle for Equality*. New York: Knopf, 1976.

Litwack, Leon. *North of Slavery: The Negro in the Free States, 1790–1860*. Chicago: University of Chicago Press, 1965.

———. *Been in the Storm So Long: The Aftermath of Slavery*. New York: Knopf, 1980.

Malcomson, Scott L. *One Drop of Blood: The American Misadventure of Race*. New York: Farrar, Straus & Giroux, 2000.

McPherson, James M. *Struggle for Equality: Abolitionists and the Negro in the Civil War and Reconstruction*. Princeton: Princeton University Press, 1964.

Reimers, David M. *Still the Golden Door: The Third World Comes to America*. 2nd ed. New York: Columbia University Press, 1992.

Stampp, Kenneth M. *The Era of Reconstruction: 1865–1877*. New York: Random House, 1965.

Woodward, C. Vann. *The Strange Career of Jim Crow*. 3rd ed. New York: Oxford University Press, 1989.

The Internet is a vast source of information on U.S. immigration, slavery, the civil rights movement, and the history and experience of ethnic groups in America. Government agencies such as the U.S. Census Bureau (www.census.gov) and U.S. Immigration and Naturalization Service (www.ins.gov) provide in-depth statistics and policy background, both historical and current. The National Archives and Records Administration (www.nara.gov) and Library of Congress (www.loc.org) offer extensive materials; the latter features two relevant exhibitions—"The African-American Odyssey: A Quest for Full Citizenship" and "African-American Mosaic: A Resource Guide"—and the American Memory visual archive. Here are a few of the many other websites that may assist your research.

Statue of Liberty and Ellis Island National Monuments (www.nps.gov/stli): official site of the National Park Service.

NAACP (www.naacp.org): official site of the National Association for the Advancement of Colored People.

The Schomburg Center for Research in Black Culture (www.nypl.org/research/sc/sc.html): national research center of the New York Public Library, devoted to collecting, preserving and providing access to resources documenting the experiences of peoples of African descent throughout the world. Digital Schomburg provides access to extensive materials in, and catalogues to, the major divisions.

Smithsonian Institution (www.si.edu/resource/faq/nmah/afroam.htm): index of the Smithsonian's extensive resources on African American history and culture.

The New Americans: Immigration, America's Story (www.pbs.org/kcet/newamericans): an in-depth PBS research project.

CHAPTER 5

Ambrose, Stephen E. *D-Day, June 6, 1944: The Climactic Battle of World War II.* New York: Simon & Schuster, 1995.

Catton, Bruce. *The Centennial History of the Civil War,* 3 vols. New York: Doubleday, 1961–65; reprint 2000.

Coffman, Edward M. *The War to End All Wars: The American Military Experience in World War I.* Madison: University of Wisconsin Press, 1968; reprint 1998.

Commager, Henry Steele, and Richard B. Morris, eds. *The Spirit of 'Seventy-Six: The Story of the American Revolution as Told by Participants.* Indianapolis: Bobbs-Merrill, 1958; New York: DeCapo Press, reprint 1995.

Daniels, Roger. *Concentration Camps North America: Japanese in the United States and Canada During World War II.* Malabar, Fla.: Krieger, 1981; reprint 1993.

Eisenhower, Dwight D. *Crusade in Europe.* New York: Doubleday, 1948; reprint 1997.

Fehrenbach, T. R. *This Kind of War: The Classic Korean War History.* Washington, D.C.: Brassey's, 1963; reprint 2000.

Foote, Shelby. *The Civil War: A Narrative.* 3 vols. New York: Random House, 1974.

Freeman, Douglas S. *Lee's Lieutenants.* 3 vols. New York: Scribner's, 1986; reprint 1997.

Fussell, Paul. *The Great War and Modern Memory.* New York: Oxford University Press, 1975; reprint 2000.

Grant, Ulysses S. *Personal Memoirs.* 1885–86; numerous reprints.

Herring, George C. *America's Longest War: The United States and Vietnam, 1950–1975.* 3rd ed. New York: McGraw-Hill, 1995.

Hickey, Donald. *The War of 1812: A Forgotten Conflict.* Champaign: University of Illinois Press, 1989.

Iriye, Akira. *Power and Culture: The Japanese-American War, 1941–1945.* Cambridge: Harvard University Press, 1981.

Isaacs, Arnold R. *Without Honor: Defeat in Vietnam and Cambodia.* Baltimore: Johns Hopkins University Press, 1983; reprint 1999.

Johannsen, Robert W. *To the Halls of the Montezumas: The Mexican War in the American Imagination.* New York: Oxford University Press, 1985; reprint 1988.

Karnow, Stanley. *Vietnam: A History.* 2nd. ed. New York: Penguin, 1997.

Keegan, John. *The Second World War.* New York: Viking, 1989.

———. *The First World War.* New York: Knopf, 1999.

Kennedy, David. *Over Here: The First World War and American Society.* New York: Oxford University Press, 1988.

Marshall, S. L. A. *The American Heritage History of World War I.* New York: Random House, 1964; Reissued as *World War I.* New York: Houghton Mifflin, 2001.

McPherson, James M. *Battle Cry of Freedom: The Era of the Civil War.* New York: Oxford University Press, 1988.

Middlekauff, Robert. *The Glorious Cause: The American Revolution, 1763–1789.* New York: Oxford University Press, 1985.

Oates, Stephen B. *The Approaching Fury: Voices of the Storm, 1820–1861.* New York: HarperCollins, 1991.

Sheehan, Neil. *A Bright Shining Lie: John Paul Vann and America in Vietnam.* New York: Random House, 1988.

Sifry, Micah L., and Christopher Cerf, eds., *The Gulf War Reader: History, Documents, Opinions.* New York; Random House, 1991.

Weigley, Russell Frank. *The American Way of War: A History of United States Military Strategy and Policy.* Bloomington: Indiana University Press, 1978.

Wood, Gordon. *The Creation of the American Republic, 1776–1787.* Chapel Hill: University of North Carolina Press, 1969; reprint 1998.

Woodward, C. Vann, ed. *Mary Chesnut's Civil War.* New Haven: Yale University Press, 1981.

Websites of prominent government facilities and historical institutions—such as the Library of Congress (www.loc.gov), National Archives and Records Administration (www.nara.gov), and Smithsonian Institution (www.si.edu)—are excellent places to begin Internet research on U.S. military history. Sites devoted to specific wars—such as CivilWar.com (www.civilwar.com)—or battles, military leaders, and other subjects of interest can be found using your Internet index and search engine of choice. For general background and links, the following are recommended.

U.S. Department of Defense (www.defenselink.mil): comprehensive official website, with armed forces and defense news, special reports, historical background, and links to sites for individual services, departments, and offices.

National Park Service (www.nps.gov): "Parknet" portal of the NPS. Select "Links to the Past" and "Military History" for extensive information, tours, special collections, and links to individual sites on historic battlefields, memorials, and military cemeteries from the eighteenth to the twentieth centuries. (The NPS is dedicated to preserving and protecting these landmarks.)

Naval Historical Center (www.history.navy.mil): official home page of facility at Washington Navy Yard; rich in information and links.

U.S. Army Center of Military History (www.army.mil/cmh-pg): official home page and link index of programs, resources, and facilities.

The American War Library (http://members.aol.com/veterans/index.html): vast online veterans registry, with links to thousands of other military and veterans websites.

CHAPTER 6

Abraham, Henry J. *Freedom and the Court.* 7th ed. New York: Oxford University Press, 1998.

———. *Justices and Presidents.* 2nd ed. New York: Oxford University Press, 1985.

Adams, Henry. *The History of the United States During the Administrations of Jefferson and Madison.* New York: Library of America, 1986.

Bailyn, Bernard. *The Origins of American Politics.* New York: Knopf, 1970.

Cardozo, Benjamin. *The Nature of the Judicial Process.* New Haven: Yale University Press, 1921; reprint 1985.

Corwin, Edward Samuel. *Edward S. Corwin's Constitution and What It Means Today.* 14th ed. Princeton: Princeton University Press, 1978.

Cox, Archibald. *The Court and the Constitution.* Boston: Houghton Mifflin, 1987.

Ellis, Joseph J. *Founding Brothers: The Revolutionary Generation.* New York: Knopf, 2000.

Foner, Eric. *Politics and Ideology in the Age of the Civil War.* New York: Oxford University Press, 1992.

———. *Reconstruction: America's Unfinished Revolution, 1863–1877.* New York: HarperCollins, 1989.

Hall, Kermit. *The Oxford Companion to the Supreme Court of the United States.* New York: Oxford University Press, 1992.

Hofstadter, Richard. *The American Political Tradition.* New York: Random House, 1989.

Kammen, Michael. *A Machine That Would Go of Itself: The Constitution in American Culture.* New York: Knopf, 1986.

Kluger, Richard. *Simple Justice: The History of Brown v. Board of Education.* New York: Random House, 1977.

Lewis, Anthony. *Gideon's Trumpet.* New York: Vintage, 1966; reprint 1989.

Madison, James, Alexander Hamilton, and John Jay. *The Federalist,* 1788; numerous reprints.

Neely, Mark E. Jr. *The Fate of Liberty: Abraham Lincoln and Civil Liberties.* New York: Oxford University Press, 1992.

Neustadt, Richard. *Presidential Power and the Modern Presidents.* New York: Free Press, 1991.

Rakove, Jack N. *Original Meanings: Politics and Ideas in the Making of the Constitution.* New York: Vintage Books, 1997.

Rehnquist, William H. *The Supreme Court.* New York: Knopf, 2001.

Tocqueville, Alexis de. *Democracy in America.* 1835–40; numerous reprints.

Tribe, Laurence H. *American Constitutional Law.* 3rd ed. New York: Foundation Press, 2000.

Wills, Gary. *Inventing America: Jefferson's Declaration of Independence.* New York: Random House, 1979.

The main branches of the U.S. federal government maintain informative (and highly popular) websites that provide extensive background on issues and proceedings regarding legislation, politics, and judicial review. These include:

The White House and Executive Branch: www.whitehouse.gov
The Senate: www.senate.gov
The House of Representatives: www.house.gov
Supreme Court: www.supremecourtus.gov

The Library of Congress maintains an extensive online database of legislative information called Thomas (http://thomas.loc.gov). A number of private and educational Internet initiatives provide in-depth political information, critical analyses, and rich historical archives. Among these are:

PoliSci.com (www.polisci.com): a vast resource with a strong links directory.
Legal Information Institute (http://supct.law.cornell.edu/supct): includes a searchable database of Supreme Court rulings and case summaries, past and pending.

CHAPTER 7

Barton, Josef J. *Peasants and Strangers: Italians, Rumanians, and Slovaks in an American City, 1890–1950.* Cambridge: Harvard University Press, 1975.

Bissinger, Buzz. *A Prayer for the City.* New York: Vintage Books, 1999.

Blumin, Stuart. *The Emergence of the Middle Class: Social Experience in the American City, 1760–1900.* Cambridge: Cambridge University Press, 1989.

Bremner, Robert H. *From the Depths: The Discovery of Poverty in the United States.* New York: New York University Press, 1956.

Bridges, Amy. *A City in the Republic: Antebellum New York and the Origins of Machine Politics.* Cambridge: Cambridge University Press, 1984.

Burrows, Edwin G., and Mike Wallace. *Gotham: A History of New York City to 1898.* New York: Oxford University Press, 1998.

Gans, Herbert. *The Levittowners: Ways of Life and Politics in a New York Suburban Community.* New York: Columbia University Press, 1967; reprint 1982.

Jackson, Kenneth T. *Crabgrass Frontier.* New York: Oxford University Press, 1985.

———, ed. *Encyclopedia of New York.* New Haven: Yale University Press, 1995.

Lynd, Robert, and Helen Lynd. *Middletown: A Study in American Culture.* New York: Harcourt, Brace & World, 1959.

———. *Middletown in Transition: A Study in Cultural Conflicts.* New York: Harvest Books, 1982.

Osofsky, Gilbert. *Harlem: The Making of a Ghetto, 1890–1930.* New York: Harper & Row, 1966; 2nd reprint ed., 1996.

Schiesl, Martin J. *The Politics of Efficiency: Municipal Administration and Reform in America, 1880–1920.* Berkeley: University of California Press, 1977.

Warner, Sam B. Jr. *Streetcar Suburb: The Process of Growth in Boston, 1870–1900.* 2nd ed. Cambridge: Harvard University Press, 1978.

———. *The Urban Wilderness: A History of the American City.* New York: Harper & Row, 1972; reprint 1995.

Wilentz, Sean. *Chants Democratic: New York City and the Rise of the American Working Class, 1788–1850.* New York: Oxford University Press, 1983; reprint 1986.

Information regarding U.S. urban policy can be found at the Internet site for the Department of Housing and Urban Development (www.hud.gov), and regarding farm programs at the Department of Agriculture site (www.usda.gov); both sites also provide background on their respective bureaus, agencies, and offices, as well as statistics and extensive links.

For historical background on major cities, websites for local historical societies are a good place to start. The New York Historical Society (www.nyhistory.org) and Chicago Historical Society (www.chicagohs.org) maintain especially rich and informative web pages. The following are among the many other fascinating Internet resources to explore:

Los Angeles: Past, Present, and Future (www.usc.edu/isd/archives/la): based on archival resources of the University of Southern California.
Exploredc.org: Gateway to America's Capital (www.exploredc.org): covering the history, heritage, and culture of Washington, D.C., and surroundings—includes text, pictures, audio, and virtual tours.
"100 Years of New York City" (www.nytimes.com/specials/nyc100): a special collection from *The New York Times.*

CHAPTER 8

Ambrose, Stephen E., and Douglas G. Brinkley. *Rise to Globalism: American Foreign Policy Since 1938.* 8th ed. New York: Penguin, 1997.

Blum, John Morton. *Woodrow Wilson and the Politics of Morality.* Boston: Addison-Wesley, 1998.

Dougherty, J. E., and R. L. Pfaltzgraff Jr. *Contending Theories of International Relations.* 4th ed. Boston: Addison-Wesley, 1996.

Gaddis, John Lewis. *The United States and the Origins of the Cold War: 1941–1947.* Rev. ed. New York: Columbia University Press, 2000.

Hogan, Michael J. *The Marshall Plan: America, Britain, and the Reconstruction of Europe, 1947–1952.* Cambridge: Cambridge University Press, 1989.

Kennedy, Robert F., and Arthur Schlesinger Jr. *Thirteen Days: A Memoir of the Cuban Missile Crisis.* New York: Norton, 1999.

Kissinger, Henry A. *White House Years.* Boston: Little Brown, 1980.

———. *Years of Upheaval.* Boston: Little Brown, 1982.

———. *Years of Renewal.* New York: Simon & Schuster, 1998.

LaFeber, Walter. *Inevitable Revolutions: The United States in Central America.* 2nd rev. ed. New York: Norton, 1993.

Langley, Lester D. *America and the Americas: The United States in the Western Hemisphere.* Athens: University of Georgia Press, 1989.

McCullough, David. *Path Between the Seas: The Creation of the Panama Canal, 1870–1914.* New York: Simon & Schuster, reprint 1999.

Pastor, Robert, and Jorge Castaneda. *Limits to Friendship: The U.S. and Mexico.* New York: Random House, 1989.

Perkins, Bradford, Akira Iriye, and Warren I. Cohen. *The Cambridge History of American Foreign Relations.* 4 vols. Cambridge: Cambridge University Press, 1993–95.

Powaski, Ronald E. *The Cold War: The United States and the Soviet Union, 1917–1991.* New York: Oxford University Press, 1997.

Smith, Robert Freeman. *The Caribbean World and the United States.* New York: Macmillan, 1994.

Walker, Martin. *The Cold War: A History.* New York: Henry Holt, 1995.

The U.S. Department of State maintains an elaborate and up-to-date website (www.state.gov) that includes extensive sections on diplomatic history, educational and cultural affairs, geographical studies, and official documents. The National Security Archive (www.gwu.edu/~nsarchiv) at the George Washington University collects and publishes declassified documents acquired through the Freedom of Information Act. The prestigious journal *Foreign Affairs* (www.foreignaffairs.org) offers online summaries of recent articles, book reviews, and other materials on contemporary issues. Its parent organization, the Council on Foreign Relations, also maintains an informative site (www.cfr.org), including newspaper clippings and an in-depth "Resource Center."

Notable sites on specific historical subjects include:
The Louisiana Purchase, 1803
(www.yale.edu/lawweb/avalon/diplomacy/fr1803m.htm): part of the Avalon Project at the Yale Law School—treaties, speeches, and other primary source materials.
The Age of Imperialism (http://smplanet.com/imperialism/toc.html): an online history project from Small Planet, an Internet resource for teachers and publishers.
The Cold War Museum (www.coldwar.org): in-depth information, online exhibits, links, and more.

CHAPTER 9

Atack, Jeremy, and Peter Passell. *A New Economic View of American History: From Colonial Times to 1940.* 2nd ed. New York: Norton, 1994.

Bluestone, Barry, and Bennett Harrison. *The Deindustrialization of America.* New York: Basic Books, 1982.

Chandler, Alfred D. Jr. *The Visible Hand: The Managerial Revolution in American Business.* Cambridge: Harvard University Press, 1977.

Denby, Charles. *Indignant Heart: A Black Worker's Journal.* Boston: South End Press, 1978; Detroit: Wayne State University Press, reprint 1989.

Dulles, Foster R., and Melvyn Dubofsky. *Labor in America: A History.* 6th ed. Wheeling, Ill.: Harlan Davidson, 1999.

Galbraith, John Kenneth. *The Great Crash of 1929.* 3rd ed. Boston: Houghton Mifflin; reprint 1997.

———. *The Affluent Society.* 40th anniversary ed. Boston: Houghton Mifflin, 1998.

Gates, Paul W. *The Farmer's Age: Agriculture, 1815–1860.* Armonk, N.Y.: M. E. Sharpe, 1977.

Green, James. *The World of the Worker: Labor in Twentieth-Century America.* New York: Hill and Wang, 1980; Champaign: University of Illinois Press, reprint 1998.

Kennedy, David M. *Freedom from Fear: The American People in Depression and War, 1929–1945.* New York: Oxford University Press, 1999.

Kessler-Harris, Alice. *Out to Work: A History of Wage-Earning Women in the United States.* New York: Oxford University Press, 1982.

Leuchtenberg, William E. *The Perils of Prosperity, 1914–32.* 2nd ed. Chicago: University of Chicago Press, 1993

Martin, John Frederick. *Profits in the Wilderness: Entrepreneurship and the Founding of New England Towns in the Seventeenth Century.* Chapel Hill: University of North Carolina Press, 1991.

McElvaine, Robert S. *The Great Depression: America, 1929–1941.* New York: Times Books, 1984; reprint 1994.

Noble, David F. *America by Design: Science, Technology, and the Rise of Corporate Capitalism.* New York: Oxford University Press, 1979.

Phillips, Kevin P. *The Politics of Rich and Poor.* New York: Random House, 1990.

Schumacher, E. F. *Small Is Beautiful: Economics As If People Mattered.* New York: HarperCollins, 1989.

Temin, Peter, ed. *Engines of Enterprise: An Economic History of New England.* Cambridge: Harvard University Press, 2000.

Terkel, Studs. *Hard Times: An Oral History of the Great Depression.* New York: Pantheon, 1970; New York: New Press, reprint 2000.

———. *Working: People Talk About What They Do All Day and How They Feel About What They Do.* New York: Pantheon, 1974; New York: New Press, reprint 1997.

Thurow, Lester. *Building Wealth: The New Rules for Individuals, Companies, and Nations in a Knowledge-Based Economy.* New York: HarperBusiness, 2000.

Trachtenberg, Alan. *The Incorporation of America: Culture and Society in the Gilded Age.* New York: Hill & Wang, 1982.

Veblen, Thorstein. *Theory of the Leisure Class,* 1899; reprint ed. Amherst, N.Y.: Prometheus Books, 1998.

Woodward, Bob. *Greenspan's Fed and the American Boom.* New York: Simon & Schuster, 2000.

The websites of the U.S. Department of Commerce (www.doc.gov), Department of Labor (www.dol.gov), and Department of the Treasury (www.ustreas.gov) all provide historical background, as well as current information, on their respective functions, policies, programs, and agencies, with extensive statistics and links to other relevant sites. The web pages of the U.S. Mint (www.usmint.gov) and Bureau of Printing and Engraving (www.bep.treas.gov) provide in-depth information on coinage and the printing of money. In addition, the White House home page (www.whitehouse.gov) provides easy access to the sites of such other government agencies and offices as the Bureau of Labor Statistics, Federal Reserve, and Federal Trade Commission, among many others. The "American Memory" archive and special exhibitions at the Library of Congress site (www.loc.gov) provide a treasure trove of visual material, oral histories, and other primary source materials on every period of U.S. economic history. Informative educational and commercial sites include:
"Between a Rock and a Hard Place: A History of American Sweatshops, 1820–Present" (http://americanhistory.si.edu/sweatshops): a special exhibition of the Smithsonian Institution.
New York Times: The Crash of '29 (www.nytimes.com/library/financial/index-1929-crash.html): a special report featuring coverage from the newspaper's archives.
New Deal Network (http://newdeal.feri.org): includes a documentary library of more than 700 speeches, letters, and other texts; photo gallery; lesson plans and bibliographies; moderated discussions; and scholarly essays.
New York Stock Exchange (www.nyse.com): the official website—operations, regulation, history, market information, etc.
AFL-CIO (www.aflcio.org): official website of the nation's largest trade-union confederation.

CHAPTER 10

Bailyn, Bernard. *Education in the Forming of American Society: Needs and Opportunity for Study.* New York: W. W. Norton, reprint 1972.

Barzun, Jacques. *Begin Here: The Forgotten Conditions of Teaching and Learning.* Chicago: University of Chicago Press, 1991.

———. *The American University: How It Runs, Where It Is Going.* 2nd ed. Chicago: University of Chicago Press, 1993.

Cremin, Lawrence A. *American Education: The Colonial Experience, 1607–1783.* New York: Harper & Row, 1970.

———. *American Education: The National Experience, 1783–1896.* New York: Harper & Row, 1980.

———. *American Education: The Metropolitan Experience, 1876–1980.* New York: Harper & Row, 1988.

Dewey, John. *Democracy and Education: An Introduction to the Philosophy of Education, 1916.* New York: Macmillan, 1916; New York: Simon & Schuster, reprint 1997.

———. *The School and Society and the Child and the Curriculum.* 1899. Mineola, N.Y.: Dover, reprint 2001.

Du Bois, W. E. B. *The Souls of Black Folk.* 1903. New York: Penguin, reprint 1996.

Gardner, Howard. *The Unschooled Mind: How Children Think and How Schools Should Teach.* New York: Basic Books, 1993.

Hirsch, E. D. *Cultural Literacy: What Every American Needs to Know.* New York: Vintage Books, 1988.

Hofstadter, Richard. *Anti-Intellectualism in American Life.* New York: Random House, 1966.

Karier, Clarence J. *The Individual, Society, and Education: A History of American Educational Ideas*. 2nd ed. Champaign: University of Illinois Press, 1986.

Nasaw, David. *Schooled to Order: A Social History of Public Schooling in the United States*. New York: Oxford University Press, 1981.

Pulliam, John D., and James J. Van Patten. *History of Education in America*. 7th ed. Upper Saddle River, N.J.: Prentice Hall, 1998.

Ravitch, Diane. *Left Back: A Century of Failed School Reforms*. New York: Simon & Schuster, 2000.

The following institutions and organizations maintain informative websites on conditions, policies, and issues in contemporary American education, with respective emphasis on federal programs, the role of teachers, curricula, standards and assessment, and other aspects: the U.S. Department of Education (www.ed.gov); National Center for Education Statistics (http://nces.ed.gov); American Federation of Teachers (www.aft.org); and National Education Association (www.nea.org). Internet sites for major colleges and universities, school boards, and regional districts are another valuable source of information on public and private education today.

A number of scholars, students, libraries, and independent web developers have compiled online materials covering the history of education. These are best identified by conducting word searches and browsing your index of choice. One primary source archive you may find interesting, for example, is a collection of nineteenth-century schoolbooks, in searchable format, collected by the Digital Research Project at the University of Pittsburgh (http://digital.library.pitt.edu/nietz).

CHAPTER 11

Bruce, Robert V. *The Launching of American Science, 1846–1876*. New York: Knopf, 1987.

Howard Hughes Medical Institute and Robert A. Potter, eds. *Exploring the Biomedical Revolution*. Baltimore: Johns Hopkins University Press, 2000.

Hughes, Thomas P. *American Genesis: A Century of Invention and Technological Enthusiasm,1870–1970*. New York: Viking, 1989.

Josephson, Matthew. *Edison: A Biography*. New York: John Wiley, 1992.

Kohlstedt, Sally Gregory, and Margaret W. Rossiter, eds. *Historical Writings on American Science: Perspectives and Prospects*. Baltimore: Johns Hopkins University Press, 1985.

Kolata, Gina Bari. *Flu: The Story of the Great Influenza Pandemic of 1918 and the Search for the Virus That Caused It*. New York: Farrar, Straus & Giroux, 1999.

Larson, Edward J. *Summer for the Gods: The Scopes Trial and America's Continuing Debate Over Science and Religion*. New York: Basic Books, 1997.

Marcus, Alan I., and Howard P. Segal. *Technology in America: A Brief History*. 2nd ed. New York: Harcourt Brace Jovanovich, 1999.

Murphy, Lamar Riley. *Enter the Physician: The Transformation of Domestic Medicine, 1760–1860*. Tuscaloosa: University of Alabama Press, 1991.

Noble, David F. *America by Design: Science, Technology, and the Rise of Corporate Capitalism*. New York: Oxford University Press, 1979.

Pursell, Carroll W. Jr., ed. *Technology in America*. 2nd ed. Cambridge: MIT Press, 1990.

———. *The Machine in America: A Social History of Technology*. Baltimore: Johns Hopkins University Press, 1995.

Rhodes, Richard. *The Making of the Atomic Bomb*. New York: Simon and Schuster, 1986; New York: Touchstone Books, reprint 1995.

Starr, Paul. *The Social Transformation of American Medicine*. New York: Basic Books, 1982.

Weiner, Jonathan. *Time, Love, and Memory: A Great Biologist and His Quest for the Origins of Behavior*. New York: Knopf, 1999.

Williams, Trevor I. *Science: A History of Discovery in the Twentieth Century*. New York: Oxford University Press, 1990.

The relevant departments, agencies, and offices of the federal government maintain extensive sites on the Internet. Among these are the Department of Health and Human Services (www.dhhs.gov), National Science Foundation (www.nsf.gov), Centers for Disease Control and Prevention (www.cdc.gov), and Food and Drug Administration (www.fda.gov). Of particular interest to anyone investigating the history of medicine is the National Library of Medicine, History of Medicine Division (www.nlm.nih.gov/hmd/hmd.html).

The websites of nonprofit organizations and professional societies, including the American Medical Association (www.ama-assn.org), American Association for the Advancement of Science (www.aaas.org), Smithsonian Institution (www.si.edu), and associations dedicated to specific subject disciplines also provide a wealth of information.

Among the many online initiatives dedicated to the history of American science and medicine, the Center for History and New Media at George Mason University maintains an extensive catalogue of links, fully annotated and reviewed—ECHO: Exploring and Collecting History Online (http://chnm.gmu.edu/echo). The site also includes a "Memory Bank" of firsthand accounts and special collections on advances, setbacks, and events in the history of science and technology.

CHAPTER 12

Barnouw, Erik. *A Tower in Babel: A History of Broadcasting in the United States to 1933*. New York: Oxford University Press, 1966.

———. *The Golden Web: A History of Broadcasting in the United States, 1933–1953*. New York: Oxford University Press, 1968.

———. *The Image Empire: A History of Broadcasting in the United States from 1953*. New York: Oxford University Press, 1970.

———. *Tube of Plenty: The Evolution of American Television*, 2nd rev. ed. New York: Oxford University Press, 1990.

Bilstein, Roger. *Flight in America: From the Wrights to the Astronauts*. 3rd ed. Baltimore: Johns Hopkins University Press, 2001.

Chandler, Alfred D., and James W. Cortada, eds. *A Nation Transformed by Information: How Information Has Shaped the United States from Colonial Times to the Present*. New York: Oxford University Press, 2000.

Goodrich, Carter, ed. *Canals and American Economic Development*. Port Washington, N.Y.: Kennikat Press, 1961.

Jenkins, Dennis R. *Space Shuttle: The History of the National Space Transportation System: The First 100 Missions*, Cape Canaveral, Fla.: D. R. Jenkins, 2001.

Jensen, Oliver. *The American Heritage History of Railroads in America*. New York: McGraw-Hill, 1975.

Lewis, D. L., and Laurence Goldstein, eds. *The Automobile and American Culture*. Ann Arbor: University of Michigan Press, 1984.

Morrison, Samuel Eliot. *The Maritime History of Massachusetts, 1783–1860*. Boston: Houghton Mifflin, 1961.

Rowland, Wade. *Spirit of the Web: The Age of Information from Telegraph to Internet*. Toronto: Somerville House, 1997.

Sklar, Robert. *Movie-Made America: A Cultural History of American Movies*. Rev. ed. New York: Vintage Books, 1994.

Standage, Tom. *The Victorian Internet: The Remarkable Story of the Telegraph and the Nineteenth Century's On-Line Pioneers*. New York: Walker, 1998.

Sterling, Christopher, and John Kittross. *Stay Tuned: A Concise History of American Broadcasting*. 3rd ed. Mahwah, N.J.: Lawrence Erlbaum, 2001.

Stover, John F. *American Railroads*. 2nd ed. Chicago: University of Chicago Press, 1998.

Summers, Mark W. *Railroads, Reconstruction, and the Gospel of Prosperity*. Princeton: Princeton University Press, 1984.

Taylor, George Rogers. *The Transportation Revolution, 1815–1860*. New York: Rinehart, 1951; White Plains, N.Y.: M. E. Sharpe, reprint 1977.

Wolfe, Tom. *The Right Stuff*. New York: Farrar, Straus & Giroux, 1979; numerous reprints.

Perhaps no fields of interest are better represented on the Internet than those of communication and transportation. The departments and agencies of the federal government are one good place to start an online investigation of these subjects. The Federal Communications Commission (www.fcc.gov) maintains an extensive website, as does the

Department of Transportation (www.dot.gov); the latter includes links to the Federal Aviation Administration (FAA), Federal Highway Administration (FHWA), National Highway Traffic Safety Administration (NHTSA), Federal Railroad Administration (FRA), and other regulatory bodies. Here are some other compelling and informative sites maintained by government, commercial, educational, and nonprofit organizations:

ERAU Virtual Libraries: Aerospace and Aviation (www.erau.edu/libraries/virtual): two vast, well-organized indexes of links to websites of historical and contemporary information.

How Stuff Works (www.howstuffworks.com): a selection of articles and diagrams on the workings of everything from cars and space vehicles to televisions, telephones, and computers.

National Transportation Library (http://ntl.bts.gov): statistics, history, regulations, and more.

NASA (www.nasa.gov): still one of the all-time great sites on the Net!

Motion Picture Association of America (www.mpaa.org): site of the industry's governing body.

Museum of Television and Radio (www.mtr.org): the New York City museum online.

Virtual Museum of Computing (http://vmoc.i.am): a rich collection of links and other material.

CHAPTER 13

Frazier, E. Franklin. *The Negro Church in America.* Rev. ed. New York: Schocken, 1989.

Handy, Robert. *A History of the Churches in the United States and Canada.* New York: Oxford University Press, 1977.

Herberg, Will. *Protestant, Catholic, Jew: An Essay in American Religious Sociology.* New York: Doubleday, 1955; Chicago: University of Chicago Press, reprint 1983.

Larson, Edward J. *Summer for the Gods: The Scopes Trial and America's Continuing Debate Over Science and Religion.* New York: Basic Books, 1997.

Lincoln, C. E., and L. H. Mamiya. *The Black Church in the African-American Experience.* Durham, N.C.: Duke University Press, 1990.

Middlekauff, Robert. *The Mathers: Three Generations of Puritan Intellectuals, 1596–1728.* New York: Oxford University Press, 1971; Berkeley: University of California Press, reprint 1999.

Neuhaus, Richard John. *The Naked Public Square: Religion and Democracy in America.* 2nd ed. Grand Rapids, Mich.: Eerdmans, 1986.

Noll, Mark. *A History of Christianity in the United States and Canada.* Grand Rapids, Mich.: Eerdmans, 1992.

Queen, Edward L., Stephen R. Prothero, and Gardiner H. Shattuck Jr., eds. *The Encyclopedia of American Religious History.* New York: Facts on File, 1996.

Rosten, Leo, ed. *Religions in America: Ferment and Faith in an Age of Crisis.* New York: Simon & Schuster, 1975.

Silverman, Kenneth. *The Life and Times of Cotton Mather.* New York: HarperTrade, 1985.

Stegner, Wallace. *Mormon Country.* Lincoln: University of Nebraska Press, 1981.

Warner, Michael, ed. *American Sermons: The Pilgrims to Martin King, Jr.* New York: Library of America, 1999.

The major religious organizations and churches of the United States all maintain up-to-date sites on the Internet. Examples include the National Conference of Catholic Bishops (NCCB) and United States Catholic Conference (USCC) (www.nccbuscc.org), and the National Council of the Churches of Christ in the U.S.A. (www.ncccusa.org). The latter site, titled ElectronicChurch.org, includes comprehensive links to the home pages of affiliated churches. A variety of educational and nonprofit organizations maintain highly informative and well-indexed sites focused specifically on the history of religion in America. Among these are:

"The American Religious Experience" (http://are.as.wvu.edu): a collaborative online publication and scholarly exchange project involving the University of North Carolina at Chapel Hill, Louisiana State University, and West Virginia University. Includes a course syllabus, film archive, and other special features.

"The Material History of American Religion Project" (www.materialreligion.org): documents, online discussion, and other resources mounted by the Divinity School of Vanderbilt University.

Religion and the Founding of the American Republic (http://lcweb.loc.gov/exhibits/religion): a Library of Congress exhibit.

Jewish-American History on the Web (www.jewish-history.com): a privately maintained site dedicated to nineteenth-century Jewish American history, poetry and fiction, polemics and philosophy.

CHAPTER 14

Barden, Romare, and Harry Henderson. *A History of African-American Artists: From 1792 to the Present.* New York: Pantheon, 1993.

Basinger, Jeanine. *American Cinema: One Hundred Years of Filmmaking.* New York: Rizzoli, 1994.

Baym, Nina, ed. *The Norton Anthology of American Literature.* 5th ed. New York: W. W. Norton, 1998.

Bercovitch, Sacvan, ed. *Cambridge History of American Literature.* 7 vols., Rev. eds. New York: Cambridge University Press, 1995–2001.

Bordman, Gerald Martin. *The Oxford Companion to American Theater.* 2nd ed. New York: Oxford University Press, 1992.

Brustein, Robert. *Reimagining the American Theatre.* New York: Hill & Wang, 1991.

Davis, Keith F. *An American Century of Photography: From Dry Plate to Digital: The Hallmark Collection.* Rev. ed. New York: Harry N. Abrams, 1999.

de Mille, Agnes. *Book of the Dance.* New York: Golden Press, 1963.

Elliott, Emory, ed. *Columbia Literary History of the United States.* New York: Columbia University Press, 1988.

Gates, Henry Louis Jr., and Nellie Y. McKay, eds. *The Norton Anthology of African American Literature.* New York: W. W. Norton, 1996.

Green, Jonathan. *American Photography: A Critical History, 1945 to the Present.* New York: Harry N. Abrams, 1985.

Hart, James David. *The Oxford Companion to American Literature.* 6th ed. New York: Oxford University Press, 1995.

Haskell, Barbara. *The American Century: Art and Culture, 1900–1950.* New York: Whitney Museum of Art, 1999.

Hughes, Robert. *American Visions: The Epic History of Art in America.* New York: Knopf, 1997.

Kammen, Michael G. *Mystic Chords of Memory: The Transformation of Tradition in American Culture.* New York: Vintage Books, 1993.

———. *American Culture, American Tastes: Social Change and the 20th Century.* New York: Basic Books, 2000.

Kasson, Joy S. *Marble Queens and Captives: Women in 19th-Century American Sculpture.* New Haven, Conn.: Yale University Press, 1990.

Kirstein, Lincoln. *Dance.* 1935; Westport, Conn.: Greenwood Press, reprint 1970.

Magill, Frank N. *Masterpieces of African-American Literature.* New York: HarperCollins, 1992.

Mumford, Lewis. *Roots of Contemporary American Architecture.* Mineola, N.Y.: Dover, 1972.

Nicholls, David, ed. *The Cambridge History of American Music.* New York: Cambridge University Press, 1999.

Phillips, Lisa, et al. *The American Century: Art and Culture, 1950–2000.* New York: Whitney Museum of Art, 1999.

Scully, Vincent. *American Architecture and Urbanism.* Rev. ed. New York: Holt, 1988.

Skillion, Anne. *The New York Public Library Literature Companion.* New York: The Free Press, 2001.

Terry, Walter. *The Dance in America.* Rev. ed. New York: Da Capo, 1981.

Tyrrell, John, and Stanley Sadie, eds. *The New Grove Dictionary of Music and Musicians.* 30 vols., 2nd ed. New York: Grove's Dictionaries, 2001.

The immediacy and multimedia capability of the Internet make it an ideal medium for conveying information on American culture, the arts, and entertainment media. Here is a small sampling:

National Endowment for the Arts (http://arts.endow.gov): site of the federal arts-funding body.

Bartleby.com: Great Books Online (www.bartleby.com): a searchable database of literature, poetry, and literary reference materials; the site offers a vast selection of classics to download for free and contemporary works to order.

ArtSource (www.ilpi.com/artsource): a vast index of Internet resources on art and architecture—museums, libraries, organizations, special exhibits, image collections, projects, and programs.

Historic American Sheet Music Project (http://scriptorium.lib.duke.edu/sheetmusic): from the archives of Duke University, provides access to lyrics, photos, and background information on more than 3,000 pieces from 1850 to 1920.

American Theater Web (www.americantheaterweb.com): listings of more than 1,000 U.S. theaters and nonprofit performing arts groups, with summaries of productions and links to many individual websites; little history but a valuable resource for theatergoers.

American Museum of Photography (www.photographymuseum.com): an online "museum without walls," featuring numerous special collections, tours, information, and a research center.

The Internet Movie Database (www.imdb.com): a comprehensive source of movie information on the Internet, including reviews, filmographies, and biographies of actors, writers, directors, and others, as well as listings of current feature releases and special collections of vintage images. The Internet Broadway Database (www.ibdb.com) is a similar site that provides extensive information on Broadway theater, from actors' Broadway credits and production values of shows to season lineups of theater companies and the histories of Broadway theaters.

INDEX

L

PHOTO CREDITS

THE NEW YORK PUBLIC LIBRARY HUMANITIES AND SOCIAL SCIENCES LIBRARY:
Arents Collection on Tobacco: **469**
Art and Architecture Collection, Miriam & Ira D. Wallach Division of Art, Prints and Photographs: **511**
General Research Division: **83, 85, 207, 253, 283, 360**
Irma and Paul Milstein Division of United States History, Local History and Genealogy: **49, 81, 159, 252, 340, 432**
Manuscripts and Archives Division: **222**
The New York Public Library Archives: **247, 260**
Photography Collection, Miriam & Ira D. Wallach Division of Art, Prints and Photographs: **11, 31, 86, 116, 157, 161, 164, 192, 225, 237, 266, 282, 286, 357, 417, 443, 461, 491, 520, 523**
Prints Collection, Miriam & Ira D. Wallach Division of Art, Prints and Photographs: **62, 69, 78, 80, 96, 147, 197, 232, 235, 244, 251, 325, 381, 383, 386, 388, 420, 425**
Rare Books Division: **15, 26, 41, 470, 488**

THE NEW YORK PUBLIC LIBRARY SCHOMBURG CENTER FOR RESEARCH IN BLACK CULTURE:
Art and Artifacts Division: **105**
Manuscripts, Archives and Rare Books Division: **365**
Photographs and Prints Division: **64, 121, 127, 145, 153, 485, 498**

THE NEW YORK PUBLIC LIBRARY FOR THE PERFORMING ARTS, DOROTHY AND LEWIS B. CULLMAN CENTER:
Billy Rose Theatre Collection: **517**
Music Division: **160, 504**

THE NEW YORK PUBLIC LIBRARY, THE BRANCH LIBRARIES
Picture Collection: **29, 43, 59, 67, 82, 317, 338, 362, 456, 460, 499**

AP/WIDE WORLD PHOTOS: **129 (bottom), 370**

BETTMAN/CORBIS: **28, 130, 140, 211, 224, 355, 368, 377, 475, 476**

BROWN BROTHERS, STERLING, PA: **311, 341, 343**

CORBIS: **123, 290, 296**

COURTESY OF THE ARCHIVES, CALIFORNIA INSTITUTE OF TECHNOLOGY: **406**

DAVID TURNLEY/CORBIS: **100, 132, 274, 293**

FBI FUGITIVE PUBLICITY SPECIAL SERVICES UNIT: **128**

HENRY DILTZ/CORBIS: **220**

HULTON-DEUTSCH COLLECTION/CORBIS: **289**

LIBRARY OF CONGRESS: **71, 90, 119, 267, 268, 474**

NASA (NATIONAL AERONAUTICS AND SPACE ADMINISTRATION): **443, 448**

NATALIE FOBES/CORBIS: **93**

NATIONAL ARCHIVES AND RECORDS ADMINISTRATION, COURTESY AIP EMILIO SERGE VISUAL ARCHIVES: **402**

NATIONAL ARCHIVES AND RECORDS ADMINISTRATION: **393, 394**

NEIL HEILPERN/GLOBE PHOTOS, INC.: **129 (top)**

REUTERS NEW MEDIA INC./CORBIS: **134, 179**

WALLY McNAMEE/CORBIS: **299**